The Adams Papers

L. H. BUTTERFIELD, EDITOR IN CHIEF

SERIES III

GENERAL CORRESPONDENCE
AND OTHER PAPERS
OF THE ADAMS STATESMEN

Legal Papers of John Adams

Legal Papers of
John Adams

L. KINVIN WROTH and HILLER B. ZOBEL

EDITORS

———————— ☆ ————————

Volume 1 · *Introduction* · *Cases* 1–30

THE BELKNAP PRESS
OF HARVARD UNIVERSITY PRESS
CAMBRIDGE, MASSACHUSETTS

1965

Distributed in Great Britain by Oxford University Press · London

Funds for editing *The Adams Papers* have been provided by Time, Inc., on behalf of *Life*, and by the Ford Foundation, to the Massachusetts Historical Society, under whose supervision the editorial work is being done.

The William Nelson Cromwell Foundation has made possible the editing of the *Legal Papers* by means of a grant to the Harvard Law School.

Library of Congress Catalog Card Number 65-13855 · Printed in the United States of America

This edition of *The Adams Papers*
is sponsored by the MASSACHUSETTS HISTORICAL SOCIETY
to which the ADAMS MANUSCRIPT TRUST
by a deed of gift dated 4 April 1956
gave ultimate custody of the personal and public papers
written, accumulated, and preserved over a span of three centuries
by the Adams family of Massachusetts

The acorn and oakleaf device on the preceding page is redrawn from a seal cut for John Quincy Adams after 1830. The motto is from Cæcilius Statius as quoted by Cicero in the First Tusculan Disputation: *Serit arbores quæ alteri seculo prosint* ("He plants trees for the benefit of later generations").

The Adams Papers

Foreword

Practitioners of the common law have often tried to utilize the civilian's comfortable distinction between the private and the public law. They have not often found satisfaction in the effort. It is not my purpose to search out the reasons why a continental concept does not easily fit the form of Anglo-American reality. All that I can do is suggest that the story of John Adams' career at the Massachusetts bar, as that story is revealed in these remarkable volumes, may help us to understand why common-law lawyers have tended to see so many bright colors of statecraft in the petty disputes of neighbors, and so many dull tones of legalism in the great cases of public moment. In any event, it seemed quite clear to the Trustees of the William Nelson Cromwell Foundation that they should give their support to a venture in scholarship which would encourage understanding of the intimate relations between the small details of private controversy and the larger design of public order. The progression of John Adams from a craftsman of laws to an architect of governments is a significant and exciting chapter in the history of American law and the chronicle of our public affairs.

BRUCE BROMLEY

Contents

Contents

Contents

Contents

G. DOMESTIC RELATIONS

H. ADMINISTRATIVE LAW

Descriptive List of Illustrations

Preface

Until recently the study of American legal history, except for legislative and constitutional developments involving public law, has not been considered academically respectable. Inquirers have had to make do with pious "Notices of Eminent Lawyers and Judges" in works of local history and "Historical Addresses on the Bench and Bar" of such-and-such a county—works which are occasionally useful but are always long on sentiment and anecdote and short on documentation.

Whatever the explanation may be, the result has been that we have known little about what colonial lawyers actually did as they earned their daily living and adapted to transatlantic conditions and purposes the British and still older legal institutions that they had inherited. To be sure, some advances into this *terra incognita* have lately been made, with the publication of early court records and of a few—too few—specialized studies. But general histories still usually ignore law as argued and adjudicated in the courts, and with few exceptions biographers of lawyers and judges famous in their time hurry over the legal chapters in their subjects' lives in order to get them into the more familiar and hence more comfortable arena of politics.

John Adams is a conspicuous example of this treatment. Everyone who has written about him has agreed with each other and with Adams himself that he was a hard-working, learned, and able lawyer, and that his reading and training in the law furnished him a firm base for his rise to the highest offices in the land. But surprisingly few details have been put forward, and only meager documentation for his practice has been published. In Charles Francis Adams' mid-19th-century edition of his grandfather's writings, hardly half a dozen of the sixty-four cases set out in the present volume were printed even in part, and only a few others were discussed either in the "Life" that occupies the entire first volume or in the extensive notes and appendixes in the other nine volumes. The cases partially printed in the *Works* have become the celebrated ones: the argument over Writs of Assistance in 1761, which Adams merely—though memorably—reported; Adams' defense of John Hancock against charges of smuggling in 1769; the trial later the same year of Michael Corbet for murder on the high seas; and the trials in 1770 of Captain Thomas Preston and the luckless British troops indicted for their part in what is known as the Boston Massacre. These important cases, naturally enough, have been worked hard by Adams' biographers, for every one of them has not only high human interest but large political implications. Yet taken all together they give little notion of Adams' laborious years at the bar, even when embellished with anecdotes, character sketches, and entertaining reflections on the life of a colonial lawyer drawn from Adams' Diary, Autobiography, and early letters.

The materials for doing much better than this existed but lay out of sight. In the handling of his grandfather's legal papers C. F. Adams fell signally below his own standards as a scholarly editor. He examined the voluminous and disorderly mass, printed some selected pieces, and levied on a few others for his "Life" and *Works* of John Adams. But he then gave up, bundled up the lot, and put them away for good. After the 1850's they seem to have been very seldom looked into until the Adams Papers editorial enterprise was launched in 1954 at the Massachusetts Historical Society, where the family archives had been deposited in 1902 but had not been made available to scholars.

The first inspection of them by the editor in chief of the Adams Papers was frustrating enough to evoke a certain sympathy with his predecessor, the family archivist and editor. Apart from a few bound or sewn volumes containing court dockets, commonplace-book entries, pleading forms, and records of several important cases in admiralty, John Adams' legal papers as found were a jumbled mass of stitched and loose leaves of various sizes that commonly showed wear from being carried in the lawyer's pocket. Almost all were written with the haste characteristic of an attorney under the usual pressures and distractions of courtroom and office. Many bear as a caption the name of the pertinent case, but few bear the name or term of the court, and virtually none gives the date when it was written. These orphic leaves may include copies of some of the actual documents pertaining to their respective cases and occasional scraps of correspondence and accounts with clients. But for the most part they are jottings of authorities and arguments used, or to be used, in a given trial; notes on depositions and courtroom evidence on one or both sides of a case; sometimes the judges' interjections and opinions; and, rarely, a written-up version of Adams' appeal to the jury. In short, they are Adams' working papers as a trial lawyer.

How completely or incompletely they represent the entire body of Adams' records as a lawyer is beyond conjecture. Adams himself said that he lost important papers from his house and office during the British occupation of Boston in 1775–1776. Both the fragmentary character of many of the surviving pieces and the disorder in which the corpus was found strongly suggest that these are simply what happened to survive—in effect the sweepings of his office. This suggestion is supported by the fact that the manuscripts document more or less satisfactorily only a few hundred cases among the many hundreds in which we know from other evidence that Adams was professionally concerned.

At any rate, such were the legal materials found among the Adams family manuscripts in 1954. Despite their unpromising condition, it seemed clear even to an historian without legal training that there was valuable ore in this lode which should be mined. An examination of the material by Mark DeWolfe Howe, professor of law at Harvard and a member of the Adams Papers Editorial Advisory Committee, strongly confirmed this opinion. What was needed, clearly, was an intensive study, arrangement, and cataloguing of every piece by someone who was trained in the law and who cared about the history of the law in early America. These qualifications are not commonly found in combination, but beginning in 1957, with the active encouragement of Dean Erwin N. Griswold, arrangements were made for a pair of third-year Harvard law students to perform this task while enrolled for credit in a history course offered by the editor in chief of the Adams Papers in the Harvard Graduate School. They were Messrs. R. Tenney Johnson and Hiller B. Zobel; their work was later taken up by Mr. L. Kinvin Wroth, who had recently graduated from the Harvard Law School. In the summer of 1961, the study and arrangement of the legal papers having been substantially completed, Mr. Wroth (then assistant professor in the Dickinson School of Law, Carlisle, Pennsylvania, and now associate professor of law, University of Maine Law School) and Mr. Zobel (associated with the firm of Bingham, Dana and Gould in Boston) jointly proposed a plan for editing a selected but large-scale collection of John Adams' legal papers, the materials to be drawn not only from the family archives but from all other pertinent sources and to be accompanied by appropriate commentary and annotation. The plan was laid before the Adams Papers Administrative Board and approved in the fall after discussions with those interested at the Harvard Law School, the Harvard University Press, and the Massachusetts Historical Society.

Through the good offices of Dean Griswold another essential party was brought into the agreement early in 1962. The Trustees of the William Nelson Cromwell Foundation of New York City, an organization devoted among other good causes to furthering studies in American legal history and with a distinguished record in that field, made a grant, later supplemented, to cover the costs of editorial work. Harvard University Press undertook to publish two (later increased to three) volumes of the *Legal Papers of John Adams* under its Belknap Press imprint, as a unit—though a separable one—of *The Adams Papers.** The editors were to be, and are, Messrs. Wroth and Zobel, serving as research associates in law at Harvard University, under the general supervision of the editor in chief. Professor Howe has acted throughout the enterprise as a generous and invaluable consultant to all parties. Public announcement of the undertaking was made in March 1962. An office was made available in Austin Hall, adjacent to the Harvard Law School Library, Miss Judith Diekoff (now Mrs. Daniel J. Burton) was engaged as secretary and editorial assistant, photoduplicates of the relevant files in the Adams Papers were produced, and work on the *Legal Papers of John Adams* began in earnest in July 1962.

Figuratively, and in some respects almost literally, what the editors have carried out in the volumes now presented is an extended piece of archeological reconstruction, as imaginative in its controlling principles as it is meticulous in its scholarly details. The work could hardly have been done at all without the existence of the incomparable archives of early Massachusetts courts in the custody of the Clerk of the Supreme Judicial Court for Suffolk County in Boston. Consisting of minute books and written-up records for the highest court in all counties and of file papers for over 175,000 cases before 1800, these have been described in more detail by the editors in their Introduction. What the editors have not described is the laborious process by which every case documented even fragmentarily in the Adams Papers

---

* In the general plan of *The Adams Papers*, the present volumes, though complete in themselves, are to be considered as a supplement to the as yet unpublished *Papers of John Adams*, that is, to Part 1 of Series III, the *General Correspondence and Other Papers* of the three Adams statesmen. For the general plan of publication, necessarily though regrettably complex, see the Introduction to the *Diary and Autobiography of John Adams*, 1:xxxvii–xli. Since work is going on concurrently on several different and more or less completely independent series and parts of the edition, there can and will be no continuous volume numbering throughout *The Adams Papers*. All scholarly references to *The Adams Papers* should therefore be to the title and volume of the particular unit concerned—in this case, of course, to the *Legal Papers of John Adams*.

has been checked against the court files for its date and history and for other papers bearing on the case. The yields of information and additional documentation have been tremendous and have led on to other judicial archives and to collections of personal papers in Massachusetts and elsewhere. A large portion of the findings is now laid before the reader. Adams' condensed, cryptic, and sometimes half-legible jottings are here dated, put in context, and frequently amplified by related documents that help tell the story; and the legal and historical significance of each case has been searchingly appraised. Moreover, the technical language of an old and conservative profession—what Adams called the "lignum Vitæ words" of the law—has been explained so that laymen can understand what is going on, and the reports and statutes have been cited and quoted so that readers who care to can follow the judicial process into its last refinements. In short, the editors have brought John Adams the lawyer alive and have enabled us to watch him at work. Clearly no other method than this "documentary reconstruction" (to borrow a phrase used by Professor Goebel in his work on Alexander Hamilton's law practice) could accomplish this end so well.

One or two limitations must be mentioned. It has already been said that the materials now printed are only a selection from those extant. The editors have explained their principles of selection but would plainly admit that they have omitted some cases as worthy of editorial attention and publication as some that they have included. (*All* of those surviving in John Adams' files are available in the microfilm edition of the Adams Papers, but they are very partially and defectively identified and arranged there.) It should be added that the selection has been made within narrow bounds. Aside from the initial notes on Adams' early legal studies and his book of pleading forms, all the documents relate to actual cases or court actions. Deliberately excluded are whole classes of Adams' writing that have a different sort of legal interest, for example his papers as a town officer and as a legislator, his instructions written for the towns of Braintree and Boston to their members in the General Court, his argument against crown salaries for judges, and his numerous published and unpublished writings on constitutional issues during the ten-year public debate that preceded the Revolution. Although these have been touched on in the editors' Introduction and been drawn on in their commentary when relevant, the writings themselves have been left for presentation among Adams' papers as a statesman, which will include as well his principal contribution to public law, the Massachusetts Constitution of 1780, and his later writings on constitutional and international law. Chronologically the *Legal Papers* end with Adams' last case at the bar, the initial stage of *Penhallow v. The Lusanna* (No. 58 in these volumes) in the New Hampshire Court Maritime in December 1777. In his Autobiography Adams recalled that it was while he was speaking in that court that "Mr. Langdon came in from Phyladelphia and leaning over the bar whispered to me, that Mr. Deane was recalled [as a member of the American Commission in Paris], and I was appointed to go to France." More than two decades of continuous and all-absorbing public service followed. Upon being retired from the Presidency in 1801, Adams considered the possibility of resuming his practice or at least taking in some students to read law, but he apparently never returned to the courtroom after sailing to France in February 1778.

The papers here assembled richly reveal the life and mind of John Adams the attorney and barrister, the life of the law in his time and place, and life in New England on the eve of the Revolution. To the first two of these topics the editors have addressed themselves systematically in their general Introduction, and to the second, of course, throughout the volumes. But on the third—Adams' legal papers as materials for social history—a nonlegal historian may be permitted to enlarge a little.

The concerns of litigants in the 1760's and 1770's were, as at any other time, representative of the concerns of their contemporaries generally. But people in court talk more, or at least talk more earnestly, and they are obliged to answer questions regarding matters that vitally affect their interests. They have to *explain* things that in other situations, say in writing a letter to a friend or a relative, can be assumed and therefore do not have to be explained. Just *why* and *how* did a dispute arise over a piece of property, an unpaid loan, a mill shut down for lack of water, a meadow flooded by too much water, a sailor's right to defend himself against impressment, a printer's right not to divulge the authorship of an offending article, a Negro man or woman's rights in colonial Massachusetts, a protested tax for the support of the town minister, the eligibility of a voter in a town meeting debating a heated issue, the right to dig clams on a tidal flat, the support of an errant wife, an illegitimate child, or a destitute family? It is the fullness of detail with which the relevant circumstances must be set forth on both sides of an argument that gives court testimony its peculiar value as a transcript of life in a given place and time.

The cases in the *Legal Papers of John Adams* touch on almost every concern that 18th-century New Englanders had. The very first group of interrelated cases here printed documents a quarrel over an indentured boy among members of the great Mayhew clan of Martha's Vineyard, all of them bearing Old Testament names and many of them behaving according to the ancient code of an eye for an eye. In one of the trials Thomas Daggett, a member of the posse that had gone to serve a warrant on a particularly Amazonian Mayhew female, testified that during the melee that followed, "Bethiah said I shall go into a fit." Bassett, the deputy sheriff, then "let her go." Whereupon, "She struck him." Feelings ran so high in this complex of suits and countersuits, John Adams said, that it was literally "impossible for human Sagacity to discover on which Side Justice lay." And no wonder.

Respecting the next case, *King v. Stewart* (No. 2), we have hitherto had only a tantalizing reference in a letter John Adams wrote to his wife in 1774, on the very eve of his departure for the first Continental Congress, when traveling the "eastern circuit" for the last time. His letter expressed his detestation of "private Mobs" and described how a riffraff of merchant Richard King's disgruntled neighbors in Scarborough, Maine, "broke into his House and rifled his Papers, and terryfed him, his wife [who was well along in pregnancy], Children and Servants in the Night." Adams, who was counsel for King, called it "a famous Cause," and it was certainly a protracted one since the mobbing had occurred eight years earlier during the Stamp Act troubles. It has, however, never been documented, or more than passingly mentioned in print, until now. The materials for doing so existed, notably in the New-York Historical Society among the papers of Senator Rufus King (son of the plaintiff), where an extensive file on the elder King's efforts "to bring the Parpitrators to Justice" reposes; in the Adams Papers, which contain Adams' emotional plea to the jury fully written out; and, for the progress of the case through the courts, in the judicial archives in the Suffolk County Courthouse. These have now at length been brought together to tell a dramatic and revealing tale of rural New England.

The name of the Province in which John Adams grew up and practiced law was Massachusetts Bay, and fittingly, since the sea furnished not only a great part of the colonists' livelihood but also of their diet. And since 18th-century Boston was virtually an island, almost all of its inhabitants were in some sense seafarers. The earliest court action of historical importance in which Adams was concerned, and hence the earliest included in these volumes (*Petition of Lechmere*, No. 44), was the argument before the Superior Court of Judicature in February 1761 over the legality of writs of assistance—instruments sought by customs officials to facilitate searches for goods smuggled in by water. The celebrated case of *Sewall v. Hancock* (No. 46) over John Hancock's sloop *Liberty* also involved smuggling and, as argued by Adams in defending Hancock, raised grave constitutional issues. Two of Adams' most spectacular cases, both of which were tried in special admiralty courts and in both of which he saved his clients from hanging, were on charges of murder at sea. Concerning Michael Corbet's killing of Lieutenant Henry Panton of the Royal Navy—the latter a man of such nonchalant elegance that one would suppose him more at home in Pall Mall than off Marblehead—we know every last detail because every man jack aboard the *Pitt Packet* seems to have testified except the dead man, who had bled to death from a harpoon driven into his neck (*Rex v. Corbet*, No. 56). In the other murder case Adams himself was never able to determine the innocence or guilt of his client Nickerson, the only survivor of a peculiarly "misterious, inexplicable Affair" (*Rex v. Nickerson*, No. 57); nor shall we. But the colorful documentation for both cases prompts the observation that there are materials among Adams' legal papers that writers of historical fiction, as well as historians, have overlooked. Another example is "the Case of the Whale" (*Doane v. Gage*, No. 43), in which more than seventy witnesses furnish in their own tarry language a superlatively vivid picture of life among the whalers of the North Atlantic and a virtual textbook of whaling practices and customs. The documents prove Melville right in representing whalers as generally talkative and contentious. But not even Melville has drawn a more engagingly eccentric character than the crew member whose credibility was questioned because he had a habit of jumping into the sea with his clothes on and kept a journal which he boasted was better than the captain's.

We know from John Adams' letters and Diary that he had a special talent for rendering dialogue, and the talk of the witnesses as he recorded it in his minutes of court actions is endlessly fascinating. It is the genuine, not invented, talk of his unsophisticated neighbors. Of old Mr. Clap of Scituate, whose peculiar will full of blank pages was being contested, a defense witness rejoicing in the name of Bezaliel Curtis remarked: "He said Will [Clap's eldest son, who had been cut off in the will] had wronged him, and had Creatures [i.e. had taken or borrowed some of his father's stock or "critters"] and not returned 'em" (*Clap's Will*, No. 15). In the bastardy case of *Gage v. Headley* (No. 29), poor, confused Lydia Gage of Lincoln is a classic type of the country girl in the worst trouble she could possibly get into; in the harsher language of the day she was "a common Strum." It was agreed by all that her child was "got soon after the Trooping at Sudbury." (The clergy were always pointing out that muster days, like elections, encouraged sinfulness.) But the question was, Who was the father? Witnesses said that from time to time during her pregnancy Lydia had mentioned various candidates. "Twas a transient Person, and [Simeon] Hagar, and Pucker, a poor Toad." But some said that this was because the real offender had both bribed and threatened her to stop her from telling the truth. For example, Sufferana Hagar (could her name have been a Yankee version of Sophronia?) testified that the suspect Josiah Headley "said he would take his gun and shoot her. But I did not think, he intended to shoot deeper than some People think he had done." To establish paternity, and thus assure support for the child, the law required, among other things, that the woman accuse the man during her actual travail. Fortunately Lydia (or humanity) had a friend in Deacon Humphry Farrar, who appeared as her first witness in court and declared that "At the Groaning I heard her say that it was Josiah Headleys of Weston the Miller and Tavernkeeper." Since the records of the Middlesex Court of General Sessions have been lost, we do not know how this case came out. The Lincoln town records show that five years later the child, named Josiah "doubtless in honor of the putative father," was living in Deacon Farrar's family. This may mean any one of several things that the reader's imagination will have to supply.

For the student of language, as well as of manners, education, religion, economics, or any other facet of colonial life, the documents furnish some agreeable finds and occasional puzzles. Here are "Pampousies," probably to be equated with "pampouties," a kind of slippers from the East Indies, and "Catalaber," more or less recognizable as an early form of "cantilever," a timber bracket under a projecting roof. But sound and context alone will have to supply the meaning of a few words so far not found in any general or specialized dictionary. "Hiddalo," found in the case of *Rex v. Richardson* (No. 59) in a context suggesting uproar and confusion, may be etymologically related to our "hubbub" or "hullabaloo." "Scurlogging," the first word in Adams' minutes of the trial of Richard King's persecutors, apparently means a mobbing or a "roughing up" of some hapless victim by his neighbors. The phenomenon, if not the word itself, is no doubt related to the English "skimmington-ride," found elsewhere in Adams' legal papers and well known from Hardy's description of such a rural incident in *The Mayor of Casterbridge.*

These are mere incidental notes that could be continued indefinitely. Every document throws at least a pinpoint of light on the way people in Massachusetts Bay felt, thought, spoke, and acted two centuries ago; and some of them throw strong and steady beams of light on matters we needed to know more about. The capital example is the assemblage of material in the third volume documenting the two major trials (*Rex v. Preston, Rex v. Wemms,* Nos. 63, 64) that grew out of the mobbing and killing in King Street (present State Street), Boston, on the night of 5 March 1770.

It is astonishing, but true, that despite all the words and ink spent on the subject, no comprehensive and reliable account of the Boston Massacre and its sequels has hitherto been written. The reasons are twofold. For a long time after the Massacre occurred, few if any people would have found a reliable, that is to say an impartial, account acceptable. That the British soldiers had committed bloody butchery in King Street was one of the pieties most firmly fixed in the American mind. But as the piety faded and history began to replace propaganda and folklore, such new documentation as appeared was defectively presented and much more of the essential documentation had dropped from sight. In these circumstances the present editors very properly determined to furnish the fullest possible record of the two Massacre trials in which John Adams was concerned. They have included, in text or notes, not only the transcript of the second trial (that of the soldiers), which was contemporaneously printed and has therefore been the main reliance of historians, but also a substantial but hitherto unpublished summary of the defense evidence in the first trial (that of Captain Preston), for which no transcript of the court proceedings exists. In addition, here are notes, in large part published for the first time, of most of the lawyers who participated in the trials, on their own witnesses and arguments and on those of the other counsel. Taken all together these constitute a body of documentation that is uniquely thick-textured and that brings us as fully and continuously into the courtroom of 1770 as 20th-century readers can ever hope to be.

About 120 witnesses furnished evidence in the Preston and Wemms trials. Their testimony and the half-dozen lawyers' arguments based on it present a morbid anatomy of a town torn and harried by political strife and military occupation. Everyone of course wanted to tell his own story of the fatal night, but the very profusion of evidence makes the truth hard, perhaps impossible, to isolate. What *is* truth in such circumstances? No surviving participant or witness could tell more than a fraction of what actually happened when the townspeople and soldiers shouted, shoved, tussled, slipped, and slid on the ice and snow around the gutter that ran in front of the Custom House. But here, at any rate, is what every available witness *thought* happened, and from this abundant and conflicting evidence readers must reconstruct the events of the night and assign responsibility for them as best they can.

More important, of course, than who did precisely what, is the question of how well the leaders of the community managed to bridle their emotions and to put their minds on the administration of justice, or on what the editors call "the control of vengeance." Did anyone, in fact, really want impartial justice done? John Adams' testimony on this question is disappointingly meager and cryptic and merely contributes to the mysteries concerning the Massacre and the trials that will probably remain forever unsolved. He put down few of his private thoughts during 1770, and his reflections afterward were pervaded by a self-pity that hardly seems warranted. The known facts do not suggest that either he or Josiah Quincy lost status or suffered reprisals for their part in defending Preston and his troops. That there were threats of mob action and attempts to pack the juries is true, and it is also true that one of the judges wrote in a highly unjudicial way about "the Dishonour of the Inhabitants" while the first trial was in progress. Yet persons of both persuasions who attended that trial remarked on the "order and decorum" of the proceedings and spectators. And from a source highly placed and not likely to be prejudiced in favor of "the Inhabitants," came a clear assertion soon after the trials were over that justice had been done in spite of the inflamed state of the community. In announcing the result to an English friend, Lieutenant Governor Hutchinson said: "There certainly is a stock of Virtue in the Country though sometimes overborne by the Violent Efforts of some as bad men perhaps as any upon the Globe." However strongly feelings ran in Massachusetts Bay in 1770, they did not in this critical instance overrun the processes of law. This cannot be said of certain later and similar incidents in our history, some of them shamefully recent and even current. But if it can be said of the Boston Massacre, it restores that sad and somewhat squalid affair, considered in its larger implications, to rank among events in which Americans may take pride.

L. H. BUTTERFIELD
Editor in Chief

Introduction

John Adams was before anything else a practicing lawyer—a man of the office, the library, and the courts. Future legal historians and biographers must describe in comprehensive detail the legal system of pre-Revolutionary Massachusetts in which he studied and practiced, and the extent to which his legal training and the habits thereby developed influenced his later public service. The *Legal Papers of John Adams* is intended to furnish some of the raw material for such comprehensive studies. This Introduction seeks only to help the reader find his way into the context of 18th-century Massachusetts practice and to describe briefly Adams' legal career.

I. SOURCES FOR THIS EDITION

The Adams Legal Papers

If the effect of Adams' legal career upon his public life is still unknown, its impact upon the corpus of the Adams Papers is obvious and substantial. Adams, being a lawyer, constantly minuted and noted every variety of legal experience, from careful abstracts of reported opinions to barely legible jottings of courtroom testimony. And being an Adams, he rarely discarded any bit of writing, a trait multiplied in his descendants. The result is an accumulation of loose papers, notebooks, dockets, and miscellany that is impressive in bulk but that had remained largely unexplored until work began on the Adams Papers editorial enterprise. In arranging the family archives as a whole, the editors of the Adams Papers physically segregated these materials so far as they feasibly could. They now form a segment of the John Adams Miscellany that appears in the microfilm edition of the Adams Papers as Reels 182–186.[1] In this Introduction they are designated as the Adams Legal Papers or simply as the Legal Papers.

---

[1] In Part III of Microfilms of The Adams Papers, published by the Massachusetts Historical Society, 1954–1959, available in many libraries. Location references for materials in the Adams Papers in the present letterpress edition are normally to the microfilm edition by reel number, except for letters and documents that can readily be found by date alone, in Part IV, Letters Received and Other Loose Papers, arranged chronologically.

The order, if any, in which Adams retained his papers has not survived. Such rationality as exists in the papers resulted from Adams' not always uniform habit of recording all his courtroom minutes for any given term of court in a single booklet or leaflet of eight leaves, each leaf approximately six inches by four inches. We believe Adams made these booklets up himself as the occasion required, folding them out of a single sheet of paper, and then cutting the folds and pinning or stitching them together, if necessary. The evidence for this surmise is slender: the appearance from time to time in the Legal Papers of a leaflet with uncut pages, the writing on some pages upside down.

A combination of court materials and summaries, all relating to matters before the Court of Vice Admiralty and the Special Court of Admiralty for the Trial of Piracies, occupies a slightly larger notebook called in this edition the "Admiralty Book." It is not clear whether Adams kept these materials together by choice, as he happened to inscribe them, or whether he collected the documents and reports of his Admiralty cases at some time after the litigation. There are indications that he hoped to publish at least some of this material as a political attack on the Vice Admiralty Court.

Many of the documents in the Legal Papers are not courtroom minutes. Careful lawyer that he was, Adams frequently looked into troublesome points of law prior to the trial or hearing at which they were expected to arise. The written results of this research, which in this edition are called *notes* (as distinguished from courtroom *minutes*),[2] were usually inscribed on unfolded sheets of paper, in a much less hurried hand.

Besides the case-centered materials, the Legal Papers contain a group of office records. First, bound into two books, each about six inches by four inches, are long docket lists—lists of cases, term by court term, written in a clerk's neat hand, interspersed with Adams' notations: "to be demurred," "agreed," and so on. Second are various dockets and memoranda in Adams' hand; these are either lists of his cases to be heard at a particular session of court, or the documentary remains of his accounting system. Finally, there are fragmentary bills and accounts with sheriffs, clerks of courts, and clients.

At the start of his career, Adams kept notes of worthwhile points

[2] Robert Treat Paine's court jottings, already titled by Paine himself or by one of his descendants (see p. xxxv below), and William Wetmore's accounts of trial matters, which do not appear to have been courtroom-written (see p. xxxv below), have been given the collective titles of Paine Law Notes, Paine Massacre Notes, and Wetmore Notes. The distinction between "notes" and "minutes" has been preserved in the description of individual documents from these sources, however.

in a commonplace book; later he maintained a collection of noteworthy pleadings. Both of these remain in the Legal Papers; both have been printed in the present edition.

Court Papers

The largest source of information about John Adams' legal career exists strangely enough, not in the Legal Papers themselves, but in that legal and historical treasure which, largely unexplored by lawyers and historians alike, rests in the office of the Clerk of the Massachusetts Supreme Judicial Court for Suffolk County, Pemberton Square, Boston. Here are record books, minute books, and file papers covering, with varying degrees of completeness, the entire period from 1629 to 1800. Over 300,000 documents have been serially numbered and neatly tipped into bound folio volumes (1289 of them). Finding, preserving, and organizing this unique documentary source was largely the work of one man, John Noble, Clerk of the Supreme Judicial Court from 1875 to 1908.[3] The entire collection has been titled "Suffolk Files" in this edition.

The documentation covering the period of Adams' full-time legal practice, that is from 1758 to 1774, can be divided roughly into three groups: records, minute books, and file papers. The *Records* are folio volumes containing the "record"—the formal, official statement of the proceedings and the court's action—in each case. Substantially all the records of the Superior Court of Judicature for the period 1692–1776 are preserved in the Suffolk Files. The records for all terms of court in one calendar year are typically bound into a single volume (sometimes two or more years in a volume), where they are indexed roughly alphabetically. Nothing but fragments of the Inferior Court Records from Adams' time have survived; but from surviving records preceding and following his era, it appears that they were maintained exactly as were the Superior Court Records.[4]

Minute Books were quarto waste books maintained on a county-by-county basis. Typically, the clerks, prior to the commencement of

---

[3] Noble himself told the story in two authoritative articles: "The Early Court Files of Suffolk County," 3 Col. Soc. Mass., *Pubns.* 317 (1900); "The Records and Files of the Superior Court of Judicature, and of the Supreme Judicial Court, Their History and Places of Deposit," 5 Col. Soc. Mass., *Pubns.* 5 (1902).

[4] The Records of the Court of Vice Admiralty from 1718 to 1733, as well as its Minute Book for 1765–1772 and other papers; the Records and files of the Governor and Council sitting in Divorce, for 1760 to 1786; and the Records of the Supreme Court of Probate from 1760 to 1830 are also in the office of the Clerk of the Supreme Judicial Court for Suffolk County, as are the minute books of the Court of General Sessions of the Peace for Suffolk County.

any given term, wrote down in consecutive order, with space between each case, the names of all the civil actions pending at that term, the continued cases first, followed by the new entries. These were then numbered in two individual series. Criminal matters (not numbered) were also listed; although there appears to have been no firm practice as to the position of the criminal cases within the minute-book notations for any given term of court, they are generally found at or near the end of the term. The typical civil minute-book entry shows the full names of the parties, with each one's lawyers listed beneath his name. The name of the lawyer "entering" the case appears in the left margin; the disposition of the case at that term of court is noted in the space below the attorneys' names. It is impossible to tell from a minute-book entry just what a civil case is about. In criminal matters, by contrast, the entire indictment is usually set out, as well as the names of the jurors.

Many of the minute books for the Inferior Court, which had been missing and presumed lost, were located while the present edition was in preparation by Burnell Hersey, Esq., in the vault beneath the Old Court House Building, Pemberton Square, Boston, in the custody of the Clerk of the present Superior Court for Civil Business. The form of these books is generally similar to that used in the Superior Court except that continued and new cases are numbered in one sequence.

The *File Papers* of a given case are those documents which were figuratively, and, in matters which actually went to trial, literally, before the court. With respect to the period of Adams' practice, there are virtually complete files for those cases which came before the Superior Court, not only for Suffolk County, but for the other counties as well. The Suffolk Files contain skimpy documentation for the Suffolk Inferior Court for this period, but Mr. Hersey also discovered a substantial collection of Inferior Court file papers; it is to be hoped that these will soon receive the same careful preservation which has been bestowed on the rest of the documents.[5]

Other Manuscript Sources

In addition to documentary sources individually recognized in appropriate footnotes, the editors have drawn on the following:

Cushing Reports, a collection in the Harvard Law School Library

[5] There are also Inferior Court papers in the offices of the respective Clerks of Courts, Middlesex, Plymouth, Barnstable, and Worcester counties, Massachusetts, and York, Cumberland, and Lincoln counties, Maine. Hopefully, time and funds will some day be available to permit a thorough cataloguing and (where necessary) preservation of these untapped sources.

of copies of notes in a hand which has not been identified, originally compiled by Judge William Cushing. Some of the cases covered have been printed in the present edition. The entire collection is being edited for publication by John D. Cushing of the Massachusetts Historical Society.

The *Wetmore Notes*, a collection in four volumes, of Essex County cases in the hand of William Wetmore (1749–1830), Harvard 1770, pupil and later son-in-law of the Salem lawyer, William Pynchon, whose jottings were apparently the source of many of the collected cases. (The editors are particularly indebted to L. H. Butterfield for identification of this source, the manuscript of which bears no author's name and which, by circumstances obscure and unexplained, found its way into the Adams Legal Papers.)

The *Robert Treat Paine Papers* in the Massachusetts Historical Society, containing a bound collection of Paine's own almost indecipherable courtroom minutes.[6]

The *Adams Papers*, the chronologically arranged general correspondence and other materials beyond those segregated as John Adams' Legal Papers.

Documents in the *Public Record Office*, London, primarily from the Treasury and Colonial Office Papers, available in photostat form in the British Reproductions Collection of the Library of Congress, Manuscript Division.

National Archives microcopies of three important files of public records in that repository: the Papers of the Continental Congress, the records of the Court of Appeals in Cases of Capture, and the Appellate Case Files of the Supreme Court of the United States.

2. THE EDITORIAL METHOD

The plan of these volumes is topical. With the exception of the first two sections, which deal with law study and pleading, the materials published have been grouped under the time-honored divisions of the law—torts, contracts, property, and the rest. The headings chosen are very broad. For example, the section labeled "Property" treats numerous variants of the topic, including real estate, probate matters, and water rights. Many cases, of course, defy categorization; the ultimate location depends on what seemed to be the dominant theme. Each of the eighteen topics has been given a different alphabetical designation.

Since the Adams Legal Papers are primarily case-oriented, the

[6] For a fuller description, see Vol. 3:42–43 below.

documents published under each topical subdivision (again excepting the first two topics) have been grouped into sixty-four numbered principal cases. Within each topic the cases are usually in chronological order according to the date on which the litigation commenced.[7] The dates affixed to each case represent the inclusive dates for the litigation—the years of commencement and final disposition. As an aid in relating each case to the general pattern of Adams' practice and career, the editors have prepared a Chronology in which the numbered cases published in this edition are placed, with other cases and biographical information, in order by date.

Each principal case consists of one or more separate documents, numbered with Roman numerals if more than one document appears in a case. The editors have supplied every document with a brief title and have attributed to it a court (if appropriate) and date.

Two editorial aids accompany the documents published: introductory essays (labeled "Editorial Notes") and footnotes.

The editorial notes have been used flexibly to suit the nature of the materials covered. For example, before topics of great length or complexity the editors have summed up the historical and legal background, and the broader issues involved, in a topical editorial note. If the cases within a topic can be more effectively discussed in a single essay, this note covers all of them. In most instances, however, each case bears an individual editorial note discussing the facts of the case and problems peculiar to it. Where two cases are closely linked factually they may be covered in a single editorial note.

The footnotes are designed to permit the reader to follow the pattern of each trial or argument as closely as possible. All cases, statutes, and legal treatises cited in the documents published have been identified if possible, and relevant portions of the cited material have been quoted or summarized. Matters of historical interest not covered in the editorial notes have also been dealt with in footnotes to the documents. Finally, the documentary footnotes include editorial information necessary for full understanding of textual problems. In an effort to eliminate at least a few footnotes, the editors have supplied a Register of Bench and Bar containing biographical data on the leading lawyers and judges mentioned in these volumes.

In the editorial notes and annotation the editors have tried to explain enough of the law so that a layman could understand what he

---

[7] In order to permit inclusion of the Boston Massacre materials, Nos. 63, 64, in a single volume, cases in the "Criminal Law" section are presented out of chronological order.

was reading; but this is, after all, a casebook, and explication of every legalism would have bored the legal reader and crowded out more essential information. Non-lawyers may find some of their occasional discomfort dispelled by resort to a good legal dictionary.

The editors have followed the general textual policy laid down for *The Adams Papers* as a whole.[8] (The reader should particularly note the arbitrary italicization of speakers' names, whether lawyers, witnesses, or judges.) The editors have not attempted to regularize Adams' quotations, but have indicated in footnotes, or by bracketed insertions, major errors or omissions. It may be assumed that italics in a document printed, or in a quotation in editorial matter, reflect the existence of italics in the source, unless otherwise indicated.

The only major departure from usual Adams Papers form has been in the citations. Since so much of the material cited is legal in nature, the editors decided to render virtually all citations in the basic legal form—volume number preceding the name of the author or work and page numbers following, without punctuation or abbreviation for the word "page." The basic guide to citation form has been the Harvard Law Review's *Uniform System of Citation* (the "Blue Book"),[9] with certain variations to permit the adding of supplementary bibliographical information. Full details of the system as modified appear at the beginning of the "short title" list in the Guide to Editorial Apparatus which follows this Introduction. For cross references to materials in other principal cases in the present volumes, the number assigned to each case has been used. Unless the title of the case is material to the sense of the passage in which it appears, the form is simply "No. 2," with any appropriate cross-referenced document or footnote number added.

Unlike diary entries and letters, which are usually dated, many of the Legal Papers bear no date; those which do are usually docketed only to the term of court (i.e. the place, month, and year). Exact dating of the documents here printed has therefore often proved impossible, but an attempt has been made throughout to supply, in the italicized line following the caption of each document, the actual or approximate date of the document, together with the name of the court which was at this stage hearing the case in question. When this information is conjectural, the editors have justified the assigned date in the annotation.

Occasionally, Adams' habit of taking down his courtroom minutes

---

[8] 1 JA, *Diary and Autobiography* lv–lix; 1 *Adams Family Correspondence* xliii–xlv.

[9] *A Uniform System of Citation* (Cambridge, 10th edn., 1958).

on anything handy has rendered the dating of the given document nothing more than an educated guess, based on Court Record, Minute Book, or some such extraneous source as the Robert Treat Paine Papers. Notes of legal authorities, which could have been made any time before disposition of the case, have arbitrarily been attributed to the term of court at which the disposition actually occurred—or to the term in which it seemed most likely that the authorities were used.

The diffuse nature and great volume of the materials in the Adams Legal Papers and other sources have raised problems of selection rare in the editing of the diaries and correspondence published in Series I and II of *The Adams Papers*. Because it would have been possible fairly to justify the inclusion or omission of any case in the Legal Papers or any Adams case in the various court files, the editors—happily aware of their total vulnerability—have relied on several criteria with approximately equal emphasis: (1) Did the case in question illuminate a particular legal point? (2) Did it contain an unusual document? (3) Did it (when considered with other cases) give balance to the general picture of Adams' practice? (4) Was it interesting, historically or socially, if not legally? (5) Was there any real reason for not including it?

Once a case was selected for inclusion, two basic principles applied: (1) Any Adams document would be printed, except for such trivial or formal items as bills of costs or stereotyped pleadings—"Adams document" being defined as any paper (a) in John Adams' hand, (b) about John Adams, or (c) found in the corpus of the Legal Papers. (2) Any other document would be printed if it: (a) explained or illuminated the case, or (b) was interesting for any other reason and was not cumulative of other material.

3. PRACTICE AND PROCEDURE

The Courts of Provincial Massachusetts

It is a commentary, either on Adams' time or our own, that the court system in which he practiced was as jurisdictionally differentiated as the Massachusetts judicial system of today. The discussion which follows is not and cannot be definitive. Only enough detail has been included to permit an intelligent appreciation of the juridical framework of Adams' practice. A thorough treatment of the court system must, like so much other work on this subject, await the documentary exhumation of which the present edition is only a spadeful.

At the bottom of the judicial pyramid came the individual courts of the justices of the peace. Appointed on a county-by-county basis, these justices held one-man courts with civil jurisdiction over "debts, trespasses, and other matters" involving controversies of under forty shillings (and not involving title to land); appeal lay to the Inferior Court.[10] On the criminal side, the justices could hear complaints of breaches of the peace, violation of the Sabbath laws, and other minor offenses. A justice could impose a fine of up to twenty shillings, and could sentence a convicted prisoner to imprisonment up to twenty-four hours, to the stocks, or to be whipped.[11] Appeals in criminal cases lay to the Court of General Sessions of the Peace.[12]

All the justices of the peace in each county were, in accordance with English practice, named and appointed in a single commission, which authorized all of them, jointly or severally, to keep the peace. The justices of each county, sitting together, jointly comprised the next rung of the judicial ladder, the Court of General Sessions of the Peace. One such court sat quarterly in each county, concurrently with the Inferior Court of Common Pleas for the county.[13] It heard appeals in criminal matters from the courts of the individual justices of the peace, with the appeal apparently entailing a new trial, by jury.[14] And appeals lay from the Sessions to the Superior Court of Judicature.[15]

---

[10] Act of 18 June 1697, 1 A&R 282.

[11] Act of 1 Nov. 1692, 1 A&R 51–55; Act of 22 Oct. 1692, 1 A&R 58–59; Act of 14 July 1693, 1 A&R 122–123. For a full summary, see Joseph H. Smith, ed., *Colonial Justice in Western Massachusetts (1639–1702)* 82–88 (Cambridge, Mass., 1961).

[12] Act of 16 June 1699, 1 A&R 367, 368.

[13] Act of 16 June 1699, 1 A&R 367. See 5 *Province and Court Records of Maine* xii–xvi (Portland, Maine, ed. Neal W. Allen Jr., 1964). The commission of the peace for each county provided that the Court of General Sessions was to be held by three or more justices, including at least one from a specially designated list. Those specially designated were known as "justices of the quorum" from the language of the traditional Latin form of the commission used in England, which may be translated, "Of whom [quorum] we wish some one of you, A, B, C, D, &c., to be one." See, for example, 4 *id.* at 21–23, 245–246. By the 18th century in England, it had become customary to name virtually all the justices in the commission as of the quorum. See 1 Blackstone, *Commentaries* *351; 1 Holdsworth, *History of English Law* 290. In Massachusetts, however, only a small proportion of those commissioned were of the quorum. See, for example, Whitmore, *Mass. Civil List* 130–131. It was also customary in Massachusetts for certain leading civil officers to be appointed justices of the peace with powers running throughout the Province. This was accomplished by naming them in the commission of the peace for each county. See Book of Commissions, Proclamations, Pardons, &c., 1756–1767, fols. 264–285, M–Ar.

[14] Act of 16 June 1699, 1 A&R 367, 368. The Inferior Court and the Sessions drew jurors from a common venire. Act of 23 April 1742, 2 A&R 1090 (and extended — see Act of 22 April 1749, 3 A&R 447; Act of 26 April 1770, 5 A&R 39).

[15] Act of 16 June 1699, 1 A&R 367, 368. See also No. 24.

Administratively, the various Courts of General Sessions served their counties as regulatory agencies. An examination of the statutes and the available minute books and files shows that the Sessions supervised county finances; regulated highways; controlled the establishment of inns and liquor retailers; appointed a host of wine gaugers, sealers of leather, and the like; exercised a kind of pure-food jurisdiction; protected monopolies; supervised the operation of the poor laws; and even attended to the construction of public buildings. In the Suffolk Files, for example, are accounts and orders dealing with the construction of the new Suffolk County courthouse in the 1760's, richly illustrative, not only of the Sessions' administrative functions, but of the architectural practices of the time.[16]

Each county also had its own Inferior Court of Common Pleas, which sat quarterly, at one or more locations throughout the county. This court consisted of four judges, appointed by the governor and council, any three to be a quorum.[17] A statute provided that "all civil actions, other than such as are cognizeable before a justice of the peace, shall be originally heard and tryed in an inferiour court of common pleas, except in suits where the king is concerned which may be brought in any of his majesty's courts within this province at the pleasure of the prosecutor."[18] Writs ran throughout the province, but venue of most personal actions lay only in the plaintiff's or the defendant's home county.[19]

A dissatisfied litigant in the Inferior Court might appeal to the next term of the Superior Court where a trial *de novo* was held, with each party "allowed the benefit of any new and further plea and evidence."[20] Occasionally, the legislature would allow relief to a would-be appellant who had a justifiable reason for a late filing.[21]

The Inferior Court for each county had its own clerk, its own bar, and its own rules of practice. An interesting note from the Suffolk Files is a letter dated 10 September 1763 from Daniel Leonard to Ezekiel Goldthwait, the clerk of the court, requesting "an attested

[16] See Min. Bk., Suff. Sess. 1764–1766, *passim.* See generally, Nos. 24–30.
[17] Act of 15 June 1699, 1 A&R 369.
[18] Act of 3 June 1707, 1 A&R 459–460.
[19] Act of 15 June 1699, 1 A&R 369, 370; Act of 29 Dec. 1749, 3 A&R 481. The exceptions were trespass *vi et armis* and debts due by bond, which could be brought only in the county where the trespass had been committed or the bond had been given. Nonresidents could be sued in any county.
[20] Act of 12 June 1701, 1 A&R 464, 465–466. The appellant originally had to file written "reasons of his appeal," *ibid.*; but by JA's time this requirement had been abolished. Act of 18 Jan. 1742, 2 A&R 1086.
[21] For an excellent example, see Bicknell v. Draper, SF 84512. SCJ Rec. 1764–1765, fols. 304–306; Resolve of 23 Feb. 1763, c. 306, 17 A&R 360.

copy of the Rules of Court that were made at July Term for the Regulation of Practice."[22]

At the head of the judicial system came the Superior Court of Judicature, Court of Assize and General Gaol Delivery, a single court with five justices (any three of whom were a quorum) appointed, like all the other judges, by the governor "with the advice and consent of the Councill,"[23] sometimes from the bar, but frequently (and with notable success) from the laity. While the court in Adams' day leaned heavily for what might be called legal advice on a brilliant and learned former barrister, Edmund Trowbridge, it is also true that such non-lawyers as Peter Oliver and Thomas Hutchinson made, as far as one can tell from imperfect evidence, reasonably astute judges. Hutchinson, the Chief Justice from 1760 to 1769, diligently compensated for his lack of legal education by wide reading, common sense, and a cultivated ability to make the barristers do the legal spade-work for him. "I never presumed to call myself a Lawyer," he wrote after leaving the bench. "The most I could pretend to was when I heard the Law laid on both sides to judge which was right."[24]

It might be noted that, although special justices could be appointed by the Governor and Council to sit on specific cases where a justice might decline to act or disqualify himself,[25] the regular justices could and sometimes did hold other government positions. Hutchinson, for example, was simultaneously Chief Justice of the Superior Court, Lieutenant Governor of the province, Councilor, and Judge of Probate for Suffolk County.[26]

By statute, the Superior Court exercised jurisdiction over all actions, real, personal, or mixed, including pleas of the crown—in other words, common-law jurisdiction as full and ample as the jurisdiction the common-law courts in England "have or ought to have."[27] The court possessed original jurisdiction only over matters involving the crown.[28]

---

[22] SF 84623. The justices of the Inferior Courts, like those of the Superior Court, were statutorily authorized "to make necessary rules for the more orderly practising" in each court. Act of 12 June 1701, 1 A&R 464.

[23] Charter of 1691, 1 A&R 12.

[24] Hutchinson to John Sullivan, 29 March 1771, 27 Mass. Arch. 136. JA's comment on Oliver: "Our Judge Oliver is the best bred Gentleman of all the Judges, by far. There is something in every one of the others indecent and disagreable, at Times in Company—affected Witticisms, unpolished fleers, coarse Jests, and sometimes rough, rude Attacks, but these you dont see escape Judge Oliver." 2 JA, *Diary and Autobiography* 51.

[25] See SF 152575.

[26] See 3 JA, *Diary and Autobiography* 275.

[27] Act of 26 June 1699, 1 A&R 370.

[28] See text at note 18 above.

Under its appellate jurisdiction, the appellant could claim an entire new trial in the Superior Court.[29] The loser in an appeal, if his purse allowed, and provided he had not already lost in the Inferior Court, was entitled to bring an action of review in the Superior Court, which afforded still another opportunity for a new trial.[30] The Province Charter also permitted an appeal to the Privy Council "in any Personall Accion" where the amount in controversy exceeded £300. But the word "Personall" appears to have been construed, in England at least, to include real actions, as well.[31]

An appeal also lay to the Superior Court from the Court of General Sessions in criminal matters. By means of the writ of certiorari, the Superior Court controlled the Sessions in administrative disputes as well,[32] and, like the common-law courts in England, regulated the exercise of what was considered common-law jurisdiction by non-common-law courts. Thus the Superior Court occasionally issued a prohibition to the Royal Court of Vice Admiralty to prevent the prosecution of an action properly cognizable only at common law.[33] Finally, the judges seem occasionally to have provided the Governor, on request, with advisory opinions of law.[34]

The Superior Court rode a statutorily established and frequently revised circuit of all the counties in the Province, including the "Eastern Counties" of York and Cumberland in what is now Maine. It had its own clerks and its own bar, which was not organized on a county-by-county basis, although certain lawyers, Joseph Hawley, for example, rarely practiced before the court except in their home counties. Cases arising within a county were tried at the court's sitting

[29] See text at note 20 above. This proceeding was technically an "appeal" as that term was used in the English civil-law courts, where evidence not heard below was admissible on review. By contrast, on writ of error, the usual form of review at common law in England, the reviewing court was limited to questions of law arising on the formal record, or set forth in a bill of exceptions. See Arthur Browne, *A Compendious View of the Civil Law,* 1:494–501 (N.Y., 1st Amer. edn., 1840); Sutton, *Personal Actions* 125–127, 136–144. The Massachusetts Superior Court occasionally allowed a writ of error in cases where the time for appeal had run. See, for example, Godfrey v. Macomber, Min. Bk. 82, SCJ Plymouth, May 1768; Min. Bk. 89, SCJ Suffolk, Aug. 1769, C–26; SF 101501.

[30] Act of 18 June 1701, 1 A&R 466; Act of 23 April 1754, 3 A&R 738.

[31] Charter of 1691, 1 A&R 15; see Opinion of the Lords of Trade to the King in Council, 10 Dec. 1696, 1 A&R 145 note: "in your Majesty's Charter to that Province there is no such exclusion," i.e. of appeals to the Privy Council in real actions. See Smith, *Appeals to the Privy Council* 76–77, 162–165.

[32] See, for example, Nos. 24, 27, 28.

[33] See Wroth, "The Massachusetts Vice Admiralty Court," in George A. Billias, ed., *Law and Authority in Colonial America: Selected Essays* (Barre, Mass., in press).

[34] See Governor Thomas Pownall's "Observations" on the Bankruptcy Act, dated 11 Oct. 1757 and printed in 4 A&R 110.

in that county, but points of law could be, and frequently were, argued at sittings in other counties.

Matters involving complicated factual issues or masses of evidence were frequently heard, under order of court, by specially appointed referees, usually three in number. The process was called "referring" a case, and the matter was said to be "under reference." After taking evidence, the referees would then "report" to the court, somewhat in the manner of a jury bringing in a special verdict, and the court would then usually "accept" the report and enter judgment thereon. The Basset-Mayhew-Allen litigation, No. 1, is an excellent example of a reference.[35]

In commercial matters, or cases turning on bookkeeping or business practices, the parties were sent to panels of merchants called auditors, whose function, apparently, was similar to that of referees, although it seems to have been generally limited to the ascertainment or "auditing" of figures, rather than the finding of facts generally or specially.[36]

Although no separate court of equity or chancery jurisdiction existed, equitable concepts were apparently known and applied. Thus one action at law refers to litigation by trustees of a testamentary trust, the *res* being land in Roxbury "given to the use of the free school in said Roxbury."[37] In the absence of a chancellor, the existing legal institutions were used to apply what might be considered equitable relief. So by statute, in suits on penal bonds, the court was empowered to "chancer" plaintiff's recovery down from the amount of the bond to the actual amount of his loss.[38] In one case, a petition was made to the General Court for relief from a mistake.[39]

The common-law jurisdiction of the justice courts and of the In-

[35] The Suffolk Files are full of orders of reference and referees' reports. The mode of selecting the referees is obscure, but one document dating from 1770 suggests that one party proposed a slate of names from which the other party chose the referees. See SF 101863c. And for a case from the same period indicating that the General Court could control mistakes by referees, see SF 139436. Perjury before referees was a criminal offense. See SF 152019, SF 152216, and SF 152255.

[36] For an auditors' report, see SF 27832. John Rowe served as an auditor frequently. See Rowe, *Letters and Diary, passim.* Arbitration, or an agreement by the parties to submit their difference to a panel of nonjudicial arbiters and to abide by its decision, was another dispute-resolving technique. See No. 10. Rendering a false account to arbitrators was apparently a criminal offense. See SF 157320. The Act of 22 March 1744, 3 A&R 132, authorized the summonsing of witnesses.

[37] SF 89970.

[38] A chancery court had been set up by the Act of 5 Dec. 1693, 1 A&R 144, which had been disallowed by the Privy Council. The only subsequent statutes treating equity jurisdiction dealt with chancering penalties and the equity of redemption. Act of 10 Dec. 1698, 1 A&R 356; Act of 3 July 1735, 2 A&R 755; Act of 3 July 1735, 2 A&R 762. See No. 13.

[39] See SF 137037.

ferior and Superior Courts was supplemented by other specialized tribunals. Wills and intestacies were regulated by Courts of Probate, one to a county, presided over by a single Judge of Probate aided by a Register (i.e. Clerk) of Probate. Probate and common-law jurisdictions crossed in one recurrent way. When the personalty of an estate (that is, everything but the real property) was insufficient to pay the legacies, the Superior Court, on motion and upon presentation of a certificate from the cognizant Judge of Probate, would make an order permitting sale of so much of the real estate as was necessary to pay the legacies. But control over the various county judges of probate lay in the Governor and Council, sitting as a Supreme Court of Probate, to whom appeals from the county courts lay.[40]

The Governor and Council likewise constituted the Province's divorce court, having in this instance sole jurisdiction.[41] Here, too, the Superior Court appears to have played a supplementary role, for a Minute Book of 1773 notes the filing of a petition by John Adams on behalf of Sarah Griffin "for Alimony." [42]

Last, although in some ways highest, on the list of tribunals before which Adams practiced was the Court of Vice Admiralty, which unlike the other courts depended for its authority directly on the Crown rather than on the Massachusetts legislature.[43] It was in this court, sitting without a jury, that the great revenue battles were fought, as well as the notable Case of the Whale.[44]

The Documents of a Law Suit

A discussion of the documents found in a typical Superior Court file will serve as an introduction to the basic pleading and practice in a civil action as well as to an understanding of the limitations of the Suffolk Files as a documentary source.

A file in the Superior Court of Judicature is comprised usually of two sorts of documents, copies of papers from the Inferior Court,

[40] Act of 1 Nov. 1692, 1 A&R 43, 45. See Nos. 14 and 15. See also Charter of 1691, 1 A&R 15.

[41] Act of 3 Nov. 1692, 1 A&R 61.

[42] Min. Bk. 98, SCJ Suffolk, Aug. 1773, N-74. The matter was continued to the next term, "that the adverse party may be cited." See the petition itself in SF 91716. The disposition has not been traced. Many of the papers in divorce cases have been preserved, as well as the Records of the Court of Divorce (i.e. the Governor and Council in that capacity). But the Records contain only those matters in which a divorce was granted. See Nos. 22 and 23.

[43] Charter of 1691, 1 A&R 19.

[44] See Nos. 43–55. A special Admiralty court was occasionally convened pursuant to statute for trial of cases of piracy and quasi-piracy. See Nos. 56 and 57.

and documents newly introduced in the Superior Court itself. A typical file contains various documents:

(1) The *writ* was the initial paper commencing the action in the Inferior Court, endorsed by the party or his attorney to guarantee payment of costs if the defendant prevailed. A copy was made for the Superior Court action, because it was not the practice to file a new writ for a Superior Court proceeding. The Inferior Court writ was a printed blank, strikingly similar to that used in Massachusetts today. It read in the form of a command from the sovereign to the sheriff of the county in question, directing him to summon the defendant to appear before a given session of the court "to answer unto" the plaintiff "in a plea of" whatever the form of action was. On the back of the writ the officer who had served the defendant made a "return," that is, indicated in a brief sentence that he had complied with the command. If the plaintiff requested it, the officer might either take the defendant bodily, or attach his goods.

(2) In the body of the writ, the plaintiff set forth his *declaration*, a formalized statement of the plaintiff's claim against the defendant. Most of the forms in Adams' Pleading Book, printed below, are declarations.

(3) Further *pleadings* were generally inscribed on convenient blank places on the writ's front or back, or, if elaborate, on a separate sheet. Although the purpose of pleadings in Massachusetts, as in other courts, English and American, was to arrive at an *issue* or triable point of difference between the parties, the science of pleading in Massachusetts never reached the heights of complexity which it attained in 18th-century England.[45]

In most cases the defendant interposed a *plea in bar*, denying the facts alleged by the plaintiff, or asserting new facts in justification, either ordinarily being sufficient to bring the case to an issue of fact for the jury, and therefore to close the pleading phase of the matter.

Occasionally a defendant who disputed the legal basis for the plaintiff's claim, although admitting the existence of the facts of the matter, would file a *demurrer*. By demurring, the defendant would in effect be saying: "Everything you allege is true, but as a matter of law you are not entitled to recover anything." At this point the dispute became a purely legal issue to be determined by the court alone, after argument by counsel. Another kind of legal question could be raised by a *plea in abatement*, which attacked the technical sufficiency of the writ without reference to the merits.

[45] See p. 27–30 below.

Ordinarily the pleadings in the Inferior Court bound the parties in the Superior Court. Occasionally, to avoid the cost of two trials, a defendant in an Inferior Court action would frame a patently frivolous "sham" demurrer. In an action for trespass to land, for example, with the declaration in an acceptable form, the defendant might demur on the grounds that the plaintiff had no cause of action. The plaintiff would thereupon pray judgment, which would be allowed by the court.

Under appropriate circumstances, plaintiffs, as well as defendants, could set up one of these apparently frivolous objections. Thus, in the hypothetical trespass-to-land case mentioned earlier, the defendant's answer might be in proper form, but the plaintiff would demur, alleging that the plea was "insufficient in law." Judgment would thereupon be rendered for the defendant.

In a variant of this procedure, the defendant, instead of demurring to the declaration, might answer legal gibberish. Thus, in the trespass case we have been considering, where the proper plea was "not guilty of the trespass in the form and manner as aforesaid," the defendant might answer "that he never made the contract," or even "that the defendant is an honest man." Plaintiff would thereupon demur to the plea, and would receive judgment. Generally the party demurring took the precaution of expressly reserving his right to waive the demurrer in the Superior Court and plead over. When the matter came up before the Superior Court, he would file a pleading sufficient properly to raise the triable issue.

(4) Whether the action in the Inferior Court went on to trial or came up on one of the forms of demurrer, the court entered judgment for the prevailing party. An appropriate notation, reciting the writ, the subsequent pleadings, and the judgment, was made in the *record*; a certified copy of the record entry pertaining to this action was included as part of the file sent up to the Superior Court.

(5) Ostensibly to prevent unmeritorious appeals, a statute required the losing party in the Inferior Court contemplating an appeal to post an *appeal bond*,[46] an undertaking to prosecute the appeal. The bond, signed by the party and two others, may usually be found in the Superior Court file. These obligations were apparently formal only, because the sureties almost invariably included the party's attorney, as well as other lawyers, and on occasion even one of the opposing counsel.

(6) Documents which had been put in evidence in the Inferior Court trial usually appeared in the Superior Court files, either in the

[46] Act of 3 March 1700, 1 A&R 446; Act of 12 June 1701, 1 A&R 465.

original or by certified copy. And, of course, new documentary evidence introduced in the Superior Court also remains in the files. None of the papers are "exhibits" in the modern sense; frequently they contain no indication that the court admitted them as evidence, although occasionally a paper may be endorsed or subscribed "for this court."

(7) Under a statute[47] *depositions* could be taken in civil causes under limited circumstances: if the deponent was aged or infirm; if he was bound to sea; or if he lived more than thirty miles from the place of trial. The Superior Court files frequently contain depositions from the Inferior Court proceedings, as well as depositions taken in connection with the Superior Court litigation. Sometimes a deposition will bear the notation "sworn in court," which suggests that, even when a witness was present at the trial, his previously taken deposition could be admitted, although the restrictions, if any, on its use do not appear.

(8) The jury always rendered its *verdict* written on a scrap of paper, in sentence form, as: "The jury find for the defendant costs of suit," or, "The jury find for the plaintiff, and assess the damages as 10 pounds and costs of suit." The file generally contains the Superior Court verdict, and, where the matter was tried in the Inferior Court, a copy of the verdict from that tribunal as well. Occasionally the jury found, either on its own initiative or at the request of the court, a *special verdict*. This was nothing more than the jury's finding of a specific fact or facts, leaving the legal effect to the court. In a trespass case, for example, the jury might find that the defendant had committed the acts alleged, but by special verdict leave to the court to decide whether or not plaintiff should prevail. Precisely when, if ever, the jury brought in a special verdict uninstructed, we do not know. Because some of the surviving special verdicts are in the identifiable hands of various attorneys, we know that sometimes the lawyers prepared them; it also appears that the judges sometimes participated in the process.[48]

(9) The prevailing party, at either stage of the case, was entitled to *costs*, governed by statute. These were drawn up by the party's attorney and then "taxed" (i.e. approved) by the clerk. The bills of costs, sometimes informally drawn, generally appear in the files. Costs in the Superior Court included any costs which might have been taxed against the party in the Inferior Court.

[47] Act of 12 Dec. 1695, 1 A&R 225.
[48] For an example of a special verdict, see No. 32.

(10) In cases where the losing party below had failed to prosecute his appeal, the Court, on prayer of the appellee, would *affirm* the Inferior Court judgment. The *complaint*, the document praying *affirmation* (usually a printed form), is frequently found in the files, because there seem to have been almost as many such cases as there were fully prosecuted appeals.

(11) If the losing party failed to satisfy the judgment voluntarily, the prevailing party could obtain from the clerk an *execution*, a writ directing the sheriff to seize the losing party's property, sell it, and turn the proceeds (up to the amount of the judgment) over to the winner. If the sheriff could find no property, he could jail the losing party until the judgment was satisfied.

The Courtroom

Of most of the actual courthouses where Adams practiced we know little, much of it trivial. The Cambridge courthouse, for instance, occupied the present site of the Harvard Trust Company in Harvard Square; at Falmouth (now Portland), court was held in a church.[49] Details of the courts' seat in Boston are a bit more precise. From 1747 to 1769, the courts sat in the Town House (today the Old State House); in the latter year, a new courthouse—on Queen (now Court) Street—costing over £2400 in Massachusetts currency, was completed under the supervision of the Suffolk Sessions.[50] It was a three-story building, with the Superior Court clerk's office at the east end of the ground floor, and the Inferior Court clerk's office at the west end. The courtroom itself was on the second floor, with a chimney and fireplace behind the "judges' seat."[51] The reported events of the Richardson trial, No. 59, suggest that the jail was located at some remove from the courthouse. This building had been reconstructed in 1766, and the prisoners moved in the meantime to the Cambridge jail.[52]

We have embarrassingly little knowledge of the way in which the Massachusetts courts regulated their business and conducted their trials. Litigation was certainly more peremptory than it is today; the

[49] See the diorama of Cambridge in 1775 in Widener Library, Harvard; see also Bolster, "Cambridge Court Houses," 39 Cambridge Hist. Soc., *Procs.* 55 (1964). On the Falmouth (Maine) court, see JA to AA, 6 July 1774, 1 *Adams Family Correspondence* 128.

[50] See Noble, "The Records and Files of the Superior Court of Judicature, &c.," 5 Col. Soc. Mass., *Pubns.* 5, 22 (1902).

[51] See John Mein and John Fleeming, *Register for New England and Nova Scotia ... 1768* 51 (Boston, n.d.); *Boston Gazette*, 29 March 1773, p. 3, col. 1.

[52] See SF 87365.

Minute Books show that the Superior Court would dispose of as many as six jury trials (using only two twelve-man juries) in a single day, and the Massacre Trials, Nos. 63, 64, were said to have been the first criminal matters to require more than one day for trial in the history of Massachusetts.[53] But even so, the court seems to have faced the problem of clogged dockets:

At Plymouth Court April Term 1763. Ordered—That for the future in all the Courts except for the County of Suffolk the continued Actions be first tried in the order they shall stand entered and then the new entries in the same order and in case of the continuance of any Action upon sufficient Reason offered the next Action in order shall be immediately called and brought to trial.[54]

What might constitute "sufficient Reason" is suggested by an entry in the Suffolk Inferior Court Minute Book: "Cont[inue]d by Order on the Motion of the Def[endan]t W. Story, he having made Oath that he has a material Witness absent, whose Evidence [i.e. deposition] he has not been able to Procure."[55]

All issues of fact were tried to a jury; there is no presently known instance of trial to the court alone. The jury panel was assembled by the clerk of court's sending to each town in the county a document called a *venire*, requiring the inhabitants of the town to nominate a specified number of men for jury duty. Statutes regulated the entire proceedings, and failure to attend as a venireman was a fineable offense.[56]

Once assembled at court, the veniremen were divided into two panels of twelve, called respectively the first and second jury. Trials then commenced, with the juries alternating. In criminal cases, which appear from the Minute Books to have been tried in a block after the civil business, juries were apparently new-empaneled. At any rate, as some of the cases printed in this edition show,[57] the judges could exert very little control over a jury once a case had been sent to the jury room.[58]

[53] Quincy, *Reports* 383 note.
[54] SF 100432; SCJ Rec. 1763–1764, fols. 43b–44a.
[55] Min. Bk., Inf. Ct. Suffolk, July 1771, No. 239.
[56] See Act of 22 June 1698, 1 A&R 335; see also SF 148024. The documents indicate that even in the 18th century, prospective jurors sometimes sought to escape service. One man gave as his excuse that he was warden of Trinity Church and also sole proprietor of a warehouse. SF 100599. Another protested that "I have not had the mesels nor none of my famaly and I am informed that they are very much in Boston." SF 79404.
[57] Nos. 12 and 59.
[58] But see SF 157569, where a new trial was ordered after six jurors reported that they had agreed to a verdict for defendant on the erroneous assumption that,

The judges of the Superior Court rendered few opinions in writing, none on any regular or formal basis, although they seem occasionally to have reduced the reasoning in selected cases to writing and caused the "report" to be filed with the papers of the case.[59] Sometimes matters presented to the court were considered so important that an attested memorandum was filed by leave of court, presumably as a guide for the future. In one case, for example, plaintiff's bookkeeper was testifying on his employer's behalf. Defendant's counsel on cross-examination asked if it were not true that some of plaintiff's goods had been seized by the customs officers for being unlawfully imported. Plaintiff's counsel objected to the question as being "impertinent to the Issue and tending to charge the plaintiff with an offence against which he was not prepared to Defend himself." The four-judge Superior Court split, the objection was sustained, and the report filed.[60]

Whether the Inferior Courts followed the practice of memorandum opinions is not known, although on one notable occasion, "After the Court had given Judgment Mr. Gridley moved for a Minute of the Reasons of the Judgment. [*Judge*] Wells said the Court was not accountable to the Bar for their Reasons." But, "after some Debate, the Clerk was ordered to minute the Reason." [61] Generally, however, except for such private and unofficial collections of arguments and decisions as that compiled by Josiah Quincy Jr., and the memory of bench and bar, little in the way of precedent and *stare decisis* bound the judges. A fine example of informal adherence to a prior decision is *Alcock v. Warden*, No. 8. But even English authority, cited so regularly, seems to have been only of persuasive, rather than binding, force. And, where the Massachusetts conditions seemed to justify the modification of an English rule, the local judges apparently innovated as necessary.[62] But certainly the constant citation of so much English legal material, treatises as well as reports, suggests that the Massachusetts judges did not regard themselves as free to write on a blank slate.

---

even if the jury had reported itself unable to agree, defendant would still have been awarded costs. See also No. 37, note 8.

[59] See opinion of Trowbridge, J., in No. 17; see also No. 28, Doc. IV.

[60] SF 26290. And see also SF 27639, the famous case of Erving v. Craddock, Quincy, *Reports* 553, where defendant, seeking to justify a customs seizure, offered unsuccessfully to prove that it was a common practice of the illicit trade with Holland to clear for St. John's in the West Indies, and that this was plaintiff's practice too. The memorandum, apparently in Edmund Trowbridge's hand, is attested by Clerk Samuel Winthrop. For a similar example, see SF 100949.

[61] 1 JA, *Diary and Autobiography* 231.

[62] See Nos. 17 and 27, notes 4–9.

In the absence of a comprehensive set of reported decisions or a complete analysis of the Suffolk Files, it is difficult to generalize about the litigatory diet of the Massachusetts judicial system. The cases printed in this edition suggest that virtually every kind of action known to the common law came before the courts. Simple contracts and commercial relations were the most frequent types of litigation, with land cases second. Except for defamation and injuries to property, tort law seems to have been embryonic, as it was in England. Even in the Suffolk Files, very few "personal injury" actions (except assault) have come to light, although actions against physicians for malpractice seem to have been known, and several esoteric tort theories have been unearthed.[63]

Massachusetts had an exceptionally detailed approach to criminal law. In addition to what might be called "ordinary" offenses, such as murder, manslaughter, rape, burglary, forgery, and arson, the Massachusetts courts were concerned with punishing a host of somewhat more unusual crimes.[64] Moreover, criminal procedure had many present-day features, such as extradition,[65] habeas corpus,[66] petition for change of venue,[67] and appointment of counsel. This last was apparently an established practice, although it is not yet clear whether the practice was limited to capital cases. In an undated document one Hindrick Hirsst, "a Sweed by birth, not well acquainted with the English tongue," petitioned the Superior Court for "an attorney to make his defense as in such Cases is usual in the Law."[68] And at

---

[63] Possible personal injury, SF 85987, SF 101586, SF 132065; medical malpractice, SF 26202, SF 157569; unlawful taking of property by a provincial military officer, SF 100627; selectmen's placing persons diseased with smallpox in plaintiff's house, SF 145568; collision between a cart and a cow, SF 145768; knowingly keeping a dangerous cow which gored plaintiff's horse, SF 157396.

[64] Aggravated trespass, SF 83625; the "buried treasure" swindle, SF 83626; deer-shooting, SF 84551, SF 131268; challenge to a duel, SF 84643, SF 172086; being a "common drunkard," SF 84945; attempting to spread smallpox, SF 85237; cruelty to apprentice, SF 172740, SF 173312; fornication with fiancée, SF 173878; slander, SF 26306; libel, SF 28837; tarring and feathering, SF 131971; mobbing, SF 147775; seeking to procure a soldier's desertion, SF 101238; improper imprisonment, SF 102458a; assisting a jailbreak, SF 157386; town's failure to maintain a school, SF 152521, SF 157337; sale of inferior grade of shoes (the goods being seized, examined by experts, and condemned), SF 79445; sale of a "putrid and corrupted Hog" which had "dyed of a mortifying Distemper," SF 83205.

[65] SF 80864.

[66] SF 100579. This dates from 1765 and is particularly significant, because the Massachusetts Habeas Corpus Act, enacted 14 Dec. 1692 on the model of the English act, 31 Car. 2, c. 2 (1679), was disallowed (because "the privilege has not as yet been granted in any of His Ma[jes]ty's Plantations," see 1 A&R 95, 99) and never reenacted.

[67] SF 25115.

[68] SF 173884. Hirsst's crime is not specified.

Worcester, in September 1768, Adams himself represented such a defendant. Samuel Quinn, accused of rape, "named me to the Court for his Council. I was appointed, and the Man was acquitted, but remanded in order to be tryed on another Indictment for an assault with Intention to ravish. When he had returned to Prison, he broke out of his own Accord—God bless Mr. Adams. God bless his Soul I am not to be hanged, and I dont care what else they do to me." [69]

Despite these manifestations of judicial sophistication, 18th-century Massachusetts law could be barbarous. A convicted counterfeiter might have his ear cut off, and a convicted thief, unable to pay for the goods stolen, might be sold for a term of years to one of His Majesty's subjects. [70]

4. JOHN ADAMS THE LAWYER

The Legal Education of John Adams

"Let us look upon a Lawyer," wrote John Adams to his college classmate Charles Cushing in April 1756.

In the beginning of Life we see him, fumbling and raking amidst the rubbish of Writs, indightments, Pleas, ejectments, enfiefed, illatebration and a 1000 other lignum Vitæ words that have neither harmony nor meaning. When he gets into Business he often foments more quarrels than he composes, and inriches himself at the expense of impoverishing others more honest and deserving than himself. Besides the noise and bustle of Courts and the labour of inquiring into and pleading dry and difficult Cases, have very few Charms in my Eye. [71]

These seem to have been the last brave arguments of a young man about to enter upon a course which he has known for some time that he will take. Adams' family had assumed when he went to Harvard, at some sacrifice to them, that he would enter the Congregational ministry, following in the footsteps of his uncle Joseph, Class of 1710, an eminent New Hampshire clergyman. [72] Upon graduation in 1755,

[69] 1 JA, *Diary and Autobiography* 353. See Min. Bk. 83, Worcester SCJ, Sept. 1768; SF 152338. Obtaining counsel was not always so easy. See No. 59.

[70] *Boston Gazette*, 10 Mar. 1772, p. 3, col. 1 (sale of thief); *Boston Gazette*, 10 May 1773, p. 2, col. 3 (ear-removal). See also Rex. v. Moyse and Reader, No. 61. But note the vote of the Suffolk Court of General Sessions of the Peace in Jan. 1769 discharging from jail those prisoners too poor to pay their fines. The statute regulating the involuntary servitude was the Act of 1 Nov. 1692, 1 A&R 51, 52.

[71] JA to Charles Cushing, 1 April 1756. MS not located; facsimile in *The Month at Goodspeed's*, vol. 19, no. 5 (Feb. 1948) frontispiece. Printed in 46 MHS, *Procs.* 410–412 (1912–1913).

[72] See 1 JA, *Diary and Autobiography* 355 note; 3 *id.* at 263.

however, Adams put off the moment of decision by undertaking to keep a school in Worcester. There he had at first spent his leisure hours in reading and copying out sermons—an occupation which he found "worth while for a candidate for the ministry"—and in long evenings of theological discussion.[73]

Despite these activities, and letters of encouragement from his classmates, his resolve began to waver. In his Autobiography, written nearly fifty years later, Adams said that his "Inclination was fixed upon the Law" while he was still a student at Harvard through participation in readings and debates.[74] Certainly at Worcester he seemed in no hurry to follow the paths of ministerial righteousness. He started to read works of political and natural, as well as moral, philosophy, and his evening conversations began to turn more and more toward practical affairs.[75] And there was ample stimulus for one interested in the law. A leading member of Adams' social circle was James Putnam, Harvard 1746, a successful lawyer and an eager disputant on the topics of the day. Moreover, amidst rural boredom, the law was hardly an arid study but the principal entertainment after church-going—other pastimes being frowned upon by the godly and prohibited by the legislature. The county Inferior Court and Court of Sessions sat in Worcester four times a year, and every September the Superior Court, with its train of lawyers from Boston, came there on circuit.

In his April letter to Cushing, although Adams had pointed out as a serious drawback of the ministry the church's constant internal wrangling, he had concluded that it was still the most desirable of the professions. But he was "as yet very contented in the place of a School Master" and would "not therefore very suddenly become a preacher." This phrase should have warned all his solicitous friends. After a

[73] 1 JA, *Diary and Autobiography* 10 (24 Feb. 1756). JA's activities at Worcester from Jan. through Aug. 1756 are chronicled in *id.* at 1–44.

[74] 3 JA, *Diary and Autobiography* 262–263. For references to letters from classmates, see JA to Cushing, 1 April 1756, 19 Oct. 1756 (sources in note 71 above). See also Richard Cranch to JA, Oct. 1756, Adams Papers. On seeing his letters to Cushing in print sixty years later, JA wrote to Cushing's son, "I was like a boy in a country fair, in a wilderness, in a strange country, with half a dozen roads before him, groping in a dark night to find which he ought to take. Had I been obliged to tell your father the whole truth, I should have mentioned several other pursuits. Farming, merchandise, law, and above all, war. Nothing but want of interest [i.e. influence] and patronage prevented me from enlisting in the army." JA to Cushing, 13 March 1817, Adams Papers, printed in 1 JA, *Works* 38 note. JA similarly spoke of the attractions of military life in his letter to Jonathan Mason in 1776, note 185 below.

[75] See, for example, 1 JA, *Diary and Autobiography* 2, 7, 11, 16, 18, 20, 22, 31. JA's later recollection that he had thought also of becoming a physician (3 JA, *Diary and Autobiography* 264) is supported by a brief discussion of the possibility in JA to Cushing, 1 April 1756, note 71 above.

spring in which "Company, and the noisy Bustle of the publick Occasion" engendered by the May term of the Inferior Court had interrupted his meditations,[76] and a summer in which he achieved nothing worth speaking of, he made the decision that he had been resisting for a year. On 21 August 1756 he "compleated a Contract with Mr. Putnam, to study Law under his Inspection for two years," and on the following day he "Came to Mr. Putnams and began Law. And studied not very closely this Week."[77]

Adams kept no diary during his two years with Putnam, but his course of study can be pieced together from other sources. The bulk of the curriculum seems to have been readings in the traditional masters of the common law. Two years after the completion of his studies, he wrote:

Wood. Coke. 2 Vols. Lillies Ab[ridgemen]t. 2 Vols. Salk[eld's] Rep[orts]. Swinburne. Hawkins Pleas of the Crown. Fortescue. Fitzgibbons. Ten Volumes in folio I read, at Worcester, quite thro—besides Octavos and Lesser Volumes, and many others of all sizes that I consulted occasionally, without Reading in Course as Dictionaries, Reporters, Entries, and Abridgements, &c.[78]

Putnam seems to have done little in the way of active teaching. Soon after his admission to the bar Adams complained: "Now I feel the Dissadvantages of Putnams Insociability, and neglect of me. Had he given me now and then a few Hints concerning Practice, I should be able to judge better at this Hour than I can now."[79] Improvements in methods of legal instruction have not altogether eliminated this problem.

His apprenticeship completed, Adams came home in the fall of 1758, despite the urgings of friends in Worcester that he remain there. He was determined to settle in Braintree, there being no other practitioner in Suffolk County established outside of Boston. Because he had not been admitted to the bar of the Inferior Court in Worcester, he had to present himself to the leading lawyers in Boston, who subjected him to a series of oral quizzes in order to ascertain his qualifica-

---

[76] 1 JA, *Diary and Autobiography* 27. Compare 3 *id.* at 264.

[77] 1 JA, *Diary and Autobiography* 42, 44. See also JA to Richard Cranch, 29 Aug. 1756, Adams Papers; JA to John Wentworth, Sept. 1756 (original owned by Gilbert H. Montague, 1960). For Cranch's disapproval of Adams' decision, see Cranch to JA, Oct. 1756, Adams Papers.

[78] 1 JA, *Diary and Autobiography* 173. Although JA may have labored for Putnam "amidst the rubbish of Writs," only one such document has come to light. SF 26778.

[79] 1 JA, *Diary and Autobiography* 63.

tions for practice. There were giants at the bar in those days—at least in the eyes of a raw young lawyer. On his first appearance in the court house he "felt Shy, under Awe and concern, for Mr. Gridley, Mr. Prat, Mr. Otis, Mr. Kent, and Mr. Thatcher were all present and looked sour."[80] Mastering his fears, however, he proceeded to call on these men, seeking their approval.

For Adams, the most meaningful of these interviews was that with Jeremiah Gridley, dean of the Massachusetts bar. After asking the candidate about his studies, Gridley urged upon him a broad course, covering not only the common law, but also "civil Law, and natural Law, and Admiralty Law," and gave him directions for study in each. Then came timeless words of counsel:

I have a few Pieces of Advice to give you Mr. Adams. One is to pursue the study of the Law rather than the Gain of it. Pursue the Gain of it enough to keep out of the Briars, but give your main Attention to the study of it. The next is, not to marry early. For an early Marriage will obstruct your Improvement, and in the next Place, twill involve you in Expence. Another Thing is not to keep much Company. For the application of a Man who aims to be a lawyer must be incessant. His Attention to his Books must be constant, which is inconsistent with keeping much Company.[81]

Adams took these words as his guide. Gridley's approach fitted his own intellectual inclinations precisely, so that throughout his life he remained a student, considering all legal learning his domain, and from that moment looked to Gridley as his master. His wry comment years later indicates that Gridley's philosophy had its disadvantages:

His Advice made so deep an Impression on my mind that I believe no Lawyer in America ever did so much Business as I did afterwards in the seventeen Years that I passed in the Practice at the Bar, for so little profit: and although my Propensity to marriage was ardent enough, I determined I would not indulge it, till I saw a clear prospect of Business and profit enough to support a family without Embarrassment.[82]

Upon the recommendations of Gridley and others, Adams was sworn an attorney in the Suffolk County Inferior Court on 6 November 1758, taking substantially the same oath still given at the Massachusetts bar.[83] He then settled down in Braintree to pursue the lonely

---

[80] 1 JA, *Diary and Autobiography* 54. See 3 *id.* at 270.

[81] 1 JA, *Diary and Autobiography* 54–55. Compare the account of the interview in 3 *id.* at 271–272.

[82] 3 JA, *Diary and Autobiography* 272.

[83] Min. Bk., Inf. Ct. Suffolk, Oct. 1758, following No. 221. See 1 JA, *Diary and Autobiography* 58–59. Compare 2 *id.* at 12; 3 *id.* at 273. For the oath which

and arduous routine of any young lawyer starting out for himself. Since he was not at once overrun with clients, he was able to devote much of his time to the furtherance of his legal education. Following Gridley's advice, he embarked upon an impressive course of reading in the civil law, reporting in November 1760 that, in spite of occasional lapses for which he constantly chided himself, "Justinian's Institutes I have read, thro, in Latin with Vinnius's perpetual Notes, Van Muydens Tractatio Institutionum Justiniani, I read thro, and translated, mostly into English, from the same Language. Woods Institute of the Civil Law, I read thro. These on the civil Law." In the same period, he had read four common-law treatises, as well as "some Reporters" and "a general Treatise of naval Trade and Commerce." [84] One product of this enterprise was certainly his Commonplace Book, printed in the present edition,[85] which he filled with abstracts drawn from his reading.

Not all learning came from books. Adams was barely back in Braintree before he attended a trial before Col. Josiah Quincy, one of the local justices of the peace, and he went to court in Boston even before he was admitted to the bar.[86] His diary shows that after his admission he was in frequent attendance on both the Inferior and Superior Courts, making notes of the arguments which he heard, digesting the authorities cited in these arguments, and elaborating in his own words upon the points raised. He also sought practical information from all available sources. While reading the treatise on naval trade, for example, he asked the master of a ship "what is a Bill of Lading, what the Pursers Book. What Invoices they keep. What Account they keep of Goods received on Board, and of Goods delivered out, at another Port. &c." [87] On another occasion, after a discussion of real-estate leases with several Braintree neighbors, he wrote: "I find that as much knowledge in my Profession is to be acquired by Conversing with common People about the Division of Estates, Proceedings of Judge of Probate, Cases that they have heard as Jurors, Witnesses, Parties, as is acquired by Books." [88]

JA took, see Act of 20 June 1702, c. 7, §2, 1 A&R 467. The present oath is in Mass. G.L., c. 221, §38 (Ter. edn., 1932).

[84] 1 JA, *Diary and Autobiography* 173–174. This course of study has been said to have exceeded "that of any other law student of the time." Charles Warren, *A History of the American Bar* 171 (Cambridge, Mass., 1912). As to colonial law study generally, see *id.* at 157–187.

[85] P. 4–25 below.

[86] See 1 JA, *Diary and Autobiography* 48–50, 54, 56–57.

[87] 1 JA, *Diary and Autobiography* 53–54.

[88] 1 JA, *Diary and Autobiography* 100.

However knowledgeable the litigious yeomanry of Braintree may have been, the bar was undoubtedly an educational resource of more lasting value. Adams took frequent opportunity to ask his seniors questions "concerning some Points of Practice in Law" that puzzled him, and to record their conversations upon such matters. On at least one occasion he sought advice more formally, asking Gridley for specific criticism of a declaration which he had drawn.[89] Further self-education resulted from correspondence with lawyers of his own generation on interesting points which each had come upon.[90]

The Development and Extent of Adams' Practice

Less than two months after his admission to practice, Adams drew his first writ, a "Declaration in Trespass for a Rescue." This suit, before a local justice of the peace, arose between two Braintree neighbors, one of whose cattle grazed on the field of the other. Unfortunately, Adams' declaration was defective and the writ abated. In his diary he bemoaned his "Precipitation" in taking the case, blaming "the cruel Reproaches" of his mother, "the Importunity" of the client, and "the fear of having it thought I was incapable of drawing the Writt." [91] He was sure that the episode would make him a laughingstock and drive away potential clients, but the next month he appeared again before a justice, and in July 1759 he entered his first action in the Inferior Court.[92] His diary entries for the year reflect other business as well.

Early in 1760, Adams took positive steps to bring himself to the attention of potential clients. In May he wrote an essay decrying the number of alehouses in Braintree. After a year's campaign, he succeeded: the town meeting passed a resolution limiting the number of liquor licenses to three.[93] At about the same time he launched another reform movement, this time against "pettyfoggers," local deputy sheriffs and scriveners who gave bad legal advice and fomented

---

[89] 1 JA, *Diary and Autobiography* 76, 109–110, 157–159.

[90] See JA to Peter Chardon, Jan. 1761, 1 JA, *Diary and Autobiography* 196–197; Jonathan Sewall to JA, 29 Sept. 1759, Adams Papers; JA to Sewall, Feb. 1760, Adams Papers; Sewall to JA, 13 Feb. 1760, Adams Papers. Compare 3 JA, *Diary and Autobiography* 278.

[91] 1 JA, *Diary and Autobiography* 64. See *id.* at 48–50, 57–58, 62–63, 65. After the present edition was in page proof, JA's draft of the defective writ and his thoughts on the case were found in the Royall Tyler Collection, Gift of Helen Tyler Brown, VtHi.

[92] Field v. Thayer, Min. Bk., Inf. Ct., Suffolk, July 1759, No. 163. For the appearance before the justice, see 1 JA, *Diary and Autobiography* 69–71. JA drew at least one other writ for the July 1759 court. See Spear v. Hayward, SF 79783.

[93] 1 JA, *Diary and Autobiography* 128–130, 151–152.

litigation.[94] Perhaps because of these activities, he was able to report in June 1760 that he "had secured 6 Actions" for the July Inferior Court, and a day later "3 entirely new clients."[95] From that point on, his diary contains numerous drafts of arguments and other notes which indicate a steadily developing practice. His fragmentary lists of writs drawn, beginning in January 1761, show that he soon had from ten to twenty writs per term in the Inferior Court in the years before 1763.[96]

In November 1761 Adams was admitted an attorney in the Superior Court.[97] The following year, in a move attributed to Chief Justice Thomas Hutchinson's desire to add dignity to the proceedings of that court, all members of its bar were formally called as barristers at the August term. Adams was among those who thereafter appeared in "Gowns and Bands and Tye Wiggs."[98] This marked the beginning of his practice in the Suffolk Superior Court, where, according to the Minute Books, for the next two or three years he was of counsel in from one to five actions at each term. For the time being, however, his principal concern remained the Common Pleas. In January 1763, for example, he had thirty-six actions at the Suffolk Inferior Court.[99] It was not until 1765 that he seems to have made any significant progress in the Superior Court. In March of that year he appeared in at least five actions there, two of which he tried to a jury without success. He was of counsel in eight actions at the August term, prevailing in two of four jury actions.

As he became better established, Adams' business began to expand outside Suffolk County. As early as June 1762, his diary records that he journeyed "To the Land of the Leonards" (Bristol County, a region populated by lawyers and judges of that name) to attend the Inferior Court at Taunton.[100] His surviving docket lists for the years 1764 to 1768 show that he attended the Taunton Inferior Court frequently

[94] See 1 JA, *Diary and Autobiography* 135–138, 159, 205–206. As part of this campaign, JA obtained an appointment for his brother, Peter Boylston Adams, as deputy sheriff, thus ending the need to rely on "pettyfoggers" for the service of writs. See *id.* at 216–217; 3 *id.* at 277.

[95] 1 JA, *Diary and Autobiography* 135.

[96] See text at note 146 below. See also 2 JA, *Works* 237 note.

[97] 1 JA, *Diary and Autobiography* 224.

[98] 3 JA, *Diary and Autobiography* 276. See Min. Bk. 79, SCJ Suffolk, Aug. 1762; Quincy, *Reports* 35. Actually, JA's first appearance in the Superior Court was in Feb. 1761, when he filed a prayer for affirmation, a privilege apparently allowed to Inferior Court attorneys. See Lambard v. Tirrell, SF 172280.

[99] JA, Docket, Inf. Ct. Suffolk, Jan. 1763. Adams Papers, Microfilms, Reel No. 182.

[100] 1 JA, *Diary and Autobiography* 227. He had prepared at least one writ for the July 1761 Plymouth Inferior Court, but there is no evidence that he attended the court. See JA's record book, described in note 146 below.

and had cases at nearly every term of the Plymouth Inferior Court during this period. In addition, he was sometimes present at the Barnstable and Middlesex Inferior Courts and even traveled at least once to the Inferior Court at Pownalborough in Lincoln County, District of Maine, the farthest extent of Massachusetts justice to the eastward.[101] At the same time, he rode circuit with the Superior Court, appearing at Bristol in October 1764 and subsequent terms, at Plymouth for the first time in 1765, Worcester and Essex in 1766, Barnstable and Middlesex in 1767, Hampshire in 1768, and Cumberland and Lincoln in 1769.

Adams entered the most active phase of his career in 1768. He appeared in a total of 110 cases entered at nine different terms of the Superior Court (nearly double his previous best annual total) and about 200 cases in various Inferior Courts; he also began to practice in the royal Vice Admiralty Court, where he had one civil case and several important actions for breach of the Acts of Trade.[102] His practice seems to have reached a peak in 1772 and 1773. In 1772 he appeared in 202 Superior Court cases in all counties. The next year he drew 262 writs in the Suffolk Inferior Court (not all of which were served or entered) and in 38 more cases there represented the defendants.[103] In these years he was certainly the busiest lawyer in the Province, being engaged in 85 entries at the August 1772 Suffolk Superior Court. Thereafter he had fewer cases, because political developments in 1773 and 1774 hurt all lawyers' business. After 1774 his political activities kept him out of what little law business there was until his retirement from Congress at the end of 1777. He then returned to Massachusetts, fired by tales of prosperity at the bar and full of expectations of profit. But he was almost immediately appointed Joint Commissioner to France. His departure for that post in February 1778 after only one known court appearance marked the end of his career as a practicing lawyer.[104]

[101] 1 JA, *Diary and Autobiography* 258–259; 3 *id.* at 281–282. The dockets referred to in the text are in Adams Papers, Microfilms, Reel No. 184.

[102] See Nos. 43, 45–49. The continuing increase in JA's practice the following year brought the unhappy comment from James Otis that he had "become the Sport of the young Gentlemen of the Bar, and he was greatly mortified on looking over the Entries this present term of the Superior Court [Aug. 1769] to find he had but 4 when the youngest *Quincy* had 9 and *John Adams* had 60." Andrew Oliver to Governor Bernard, 3 Dec. 1769, 12 Bernard Papers 163–164, MH, printed in Quincy, *Reports* (Appendix) 464. The Minute Book and JA's docket for this term (Adams Papers, Microfilms, Reel No. 184) show that he was indeed engaged in sixty civil actions, as well as in three criminal cases.

[103] JA, Office Book, Jan., April, July, Oct. 1773. MQA.

[104] His court appearance was in Penhallow v. The *Lusanna*, No. 58. For further details of his homecoming and departure, see *id.*, text at notes 11, 45, 64–66. As to lawyers' prosperity, see also AA to JA, 1 June 1777, 2 *Adams Family Correspond-*

The content of Adams' practice has not yet been analyzed in detail, but it is safe to say that it covered almost every public and private activity carried on in the Province. The majority of his cases arose out of the simpler financial transactions of trade and commerce, being suits to recover obligations embodied in promissory notes, bonds, or accounts. The more complicated suits of this variety stemmed from the involved affairs of Boston's merchants and their European and West Indian correspondents. Another significant group of cases concerned real estate. Land was one of the principal elements of provincial wealth, and land speculation was a major stimulus to settlement and exploitation of the still empty back country. In the realm of tort, the majority of cases seemed to involve injury to property interests, whether real or personal. Adams also had many suits for defamation in an era of strict honor and tender feelings, as well as a number of actions for assault and battery.

Public matters, too, produced a substantial amount of litigation. Adams devoted much time to suits to collect taxes, to enforce other Province laws, and to protect town interests in land. Other town matters—proceedings under the poor laws, on highway regulation, and the like—brought him often before the county courts of general sessions of the peace, which were charged with administering the great bulk of local regulation. As an active trial lawyer, Adams also had many criminal cases. This branch of the practice involved a familiar range of ills—murder, rape, larceny, assault, counterfeiting—and some more peculiar to Adams' times, such as rioting, mobbing, and tarring and feathering.

Although most of Adams' cases were in the courts of common law, he ventured into every other type of court held in the Province. His practice in the Vice Admiralty Court, almost entirely limited to actions under the Acts of Trade, has already been mentioned. He also appeared in special courts of admiralty called for the trial of felonies committed at sea; in the county courts of probate, as well as before the Governor and Council sitting as the Supreme Court of Probate; and before Governor and Council in their capacity as a court of divorce.

Adams spent most of his time in the trial of cases. In 18th-century Massachusetts much of the office work that today occupies many lawyers almost exclusively—the drafting of wills, deeds, and con-

---

ence 251. Two cases in which JA is known to have been engaged for the Feb. 1778 term of the Superior Court are discussed in No. 58, note 66. See also 2 *Adams Family Correspondence* 395 note. The Suffolk Inferior Court Minute Book for January 1778 reveals that he entered no actions at that term. No other court sessions were scheduled during his brief stay in Massachusetts.

tracts—seems to have been performed by such non-lawyers as scriveners, notaries, or the parties themselves. The bar apparently claimed no monopoly in these matters, trying to protect itself only from unauthorized practice in the courts. Nevertheless, Adams did on occasion perform counseling and drafting services for his clients in matters not directly connected with litigation.

In his diary for 1759–1760 appear entries which show that he had been called upon to draft a deed, to give advice orally to several "Consultors" who came to his office, and to render a written opinion to a client contemplating suit on an obligation owed to an apprentice.[105] Thereafter, such matters continued to form a small but steady part of Adams' practice. For example, his dockets for the southern counties to which he rode circuit contain occasional entries for fees received for "advice" apparently rendered from the saddlebag. Adams' account with John Hancock, receipted in December 1771, contains two items for "advice" and one for drawing a bill of sale.[106] Documents pertaining to the Boston Tea Party in 1773 show that Adams and another lawyer were retained by the owners of one of the tea ships to give legal advice just before the events which made their queries moot.[107] Letters in the Adams Papers indicate also that clients sometimes sought counsel in a formal way. In March 1773, one W. L. Morgan, who said that he had previously conducted certain "Evening Amusements" at Portsmouth and now wished to put on his entertainment in Boston, wrote for a legal opinion on his plans. He enclosed a proposal, evidently for a kind of private subscription arrangement, which he hoped would "secure me and my necessary Assistants from being troubled by the Act of the Province (if it now exists) against Theatrical Entertainments."[108] Adams' reply unfortunately has not been found.

[105] 1 JA, *Diary and Autobiography* 88, 98, 143, 145, 175. For an instance of drafting by a non-lawyer, see Rowe, *Diary* 64.

[106] Reproduced as an illustration in the present edition. Discussed further, text at note 137 below. JA's account with the Kennebec Co., note 139 below, contains similar entries.

[107] Vol. 2:105 below.

[108] W. L. Morgan to JA, 4 March 1773, Adams Papers. For other examples, see Jacob Rowe to JA, 24 Dec. 1773, Adams Papers; JA to Samuel Tufts, 8 Feb. 1773, Adams Papers. The statute referred to by Morgan was the Act of 11 April 1750, c. 24, 3 A&R 500, providing penalties of £20 against anyone who established a theater for "stage-plays, interludes or other theatrical entertainments," and £5 for any actor or spectator in any such event where the audience exceeded twenty. It had been renewed until 1 Nov. 1775 by Act of 15 Nov. 1770, c. 5, 5 A&R 86, provoking from Lieutenant Governor Hutchinson the comment that, although the act had "been complained of as unnecessarily restraining the use of innocent amusements," he felt it wiser to consent in its passage and not "thereby increase the ill humors among the People." *Id.* at 141. See also *id.* at 62.

On at least one occasion Adams served as administrator of the estate of a deceased intestate, as is evidenced by a copy of the letters of administration in the Adams Papers.[109] Litigation itself produced a certain amount of activity more in the nature of negotiation than advocacy. In January 1767, for example, Adams informed his friend and brother-in-law, Richard Cranch, that, rather than again sue a "miserable animal" of a debtor who would be badly hurt by the costs, he had taken the debtor's note for the amount of a debt owed Cranch on a previous judgment and was forwarding the note with an account that the debtor claimed Cranch owed him.[110] Satisfaction of a judgment could lead a lawyer to extraordinary efforts. On 1 April 1770 Adams wrote to George Hayley, London merchant and correspondent of John Hancock, that he had been obliged to travel to Gloucester with an execution in Hayley's favor, which he was there able to satisfy out of the real estate of the debtor, who had absconded. The letter describes the problems and mechanics of sale, concluding with a request that someone else be given charge of the property, because "it lies so far out of my Province, both in the Nature and Situation of it." [111]

Adams' clients came from all segments of Massachusetts society. Probably the majority of them were the solid yeomen of Suffolk County—particularly those in the Braintree area—who year in and year out were constantly bringing one another into court to resolve petty differences. A number of his relatives, of whom he had many, appear regularly as clients. As his reputation increased, however, Adams began more and more to draw his business from the upper ranges of the social and financial order. In his diary for 30 June 1772 he catalogued some of the leading citizens who had been his clients: Silvester Gardiner, James Bowdoin, James Pitts, John Hancock, John Rowe, Jeremiah Lee, Daniel Sargeant, Robert Hooper, and Elisha Doane—all men of great wealth, many of whom were engaged in politics as well.[112]

[109] Letters of administration for the estate of Benjamin Hunt Jr., Braintree, granted 23 July 1762. For a case in which JA acted as a referee, see Ingersole v. Viscount, Min. Bk. 81, SCJ Suffolk, March 1765, C–34; Min. Bk. 89, SCJ Suffolk, March 1769, C–1. SF 101329.

[110] JA to Cranch, 5 Jan. 1767, Adams Papers. For another example, see 1 JA, *Diary and Autobiography* 182–183.

[111] JA to Hayley, 1 April 1770, Adams Papers.

[112] 2 JA, *Diary and Autobiography* 61. Through politics JA was to lose the business of Gardiner and Harrison Gray. See JA to AA, 6 July 1774, 1 *Adams Family Correspondence* 128–129; 2 JA, *Diary and Autobiography* 11. In Dec. 1772 he said "Farewell" to Hancock also. *Id.* at 72. The breach seems to have been healed by

Other clients of importance included Governor John Wentworth of New Hampshire; Harrison Gray, Treasurer of the Province; William Story, Deputy Register of the Vice Admiralty Court; Benjamin Hallowell, a commissioner of the customs; and, on at least one occasion, ex-Governor Sir Francis Bernard. The names of others known to history as well as to their contemporaries appear in his cases—for example, Paul Revere, Joseph Warren, and Benjamin Church. There was also the Kennebec Company, consisting of Gardiner, Bowdoin, Pitts, and Hallowell, proprietors of a vast tract in the Kennebec Valley in Maine, whose interests Adams served for many years. In addition, Adams acted in behalf of many towns, including Boston, a name appearing frequently in his accounts.

Many of Adams' cases are important today because of their connection with the dynamic political forces at work in pre-Revolutionary Boston. Among such cases printed in the present edition are the trials in which Adams and others braved public opinion to defend the British officer and soldiers charged with the killings known as the Boston Massacre (Nos. 63, 64); the argument of James Otis against writs of assistance, which was later much circulated as reported by Adams (No. 44); numerous suits for violation of the British Acts of Trade, including the prosecution of John Hancock for the alleged smuggling of prohibited wine in his sloop *Liberty* (No. 46); the suits brought by Hancock on behalf of certain London creditors of tory printer John Mein, an effective opponent of the nonimportation movement (No. 12); and the trial of Michael Corbet and other seamen before a special court of admiralty for the killing of a British naval officer who had boarded their merchant vessel at sea allegedly to impress them (No. 56). In cases not reported in these volumes, Adams represented James Otis in his suit against John Robinson, a customs commissioner who had seriously injured Otis in a tavern brawl,[113] and took the case of two county officers sued by merchant Ebenezer Cutler for assisting a mob to harass him when he had transported British goods in defiance of the nonimportation agreement.[114]

Without a more elaborate analysis of the substantive law of 18th-century Massachusetts than the editors have been able to undertake,

---

1774, when JA again began representing Hancock. See SF 92302; Min. Bk. 98, SCJ Suffolk, Aug. 1774, N–65.

[113] See Otis v. Robinson, 2 JA, *Diary and Autobiography* 47–48 (25–27 July 1771); Zobel, "Law under Pressure: Boston 1769–1771," paper given at the Conference on Colonial History, Worcester, Mass., April 1964, to be published in George A. Billias, ed., *Law and Authority in Colonial America: Selected Essays* (Barre, Mass., in press).

[114] See Pierpont v. Cutler, 2 JA, *Diary and Autobiography* 8–9.

it is not possible to define fully or accurately Adams' contribution to legal development. Isolated instances of influence may be found, however. His cases in the field of administrative law, for example, helped to define the Superior Court's scope of review over the courts of sessions, one decision in his favor even leading to a legislative change (No. 27). In two of Adams' cases the opinions of Judge Edmund Trowbridge on questions having to do with levy of execution were considered significant enough to be printed in the 19th-century Massachusetts reports.[115] Certain of the forms copied into his Pleadings Book, printed elsewhere in this volume,[116] were included in a form book published in successive editions between 1802 and 1905.

Some of Adams' cases also had a bearing on later developments in constitutional law. Several suits in which slaves sued for their freedom were decided on technical rather than humanitarian considerations, but they mark the first stirrings of a later movement (Nos. 38–42). Adams was of counsel in a number of cases arising out of the struggles of Baptists and other dissenters against the Congregational religious "establishment." The concessions won by the dissenters in these suits surely prepared the ground for the intensified battles over religious liberty which followed the Revolution (No. 37). One of Adams' last cases, a prize suit in the New Hampshire state admiralty court, went through a series of appeals and countersuits that finally brought it before the United States Supreme Court in 1795 (No. 58). The decision there, long after Adams had severed all connection with the case, treated important questions of federal and state power that were but dimly perceived in 1777.

The Mechanics of Practice

Adams and his contemporaries at the bar were sole practitioners, partnerships in the modern sense being unknown. The informality and closeness of the bar supplied many of the advantages of partnership, however. For instance, lawyers freely loaned books to those who lacked them.[117] They also seem commonly to have assisted one another in such matters as court appearances. Adams wrote to Samuel Quincy, asking him to enter some forty actions at the current Suffolk Inferior

[115] Richmond v. Davis, Quincy, *Reports* 279 (Suffolk SCJ, 1769); Hooton v. Grout, *id.* at 343, 368–369 (Worcester SCJ, 1772). See 8 Mass. 554; 14 Mass. 473.

[116] P. 26–86 below.

[117] See, for example, 1 JA, *Diary and Autobiography* 52, 56, 169, 199, 251. Compare *Boston Gazette*, 24 Oct. 1768, p. 3, col. 3: "Any person possessed of Jacob's Law Dictionary, or any other books belonging to the subscriber is desired to return the same. James Otis."

Court, "and answer for me in all things once more, and to write me one Line to let me know my Fate, as usual."[118] Adams' dockets in later years show that he would on occasion divide up his entries at a particular term among several lawyers when he was unable to attend.[119]

It was usual for two lawyers to argue on each side in a case, but we do not know whether such arrangements represented the choice of the client or of the lawyers. In any event these pairings were too fluid to be called partnerships. The Superior Court Minute Books show that Adams more frequently appeared alone than with co-counsel. When he was not alone, Jonathan Sewall, Robert Treat Paine, Josiah Quincy Jr., and three or four others were the lawyers most often paired with him. But he appeared in one or more cases with at least thirty lawyers between 1762 and 1774 and was opposed even to Sewall, Paine, and Quincy far more often than he was joined with them.[120]

Adams established his office in Braintree at the beginning of his career and remained there until 1768.[121] In the latter year, finding that he was spending more time traveling than in court, he moved with his family to Boston, where both the bulk of his practice and the political events which were demanding more and more of his time were concentrated. Between 1768 and 1771 he changed his Boston residence three times. He may have had an office in his first house at Brattle Square not far from the Court House. In the spring of 1769 he moved his family to Cole Lane, some distance away. He then probably took the office "near the steps of the Town house Stairs" where, according to his Autobiography, he was sitting on the morning after the Boston Massacre in 1770 when approached by Captain Preston's representative.[122]

In 1771, wearied by the pace of life in town, Adams brought his family back to Braintree to live, becoming for a while virtually a commuter. He then took an office in Queen (now Court) Street, at

[118] JA to Samuel Quincy, 2 Jan. 1764, MHi:Misc. Bound MSS.

[119] See JA, Docket, Inf. Ct. Suffolk, Oct. 1769; SCJ Suffolk, Feb. 1774. Adams Papers, Microfilms, Reel Nos. 182, 183.

[120] In addition to Sewall, Paine, and Quincy, the lawyers with whom JA was most frequently joined were James Otis, Benjamin Kent, James Putnam, and Daniel Leonard. Others with whom he was paired at least once include Robert Auchmuty, Jeremiah Gridley, Richard Dana, Francis Dana, Samuel Quincy, James Hovey, John Worthington, Simeon Strong, Samuel Fitch, Andrew Cazneau, Daniel Farnham, John Lowell, William Cushing, David Wyer, Sampson Salter Blowers, Samuel Swift, Pelham Winslow, Theophilus Bradbury, William Pynchon, Oakes Angier, James Sullivan, Nathaniel Peaslee Sargeant, and Jeremiah Dummer Rogers.

[121] See 1 JA, *Diary and Autobiography* 225 note; 1 *Adams Family Correspondence* 23 note.

[122] 3 JA, *Diary and Autobiography* 292. The move in 1768 and those thereafter until 1771 are described in *id.* at 286–287, 291; 2 *id.* at 68.

which he was in steady attendance while the court was in session. Sometimes he traveled back and forth between Boston and Braintree in the same day; at other times he stayed with friends or relatives.[123] In this routine he apparently found some relief for a while, but business—public and private—soon called him back to Boston. In the fall of 1772 he bought a house in Queen Street, "near the Scæne of my Business, opposite the Court house . . . and inconvenient and contracted as it was I made it answer both for a Dwelling and an Office, till a few Weeks before the 19th of Appril 1775 when the War commenced."[124]

As the account of his practice suggests, Adams must have spent nearly as much time in the saddle, riding circuit, as he did at his desk. These trips to Taunton, Plymouth, Worcester, Salem, Falmouth (now Portland), and other places were often unproductive and always arduous. In his diary and letters Adams spoke frequently of the expense of travel and the potentially more rewarding practice which he was missing at Boston. He spoke too of the boredom and discomfort of his trips and of his ardent longings for familiar scenes and faces. The long eastern circuit to Ipswich and down to Maine which the Superior Court made each June seemed particularly painful, doubtless not only because it entailed a two- or three-week separation from his family but because of the long distances and rude living conditions involved.

Adams' trip on the eastern circuit in 1771 is typical.[125] On 17 June he set out from Braintree "in a Cloth Coat and Waiscoat, but was much pinched with a cold, raw, harsh, N.E. Wind. At Boston I put on a thick Flannel Shirt, and that made me comfortable, and no more— So cold am I or so cold is the Weather." After the stop in Boston and dinner in Malden, he pressed on, riding for a while in company with Judge Cushing of the Superior Court. The two stopped briefly in Lynn, but Adams went on to spend the night in Salem, complaining that "I have hurt myself today, by taking cold in the forenoon, and by drinking too much Wine" at his various way stops. No relief was immediately at hand, however. A friend, grief-stricken at the recent loss of his wife, shared Adams' chamber, keeping him awake for hours with his woes.

[123] For the move in 1771 and the life of a commuter, see 2 JA, *Diary and Autobiography* 6–11, 45–50. The office in Queen Street is described in a notice in the *Boston Gazette*, 22 April 1771, p. 3, col. 2: "John Adams Notifies the Removal of his Office to a Room in Queen-Street, in the House of Mr. John Gill, within a few Steps of the New Court-House, but on the opposite Side of the Street."

[124] 3 JA, *Diary and Autobiography* 296–297. For the move, see 2 *id.* at 63, 67–68.

[125] The following account is based on diary entries from 17 June to 5 July in 2 JA, *Diary and Autobiography* 35–45.

The next day Adams arrived at Ipswich, where he remained in reasonably comfortable surroundings for the week that the court sat there. Then came a day's ride to York, with a lengthy stop on the way in Portsmouth, New Hampshire. After four days in York, Adams and several other lawyers departed for Falmouth, spending the night at Biddeford. Rain delayed the party for a day, but on Sunday they went on to Scarborough, and, after going "to meeting forenoon and afternoon," proceeded to Falmouth. There, on 2 July, Adams expressed his disgust in his diary: "This has been the most flat, insipid, spiritless, tasteless Journey that ever I took, especially from Ipswich. I have neither had Business nor Amusement, nor Conversation. It has been a moping, melancholly Journey upon the whole." Yet he was still there on 5 July, having argued at least one case in a manner which brought him what he felt to be ill-deserved compliments. His diary breaks off at this point, but presumably he then began the homeward trip, which would have taken him at least three more days of riding—a total elapsed time of over three weeks.

Despite their inconveniences these trips had certain advantages. In the first place, they must have produced a favorable financial balance. The trips to Bristol and Plymouth always resulted in much business, and the journeys to the eastward usually concerned the affairs of the Kennebec Company, one of Adams' most lucrative connections. Riding circuit must have had a major effect on the atmosphere in which practice was conducted. As Adams' 1771 trip shows, judges and lawyers often traveled together, finding lodgings at the same inn and frequently spending the evenings in mild conviviality. There were also chances for more serious discussion. On the trip just described, for example, Adams spent two evenings in conversation with Judge Trowbridge, one of the foremost legal minds in the province.[126] Men thus thrust together in common discomfort must inevitably have developed an easy familiarity that made their professional relations closer and more relaxed.

The routine of litigation varied with Adams' location. In Suffolk County the practice centered on the paperwork of an action in the Inferior Court. Adams apparently obtained blank writ forms from the clerk prior to the beginning of each term of court. A client would request that Adams draw a writ as the first step in what was, for many simple notes and accounts, just another coercive measure in the collection process, intended to force payment from a reluctant debtor. The small number of writs which actually led to litigation attests this fact. Often a settlement satisfactory to the plaintiff occurred before

[126] 2 JA, *Diary and Autobiography* 38–39, 41–42.

the defendant was served. Where more pressure was necessary, Adams or his client delivered the writ to the sheriff; service on the defendant had to be accomplished at least fourteen days before the court sat.[127] Service led to a few more settlements. If the action was to proceed, Adams entered it on the docket of the court, a step which had to be taken on or before the first day of the term.[128] The clerk of the court prepared lists of all the entries and distributed them to the lawyers. But many cases on these lists were never tried, either because the writ could not be served or because of a late compromise by the parties.

Adams was retained by defendants in relatively few cases, but a far greater proportion of these matters was actually tried than was true of cases in which he represented plaintiffs. This fact suggests that, unlike his modern counterpart, the 18th-century defendant did not obtain counsel until just before trial. Once a case reached the trial stage, it no longer fitted into the paperwork routine. It might be continued (that is, put over) for several terms, demurred, or tried to a jury. If there was a judgment, execution would issue, or an appeal might be taken to the Superior Court. The appeal itself might be dropped, in which case a complaint for affirmation had to be filed; or it might be continued or tried. At these later stages, Adams might be engaged to try or argue a case with which he had not been previously connected.[129]

On circuit, the routine was like that after entry in Suffolk. The drawing of writs and entering of actions in the Inferior Court seems to have been accomplished by local counsel; when Adams took a case, it was usually either to replace the local man or to join with him.[130] He tried some of his circuit cases by prearrangement with Boston

---

[127] Act of 26 June 1699, c. 3, §4, 1 A&R 370.

[128] Act of 15 Jan. 1743, c. 13, §2, 3 A&R 29. A lawyer with a substantial number of cases entered them all at once by submitting a list of them to the clerk. See JA to Samuel Quincy, note 118 above. See several lists of JA's entries in SF 26254, SF 26478, SF 26958, SF 175190, SF 175257, SF 175289.

[129] The sheer number of cases sometimes led to error. In June 1765 the General Court granted the petition of Thomas Torrey of Plymouth for a stay of execution on a judgment recovered against him at the July 1764 Suffolk Inferior Court, where he had been unable to appear on account of the smallpox, "but employed Mr. Adams to appear as his Attorney, [but] the petitioner . . . was called out [i.e. the case was called for trial] before Mr. Adams got to Boston." Resolve of 13 June 1765, c. 25, 18 A&R 17.

[130] On rare occasions the situation might be reversed. In April 1773 Adams drew a "Writ of Ejectment" for one of the Kennebec Company's actions at Pownalborough Inferior Court. JA's account with Kennebec Co., 5 Feb. 1774, MeHi: Kennebec Papers. JA did not attend the court, however. Occasionally, he did draw writs for the Plymouth Inferior Court. See JA, Dockets, Adams Papers, Microfilms, Reel No. 184.

clients who had business in the outlying counties. Other cases came to him after his arrival in the shire town—virtually at the courthouse door. This feature of ambulatory law practice is perhaps best illustrated by Adams' comment in a letter written during a halt en route to Falmouth from York in July 1774, that Josiah Quincy Jr. "would not stop, but drove forward, I suppose that he might get upon the Fishing Ground before his Brother Sam, and me."[131]

The account books necessary for an estimate of Adams' income from the practice of law are missing, and there are no other comparable sources. If we are to take him at his word, we must conclude that he made no fortune at the bar. But he was able to purchase modest real-estate holdings in Braintree and a house in Boston, as well as to spend "an Estate in Books [and] a Sum of Money indiscreetly in a Lighter, another in a Pew."[132] It was not from such modest investments, or his conservative speculations in mortgages, that wealth came in 18th-century Boston, however. Adams recognized this in his Autobiography: "I was too much enamoured with Books, to spend many thoughts upon Speculation on Money. . . . I was more intent on my Business than on my Profits, or I should have laid the foundation of a better Estate."[133]

Even at the peak of his career, Adams owed any financial success more to quantity of business than to high fees. His charges seem to have been standard for nearly all clients and in many cases were governed by statute. The minimum for drawing a writ was seven shillings, but in cases where a complex declaration was required the figure might go as high as eighteen shillings. The average seems to have been about twelve shillings. Adams often bore the cost of service (usually three or four shillings) in the first instance, as existing accounts with sheriffs for their labors show.[134] When an action was entered in the Inferior Court, there were clerk's, justices', and other fees totaling 9s. 8d.[135] In many cases Adams received twelve shillings from the client for entry, treating the difference as an advance to be

---

[131] JA to AA, 4 July 1774, 1 *Adams Family Correspondence* 122.

[132] JA to AA, 29 June 1774, 1 *Adams Family Correspondence* 114. See 2 JA, *Diary and Autobiography* 62–63, 87–88.

[133] 3 JA, *Diary and Autobiography* 286.

[134] See JA's account with Moses French, 1763–1764. Adams Papers, Microfilms, Reel No. 185. JA's account with his brother, Peter Boylston Adams, 26–27 Sept. 1766, Adams Papers. Some sheriffs' accounts remained unpaid as late as 1790. See Cotton Tufts to JA, 18 Sept. 1790, Adams Papers. Figures in this and the next paragraph are based on a study of the accounting devices described in text at notes 146–151 below.

[135] Act of 5 March 1765, c. 26, §2, 4 A&R 746; Act of 26 Feb. 1773, c. 42, §2, 5 A&R 243.

credited later. If Adams obtained judgment in his client's favor, charges for service and entry were taxed as costs against the losing defendant. These charges were often also paid by the defendant when an action was settled, although it seems to have been more common for the plaintiff to bear his own costs in such cases, as is usual today.

Once the case was entered, most of the fees were limited by statute. A lawyer could charge twelve shillings for a trial in the Superior Court and six shillings for an Inferior Court trial. In addition, whether or not the case came to trial, Adams charged his clients 1s. 6d. per day for "attendance," that is, presence in court until the case was disposed of. These sums were also taxed as costs.[136] In cases where points of law were argued separately from the trial, a matter not covered by statute, Adams, at least later in his career, charged an extra five-shilling "arguing fee." The usual charge for "advice," when distinct from litigation, seems to have been about twelve shillings.

Most of Adams' income seems to have come to him through these small increments—a great many twelve-shilling writs and a substantial number of litigated matters that brought him no more than a pound or two. More rarely a single case might be complicated enough to bring a larger fee, but usually the figure would have been earned shilling-by-shilling through the same painstaking series of small steps that made up the lesser business.

John Hancock's account with Adams, rendered and paid in December 1771, is a good demonstration of the economics of practice.[137] It covers the period March 1769 to December 1771 (the month in which writs for the January 1772 Inferior Court were drawn) and contains twenty-five items in nineteen different matters, amounting to a total charge of some £55. Of these twenty-five items, seventeen are under a pound, and only two exceed £2 10s. Of the nineteen matters, twelve produced fees amounting to less than a pound. The cases producing higher fees had been entered on the docket and involved one or more trial fees and numerous days' attendance. The only two really substantial sums were fees in the two suits against John Mein which Hancock had managed; these came to £34. The Mein actions, as the discussion of them in this volume shows, were continued several times in both the Inferior and Superior Courts. Lengthy accounts had to be procured and annexed to the writs, and elaborate

[136] Act of 5 March 1765, c. 26, §2, 4 A&R 747; Act of 26 Feb. 1773, c. 42, §2, 5 A&R 243.
[137] This account, a MS owned by Nathaniel E. Stein of New York City, 1964, is reproduced as an illustration in the present edition.

new pleadings were filed on appeal. The fees here too were undoubtedly made up of a multitude of small items.[138]

Adams' fees were not always measured by this scale, however, and there were occasionally other sources of income. The Kennebec Company paid him a flat sum of £30 annually to cover fees and expenses on each of his trips to Falmouth from 1769 to 1771; his account with the company, receipted in February 1774, shows an item in June 1772 for "a Journey to Falmouth in Casco Bay and Fees in your Causes and Concerns at that Court by agreement for" £15.[139] In January 1778, just before Adams' departure for France, the grateful proprietors voted that the Treasurer give him "a Fee of One hundred Dollars for carrying on the Company's Cause with Coll. Tyng." This was a case for which Adams had billed earlier at the usual rates. He had apparently participated only in the preparation for trial in 1778, so that the size of the figure (inflation aside) indicates that the tales of prosperity which drew him back to practice at the end of 1777 were not unfounded.[140]

There are occasional records of other lump-sum fees which do not seem directly based on item-by-item charges for the services involved. For example, in his suit with John Robinson, James Otis made it a condition of the settlement which finally resulted that Robinson would provide a fee of £30 for each of Otis' lawyers—a sum which Adams described in a docket note as "a genteel Fee."[141] In the Boston Massacre trials, the total fees of £136 10s. to be divided among four lawyers for the two trials suggest something more than the usual charges.[142] Fees in Admiralty also seem to have been computed on a different scale. In the fall of 1772 Adams received a total of £12 for his services in the preliminary stages of the Kennebec Company's defense of its logs against Surveyor General John Wentworth (No. 55).[143] For the defense of Ansell Nickerson in a special court of admiralty, Adams received a note (never paid) for £6 13s.[144] Retaining

[138] See No. 12.

[139] Account with Kennebec Co., 5 Feb. 1774, MeHi:Kennebec Papers. The payments from 1769 to 1771 were made in cash. See Accounts of Henry Alline (Secretary of the Company), 1770, 1771; Waste Book, p. 147. MeHi:Kennebec Papers. For a summary of these trips, see Williamson, "The Professional Tours of John Adams in Maine," 1 Maine Hist. Soc., *Colls.* (2d ser.) 301–308 (1890).

[140] The 1778 vote is in 3 Kennebec Purchase Records 172, MeHi:Kennebec Papers. Adams' previous billing is in his account of 5 Feb. 1774 with the Company, note 139 above. For further discussion see No. 58, note 66.

[141] JA, Docket, SCJ Suffolk, Aug. 1772, Adams Papers, Microfilms, Reel No. 183.

[142] See editorial note to Nos. 63, 64, note 108.

[143] See vol. 2:257, note 39.   [144] See No. 57, text at note 25.

fees were also a fairly frequent source of income not regulated by statute. Sums of a pound or more might be paid to a lawyer, as much to prevent the other side from obtaining his services as anything else.[145]

It is possible to reconstruct the methods by which Adams kept his financial records. In his earliest years at the bar, he kept a single record in which he entered under the appropriate term of court each writ drawn and each suit in which he represented the defendant. Under each such entry he thereafter made a minute of his fee and of all subsequent phases of the case involving money, his receipts, and his own dealings with any funds of his clients that came into his hands.[146]

As his practice became more extensive, Adams' accounting techniques grew correspondingly more sophisticated. At first he seems to have operated entirely on a cash (or at least negotiable instrument) basis, and in the counties to which he traveled on circuit he apparently continued to use this method with all but a few major clients. After about 1768, however, the notation "posted" begins to appear beside certain entries in his lists of Suffolk County actions, indicating that his fees and other charges for those suits were being entered in an account ledger of some sort against the name of his client.[147] Surviving materials for the years after 1770 show that there were at least three accounting tools in Adams' bookkeeping system.

The basic device was the "Office Book" or "Writ Book," a term-by-term listing of writs drawn for the Suffolk County Inferior Court, in which all fees and charges for drawing, entering, and serving each writ appeared, as well as the terms of any pretrial settlement of the action or direct payment of cash to Adams by or on behalf of the client.[148] If the disposition of the case was such that no execution was to issue, then the notation "finished" would appear beside the entry if

[145] See 1 JA, *Diary and Autobiography* 223, 319; JA, Docket, SCJ Suffolk, Aug. 1770, Adams Papers, Microfilms, Reel No. 184; JA, Docket, SCJ Suffolk, Feb. 1774, Adams Papers, Microfilms, Reel No. 183. Compare No. 58, note 44; editorial note to Nos. 63, 64, note 108.

[146] This early journal was broken up for souvenirs by a granddaughter, Elizabeth Coombs Adams, sometime in the 19th century. Three fragments survive today. One fragment, of two leaves, was in the possession of Goodspeed's Book Shop, Boston, which in August 1963 offered a single leaf for sale. *The Flying Quill,* Aug. 1963. A second, of ten pages, is in MQHi. A third single leaf is owned by the Bostonian Society. The three together form more or less consecutive parts of a single journal covering the period Jan. 1761 to Jan. 1763.

[147] The first such notation is in JA, Docket, Inf. Ct. Suffolk, July 1768, Adams Papers, Microfilms, Reel No. 182. See also 1 JA, *Diary and Autobiography* 264, 344.

[148] JA's Office Book for Jan. 1770 through April 1774 is in MQA. For descriptions of it in use, see Edward Hill to JA, 29 July 1774, Adams Papers; Cotton Tufts to JA, 18 Sept. 1790, Adams Papers. JA called this document the "Writ Book," but it has also been described as the "Office Book" when cited in the present edition.

Adams had been paid in cash or by note; "posted" would appear if any unpaid balance was being transferred to the client's account; or "not to be posted" might be written, indicating that for some reason Adams was not charging for his services. Sometimes the notation would be "posted to Mr. ———," a third party who apparently was bearing the charges of a particular action.

If execution was to be levied in behalf of Adams' client, the entry "posted E.B." would appear in the Writ Book, meaning that the case had been entered in the second bookkeeping device, the "Execution Book."[149] There the amounts of the judgment, costs, and fee for the execution were entered. Upon satisfaction, Adams either received the amount of the costs (his fees and outlays) in cash, in which case the notation "finished" appears, or the balance of costs outstanding was "posted" to the client's account.

Debtor and creditor ledgers in which each client had a separate account were the third device. Here were posted entries from the writ and execution books. Other fees and charges, such as those for attendance at court, arguing and trying cases, and obtaining copies of the record and papers in appealed cases, were entered separately in the ledgers when the matter was such that no bill of costs embodying these charges could be taxed against the other party. Credits, such as payments on account, were also entered.[150] The means which Adams used for keeping track of these last billable items is not entirely clear. He was charged for copies of records by the court clerk who prepared them, and he posted such charges from the bill to the appropriate accounts.[151] The other matters are occasionally noted in the docket lists supplied by the clerk each term, which Adams used as a kind of running register of the disposition of his cases. Inconsistency in such entries suggests the existence of still a fourth bookkeeping tool, a case-by-case record in which attendance and like matters were recorded systematically. Occasional mentions of "minute books" in the docket lists may refer to such a device.[152]

[149] No copy of an "Execution Book" has survived. The description which follows in the text is based on several leaves found in the Writ Book, note 148 above, which had evidently served as an overflow execution book.

[150] None of these ledgers has survived. The description which follows in the text is based on copies of accounts rendered to clients by JA which were evidently drawn from such ledgers. See materials cited in notes 137, 139, above. See also JA's account with the estate of John Ruddock, 1770–1772, Adams Papers, Microfilms, Reel No. 185.

[151] See Middlecott Cooke's account with JA, March 1770, Adams Papers. See 1 JA, *Diary and Autobiography* 350 note.

[152] See JA, Docket, Inf. Ct. Suffolk, Jan. 1772; SCJ Suffolk, Feb. 1774, Adams Papers, Microfilms, Reel No. 183.

Since Adams' receipts tended to take the form of promissory notes or accounts receivable, collection was a serious problem. Part of the difficulty lay in Adams' extreme slowness about calling his debtors to book, a trait probably resulting from press of business, rather than generosity. For example, Hancock's account, already described, covered a period of over two years when rendered, and in the Adams Papers there are still a number of unreceipted notes for legal fees given by various impoverished clients.[153] In 1790, when he was serving in Philadelphia as the nation's first Vice President, accounts both for and against him, dating from his pre-Revolutionary law practice, were still outstanding.[154] Adams was not always so slow, however, and was, in fact, one of his own best clients. Nearly forty actions in which he was plaintiff have been identified in the court files. Although many of them are suits on notes or bonds which could have arisen in other ways, several are on accounts which clearly show that the defendant was a defaulting client.[155]

The Intellectual Side

Amidst the confusion and detail of his extensive practice, Adams never lost sight of the one element in his professional make-up which raised him above so many of his contemporaries at the bar. His questing, Harvard-opened mind, stimulated by the example of Putnam, and to a far greater extent by Gridley, always approached the law on the highest possible plane as an intellectual discipline—one of the humanities. As he read the dry and endlessly annotated texts of the civil law and the ancient common-law classics urged upon him by Gridley, he also worked his way through the philosophers of the Enlightenment, who spoke so much in jurisprudential terms. Justinian, Vinnius, Bracton, Coke, Bolingbroke, Montesquieu, and Rousseau mingle in the early diary entries that record his reading. From this course of study came the appreciation of law as politics, law as philosophy, and law as jurisprudence which so colored Adams' later approach to the problems of his time and was so much a part of his contribution to their solution.

Gridley's original inspiration had been a critical factor in the

[153] See text at note 144 above. These notes are filed under date in the Adams Papers.

[154] Cotton Tufts to JA, 18 Sept. 1790, Adams Papers.

[155] See, for example, Adams v. Bowditch, Inf. Ct. Suffolk, Jan. 1773, SF 91541; Adams v. Brown, Inf. Ct. Suffolk, Jan. 1773, SF 91520; Adams v. Eddy, Inf. Ct. Suffolk, July 1770, SF 89715; Adams v. Whitmarsh, Inf. Ct. Suffolk, April 1771, SF 90271, reproduced as an illustration in this volume.

formation of this intellectual interest, and Gridley was to be instrumental in reviving it and directing it at its maturity. In January 1765 the older lawyer brought Adams and two or three contemporaries together in a legal study and discussion group, which Adams called the "sodality," or "Sodalitas, A Clubb of Friends."[156] The group does not seem to have lasted long, but while it flourished, Adams found it highly stimulating and rewarding. The readings in the ancient English and Roman law were such as he might have pored over alone, but the sodality changed what had been dutiful labor into a source of heightened comprehension, as the "Friends" explored thoroughly the philosophical and historical roots of their legal system. Out of this exploration came Adams' first major piece of writing, later called "A Dissertation on the Canon and Feudal Law," which is discussed more fully below.

An important manifestation of Adams' intellectual approach to the law was the size and breadth of his law library. Naturally, a busy and prosperous lawyer would require a full collection of reports, treatises, abridgments, collections of precedents, and statute books. These were stock in trade, but the expansion of Adams' library into what he later described as "the best Library of Law in the State"[157] was in great measure a part of his broader intellectual development.

As early as 1761 Adams could report that he had "bought some Books &c.," and there is evidence of sporadic purchases after that, but for many years he could satisfy his appetite only through borrowing from others. Harvard College, Gridley, Otis, and Samuel Quincy were among those who lent him books too esoteric and expensive for a young lawyer to buy, even if he could have found them in the bookstalls of Boston.[158] He apparently bought many of Gridley's books at auction after the latter's death, a solid start for a substantial collection.[159] In 1768, when his practice had begun to bring him significant returns, he wrote in his diary on the eve of the Gridley sale that he was "mostly intent at present, upon collecting a Library," a project which he found took "a great deal of Thought, and Care, as well as Money."[160] The source of his later complaints that he had "spent an

---

[156] See 1 JA, *Diary and Autobiography* 251–258; compare 3 *id.* at 285–286.

[157] 3 JA, *Diary and Autobiography* 274.

[158] See 1 JA, *Diary and Autobiography* 224, 317; see also note 117 above.

[159] See the large number of books bearing Gridley's autograph in *Catalogue of JA's Library, passim.* See, for example, 1 JA, *Diary and Autobiography* 57 note, 199 note. Gridley's library, "consisting of Law, History, Divinity, &c.," was sold on 2 Feb. 1768 with a printed catalogue. See *Boston Gazette*, 25 Jan. 1768, p. 4, col. 2; 1 Feb. 1768, p. 3, col. 2.

[160] 1 JA, *Diary and Autobiography* 337. For law books on sale in Boston at this

Estate in Books" is apparent in his efforts in 1771 to open a "Correspondence" with Messrs. Dilly, London booksellers. He expected to spend £20 or £30 a year on books and wanted sent to him "every Book and Pamphlet, of Reputation, upon the subjects of Law and Government as soon as it comes out—for I have hitherto been such an old fashiond Fellow, as to waste my Time upon Books, which noBody else ever opened here, to the total Neglect of spick and span." [161]

The editors have not attempted to produce a detailed bibliography of Adams' law books, or even to identify them consistently in footnotes. The sources for a bibliographical study exist, and it is to be hoped that one may be forthcoming, either as part of a larger study of the successive and cumulative Adams family libraries to be prepared by the Adams Papers editors, or as a separate essay. The best existing source is the printed *Catalogue* of John Adams' books as they now stand in the Boston Public Library.[162] This work shows, for example, that he owned at least nineteen volumes of reports, including Barnardiston, Burrow, Coke, Croke, Hobart, Kelyng, Lord Raymond, Salkeld, Saunders, and Vernon; Bacon's and Viner's *Abridgments*; Ruffhead's English *Statutes at Large*; Rastell's, Coke's, and Lilly's books of entries; and a large number of treatises and general works on common law, civil law, the law of nations, and more general jurisprudential topics. Among the treatises were Gilbert's works on the Exchequer, the Court of Chancery, and feudal tenures; Barrington, *Observations on the Statutes*; Godolphin, *Orphans' Legacy* and *Repertorium Canonicum*; Foley, *Poor Laws*; Fortescue, *De Laudibus Angliæ*; Calvinus, *Lexicon Juridicum*; Gardiner, *Instructor Clericalis*; Hale, *History of the Pleas of the Crown*; Hawkins, *Pleas of the Crown*; the *State Trials*; Selden, *Opera Omnia*; Malynes, *Lex Mercatoria*; Swinburne, *Testaments and Last Wills*; Blackstone, *Commentaries*, in English and American editions (to the latter of which Adams was a subscriber);[163] and many other 18th-century legal works.

The *Catalogue* cannot be relied upon as accurate for two reasons. First, it does not represent the entire Adams family library by any means. Among John Quincy Adams' books in the Stone Library at Quincy are undoubtedly books once belonging to the elder Adams

time, see bookseller John Mein's advertisement of Burrow's *Reports*, Blackstone's *Commentaries*, and other legal works. *Boston Chronicle*, 2 May 1768, Supplement, p. 183.

[161] 1 *Adams Family Correspondence* 74–75; see also *id.* at 72–73, 80.

[162] *Catalogue of the John Adams Library in the Public Library of the City of Boston* (Boston, 1917).

[163] *Catalogue of JA's Library* 28; see Charles Warren, *A History of the American Bar* 178 (Cambridge, 1912).

that were appropriated by the younger, who also had a brief legal career.[164] Secondly, Adams remained interested in the law for nearly fifty years after he left active practice, and in many cases it cannot be determined when a given book in the *Catalogue* was purchased. There are specific references to a few books in Adams' diary and correspondence which permit such a dating,[165] and occasionally a book itself bears a date of acquisition. There are also countless citations of legal works, not only in the present edition, but throughout the diary as well. Although these citations are a great aid in determining the content of Adams' library, they present certain pitfalls. Since lawyers frequently lent one another books, a particular citation may mean only that the cited work was owned by someone in Boston. It may not mean even that much. Careful scrutiny will reveal that citations have often been lifted bodily from another source, such as a treatise or abridgment. This is especially true of references to the more obscure English reports. The final compilation of an Adams legal bibliography will thus involve a careful process of study of the available books themselves and contemporary references to them, combined with a weighing of the probabilities that Adams used a given work.

The Legal Profession

Adams' awe before the leaders of the bar at the time of his admission in 1758 has been described. His own professional maturing can perhaps be measured in the speed with which awe and the desire to attract and please turned into critical evaluation. His keen eye soon caught their foibles: Gridley's "great Learning, his great Parts and his majestic Manner ... diminished by stiffness and affectation"; Prat, with "a strong, elastic Spring, or what we call Smartness, and Strength in his Mind"; Otis, "extremely quick and elastic," who "springs, and twitches his Muscles about in thinking"; Thatcher, lacking "this same Strength and Elasticity ... sensible, but slow of Conception and Communication ... queer, and affected." [166] Kent, "for fun, Drollery, Humour, flouts, Jeers, Contempt ... an irregular

---

[164] As to the Adams' libraries generally, see 1 JA, *Diary and Autobiography* xxxvii note.

[165] For example, on 23 Sept. 1775 Joseph Hawley wrote to AA that "The Publick have great Need of two Vols. of Mr. Adams *English Statutes at large.* The edition which Mr. Adams owns is (if I don't mistake) Ruffhead's." 1 *Adams Family Correspondence* 283. See also the memo in JA's account with John Hancock of Dec. 1771, note 137 above, indicating that Hancock had procured for JA a set of the *State Trials.*

[166] 1 JA, *Diary and Autobiography* 83–84.

immethodical Head, but his Thoughts are often good and his Expressions happy." [167] Younger men, too, came under his critical gaze. Fitch was "not Steady," with "a look of Conceit, affectation, Suspicion, and Diffidence. His swell. His Puff." [168] Auchmuty argued with "voluble Repetition and repeated Volubility." How was "this Man conspicuous? in Reasoning? in Imagination? in Painting? in the Pathetic? or what? In Confidence, in Dogmatism, &c." To call him a leader of the bar was "a Libel upon it—a Reproach and disgrace to it." [169] And through all runs the tragic decline of Otis, once "Nervous, Concise, and pithy," now (in 1770) "verbose, roundabout and rambling, and long winded ... an Object of Admiration, Reverence, Contempt and Compassion all at once." [170]

As his personal evaluations of the bar sharpened, his collective judgment of his colleagues grew more dispassionate. In 1766, he could, without comment, rank himself and two contemporaries among the leaders and calmly wonder which of them would be gone four years later.[171] That he had taken his colleagues' measure is perhaps most clearly expressed in his description of them in 1769: "I don't think the World can furnish a more curious Collection of Characters" than Otis, Kent, Dana, Gridley, Fitch, and the others.[172]

The informal manner in which Adams was examined and recommended for admission to the bar in 1758 suggests that this "curious Collection of Characters" was at that time very loosely organized, with rather ill-defined requirements of study and apprenticeship. The beginnings of a more formal organization may stem from Hutchinson's creation of the grade of barrister and the formalities of gown and wig in 1762. In any event, an actual bar association is known to have met thereafter. In February 1763 the bar agreed upon rules limiting practice in the Inferior Court to a "sworn attorney," only to see the court reject the proposals when Otis, who had apparently kept silent before, opposed them on presentation. "Thus," reported Adams, no doubt particularly aroused because of his long campaign against

[167] I JA, *Diary and Autobiography* 110.
[168] I JA, *Diary and Autobiography* 242.
[169] I JA, *Diary and Autobiography* 317.
[170] I JA, *Diary and Autobiography* 348–349. In May 1771 JA recorded his pleasure at being able to repay the favor which Otis had done him years ago in recommending him for admission to the bar. JA "strongly recommended 14 clients from Wrentham and 3 or 4 in Boston to him, and they have accordingly by my Perswasion engaged him in their Causes, and he has come out to Court And behaved very well, so that I have now introduced him to Practice." 2 *id.* at 12. Compare note 102 above.
[171] I JA, *Diary and Autobiography* 316.
[172] I JA, *Diary and Autobiography* 347.

pettifoggers, "with a whiff of Otis's pestilential Breath, was this whole system blown away." [173]

At another meeting described by Adams in July 1766, the bar met formally to vote upon the admission of "3 young Gentlemen"—a significant advance over the private consultations with which Adams was ushered into practice. Still more important, at this meeting "the Bar has at last introduced a regular Progress, to the Gown, and seven Years must be the State of Probation." [174] The new rule seems to have meant three years of study, two years as an Inferior Court attorney, and two years as an attorney in the Superior Court—a "Progress" slow enough to meet the twin aims of assuring adequate preparation and hindering the development of competition.

In January 1770, for reasons that are obscure, a number of Suffolk County barristers and attorneys formed a new bar association in which Adams was to play a leading part. At the first meeting he was elected secretary and directed to "wait on Judge Auchmuty, and request of him, the records of a former Society of the Bar in this County." [175] The new group continued to meet regularly thereafter until July 1774, when the closing of the courts and the departure of many members (including the secretary) for other concerns brought a temporary halt. By 1778 the Society had begun to meet again, and, as the first Boston Bar Association, continued in existence until 1835. [176]

Like its predecessor, the new association concerned itself with rules of practice, but most of its deliberations were devoted to the regulation of law study and admission to the bar. At the start, prior practices were followed. For example, in October 1770 it was voted that Josiah Quincy Jr., Sampson Salter Blowers (two of the "3 young Gentlemen" admitted in 1766), and Francis Dana "be admitted as barristers, they having studied and practised the usual time." [177] In

[173] 1 JA, *Diary and Autobiography* 235–236. See, generally, 3 *id.* at 274.

[174] 1 JA, *Diary and Autobiography* 316.

[175] Suffolk County Bar Book, MHi, printed in 19 MHS, *Procs.* (1st ser.) 147 (1881–1882). The first sixteen pages of the MS (covering 3 Jan. 1770–26 July 1774) are in JA's hand.

[176] Hollis R. Bailey, *Attorneys and Their Admission to the Bar in Massachusetts* 58, 65 (Boston, 1907). JA attended meetings of the bar in other counties as well. See 2 JA, *Diary and Autobiography* 44 (Cumberland Co.), 94 (Essex Co.).

[177] Suffolk County Bar Book, 19 MHS, *Procs.* 148. Blowers and Dana were not called by the court until Sept. 1772. Min. Bk. 79, SCJ Suffolk. Quincy was never called, perhaps because of his political views, but this did not hinder him in the development of an active practice. As early as April 1769 he had tried a case to the jury, and at the Aug. 1769 Suffolk Superior Court he began "to manage all [his] own Business . . . though unsanctified and uninspired by the Pomp and Magic of—the Long Robe." Quincy, *Reports* 317. The intent of the distinction between

February 1771 the bar accepted the report of a committee of which Adams was a member, recommending adoption, with amendments, of certain rules of the Essex County bar. The new Suffolk rules embodied the requirement of a total of seven years' "Progress to the Gown," but added certain qualifications. No member was to take a student without consent of the bar, nor was anyone to be recommended for admission to the Inferior Court who had not studied with a barrister for at least three years. The consent of the bar was to be given only at a general meeting, and was not to be given to one who had "not had an education at college, or a liberal education equivalent in the judgment of the bar." [178]

Adams had more than a casual interest in the rules he helped to formulate, for one of his own significant contributions to the development of the legal profession was his role as teacher of the students who served as clerks in his office. When the new rules were adopted he already had two clerks and had seen at least one earlier student enter upon a successful career at the bar. He considered preceptorship a serious responsibility, for, he said on taking two clerks in 1769, "[M]y own Honour, Reputation and Conscience, are concerned in doing my best for their Education, and Advancement in the World. For their Advancement I can do little, for their Education, much, if I am not wanting to myself and them." [179] That he found it a responsibility worth bearing, however, appears in his comment in 1778 that "Few Things ever have given me greater Pleasure than the Tuition of Youth to the Bar, and the Advancement of Merit." [180]

In his Autobiography, Adams recalled that, from 1769 until the

---

attorneys and barristers seems to have been that only barristers should manage litigation and argue to court or jury. See Alger, "Barristers at Law in Massachusetts," 30 *NEHGR* 206 (1877). In general this seems to have been the practice, but the Minute Books show that occasionally attorneys joined barristers as co-counsel and more rarely emulated Quincy by appearing alone in a case. Lack of statutory authority for the distinction may have prevented both bench and bar from objecting or seeking to apply sanctions.

[178] Suffolk County Bar Book, 19 MHS, *Procs.* 149–150. A further rule provided that students of those whom the association had recommended as barristers would have the same status as students of those whom the court had called to the bar. *Id.* at 150. This provision seems to have been aimed at the situation of Quincy, Blowers, and Dana, note 177 above, who had been recommended but not called.

[179] 1 JA, *Diary and Autobiography* 338. JA charged William Tudor, one of the two, £10 sterling as a fee. *Id.* at 339–340.

[180] 2 JA, *Diary and Autobiography* 273. Compare JA to Jonathan Mason, 18 July 1776, Adams Papers, printed in 9 JA, *Works* 424. When his own sons were contemplating law study, JA wrote that he ought to come home and take them into his office, for he "was once thought to have a tolerable Knack at making Lawyers, and now would save a large sum by it." JA to Cotton Tufts, 2 June 1786, LbC, Adams Papers, printed in 9 JA, *Works* 549.

Revolution, he "had never been without three Clerks in my Office."[181] The following chronological listing of the ten men known to have clerked for him shows that this recollection is substantially correct:

Oakes Angier	ca. 1766–1768
Jonathan Williams Austin	August 1769–July 1772
William Tudor	August 1769–July 1772
Elisha Thayer	May 1771–February 1773
Jonathan Williams	September 1772–ca. October 1774
Edward Hill	October 1772–ca. January 1775
John Trumbull	December 1773–September 1774
Nathan Rice	July 1774–May 1775
John Thaxter	July 1774–July 1777
Jonathan Mason	September 1775–August 1776

There may possibly have been others who entered his office, but it seems probable that this list is nearly complete. Because in 1769 Adams had been reluctant to take even two clerks, it is unlikely that he would have carried any greater number than that appearing here in later years. As to the period before 1769, it seems probable that Angier, who was subsequently admitted in Plymouth County, was Adams' only student before he moved his office to Boston in 1768.[182]

Biographical details on Adams' clerks appear under their names in the Register of Bench and Bar. In summary, they were a group of young men of brilliant promise which most of those who survived the Revolutionary decade went on to fulfill in public service. Eight

[181] 3 JA, *Diary and Autobiography* 419.

[182] Among those who have been suggested as possibly having studied with JA is Royall Tyler, later Chief Justice of Vermont. See Tyler, "Royal Tyler," 1 Vt. Bar Assoc., *Procs.* 44 (1876). This is an evident error, probably based on the fact that Tyler, Harvard 1776, lived briefly in Braintree toward the close of the Revolution. He had already been admitted to the Inferior Court in 1780 on motion of Benjamin Hichborn, who was probably his preceptor. Suffolk County Bar Book, 19 MHS, *Procs.* 154. Moreover, his subsequent relations with the Adams family, arising out of his unsuccessful courtship of AA2, give no hint that he had formerly been in the intimate position of a clerk. See 3 JA, *Diary and Autobiography* 160–161, 192–193; Mayo, "Miss Adams in Love," 16 *American Heritage* 36 (1965). Another candidate is Israel Keith, Harvard 1771, who possessed a commonplace book containing notes directly attributable to JA, including a copy of the "Abstract" on writs of assistance. See No. 44, note 103; Quincy, *Reports* (Appendix) 478. Since Keith was admitted to the Superior Court as an attorney in 1780, the timing makes it possible that he clerked for JA, but there is no direct evidence. He probably was a student of one of JA's former clerks. JA refused to accept one William Lithgow in 1771 as not having been to college. 2 JA, *Diary and Autobiography* 19; compare Suffolk County Bar Book, 19 MHS, *Procs.* 150–151. JA also successfully recommended Levi Lincoln to Joseph Hawley as a student in 1773, indicating that perhaps Lincoln had wished to study with JA. Hawley to JA, 30 June 1773, Adams Papers.

were Harvard graduates, one was a Yale man, and one came from Princeton. Austin, Thayer, Williams, and Hill had all died by 1780, Hill while in the army, and Austin after two years of service. Angier, before his death in 1786, had amassed a considerable fortune in practice and had served in the first General Court elected after Independence. Trumbull, early American poet and wit, became a successful lawyer and judge in Connecticut. Tudor and Mason went on to long and productive careers in private practice and in state and federal government. Thaxter, who became an intimate of the whole family, was Adams' private secretary in Europe from 1779 to 1783. Rice served ably in the Continental Army through the Revolution and was a lieutenant colonel in the Provisional Army from 1799 to 1800.

The documentary remains of Adams' practice show that his students, like many others before and since on both sides of the Atlantic, did their share of "raking amidst the rubbish of Writs." The writs filed in his cases, notations in his dockets and account books, forms copied into his Pleadings Book, are more often than not in the handwriting of one or another of his "young Gentlemen." Perhaps remembering the dissatisfactions of his own student days, Adams gave his clerks much more than this fundamental 18th-century course of law study. In the first place, he expressed great personal warmth toward them, bringing some of them into his family and developing lifelong personal friendships with them.[183] Secondly, he gave them much responsibility for the conduct of the lesser phases of his practice—drawing writs, entering actions, keeping track of the court docket, and collecting fees from clients.[184]

Most important was the intellectual approach to the law, learned from Gridley and painstakingly developed further on his own initiative, which Adams sought to instill in his students. By personal example and teaching, he undoubtedly encouraged them to make constant use of his ample library. His diary and letters contain many references to the need for steady application to study. His views appear most strongly in two letters to Jonathan Mason written in 1776 when

[183] See, for example, 2 JA, *Diary and Autobiography* 9; 1 *Adams Family Correspondence* 145–146; JA to John Tudor (father of JA's student William Tudor), 23 July 1774, Tudor Papers, MHi, printed in 9 JA, *Works* 340–342. This personal relationship appears most clearly in the case of John Thaxter, Nathan Rice, and Jonathan Mason, who tutored the Adams children and were full members of the household during the trying days at the beginning of the Revolution. See 1, 2 *Adams Family Correspondence, passim.*

[184] See Jonathan Williams to JA, 28 June 1774; William Tudor to JA, 3 Sept. 1774; Edward Hill to JA, 4 Sept. 1774, all in Adams Papers. JA's dockets, cited in note 119 above, seem to contain instructions to a clerk, or clerks, for the management of litigation in his absence.

Mason had nearly completed a frustrating year in what was left of Adams' office and was contemplating abandoning study for more worldly pursuits. Adams advised his student against going into practice.

[I]t is of more Importance that you read much, than that you draw many Writts. The common Writts upon Notes, Bonds and Accounts, are mastered in half an Hour. Common Declarations for Rent, and Ejectment and Trespass, both of Assault and Battery and *Quare Clausum fregit*, are learn'd in very near as short a Time. The more difficult special Declarations, and especially the Refinements of Special Pleadings, are never learnd in an office. They are the Result of Experience, and long Habits of Thinking.

To learn the art of pleading, Mason was advised to read Plowden, *Instructor Clericalis*, Mallory, Lilly, Rastall, and Coke. "Your time will be better spent upon these authors than in dancing attendance upon a Lawyer's office and his Clients."[185] But this was only a beginning. The student must read all of the amassed wisdom of the common law to be found in Coke's *Institutes, Entries,* and *Reports*; in Horne, Bracton, Britton, Fleta, Glanville, and other ancient masters; and in the yearbooks, the earliest common-law reports. In addition, the great works of the civil law should be studied—not only Justinian and his commentators, but Wood, Domat, Ayliffe, and Taylor—because this was a study "so interspersed with History, Oratory, Law, politics, and Warr, and Commerce, that you will find Advantages in it, every day."[186]

If this was a course of study which might have caused the hardiest enthusiast to wonder when he would have time to eat and sleep, it was no more than Adams had set for himself and largely accomplished in the years since Worcester. If, as a practical matter, even Adams could not have allowed a clerk the time to get through such a curriculum, nevertheless, the very fact that such a challenge could be made must have opened the minds of his students to the broader meaning of the law.

[185] JA to Jonathan Mason, 18 July 1776, LbC, Adams Papers, printed in 9 JA, *Works* 423–424.

[186] JA to Jonathan Mason, 21 Aug. 1776, LbC, Adams Papers, printed in 9 JA, *Works* 432–433. There is little evidence that JA was familiar with the yearbooks. They were seldom cited in his cases and then probably only from secondary sources. In conversation with James Duane of New York in Philadelphia during Oct. 1775, however, he had learned that New York lawyers studied law by translating yearbooks. 2 JA, *Diary and Autobiography* 217–218. For details of clerkship under a regime similar to JA's, see JQA's account of his studies with Theophilus Parsons in 1787–1788. "Diary of John Quincy Adams," 16 MHS, *Procs.* (2d ser.) 295–464 *passim*, but especially 349, 351, 358 (1902).

Law and Public Life

John Adams brought two great qualities to public life from his legal training and experience. The first was a lawyer's natural aptitude for the business of government. The analytical and organizational abilities, the knowledge of the workings of daily affairs, which the study and practice of law develop in a lawyer, make him an instinctive specialist in administration and legislation. The second, perhaps more peculiarly Adams' own, was a broad understanding of the law as political philosophy. His extensive knowledge of comparative law and constitutional theory, a product of his years of reading, was an ideal background for the political crises of the times.

Adams put the first of these qualities into practice early in his career. After attracting attention in Braintree with his campaigns against alehouses and pettifoggers, he found as early as 1761 that he was being consulted on the town's highway problems. For several years thereafter, he served on committees having to do with such matters, as well as with the sale of town lands, and in March 1765 he was chosen surveyor of highways.[187] The "Abstract" of the writs of assistance argument which Adams prepared in 1761 (No. 44, Document II) was his first significant demonstration of the second quality. In 1765 the fortunate coincidence of developments in his private intellectual life and the passage of the Stamp Act by Parliament gave him an opportunity to bring the broader resources of his legal background directly to bear in a matter of great public importance. From that point on, the roles of lawyer, public servant, publicist, and political philosopher were inextricably mixed.

In January 1765 Adams' participation in Gridley's "sodality" had led him to contemplate, through the medium of legal history, the oppressive nature of the basic institutions of English government. His paper on the canon and feudal law, apparently first prepared for a meeting of the group sometime in the spring, described those oppressions at length and compared them most unfavorably with the efforts of the Puritan settlers of Massachusetts to escape the old ways and establish their own form of government in the New World.[188] Late in the spring came news of the Stamp Act, which Adams, bemoaning the damage it had done to his practice, called "this execrable Project . . . set on foot for my Ruin as well as that of America in General, and of Great Britain." [189]

---

[187] See 1 JA, *Diary and Autobiography* 201, 203, 226, 252 note, 261 note, 263; 3 *id.* at 278–280.

[188] 1 JA, *Diary and Autobiography* 255–258.

[189] 1 JA, *Diary and Autobiography* 265.

But, as Bernard Bailyn has pointed out, far from bringing him to "Ruin," the Stamp Act brought Adams for the first time into the affairs of province and empire.[190] His essay on the canon and feudal law now took on new meaning as he revised and expanded it for publication in the *Boston Gazette*. It appeared there in four installments between August and October 1765, with a conclusion characterizing the Stamp Act as a measure born of the old feudal tyranny and intended to aid in the suppression of hard-won colonial liberties.[191]

At about the same time Adams made his first official pronouncement on public issues. As a member of a town committee, he drafted Braintree's Instructions to its Representatives in the General Court, attacking a vice in the Act of particular concern to a lawyer—trial of offenses in admiralty without a jury—with supporting authority from Magna Charta.[192]

In December, Adams brought his legal talents directly into play when he argued before the Governor and Council in behalf of the town of Boston that the courts should be opened for business despite the lack of stamps. Adams' notes show that although his speech, like a courtroom argument, was narrowly phrased, it called for action in the broadest language, citing Coke and other authorities which supposedly demonstrated the limited power of Parliament.[193] His "Clarendon" letters, published in the *Boston Gazette* in January 1766, with their elaborate description of the British constitution, relied heavily on Coke, both as authority and inspiration.[194]

Riding the crest of the notoriety which the Stamp Act had brought him, Adams was elected a Braintree selectman in March 1766, defeating a candidate supported by the pro-government faction.[195] He then apparently campaigned for the General Court in May, but, while the rest of the Province rewarded the recent opponents of Parliamentary rule, Braintree, "insensible to the Common Joy" at repeal of the Stamp Act, returned a Crown supporter to the legislature.[196] Adams consoled himself in the office of selectman, where for two years he served the public in a more workaday fashion, becoming immersed in the perennial problems of local government—schools, poor relief, taxes,

[190] Bailyn, "Butterfield's Adams: Notes for a Sketch," 19 *WMQ* (3d ser.) 250 (1962).

[191] Printed under its later title, "Dissertation on the Canon and Feudal Law," with CFA's comment, in 3 JA, *Works* 447–464.

[192] Printed in 3 JA, *Works* 465–468. See 1 JA, *Diary and Autobiography* 265 note.

[193] See 1 JA, *Diary and Autobiography* 265–268; 2 JA, *Works* 159 note; No. 44, text at note 48; No. 46, text at note 68; Quincy, *Reports* 202–214.

[194] Printed, with CFA's comment, in 3 JA, *Works* 469–483. See also 1 JA, *Diary and Autobiography* 272–277, 281–282, 286–292, 296–299; No. 46, notes 76, 102.

[195] 1 JA, *Diary and Autobiography* 302–304.

[196] 1 JA, *Diary and Autobiography* 312–313.

and roads. In later years, when he tried many cases under the poor and tax laws, he was undoubtedly grateful for this exposure to local problems from the administrative viewpoint.[197]

In 1768 Adams declined to run for selectman again and moved to Boston, where he at once became involved in the clubs and caucuses of urban politics. Events soon brought his law practice and his political activities into phase. In the turmoil after the seizure of John Hancock's *Liberty* in June 1768, he drafted Boston's Instructions to its representatives, putting forward legal arguments against the presence of H.M.S. *Romney* in Boston Harbor and the impressment activities of her captain. His defense of Hancock in suits for penalties for alleged smuggling in the *Liberty* was the source for a second set of Boston Instructions in March 1769 and several contributions to "A Journal of the Times," a patriotic propaganda column which appeared in both Boston and other colonial newspapers. These writings again drew heavily on Coke and his interpretation of Magna Charta, as well as on a number of civil-law authorities.[198] At about this time Adams achieved enough prominence to lead various Crown adherents into unsuccessful efforts to draw him to the royal side.[199]

Adams was elected to the House of Representatives from Boston in June 1770,[200] despite his having agreed to defend Preston and the British troops after the Massacre (Nos. 63, 64). There he served with great industry for a year, apparently acting as legal adviser to the patriot faction in its clashes with Lieutenant Governor Hutchinson. He was a member of several committees formed to protest Hutchinson's order that the House sit in Cambridge, and he helped to prepare the final resolution which the House defeated in preference to dissolution.[201] Hutchinson reported that "the members of the first character for knowledge in the law were much engaged in" a subsequent controversy over the form of the enacting clause in legislation regulating provincial salaries. Adams, Joseph Hawley, and Daniel Leonard were members of a committee appointed to report on the matter.[202]

---

[197] 1 JA, *Diary and Autobiography* 304–305, 332–333. See warnings under the poor laws signed by JA and other selectmen in SF 87296, SF 87538, SF 87540. For his involvement as counsel in such local matters, see Nos. 24–33, 37. JA's client John Ruddock, note 150 above, was a Boston tax collector.

[198] See No. 46.

[199] See vol. 2:102–103 below.

[200] 3 JA, *Diary and Autobiography* 294.

[201] See 3 JA, *Diary and Autobiography* 295; 2 JA, *Works* 233–235 note; 5 A&R 138–139.

[202] See 2 JA, *Works* 235 note; 3 JA, *Diary and Autobiography* 295; 5 A&R 139–

A number of nonpolitical measures dealt with matters of importance to Adams then or later in his legal career. Among several new towns which the House carved out of hitherto unincorporated districts were four within the propriety of the Kennebec Company along the Kennebec River in Maine.[203] Because Adams had been active in litigation for the Company since 1769, it seems probable that he had a part in the passage of these acts. In November 1770 a committee of which he was a member brought in a bill, ultimately enacted, for a new statute of limitations, ending a twenty-year suspension of the limitations on certain actions. Adams must have found his acquaintance with this act useful when its construction became an issue in a case which he argued the next June.[204] Another measure arose out of a matter in which he had been concerned as counsel—the efforts of Baptists and Quakers to avoid taxation for support of the ministry. An act renewing exemptions for the dissenters, with "some small alteration in favour to the Baptists," included a provision of former acts, missing in the immediately previous one, that those exempted from taxation could not vote in town meeting on church matters. An election case which Adams had argued in 1769 demonstrated this gap in the existing statute.[205]

The combination of a hectic legislative term and a busy law practice, which had included the Boston Massacre trials, led Adams to leave not only the House but the town in April 1771, complaining that both his health and his business had suffered in the public service. When he brought his family back to Boston in the fall of 1772, it was with a firm resolve to stay out of politics altogether.[206] In this effort he was for a time successful, at least as far as elective office was concerned. The House chose him to sit on the Council in 1773 and

---

140. Hutchinson's comment appears in 3 Hutchinson, *Massachusetts Bay*, ed. Mayo, 227. For other public matters in which JA was involved at this session, see 2 JA, *Works* 235 note; 2 JA, *Diary and Autobiography* 2.

[203] See Acts of 26 April 1771, cc. 27, 30, 33, 34, 5 A&R 129, 132, 135–136. See also vol. 2:258, note 41, below.

[204] See Act of 20 Nov. 1770, c. 9, 5 A&R 109–111, 143; Smith v. Fuller, No. 21, note 21. For the activities of the committee, see *Mass. House Jour., 1770–1771* 98, 133, 140, 141, 157 (Boston, 1770–1771).

[205] See Act of 20 Nov. 1770, c. 10, §5, 5 A&R 113; Pingry v. Thurston, No. 31, note 11. For JA's other cases on this point, see No. 37, note 8. In April 1771 a resolve was passed having to do with the statute levying ministerial taxes in the town of Ashfield, an important controversy which reached the Privy Council and had ramifications in Philadelphia in 1774. *Id.*, notes 9–14; Resolve of 12 April 1771, c. 62, 18 A&R 495. The statute concerning theatrical entertainments, about which JA was called upon to give advice in 1773, had also been renewed while he was in the House. See note 108 above.

[206] For the moves see notes 123, 124, above.

again in 1774, but he was negatived on both occasions by the Governor.[207]

Adams did engage in one piece of public service of at least superficially a nonpolitical character. On 1 March 1774 the General Court appointed him, with James Bowdoin, a committee to prepare a statement of Massachusetts' claim to the "western lands," territory extending westward to the Pacific Ocean, which the province claimed under the terms of the old Bay Colony charters. According to his later account, Adams produced a brief supporting the Massachusetts position, which was not acted upon in 1774 because of sudden changes in the political scene, but which was rediscovered and used by the Massachusetts representatives in boundary negotiations with New York after the Revolution. A copy of this document, as supplemented by a committee in 1783, has survived, together with Adams' notes for it and materials he assembled to refute the New York claims.[208] Since the arguments seem to have been based on the terms of the various royal charters and confirmatory legislation, he must have found his work of the preceding year on the Kennebec Company's claim to mast trees cut on its lands (No. 55) a useful preparation.

In matters of more immediate political importance, Adams' resolve to avoid involvement soon weakened, but his role was to be unofficial. When Governor Hutchinson, addressing the House in January 1773, announced that Parliament could bind the colonies by legislation "in all cases whatsoever," the House felt obliged to reply. Adams supplied the authorities and reasoning underlying the paper delivered to the Governor on 26 January.[209]

More critical were questions concerning the judiciary. Since Thomas Hutchinson's appointment as Chief Justice in 1760 at the expense of the elder James Otis' claims to the post, the Superior Court bench had been involved in controversy. Hutchinson's plural office-holding, the appointment of his brother Foster to the bench after the

---

[207] 2 JA, *Diary and Autobiography* 82–83, 96 note.

[208] See 3 JA, *Diary and Autobiography* 302–304; 2 *id.*, at 95–96; 1 *The Law Practice of Alexander Hamilton* 553–561, 564–565 (N.Y., ed. Julius Goebel Jr. et al., 1964). The copy of JA's brief, in MHi, is printed in *id.* at 631–650. It has been asserted that this was not a partisan question. At the meeting of the joint boundary commission at Hartford in May 1773, however, it was patriot Joseph Hawley who sought to advance Massachusetts' western claims, and Governor Thomas Hutchinson who brought about an agreement that avoided the issue. The appointment of Adams and Bowdoin in 1774 thus may have been one more effort to embarrass the Governor. Compare 8 Sibley-Shipton, *Harvard Graduates* 200, with 1 Hamilton, *Law Practice*, ed. Goebel, 559–560.

[209] See 2 JA, *Diary and Autobiography* 78 note; 3 *id.* at 304–305; 2 JA, *Works* 310–311 note; 8 Sibley-Shipton, *Harvard Graduates* 199.

Governor resigned, the appointment as Chief Justice of Judge Peter Oliver (a relative by marriage of the Hutchinsons and brother of Andrew Oliver, Secretary of the Province), the fact that neither Oliver nor the Hutchinsons had received formal legal training, had all aroused criticism from the patriot side for years. Crisis finally came with the proposal of the Crown to make the judges of the Superior Court independent of the provincial legislature by paying them salaries out of revenues collected in the colonies.[210] At a Cambridge town meeting in December 1772, William Brattle, a member of the Council, had argued that the proposal was harmless, because the judges, having life tenure during good behavior, would not be influenced by the source of their salaries. Brattle then challenged Adams by name to debate the point and proceeded to have his argument published in the *Boston News Letter*.

Adams, fearful that, as a result of "These vain and frothy Harrangues and Scribblings," Brattle's "Ignorant Doctrines were taking Root in the Minds of the People," wrote a series of seven articles in reply, evoking a single rebuttal from Brattle. Adams contended that, unless a statute altered the common law, judges held office only at the King's pleasure, arguing that this was the rule in England until the Act of Settlement in 1701 gave judges life tenure. The authority which he cited to support this position is a good demonstration of his weapons for such a controversy. Besides citations from numerous reporters and the *State Trials*, he brought to bear not only such common-law authorities as Bracton, Coke, Fortescue, Bacon, Gilbert, Hawkins, and Blackstone, but also historians Hume, Rapin, Rushworth, and Stryk.[211]

These articles did not themselves end the controversy over judges' salaries, but they put Adams in a position to prepare the measure which did. According to his Autobiography, to avoid mob violence against the judiciary, he proposed that judges taking royal grants be impeached by the House and tried by the Council. He recalled that

---

[210] See vol. 2:101, 104; 8 Sibley-Shipton, *Harvard Graduates* 198–199; 2 JA, *Diary and Autobiography* 65–66. For examples of JA's feelings on the questions of nepotism and lack of law training among the Hutchinsons and Olivers, see 1 *id.* at 167–168, 259–261, 332; 2 *id.* at 90. As to Otis, see No. 44, note 21.

[211] Printed, with the Cambridge Instructions and Brattle's articles, in 3 JA, *Works* 513–574; see 2 JA, *Diary and Autobiography* 77–79. Samuel Stryk's *Examen Juris Feudalis* had been part of the reading of the sodality in Jan. 1765. *Id.* at 252–255. The provision of the Act of Settlement, 12 June 1701, was 12 & 13 Will. 3, c. 2, §3. On the question of judicial tenure in the colonies, see Edward Dumbauld, *The Declaration of Independence and What It Means Today* 112–115 (Norman, Okla., 1950).

he had supplied the authorities on which the proceedings were based, had developed arguments based on those authorities to convince the waverers that the power thus claimed existed, and had advised the committee of the House finally chosen to draft articles of impeachment against Peter Oliver, the Chief Justice, who alone had not renounced the royal salary. At the end of February the House adopted the articles and the matter went to the Council. There it remained unacted upon, despite further encouragement from Adams, because Hutchinson refused to preside.[212]

Although impeachment failed, its real purposes were ultimately achieved. Refusals of juries to serve if Oliver appeared, and threats of violence in the shire towns, had kept him from the bench through the spring of 1774. At the August term of the Superior Court in Boston he determined to face the issue and took his place with the court. As the mob, held back only by the fear of troops, roamed Boston, the jurors to a man refused to take the oath while Oliver, under impeachment, sat as Chief Justice. The court therefore heard only non-jury business for the brief remainder of the term. When it sat again in February 1775, with Oliver presiding in a now safely loyalist Boston, only a single case was called, and the history of royal justice in Massachusetts came to an end.[213] The courts in effect were closed, and the breakdown of civil order which could end only in Revolution had begun.

Adams characteristically bemoaned the effects upon his practice of these events and the passage by Parliament of the Coercive Acts,[214] but he had little time to spare in regrets. In June 1774 he was appointed to what became known as the First Continental Congress, and he left for its meeting at Philadelphia early in August. There he

[212] See 8 Sibley-Shipton, *Harvard Graduates* 518, 748–751. For JA's role, see 2 JA, *Diary and Autobiography* 88–89, 3 *id.* at 298–302. The idea of impeachment was suggested and some of the same authority cited in an attack on Hutchinson published in the *Boston Gazette*, 4 Jan. 1768, attributed to Josiah Quincy Jr. It is reprinted in Quincy, *Reports* (Appendix) 580–584.

[213] SCJ Rec., Aug. 1774, fols. 238–244; Feb. 1775, fol. 1. See 8 Sibley-Shipton, *Harvard Graduates* 751–754; JA to AA, 29 June 1774, 1 *Adams Family Correspondence* 109–110; same to same, 29 June 1774, *id.* at 111–112: William Tudor to JA, 3 Sept. 1774; Edward Hill to JA, 4 Sept. 1774, both in Adams Papers; *Catalogue of Early Court Files* 93–94 (Boston, 1897). The case in Feb. 1775 was Walker v. Parker, SCJ Rec. 1775–1778, fol. 1, formerly a JA case. See SF 92367. A referees' report for Walker was entered. In Aug. 1777, however, the case, still on the docket, was dismissed, the appellant being dead. Min. Bk. 103, SCJ Suffolk, Aug. 1777, C–60. Apparently no judgment had been entered on the report in 1775.

[214] JA to AA, 29 June 1774, 1 *Adams Family Correspondence* 113–114; see also *id.* at 117, 123. For the Coercive Acts, see vol. 2:105–106 below; Ross' Case, No. 53.

found that nearly half the delegates were lawyers.[215] Like him they were experienced in public service of the conventional sort, and many of them had also spent the last decade advocating opposition to the Crown on grounds in large measure drawn from the knowledge of legal history and constitutional theory that was part of the learning of their profession. With these arguments the lawyers had made a revolution. Now they were faced with the tasks of turning arguments into the constitutional basis of a new government and applying their talents for public service to make that government work.

Accordingly, after August 1774 Adams devoted his legal knowledge and abilities very largely to the development and operation of the governments of Massachusetts and the United States. In Massachusetts he sat in the Provincial Congress and on the Council, but his most important role was in the judiciary. He was made a justice of the peace for Suffolk County in September 1775, presumably the same kind of courtesy appointment that had been one of the old regime's major sources of patronage. On 28 October 1775 the Council notified him that he had been appointed Chief Justice.[216] This position might have seemed to him the peak of achievement in other times, but, with his constant absences to attend Congress, it proved a source of more vexation than pleasure. After much soul-searching Adams finally resigned the office in February 1777 on the grounds that he was unable to perform his duties and that he was being charged with the same kind of plural office-holding that he had found so obnoxious in the Hutchinsons and the Olivers before the Revolution.[217]

While he held judicial office, Adams worked steadily for the restoration of the judiciary and regular court sessions. He viewed these as essential to the establishment of a stable state government, not only because the judicial system was the part of government with which he was most familiar, but because he knew that it was through the

[215] 2 JA, *Diary and Autobiography* 96–97, 115. JA's conversations with his colleagues from other provinces are an interesting combination of mutual education and feeling-out. See *id.* at 98–127, *passim.*

[216] 2 JA, *Diary and Autobiography* 161 note, 166 note. See JA's commissions as justice of the peace and of the quorum, 6 Sept. 1775, and as justice of the peace throughout the Province, 8 Nov. 1775, both in the Adams Papers. See also AA to JA, 25 Oct. 1775, 1 *Adams Family Correspondence* 314. As to the patronage aspects of such appointments under the Crown, see JA to AA, 30 June 1774, *id.* at 116–117. The notification from the Council, 28 Oct. 1775, is in the Adams Papers.

[217] For JA's doubts about holding the office, see JA to AA, 18 Nov. 1775, 1 *Adams Family Correspondence* 327–328; same to same, 12 May 1776, *id.* at 406; same to same, 3 July 1776, 2 *id.* at 27; same to same, 18 Aug. 1776, *id.* at 99–100. For his resignation, see same to same, 10 Feb. 1777, *id.* at 159. See 3 JA, *Works* 23–25; 3 JA, *Diary and Autobiography* 359–360. JA had earlier resigned from the Council for similar reasons. See 1 *Adams Family Correspondence* 421 note.

courts that most people, especially in the remote parts of the state, received their principal contact with the central authority. His letters written from Philadelphia to his friends and judicial colleagues at home were filled with urgings and questions about the preparations for reopening the courts. On a brief visit to Massachusetts in the winter of 1775–1776, he drafted a proclamation for the General Court which was to be read in town meetings and at the opening of the courts—perhaps as part of the charge to the grand jury, a common vehicle for political pronouncements at this time.[218] In this document Adams set forth briefly the justifications for independence and for the establishment of a state government and called upon all to support the new institutions. He gave particular emphasis to the "magistrates and courts of justice," who were "to see those laws enforced, which are necessary for the preservation of peace, virtue, and good order." [219]

Adams' only direct participation in the return of justice to Massachusetts was literally nominal: his name was "tested" (i.e. signed) as Chief Justice by the clerk on the venires for each county. When the courts finally did reopen in June 1776, however, his spirit was behind the careful dignity with which the judges proceeded, and his eager queries as to their success were in their hands almost as soon as the terms were over. Only after he was satisfied that the people had accepted the new system did he feel that he had sufficiently discharged his trust to be able to resign his office.[220]

Countless legislative and administrative labors which cannot be detailed here occupied Adams in the Continental Congress. Two in particular seem directly related to his previous career at the bar. He was on committees assigned to draft rules for the government of the navy in 1775 and to revise the articles of war in 1776. These military codes were largely based on the British articles of war and certain provisions of the Mutiny Acts, with which he must have been familiar

[218] See Cushing, "The Massachusetts Judiciary and Public Opinion," paper given at the Conference on Colonial History, Worcester, Mass., April 1964, to be published in George A. Billias, ed., *Law and Authority in Colonial America: Selected Essays* (Barre, Mass., in press). As to JA's concern for the opening of the courts, see JA to AA, 27 May 1776, 1 *Adams Family Correspondence* 420–421; same to same, 7 July 1776, 2 *id.* at 38; JA to William Cushing, 9 June 1776, Adams Papers, printed in 9 JA, *Works* 390.

[219] See facsimile of the proclamation, 23 Jan. 1776, in Worthington C. Ford, comp., *Broadsides, Ballads, &c. Printed in Massachusetts, 1639–1800* (75 MHS, Colls.), No. 1973 (Boston, 1922). The passage in text is quoted from the version printed in 1 JA, *Works* 193–196, from a MS in JA's hand then in M-Ar. See generally 2 JA, *Diary and Autobiography* 226 note; 1 *Adams Family Correspondence* 360 note.

[220] See AA to JA, 15 Sept. 1776, 2 *Adams Family Correspondence* 125; 3 JA, *Diary and Autobiography* 363. See, generally, Quincy, *Reports* 340–342. For the venire for the June 1776 Essex Superior Court, bearing JA's name, see SF 132468.

from his experiences with the British forces in Boston, not only at the time of the Boston Massacre, but during the months of occupation that preceded Lexington and Concord.[221] Adams' other service of a distinctly legal nature was his membership from March 1777 until his retirement in November of that year on the congressional committee formed to decide appeals from the newly formed state admiralty courts in cases of prize. In this role he sat on what was essentially a judicial body, clearly bringing to bear all his long courtroom experience.[222]

Adams' most significant services on the national level are beyond the scope of this essay. As a framer of and apologist for the constitutional basis of revolution, he put his broad understanding of law and politics and his personal experience with many of the critical issues to constant use in the congressional debates which formulated the theoretical consensus leading to the Continental Association in 1774 and the Declaration of Independence in 1776. The consensus was supported by his "Novanglus" papers (1775), a definitive statement of the colonial position, in which he cited an array of common-law and civil-law authorities, as well as writings in political philosophy.[223] Adams made another important contribution to the growth of the new nation with his works on the constitutions of the state governments formed as a necessary part of national development. The Massachusetts Constitution of 1780, which he drafted, was a vivid example for other states of theory being put into practice.[224] All of these activities, as well as his diplomatic career and his subsequent service as Vice President and President, drew to a greater or lesser extent on his background as a lawyer and student of law.

Detailed discussion of the relation between Adams' legal back-

[221] See 3 JA, *Diary and Autobiography* 346, 409–412; Nos. 60, 61, 63, 64; AA to Mercy Otis Warren, 25 Jan. 1775, 1 *Adams Family Correspondence* 179–181. JA also may have gained some knowledge of naval justice from the proceedings of the special courts of admiralty before which he had appeared, since these bodies followed substantially the procedure of a naval court-martial. See No. 56, note 17. See, generally, William Winthrop, *Military Law and Precedents* 21–22, 929–971 (Washington, 2d edn., 1920).

[222] See No. 58, text at notes 4–10.

[223] Reprinted in 4 JA, *Works* 1–177. See JA's notes of the debates in Congress in 2 JA, *Diary and Autobiography* 122–250, *passim*. For a discussion of the relation between the text of the Declaration of Independence and the political crises of the preceding decade, see Dumbauld, *Declaration of Independence*, *passim*. The link between JA's role as lawyer, legislator, and polemicist in many of these crises, and his service on the committee which drafted the Declaration, is a particularly fruitful subject for further study.

[224] See JA, *Thoughts on Government* (1776), reprinted in 4 JA, *Works* 193–201; JA, *Report of a Constitution* (1779), reprinted, with extensive commentary by CFA, in 4 JA, *Works* 213–267; JA, *Defence of the Constitutions of Government of the United States of America* (1787–1788), reprinted, with a preface by CFA, in 4 JA, *Works* 273–588; 5 *id.* at 1–490; 6 *id.* at 1–220.

ground and his life in public service must await publication of his political and philosophical writings and public papers in later volumes of *The Adams Papers*. From even this bare summary, however, we may conclude that, in the practice of law and, most of all, in his own profoundly intellectual approach to the law, Adams found the great sources of inspiration which shaped and directed his contribution to the founding of this nation. In translating the residue of so many centuries of legal development into new ideas and forms of government that were to alter the course of world history, Adams stands as a classic demonstration of the wisdom of his guiding genius, Coke, who urged modern readers not to neglect the ancient yearbooks, because, "Out of the old fields must spring and grow the new corn." [225]

L. KINVIN WROTH
HILLER B. ZOBEL

[225] Preface, 1 Co. Rep. [ix] (Dublin, ed. George Wilson, 1793).

The Massachusetts Bench and Bar:
A Biographical Register of
John Adams' Contemporaries

Here follow brief biographical sketches of seventy-two judges, lawyers, and law students who were active during the period of John Adams' career as a practicing lawyer. The list includes: (1) all justices who sat on the royal Superior Court of the Province between 1758 and the closing of the courts in 1774; (2) all lawyers called to the Superior Court as barristers from 1762, when the degree was first adopted, until 1774; (3) a few important figures among the many lawyers who were admitted as attorneys in the Inferior or Superior Court from 1758 to 1774, but either were never barristers, or were called later; (4) the ten men who are known to have clerked for Adams from 1766 to 1777, regardless of when, where, or whether they were admitted to practice. It should be assumed that a lawyer practiced primarily in Suffolk County unless another county is mentioned in the sketch.

Since these sketches are intended primarily for identification, there has been no attempt at either bibliographical or factual completeness. In many cases the only reference given is to a standard source, such as the *DAB* or Sibley-Shipton, *Harvard Graduates*, where the reader will find citations to full-length biographies and other biographical works, as well as listings of the subject's own writings and manuscripts. Fuller references have been supplied only when there is no standard source on a subject, or important information does not appear in the standard source. It should go without saying that a great many of the sketches could be amplified by consulting the indexes to the present and preceding volumes of *The Adams Papers*.

In many of the sketches factual data, such as dates of admission to the bar, appointment to judicial or other civil office, and service in the legislature, have been supplied without citation from a variety of additional sources, including the Minute Books of the Superior Court; Whitmore, *Mass. Civil List*; the legislative lists contained in A&R; the Suffolk County Bar Book, MHi, printed in 19 MHS, *Procs.* (1st ser.) 147 (1881–1882); and the civil, legal, and legislative lists appearing in a series of almanacs published at Boston and variously titled, *A Pocket Almanack* (1780–1787), *Fleets Pocket Almanack [and] Massachusetts Register* (1788–1797), *Fleets' Register, and Pocket Almanack* (1798–1800), and *The Massachusetts Register and United States Calendar* (1801–1821). Many of these references, particularly those to the Minute Books, came from the Adams Papers Editorial Files.

Each of the sketches has been indexed under the subject's name, where it appears first among the entries, with the rubric "sketch of."

OAKES ANGIER (1745–1786). Harvard 1764. Studied law with JA, ca. 1766–1768. Admitted attorney, SCJ, May 1771; barrister, Aug. 1773.

Practiced in Plymouth Co. Represented Bridgewater in the House, 1776, 1778, 1779, despite his somewhat equivocal political stance. Amassed a sizable fortune in practice before his death. See 1 *Adams Family Correspondence* 84 note, 140–141; 2 *id.* at 4, 13.

ROBERT AUCHMUTY (ca. 1723–1788). Admitted to Harvard, class of 1746, but never matriculated. Admitted attorney, SCJ, Feb. 1752; barrister, Aug. 1762.

Advocate General in Admiralty, 1762–1767. Judge of the Massachusetts Vice Admiralty Court, 1767–1776, a post held by his father, Robert Auchmuty (d. 1750), from 1733 to 1747. Judge of the new District Court of Vice Admiralty at Boston from its creation in 1768 until 1776. Appointed Justice of the Peace and of the Quorum, 1769. Counsel with JA and Josiah Quincy Jr., q.v., in the trial of Captain Preston after the Boston Massacre, 1770 (No. 63). A leading loyalist; one of his letters to officials in England was among those published in Boston by the patriots in 1773. An addresser of Hutchinson, 1774. Sailed to Halifax and then England in 1776. Proscribed, 1778. 12 Sibley-Shipton, *Harvard Graduates* 12–16.

JONATHAN WILLIAMS AUSTIN (1751–1779). Harvard 1769. Studied law with JA, 1769–1772. Admitted attorney, Suffolk Inferior Court, July 1772; attorney, SCJ, Aug. 1778.

Witness in Boston Massacre trials, 1770 (Nos. 63, 64). Major in the Massachusetts forces and in the Continental infantry, 1775–1776. See 1 *Adams Family Correspondence* 81 note.

DANIEL BLISS (1740–1806). Harvard 1760. Admitted attorney, SCJ, Sept. 1768; barrister, Sept. 1772.

Brother of Jonathan Bliss, q.v. Practiced in Middlesex Co. Appointed Justice of the Peace, Worcester, 1767; Middlesex, 1773. An addresser of Hutchinson, 1774. Proscribed, 1778. Commissary in the British army during the Revolution. Thereafter member of the Council and Judge of the Court of Common Pleas in New Brunswick, where he remained until his death. Jones, *Loyalists of Mass.* 35–36.

JONATHAN BLISS (1742–1822). Harvard 1763. Said to have studied law with Thomas Hutchinson, q.v. Admitted attorney, SCJ, Sept. 1768; barrister, Sept. 1772.

Brother of Daniel Bliss, q.v. Practiced in western Massachusetts. Represented Springfield and Wilbraham in the House, 1768, 1769. One of the 17 "Rescinders" who voted to withdraw resolutions protesting the Townshend Acts, 1768. Appointed Justice of the Peace, 1770. Departed for England at the start of the Revolution and was proscribed in 1778. In 1785 appointed Attorney General of the newly formed province of New Brunswick. Served in the assembly there and was Chief Justice from 1809 to 1822. *DAB.*

MOSES BLISS (1736–1814). Yale 1755. Studied law with John Worthington, q.v. Admitted attorney, Hampshire Inferior Court, Nov. 1761; attorney, SCJ, Sept. 1763. Listed as a barrister in *A Pocket Almanack . . . 1780* (Boston, no date).

Began study of theology, being licensed to preach, 1757. Practiced in Hampshire Co. until 1793. Appointed Justice of the Peace, 1769; of the Quorum, 1771. Prominent in town affairs until the Revolution, when he withdrew, lacking sympathy for the popular cause. Represented Springfield in the House, 1796, 1797. Served as Judge, Hampshire Inferior Court, 1798–1810. 2 Dexter, *Yale Graduates* 365–366.

SAMPSON SALTER BLOWERS (1742–1842). Harvard 1763. Said to have studied law with Thomas Hutchinson, q.v. Admitted attorney, Suffolk Inferior Court, July 1766; attorney, SCJ, Aug. 1768; barrister, Sept. 1772.

Married daughter of Benjamin Kent, q.v. Associated with JA and Josiah Quincy Jr., q.v., in the trial of the soldiers after the Boston Massacre, 1770 (No. 64). Loyalist. An addresser of Hutchinson, 1774. Went to England in 1774. Proscribed in 1778 and imprisoned briefly (by Kent) on his return to Boston. Served as judge of the royal Court of Vice Admiralty at Newport, Rhode Island, in 1779 and as Solicitor General of New York, 1780–1783. Moved permanently to Halifax in 1784, where he was Attorney General, Speaker of the House, Councilor, and, from 1797 to 1833, Chief Justice and President of the Council. *DAB.*

SHEARJASHUB BOURNE (1746–1806). Harvard 1764. Admitted attorney, SCJ, May 1767; barrister, Sept. 1772.

Practiced in Barnstable Co. Appointed Justice of the Peace, 1773. Addresser of Hutchinson, 1774. Recanted. Involved in the affair of the *Lusanna*, 1775–1802 (No. 58). Represented Barnstable in the House, 1782–1785, 1788–1790. Member of the Massachusetts Ratification Convention, 1788. Served in Congress, 1791–1795. Chief Justice, Suffolk Inferior Court, 1799–1806. *Biog. Dir. Cong.*

THEOPHILUS BRADBURY (1739–1803). Harvard 1757. Admitted attorney, Cumberland Inferior Court, May 1762; attorney, SCJ, June 1765; barrister, June 1767.

xcvii

Practiced in Falmouth (now Portland, Maine) until 1779, thereafter in Newburyport. Appointed Justice of the Peace, 1768. Attorney General, Cumberland Co., 1777–1779. Served in the Massachusetts Senate, 1791–1792. Elected to Congress in 1795–1796. Sat on the Supreme Judicial Court from 1797 until his removal by legislative address in 1803 after a paralytic stroke. *DAB.*

WILLIAM BROWNE (1737–1802). Harvard 1755. Studied law with Edmund Trowbridge, q.v., but never practiced.

Appointed Justice of the Peace and of the Quorum, 1761. Briefly Collector of the Port of Salem, 1764, but dismissed, apparently in scandal over counterfeit clearances. Represented Salem in the House, 1762–1768. One of the seventeen "Rescinders" who voted to withdraw resolutions protesting the Townshend Acts, 1768. Judge, Essex Inferior Court, 1770–1774. Addresser of Gage, 1774. Appointed Judge of the Superior Court and a Mandamus Councilor, 1774. Took refuge in Boston. In 1776 sailed for England. Proscribed, 1778. Governor of Bermuda, 1781–1788. 13 Sibley-Shipton, *Harvard Graduates* 551–560.

ANDREW CAZNEAU (d. 1792). Admitted attorney, SCJ, May 1765; barrister, June 1767.

Brother-in-law of Daniel Leonard, q.v. Addresser of Hutchinson, 1774, and Gage, 1775. Sailed for Halifax, 1776, and thence to New York, where he fought in defense of the city. Proscribed, 1778. Marshal of the Rhode Island Vice Admiralty Court, Newport, 1780. Judge of the Vice Admiralty Court and member of the Council, Bermuda, 1780–1783. Returned to Boston, 1788. Died at Roxbury. Jones, *Loyalists of Mass.* 78–79.

PETER CHARDON JR. (d. 1766). Harvard 1757. Admitted attorney and barrister, SCJ, March 1763.

Early friend and correspondent of JA. Son of prominent Boston merchant. A namesake was Peter Chardon Brooks (1767–1849), leading Massachusetts capitalist and father-in-law of CFA. See "Memoir of Peter Chardon Brooks," 8 *NEHGR* 298 (1854); 1 JA *Diary and Autobiography* 47–48, 196–197.

JOHN CHIPMAN (1722–1768). Harvard 1738. Admitted attorney, SCJ, Oct. 1751; barrister, Aug. 1762.

Practiced in Essex Co. Appointed Justice of the Peace, 1761. Member of committee to instruct the representatives of Marblehead on the Stamp Act, 1765. While arguing in the Superior Court, Falmouth (now Portland, Maine), 1 July 1768, seized with an "Apoplectic Fit" and died a few hours later. 10 Sibley-Shipton, *Harvard Graduates* 276–277.

JOHN CUSHING (1695–1778). Had no formal legal training.

Resident of Scituate. Representative in the House frequently after 1721. Councilor, 1746–1763. Plymouth Co. Judge of Probate and Inferior Court Judge, 1738–1746. Justice of the Superior Court, 1748–1771, a post held previously by his father, John Cushing (1662–1737), and subsequently by his son William Cushing, q.v. Washburn, *Judicial History of Mass.* 298–299.

WILLIAM CUSHING (1732–1810). Harvard 1751. Studied law with Jeremiah Gridley, q.v. Admitted attorney, SCJ, Feb. 1758; barrister, Aug. 1762.

Practiced in Scituate from 1755 to 1760 and in Pownalborough (now Dresden, Maine) from 1760 to 1772, serving not only as Justice of the Peace and of the Quorum, Register of Deeds, and Judge of Probate, but as general counsel of the Kennebec Company during the latter period. In 1772 appointed Judge of the Superior Court, a post held by his father (John Cushing, q.v.) and grandfather (John Cushing, 1662–1737) before him. Only royal judge to be appointed to the Superior Court established by the Revolutionary Council in 1775. Presided at its first sessions and succeeded JA as Chief Justice of Massachusetts in 1777, serving until 1789. A member of the Massachusetts Constitutional Convention of 1779 and vice president of the state Ratification Convention in 1788. Appointed first Associate Justice of the Supreme Court of the United States in 1789, serving until his death. Appointed Chief Justice in 1796, but resigned the commission after a week for reasons of health. 13 Sibley-Shipton, *Harvard Graduates* 26–39. His MS Reports (MH-L) and other papers pertaining to his judicial service in Massachusetts are being edited for publication by John D. Cushing of the Massachusetts Historical Society.

FRANCIS DANA (1743–1811). Harvard 1762. Studied law with his maternal uncle, Edmund Trowbridge, q.v. Admitted attorney, SCJ, Aug. 1768; barrister, Sept. 1772.

Son of Richard Dana, q.v. After an unsuccessful private reconciliation mission in England, 1775–1776, served as a member of the Massachusetts Council, 1776–1780, and a delegate to the Continental Congress, 1777–1779. Secretary to JA's legation in France, 1779–1780. Minister (unrecognized) to Russia, 1781–1783, with JQA as his private secretary. Appointed to the Massachusetts Supreme Judicial Court in 1785. Chief Justice, 1791–1806. *DAB*. For a more detailed biography, see W. P. Cresson, *Francis Dana* (N.Y., 1930). His papers are in MHi.

RICHARD DANA (1700–1772). Harvard 1718. Admitted attorney, SCJ, May 1734; barrister, Aug. 1762.

Married a sister of Edmund Trowbridge, q.v. Practiced in Essex and Middlesex cos. before moving to Boston. Represented Marblehead in the House, 1738. Active in the affairs of the town of Boston, serving in various offices and as counsel. Appointed Justice of the Peace, 1756; of the Quorum, 1757. An active Son of Liberty, especially during the Stamp Act and Boston Massacre crises. Father of Francis Dana, q.v. 6 Sibley-Shipton, *Harvard Graduates* 236–239.

JOSEPH DUDLEY (1732–1767). Harvard 1751. Apparently studied with Jeremiah Gridley, q.v. Admitted attorney and barrister, SCJ, Aug. 1762.
Married Gridley's daughter. Participant with JA in Gridley's "sodality," 1765. Appointed Justice of the Peace, 1761. 13 Sibley-Shipton, *Harvard Graduates* 39–40.

DANIEL FARNHAM (1719–1776). Harvard 1739. Studied law with Edmund Trowbridge, q.v. Admitted attorney, SCJ, Nov. 1745; barrister, Aug. 1762.
Practiced in Newburyport. Appointed Attorney General for York Co., 1744; Justice of the Peace, Essex Co., 1752. Loyalist in sympathy, but did not go into exile. 10 Sibley-Shipton, *Harvard Graduates* 364–366.

SAMUEL FITCH (1724–1799). Yale 1742. Admitted attorney, SCJ, Aug. 1754; barrister, Aug. 1762.
Participant with JA in Jeremiah Gridley's "sodality," 1765. Appointed Justice of the Peace, 1762. Advocate General in Admiralty, 1770–1776. Appointed Deputy Judge, 1768. Solicitor to the American Board of Customs Commissioners, he was an Addresser of Hutchinson in 1774, and Gage in 1775, and left for Halifax and England in 1776. Proscribed, 1778. 1 Dexter, *Yale Graduates* 706–707; 11 Sibley-Shipton, *Harvard Graduates* 144–147; *DAB*.

EDMUND GOFFE. *See* EDMUND TROWBRIDGE.

DAVID GORHAM (1712–1786). Harvard 1733. Admitted attorney, SCJ, May 1766.
Practiced in Barnstable Co., but concentrated on office-holding. Appointed Register of Probate, 1740, and Justice of the Peace and of the Quorum, 1753. Addresser of Hutchinson, 1774, but recanted with Shearjashub Bourne, q.v. Continued practice and held minor offices after the Revolution, but denied commission as Justice of the Peace. 9 Sibley-Shipton, *Harvard Graduates* 300–303.

BENJAMIN GRIDLEY (1732–before 1800). Harvard 1751. Admitted attorney and barrister, SCJ, Aug. 1762.
Nephew of Jeremiah Gridley, q.v. Did not practice law extensively. Appointed Justice of the Peace, 1774. Addresser of Hutchinson, 1774, and Gage in 1775. Appointed judge of Suffolk Inferior Court by Gage, June 1775. Sailed to Halifax in 1776, and then to England. 13 Sibley-Shipton, *Harvard Graduates* 90–94.

JEREMIAH GRIDLEY (1702–1767). Harvard 1725. Admitted attorney, SCJ, Feb. 1732; barrister, Aug. 1762. (Sometimes called Jeremy.)

The leading lawyer of his time. Many of the outstanding lawyers of the next generation studied under him, including William Cushing, James Otis, Benjamin Prat, and Oxenbridge Thacher, qq.v. Others, notably JA, were deeply influenced by his knowledge of the law. Founder of the "sodality," a legal discussion group in which JA participated, 1765. Broadly interested in literary matters as well, founding the *Weekly Rehearsal* (1731) and (with others) the *American Magazine* (1743). Appointed Justice of the Peace and of the Quorum, 1746. Represented Brookline in the House frequently, 1755–1767. Appointed Attorney General, 1767. Represented the Crown in the argument on writs of assistance in 1761 (No. 44), but appeared with JA before the Council in 1765 to argue on behalf of the merchants of Boston that the courts be opened during the Stamp Act crisis. 7 Sibley-Shipton, *Harvard Graduates* 518–530.

JOSEPH HAWLEY (1723–1788). Yale 1742. Studied law with Phineas Lyman, Yale 1738, of Suffield, Massachusetts (now Connecticut). Admitted attorney, SCJ, Sept. 1751; barrister, Aug. 1762. "Silenced" (disbarred) Oct. 1767 for newspaper publications "containing divers injurious and scandalous Reflections on several of the Justices of this Court, for what they did in Court, and as Justices thereof." Restored on his petition and promise of future good behavior, Oct. 1769. SCJ Rec. 1767–1768, fol. 46; Min. Bk. 90, SCJ Hampshire, Oct. 1769; SF 157477, 157559.

Practiced in Hampshire Co. Appointed Justice of the Peace, 1749; of the Quorum, 1762. Principal spokesman of patriot party in western Massachusetts. Frequently represented Northampton in the House, participating with JA and others in many of the legislative battles preceding the Revolution. Elected to the Council in 1769. Declined to serve in Continental Congress, 1774, but maintained an active correspondence with JA and other members, urging independence. Elected to the House, 1775–1777. Developing mental illness caused him gradually to withdraw from public life after 1776. Critic of the Massachusetts Constitution of 1780, declining to serve in the state Senate because of the religious test imposed. *DAB*; 1 Dexter, *Yale Graduates* 709–712. For a more recent biography, see E. Francis Brown, *Joseph Hawley, Colonial Radical* (N.Y., 1931). Portions of his papers are in NN.

EDWARD HILL (1755–1775). Harvard 1772. Studied law with JA, 1772–1775.

Son of Alexander Hill, Boston merchant. Took a sum of money from JA's office, July 1774, in course of departure from Boston for personal reasons. JA apparently accepted his apology, because he is mentioned as in the office as late as Oct. 1774. Enlisted in the army and died of "camp fever," March 1775. 1 *Adams Family Correspondence* 146 note, 173; see letters of Hill to JA, July–Sept. 1774, Adams Papers.

JAMES HOVEY (1712–1781). Admitted attorney, SCJ, May 1752; barrister, Aug. 1762.

Practiced in Plymouth Co. Appointed Justice of the Peace, 1760; of the Quorum, 1764. See Washburn, *Judicial History of Mass.* 238; *The Hovey Book* 76–78 (Haverhill, 1913).

FOSTER HUTCHINSON (1724–1799). Harvard 1743. Had no formal legal training.

Brother of Thomas Hutchinson, q.v. Appointed Justice of the Peace, 1752; of the Quorum, 1761. Judge, Suffolk Inferior Court, 1758–1771. Justice, Superior Court, 1771–1775. Deputy Judge of Probate, Suffolk Co., 1765–1769; Judge, 1769–1775. Rejected the royal salary grant, but accepted appointment as Mandamus Councilor, 1774. Sailed for Halifax, 1776, remaining there until his death. Proscribed, 1778. Took no part in public life in Halifax, but claimed that he was still Suffolk Co. Judge of Probate and retained custody of the probate records until 1784, when Benjamin Kent, q.v., was able to procure their surrender. His son, Foster Jr. (d. 1815), was a Judge of the Nova Scotia Supreme Court. 11 Sibley-Shipton, *Harvard Graduates* 237–243.

THOMAS HUTCHINSON (1711–1780). Harvard 1727. Had no formal legal training.

The most important figure on the loyalist side in pre-Revolutionary Massachusetts. Appointed Justice of the Peace, 1740. Served in the House, 1739–1749, and on the Council, 1749–1766. Expert on provincial currency and credit. Lieutenant Governor, 1758–1771, serving as acting Governor from 1769 until his appointment as Governor in 1771. Chief Justice, 1760–1771 (did not sit after 1769). Also served as judge of the Suffolk Inferior Court, 1752–1758, and as Suffolk County Judge of Probate, 1752–1769. As judge and Governor, involved in the major political events of the period, including the arguments on writs of assistance (No. 44), the Stamp Act crisis, the Boston Massacre (Nos. 63, 64), the burning of the *Gaspee*, and the Boston Tea Party. Called to England in 1774 and relieved as Governor; never returned to Massachusetts. Author of *History of the Colony and Province of Massachusetts Bay*, a thoughtful and scholarly work, of principal value for its account of his own administration (first published in 3 vols., 1764–1828; ed. Lawrence Shaw Mayo, Cambridge, Mass., 1936, 3 vols.). 8 Sibley-Shipton, *Harvard Graduates* 149–215.

BENJAMIN KENT (1708–1788). Harvard 1727. Admitted attorney, SCJ, ca. 1739; barrister, Aug. 1762.

Began career as a Congregational minister. Dismissed by an ecclesiastical council after a heresy trial in 1735, but won a lengthy civil suit for his back salary in 1737. A Son of Liberty and correspondent of John Wilkes. Appointed state Attorney General, 1776. Served as Attorney

General for Suffolk Co., 1777–1785. Under the influence of his loyalist son-in-law, Sampson Salter Blowers, q.v., joined family in Halifax in 1785. 8 Sibley-Shipton, *Harvard Graduates* 220–230.

DANIEL LEONARD (1740–1829). Harvard 1760. Studied law with Samuel White, q.v. Admitted attorney, SCJ, May 1765; barrister, Aug. 1767.

Married White's daughter and succeeded to his practice in Bristol Co. Appointed Justice of the Peace, 1767; King's attorney for Bristol Co., 1769. Represented Taunton in the House, 1769–1772, 1773–1774. Addresser of Hutchinson and Mandamus Councilor, 1774. Author of "Massachusettensis" papers, seventeen pseudonymous newspaper essays defending the Crown, to which JA replied as "Novanglus," 1774–1775. Took shelter in Boston, 1774, where he was appointed solicitor to the Customs Commissioners in 1775. Sailed to Halifax in 1776, giving his legal services to the Crown there and in England, where he continued to act for the Commissioners. Proscribed, 1778. Admitted to the Inner Temple, 1779. Chief Justice of Bermuda, 1782–1806. Returned to practice in England, where he was a leading barrister until his death. *DAB.*

JOHN LOWELL (1743–1802). Harvard 1760. Studied law with Oxenbridge Thacher, q.v. Admitted attorney, SCJ, May 1765; barrister, June 1767.

Practiced in Newburyport until 1777, thereafter in Boston. Appointed Justice of the Peace, 1769. Addresser of Hutchinson, 1774, recanting several months later. Represented Newburyport in the House, 1776; Boston, 1778, 1780. Delegate to Massachusetts Constitutional Convention, 1779–1780. Served in Continental Congress, 1782–1783. Appointed to federal Court of Appeals in Cases of Capture, 1782. Judge, United States District Court, Massachusetts, 1789. Appointed Chief Judge of the First Circuit in Feb. 1801 by JA — one of the "midnight judges." *DAB;* 1 *Adams Family Correspondence* 405–406. His papers are in MHi.

BENJAMIN LYNDE (1700–1782). Harvard 1718. Studied law with Judge Samuel Browne, Essex Inferior Court, his uncle.

Son of Chief Justice Benjamin Lynde (1666–1745), who had studied at the Inns of Court. Naval Officer, Port of Salem, 1721–1729. Represented Salem in the House, 1728–1731. Served on the Council, 1737–1741, 1743–1766, declining to run thereafter because his efforts in favor of the Stamp Act meant certain defeat. Appointed Justice of the Peace, 1729. Judge, Essex Inferior Court, 1739–1746. Justice, Superior Court, 1746–1771; Chief Justice, 1771–1772. Presided at the Boston Massacre trials, 1770 (Nos. 63, 64). Essex Co. Judge of Probate, 1772–1775. Loyalist in sympathy (addresser of Gage, 1774), but managed to maintain a neutral position. 6 Sibley-Shipton, *Harvard Graduates* 250–257.

His diary is a most useful account of his activities on the Bench. See vol. 3:39 below.

JONATHAN MASON (1756–1831). College of New Jersey (Princeton) 1774. Studied law with Josiah Quincy Jr., q.v., 1774–1775; with JA, 1775–1776; with Perez Morton, 1776. Admitted attorney, SCJ, 1779.

Son of Jonathan Mason, who was a prominent Boston merchant, Son of Liberty, and witness in the Boston Massacre trials (Nos. 63, 64). Federalist. Served in the Massachusetts House and Senate periodically, 1786–1800, 1803–1808, and as interim U.S. Senator, 1800–1803. Thereafter withdrew from politics, but was elected to Congress, 1816, 1818. *DAB.*

DANIEL OLIVER (1743–1826). Harvard 1762. Admitted attorney, Suffolk Inferior Court, July 1766; attorney, SCJ, Aug. 1768; barrister, Sept. 1772.

Nephew of Chief Justice Peter Oliver, q.v. Practiced in Worcester Co. Appointed Justice of the Peace, 1768. Represented Hardwick in the House, 1770–1771. Addresser of Hutchinson, 1774. Sailed to Halifax, 1776, then to England, where he remained until his death. Proscribed, 1778. Jones, *Loyalists of Mass.* 222.

PETER OLIVER (1713–1791). Harvard 1730. Had no formal legal training.

Early Plymouth Co. industrialist, with poetic talent. Leading loyalist. Related to the Hutchinsons by marriage. Appointed Justice of the Peace, 1744. Judge, Plymouth Inferior Court, 1747–1756. Justice, Superior Court, 1756–1772; Chief Justice, 1772–1775. Represented Middleboro in the House, 1749, 1751, and sat on the Council, 1759–1766, upholding the Crown position. Impeached as Chief Justice by the House, 1774, for refusing to reject the royal salary grant. Jurors refused to serve under him thereafter. Appointed a Mandamus Councilor, 1774, and served on that body, taking refuge in Boston. Sailed to Halifax, 1776, and then to London. Proscribed, 1778. In retirement wrote *Origin and Progress of the American Rebellion*, a lengthy and very partisan account of the political events which he had witnessed (ed. Douglass Adair and John A. Schutz, San Marino, Calif., 1963). 8 Sibley-Shipton, *Harvard Graduates* 737–763.

JAMES OTIS SR. (1702–1778). Admitted attorney, SCJ, April 1731; barrister, Aug. 1762.

Father of James Otis Jr., q.v. Practiced in Barnstable and Plymouth cos. Appointed Justice of the Peace, 1734; of the Quorum, 1748. Attorney General, 1748. Disappointed in his aspirations to the Chief Justiceship by the appointment in 1760 of Thomas Hutchinson, q.v. — supposedly a cause of the younger Otis' enmity toward the Crown. Represented Barnstable in the House, 1745–1756; Speaker, 1760–1761. Councilor,

1762–1774 (negatived, 1767–1769). On the first Revolutionary Council, 1775–1776. Appointed Chief Justice, Barnstable Inferior Court, and Judge of Probate, 1764. Washburn, *Judicial History of Mass.* 212–213; see 11 Sibley-Shipton, *Harvard Graduates* 250–252.

JAMES OTIS JR. (1725–1783). Harvard 1743. Studied law with Jeremiah Gridley, q.v. Admitted attorney, SCJ, May 1750; barrister, Aug. 1762.

Leading pamphleteer, politician, and lawyer for the patriot side in the 1760's. Son of Col. James Otis Sr., q.v. Practiced first in Plymouth, but in 1749 moved to Boston. One of the most learned and successful lawyers of the period, with serious literary pretensions as well. Appointed Justice of the Peace in 1756, and at about the same time Advocate General in Admiralty. Turned against the Crown in 1760, allegedly because Thomas Hutchinson, q.v., was appointed Chief Justice in preference to James Otis Sr. at the death of Stephen Sewall, q.v. Resigned as Advocate General and in 1761 argued against the application of the customs officers for writs of assistance (No. 44). His argument, as recorded and circulated by JA, became an important piece of patriot propaganda and may have inspired Otis' *Rights of the British Colonies* (1764) and later pamphlets, which were of major significance in the Revolutionary movement. Represented Boston in the House, 1761–1769, despite growing doubts of his sincerity in the patriot cause, arising from the tortured course both of his political dealings and of the logic of his pamphlets. With Samuel Adams and Joseph Hawley, q.v., acted as a leader of the patriot majority of the House, attending the Stamp Act Congress in 1765. In Sept. 1769, struck on the head in a scuffle with Customs Commissioner John Robinson, an incident leading to protracted litigation, in which JA represented Otis. Thereafter, madness, occasionally apparent earlier, overtook him. Elected in 1771 to the House, but spent the greater part of his remaining years in confinement, or at least retirement, reappearing for brief lucid intervals succeeded by displays of obvious insanity. Killed by a bolt of lightning as he stood in his doorway watching a storm. *DAB*; 11 Sibley-Shipton, *Harvard Graduates* 247–287. See also Bernard Bailyn, *Pamphlets of the American Revolution*, 1:410–417, 546–552 (Cambridge, Mass., 1965).

ROBERT TREAT PAINE (1731–1814). Harvard 1749. Studied law with Benjamin Prat, q.v. Admitted attorney, Suffolk Inferior Court, May 1757; attorney, SCJ, Feb. 1758; barrister, Aug. 1762.

From 1749 until 1757, variously schoolteacher, merchant, whaler, preacher, and law student. Practiced in Boston until 1761, thereafter primarily in Taunton until 1781, when he returned to Boston. Appeared for the prosecution in the Boston Massacre trials, 1770. (Nos. 63, 64). Appointed Justice of the Peace, 1763. Represented Taunton in the House, 1773–1775, 1779. Speaker, 1777–1778. Declined seat on the Superior Court, 1775. Elected a delegate with JA to the Continental Congress,

1774; signer of the Declaration of Independence. Declined re-election to Congress in 1777, and chosen Attorney General of Massachusetts, serving until 1790. Councilor, 1775, 1780. On drafting committees for the Massachusetts Constitution of 1780. Sat on the Supreme Judicial Court, 1790–1804. 12 Sibley-Shipton, *Harvard Graduates* 462–482. His diary, extensive law notes, and other papers are in MHi and are a principal source for the present work. His correspondence is being edited for publication by Stephen T. Riley, Director of the Massachusetts Historical Society.

THEOPHILUS PARSONS (1750–1813). Harvard 1769. Studied law with Theophilus Bradbury and Edmund Trowbridge, qq.v. Admitted attorney, Cumberland Inferior Court, July 1774; attorney, SCJ, June 1776; barrister, ca. 1784.

Practiced in Essex Co. Leading lawyer of the post-Revolutionary generation, having many later distinguished students, including JQA. Interested in science as well, producing essays on astronomy and geometry. Author of the *Essex Result*, report of the Essex Convention in opposition to the proposed Massachusetts Constitution of 1778. A leader in the Essex Junto at the Massachusetts Constitutional Convention of 1779. Delegate to the Massachusetts Ratification Convention, 1788. Elected to the House, 1779, 1787–1791, 1805. Appointed Chief Justice of Massachusetts, 1806, serving until his death. *DAB.*

SAMUEL PORTER (1743–1798). Harvard 1763. Studied law with Daniel Farnham, q.v. Admitted attorney, SCJ, Nov. 1768; barrister, Sept. 1772.

Practiced in Essex Co. Addresser of Hutchinson, 1774, and of Gage, 1774. Fled from Salem in May 1776 overland to New York and thence to England, where he remained until his death. Proscribed, 1778. Jones, *Loyalists of Mass.* 237–238.

BENJAMIN PRAT (1711–1763). Harvard 1737. Studied with Jeremiah Gridley, q.v., and Robert Auchmuty Sr. Admitted attorney, SCJ, ca. 1746.

Leg amputated as result of accident, 1729. Married Auchmuty's daughter. Leading lawyer in Boston; minor poet. Moderator of the Town Meeting, 1757. Representative in the House, 1757–1759, but fell from favor with departure of Governor Pownall. Appointed Chief Justice and Councilor, province of New York, 1761. Returned briefly to Massachusetts during struggle over source of judges' salaries in New York, 1762. Went back to bench when struggle was resolved in Crown's favor. 10 Sibley-Shipton, *Harvard Graduates* 226–239. His law library of 115 volumes is itemized in the inventory of his estate filed in Suffolk Co. Probate Court, 8 July 1763, printed in Abbott Lowell Cummings, ed., *Rural Household Inventories* 202–206 (Boston, 1964).

JAMES PUTNAM (1726–1789). Harvard 1746. Studied law with Edmund Trowbridge, q.v. Admitted attorney, SCJ, Sept. 1749; barrister, Aug. 1762.

Practiced in Worcester. JA studied law in his office, 1756–1758. Appointed Justice of the Peace and of the Quorum, 1762. Addresser of Hutchinson, 1774, and Gage, 1775. Took refuge in Boston, 1774, and appointed Attorney General, 1775. Sailed for Halifax, 1776, then to New York, where he held a military post. Proscribed, 1778. Lived in England, 1779–1784. Then moved to New Brunswick as Judge of the Supreme Court and member of the Council. 12 Sibley-Shipton, *Harvard Graduates* 57–66.

WILLIAM PYNCHON (1723–1789). Harvard 1743. Studied law with Mitchell Sewall, Essex Co. Clerk of Courts and Register of Deeds. Admitted attorney, SCJ, June 1757; barrister, Aug. 1762.

Practiced in Essex Co. Had many students, including William Wetmore, q.v., later his son-in-law. Appointed Justice of the Peace, 1761. Addresser of Hutchinson, 1774, but recanted. Addresser of Gage, 1774. Although remaining firmly loyalist in sympathy, he braved out the Revolution in Salem, continuing to practice law in partnership with Wetmore, and finally being appointed a Justice of the Peace and of the Quorum in 1786. 11 Sibley-Shipton, *Harvard Graduates* 295–301.

JOSIAH QUINCY JR. (1744–1775). Harvard 1763. Studied law with Oxenbridge Thacher, q.v. Admitted attorney, Suffolk Inferior Court, July 1766; attorney, SCJ, Aug. 1768. Never called as a barrister, perhaps because of political beliefs, but practiced unhindered.

Radical leader, newspaper writer, pamphleteer, orator, and successful lawyer. Often called "the Patriot" to distinguish him from his father ("the Colonel") and son ("the President"–of Harvard), both also named Josiah. Brother of Samuel Quincy, q.v. At Thacher's death, continued law studies, taking over the office and retaining much of his late mentor's practice. Counsel for the defense with JA in the second Boston Massacre trial, 1770 (No. 64). Also represented an unpopular defendant in *Rex v. Richardson*, No. 59. Always frail in health, he died of tuberculosis aboard ship in sight of Massachusetts, returning from a secret, high-level, and unsuccessful, reconciliation mission to England in April 1775. *DAB.* Selections from his courtroom notes, started during his student days and now with other family papers in MHi, were published in 1865 as Quincy, *Reports.*

SAMUEL QUINCY (1734–1789). Harvard 1754. Studied law with Benjamin Prat, q.v. Admitted attorney, Suffolk Inferior Court, Nov. 1758; attorney, SCJ, Nov. 1761; barrister, Aug. 1762.

Early friend of JA. Brother of Josiah Quincy Jr., q.v. Counsel for the Crown in the Boston Massacre trials, 1770 (Nos. 63, 64). Appointed

Justice of the Peace and Solicitor General, 1771. Addresser of Hutchinson and Gage, 1774. Sailed for England, May 1775. Proscribed, 1778. Customs officer and successful barrister in Antigua and elsewhere in the West Indies, 1779–1789. 13 Sibley-Shipton, *Harvard Graduates* 478–488.

WILLIAM READ (1710–1780). Admitted attorney, SCJ, Feb. 1759; barrister, Aug. 1762.

Son of "Father Read," i.e., John Read (1680–1749), leading Massachusetts lawyer of the first half of the 18th century. Appointed Deputy Judge of the Vice Admiralty Court, 1766. Judge, Suffolk Inferior Court, 1770–1775. Appointed to state Superior Court, 1775, but declined. See 4 Sibley-Shipton, *Harvard Graduates* 369–377; Washburn, *Judicial History of Mass.* 184, 319; 1 *Adams Family Correspondence* 404.

NATHAN RICE (1754–1834). Harvard 1773. Studied law with JA, 1774–1775.

Joined Continental Army, 1775. Served during the war as aide to General Benjamin Lincoln and with Lafayette, attaining the rank of major. Settled in Hingham, which he represented in the House, 1801–1805. He seems never to have practiced law, but was active in town business. Colonel in the Provisional Army, 1799–1800, serving at Oxford, Massachusetts. Apointed Justice of the Peace, 1803; of the Quorum, 1810. Moved to Burlington, Vermont, 1811, where he remained as a leading citizen until his death. See 1 *Adams Family Correspondence* 142 note; Abby Maria Hemenway, ed., *The Vermont Historical Gazetteer*, 1:544 (Burlington, 1867).

JEREMIAH DUMMER ROGERS (d. 1784). Harvard 1762. Studied law with Robert Auchmuty, q.v. Admitted attorney, SCJ, Oct. 1769; barrister, Oct. 1772.

Practiced in Middlesex Co. Appointed Justice of the Peace, 1766. Addresser of Hutchinson, 1774. Took refuge in Boston, 1775. Sailed for Halifax, 1776, where he was a wine merchant until his death. Proscribed, 1778. Jones, *Loyalists of Mass.* 246.

NATHANIEL ROPES (1726–1774). Harvard 1745. Had no formal legal training.

Represented Salem in the House, 1760–1761. Councilor, 1762–1769, supporting policies of Hutchinson. Appointed Justice of the Peace and of the Quorum, 1761. Judge, Essex Inferior Court, 1761–1772. Essex Co. Judge of Probate, 1766–1772. Justice, Superior Court, 1772–1774. His death was hastened by the agitation over the royal salary grant, which he renounced on his deathbed. 11 Sibley-Shipton, *Harvard Graduates* 572–574.

CHAMBERS RUSSELL (1713–1766). Harvard 1731. Had no formal legal training.

Appointed Justice of the Peace, 1740. Judge, Massachusetts Vice Admiralty Court, 1746–1766. Judge, Middlesex Inferior Court, 1747–1752. Justice, Superior Court, 1752–1766. Jonathan Sewall, q.v., studied in his office. Frequently elected to the House from Concord or Charlestown, 1740–1754. Founder of the town of Lincoln, 1754, and its Representative thereafter. Member of the Council, 1759–1761. Supported the Stamp Act as judge and legislator. Died in England while apparently on a mission concerning the New York–New Jersey boundary dispute. 9 Sibley-Shipton, *Harvard Graduates* 81–87.

NATHANIEL PEASLEE SARGEANT (1731–1791). Harvard 1750. Admitted attorney, SCJ, Oct. 1764; barrister, June 1767.

Practiced in Haverhill. Appointed Justice of the Peace, 1767. Delegate to Second Provincial Congress, 1775. Represented Haverhill in the House, 1776. Declined appointment to the Superior Court, Oct. 1775, but accepted appointment, Sept. 1776. Delegate to the Massachusetts Constitutional Convention of 1779. Appointed Chief Justice, 1790. 12 Sibley-Shipton, *Harvard Graduates* 574–580.

DAVID SEWALL (1735–1825). Harvard 1755. Studied law with Judge William Parker, Portsmouth, New Hampshire. Admitted barrister, June 1763.

Married Judge Parker's daughter. Practiced in York Co., beginning 1760. Appointed Register of Probate, 1766; Justice of the Peace, 1767. Politically moderate, but reappointed to these offices, 1775, and served on Council, 1776–1778. Associate Justice, Superior Court and Supreme Judicial Court, 1777–1789. Member, Massachusetts Constitutional Convention, 1779. Judge, United States District Court for the District of Maine, 1789–1818. 13 Sibley-Shipton, *Harvard Graduates* 638–645.

JONATHAN SEWALL (1729–1796). Harvard 1748. Studied law with Chambers Russell, q.v. Admitted attorney, SCJ, Jan. 1757; barrister, Aug. 1762.

Practiced primarily in Middlesex Co. Early correspondent and friend of JA. Gradually increasing political differences led to a dramatic parting at Falmouth (now Portland, Maine) in 1774, but they were reunited warmly, if briefly, in London in 1787. Said to have turned to the Crown side when a petition to clear the bankrupt estate of his uncle, late Chief Justice Stephen Sewall, q.v., was rejected by the General Court after the Otises, qq.v., had promised to secure its passage. Appointed Justice of the Peace, 1762. As "Philanthrop," participated in newspaper controversy with JA over attacks on Governor Bernard, 1766–1767. Appointed Solicitor General, Attorney General, and Advocate General in Admiralty, 1767. "Informer" and counsel for the Crown in *Sewall v. Hancock*, No. 46, suit for penalties arising out of alleged smuggling in John Hancock's sloop *Liberty*, 1768–1769. Appointed Judge of the new District Vice Admiralty Court to sit at Halifax in 1769. Drew the Boston Massacre indictments (Nos. 63, 64), but withdrew from the prosecution, 1770. Addresser of Hutchinson, 1774, and of Gage, 1775. Took refuge in Boston, 1774. Sailed for London, Aug. 1775. Proscribed, 1778. Sailed to New Brunswick, 1787, where he practiced law, the Halifax Vice Admiralty Court having been abolished. His son Jonathan (1766–1840) was Chief Justice of Lower Canada, 1808–1838. 12 Sibley-Shipton, *Harvard Graduates* 306–324; see Stark, *Loyalists of Mass.* 456.

STEPHEN SEWALL (1702–1760). Harvard 1721.
Nephew of Chief Justice Samuel Sewall (1652–1730). Librarian and tutor at Harvard, 1726–1739. Achieved such renown for knowledge of the law gained through private study that he was appointed a justice of the Superior Court in 1739. Chief Justice, 1752–1760. Councilor, 1752–1760. Uncle of Jonathan Sewall, q.v. 6 Sibley-Shipton, *Harvard Graduates* 561–567.

SIMEON STRONG (1736–1805). Yale 1756. Studied law with John Worthington, q.v. Admitted attorney, SCJ, Sept. 1765. Listed as a barrister, *A Pocket Almanack . . . 1786.* Not on similar lists as either attorney or barrister, 1780–1785, indicating temporary withdrawal from practice.
Practiced in Hampshire Co. Represented Hadley and South Hadley in the House, 1767–1768, 1769–1770. In Massachusetts Senate, 1793. Justice, Supreme Judicial Court, 1800–1805. 2 Dexter, *Yale Graduates* 437–439.

JAMES SULLIVAN (1744–1808). Studied law with his brother, John Sullivan, q.v. Admitted attorney, SCJ, June 1770; barrister, Sept. 1772.
Practiced in York Co. until 1778; thereafter in Groton and Boston. King's attorney for York Co. Appointed Justice of the Peace, 1774. Served in the Provincial Congress and in the House, periodically, 1775–1784. Justice, Superior Court and Supreme Judicial Court, 1776–1782. Elected to Continental Congress, 1783. Massachusetts Attorney General, 1790. Defeated by Federalist candidate in race for governor, 1797, but elected to the office in 1807 and, narrowly, in 1808. Author of several works on legal and historical topics. *DAB.*

JOHN SULLIVAN (1740–1795). Studied law with Samuel Livermore. Portsmouth, New Hampshire. Admitted attorney, SCJ, June 1767.
Brother of James Sullivan. q.v. Practiced in New Hampshire. Delegate to First and Second Continental Congresses. Appointed Brigadier General, 1775, Major General, 1776, fighting in many of the major campaigns of the Revolution until his resignation in 1779 for health reasons. Attorney General of New Hampshire, 1782–1786. Served in state Assembly (Speaker, 1785). Elected "President" (governor) of New Hampshire, 1786, 1787, 1789. Judge, United States District Court, New Hampshire, 1789–1795. *DAB.*

SAMUEL SWIFT (1715–1775). Harvard 1735. Studied law with Jeremiah Gridley, q.v. Admitted attorney, SCJ, Aug. 1761; barrister, Aug. 1762.

In office of Suffolk Co. Clerk of Courts, ca. 1736–1744; thereafter in practice in Boston. Appointed Justice of the Peace, 1741. Not reappointed after accession of George III, 1760. Leading Son of Liberty. Said to have been a manager of the Boston Tea Party. Served on Committee of Correspondence and on a Committee appointed in 1773 to prepare a vindication of Boston. Moderator of the Town Meeting, April 1775. Caught in Boston by the British; died under house arrest, Aug. 1775. 9 Sibley-Shipton, *Harvard Graduates* 580–583.

OXENBRIDGE THACHER (1719–1765). Harvard 1738. Said to have studied law with Jeremiah Gridley, q.v. Admitted attorney, SCJ, Feb. 1752; barrister, Aug. 1762.

Leading lawyer, whig politician, and pamphleteer. Served on numerous Boston committees. Argued with Otis in 1761 against the application of the customs officers for writs of assistance (No. 44). Appointed Justice of the Peace, 1761. Represented Boston in the House, 1763–1765, leading the opposition to the American Act of 1764 with his pamphlet, *Sentiments of a British American.* 10 Sibley-Shipton, *Harvard Graduates* 322–328. See also Bernard Bailyn, *Pamphlets of the American Revolution,* 1:484–488 (Cambridge, Mass., 1965).

JOHN THAXTER (1755–1791). Harvard 1774. Studied law with JA, 1774–1777. Admitted attorney, Suffolk Inferior Court, July 1777; attorney, SCJ, ca. 1784.

First cousin of AA. During his clerkship, tutored JA's sons and became virtually a member of the family. Clerk in the office of the Secretary of the Continental Congress at York and Philadelphia, 1778. JA's private secretary in Europe, 1779–1783. Subsequently settled in Haverhill, where he practiced law. 2 JA, *Diary and Autobiography* 402 note. A small group of his papers is in MHi, and his extensive correspondence with JA and other members of the family is in the Adams Papers.

ELISHA THAYER (d. 1774). Harvard 1767. Studied law with JA, 1771–1773. Excused from third year of clerkship by the bar because of ill-health.

Son of JA's old Braintree rival, Capt. Ebenezer Thayer. 2 JA, *Diary and Autobiography* 10.

EDMUND TROWBRIDGE (1709–1793). Harvard 1728. Used the name "Goffe" until well into middle life, after his uncle and guardian, Col. Edmund Goffe. Admitted attorney, SCJ, July 1732; barrister, Aug. 1762.

Practiced primarily in Middlesex Co. Considered the most scholarly lawyer and judge of the pre-Revolutionary period. Many of his students went on to great success at the bar. Appointed Justice of the Peace and of the Quorum, 1739. Attorney General, 1749–1767. Represented Cambridge in the House, 1750–1752, 1755, 1763. Member of the Council, 1764–1766, where he supported Crown policies. Justice of Superior Court, 1767–1775, bringing to the bench legal knowledge which many of his fellow judges lacked. Pleadings and opinions in the field of real property reprinted and cited by Massachusetts lawyers into the 19th century. Renounced the royal salary grant, 1774, and thereafter remained a neutral, withdrawing from public life to devote himself to legal research and study. 8 Sibley-Shipton, *Harvard Graduates* 507–520; *DAB*.

JOHN TRUMBULL (1750–1831). Yale 1767. Studied law with JA, 1773–1774. Admitted to practice in Connecticut, 1773.
Wit and jurist. Cousin of Jonathan Trumbull (1710–1785), who was Revolutionary governor of Connecticut, and John Trumbull (1756–1842), American painter. Began career as a poet while an undergraduate. Studied literature and law in Connecticut, 1767–1773, serving as a Yale tutor, 1772. His first major satirical work, *The Progress of Dulness*, was written and published at this time. In Aug. 1774 returned to New Haven to practice law, moving to Hartford in 1781. *M'Fingal*, satirical epic on the Revolution, published 1775–1782, was the basis of his later literary reputation. State's attorney, Hartford Co., 1789. Served in the legislature, 1792, 1800. Judge of the Connecticut Superior Court, 1801–1819, and of the Supreme Court of Errors, 1808–1819. Died at Detroit, Michigan Territory, where he had moved in 1825. *DAB*.

WILLIAM TUDOR (1750–1819). Harvard 1769. Studied law with JA, 1769–1772. Admitted attorney, Suffolk Inferior Court, July 1772; attorney, SCJ, Aug. 1778; barrister, Feb. 1784.
Son of Deacon John Tudor. Lifelong friend and correspondent of JA. Judge Advocate of the Continental Army, 1775–1778. Practiced law in Boston until 1796, when a substantial inheritance enabled him to retire. Thereafter he devoted his life to travel and civic enterprise. Many of his students became prominent lawyers and judges. Appointed Justice of the Peace, 1781. Represented Boston in the House, 1779, 1791–1796; Senator from Suffolk Co., 1801–1803. Massachusetts Secretary of State, 1809–1810. Clerk of the Supreme Judicial Court, 1811–1819. "Memoir of Hon. William Tudor," 8 MHS, *Colls.* (2 ser.) 285–325 (1819). His papers are in MHi.

JOSHUA UPHAM (1741–1808). Harvard 1763. Admitted attorney, SCJ, Sept. 1768; barrister, Sept. 1772.
Practiced in Worcester Co. Appointed Justice of the Peace, 1769. Loyalist in sympathy, but recanted in May 1775. Nevertheless, proscribed in 1778. Appointed Advocate General of the Rhode Island Vice Admiralty Court, 1779, but never served, Newport being evacuated by the

British. Served in loyalist forces around New York, 1781–1782. Judge, Supreme Court of New Brunswick, and Councilor, ca. 1785–1808. Jones, *Loyalists of Mass.* 281–283.

WILLIAM WETMORE (1749–1830). Harvard 1770. Studied law with William Pynchon, q.v. Admitted attorney, Essex Inferior Court, April 1774; attorney, SCJ, June 1776; barrister, Feb. 1784.

Married Pynchon's daughter. Practiced with Pynchon in Salem until 1785, thereafter in Boston. Addresser of Gage, 1774. Represented Salem in the House, 1777. Succeeded Shearjashub Bourne, q.v., as Chief Justice, Suffolk Inferior Court, 1807, serving in that post and as an associate justice of the successor Middle Circuit Court of Common Pleas until 1821. One of his daughters, Sarah Waldo, married the future United States Supreme Court Justice, Joseph Story, in 1808. James C. Wetmore, *The Wetmore Family of America* 446–448 (Albany, 1861). See also 2 JA, *Diary and Autobiography* 94. Wetmore's student notes, largely copied from Pynchon's law notes and now in the Adams Papers, are a principal source for the present work.

SAMUEL WHITE (1710–1769). Harvard 1731. Admitted attorney, SCJ, May 1752; barrister, Aug. 1762.

Practiced in Bristol Co. Appointed Justice of the Peace, 1744; of the Quorum, 1756. Appointed Judge, Bristol Inferior Court, 1756. Represented Taunton in the House, 1749–1759; Speaker, 1759. Elected and chosen Speaker again, 1764–1766; member of the Council, 1766–1769. 9 Sibley-Shipton, *Harvard Graduates* 110–112.

ABEL WILLARD (1732–1781). Harvard 1752. Studied law with Benjamin Prat, q.v. Admitted attorney, Worcester Inferior Court, Nov. 1755; attorney, SCJ, Sept. 1762.

Practiced in Worcester Co. Appointed Justice of the Peace and of the Quorum, 1769. Addresser of Hutchinson and Gage, 1774. Fled to Boston, 1775, and finally to England, where he died. Proscribed, 1778. 13 Sibley-Shipton, *Harvard Graduates* 301–303.

JONATHAN WILLIAMS (d. 1780). Harvard 1772. Studied law with JA, 1772–1774.

Son of John Williams, Inspector General of the Customs, and cousin of Jonathan Williams (1750–1815), who later became first superintendent of the military academy at West Point. Moved to Worcester, 1774, exchanging houses with James Putnam, q.v. Traveled to Europe for his health, 1779, meeting JA there. 2 JA, *Diary and Autobiography* 227–228, 356; see 12 Sibley-Shipton, *Harvard Graduates* 60–61; (Boston) *Continental Journal*, 4 May 1780.

PELHAM WINSLOW (1737–1783). Harvard 1753. Studied law with

James Otis Jr., q.v. Admitted attorney, SCJ, April 1764; barrister, May 1767.

Practiced in Plymouth Co. Appointed Justice of the Peace, 1771. Took refuge in Boston, 1774. Sailed for Halifax, 1776, then to New York, where he served the Crown as paymaster and commissary. He saw some naval service with a loyalist fleet out of Newport in 1779, but returned to New York, where he died. 13 Sibley-Shipton, *Harvard Graduates* 374–377.

JOHN WORTHINGTON (1719–1800). Yale 1740. Studied law with Phineas Lyman, Suffield, Massachusetts (now Connecticut). Admitted attorney, SCJ, Sept. 1749; barrister, Aug. 1762.

Practiced in Springfield. King's attorney. Represented Springfield in the House, 1747–1768, 1770–1774. Commissioner, Albany Congress, 1754. Approved of the Stamp Act Congress, 1765, but declined to be a delegate. Member of the Council, 1767–1768, favoring Crown policies. Appointed Mandamus Councilor, 1774, but declined to serve. Reconciled by 1778 and active again in politics and practice. *DAB*.

DAVID WYER JR. (1741–1776). Harvard 1758. Admitted attorney, SCJ, June 1765; barrister, June 1767.

Practiced in Falmouth (now Portland, Maine). Occasionally acted as King's attorney. Died in epidemic following the burning of Falmouth. Others of his family were loyalists. Stark, *Loyalists of Mass.* 466.

Acknowledgments

That any of John Adams' legal papers appear in print is a tribute to the energy and devotion of many more people than the names which happen to appear on the title page. In the preparation of these volumes, more perhaps than in any earlier productions in *The Adams Papers*, the principle of the iceberg has applied. It is a double pleasure, therefore, to mark the end of the editing, and the beginning of the text, with a modest recognition of encouragement and aid received from many sources.

Mark DeWolfe Howe, Professor of Law, Harvard University, is, more than anyone else, responsible for the publication of this edition. It was he who successively steered the present editors toward the editor-in-chief when each was still a student at the Harvard Law School; it was he who fanned the editors' tentative spark and initiated arrangements not only for funds to fuel the editorial fire, but for a proper hearth for it at Harvard; and finally, as the material has taken semi-literate shape, he has continued to afford the editors the privilege of submitting their drafts and proofs to him for criticism and improvement.

Lyman H. Butterfield, editor-in-chief in every sense, has conferred on the editors in bountiful measure his meticulous attention to detail, his matchless understanding of the craft of editing, and, most important of all, his confidence. They can only hope that they have been able to approach his standards.

Wendell D. Garrett, associate editor of the Adams Papers, has, with unfailing good taste and humor, guided the editors through a mass of intricacies.

Dean Erwin N. Griswold of the Harvard Law School is *hors concours* at encouraging young lawyers to hurdle difficulties apparently insurmountable; thus it has been with this work.

The trustees of the William Nelson Cromwell Foundation have in their collegiate capacity generously stimulated the production of this edition with two grants, *sine qua non*.

Stephen T. Riley, Director of the Massachusetts Historical Society, has read and criticized the galley proofs and has at all times eased the editors' burden by sharing with them his special knowledge of the Papers of Robert Treat Paine.

Clifford K. Shipton, Director of the American Antiquarian Society, Archivist of Harvard University, and Sibley Editor of the Massachusetts Historical Society, has read and criticized the galley proofs and has at various times in the course of the project added blue pencil and removed red tape.

Other contributory critics and proofreaders included John D. Cushing and Malcolm Freiberg of the Massachusetts Historical Society, Professor Robert E. Moody of Boston University, and Professor Samuel E. Thorne of the Harvard Law School.

Walter M. Whitehill, Director of the Boston Athenæum, graciously increased the editors' knowledge of John Adams' Boston; he and his assistant, Jane N. Garrett, also made the Athenæum's volumes and manuscripts freely available.

No project of this sort could long exist without a talented, understanding editorial assistant. To say that the functions of Mrs. Daniel J. Burton (who started with us as Miss Judith A. Diekoff) encompassed documentary transcription and historical and bibliographical research is only to give the barest suggestion of her value to the venture. Mrs. Burton, Michael E. Hager, Esq., and Deborah B. Zobel also provided most of the Latin translations, for which the editors have taken credit—and responsibility.

Mrs. Carl A. Pitha lent us her exceptional talents as an indexer; dealing with unfamiliar material, she was nonetheless able to reduce the task first to manageable size, and then, assisted by Mrs. Douglas Craib, to smooth order. Miss Virginia Casey, Mrs. James Nichols, Mrs. Paul Norton, and Mrs. Philip R. Peters patiently typed and retyped large portions of the manuscript. Mrs. William Foresta and Miss Susan I. Hitchcock provided outstanding secretarial support.

It is customary for editors to thank their wives last, but Susan C. Wroth and Deborah B. Zobel contributed not merely the traditional uxorial encouragement, aid, and comfort, but also essential clerical and investigatory skills.

Advice and consent, both equally important to the edition, came from many sources, of which the editors wish particularly to mention: Professors Bernard Bailyn, Stanley N. Katz, Arthur A. Maass, and Frank Michelman, Harvard; Professors Carl Bridenbaugh, James Hedges, William G. McLoughlin, and Lawrence C. Wroth, Brown; Professor George A. Billias, Clark; Professor Katherine Turner, Wellesley; Dean Benjamin W. Labaree, Williams; Professor William Hedges,

Acknowledgments

Goucher; Professor Thomas C. Barrow, University of Missouri; Seymour P. Edgerton, Esq., and Robert J. Hallisey, Esq., Bingham, Dana & Gould; Marcus A. McCorison, American Antiquarian Society; and Mrs. Katherine A. Kellock, Washington, D.C.

Dean Edward S. Godfrey and the faculty and staff of the University of Maine School of Law demonstrated limitless patience during the travail necessary to bring forth these volumes.

The staff of the Massachusetts Historical Society and The Adams Papers assisted materially in various ways and at all times; the editors wish particularly to thank: The Misses Winifred Collins, Amber Cox, Anna Moses, and Marjorie Sprague; Mrs. David R. Riggs Jr.; and (especially) R. Tenney Johnson, Esq., whose ground breaking in the Legal Papers and the Suffolk Court Files made the editors' road not merely passable but possible.

Through the efforts of the staff of the Harvard Law School and its Library, the editors were able to establish and maintain a collection of 18th-century law books which even John Adams might have envied. This happy circumstance depended on the friendly cooperation of Librarian Earl M. Borgeson, Miss Edith G. Henderson, Philip Putnam, and George Strait. Vice Dean Louis A. Toepfer and Miss Mary Conlan assisted the editors in the solution of countless administrative dilemmas.

The editors have received, in the course of their work, much more than the usual courtesies from the respective staffs of Widener Library; Houghton Library; the Harvard University News Office; the Harvard University Archives; the Massachusetts Archives; the Essex Institute; the Office of the Collector of Customs, Boston; the National Historical Publications Commission; the Manuscript and Interlibrary Loan Divisions of the Library of Congress; the New-York Historical Society; the New York Public Library; the Historical Society of Pennsylvania; the Portland, Maine, Public Library; the Maine Historical Society; Fogler Library, University of Maine; and the University of Maine Law School Library.

We wish to express thanks to the Council of the Massachusetts Historical Society for permission to print several important items from the Robert Treat Paine Papers, and to the Public Record Office, London, for allowing us to reproduce certain documents from the Treasury and Colonial Office Papers. Crown Copyright material in the Public Record Office is printed by permission of the Controller of Her Majesty's Stationery Office.

Hon. Raymond S. Wilkins, Chief Justice of the Supreme Judicial

Court, and Hon. G. Joseph Tauro, Chief Justice of the Superior Court, encouraged the editors by their interest in the project and their willingness to favor the editors' use of court sources.

Chester Dolan, Esq., Clerk of the Supreme Judicial Court for Suffolk County during most of the work on these volumes, has always shown the deepest interest in and understanding of the historical value of the old papers entrusted to his care. Mr. Dolan obtained funds and personnel to commence microfilming each document, and he also arranged for the restoration and preservation of the Superior Court Minute Books, which were starting to disintegrate from age and neglect. To the present editors, he always gave ready assistance and earnest encouragement. It is a particular pleasure to state our gratitude to him and to his assistants, Richard McLaughlin (now Clerk of the Supreme Judicial Court for the Commonwealth), Daniel Donnelly, and Misses Virginia Lynch, Eileen Kennedy, Theresa McLaughlin, Rita McMillan, and Dorothy Viano. And it is also a pleasure to note that the present Clerk of the Supreme Judicial Court for Suffolk County, John E. Powers, Esq., is continuing Mr. Dolan's work.

The editors wish also to thank Thomas Dorgan, Esq., Clerk of the Suffolk Superior Court, Deputy Clerk Michael Sclafani, and acting clerk John Donahue; and Edward Sullivan, Esq., Clerk of the Middlesex Superior Court, for courtesies extended during the search among the papers of the Inferior Court of Common Pleas.

This enterprise depended heavily on the contribution of numerous students and scholars of law, history, biography, and geography: John W. Bethell; Miles Bradbury; Burnell Hersey, Esq., Dale Hershey, Esq., Justin Kimball, Esq., and William B. Parks Jr., Esq. On the basis of Cornelius Minihan's preliminary research, Mrs. Lovell Thompson and Susan C. Wroth prepared rough drafts of many of the sketches in the Register of the Massachusetts Bench and Bar.

In various matters of art, photography, and bibliography, the editors received abundant aid from John E. Alden of the Boston Public Library; Mrs. John W. Bethell; George M. Cushing Jr. (whose magnificent photographs of the courthouse materials enlighten as they delight); the staff of the Fogg Art Museum; Thomas Maytham and Miss Laura Luckey of the Boston Museum of Fine Arts; Miss Emma Papert of the Metropolitan Museum of Fine Arts; Professor Jules D. Prown, Yale (whose generous willingness to share his knowledge of matters pertaining to John Singleton Copley made possible the portrait gallery which leavens these legalistic volumes); and Mildred Steinbach and the staff of the Frick Art Reference Library.

Guide to Editorial Apparatus

1. TEXTUAL DEVICES

The following devices are used throughout *The Adams Papers* to clarify the presentation of the text.

[...], [....]	One or two words missing or illegible and not conjecturable.
[...]¹, [....]¹	More than two words missing or illegible and not conjecturable; subjoined footnote estimates amount of matter represented by suspension points.
[ ]	Number or part of a number missing or illegible. Amount of blank space inside brackets approximates the number of missing or illegible digits.
[roman]	Conjectural reading for missing or illegible matter. A question mark is inserted before the closing bracket if the conjectural reading is seriously doubtful.
⟨*italic*⟩	Matter canceled in the manuscript but restored in our text.
[*italic*]	Editorial insertion in the text.

2. ADAMS FAMILY CODE NAMES

In conformity with practice elsewhere in *The Adams Papers*, the editors have avoided constant and confusing repetition of names of members of the Adams family throughout the annotation by using the following short but unmistakable forms for the names of those principally concerned:

First Generation

JA	John Adams (1735–1826)
AA	Abigail Smith (1744–1818), *m.* JA 1764
PBA	Peter Boylston Adams (1738–1823), JA's brother

Second Generation

JQA	John Quincy Adams (1767–1848), son of JA and AA
AA2	Abigail Adams (1765–1813), daughter of JA and AA

Third Generation

CFA   Charles Francis Adams (1807–1886), son of JQA

Fourth Generation

BA   Brooks Adams (1848–1927), son of CFA

3. DESCRIPTIVE SYMBOLS

The following symbols are employed throughout *The Adams Papers* to describe or identify in brief form the various kinds of manuscript originals.

Dft	draft
FC	file copy (Ordinarily a copy of a letter retained by a correspondent *other than an Adams*, since all three of the Adams statesmen systematically entered copies of their outgoing letters in letterbooks.)
Lb	Letterbook (Used only to designate Adams letterbooks and always in combination with the short form of the writer's name and a serial number, as follows: Lb/JQA/29, i.e. the twenty-ninth volume of John Quincy Adams' Letterbooks.)
LbC	letterbook copy
MS, MSS	manuscript, manuscripts
RC	recipient's copy

4. LOCATION SYMBOLS

Locations of documents privately owned and of documents in public institutions outside the United States are to be given in expanded or at least completely recognizable form. Locations of documents held by public institutions in the United States are to be indicated by the short, logical, and unmistakable institutional symbols used in the National Union Catalog in the Library of Congress. The following list gives the symbols and their expanded equivalents for institutions in the United States owning originals drawn upon in the *Legal Papers of John Adams*.

DLC	Library of Congress
DNA	The National Archives
M-Ar	Massachusetts Archives
MB	Boston Public Library

MBAt	Boston Athenæum
MeHi	Maine Historical Society
MH	Harvard College Library
MH-Ar	Harvard Archives
MH-BA	Harvard Graduate School of Business Administration
MH-L	Harvard Law School
MHi	Massachusetts Historical Society
MQA	Adams National Historic Site, Quincy, Massachusetts
MQHi	Quincy Historical Society
MSaE	Essex Institute, Salem, Massachusetts
NHi	New-York Historical Society
NN	New York Public Library
RPB	Brown University Library, Providence, Rhode Island
VtHi	Vermont Historical Society

5. OTHER ABBREVIATIONS AND CONVENTIONAL TERMS

Adams Papers

Manuscripts and other materials, 1639–1889, in the Adams Manuscript Trust collection given to the Massachusetts Historical Society in 1956 and enlarged by a few additions of family papers since then. Citations in the present edition refer almost always to the microfilm reel number where the manuscript may be found.

Adams Papers Editorial Files

Other materials in the Adams Papers editorial office, Massachusetts Historical Society. These include photoduplicated documents (normally cited by the location of the originals), photographs, correspondence, and bibliographical and other aids compiled and accumulated by the editorial staff.

Adams Papers, Microfilms

The corpus of the Adams Papers, 1639–1889, as published on microfilm by the Massachusetts Historical Society, 1954–1959, in 608 reels. Cited in the present work by reel number, in almost all references to the Adams Papers.

Bernard Papers

The collected papers of Massachusetts Governor Francis Bernard, in volumes 4, 10, and 43 of the Sparks Manuscripts, MH.

Ch.
 English court of Chancery.

C.J.
 Chief Justice.

C.P.
 English court of Common Pleas.

Cushing Reports
 "Notes of Cases decided in the Superiour and Supreme Judicial
 Courts of Massachusetts from 1772 to 1789—taken by the
 Honorable William Cushing one of the Judges during that period
 and most of the time Chief Justice." MH-L.

Divorce Recs.
 Records of the Governor and Council sitting as Court of Divorce.
 1760–1786, in the Office of the Clerk of the Supreme Judicial
 Court for Suffolk County, Suffolk County Court House, Boston.

Exch.
 English court of Exchequer.

H.L.
 House of Lords.

Hancock Papers
 Hancock Papers, Baker Library, MH-BA.

Inf. Ct.
 Massachusetts Inferior Court of Common Pleas.

J.
 Justice.

JA, Office Book, MQA
 John Adams' office book or writ book, MQA.

K.B.
 English court of King's Bench.

Mass. Arch.
 Massachusetts Archives, State House, Boston.

Middlesex Reg. Deeds
> Registry of Deeds, Middlesex County, Cambridge, Massachusetts.

Min. Bk. . . . SCJ
> Minute Books of the Massachusetts Superior Court of Judicature in the Office of the Clerk of the Supreme Judicial Court, Suffolk County, Suffolk County Court House, Boston. Case numbers prefixed by "C" are continued actions; those prefixed by "N" are new actions.

Min. Bk. . . . Inf. Ct.
> Minute Books of the Massachusetts Inferior Court of Common Pleas for Suffolk County, in the custody of the Clerk of the Massachusetts Superior Court for Civil Business, Suffolk County Court House, Boston.

N.P.
> Nisi Prius

Paine Diary
> MS diary of Robert Treat Paine, dating from 25 March 1756 to 8 May 1814, Paine Papers, MHi.

Paine Law Notes
> MS volumes of notes on contemporary cases, Paine Papers, MHi.

Paine Massacre Notes
> MS notes on the Boston Massacre trials, Paine Papers, MHi.

Paine Papers
> MS collected papers of Robert Treat Paine, other than diary or law and Massacre notes, MHi.

PCC
> Papers of the Continental Congress. Originals in the National Archives; microfilm edition in 204 reels. Usually cited in the present work from the microfilms, but according to the original series and volume numbering devised in the State Department in the early 19th century; for example, PCC, No. 93, III, i.e. the third volume of series 93.

PRO
    Public Record Office, London.

Q.B.
    English court of Queen's Bench.

Revere Plan
    Plan of the scene of the Boston Massacre, supposedly drawn by
    Paul Revere. Chamberlain Collection, MB.

RG
    Record Group. Used, with appropriate numbers, to designate the
    location of documents in the National Archives.

SF
    Suffolk County Court House, Early Court Files and Miscellaneous
    Papers in the Office of the Clerk of the Massachusetts Supreme
    Judicial Court for Suffolk County, Suffolk County Court House,
    Boston.

SCJ Rec.
    Massachusetts Superior Court of Judicature Records, in the
    Office of the Clerk of the Supreme Judicial Court for Suffolk
    County, Suffolk County Court House, Boston. Volumes are cited
    by inclusive dates.

SJC Rec.
    Massachusetts Supreme Judicial Court Records, in the Office of
    the Clerk of the Supreme Judicial Court for Suffolk County,
    Suffolk County Court House, Boston. Volumes are cited by in-
    clusive dates.

Supreme Ct. Probate Rec. 1760–1830
    Massachusetts Supreme Court of Probate and Supreme Judicial
    Court Probate records, in the Office of the Clerk of the Supreme
    Judicial Court for Suffolk County, Suffolk County Court House,
    Boston.

Thwing Catalogue, MHi
    Annie Haven Thwing, comp., Inhabitants and Estates of the
    Town of Boston, 1630–1800; typed card catalogue, with supple-
    mentary bound typescripts, MHi.

U.B.
    Upper Bench. (The equivalent during the Commonwealth,
    1649–1660, of the English court of King's Bench.)

Vice Adm. Min. Bk.

> Minute Book of the Massachusetts Court of Vice Admiralty, Boston, in the Office of the Clerk of the Supreme Judicial Court for Suffolk County, Suffolk County Court House, Boston.

Vice Adm. Rec.

> Records of the Massachusetts Court of Vice Admiralty, 3 vols., 1718–1745, in the Office of the Clerk of the Supreme Judicial Court for Suffolk County, Suffolk County Court House, Boston.

Wetmore Notes

> William Wetmore, Reports on Essex County Legal Cases, 1771–1778, Adams Papers, Microfilms, Reel No. 184, MHi.

6. SHORT TITLES OF WORKS
FREQUENTLY CITED

A. *Form of Citation*

In general, the guide to citation form has been *A Uniform System of Citation* (Cambridge, Mass., 10th edn. 1958), with certain modifications in the interests of harmony with other volumes in *The Adams Papers*. Principal among the modifications are:

(1) *Typography*. Titles of books and periodicals are in italics; titles of articles are in roman, enclosed in quotation marks; titles of unpublished works, e.g. dissertations, are in roman without quotation marks.

(2) *Short and full titles*. All English and American law reports are cited by one of the common abbreviations listed in Black's *Law Dictionary*. To avoid the baroque verbiage of the early English law printers, the expanded titles for the several English reports are taken verbatim from Sweet and Maxwell, *Legal Bibliography*. Other books and periodicals frequently cited have generally been assigned short titles. Abbreviations of reports, and short titles, are listed below under "C. Other Works." When any law report or short-titled work is cited, standard legal citation form is usually followed; volume number preceding author's last name or the short title; page number following title without punctuation. Works not cited often enough to merit a standard short-title form are cited in nonlegal form: author's complete name and the work's full title, followed by volume and page numbers

and place and date of publication. When such a work is cited again within the same *Legal Papers* case, it is there given a short title and standard legal form is followed.

(3) *Latin forms.* Most Latin forms, such as *supra* and *infra*, have been replaced by English equivalents.

B. *Statutes*

English statutes are cited by regnal year, chapter and section if appropriate, and year of enactment. For example, 28 Hen. 8, c. 15, §2 (1536). Unless otherwise indicated, the text of 18th-century statutes quoted or referred to is that found in *The Statutes at Large* (Cambridge, Danby Pickering, ed., 46 vols., 1762–1807). More recent acts are cited from official session-law volumes.

Massachusetts provincial statutes are cited by date of enactment, and chapter and section if applicable. Unless otherwise indicated, the text quoted or referred to is that found in *The Acts and Resolves, Public and Private, of the Province of the Massachusetts Bay* (Boston, ed. Ellis Ames, Abner C. Goodell, et al., 21 vols., 1869–1922), abbreviated A&R. For example, Act of 9 June 1693, c. 3, §8, 1 A&R 117.

Other statutes are cited in accordance with the principles of *A Uniform System of Citation.* Abbreviations appear immediately below.

C. *Other Works*

A&R
  See "B. Statutes," immediately above.

A.L.R.
  American Law Reports Annotated, Rochester, N.Y., 1919– .

Acts, Privy Council (Col.)
  Acts of the Privy Council of England. Colonial Series, 1613–1783. W. L. Grant, James Munro, eds., Hereford, 1909–1912; 6 vols.

Acts, Acts and Resolves
  Annual Massachusetts session-law volumes, Boston, 1839 to date.

Adams, *New Light*
  Randolph G. Adams, *New Light on the Boston Massacre*, Worcester, Mass., 1938.

Adams Family Correspondence
  Adams Family Correspondence, ed. L.H. Butterfield and others, Cambridge, Mass., 1963– .

T. R. Adams, "American Independence"
> Thomas R. Adams, "American Independence: The Growth of an Idea. A Bibliographical Study of the American Political Pamphlets Published between 1764 and 1766 . . . ," Colonial Society of Massachusetts, *Publications*, vol. 43 (in press). A pre-print of this bibliography was published by Brown University Press in 1965.

AHR
> *American Historical Review.*

Alden (Mass.)
> Cyrus Alden, *An Abridgment of Law, with Practical Forms, in Two Parts. Part I. An Abridgment of Blackstone's Commentaries—Massachusetts Statute Laws and Massachusetts Term Reports*, Boston, 1819.

Aleyn
> John Aleyn, *Select Cases in the King's Bench*, London, 1681.

Ambl.
> Charles Ambler, *Reports, Court of Chancery*, 2d edn., London, 1828; 2 vols.

Amer. Antiq. Soc., *Procs.*
> American Antiquarian Society, *Proceedings.*

Amer. Jour. Legal Hist.
> *American Journal of Legal History.*

Ames, *Lectures on Legal History*
> James Barr Ames, *Lectures on Legal History and Miscellaneous Legal Essays*, Cambridge, Mass., 1913.

Andrews, *Colonial Period*
> Charles McLean Andrews, *The Colonial Period of American History*, New Haven, 1934–1938; 4 vols.

Army List 1770
> *A List of the General and Field-Officers . . . in the Army . . . with The Dates of their Commissions . . . with the Uniforms to each Regiment . . . for 1770*, London, n.d.

Bacon, *Abridgment*
> Matthew Bacon, *New Abridgment of the Law*, London, 1736–1766; 5 vols.

Barn.
> T. Barnardiston, *Reports, Court of Chancery*, London, 1742.

Barn. K.B.

T. Barnardiston, *Reports of Cases in the King's Bench from 12 King George I to Trinity Term 7 King George II*, London, 1744; 2 vols.

Barn. & Ald.

R. V. Barnewall and E. H. Alderson, *Reports of Cases Argued and Determined in the Court of King's Bench*, Dublin, 1818-1822; 5 vols.

Barrington, *Observations upon the Statutes*

Daines Barrington, *Observations upon the Statutes, chiefly the more ancient from Magna Charta to 21st James the First, ch. xxvii, with appendix: a proposal for new modelling the Statutes*, London, 1766.

Barrow, Colonial Customs

Thomas C. Barrow, The Colonial Customs Service, 1660-1775 (Harvard Univ. doctoral dissertation, 1961).

Beav.

Charles Beavan, *Reports of Cases in Chancery, Rolls Court, 1838-1866*, London, 1840-1869; 36 vols.

Beccaria, *Essay on Crimes and Punishments*

Cesare Bonesana, Marchese di Beccaria, *An Essay on Crimes and Punishments*, 4th edn., London, 1775.

Bell, *Bench and Bar of N.H.*

Charles H. Bell, *Bench and Bar of New Hampshire*, Boston, 1894.

Bibb. (Ky.)

George M. Bibb, *Reports, Court of Appeals, Kentucky, 1808-1817*, Frankfort, 1815-1817; 4 vols.

Binn.

Horace Binney, *Reports* (Pennsylvania Reports, 1799-1814), Phila., 1809-1815; 6 vols.

Biog. Dir. Cong.

Biographical Directory of the American Congress, 1774-1949, Washington, 1950.

Black, *Law Dictionary*

Henry C. Black, *Black's Law Dictionary*, 4th edn., St. Paul, 1951.

H. Bl.

Henry Blackstone, *Reports, Court of Common Pleas and Exchequer Chamber, 1788-1796*, London, 1791-1796; 2 vols.

W. Bl.

William Blackstone, *Reports, Courts of Westminster Hall, 1746-*

1779, with a Preface Containing Memoirs of His Life, London, 1781; 2 vols.

Blackstone, *Commentaries*
William Blackstone, *Commentaries on the Laws of England*, Oxford, 1765–1769; 4 vols.

Boston Record Commissioners, *Reports*
City of Boston, Record Commissioners, *Reports*, Boston, 1876–1909; 39 vols.

Boston Streets, &c., 1910
City of Boston, Street Commissioners, *Streets, Alleys, Places, etc., in the City of Boston*, Boston, 1910.

Bracton
Henry de Bracton, *De Legibus et consuetudinibus Angliae Libri quinq*, London, 1569.

Browne, *Civil Law*
Arthur Browne, *Civil Law, and . . . the Law of Admiralty*, 2d edn., London, 1802; 2 vols.

Buller, *Nisi Prius*
Francis Buller, *Introduction to the Law Relative to Trials at Nisi Prius*, London, 1772.

Bulstrode
Edward Bulstrode, *Reports in King's Bench, 1609–1626*, London, 1688; 2 vols.

Burn, *Ecclesiastical Law*
Richard Burn, *Ecclesiastical Law*, 2d edn., London, 1767; 4 vols.

Burr.
James Burrow, *Reports, King's Bench, 1756–1772*, London, 1766–1780; 5 vols.

Burrell
William Burrell, *Reports, Court of Admiralty and upon Appeal, 1758–1774*, London, 1885.

Cal. State Papers (Col.)
Calendar of State Papers, Colonial Series, America and the West Indies, ed. W. N. Sainsbury and others, London, 1866–1926; 22 vols.

Catalogue of JA's Library
Catalogue of the John Adams Library in the Public Library of the City of Boston, Boston, 1917.

Chalmers, *Opinions*
George Chalmers, ed., *Opinions of Eminent Lawyers on Various Points of English Jurisprudence, Chiefly Concerning the Colonies, Fisheries, and Commerce of Great Britain*, Burlington, Vt., 1858.

Chitty, *Criminal Law*
Joseph Chitty, *The Criminal Law*, 2d edn., London, 1816; 4 vols.

Chitty, *Pleading*
Joseph Chitty, *Pleading and Parties to Actions*, 2d edn., London, 1811; 2 vols.

Co. Rep.
Edward Coke, *Reports*, London, 1727; 13 parts.

Coke, *Institutes*
Edward Coke, *Second Part of the Institutes of the Lawes of England; containing the exposition of many ancient and other Statutes*, London, 1642.

——— *Third Part of the Institutes of the Laws of England; concerning High Treason and other Pleas of the Crown, and Criminall Causes*, London, 1644.

——— *Fourth Part of the Institutes of the Laws of England; concerning the Jurisdiction of Courts*, London, 1644.

Coke, *Littleton*
Edward Coke, *First Part of the Institutes of the Lawes of England; or, Commentarie upon Littleton*, 2d edn., London, 1629.

Col. Soc. Mass., *Pubns.*
Colonial Society of Massachusetts, *Publications*.

Colum. L. Rev.
Columbia Law Review.

Comyns
J. Comyns, *Reports, King's Bench, Common Pleas, and Exchequer [with] Special Cases in Chancery and Before the Delegates*, London, 1744.

Comyns, *Digest*
J. Comyns, *Digest of the Laws of England*, London, 1762–1767; 5 vols.

Cowp.
Henry Cowper, *Reports, King's Bench, 1774–1778*, London, 1783.

Cranch (U.S.)

William Cranch, *Reports of Cases argued and adjudged in the Supreme Court of the United States*, Washington, N.Y., and Flatbush, N.Y., 1804–1817; 9 vols.

Crim. Law Quart.

Criminal Law Quarterly.

Cro. Car.

George Croke, *Reports of Cases in King's Bench and Common Bench*, Part 3, Charles, London, 1657.

Cro. Eliz.

George Croke, *Reports of Cases in King's Bench and Common Bench*. Part 1, Elizabeth, London, 1661.

Cro. Jac.

George Croke, *Reports of Cases in King's Bench and Common Bench*. Part 2, James, London, 1683.

Cunningham, *Law Dictionary*

T. Cunningham, *New and Complete Law Dictionary; or General Abridgment of the Law*, London, 1764–1765; 2 vols.

Curwen, *Journal and Letters*

The Journal and Letters of Samuel Curwen, . . . from 1775 to 1783; with an Appendix of Biographical Sketches, ed. George Atkinson Ward, 4th edn., Boston, 1864.

Cush.

Luther S. Cushing, *Reports* (Massachusetts Reports 1848–1853), Boston, 1865–1866; 12 vols.

DAB

Allen Johnson and Dumas Malone, eds., *Dictionary of American Biography*, New York, 1928–1936; 20 vols. plus index and supplements.

Dall.

Alexander J. Dallas, *Reports of Cases Ruled and Adjudged in the Courts of Pennsylvania before and since the Revolution and in the Several Courts of the United States*, Philadelphia, 1790–1807; 4 vols.

Dalton, *Country Justice*

Michael Dalton, *The Countrey Justice; containing the Practice, Duty and Power of the Justices of the Peace as well in as out of Their Sessions and . . . an Appendix . . . etc.*, London, 1746.

Dane, *Abridgment*
> Nathan Dane, *A General Abridgment and Digest of American Law*, Boston, 1824; 8 vols.

Dexter, *Yale Graduates*
> Franklin Bowditch Dexter, *Biographical Sketches of the Graduates of Yale College, with Annals of the College History*, N.Y., 1885–1912; 6 vols.

Dickerson, *Boston under Military Rule*
> Oliver M. Dickerson, ed., *Boston under Military Rule, 1768–1769, As Revealed in A Journal of the Times*, Boston, 1936.

Dickerson, *Navigation Acts*
> Oliver M. Dickerson, *The Navigation Acts and The American Revolution*, Phila., 1951.

Dickens
> John Dickens, *Reports of Cases in the High Court of Chancery (1559–1797)*, London, 1803; 2 vols.

DNB
> Leslie Stephen and Sidney Lee, eds., *The Dictionary of National Biography*, N.Y. and London, 1885–1900; 63 vols. plus supplements.

Domat, *Civil Law*
> Jean Domat, *The Civil Law in its Natural Order: Together with the Publick Law*, transl. William Strahan, London, 1722; 2 vols.

Doug.
> Sylvester Douglas, *Reports, King's Bench*, London, 1783.

Drake, *History and Antiquities of Boston*
> Samuel G. Drake, *The History and Antiquities of Boston*, Boston, 1856.

Duncombe, *Trials per Pais*
> Giles Duncombe, *Trials per Pais: or Law concerning Juries by Nisi Prius, etc.*, London, 1665.

Dyer
> J. Dyer, *Ascuns Nouel Cases. Les Reports des divers select Matters et Resolutions*, London, 1585.

Eng. Rep.
> *The English Reports*; 176 vols. A collection and translation into English of all the early English reporters.

Eq. Cas. Abr.
> *General Abridgment of Cases in Equity, argued and adjudged in the*

High Court of Chancery, etc., with several cases never before published, alphabetically digested under proper titles, London 1732–1756; 2 vols.

Everard, *History of the 29th Regiment*
> H. Everard, *History of Thomas Farrington's Regiment subsequently designated the 29th (Worcestershire) Foot 1694 to 1891,* Worcester, England, 1891.

F. 2d
> *Federal Reporter,* Second Series, St. Paul, 1925– .

F. Supp.
> *Federal Supplement,* St. Paul, 1933– .

Farr.
> Thomas Farresley, *Modern Cases,* London, 1762.

Fifoot, *History and Sources*
> C. H. S. Fifoot, *History and Sources of the Common Law,* London, 1949.

Fitzherbert, *New Natura Brevium*
> Anthony Fitz-Herbert, *New Natura Brevium,* London, 1755.

Fortescue, *De Laudibus Legum Angliæ*
> John Fortescue, *De Laudibus Legum Angliæ,* 2d edn., London, 1741.

Foster, *Crown Cases*
> Michael Foster, *A Report of Some Proceedings on the Commission of Oyer and Terminer and Goal Delivery for the Trial of the Rebels in the Year 1746 in the County of Surry, and of other Crown Cases. To Which are Added Discourses upon a few Branches of the Crown Law,* Oxford, 1762.

Gage, *Correspondence*
> *The Correspondence of General Thomas Gage with the Secretaries of State, 1763–1775,* ed. Clarence E. Carter, New Haven 1931–1933; 2 vols.

Gardiner, *Instructor Clericalis*
> Robert Gardiner, *Instructor Clericalis; or, Precedents in the Court of King's Bench and Common Pleas, for young clerks,* London, 1697–1714; 6 parts.

Gay Transcripts
> Frederick L. Gay, Transcripts Relating to the History of New England, 1630–1776, MHi.

Gray
> Horace Gray, Jr., *Reports, Supreme Court, Massachusetts, 1854–1860*, Boston, 1855–1871; 16 vols.

Gilb. Rep. Ca. Eq.
> Geoffrey Gilbert, *Reports of Cases in Equity, Courts of Chancery and Exchequer, [1705–1726; with] Cases in Equity, Court of Exchequer, Ireland*, London, 1734.

Gilbert, *Common Pleas*
> Geoffrey Gilbert, *History and Practice of the Court of Common Pleas*, Dublin, 1737.

Gilbert, *Evidence*
> Geoffrey Gilbert, *Law of Evidence by a Late Learned Judge*, London, 1756.

Gordon, *History of Independence*
> William Gordon, *The History of the Rise, Progress, and Establishment, of the Independence of the United States of America: including an Account of the late War; and of the Thirteen Colonies, from their origin to that period*, London, 1788; 4 vols.

Hale, *Pleas of the Crown*
> Matthew Hale, *Historia Placitorum Coronæ: The History of the Pleas of the Crown*, London, 1736; 2 vols.

Hale, *Pleas of the Crown (Summary)*
> Matthew Hale, *Pleas of the Crown: or, A Methodical Summary of the Principal Matters relating to that Subject*, London, 1716.

Hardw.
> *Cases temp. Hardwicke. Cases argued in Court of King's Bench, 7–10 K. George II in the time of Lord Hardwicke, and Lord Lee, also two in Equity, determined by Lord Chancellor Hardwicke*, Dublin, 1769.

Harper, *Navigation Laws*
> Lawrence A. Harper, *The English Navigation Laws*, N.Y., 1939.

Harv. L. Rev.
> *Harvard Law Review.*

Hawkins, *Pleas of the Crown*
> William Hawkins, *A Treatise of the Pleas of the Crown*, 4th edn., London, 1762; 2 vols.

Hetley
> Thomas Hetley, *Reports and Cases 3–7 Charles I, as they were argued by most of the Kings Serjeants at the Common Pleas Barre*, London, 1657.

Hob.

> H. Hobart, *Reports in the reign of James I with some few cases in the reign of Queen Elizabeth*, London, 1641.

Holdsworth, *History of English Law*

> William Holdsworth, *A History of English Law*, Boston and London, 1922–1952; 13 vols.

Holt, K.B.

> John Holt, *Report of Cases determined by Holt, 1688–1710*, London, 1738.

Hoon, *English Customs*

> Elizabeth E. Hoon, *The Organization of the English Customs System, 1696–1786*, N.Y., 1938.

Hough, *Reports*

> Charles M. Hough, ed., *Reports of Cases in the Vice Admiralty of the Province of New York and in the Court of Admiralty of the State of New York, 1715–1788*, New Haven, 1925.

Howell, *State Trials*

> T. B. and T. J. Howell, *Complete Collection of State Trials and Proceedings for High Treason and other crimes and misdemeanors from the earliest period to 1820*, London, 1809–1826; 33 vols.

Hutchinson, *Massachusetts Bay*, ed. Mayo

> Thomas Hutchinson, *The History of the Colony and Province of Massachusetts-Bay*, ed. Lawrence Shaw Mayo, Cambridge, Mass., 1936; 3 vols.

Ipswich Hist. Soc., *Pubns.*

> Ipswich Historical Society, *Publications*.

JA, *Diary and Autobiography*

> *Diary and Autobiography of John Adams*, ed. L. H. Butterfield and others, Cambridge, Mass., 1961; 4 vols.

JA, *Works*

> *The Works of John Adams, Second President of the United States: with a Life of the Author*, ed. Charles Francis Adams, Boston, 1850–1856; 10 vols.

JCC

> Worthington C. Ford and others, eds., *Journals of the Continental Congress, 1774–1789*, Washington, 1904–1937; 34 vols.

Jenk. Cent.

> David Jenkins, *Eight Centuries of Reports; or, Eight hundred cases, Exchequer-Chamber or upon Writs of Error*, London, 1734.

Jefferson, *Papers*, ed. Boyd
> *The Papers of Thomas Jefferson*, ed. Julian P. Boyd and others, Princeton, 1950– .

Johns.
> William Johnson, *Reports, Supreme Court of Judicature, New York*, N.Y., 1807–1823; 20 vols.

Johns. Ch.
> William Johnson, *Reports, Court of Chancery, Albany*, 1816–1824; 7 vols.

Jones, *Loyalists of Mass.*
> E. Alfred Jones, *The Loyalists of Massachusetts: Their Memorials, Petitions and Claims*, London, 1930.

T. Jones
> T. Jones, *Les Reports de divers Special Cases en le Common Bank et en le Court del Bank le Roy*, London, 1695.

W. Jones
> William Jones, *Les Reports de divers Special Cases cy bien in le Court de Banck le Roy, come le Common-Banck, Angleterre*, London, 1675.

Keble
> J. Keble, *Reports, King's Bench, at Westminster*, London, 1685; 3 vols.

Keilw.
> Robert Keilwey, *Reports d'Ascuns Cases . . . aux temps du Roy Henry le Septieme et du Roy Henry le Huitiesme . . . seliges hors des papieres de Keilwey, par Jean Croke*, London, 1688.

Kelyng
> John Kelyng, *Report of divers Cases in Pleas of the Crown, with Directions for Justices of the Peace*, 2d edn., London, 1739.

Kent, *Commentaries*
> James Kent, *Commentaries on American Law*, N.Y., 1826–1830; 4 vols.

Kidder, *History of the Boston Massacre*
> Frederic Kidder, *History of the Boston Massacre*, Albany, 1870.

Kirby
> Ephraim Kirby, *Reports, Superior Court, Connecticut*, Litchfield, Conn., 1789.

Knollenberg, *Origin of the American Revolution*
Bernhard Knollenberg, *Origin of the American Revolution: 1759–1766*, N.Y., 1960.

L.R.A.
Lawyers Reports Annotated, Rochester, N.Y., 1905–1918; 77 vols.

Latch
John Latch, *Plusieurs tres bons Cases, come ils estoyent adjudgees es trois premiers ans du raign du feu Roy Charles le Premier, Bank le Roy*, London, 1622.

Laws and Liberties
General Lawes and Libertyes Concerning the Inhabitants of the Massachusets, Cambridge, Mass., 1648.

Ld. Raym.
Robert, Lord Raymond, *Reports, King's Bench and Common Pleas*, 3d edn., London, 1775; 3 vols.

Leon.
William Leonard, *Reports and Cases of Law in the Courts at Westminster*, London, 1658.

Lev.
Creswell Levinz, *Reports of Cases in the Court of King's Bench and Common Pleas, during the time of Sir R. Foster, Sir R. Hyde and Sir J. Kelyng were Chief Justices: also cases in other Courts during that time*, London, 1702.

Lofft
Capel Lofft, *Reports, King's Bench, with Select Cases, Court of Chancery and of Common Pleas*, Dublin, 1790.

L.Q. Rev.
Law Quarterly Review.

Lutw.
E. Lutwyche, *Un Livre des Entries; contenant auxi un Report des Resolutions del Court sur diverse Exceptions prises as Pleadings et sur auters matters en ley, surdant (pur la plupart) en le Court de Common Bank*, London, 1704; 2 vols.

Lynde, *Diary*
The Diaries of Benjamin Lynde and of Benjamin Lynde, Jr.; with an Appendix, Boston and Cambridge, Mass., 1880.

M & M
William Moody and Benjamin H. Malkin, *Reports of Cases, De-*

termined *at Nisi Prius, in the Courts of King's Bench and Common Pleas,* London, 1831.

Macq.
John F. Macqueen, *Reports of Scotch Appeals and Writs of Error . . . in the House of Lords,* Edinburgh, 1855–1866; 4 vols.

Maine Hist. Soc., *Colls.*
Maine Historical Society, *Collections.*

Mallory, *Modern Entries*
J. Mallory, *Modern Entries in English; being a select collection of Pleadings in the Courts of King's Bench, Common Pleas and Exchequer, and also all kinds of Writs, with readings and observations on the cases in the Reports,* London, 1734–1735; 2 vols.

Mass.
Massachusetts Reports, Exeter and Boston, 1804– .

Mass. Acts
Acts and Laws of the Commonwealth, Boston, 1780–1788. (Individual session-law volumes, cited by year.)

Mass. G.L.
Massachusetts General Laws, Tercentenary Edition, Boston, 1932; 3 vols.

Mass., *House Jour.*
Journals of the House of Representatives of Massachusetts, Boston, reprinted by the Massachusetts Historical Society, 1919– . (For the years for which reprints are not yet available, the original printings are cited, by year and session.)

Mass. Laws
Laws of the Commonwealth of Massachusetts, Boston, 1789–1838. (Individual session-law volumes, cited by year.)

C. B. Mayo, ed., "Additions to Hutchinson's History"
C. B. Mayo, ed., "Additions to Hutchinson's History," 59 Amer. Antiq. Soc., *Procs.* 11–74 (1950).

MHS, *Colls., Procs.*
Massachusetts Historical Society, *Collections* and *Proceedings.*

Mich. L. Rev.
Michigan Law Review.

Miller, *Origins of the American Revolution*
John C. Miller, *Origins of the American Revolution,* Stanford and London, 1943, 1959.

Mod.

> *Modern Reports; or, Select Cases adjudged in the Courts of K.B., Chancery, C.P. and Exchequer*, London, 1682–1738; 12 parts.

Moore K.B.

> Francis Moore, *Cases collect et report per Sir Fra. Moore*, 2d edn., London, 1688.

MVHR

> *Mississippi Valley Historical Review.*

N.E.

> *Northeastern Reporter*, St. Paul, 1885– .

NEHGR

> *New England Historical and Genealogical Register.*

NEQ

> *New England Quarterly.*

Noy

> William Noy, *Reports of Cases in the time of Queen Elizabeth and King Charles*, London, 1656.

OED

> *The Oxford English Dictionary*, Oxford, 1933; 12 vols. and supplement.

Oliver, *Origin and Progress*

> Peter Oliver, *The Origin and Progress of the American Rebellion*, ed. Douglass Adair and John A. Schutz, San Marino, 1963.

Oregon L. Rev.

> *Oregon Law Review.*

Pa. Stat.

> Pennsylvania Statutes, Harrisburg, 1872– .

Paige

> Alonzo Paige, *Reports, Court of Chancery*, N.Y., 1887; 11 vols.

Paton App.

> J. Craigie, J. Stewart, and T. Paton, *Reports of Cases Decided in the House of Lords, upon Appeal from Scotland*, Edinburgh, 1849–1856; 6 vols.

Pattee, *Old Braintree and Quincy*

> William S. Pattee, *A History of Old Braintree and Quincy, with a Sketch of Randolph and Holbrook*, Quincy, 1878.

P. Wms.

> See Peere Williams.

Peere Williams
W. Peere Williams, *Reports of Cases, Court of Chancery, and of some special cases, King's Bench*, London, 1740-1749; 3 vols.

Perham, *American Precedents*
Benoni Perham, *American Precedents of Declarations*, Boston, 1802.

Pick.
Octavius Pickering, *Pickering's Reports* (Massachusetts Reports, 1822-1839), Boston, 1853-1864; 24 vols.

Plucknett, *Concise History*
T. F. T. Plucknett, *Concise History of the Common Law*, 5th edn., London, 1956.

Pollock & Maitland, *History of English Law*
Frederick Pollock and Frederic Maitland, *The History of English Law Before the Time of Edward I*, Cambridge, 1895; 2 vols.

Josiah Quincy, *Josiah Quincy, Jr.*
Josiah Quincy, *Memoir of Josiah Quincy, Junior, of Massachusetts: 1744-1775*, ed. Eliza Susan Quincy, 2d edn., Boston, 1874.

Quincy, *Reports*
Josiah Quincy Jr., *Reports of Cases Argued and Adjudged in the Superior Court of Judicature of the Province of Massachusetts Bay, between 1761 and 1772*, ed. Samuel M. Quincy, Boston, 1865.

Quincy, *Reports* (Appendix)
Appendixes to Quincy, *Reports*.

Rolle, *Abridgment*
H. Rolle, *Abridgment des plusieurs Cases et Resolutions del Common Ley*, London, 1668.

Rowe, *Letters and Diary*
Letters and Diary of John Rowe, Boston Merchant, 1759-1762, 1764-1779, ed. Anne Rowe Cunningham, Boston, 1903.

Sabine, *Loyalists*
Lorenzo Sabine, *Biographical Sketches of Loyalists of the American Revolution, with an Historical Essay*, Boston, 1864; 2 vols.

Salk.
William Salkeld, *Reports of Cases in the Court of King's Bench, with some special cases in the Courts of Chancery, Common Pleas and Exchequer, alphabetically digested under proper heads, from the 1st of William and Mary to the 10th of Anne*, London, 1721-1724; 3 parts.

Saund.

E. Saunders, *Les Reports des Divers Pleadings et Cases en le Court del Bank le Roy en le temp del Reign de le Roy Charles II*, London, 1686–1687; 2 vols.

Savile

J. Savile, *Les Reports de divers Special Cases cybien en le Court de Common Bank come l'Exchequer*, London, 1688.

Scott, *Civil Law*

S. P. Scott, transl., *The Civil Law*, Cincinnati, 1932; 17 vols.

Shipman, *Common-law Pleading*

Benjamin J. Shipman, *Hand-book of Common-law Pleading*, 3d edn., Ballantine, 1923.

Sibley-Shipton, *Harvard Graduates*

John Langdon Sibley and Clifford K. Shipton, *Biographical Sketches of Graduates of Harvard University, in Cambridge, Massachusetts*, Cambridge and Boston, 1873– .

Siderf.

T. Siderfin, *Les Reports des divers Special Cases, Bank le Roy, Co. Ba., & L'Exchequer*, London, 1683–1684; 2 vols.

Skin.

Robert Skinner, *Reports of Cases adjudged in the King's Bench; with some arguments in special cases*, London, 1728.

Smith, *Appeals to the Privy Council*

Joseph H. Smith, *Appeals to the Privy Council from the American Plantations*, N.Y., 1950.

Stat.

United States Statutes at Large, Boston and Washington, 1850– .

State Trials

A Collection of State-Trials, and Proceedings, upon High Treason, and other Crimes and Misdemeanours, from The Reign of Queen Anne, to the Present Time, London, 1766; 10 vols.

Stark, *Loyalists of Mass.*

James H. Stark, *The Loyalists of Massachusetts and the Other Side of the American Revolution*, Boston, 1910.

Stephen, *History of Criminal Law*

J. Fitzjames Stephen, *History of the Criminal Law of England*, London, 1883; 3 vols.

Stephen, *Pleading*
Henry John Stephen, *A Treatise on the Principles of Pleading in Civil Actions*, London, 1824.

Stiles, *Literary Diary*
The Literary Diary of Ezra Stiles, D.D., LL.D., President of Yale College, ed. Franklin Bowditch Dexter, N.Y., 1901; 3 vols.

Str.
John Strange, *Reports of Cases in the courts of Chancery, King's Bench, Common Pleas and Exchequer*, London, 1755; 2 vols.

Style
W. Style, *Narrationes Modernæ, or, Modern Reports, Upper Bench Court at Westminster, as well on the Criminall as on the Pleas Side*, London, 1658.

Sutton, *Personal Actions*
Ralph Sutton, *Personal Actions at Common Law*, London, 1929.

Sweet and Maxwell, *Legal Bibliography*
W. Harold Maxwell and Leslie F. Maxwell, comps., *A Legal Bibliography of the British Commonwealth of Nations: Vol. 1; English Law to 1800*, 2d edn., London, 1955; C. R. Brown, P. A. Maxwell and L. F. Maxwell, comps., *Vol. 3: Canadian and British-American Colonial Law*, London, 1957.

T.R.
See Term Rep.

Talb.
Cases in Equity, during the Time of Chancellor Talbot, London, 1741.

Taunt.
William P. Taunton, *Reports of Cases Argued and Determined in the Court of Common Pleas, and Other Courts*, London, 1810–1823; 8 vols.

Term Rep.
C. Durnford and E. H. East, *King's Bench Reports*, London, 1787–1800; 8 vols.

Thorpe, *Federal and State Constitutions*
Francis N. Thorpe, ed., *The Federal and State Constitutions, Colonial Charters, and Other Organic Laws of the States, Territories, and Colonies Now or Heretofore Forming the United States of America*, Washington, 1909; 7 vols.

Thwing, *Crooked and Narrow Streets*
    Annie Haven Thwing, *The Crooked and Narrow Streets of the Town of Boston, 1630–1822*, Boston, 1920.

Ubbelohde, *Vice Admiralty Courts*
    Carl Ubbelohde, *The Vice-Admiralty Courts and the American Revolution*, Chapel Hill, 1960.

UCC
    Uniform Commercial Code, American Law Institute, National Conference of Commissioners on Uniform State Laws, N.Y., 1962.

U.S.
    United States Reports, Supreme Court, Boston, N.Y., and Washington, 1875– .

U.S.C.
    United States Code.

Va. L. Rev.
    Virginia Law Review.

Vaughan
    J. Vaughan, *Reports and Arguments in the Common Pleas, being all of them Special Cases and many wherein he pronounced the resolution of the whole Court of Common Pleas at the time he was Chief Justice there; to which is added a Tract concerning Process out of the Courts at Westminster into Wales*, London, 1677.

Vent.
    P. Ventris, *Reports in two parts. Part I containing cases in the King's Bench with three learned arguments . . . Part II containing cases in the Common Pleas with special Pleadings in the same; together with . . . cases in the Court of Chancery*, London, 1696.

Vern.
    Thomas Vernon, *Cases argued and adjudged in the High Court of Chancery*, 3d edn., London, 1828; 2 vols.

Ves. Jun.
    Francis Vesey, jun., *Reports of Cases argued and determined in the High Court of Chancery*, 2d edn., London, 1827; 20 vols.

Viner, *Abridgment*
    C. Viner, *General Abridgment of Law and Equity*, Aldershot, 1741–1753; 23 vols.

Wemms Trial
    The Trial of William Wemms, James Hartegan, William M'Cauley, [and others] . . . for the Murder of Crispus Attucks, [and others],

... *Superior Court of Judicature, Court of Assize, and General Goal Delivery ... taken in Short-Hand by John Hodgson*, Boston, 1770.

Wheat.
Henry Wheaton, *Reports, Supreme Court of the United States, 1816–1827*, Phila., 1816–1827; 12 vols.

Whitehill, *Boston, A Topographical History*
Walter M. Whitehill, *Boston, A Topographical History*, Cambridge, Mass., 1959.

Whitmore, *Mass. Civil List*
William H. Whitmore, comp., *The Massachusetts Civil List for the Colonial and Provincial Periods, 1630–1774*, Albany, 1870.

Wils. K.B.
G. Wilson, *Reports, King's Courts at Westminster*, London, 1770–1775; 2 vols., 3 parts.

WMQ
William and Mary Quarterly.

Wood, *Institute of the Laws of England*
Thomas Wood, *An Institute of the Laws of England; or, the Laws of England according to Common Use*, London, 1720; 4 vols.

Wood, *New Institute of the Civil Law*
Thomas Wood, *New Institute of the Imperial or Civil Law, with notes*, 3d edn., London, 1721.

Yelv.
Sir H. Yelverton, *Reports of divers special Cases, King's Bench*, 3d edn., London, 1735.

Legal Papers

Cases 1–30

Legal Papers of John Adams

A. Law Study

EDITORIAL NOTE

The two documents which follow are virtually all that have survived pertinent to Adams' early law studies, except for accounts in his diary. Document I, a fragment entitled "Ld Cokes Sayings," cannot be dated with certainty, but the content suggests that it is some kind of epitome made by Adams during his early reading of Coke on Littleton.[1]

Document II is Adams' Commonplace Book, a compendium of hypothetical cases and bits of legal wisdom arranged on a topical plan. In October 1758 Adams recorded in his diary that Peter Chardon, a rising young lawyer, "transcribes Points of Law into a Common-Place Book on Locks Modell." The "Modell" was a plan devised by John Locke for arranging quotations under topical headings.[2] Some time thereafter Adams began to keep the small notebook printed here. It has been tentatively dated 1759, partly on the basis of the Chardon remarks, and partly by the fact that it contains references to Adams' neighbors in Braintree at this time, and to his father, who died in 1761. Moreover, the handwriting is the same as that of Adams' diary entries of 1759.[3]

Adams did not collect quotations in his Commonplace Book, but what appear to be abstracts of pertinent passages drawn either from his reading in legal works such as *Doctor and Student, Instructor Clericalis,* and the reports, or from the notebooks of others at the bar. These abstracts Adams occasionally enlivened with hypothetical cases in which he substituted the names of family, neighbors, and acquaintances for the Does and Roes of the law. The passages are arranged alphabetically under key words; thus, an abstract involving more than one point of law may appear in several places in the book, perhaps in slightly different form each time.

The topics covered are a revealing portrayal of the interests of a young lawyer fresh from the traditional struggle with Coke and other repositories of the law of real property and common-law pleading. Of the abstracts only a smattering deal with property and allied problems. There are

[1] On JA's study of Coke, see 1 JA, *Diary and Autobiography* 90–91, 133, 158, 173–174.

[2] 1 JA, *Diary and Autobiography* 47. A similar book of a more formal sort which belonged to CFA is in Adams Papers, Microfilms, Reel No. 312.

[3] See p. 7–13, notes 7, 13, 16, 17, below. In a diary kept in the summer of 1759 JA made several pages of similar notes from Wood's *New Institute of the Civil Law* and Johannes van Muyden's *Compendiosa Institutionum Justiniana Tractatis.* See 1 JA, *Diary and Autobiography* 104–106, 122 note.

numerous passages dealing with the sufficiency of pleadings, but the bulk
of these, and indeed of the whole book, involve matters of contract—
sufficiency of consideration and the nature of the actions of debt, covenant,
and assumpsit. Adams also devoted much space to the Roman-law
concepts of bailment and pledge, which in refined form were an important
element of England's developing commercial law.[4] Whether Adams'
interest in these matters was purely practical, or marked the beginning of
his later serious study of the civil law,[5] their presence in his Commonplace
Book suggests an awareness that the life of the law is less reason or
experience than trade. That commercial matters were his principal field of
study is confirmed by the complete absence of anything relative to torts
outside of this area, or to criminal law.

I. ADAMS' STUDENT NOTES[1]

Ca. 1758

Nunquam prospere succedunt Res humanæ, ubi negliguntur
divinae.[2]

Sex horas somno, totidem des Legibus æquis;

Quatuor orabis, des Epulisque duas.

Quod superest ultro sacris largire Camenis. Co. Lit. sec. 85.[3]

The student must know how to work into, with Delight these rough
Mines of hidden Treasure.[4]

En la Ley. There be diverse Laws within the Realm of England.[5]

[4] See Plucknett, *Concise History* 479–480. See also p. 6, note 5, below.

[5] See Nos. 43, 46, 56, 57; 1 JA, *Diary and Autobiography* 173–174.

[1] In JA's early hand. Adams Papers, Microfilms, Reel No. 185. A single leaf,
docketed by JA: "Ld Cokes Sayings."

[2] Coke, *Littleton* 64b. Part of a discussion of the feudal tenure called frankal-
moign, "service due to Almighty God," which was, according to Coke, the most
important tenure, because the other tenures "must all become prosperous and useful,
by reason of Gods true religion and service." Then follows the line in the text, which
in translation is "Human affairs never prosper where divine affairs are neglected."
See Black, *Law Dictionary.*

[3] Following the passage in note 2 above, Coke stated "Wherein I would have our
Student follow the Advice given in these Ancient Verses, for the good spending of
the day." The lines in the text are then set out. Coke, *Littleton* 64b. Editors' translation: "Give six hours to sleep, as many to just laws. Pray for four and give two to
feasting. What is left over at the end bestow on the sacred muses."

[4] Coke, *Littleton* 5b–6a: "Of all these [ancient terms for topographical features]
you shall read in ancient books, charters, deeds, and records, and to the end that our
student should not be discouraged for want of knowledge when he meeteth with
them ... we have armed him with the signification of them, to the end he may
proceed in his reading with alacrity, and set upon and know how to work into with
delight these rough mines of hidden treasure." A line is drawn across the page in the
MS at this point.

[5] The fifteen "Laws" that follow are recited by Coke in substantially this form in
Coke, *Littleton* 11b.

1. Lex Coronæ. 2. Lex et Consuetudo Parliamenti. Ista Lex est ab omnibus quærenda, a multis ignorata, a paucis cognita.[6]

3. Lex Naturæ. 4. Communis Lex Angliæ, or Lex Terræ.

5. Statute Laws.

6. Consuetudines. Customs reasonable. 7. Jus Belli. The Law of Arms, War and Chivalry, in Republica Maximæ Conferoanda, sunt Jura Belli.

8. Ecclesiastical or Canon Law, in Courts in certain Cases.

9. Law Civil, in certain Cases, not only in Courts Ecclesiastical, but in the Court of the Constable and Marshal, and of the Admiralty; in which Court of the Admiralty is observed, la ley Olyron. An. 5. R. 1, because it was published in the Isle of Oleron.[7]

10. Lex Forestæ. 11. The law of Marque and Reprisal. 12 Lex Mercatoriæ.

13. The Laws and Customs of the Isles of Jersey, Guernsey and Man.

14. The Law and Priviledge of the stannaries.[8]

15. The Laws of the East, West and Middle Marches, now abrogated.

A precious Collection of Cokes sayings.[9]

Nullum simile quatuor Pedibus currit. Utile per Inutile non vitiatur. Qui ex damnato Coitu nascientur, inter Liberos non computentur.

[6] Editors' translation: "This law is inquired into by all, unknown to many, understood by few."

[7] JA had occasion to take note of this principle in several of his major cases. See Nos. 46, 56, 57. On 29 March 1778, after his hazardous crossing to France, JA lay "becalmed all day in Sight of Oleron," and not unnaturally expressed "a Curiosity to visit this Island of Oleron so famous in Antiquity for her Sea Laws." 2 JA, *Diary and Autobiography* 291. Oleron was the source of a code which became the basis of English maritime law. See 1 Holdsworth, *History of English Law* 526–527; 5 *id.* at 120–125.

[8] That is, the customary local law and courts of English mining communities, privileged by the Crown. See 1 Holdsworth, *History of English Law* 151–165.

[9] The "Sayings," rendered more or less accurately by JA, are found scattered in Coke, *Littleton* 3a–10a. Translations from Black, *Law Dictionary* (with one indicated exception), follow in the same order: "No simile runs upon all fours. The useful is not vitiated by the useless. Those who are born of an unlawful intercourse are not reckoned among the children. Whose is the soil, his it is up to the sky. A cultivated mind does not know how to endure ignorance [editors' translation]. That is certain which can be rendered certain. From length of time all things are presumed to have been done in due form.

"Related words [words connected with others by reference] have this particular operation by the reference, that they are considered as being inserted in those [clauses which refer to them].

"The laws themselves require that they should be governed by right. Where the same reason exists, there the same right prevails."

Cujus est solum, ejus est usque ad Cælum. Nescit generosa Mens Ignorantiam pati. Certum est, quod certum reddi potest. Ex Diuturnitate Temporis, omnia presumuntur solemniter esse Actæ.

Verba relata hac maxime operantur per Referentiam ut in esse videntur.

Ipsæ Legis cupiunt ut jure regantur. Ubi eadem Ratio ibi idem jus.

II. ADAMS' COMMONPLACE BOOK [1]

Ca. *1759*

A

Assumpsit. Sometimes signifies not only a Promise but an Actual Undertaking of the Business, an Actual Entry, upon the Execution of the Promise.

Ass[umpsit] Ind[ebitatus] will lie against A.B. upon such a Promise as this viz. "my Brother will give you an handsome gratuity, for the Trouble you shall be at in that affair which I promise you shall not be less than £300."

Assumpsit. In Assumpsit we ought to declare as the Agreement was.

Agreement. If the Agreement is to deliver 6 Sieves, part of one sort and part of another, it is not necessary in the Declaration in Assumpsit to say how many of one sort and how many of the other. The Defendant shall have his Election to deliver as many of one sort and of the other as he will.

Every Mans Agreement or Bargain ought to be performed as he understood it. And if a Man will agree to Pay his Money, before he had the Thing for which he ought to pay it, and will rely upon his Remedy to recover that Thing, he ought to perform his Agreement. But He ought not to be compelled to give Credit when he did not intend it. Therefore, if 2 Men, A and B, agree, A that B shall have his Horse, and B that he will pay 10s. to A for him: because B may have an Action for the Horse, yet there is no reason that A should have an Action for the Money before the Horse is deliverd.

In executory Agreements, if the Contract be, that one shall do an Act, and for the doing thereof, the other shall pay &c. the Performance of the Act is a Condition preecedent to the Payment. Except

---

[1] In JA's early hand. Adams Papers, Microfilms, Reel No. 184. A small, coverless, stitched booklet consisting of eighty pages, of which nearly half are blank. The writing is in a miniscule hand, and the ink on some pages has faded badly. For the dating, see p. 1, text at note 3, above.

1, a Day appointed for Payment of the Money happen before the Thing can be performed. For in this case it is plain the Party relied upon his Remedy. 2, The day appointd for Payment is to happen subsequent to the Performance. In this Case Performance is a Condition preecedent, and must be averred in an Action for the Money.

Averment. There must be an Averment of Performance of the Act or Thing to be done in a Declaration on a Promise to pay Money that was made in Consideration of that Act or Thing.

Assumpsit. May be brought for Money paid upon a Policy of Insurance by Mistake (thinking the ship to be lost when it was not).[2] But assumpsit will not lie, against a solicitor for Money given him, to bribe the Custom House Officers and laid out by him accordingly. Yet assumpsit may be brought for Money paid by Mistake on an Account.

Averment. If I am bound in a Recognisance that Mr. Foreman[3] shall appear to an Action upon 8 days Warning, and if he is condemned to satisfy the Debt. It should be averred that Mr. Foreman had 8 days Warning, because I, a stranger am to be affected with the Appearance. And tho Mr. Foreman should appear on other Terms, i.e. without 8 days Warning, that Appearance would not charge me a stranger, [or?] 3rd Person, with the Payment of the Debt in Case of Mr. Foremans Condemnation.

Suppose Assumpsit in Consideration that Mr. Foreman at Plaintiff's Request, should relinquish Ad[ministratio]n and Permit Defendant to have it to do such an Act. It must be averred not only that Mr. Foreman relinquished Ad[ministratio]n but that he relinquished it at Plaintiffs Request, for the Request is an Act to be done by Plaintiff and if he did it not, there is no Reason that he should have the Recompence.[4]

Award. If A enters into Bond to perform the award of B and C, and B and C will not make any award, A can not be liable to forfeit his Bond.

Arrest of Judgment. Judgment shall be arrested, after Verdict for Plaintiff in Indebitatus Assumpsit for a Wager or on mutual Promises, for Want of a Consideration. For neither Indebitatus Assumpsit nor

---

[2] See Nos. 10 and 11.

[3] "Mr. Foreman" has not been identified. He appears again. See, for example, text at note 33 below. He may be a neighbor, client, or friend, or perhaps this is an abstract of a jury address in which the lawyer used the foreman of the jury for rhetorical purposes.

[4] The three following paragraphs are from a second "overflow" alphabet at the back of the book.

5

Debt will lie on a Wager or on mutual Promises for Want of a real Consideration.

Judgment was arrested, because the Promise of Defendant appears by the Plaintiffs own shewing to be grounded on a Consideration, which Plaintiff had not Power to perform. The Consideration was that Plaintiff should permit Defendant quietly to enjoy when he had no Right to disturb him.

B

Bailment. There are 6 Sorts of Bailment. 1. a Depositum. 2. Commodatum. 3 Locatio et conductio. 4. Vadium or Pignus. 5. a Factorage. 6. Mandatum.[5]

Breach of Assumpsit or Promise, Defendant's assumpsit to deliver to Plaintiff, at or before 8th of Jan. '45 &c. out of a ship into a Barge to be brought by Plaintiff for the Purpose, and Plaintiff avers that he bro't his Barge, and that Defendant non deliberavit on the Eighth of Jany. Adjudged a sufficient Allegation of a Breach. 'Tho it was not alledgd that he did not deliver them before the 8th day which would have been a good Performance.

Leaving of Mill stones damnified, without making satisfaction is a Breach of a Covenant to leave those Mill stones in as good Condition as he found them or to pay the Plaintiff so much as they should be damnified, the Damages to be estimated by A and B, and altho Defendant pleads that A and B have not estimated he will not be excused. For he ought to produce the Estimation himself. If indeed the Estimation ought to be made by such Persons as the Obligee should appoint, and the Obligee had refused to appoint, this would excuse.

The Breach in an Action of Covenant may be assigned as large as the Covenant is; but a precise Breach must be shown in an Action of Debt upon a Bond conditiond to perform Covenants in a certain Judicature specified, Because a Breach is the Forfeiture of the whole Bond. This Distinction between a Bond and a Covenant and the Reasons of it ought to be carefully attended to.

If the Breach is assigned in the Words of the Covenant in an action of Covenant, it is well assigned. But in Debt on a Bond conditiond to perform Covenant a precise Breach must be shewn.

Blood. Whole Blood and half Blood. There has been a great Controversy whether the half Blood shall have a whole share, or but an half share.

---

[5] These terms are defined by JA below in alphabetical order. The "6 Sorts" are outlined by Holt in Coggs v. Bernard, 2 Ld. Raym. 909, 912–913, 92 Eng. Rep. 107, 109–110 (K.B. 1703).

6

In Case of Inheritances, and Descents the whole Blood is preferred, but this say the Advocates for the half Blood is only on Account of a maxim in Law:

Q. Is a Brother or sister of the half Blood, in the same Relation with a Brother or sister of the whole Blood? I think not.

It has been held, that a sister of the half Blood is in equal Degree with a sister of the whole Blood.

"Every Brother and sister I have living" has been adjudgd to include the half Blood as well as the whole.

The statute of Jac. 2. enacts that, if after the Death of the Father any of his Children shall die intestate, without Wife or Children, in the Life Time of the mother every Brother and sister and the Representatives of them, shall have an equal share.[6] Now it has been argued that a Brother of the half Blood is a Brother to the Intestate, as well as one of the whole Blood, and therefore should have an equall share.

C

Commodatum, i.e. cum modo datum. A Contract by which a Thing is granted, without Reward, to another for a certain Use, on Condition that the same Thing shall be returned, after the Use of it, in as good a Condition, as when deliverd.

—In this Contract the same Person continues to be owner, and the same Thing is to be returned; ergo Things that perish in the using, as Wine, Oyl &c. are not commodata.

—The Borrower is holden to the Strictest Diligence and Care, because the Contract is for his Benefit, not for that of the Lender.

—If the Borrower is guilty of the least Neglect, levissima Culpa, he is chargeable; e.g. I lend the Dr.[7] my Horse to go to Boston, and he ride him to Weighmouth, or if I lend him for 2 days, and he keeps him 3, if any Accident befalls the Horse, upon the third day, or in the Journey to Weighmouth, the Dr. will be chargeable. For perhaps the Horse would not have been hurt if he had been usd only at such Time and Place as I lent him to be usd.

—But if the Borrower observes the Conditions that the Lender shall impose, and the Horse or Goods are destroyd or damagd by any inevitable Accident as by Light[n]ing, by Fire, by Robbers &c. he shall not be chargeable. The Lender must bear the Loss 'tho he is to have no Reward for the Use of his Goods. But if the Goods suffer by

[6] 1 Jac. 2, c. 17 (1685).
[7] Presumably Dr. Elisha Savil, JA's neighbor at Braintree. See 1 JA, *Diary and Autobiography* 15.

the lightest Neglect in the Borrower, as if his servants leave the stable Door open, which gives occasion to the Thief to enter and steal the Horse, he shall be chargeable.

Consideration. If it be alledged, that whereas the Plaintiff vendidisset &c. the Defendant Promised; this imparts a Consideration and Request, for the vendidisset takes in the Concurrence of both Parties.

—An Action may be grounded on a Promise made for a past Consideration, but a previous Request must be alledgd, or else a subsequent Benefit to the Defendant.

—A past Consideration ought to be coupled with a Request.

—In Consideration the Plaintiff had at his own Charge buried Defendants Child, the Defendant promised to pay him his Charges. In Consideration that Plaintiff had served the Defendant and Ux; the Defendant after the Death of the Wife, promised to pay, &c. In Consideration the Plaintiff had married the Daughter of Defendant. In Consideration, that Plaintiff had been Defendants surety Defendant promisd to save Plaintiff harmless; so in Consideration that Plaintiff was Bail for Defendant, he promised to give him a Horse. So in Consideration that S.S. being a Carpenter had well built my House, I promise to give him £5. All these are good Considerations, and it is not necessary in any of these Cases to alledge a Request, because the Benefit which Defendant receives is a good Consideration, and necessarily implies a Request.

—In Consideration, that Plaintiff, at the Special Instance and Request of Defendant, would forbear to arrest Defendants son, till after 23d. of October, the Plaintiff promised to pay, on or before that day. This is a good Consideration, for the Plaintiff might be obliged to fullfill the Consideration by Defendants not paying till the last Instant of the 23d.

—A Woman promises to marry a Man, and the Man in Consideration thereof promises to marry her. This Consideration is good and this Promise is binding, for, Marriage is as much an Advancement to the Man as to the Woman.

—A Release of an Equity of Redemption is a very good Consideration, and the Common Law will take Notice that the Mortgagor has an Equity to be [redeemd?] in Chancery. A Release, which is the Consideration to maintain an action ought to be set forth Specially when and where it was made.[8]

Condition præceedent. The Contract is that one Party shall do an Act, as build a House, Deliver a Horse &c. and that the other Party

[8] The remaining entries under "C" are from the overflow alphabet.

for the Doing thereof shall pay Money. In this Case the Performance of the Act is a Condition præceedent to the Payment of the Money, unless a certain Day is appointed for the Payment, which will happen before the thing can be performed. For in this Case it is plain the Party relies upon his Remedy, and intended not to make Performance a Condition preceedent, and therefore an Action will lie against him, after the Day appointed for the Payment of the Money, before the Thing to be performed is performed.

—When a certain Day appointed for Payment is to happen after the Performance of the Thing to be done by the Contract, Performance is a Condition præceedent and must be averred in an Action for the Money. Where there is a Condition præcedent to be performd by Plaintiff Performance of that Condition must be set forth, in a Declaration on that Promise which was made on that Condition.[9]

Covenant lies vs. the Lessee in his Life time, or his Executors after his Death, even after assignment, altho the Lessor had Notice, and accepted Rent of the assignee but not Debt.

—Covenant lies not against Executors by Reason of the general Coven[an]t in Law, by Virtue of the Words Demise and Grant; but It lies vs. Executors on an express Covenant.

—Upon mutual and independent Covenants the Parties may have reciprocal Actions. E.g. It was covenanted by Articles that S. should assign to D. his Interest in a House &c. and that D. should pay to S. £30. Plaintiff assigns for Breach that D. has not paid the £30. Defendant pleads that S. did not assign. Plaintiff demurrs. And adjudged for him, for the Plaintiff may bring his Action before the Assignment of the House, and Defendant has a Remedy after, if the other Party performs not his Part.

Consideration. When one pays Money knowingly on an illegal Consideration, the Party that receives it ought to be punished for his offence, and the Party that pays it is Particeps Criminis.

—No Consideration, or an insufficient Consideration, a good Cause of Motion in Arrest of Judgment.

—If the Consideration, on which a Promise is made, be a Benefit to the Defendant or any Trouble or Prejudice to the Plantiff, it is sufficient.

Covenant. Defendant covenanted to leave Millstones in as good Condition as he found 'em, or to pay the Plaintiff so much as they should be damnified; the Damage to be estimated by A. and B. Plain-

---

[9] The preceding sentence is a subsequent addition by JA, since it is in a darker ink and is inserted between two paragraphs in a lighter hand.

tiff assigns for Breach that Defendant had left the Mill stones damnified, and had not made Satisfaction. Defendant pleads that A. and B hadnt estimated the Damage. Plaintiff demurred and adjudgd for him. For this Covenant is disjunctive, either to leave as good as he found, or to pay the Damages to be estimated by A and B and the latter Part of it viz. the Payment of Damages to be estimated by A and B is for the safety of Defendant, it belongs to him to procure the estimation, or otherwise he shall be liable.

Consideration. Forbearance by the Husband of Executrix to sue for Rent arrear incurred in the Lifetime of Testator, a good Consideration to maintain Assumpsit for the whole Ad[ministratio]n devolves, by the Marriage upon the Husband, and he might have releasd this Debt.

—A Promise not to do a Thing, which the Person who makes the Promise cannot do; is nothing, no Consideration; But the Promise granted on that is merely nudum Pactum.

—A Consideration perfectly past or entirely executed is no Consideration. Dr. and student Page 196.[10]

—Yet, if the service done or Thing sold, is alledged to be done or sold at the Defendants Special Instance and Request the Consideration doth continue. Croke. Eliz. 282.[11]

Covenants. In a Declaration on an independent Covenant, the Plaintiff need not set forth, that he tendered to transfer &c., because the stock was to be transferrd upon Payment of the Money; so that if Defendant has by his Agreement made himself the first Agent, he is obliged to pay the Money, before the Plaintiff is to transfer.

D

Depositum. Is a Contract by which a Man takes Goods into his Custody, to keep for the Use of the Deponent. The Person delivering the Goods is called the Deponent, and the Person receiving them the Depositary.

—The Depositary is answerable for the Goods if he keeps them with gross Negligence, but not if he keeps them as safely, and care-

[10] The edition of Christopher St. Germain's *Doctor and Student* cited here has not been identified. A passage concerning past consideration appears at p. 179–180 of the 1874 reissue of William Muchall's 18th-century edition of this famous work.

[11] Beauchamp v. Neggin, Cro. Eliz. 282, 78 Eng. Rep. 536 (Q.B. 1592). The declaration alleged that B had promised to repay £10 to N "in consideration that the said N. had paid for him, and at his request to C," £10 on a date a year before the promise. Held, there was consideration, because "when the payment is laid to be at his request, the consideration doth continue, and so is the common course."

fully as he keeps his own Goods, tho he neglected to accept them Specially.

—The Depositary has no Reward for receiving and keeping the Goods, and if the Goods are destroyed by Fire, or Stolen by Thieves, or taken away in any other manner without any Gross fault or Negligence in the Depositary, the Deponent must bear the Loss. The Depositary is not chargeable. But if they are stolen or destroyd by any gross Negligence or Mismanagement in the Depositary, such a Negligence as he never keeps his own Goods with, he is answerable because such a distinguishing Negligence is esteemd an Evidence of Fraud.

—A Depositary is the least responsible for Neglect of any of the Bailees. For he is not answerable for Goods that are lost by his Negligence, how gross soever that may be, if he keeps his own Goods with the same Negligence, and does not prove him self a Knave, by keeping the Goods deposited with greater Negligence than he does his own. For qui negligenti Amico, Rem custodiendam tradit, sibi ipsi, et propriae fatuilati, hac debit imputare.

—If a Depositary should promise expressly to redeliver Goods safely, yet he would not be answerable for 'em if stolen or destroyd without his fault. No, not if the Promise was committed to Writing.

Debt is upon the Contract or sale; but Indebitatus Assumpsit is upon the Promise.

If Debt is brought on a Contract for the sale of an Horse for £10; if it turns out that he was sold for more or less, the Plaintiff cannot recover; for it is a Precipe quod reddat, so much Money in particular.[12]

Deed. Every Mans Deed shall be taken most strongly against himself. Or rather this is the Distinction. Where there are general Words all alone in a Deed of Release, they shall be taken most strongly against the Releasor; But where there is a particular Recital, in a Deed, and then general Words follow, the general Words shall be qualified by the particular Recital.

Debt lies not on a Wager, nor on a mutual Assumpsit, nor against the Acceptor of a Bill of Exchange. But it lies vs. the Drawer for he was really a Debtor by the Receipt of the Money.

—If A lends Money to B, C's Request and upon his Promise to pay it, C cant be charged in an Indebitatus Assumpsit as for a Debt, but must be chargd in a special Assumpsit as being but collaterally bound by his Promise. Otherwise if the Money had been only deliverd

---

[12] That is, the form of the writ of debt, ordering the defendant to render a sum certain. See Stephen, *Pleading* 12–13; Fitzherbert, *New Natura Brevium* 263–264 (1704).

to, or had and receivd by, B at C's Request, for then the Loan would have been to C.

—If I enter Mr. Handcocks[13] Warehouse, and say to him deliver such Goods to E.B. a Carter, and I will pay you; This Promise will raise a Debt in me, and E.B. is not to pay for the Goods, nor is he liable for It may be a Gift from me to E.B. and a Debt for them from Me to Mr. Handcock.

—Debt will not lie, nor Indebitatus Assumpsit in Consideration that Plaintiff would sell to D. the Defendant's factor, at Defendant's Instance 200 Hogs to the Use of Defendant. There is a Repugnancy in this Declaration, for Defendant is chargd in Debt for Goods sold to his factor, whereas it should have been sold to him and deliverd to his factor.[14]

Declaration. General Declarations are often aided by pleading over. Plaintiff in Indebitatus Assumpsit declared that he contracted to release to Defendant his Equity of Redemption of Mortgaged Lands and that Defendant contractd in Consideration thereof to pay £7. And avers generally q[uoa]d Plaintiff performavit omnia, sua pote performanda, but Defendant has not paid the £7. This Declaration would be ill upon Demurrer, for the Plaintiff should have shewn the Time and Place when and where the Release of the Equity of Redemption was executed; Yet by Pleading a Release of all Demands, in Discharge of the seven Pounds, the Defendant admits and aids the Declaration.

—A sufficient Promise i.e. a Promise grounded on a sufficient Consideration must be alledgd in the Declaration.

Delivery. A Delivery in Consideration of being paid the Value, is a sale.

Disjunctive. If a Man makes a Promise or a Covenant in the Disjunctive, he must perform one Part or the other. E.g. A, in Consideration of £100, bound himself in a Bond, with a disjunctive Condition either to make a Lease L. of the Obligee, before such a Day, or to pay him £100. The Obligee died before the day, yet adjudged the Obligor should pay the £100.

Disceit. When a Man pays Money by a meer Disceit, 'tis reasonable he should have his Money again;

Deed. Where there are general Words only in a Deed of Release they shall be taken most strongly against the Releasor as where a Release is made to Dr. Savel[15] and me of all Actions, it releases all

---

[13] Presumably Thomas Hancock, founder of the fortune which his nephew John Hancock, of Braintree, inherited at the former's death in 1764.

[14] The remaining entries under "D" are from the overflow alphabet.

[15] See note 7 above.

several Actions which the Releaser has against us, as well as all joint Actions; so If an Executor releases all Actions, it will extend to all Actions that he has in both Rights, i.e. as Executor, and in his private Capacity too. But where there is a particular Recital in a Deed and then general Words follow, the general Words shall be qualified by the Special Words. E.g. My Father recovered against Dr. Savel a Judgment for £6000 and made Peter [16] and me his Executors and died. Dr. Savel made Mrs. Savel [17] his Executrix and devisd a Legacy of £5 to me and died; I, by Deed acknowledgd the receipt of the £5 of Mrs. Savell, and thereby released the said Legacy, and all Actions and Demands which I had against Mrs. Savel as Executrix to the Dr. After Argument in B[anco] R[egis], adjudged that nothing was released but the £5.[18]

Debt. Lies not against a Lessee, after an Assignment of his Term, if the Lessor had Notice, and accepted of the Assignee. But Covenant does.

—If you bring an Action of Debt for Rent, and demand less than is due, you cannot recover, but it is otherwise in Covenant.

—Debt lies where any sum of Money is due, for Money lent, or for Contract, Obligation or other specialty to be paid at a certain Time; and the same not being paid accordingly, Plaintiff shall have this Action for the Recovery of it.

Damages. In an Action of Covenant, all is recoverable in Damages, and those Damages shall be for the real Damages, which the Party can prove that he has actually sustained. Therefore a precise Breach of the Covenant need not be shewn but the Breach may be assignd, in as general Words, as the Covenant is in. Tho in Debt on a Bond or Performance of Covenants, a precise certain determinate Breach as the taking of some particular or the Building of a House with Catalabers [19] of a particular Length and Thickness less than that prescribed by Parliament, &c. must be assignd, because not the damages actually sustaind is to be recoverd by this Action but a forfeiture of the whole Bond.

Devastavit.[20] Defendant promises the Husband of Executrix, that in Consideration he will forbear to sue for Rent Arrear in the [Life of?] Testator till Mich[aelmas] &c. Defendant will pay it to the

---

[16] JA's brother, Peter Boylston Adams.

[17] Dr. Savil's wife, Ann, to whom on one occasion in 1758 JA planned to read Ovid amidst his law studies. See 1 JA, *Diary and Autobiography* 45.

[18] It is not clear whether JA has here peopled an actual case with family and friends, or whether this is a purely spontaneous flight of irony.

[19] Thus in MS, doubtless for "cantilevers." See *OED*.

[20] "He has wasted." The act of an executor, trustee, or the like, which wastes the estate. Black, *Law Dictionary*.

husband. The Husband sues Defendant on this Promise. A Recovery in this Action, would make a new Contract that would amount to a Devastavit. It will not be assetts of the Testators estate; for if Husband dies before Ex[ecutio]n, the Ex[ecuto]r or Adm[inistrato]r of Husband, and not the Wife shall sue Execution and it will be unlike a Recovery by both. The Husband will be chargeable to pay out of his own Estate, as much as he has recoverd. But the old Debt is not extinguished, untill the Money be paid to the Husband.

Demurrer. A General Demurrer will Aid a Plea with an immaterial Traverse tho an immaterial Traverse shewn for Cause upon material Demurrer, would vitiate the Plea.

On Demurrer, a Plea of Tender, when both the Parties meet at Time and Place without Pleading a Refusal, is naught, tho such a Plea is good after Verdict.

Day certain. A Person hired for a Year, can have no Action for his Wages, till the Year is expired; but if the Master covenants to pay the Wages on a certain day within the Year, an Action will lie before the Year is ended.

Distribution of Intestates Estates. The half Blood are in equal Degree, and as near a Kin as the whole Blood.

It has been adjudged several Times, since the statute for the half Blood, by Sir Richard Lloyd,[21] that the half Blood shall have but an half share. But Sir Richd. Lloyd alone, decreed in favour of the whole Blood and against the half Blood.

The true Reason, the true Principle of Distribution, is this. The Law is to give, as the Intestate might reasonably be supposed willing to have given, his Estate in Case he had made a Will, and had not been surprised by a sudden Death.

Now, Is not the natural Love of a Person to his Brothers and sisters of the whole Blood, greater than that to Brothers and sisters of the half Blood, and must we not suppose a Mans Inclinations would be to bestow his Estate upon his whole Brothers and sisters in Preference to his half Brothers and sisters? I appeal to Experience, whether Brothers and sisters of the half Blood, have half so strong an affection for each other as Brothers and sisters of the whole Blood. On the Contrary there are very often Grudges and Miffs and Misunderstandings between the second Crop of Children and the first.

---

[21] Sir Richard Lloyd (1634–1686) was Dean of the Arches (Judge of the Court of Arches) from 1684 to 1686. *DNB, sub nom.* Sir Nathaniel Lloyd. The Court of Arches had jurisdiction of appeals from all the inferior ecclesiastical courts within the province of the Archbishop of Canterbury. This jurisdiction would have included probate matters of the sort mentioned in the text. See 3 Blackstone, *Commentaries* *64–65; No. 16, text at note 1.

Duress. If a Man is induced to make a Deed, by Duress to his Property, he shall avoid it, as much as if it had been made by Duress to his Person. Strange, V[ol]. 2. Page. 915.[22]

E

Evidence. At this day Performance is given in Evidence upon Non Assumpsit.[23]

Exchange. Neither Debt nor Ind[ebitatus] Ass[umpsit] will lie against the Acceptor of a Bill of Exchange; for his Acceptance is but a collateral Engagement.

—But it lies vs. the Drawer himself, for he was really a Debtor by Receipt of the Money.

—Ind[ebitatus] Ass[umpsit] will lie vs. the Drawer of a Bill of Exchange for so much Money and receiv'd to the Plaintiffs Use. And Plaintiff may give the Note in Evidence.

Inland Bills of Exchange are on the same foundation with foreign Bills,[24] and Notes of Hand are on the same foundation with Inland Bills.

Quære. Is it necessary to set forth, in a Declaration upon a Bill of Exchange vs. the Drawer, that the Drawer had Notice of the Default of Payment by the Endorsor?

Error. Insufficient Consideration to support a Promise is a good Cause of Error of a Judgment for Performance of the Promise.

F

Factorage, or Carriage. A Delivery of Goods to be carried or otherwise managed, for a Reward to be paid to the Bailee.

—There are 2 sorts of Cases of Delivery and Acceptation to carry or manage for a Reward—either

—1. a Delivery to one that exercises a public Employment as a Common Carrier, common Hayman, Master of a ship &c. The Law charges these Persons thuss intrusted to carry Goods, against all Events but Acts of God and of the King's Enemies, for he is chargeable tho an irresistable Multitude of People should rob him. This Establish-

---

[22] Astley v. Reynolds, 2 Str. 915, 93 Eng. Rep. 939 (K.B. 1731), an action of assumpsit for money had and received in which the plaintiff claimed that the defendant had refused to surrender goods pawned except upon payment of more than legal interest. JA here has taken part of the plaintiff's argument that "a man shall avoid a deed by duress of his goods as well as of his person." *Id.* at 916, 93 Eng. Rep. at 939. The court upheld the plaintiff on this point.

[23] That is, upon the plea of the general issue ("he did not promise") in the action of assumpsit.

[24] See No. 8.

ment was continued by the Policy of the Law, for the security of all Persons, whose Affairs oblige them to trust these sorts of Persons, who might without such an Establishment, undo all Persons who had Dealings with Them, by Correspondencies with Thieves.

or

—2. To a Bailiff, Factor, and such like. Altho a Bailie [25] is to have a Reward for his Management yet he is only to do the best he can; and if he be robbd it is a good Account.

—It would be unreasonable to charge a Bailie or Factor with a Trust further than the Nature of the Thing puts it in his Power to perform it; tho the Necessity of the Cases of common Carriers, Masters of ships &c. makes such a Charge allowable in those Cases.

—If a Bailie receives his Masters Money and keeps it locked up, with a reasonable Care, he shall not be answerable for it, altho it be stolen.

G [26]

H

I

Indebitatus Assumpsit will not lie upon a Special Agreement, till the Forms of it are performed; but when that is done it raises a Duty, for which a general Ind. Ass. will lie.

Ind. Ass. is an Action upon the Promise. If you bring Ind. Ass. for £10 for a Horse sold, if he was sold for more or Less than £10, yet the Plaintiff shall recover what he was sold for; but if Debt be brought on that Contract; if it turn out more or less then Plaintiff cannot recover; for it is a Precipe quod reddat so much Money in particular.

—An Ind. Ass. will not lie, but for a sum certain.

—An Ind. Ass. does not lie for Rent secundum Ratam. But upon an express Promise for Easement, Ind. Ass. is the proper Action.

—A Permission by Plaintiff for Defendant to kill sheep in his Passage [Pasture?], is not a Lease, which passes any Interest or Property in the Soil. Tis only an Easement, and Ind. Ass. is the proper Action, grounded on an express Promise to pay for such an Easement.

—Ind. Ass. will not lie for a fine imposed on Defendant for not serving the office of sheriff of a City.

---

[25] Obsolete form of "bailiff." OED.

[26] The leaf lettered "G" is blank in the MS, as are the leaves under other letters for which no entries are printed here.

—Plea to Ind. Ass. that the Plaintiff and Defendant had accounted and the Plaintiff was found in Arrears 5s., and it was then agreed that one should be quit vs. the other except the 5s. This settlement ought not to be pleaded Specially. It may be given in Evidence on the General Issue.

—Ind. Ass. will not lie for the Repayment of £6 back to Walter by Acton (2 Parishes), on the Reversal of an order of sessions that Walter should pay to Acton £6, which it accordingly paid. Nor will Ind. Ass. lie for Money paid upon a Judgment, after the Reversal of that Judgment for Error.

—Ind. Ass. will lie in no Case, but where Debt lies. It lies not therefore on a Wager, nor upon a mutual assumpsit nor against the Acceptor of a Bill of Exchange; for this Acceptance is but a collateral Engagement. But Ind. Ass. or Debt will lie vs. the Drawer for he was really a Debtor, by the Receipt of the Money.

Ind. Ass. will not lie for an Obligor who has paid against an Obligee who has received Money on an usurious Obligation, to recover back that Money. For the Obligor is Particeps Criminis, and paid the Money voluntarily and Volenti non fit Injuria.

Ind. Ass. for Money had and received to Plaintiffs Use will lie vs. a Defendant, who had been impowerd by Letter of Attorney from an Administrator, and receivd Money due to the Intestate, and paid the same to the Administrator after the said Administration is repealed on the finding of a Will. For such an Administration is void and of Consequence the Defendant acted without Authority, and therefore an implied Contract shall be raised to charge Defendant by Ind. Ass. to the Executor.

—Ind. Ass. will lie for Money lent, or for Money laid out for Defendants Use. But Buying a Note of Defendant, upon his Warranty to make it good, is not laying out the Value of that Note for his Use, nor lending that sum to him.

—Ind. Ass. will well lie for that the Defendant being indebted to Plaintiff in £20 for [...] [27] cujusdam E. by Plaintiff at Defendants Request he assumed to pay.

—Ind. Ass. lies only when Debt lies. Debt will not lie on a Wager, on mutual Promises, &c., 'tho a special Assumpsit may.

Joindre. The Wife cannot be joined with her Husband in an Ass[umpsit] on a Promise made to the Husband, that in Considera-

[27] The word is illegible in the MS. The sentence seems to be an assertion that assumpsit lies for money paid or goods or services furnished to a third party at the defendant's request. See 1 Chitty, *Pleading* 339–340.

tion by the Husband would forbear to sue Defendant at his Request, for Money which Defendant owed the Plaintiff's Wife as Executrix to J.S. for arrears of Rent incurrd in the Life Time of J.S., till Mickaelmas following he would pay the Money to Plaintiff for she is neither privy to the Contract nor the Person to whom the Money is to be paid.[28]

Issue. The Law will always have the Issue a single Point if possible; and for that Reason will never permit a Man to plead the general Issue to a Specialty.

K

L

Locatio et Conductio. Letting, and hiring.

Locatio Conductio is a Contract by which the Use of a Thing, or the service of a Person, is gaind for some Time for a certain Reward.

—Locatio as a Bailment is confind to the Letting of Goods and is not extended to the Letting and hiring of services.

—The Hirer is obliged to the Utmost Diligence, such as the most diligent Father of a Family uses, and if he uses that, he shall be discharged. For the most diligent Man cannot always secure his Goods against Lightning, ship wreck, the Incursions of Robbers or Enemies, but if he uses his best Endeavours against them he shall be discharged.

M

Mandatum. An Acting by Commission. An Authority. A Contract by which an Affair is committed to the Management of another, and by him undertaken to be performed gratis.

—The Commissioner must Act gratis, but if he undertakes to act, he may be compelled, notwithstanding he receives no Consideration, to Act carefully, and is responsible for the Consequences of his Negligence.

—The Confidence reposed in the Commissioner by his Constituent, shall be deemd a sufficient Consideration, to support an Action to compell him to answer the Effects of his Neglect to do what he undertook.

—When one undertakes to carry or manage Goods gratis, and does the Bailor a Damage by his Neglect, he shall be chargeable, for such a Neglect is a Deceit. Let not Friendship be made the Cloak of Malice and Fraud.

[28] The following paragraph is from the overflow alphabet.

—If I make an Executory Contract, without Consideration, to carry a Cask of Brandy, from a Ware house to a ship, next Monday, I cannot be compelled, to carry this Cask, because the agreement was nudum Pactum. But if I not only agree but actually undertake to carry by taking the Cask, upon my Trucks, and then drive my Horses so carelessly that they overturn the Trucks and burst the Cask, I shall be answerable for the Brandy.

—But if the Trucks are overthrown and the Brandy Spilled, by any unavoidable Accident, e.g. if a drunken Person had met the Horses and frighted them, or had pierced the Cask and let out the Brandy, The Mandatum would not be chargeable.

N

Notes promissory. All Notes signed by any Person promising to pay to another, or order, or Bearer, the Money mentiond in the Note shall be construed to be due and payable to such Person, to whom it is made payable. Yet 'tho due and payable a General Indebitatus Assumpsit will not lie for it vs. the Indorsor, 'tho it may against the Drawer for Want of a Consideration.

Nudum Pactum. A Promise not to do a Thing which the Person that made the Promise cannot do, is nothing, no Consideration; but the Promise made, in Consideration of that Promise is merely nudum Pactum.

A Bill of Exchange is no more than Nudum Pactum. 'Tis only an Evidence of a Promise to pay.[29]

Nil Debet.[30] Nil Debet is no good Plea to an Action of Annuity.

—Nil Debet is no good Plea to an Action of Debt on a Bond, bro't by an Administrator.

—Nil Debet is a good Plea to an Action of Debt brot for Rent reserved.

—Tis a good Plea to an Action of Debt bro't on Penal Statutes..

—Tis a good Plea to Actions of Debt bro't upon awards; or to Account before Auditors.

—The Reason is these are not the Deeds of the Parties.

—Tis no good Plea on a Policy of Insurance.

—Tis no good Plea to an Action on a Bail Bond.

—Nil Debet is a good Plea where the Action is founded on a Collateral Matter, and not comprized in the Deed.

---

[29] The remaining entries under "N" are from the overflow alphabet.
[30] "He owes nothing," the plea of the general issue in the action of debt.

P

Promises. An Action for a Breach of Promise of Marriage is founded upon mutual Promises.

—It is dangerous to admit Proofs of mutual Promises unless they are committed to Writing.

—In Case of mutual Promises, one Promise is the Consideration of the other. And in these Cases the Plantiff is not obliged to aver Performance of his Part. If there is a positive Agreement that the Plaintiff should release, and that Defendant should pay £7. The Plaintiff might have maintaind an Action before he had made the Release. But if the Promise to pay the Money had been in Consideratione Cujus i.e. of the Release, the Release on the Part of the Plaintiff would have been a Condition preceedent.

—Vid. next Page but one under the Word Payment.[31]

Mutual Promises must be known by the Words of the Agreement. If I covenant with the Dr. that my father shall convey Land to him, and the Dr. pro Consideratione predicta covenants to pay to my father £160. It is held that the Dr. is obliged to pay the Money, altho my father does not convey. Here is an express Covenant by me that my father shall convey to the Dr. and then pro Consideratione predicta must not be understood in Consideration of the Conveyance, but in Consideration of my Covenant that my father should convey. For as I in Consideration of the Drs. Covenant to pay, without an Actual Payment made my Covenant, so he in Consideration of mine without an Actual Conveyance shall be construed to have made his.

—Plaintiff agreed to make a Release, in Consideratione Cujus the Defendant agreed to pay Plaintiff £7. Holt says, this, Cujus, signifies of the Execution of the Release, not of the Promise.[32] But what distinguishes this from the foregoing Case I dont see.

—An Action of Debt, nor of Indebitatus Assumpsit cant be brought on a mutual Assumpsit.

—Suppose I was indebted to Mr. Foreman, and I should go to Mr. Thatcher[33] and intreat him to pay Mr. Foreman and should promise Mr. Thatcher to pay him again, and thereupon Thatcher should

[31] An insertion by JA in a smaller hand. The passage to which he refers is on p. 21 below.

[32] Probably a reference to Thorpe v. Thorpe, 1 Ld. Raym. 662, 665, 91 Eng. Rep. 1341, 1343; 12 Mod. 455, 460, 88 Eng. Rep. 1448, 1450–1451 (K.B. 1701), where Holt states the proposition attributed to him by JA although not in the same words.

[33] Presumably Oxenbridge Thacher, the lawyer. Other lawyers whose names appear in succeeding passages are Robert Treat Paine, James Otis, and Benjamin Kent.

promise to pay the Debt to Mr. Foreman and afterwards refuse or neglect it: I may have an Action vs. Mr. Thatcher on the Promise because of my mutual Promise to him he may be indemnified.

Performance. Performance of the Act or Thing to be done is a Condition preceedent to the Payment of the Money to be paid, when the Agreement is that one shall do such an Act, and that for the doing thereof the other shall pay, unless a day be appointed for the Payment of the Money and that day is to be before the Thing to be done, can be performed. If Performance of a Covenant is rendered impossible by the Act of the Obligee, the Obligor is excused.

Pawn or Pledge. Redemption is incident to the Nature of a Pledge.

The Pawn is a security to the Pawnee, that he shall be repaid his Debt, and therefore he has a Special Property in the Thing pawned.

If Things that wear or suffer by Use as Cloaths &c. are pawnd the Pawnee must not use them, but if Things are pawnd that will be nothing the worse for Use as Jewells to a Lady &c. she may use them. But she must use them at her own Risque. For if she wears them abroad, and is there robbed of them, she will be answerable for them, whereas if she keeps 'em locked in her Cabinett, if her Cabinet should be broke open and the Jewells stolen, she would be excused.

A Pawn is in Nature of a Deposit, and as such is not liable to be usd. —But

If a Horse or Cow or any other Thing whose Maintenance is chargeable to the Pawnee be pawned, then the Pawnee may milk the Cow, or use the Horse in a reasonable Manner, in Recompence of his meat.

—The Creditor who takes a Pawn is bound to restore it upon the Payment of his Debt; i.e. if the Pawn is safe, but if the Creditor has used an ordinary Care to preserve the Pawn, but it has been not withstanding stolen or destroyd, he shall not loose his Debt.

—The Law requires nothing of the Pawnee, but an ordinary Care for Restoring the Goods.

—If the Pawnee detain the Goods pawnd, after a Tender of the Money for which they were pawnd, he is a Wrong Doer. And should be answerable for them, if lost.

Payment. An agreement was made that Defendant should pay £20 in 6 months, the Plaintiff transferring stock, which Plaintiff agreed to do, Defendant paying the £20. These are mutual Promises. Yet the Payment of the Defendant is a Condition præcedent to the Transfer of the Plantiff, and the Transfer of the Plantiff is a Condition præcedent to the Payment of Defendant, so that these are mutual Promises and Conditions præcedent too. This is to be understood, unless a Day certain be appointed either for Performance or Payment.

Pro. The Word Pro, (in Pro Consideratione inde) makes Condition præceedent in all executory Agreements, unless there is a certain day appointed for the Performance. But, yet the Word Pro does not always make a Condition præceedent so that the Plaintiff is not intituled to an Action without averring Performance on his Part, for sometimes the Word Pro makes the Covenants mutual e.g. The Plaintiff is to transfer pro the Money, which the Defendant is to pay pro the Transfer.

R

Request. An assumpsit for Work and Labour done as laid in this Case viz. quod performasset et per ferisset cannot imply a Request, because it might be done without the Knowledge or Privity of the Defendant: and such an Action will not lie, unless it be expressly averrd to have been done ex Requisitione of the Defendant.

—Work may be done for a Man without his Request or Privity; if a Man will enter on my Land, pull down my House, and build up a new one without my Consent and Approbation, the Law [. . .] the House; and the Plaintiff has no Remedy for the Work and Labour done; for

—An Action will not lie unless the Consideration is grounded on a preceedent Request or a subsequent Benefit and approbation.

—A Benefit by Implication carries a Request along with it. Hays vs. Warren.[34]

—A Delivery and Acceptance necessarily imports a Request and Privity in Defendant.

—A Man cannot be liable for Work and Labour done for a 3d. Person, unless it was done at his Request.

Repugnancies. Indebitatus Assumpsit for Money had and receivd by the Defendant for the Plantiff, ad usum of Defendant. Judgment shall not be arrested; those insensible, repugnant Words, "Ad Usum of Defendant" shall be rejected.

—Indebitatus Assumpsit in Consideration that Plaintiff would sell to D, the Defendants factor, at the Instance of the Defendant, 200 Hoggs to the use of Defendant. Debt nor Indebitatus Assumpsit will lie, for if the Defendant only promised, collaterally as a security a

[34] See Hayes v. Warren, 2 Barn. K.B. 140, 141, 94 Eng. Rep. 407, 408 (1732), an action of assumpsit for work and labor, in which a request that the work be done was not alleged. The court said that a request might be implied from certain acts, such as "the being Bail for one, curing one's child of a sudden Sickness, performing the Part of a Servant, &c.," but no such acts were found here.

Warranty for the Payment of his factor, a Special Action of the Case not Indebitatus Assumpsit nor Debt is the proper Action, but if he promised as the Principal Debtor he ought to have been chargd as the Vendee and the Goods should have been said to be deliverd not sold to his factor. So that here is a Repugnancy in this Declaration.

Rent. A.B. covenanted to pay Rent to B.C. Now if B.C. should enter by Virtue of a Power reservd in this Covenant, or if he enterd as a meer Trespasser, this is no suspension of the Rent.

S

Stranger. 3rd. Person &c. Suppose I should be bound in a Recognisance, that Mr. Foreman should appear to an Action upon 8 Days Warning and if he should be condemnd that I would Satisfy the Debt. Here as a stranger is to be affected by the Appearance there ought to be precisely such an Appearance sett forth, as was mentioned in the Condition of the Recognisance. As if I am bound in a Bond to Mr. Foreman to pay Mr. Foreman Money; Mr. Foreman may accept a Horse instead of it: But If I am bound to Mr. Foreman to pay Mr. Otis, Paine, &c. money; Mr. Otis cannot accept a Horse.

—If I promise Mr. Foreman to pay Money to a Stranger as Mr. Paine, that stranger Mr. Paine may have an Action against me for this Money. For here tho Mr. Paine is not privy, is not a Party to the Contract, yet the Payment is to be made to him.

—Suppose I owed Mr. Foreman, and should go to a 3rd. Person Mr. Kent and intreat him to pay Mr. Foreman for me, and should promise to pay him again, and thereupon Mr. Kent should promise to pay Mr. Foreman, and afterwards should neglect or refuse it; I may have an Action vs. Mr. Kent on the Promise, because of the mutual Promise from me to him, whereby he may be indemnified, and an Action will lie for Mr. Kent vs. me, even without averring Payment to Mr. Foreman. And it seems also that Mr. Foreman, being the Person for whose Benefit the Promise was made, may have an Action vs. Mr. Kent, on his Promise to me.

T

Tender. Defendant, in Consideration of £20 assumed to deliver to the Plantiff, at or before the Eighth day of Jany. 45 Qu[arte]rs of oat meal out of a ship into a Barge to be brought there by Plaintiff for said Purpose. The Defendant cant make a Tender before the last day to oblige the Plaintiff to accept them, altho he had his Election to deliver before the 8th day.

Trespass. In Trespass or Trover, for 6 sieves of diverse sorts, the Plaintiff must declare how many of each sort. But in Assumpsit we must declare as the Agreement was.

Tender. When both Parties, (Plaintiff and Defendant) meet at Time and Place, he that pleads a Tender, must also plead a Refusal; otherwise such a Plea is naught on Demurrer.

—He that pleads a Tender at the Time and Place and no one there to receive, must shew at what Time of the Day, he was there, and how long he staid.

—The last of the Day is the Time the Law appoints for a Tender but it must be time enough before sun set to [...] at the Matter.

Trover. An Administrator recovered, in an Action of Trover for Goods. And after Judgment, but before Execution The Administration was repealed. Upon this the Defendant brought Audita Querela, and adjudged that it lay.

Traverse. Where a Traverse is immaterial the Adverse Party is not excluded from an Answer; but may reply and traverse the material Part of the Plea.

U

Undertaking. There is a Difference between a Conditional and an absolute Undertaking: as if A promise to pay B such a sum, if C does not. There A is but a Security for C, but if A promise that C will pay such a sum, A is the Principal Debtor; for the Act done was upon his Credit, and no Way upon C.

V

Vadium. A Pawn. A Contract, by which a Thing is given by the Debtor to the Creditor, for security of his Debt, on Condition, that, when the Debt is paid the same Thing, in Specie should be returned.

—The Pawnee has a Special Property in the Goods. For the Pawn is a security to the Pawnee that he shall be repaid his Debt, and to compell the Pawner to pay him.

—If Cloaths &c. or any other Thing that will be the worse for Using, be pawned, the Pawnee may not use them. But if Jewells or any other Thing that will not be the worse for Use, be pawned, the Pawnee may use it but then he must use them at his own Hazard. For

—If a Lady shall lock a sett of Jewels, that have been pawnd to her, in her Cabinet, Altho her Cabinet should be broke open, and the Jewells stolen, she would be excused, but if she wears them abroad, and is there robbed of them, She will be answerable for them.

24

—A Pawn is in Nature of a Deposit, and as such is not liable to be used.

—But if a Horse, or Cow, or any other Creature or Thing whose sustenance is chargeable, be pawned, The Pawnee may ride the Horse, or Milk the Cow in a reasonable Manner, in Reward of his Keeping.

—If a Creditor takes a Pawn he is obliged to restore it, upon Payment of the Debt.

—The Law requires Nothing extraordinary of the Pawnee, but only that he shall use an ordinary Care for restoring the Goods.

—It is sufficient if the Pawnee use true Diligence, and not withstanding the Loss, he shall resort to the Pawner for his Debt, if he has usd such Diligence.

—If the Money for which Goods were pawned, were tendered to the Pawnee, before they are lost, then the Pawnee shall be answerable for them; because the Pawnee by detaining them, after the Tender of the Money, is a Wrong Doer; it is a wrongful Detainer of the Goods, and the Special Property of the Pawnee is determined, and a Man that keeps Goods by Wrong must be answerable for them at all Events: for the Detaining of them is the Reason of the Loss.

—Goods found, are governd by the same legal Distinctions with Pawns.

Verdict. Defendant assumed to pay as much as his son should be indebted to Plaintiff. Ballance of the Account to be stated between the Defendant's son, and the Plantiff. And the Plaintiff averred that an Account was stated of all Debts, owing by the Defendants son to the Plantiff, and the Defendants son was found on that Account to be indebted £20. Judgment shall not be arrested, because nothing is averred to be due and so allowd for, from the Defendants son to the Plaintiff, because it shall not be intended after Verdict that any Thing was due, from Plaintiff to Defendants son.

W

Warranty. If Upon a sale of Goods from a Merchant A.B. to my Friend C.D., I only make a collateral Promise as a surety or Warrantee to pay in Case my friend does not, I cant be chargd in Indebitatus Assumpsit but only in a Special Action of the Case.

X

Y

Z

B. Adams' Pleadings Book

EDITORIAL NOTE

In common with most lawyers John Adams maintained a collection of pleading forms to help in future drafting. A number of such forms exist in the Adams Papers as loose sheets among the case notes and other legal materials, but the majority of those which have survived were entered by Adams or one of his clerks in an untitled small quarto volume bound in law calf, which is referred to in the present edition as the Pleadings Book. The order of the forms, and the dates of Adams' involvement with most of the cases from which they come, indicate that he used the volume for this purpose from 1771 to 1773.[1] Adams was of counsel in at least 23 of the 29 cases represented in the Pleadings Book, but he probably drafted only 7 of the forms. The rest are the work of his contemporaries at the bar. The forms are printed here as they appear in the manuscript, except

---

[1] Adams Papers, Microfilms, Reel No. 186. In subsequent footnotes the editors have identified as far as possible the hands of JA's law clerks, but the identifications are all tentative. Inside the front cover of the Pleadings Book JA wrote this motto: "Vitanda est improba Siren, Desidia," from Horace, *Satires*, bk. II, Satire 3, lines 14–15 ("You must shun the wicked siren Indolence"). Pages 2–31 of the volume were numbered by JA. The editors have supplied page numbers in square brackets for citations of the pleadings from page [32] to page [62], where JA's forms end. The remainder of the volume is largely blank, but toward the middle are some additional pleading forms, which from internal evidence seem to have been copied in after the Revolution. These forms and a few pages of notes on astronomy are all in a later, unidentified hand, possibly in more than one hand. At the back, and running the other way in the volume, are four pages of pleadings in the hand of John Quincy Adams, including the form for a libel in Admiralty for seamen's wages in the United States District Court for the District of Massachusetts, dated 5 Nov. 1793.

The separate pleadings forms found in the Adams Papers include Roby v. Stone (declaration in trespass for mesne profits); Reading v. Framingham (plea to complaint under the poor laws); Potter v. Burchsted (double pleas of justification by leave of court in suit by widow of *non compos mentis*: (1) sale by guardian; (2) dower in deceased's mother); Hoyt v. Brown (declaration in case against deputy sheriff for failure to keep vessel under attachment); Apthorp v. Stanbridge (plea of tender in indebitatus assumpsit); Capen v. Spear (declaration in trespass for cutting trees and plea of justification); Church v. Bunney (form of summons where goods are attached); Epes v. Flagg (Latin form of plea of non cepit, the general issue in replevin). All are in Adams Papers, Microfilms, Reel No. 185. Pleadings from the Adams Papers and the court files are printed as documents in the following cases in the present work: King v. Stewart, No. 2; Apthorp v. Gardiner, No. 9; Prout v. Minot, No. 13; Chelsea v. Boston, No. 26; Brookline v. Roxbury, No. 27; Essane v. Dotey, No. 28; Josselyne v. Harrington, No. 30; Emmons v. Brewer, No. 33; Pierce v. Wright, No. 36; Margaret v. Muzzy, No. 40; Petition of Lechmere, No. 44; Sewall v. Hancock, No. 46; Dowse v. 33 Hogsheads of Molasses, No. 47; Dowse v. 19 Casks of Molasses, No. 49; Surveyor General v. Logs, No. 54; Rex v. Corbet, No. 56; Rex v. Preston, No. 63.

that the editors have given each case an identifying roman numeral and have supplied descriptive captions and titles where Adams omitted them. For each case, the facts and disposition, so far as they are known, and a brief summary of any matters of historical or legal significance are given in footnotes.

At first glance a collection of pleading forms looks like dull reading. The facts that lie behind the forms are seldom dull, however. For example, many of the cases presented here involve important historical events and personalities. The declarations in *Richards v. Doble* (Form VI) and *Gailer v. Trevett* (Form VII), for all their stilted technical phraseology, offer grisly accounts of the Boston mob in action, with particular emphasis on the mechanics of tarring and feathering. These two pleadings, with *Palmes v. Greenleaf* (Form XVI), serve as footnotes to several major Adams cases dealt with elsewhere in these volumes. There are also pleadings which show Paul Revere having trouble with an apprentice (Form XI), the maternal and paternal ancestors of Oliver Wendell Holmes engaged in a joint real estate venture (Form XIII), Adams' wealthy client Elisha Doane successfully avoiding taxes (Form VIII), and the family of Fisher and Nathaniel Ames engaged in an intramural dispute (Form XX). Many of Massachusetts' more litigious, if less well-known, citizens also make their contentious, cantankerous way through these pages. Braytons, Robinsons, Needhams, Kingsburys, Metcalfs, Halls, Greens, and Lorings were all involved in feuds that found expression in the courts.[2]

The pleadings, in conjunction with the other cases in these volumes, are also of interest in helping to define the scope of Adams' practice. He is widely and justly known for his defense of the British soldiers after the Boston Massacre (Nos. 63, 64), and of John Hancock in the affair of the sloop *Liberty* (No. 46). These and other similar matters made up only a small proportion of his cases. Day in and day out during his fifteen active years at the bar, even while occupied with affairs of great public significance, he was constantly concerned with a vast flow of actions on the order of those which make up the Pleadings Book. They ranged from minor loan transactions to the relatively large sums involved in the management of an estate or the winding up of a major business, and they involved all of the activities of colonial life. Here are cases arising from shipping, commerce, agriculture, the use and conveyance of land, the paper and iron industries, retail trade, crafts, death, and taxes. Such matters were the materials from which a lawyer gained his livelihood.[3]

The primary significance of the Pleadings Book is the cross section of the law in 18th-century Massachusetts which it provides. Pleading was the heart of the traditional common-law jurisprudence under which Adams practiced. No claim could be redressed unless the facts giving rise to it could be made to fit one of the common law forms of action, the centuries-old classifications in which the substantive law of England had grown up.

[2] See Forms XV, X, XXIII, IX, XVIII.
[3] For further discussion of JA's practice, see Introduction.

It was through the pleadings that substantive rights were stated in terms appropriate to one of these forms. Many of the decided cases that make up the common law are determinations of the adequacy of such statements. Further, it was the pleadings which determined the facts which the parties had to establish at the trial. Great numbers of other cases concern the relations between pleadings and facts. The 18th century marked the zenith of the formulary system. The law which Adams knew was the natural end product of a development in which "substantive law has at first the look of being gradually secreted in the interstices of procedure; and the early lawyer can only see the law through the envelope of its technical forms." [4]

The pleadings which Adams collected show nearly all of the remedies given by the forms of action being applied in Massachusetts, with some changes to take account of local practices or needs. There are declarations in most of the usual English actions, including account, special and general assumpsit, several varieties of debt, ejectment, replevin, trespass to person and to lands, trespass on the case for various wrongs, and writs of entry asserting title to lands. The most significant changes were in the last class of actions, where only the rudiments of the ancient and complex English forms were retained in a simplified system that served as the basis of the Massachusetts law of real actions for a century afterward.[5] Other alterations included the use of account, debt, and assumpsit for matters that in England would have been within the jurisdiction of the court of equity or the ecclesiastical courts, neither of which existed in Massachusetts, and the adaptation of replevin to do the work of a libel *in rem* at a time when the court of Admiralty was in great disfavor for political reasons.[6]

Adams' forms suggest that the Massachusetts practitioners were deficient in one important aspect of the English system—special pleading, the devious art of narrowing the issue through a series of successive pleadings.[7] The Pleadings Book contains only three examples of pleas other than the general issue or a general demurrer, and in those cases there were no further pleadings beyond the replication. A study of other Massachusetts cases indicates that this was generally so. The rejoinders and surrejoinders, rebutters and surrebutters that were the glory of the English system were virtually unknown in Massachusetts. Since occasional examples of special pleading are found,[8] it would seem that a taste for simplicity and a

[4] Sir Henry S. Maine, *Dissertations on Early Law and Custom* 389 (N.Y., 1886). As to the forms of action generally, see Frederic W. Maitland, *The Forms of Action at Common Law* 1–11 (Cambridge, 1936); Fifoot, *History and Sources, passim*; Sutton, *Personal Actions* 1–33, 46–71; Plucknett, *Concise History* 353–377.

[5] See Forms IV, XIII, XV.

[6] See Forms IX, XVIII, XIX, XXIV.

[7] See Sutton, *Personal Actions* 72–193; Plucknett, *Concise History* 399–423.

[8] See, for example, the pleadings in Ware v. Brick, a case in which Jonathan Sewall and Francis Dana were of counsel, in Theophilus Parsons, Precedents (MS) 58–61, MH–L.

desire to get on with the matter, rather than ignorance, account for the Massachusetts practice.

In 1859 Theophilus Parsons Jr. wrote, "In my father's time, there was a very general ignorance on this subject [pleading]. Only a few of the leading lawyers pretended to be good pleaders; and the inaccuracy or insufficiency of the pleading was one of the causes of the disorder and confusion which prevailed in the courts." [9] Since Theophilus Parsons Sr., Chief Justice of Massachusetts from 1806 to 1813, was a law student from 1770 until his admission to the bar in 1774,[10] his "time" may be said to have included the years which the Pleadings Book covers. Whatever laxity developed in the aftermath of the Revolution, Adams' forms and those seen in other cases of the period do not merit Parsons' criticism in an important sense. Most of them, both in substance and formal parts, were consistent with examples found in contemporary or later English books of forms (or "precedents" as they were called); and the bar and the courts were aware of technical rules such as those against duplicity and argumentativeness. In some respects, however, the practice of Adams' day did not meet 19th-century standards. Commentators found a few of the old forms confused and oversimplified,[11] and the lack of special pleading was a defect at what even American lawyers of this period considered the heart of the matter. Nevertheless, as far as they go, Adams' pleadings show that the Massachusetts bar before the Revolution was true to the English system in general, and capable of applying it in detail when pressed.

Even Parsons presumably would have found at least some of the Pleadings Book forms acceptable. After the passage just quoted, he went on to recount that his father "was himself a very good pleader, having devoted much time to the science. When he had students, every one was expected to write out, in a book prepared for that purpose, declarations, pleas, and forms, which my father had prepared or adopted. I have some of these books now; and the volumes of precedents, afterwards published for the use of the profession, by Anthon, Story, Oliver, and others, were compiled in a good degree from these books." [12]

Whatever one may think of the copying out of pleadings as a method of law study, it was a means of preserving and passing on forms from one generation to the next. Undoubtedly Adams' students and other lawyers copied forms from the Pleadings Book. By some such means a few of Adams' pleadings survived to appear in the numerous "volumes of precedents" which the 19th century brought forth. In 1802, Benoni Perham, a young Massachusetts law student, compiled and published at Boston the first of these works, *American Precedents of Declarations, Collected Chiefly*

[9] Theophilus Parsons, *Memoir of Theophilus Parsons* 221 (Boston, 1859).

[10] See Parsons, *Memoir* 23–24.

[11] See notes 17, 56, 93, below. As to the technical rules in Massachusetts, see No. 9.

[12] Parsons, *Memoir* 221. See the elder Parsons' own MS book of "Precedents" in MH–L.

from Manuscripts of Accomplished Pleaders; Digested and Arranged under Distinct Titles and Divisions; and Adapted to the Most Modern Practice. The volume contained the declarations in *Holden v. Conner* (Form I), *Waldo v. Gridley* (Form II), *Hill v. Whiting* (Form IV), and *Richards v. Doble* (Form VI). These pleadings appeared with only slight changes, and all but *Waldo* were attributed (with some unfairness to their real drafters) to "J. Adams." In addition, numerous similarities may be observed between forms in the Pleadings Book and those taken by Perham from Parsons and other lawyers.

Perham's work, revised by John Anthon, appeared in at least two later editions.[13] In 1828 at Boston, Benjamin Lynde Oliver brought out an enlarged version of *American Precedents* entitled *Forms of Practice; or American Precedents in Actions, Personal and Real.* Anthon and Oliver both reprinted Adams' pleadings with Perham's other forms. In the fifth revised edition of *Forms of Practice,* published in 1905 when the old system had all but run its course, those forms still appeared.[14]

In the 19th century, as the practice of law in the United States grew more sophisticated, the works of the great English pleading authorities—Chitty, Stephen, and others—were published in numerous American editions and became the standard for several generations of lawyers.[15] Under this influence American pleading developed into a science that rivaled or even exceeded the English practice in complexity. At the same time the native tradition of simplicity and adaptability derived from the 18th-century forms was preserved in *American Precedents* and its successors. Native jurists like Stearns and Dane cited the work. In at least one instance, one of the Adams pleadings appearing in it was discussed at some length as a useful and unique Massachusetts practice still followed there.[16] Adams' Pleadings Book thus helped to carry forward into the busy 19th century the law of an earlier era in which flexibility was as important as technicality.

[13] *American Precedents of Declarations* (N.Y., 2d edn., John Anthon, 1810); (Brookfield, Mass., 3d edn., John Anthon, 1821). Perham (1777–1804), Harvard 1800, had assistance from an unnamed young lawyer who was probably Joseph Story. See Benjamin L. Oliver, *Forms of Practice; or, American Precedents, in Actions, Personal and Real* vi (Boston, 1828); MH–Ar. Anthon (1784–1863), Columbia 1801, was a leader of the New York bar who assisted in founding the New York Law Institute in 1830. *DAB.*

[14] Benjamin L. Oliver, *Forms of Practice; or, American Precedents, in Personal and Real Actions* 37, 281–282, 578 (Boston, 5th rev. edn., 1905).

[15] See, for example, Joseph Chitty, *Treatise on Pleading and Parties to Actions* (N.Y., 1809); *id.* (Springfield, Mass., 16th Amer. edn., 1879, 1882–1885); Henry J. Stephen, *Principles of Pleading in Civil Actions* (Phila., 2d Amer. edn., 1831); *id.* (Phila., 9th Amer. edn., 1867); Edward H. V. Lawes, *An Elementary Treatise on Pleading in Civil Actions* (Portsmouth, N.H., 1808); John F. Archbold, *Practice of the Court of King's Bench in Personal Actions, and Ejectment* (N.Y., 1823); *id.* (N.Y., 2d Amer. edn., 1827).

[16] See Asahel Stearns, *A Summary of the Law and Practice of Real Actions* 178–179 (Boston, 1824), discussed in note 29 below. For other examples of the citation of *American Precedents,* see 1 Dane, *Abridgment* 167; 5 *id.* at 214.

I. JOHN ADAMS, BY BENJAMIN BLYTH

2. VIEW OF BOSTON, BY CHRISTIAN REMICK

THE PLEADINGS BOOK

1771–1773

[I]

CASE on a Bill of Lading vs. Master for not delivering the Plaintiff's Goods freighted on Board the Defendant's Vessell.

Asa Holden vs. Charles Conner [17]

For that the said Charles on &c.—received on board his said Ship called the X X and whereof the said Charles was Master (H[ogshea]ds, Casks &c.) containing the Goods in the schedule annexed— And on the &c.—at —— signed a certain Note in Writing called a Bill of Lading and undertook (the Dangers of the sea excepted) to deliver the said —— to the Plaintiff he paying the customary Freight and afterwards, vizt. on —— the said Charles arrived in said ship at said ——. Yet he has not delivered said Goods &c. tho the Plaintiff hath often requested it, and has been always ready to pay the Freight aforesaid, but refuses so to do.

[II]

CASE. By Freighter vs. owner for the Embezzlement of the Master upon a Bill of Lading.

Waldo vs. Gridley [18]

John Waldo of Boston &c.[19] vs. Isaac Gridley. In a Plea of Trespass on the Case, for that the said John on &c.—at Boston aforesaid, shipped

[17] In JA's hand. Pleadings Book, p. 2. Printed with some variations in Perham, *American Precedents* 135. The records and files have not been found. Perham appended the following note: "As the Dft. was to do the first act, viz. deliver the goods, it was not necessary for the Plf. to aver an offer or tender of the freight; but query, if not a time when the goods were to be delivered, and that that time was past? In order to apply the evidence, the Plf., if he cannot prove a precise time agreed on, may allege the reasonable time the law implies." The editor of the second edition of *American Precedents* revised this note to state that the plaintiff should have averred a tender, "for defendant has a *lien* upon the goods for the freight, and payment thereof is by the contract *a condition precedent.* See 3 Burr. 1499. 4 Burr. 2218. Doug. 104." He also suggested that a special request for delivery or the passage of a reasonable time might have been alleged as alternatives to a specific time of delivery. *American Precedents* 185 (New York, 2d edn., 1810). This declaration in assumpsit is one of four declarations against masters or owners of vessels on bills of lading in the Pleadings Book. See Waldo v. Gridley, Form II; Langdon v. Barber, Form III; McLean v. McEwen, Form XVII. The declaration in the last-mentioned case is a form more in accord with later practice than that printed here. See note 76 below.

[18] In JA's hand. Pleadings Book, p. 3–5. Printed with some variations in Perham,

31

on Board the said Isaac's Snow, Mermaid, then bound on a Voyage in the said Isaac's service, to Jamaica, a Quantity of Gold and silver vizt 8 Guineas, 1 Pistole, and 23 Dollars all of the Value of £19 lawfull Money with Reuben Hussey the said Isaac's servant, and Commander of said Vessell for said Voyage and for whose Conduct in said Service, the said Isaac is answerable, to be transported in said Vessell on the Plantiffs Account and Risque, to Jamaica, the Danger of the Seas only excepted, and there to be delivered to the Plantiff, his order, or assigns, he or they paying Freight therefor two Pr.Cent with Primage and Average accustomed: [20] And the said Reuben then and there in said

American Precedents 213–214. The action was filed in the Suffolk Inferior Court, where, in Oct. 1751, Jeremiah Gridley obtained a verdict in favor of Isaac Gridley for costs. See text at note 23 below. On appeal to the Superior Court in Feb. 1752 the defendant again prevailed. The Superior Court Minute Book indicates that Edmund Trowbridge filed the appeal. SCJ Rec. 1752, fol. 31; Min. Bk. 61, SCJ Suffolk, Feb. 1752, N–55. Perham put the form in a section containing actions on the case in tort, rather than under the heading "Assumpsit," where Holden v. Conner, Form I, appeared. In later practice, at least, the remedies of assumpsit and case for negligence were concurrent and the differences in form between the pleadings were slight. Among the practical differences were that in assumpsit all parties to the contract had to be joined, the agreement between the parties had to be stated in express terms, and the common counts (note 31 below) could be joined. In tort, recovery could be had against any one of the parties, only a duty need be shown, and a count in trover could be joined. See 1 Chitty, *Pleading* 92, 134–135, 138; 2 *id.* at 155–161, 319–321; Joseph K. Angell, *A Treatise on the Law of Carriers* 366–392 (Boston, 3d edn., 1857). JA probably regarded the form of action here as assumpsit. An express contract, consideration, promise, and breach are set out. Compare Angell, *Carriers* 380–392. Further, the final clause (text preceding note 22 below) in effect makes the declaration one in indebitatus assumpsit, since it alleges a sum certain owing to the plaintiff and the new defendant's presumably fictional promise to pay it. This clause does not appear in *American Precedents*. Its presence in the actual form may have been owing to a doubt as to the liability of the owner on the master's contract, or for his defaults. See authorities in notes 25, 26, below. The form was probably inserted here because of its use in Langdon v. Barber, Form III. See note 24 below.

[19] Here and elsewhere in the Pleadings Book, JA has omitted the description of the parties, known as the "addition," which in this instance was "of Boston in the County of Suffolk, merchant." SCJ Rec. 1752, fol. 31. By the English Statute of Additions, 1 Hen. 5, c. 5 (1413), in original writs and certain other processes, "in the names of defendants ... additions shall be made of their estate or degree, or mystery [i.e occupation], and of the towns, or hamlets, or places and counties, of which they were, or be, or in which they be or were conversant," or else the writ could be abated. See 1 Chitty, *Pleading* 246–247. In Massachusetts the act prescribing forms of writs provided that the plaintiff's addition should appear also. Act of 3 June 1701, c. 2, §1, 1 A&R 460. Compare Perham, *American Precedents* 90 note. The consequences of omitting the description of the plaintiff are not known, but a mistake or omission in the addition of the defendant was grounds for abatement of the writ. See Ballard v. McLean, Quincy, *Reports* 106 (SCJ Suffolk, Aug. 1764); Bromfield v. Lovejoy, Quincy, *Reports* 237 (SCJ Suffolk, March 1767).

[20] Sums paid the master by the shipper over and above the freight for his care of the goods, and to cover expenses for lights, pilotage, and wharfage. See René de Kerchove, *International Maritime Dictionary* (Princeton, 1948).

Capacity, signed a Bill of Lading, according to the Custom of Merchants,[21] thereby engaging *for the Delivery of said Gold* and Silver in manner aforesaid; and upon the Conditions aforesaid, whereby the said Isaac, according to the Custom of Merchants then and there became obliged that said Gold and Silver should be (the Danger of the seas only excepted) safely kept, transported and delivered as aforesaid, and then and there, promised the Plantiff accordingly. And the Plantiff in Fact saith, that the said Isaac's Master of said Vessell, in said Vessell and in said Isaac's Service, arrived safe at said Jamaica with said Gold and Silver, that the said Gold and Silver was not safely kept, but by the said Isaac's Master aforesaid and the Crew of the said Isaac's Vessell, for whom in such Respects he is answerable, was there on board said Vessell converted to their own Use, and imbezzled and was never delivered to the Plantiff, nor to his order nor assigns, though often requested thereto, and though the Plantiff was always ready to pay the Freight, and Primage and average aforesaid; by means whereof, the said Isaac, according to the Custom of Merchants became obliged to pay the Plantiff his Damage occasioned thereby (which the Plantiff avers, amounts to —— L.M.) on demand, and accordingly on —— &c. —— at Boston aforesaid, promised the said John to pay him the same on Demand, Yet the said Isaac, tho requested has never paid the same but neglects and refuses to do it. To the Damage &c.[22]

Octr. Court 1751 NB. This Declaration was drawn by Mr. Pratt, Mr. Gridley pleaded in Abatement, but the Plea was overruled by the Court. Issue was joined, and after a full Hearing the Case was committed to the Jury, who found for the Defendant Costs.[23]

[21] By this time the custom of merchants was a fictional allegation which need not be proved. See 5 Holdsworth, *History of English Law* 144–145.

[22] Here and in most of the forms in the Pleadings Book JA has abbreviated the formula known as the *ad damnum*, "To the Damage of the said John as he saith the sum of twenty five pounds." SCJ Rec. 1752, fol. 31. Where damages were sought such a statement had to be included, and in actions other than debt the damages claimed were the limit of the plaintiff's recovery. In debt nominal damages could be claimed, because it was the sum sued for itself, rather than damages, which was the object of the action. 1 Chitty, *Pleading* 397–400. The usual declaration in English practice concluded with the further phrase, "and therefore he brings his suit, etc." (the "etc." standing for "and good proof"). "Suit" (Latin, *sectam*) here meant followers or witnesses rather than action. Sutton, *Personal Actions* 81–82. This conclusion was not part of the form used in Massachusetts, where by statute the last phrase was "which shall then and there be made to appear with other due damages." See Act of 3 June 1701, c. 2, §1, 1 A&R 460.

[23] The proceedings in the Inferior Court. See note 18 above.

[III]

[CASE *on a bill of lading against the owner.*]

[*Langdon v. Barber*] [24]

3. Bac. 591. Bottom.[25] 3. Mod. 321. Boson vs. Sandford.[26] 1. Reading Clerk's Instructor 371. For a Precedent of a Declaration vs. Master.[27]

Summon Wm. Barber of Charlstown &c.—to answer Edward Langdon of Boston &c.—in a Plea of Trespass upon the Case for that the

[24] In JA's hand. Pleadings Book, p. 4–5. This writ, dated 29 March 1771, was probably drawn by JA, since he was of counsel for Langdon, both in the April 1771 Suffolk Inferior Court, where Barber prevailed on a demurrer to the plea, and in the Aug. 1771 Superior Court, where the jury found a verdict for Barber. Josiah Quincy Jr. was of counsel for the latter. Min. Bk., Inf. Ct. Suffolk, April 1771, No. 205; SCJ Rec. 1771, fol. 214; Min. Bk. 95, SCJ Suffolk, Aug. 1771, N–3. SF 101888. The action, like Waldo v. Gridley, Form II, was against the owner of a vessel for goods shipped on a bill of lading. This declaration does not recite the giving of a bill of lading, but sets out the contract in the language of the bill. Compare McLean v. McEwen, Form XVII; see 2 Chitty, *Pleading* 159–161. The file copy of the writ contains a second count, virtually identical to that in *Waldo*, which does recite the bill. SF 101888. Like the declaration in *Waldo*, the count here sounds in indebitatus assumpsit by virtue of the last clause.

[25] In the MS this and the following two citations appear in the margin. See 3 Bacon, *Abridgment* 591: "And as the master himself is answerable . . . so likewise hath it been held, that the owners are liable to the freighters, in respect of the freight, for the embezilments, &c. of the master and mariners." The next sentence, at p. 592, adds the qualification that "this proving a great discouragement to trade," the statute, 7 Geo. 2, c. 15 (1734), provided that the liability of the owners for the embezzlements and other defaults of master and crew done without the owners' privity should be limited to the value of the vessel and her pending freight. This Act was the ancestor of the present-day American statute limiting vessel owners' liability. Grant Gilmore and Charles L. Black Jr., *The Law of Admiralty* 664 note (Brooklyn, 1957).

[26] Boson v. Sandford, 3 Mod. 321, 323, 87 Eng. Rep. 212, 213 (K.B. 1690), holding that where goods were damaged through the neglect of the master of a vessel owned jointly by eight proprietors, all eight must be joined, and adding a dictum that the master need not, he being "no more than a Servant to the owners, [who] has no property either general or special, but the power he has is given by the civil law." The report then set out "many cases where the act of the servant shall charge the master," concluding, "Therefore though the neglect in this case was in the servant, the action may be brought against all the owners, for it is grounded *quasi ex contractu*, though there was no actual agreement between the plaintiff and them."

[27] Daniel Reading, *The English Clerk's Instructor in the Practice of the Court of King's Bench, and Common Pleas*, 1:341 (London, 1733), a declaration in assumpsit against the master of a vessel for not delivering goods loaded aboard his ship. JA's citation "371" is evidently an error, since there was only one edition of Reading's work. 1 Sweet and Maxwell, *Legal Bibliography* 277.

said Wm. at a Place called Patuxent River, in our Province of Maryland vizt. at Boston aforesaid,[28] on the 8th day of last December was
owner and Proprietor, of a Vessell, being the good Brigantine called
the Fair Lady, whereof was then Master under God for the then
present intended Voyage, Abiel Lucas, and then riding at Anchor in
Patuxent River aforesaid, in which Brigantine the said William was
used and accustomed to carry Goods, Wares, and Merchandises, for
a reasonable Hire, from Port to Port: And the said Edward, there
afterwards, on the same day, put, shipped and loaded, in good order
and well conditioned in and upon the said Brigantine, then, by Gods
Grace, bound for Boston in New England, 500 Bushells of good
merchantable Wheat, of the Value of £133 6s. 8d. L.M. to be delivered in like good order and well conditioned, at said Port of Boston,
the dangers of the Seas only excepted, unto the said Edward, or to his
assigns, he or they paying Freight for said goods with Primage and
Average accustomed, and the said William, then and there promised
the said Edward to deliver the said Wheat accordingly. Now the said
Edward in fact says, that the said Brigantine afterwards sailed from
said Patuxent River, with the said Wheat on board in good order and
well conditioned, and arrived safe at said Port of Boston with said
Wheat in like good order and well conditioned on the 17. day of
December last; yet the said William, tho often requested neither by
himself nor by any other Person for or under him, ever delivered the
said Wheat to him the said Edward, or to his assigns, tho the said
Edward was always there ready to receive the same, and to pay Freight
therefor, with Primage and Average accustomed, but the said Abiel
Lucas the said Master and Commander of said Brigantine, and in the
service of the said William, and for whose Embezzlements and Conduct in such Respects the said William is answerable, there afterwards
on the same 17th day of December last, embezzled the said 500
Bushells of Wheat and converted it to his own Use. By means whereof
the said William by Law and by the Custom and Usage of Merchants,
became obliged to pay the Plantiff his Damages occasioned thereby
(which the Plantiff avers, amount to £133 6s. 8d. L.M. [)] on demand
and promised the said Edward accordingly at said Boston on the   day
of December last, to pay him the same on demand; Yet the said Wm.
tho requested has never paid the same but neglects to do it. To the
Damage &c.

---

[28] A fictitious but nontraversable allegation intended to justify venue in Boston.
See 1 Chitty, *Pleading* 273; Fifoot, *History and Sources* 162; 5 Holdsworth, *History
of English Law* 140–142. Compare No. 4, text at note 2.

[IV]

EJECTMENT. By a posthumous Daughter, on the seizin of her Father.

Hill vs. Whiting[29]

Summon J. Whiting, to answer to Abiel Hill, &c. in a Plea of Ejectment, wherein the Plantiff demands against the said John the Possession of a certain Tract of Land containing &c. and bounded &c.

Whereupon the Plantiff saith, that Ebenezer Hill late of said Wrentham, Husbandman deceased Intestate, Father of the Plantiff, in a Time of Peace, vizt. on the 30th day of October Anno Domini 1732 was seized of the Demanded Premises in his Demesne as of Fee taking the Esplees[30] thereof to the Yearly Value of four Pounds and on the same day, afterwards at said Wrentham, the said Ebenezer died so seized thereof and Intestate, leaving Susanna his Widow pregnant with the Plantiff, who was born afterwards at said Wrentham on the sixteenth day of February Anno Domini 1733, and after the Death of the said Ebenezer Hill, Father of the Plantiff, and the Birth of the Plantiff as aforesaid, the demanded Premises, and the Right and Property thereof, descended by Law to the Plantiff, Child and Heir of the same Ebenezer deceased, and she ought accordingly to be in

[29] In JA's hand. Pleadings Book, p. 6. Printed with slight variations in Perham, *American Precedents* 301–302. JA was Whiting's counsel. For his minutes and the proceedings in the case, see No. 17. The declaration, dated 5 Dec. 1770, was probably drawn by Josiah Quincy Jr., who represented Abiel Hill. Min. Bk., Inf. Ct. Suffolk, Jan. 1771, No. 160. Although labeled "Ejectment," the action is actually one in the nature of a writ of entry, one of the ancient real actions. See note 30 below; No. 17, text at notes 3–7. Asahel Stearns, citing its appearance in *American Precedents* 362 (Brookfield, Mass., 3d edn., 1821), called this declaration a unique form developed in Massachusetts in lieu of the English action of ejectment, which supposedly was not used in the Province. Asahel Stearns, *A Summary of the Law and Practice of Real Actions* 178–179, 396–398 note (Boston, 1824). Ejectment was used on occasion, however. See No. 17, note 5; Laughton v. Pitts, Form XXVI.

[30] The products or profits of the land. This was a formal but necessary allegation in both a writ of right and a writ of entry, intended to show the substantial nature of the seisin under which the land was claimed. See Stearns, *Real Actions* 155, 364–366. The allegation "in a time of peace" was also a purely formal part of both writs, denoting activity under law at a time when the courts were open. *Id.* at 155–156. The form here differs from that usually found in a writ of entry in that it does not contain an allegation in the first paragraph detailing the particulars of the wrongful entry. In adopting JA's form, Stearns grafted such allegations on to it. *Id.* at 442–443. Although the form is not exactly a writ of entry, it is even less a writ of right. It lacks much of the latter's distinctive language, such as an allegation at the end of the land description that the lands were claimed "By writ of our lord the king of right"; a statement that the seisin "in his demesne as of fee" was also "as of right"; and the concluding clause, "and that such is his right he offers, &c." In place of the latter, this form concludes with a clause such as was ordinarily used in the writ of entry. *Id.* at 362–364. Compare Stephen, *Pleading* 37.

quiet Possession thereof, but the said John, since the Death of the same Ebenezer, hath unjustly entered into the demanded Premises, and still unjustly, deforces and holds the Plantiff out. To the Damage &c.

[V]

CASE.

[Haynes v. Shaw] [31]

Indeb. Ass. on
an Account
annexed.

Summon F.S. &c. to answer S.H. &c. in a Plea of Tres-pass on the Case, for that the said F.S. at Boston aforesaid on the 14th. day of April instant being indebted to the said

[31] In JA's hand. Pleadings Book, p. 7–9. This writ in the case of Samuel Haynes v. Francis Shaw is dated 1 April 1768, returnable to the April 1768 Suffolk Inferior Court. It was probably drafted by Robert Auchmuty, who entered the action and was Haynes' counsel at the Jan. 1769 Inferior Court, where Shaw won on a demurrer to the plea. Since only the first three counts printed here appear in the copy of the declaration in the file of the case, and there is no indication that the pleading was amended, JA may have added the others himself. Haynes' appeal was entered at the March 1769 Superior Court and continued until Feb. 1771. Then, with JA now of counsel for Haynes, the matter was submitted to referees who brought in a report awarding Shaw his costs. Min. Bk., Inf. Ct. Suffolk, April 1768, No. 198; SCJ Rec. 1771, fol. 3; Min. Bk. 89, SCJ Suffolk, March 1769, N–27; *id.,* Feb. 1771, C–14; SF 101813.

The declaration printed here is one in general assumpsit on the so-called "common counts," statements of the same underlying indebtedness made in alternative forms in order to prevent a fatal variance between pleading and proof. The counts set out and labeled in the margin by JA include four of the "indebitatus" counts, and two of the "quantum" or "value" counts, one of which JA left incomplete. The indebitatus counts alleged very generally an indebtedness in a sum certain and a fictitious promise by the defendant to pay the debt. They were: the count on an account annexed, an "immemorial practice" in Massachusetts (see Quincy, *Reports* 252 note; 1 Dane, *Abridgment* 174) which apparently replaced the counts for goods furnished or work performed used in England; counts for money paid by the plaintiff for the defendant and for money had and received by the defendant to the plaintiff's use; and the count in "insimul computassent," or on an account stated between the parties (sometimes treated as a separate variety of general assumpsit). The quantum counts were "quantum valebant" and "quantum meruit" in which the plaintiff alleged the specific goods furnished or work done and the defendant's promise to pay what the goods or services were reasonably worth. The point of this variation was that there was no need to plead and prove the precise sum involved, but as JA has set it out, the quantum valebant count concludes with a second promise to pay a sum certain, not found in the usual English forms, which seems to defeat the ostensible purpose of the pleading. The reason for this variant and its effect have not been determined. If the clause was standard form in Massachusetts, it apparently was not taken literally. Three other JA cases show that quantum meruit rather than indebitatus assumpsit was held to be the proper form where an express price was not to be pleaded and proved. Tyler v. Richards, Quincy, *Reports* 195 (SCJ Suffolk, Aug. 1765); Pynchon v. Brewster, *id.* at 224 (SCJ Suffolk, Aug. 1766); Glover v. Le Testue, *id.* at 225 note, Adams Papers, Microfilms, Reel No. 185 (SCJ Suffolk, Aug. 1770). As to the common counts generally, see Fifoot, *History and Sources* 358–371, 378–379, 391–394; Shipman, *Common-law Plead-*

S.H. in the sum of £155 19s. 9d., as by the account to the Writ annexed appears, did then and there promise the said S.H. to pay him that sum on demand. And for that the

Ind. Ass. for Money, laid out, and expended for Defendant. said F.S. afterwards, that is to say, on the same day at Boston aforesaid, was indebted to the said S.H. in another sum of £150 19s. 9d. for the like sum of Money, before that Time, at the special Instance and Request of the said Francis, and to the Use of the said Francis, paid, laid out and expended, and being so indebted, he, the said F.S. in Consideration thereof, afterwards, that is to say, the same day, at Boston aforesaid, promised the said S.H. to pay him the same on demand. And, whereas the said F.S.

Ind. Ass. for money had and received afterwards, that is to say, on the same day, at Boston aforesaid was indebted to the said Samuel H. in one other sum of one hundred and fifty two Pounds, Nineteen Shillings and Nine Pence for the like Sum of Money, by him the said F.S. before that Time had and received, to the Use of the said S.H., and being so indebted he the said Francis, in Consideration thereof, that is to say, on the same day, at Boston aforesaid, promised the said S.H. to pay him the said last mentioned sum on demand; yet the said F.S. tho requested hath not paid the said S.H. said sums.

Insim. Comp. And for that the said F.S. and S.H. at said Boston, on the day of accounted together concerning diverse sums of Money, before that Time due and owing from the said F.S. to the said S.H. and then in Arrear and unpaid, and on the Account so stated, the said F.S. was then and there found in Arrear, on the whole to the said S.H. the further sum of £200 16s. 8d. sterling, which the Plantiff avers to be equall to Lawfull Money, and the said F.S. at said Boston, on the said last mentioned day, in Consideration thereof, promised the said S.H. to pay him that sum also, on demand: And for that the said

Quant. Valebat. S.H. at said Boston, afterwards vizt. &c. had sold and delivered to the said F.S. at his special Instance and request, 13 Barrells of Flour, and other Goods, Wares and Merchandises, other than those contained in the Schedule, or Account annexed but of the same Quantity and Quality,

---

ing 152–167, 259–263; Perham, *American Precedents* 95–108. See also No. 12, text at notes 22–28, 32–36, 122–126.

and the said F.S. then and there in Consideration thereof, promised the said S.H. to pay him there for all such Sums of Money, as the said Flour, and other Goods, Wares and Merchandises in this Count mentioned were reasonably worth, whenever he should be thereto requested; Now the said S.H. in Fact saith that the said 13 Barrells of Flour last mentioned, were well worth, £22 5s. 6d. L.M., and the other Goods, Wares and Merchandises last mentioned, were well worth the several sums set against the like Articles in the annexed schedule or account amounting in the whole to   L.M. of all which the said F.S. there afterwards on the same day had due Notice from the said S.H. and thereby became obliged to pay him the same sum on demand and then and there promised so to do.

Quant. Mer.   And for that the said S.H. at said Boston on the   day of   had [32]

[VI]

TRESPASS. Assault, Battery, Wounding, Imprisonment, Tarring and Feathering.

Richards vs. Doble [33]

Attach &c. Joseph Doble of Boston &c. Mariner, to answer unto Owen Richards of said Boston Yeoman, in a Plea of Trespass, for that

---

[32] The MS breaks off here.

[33] In JA's hand. Pleadings Book, p. 10–11. Printed, with slight variations, in Perham, *American Precedents* 329–330. The writ, dated 7 Jan. 1771, and filed in April 1771 at the Suffolk Inferior Court, was presumably prepared by Samuel Fitch, who entered the action. Samuel Quincy appeared for Richards at the Jan. 1772 Inferior Court, where Doble, represented by JA, obtained a jury verdict. On appeal to the Superior Court, with Fitch now alone and JA still of counsel for Doble, Richards discontinued in Aug. 1773. Min. Bk., Inf. Ct. Suffolk, April 1771, No. 309; Jan. 1772, No. 40; SCJ Rec. 1773, fol. 104; Min. Bk. 98, SCJ Suffolk, Aug. 1773, C–33; SF 102288. See JA's minutes of the Inferior Court trial, Adams Papers, Microfilms, Reel No. 185. See also *Boston Gazette*, 24 Dec. 1770, p. 3, col. 2.
This action of trespass for assault arose out of the tarring and feathering on 18 May 1770 of Owen Richards, a minor customs official, who had been involved in the case of John Hancock's *Lydia* in 1768. See No. 46, note 2. Richards also sued at least two other assailants, whom JA represented. Benjamin Jones won a verdict against him at the July 1771 Inferior Court, the appeal being dropped in Aug. 1777. Richards v. Jones, Min. Bk. 103, SCJ Suffolk, Aug. 1777, C–19; SF 102532; see JA's minutes of the Inferior Court trial, Adams Papers, Microfilms, Reel No. 185. Against Joseph Heakley, Richards had better luck, winning a verdict at the Aug. 1772 Superior Court after losing before a jury at the Inferior Court in April 1772. Richards v. Heakley, Min. Bk. 95, SCJ Suffolk, Aug. 1772, N–27; SF 102127. JA's Office Book, April 1771 Suffolk Inferior Court, MQA, shows a fee of

the said Joseph, on the Eighteenth day of May last [1770] at Boston aforesaid, with Force and Arms an Assault on the Body of him the said Owen made and him did then and there violently beat, wound, bruise, and evil entreat, so that his Life was thereby put in great Danger, and He the said Joseph did then and there take and imprison him the said Owen, and him in Prison for a long Time, vizt. for the space of six hours, detained against Law, and the Custom of our Realm, and he the said Joseph then and there, did also grievously abuse the said Owen; forcibly took and placed him in a Cart, and stripped him naked to his Skin, and with Force as aforesaid, did tear off, from his Body, and take from him, his Hatt, Wigg, Coat, Waistcoat, and Shirt, and also a gold Sleeve Button, two Handkerchiefs, his Pocket Book, with sundrie Papers therein of the Value of   vizt. an original Note of Hand, for seven Pounds, Ten Shillings, and Sundrie, original Receipts for Moneys paid, and other Papers of Value, also one Piece of Gold Money, called a Johannes,[34] and two Spanish milled Dollars in Silver, being all of the Value of Thirty Pounds lawfull Money, none of which Things so taken from him the said Owen, have ever been returned to him again and He the said Joseph did then and there also cover and besmear the said Owen, Head, Face, and naked Body, with Tar and cover him over with Feathers, upon said Tar, and cruelly and inhumanly set fire to said Feathers; and then and there dragged said Owen in said Cart, through diverse Streets of said Town of Boston, and from one End of said Town to the other, for the Space of Six Hours, as aforesaid, and fixed a Label to his the said Owens Breast, with Writing thereon importing that he the said Owen was a common Informer, and in that Condition exposed him the said Owen

---

24s. in Doble's case and fees of 12s. and 48s. in the case of Richards v. "Joseph Aikley" [Heakley]. With the latter entry JA noted: "at Elizabeth Winship's Instance." Richards had incurred the wrath of the mob (still inflamed by the aftermath of the Boston Massacre, Nos. 63, 64), when, according to Quincy's argument for him in *Jones*, he had seized "A Vessell from Connecticutt, at noon day in the open Breach of the Acts of Trade. He was informed of it, and went to see her, and there by his own View and his oath he was obliged to seize her. In the afternoon, he was going down to the Vessell and was surrounded by a Multitude and tarred, feathered, and carted, and lost his Cloaths, Money, and Papers to the Amount of near £20 st. And in order to satiate their abandoned Brutality, they set fire to the Feathers as they stuck in the Tar, upon his naked back." JA's minutes, Richards v. Jones, cited above. See also *Boston Gazette*, 21 May 1770, p. 3, col. 1; Rowe, *Letters and Diary* 202; Esther Forbes, *Paul Revere and the World He Lived In* 208–213 (Boston, 1942); Account of the Mobbing by Richards and Others, 4 New England Papers 1–2, MH. For criminal proceedings arising from the riot, see Rex v. George Hamblin, Min. Bk. 91, SCJ Suffolk, Feb. 1771; SF 89791. (JA billed John Hancock £2 8s. 6d. for services in the latter case. See JA's account with Hancock, receipted 21 Dec. 1771, an illustration in this volume.)

34 A Portuguese gold coin, worth about 36s. OED.

to the Contempt and Resentment of our liege Subjects, and as a public Spectacle, thro said Town, and other Outrages and Enormities, on him the said Owen, He the said Joseph then and there committed, against our Peace, To the Damage &c. £1000.   7. Jan. 1771.

[VII]

TRESPASS, Assault, Battery, Wounding, Imprisonment tarring and feathering.

Gailer vs. Trevett.[35]

Attach &c. Eleazar Trevett Junior and Benjamin Trevett, Merchants, Daniel Vaun Mariner, all of Newport in the County of Newport and Colony of Rhode Island and Providence Plantation, and David Bradley, Pool Spear, Taylors, and David Provence Infant and Edward Mathews Mariner all of Boston in our County of Suffolk. To answer unto George Gailer of Boston aforesaid Mariner, in a Plea of Trespass, for that the said Eleazar Trevett Jnr., Benjamin Trevet, Daniel Vaun, David Bradley, Pool Spear, David Provence, and Edward Mathews, at said Boston in the Evening of the twenty Eighth Day of October last, together with diverse other Persons to the said George Gailer unknown, with Force and Arms, an assault, on the Body of the said George Gailer did make, and then and there with Force as aforesaid did strip the said George Gailer naked, tar and feather his Skin, and carry the said George Gailer naked, tarred and feathered, as aforesaid in a Cart about said Boston for the space of Three Hours, and with Clubbs, Staves, and a hand saw did then and there strike him the said George Gailer, sundry heavy and grievous Blows, upon the said George Gailers naked Body, and greatly bruise, and wound him and hit him the said George Gailer diverse grievous Blows, with Stones: By Reason of all which the said George Gailers Life was put into great Hazard and Danger, and greatly despaired of,

[35] In JA's hand. Pleadings Book, p. 12–13. Probably drafted by Robert Auchmuty, who entered the action at the Jan. 1770 Suffolk Inferior Court. No files for this case have been found. The tarring and feathering which it recounts took place on 28 Oct. 1769 at the hands of a mob which formed in the aftermath of John Mein's escape from Boston. See Rowe, *Letters and Diary* 194; No. 12, note 10. The case was decided in the defendants' favor on demurrer at the Jan. 1770 court. An appeal under the names of "Geo. Galer Apt. vs. Eleazr. Trivett" was entered by Robert Auchmuty at the Suffolk Superior Court in March 1770. The action was dropped at the Aug. 1771 term when neither party appeared. JA's Office Book, MQA, shows that he received a fee of 19s. 4d. from Bradley, one of the defendants, for services at the Inferior Court. See Min. Bk., Inf. Ct. Suffolk, Jan. 1770, No. 125; SCJ Rec. 1771, fol. 209; Min. Bk. 91, SCJ Suffolk, March 1770, N–33; Min. Bk. 95, SCJ Suffolk, Aug. 1771, C–38.

41

and many other Enormities, and Cruelties, the said Eleazer Trevett Jnr., Benja. Trevett, Daniel Vaun, David Bradley, Pool Spear, David Provence, and Edward Mathews, with others unknown to the said George Gailer did then and there commit, on the said George Galer, against the Peace of our Lord the King and to the Damage &c. £2000.

[VIII]

DEBT FOR TAXES, by Collector vs. an Inhabitant.

Ruggles vs. Doane.[36]

Summon Elisha Doane of Welfleet Esqr., to answer unto Samuel Ruggles of said Boston, Housewright, in a Plea of Debt, for that the said Elisha in the Year of our Lord Christ 1765 and 1766, was an Inhabitant of said Town of Boston and rateable to the Province, County and Town Taxes and was by the Assessors of said Town duely rated to Province, County, and Town Taxes, the several sums following, to wit for the Year 1765 the sum of Nine Pounds, Six Shillings and Three Pence, and for the Year 1766 the sum of £6 11s. 0d. which sums together make the sum of £15 17s. 3d. for his Proportion of Province, County, and Town Taxes in said Year, and the said Samuel was the same Year, duly chosen and sworn a Collector of Province, County and Town Taxes, in the same Town, and had the Rates aforesaid, made on the said Elisha, given him to collect; and the Time of Payment to the respective Treasurers is long since elapsed, and the said Samuel hath paid to the respective Treasurers all the sums given him to collect for those Years, and of all this the said Elisha hath had Notice from the said Samuel, whereby and by Force of an Act of this our Province, made in the fourth Year of our Reign intituled an Act to enable the Collectors of Taxes in the Town of Boston to sue for and recover the Rates and Taxes, given them to collect in certain Cases,[37] the said Elisha became indebted to the said

[36] In JA's hand. Pleadings Book, p. 14. The writ, dated 15 March 1768, may have been drafted by James Otis, who represented Ruggles in the Suffolk Inferior Court at the April 1768 term, where Doane, with Samuel Swift as counsel, prevailed on demurrer. On appeal to the Superior Court Blowers and JA appeared for Ruggles, and Auchmuty for Doane. At the Aug. 1771 term Ruggles discontinued, paying costs of £14 8s. 4d. A deposition that Doane had paid his taxes, given by a Wellfleet constable, may have been the cause. See Min. Bk., Inf. Ct. Suffolk, April 1768, No. 228; SCJ Rec. 1771, fol. 207; Min. Bk. 86, SCJ Suffolk, Aug. 1768, N–6; Min. Bk. 95, SCJ Suffolk, Aug. 1771, C–7, SF 101890.

[37] Act of 28 Jan. 1764, c. 18, 4 A&R 669, extended to 1 July 1770 by Act of 21 Feb. 1766, c. 33, 4 A&R 859. The first section of the 1764 Act gave the collectors and constables of Boston a remedy against the agents, factors and

Samuel in the said sum of £15 17s. 3d., and an action accrues to the said Samuel to recover and have the same sum, yet the said Elisha, tho often requested, hath never paid the same sum, but detains it. To the Damage &c.

Plea Nil Debet. And the said Elisha comes and defends &c. and saith, he owes nothing to the said Samuel in manner and Form as within declared and thereof puts himself on the Country.[38]

[IX]

ACCOUNT vs. Bailiff of Goods, and Receiver of Monies.

[*Green v. Green*] [39]

1. Mallory's Mod. Ent. 48. Tit. account.[40]

Summon George Green &c. to answer to Joshua Green, &c. Administrator of all and singular, the Goods and Chattells, Rights and Credits

---

trustees of an "absconding person" like that which "other creditors have for recovery of their debts." Under §2, "where any person duly rated in the said town hath removed, or shall remove, out of it, into some other town in this province, ... before payment of such rates, and where, the time for payment to the respective treasurers [i.e. province, county, and town] being elapsed, the collectors or constables in the said town shall have paid the whole sums given them to collect in each year; in all such cases it shall and may be lawful for the collectors or constables of the said town ... to sue for such rates and taxes; and they shall have all the like remedies for recovery thereof, as other creditors have for recovering their proper debts." This act was presumably passed in response to the dictum of the Superior Court in Ruddock v. Gordon, Quincy, *Reports* 58, 59 (SCJ Suffolk, Feb. 1763), that no action of assumpsit lay for the recovery of taxes by a collector when the only statutory remedy was distress. See Act of 3 Oct. 1730, c. 1, §§12–17, 2 A&R 552–554. An action of debt was the usual remedy in a right of action given by statute. See Shipman, *Common-law Pleading* 137–138. Although it is not made explicit in the pleading, it seems probable that Doane was being sued under the second section of this act as one who had "removed." Later one of JA's clients, he was an extremely wealthy man, owning property in Boston as well as in Wellfleet and elsewhere. See No. 58, note 12 and Doc. I. The tax acts in question were the Act of 21 June 1765, c. 18, 4 A&R 818, and the Act of 27 June 1766, c. 6, 4 A&R 883.

[38] The plea, nil debet (literally, "he owes nothing"), was the general issue in debt, putting in issue, "nearly everything that negatived the existence of the debt at the time of the commencement of the action." Sutton, *Personal Actions* 164. See Shipman, *Common-law Pleading* 327–328. The phrase in the plea abbreviated at the "&c." is, in full, the commonly omitted formula called the "defense": "comes and defends the wrong and injury when and where it so behoves him; and the damages, and whatsoever else he ought to defend." "Defends" in this context means "denies." See note 94 below. The concluding phrase, "puts himself on the Country," is the formal conclusion of a traverse, a pleading tendering an issue triable by jury which the other party had to accept if properly pleaded. See Sutton, *Personal Actions* 81–83. The formal acceptance of the issue, known as the similiter, is omitted here. See note 68 below.

which were of Anna Green late of said Boston, Widow deceased
intestate in a Plea of Account for that the said George at said Boston,
on the first day of July Anno Domini 1765, the said Anna being then
living, and from the said first day of July to the Thirty first day of
December Anno Domini 1768 was the Bailiff and [41] Receiver of
Monies of the said Anna, she being all that Time living, during which
Time the said George received of the Monies of the said Anna at said
Boston, one hundred Pounds, by the Hands of Samuel Cotton, Thirty
Pounds by the Hands of Thaddeus Wyman &c.   in the whole

---

[39] In JA's hand. Pleadings Book, p. 15. The writ was dated 5 March 1771,
returnable to the April 1771 Suffolk Inferior Court. It was probably drawn by
JA, who received a fee of 18s. from Joshua Green at the April 1771 court. Office
Book, MQA. At the July 1771 Inferior Court Joshua won a jury verdict, with
Samuel Quincy appearing for him. On appeal in Feb. 1772, with JA and Quincy
both as his counsel, the jury affirmed the prior verdict. See Min. Bk., Inf. Ct.
Suffolk, April 1771, No. 200; SCJ Rec. 1772, fol. 17; Min. Bk. 95, SCJ Suffolk,
Aug. 1771, N–5; Feb. 1772, C–56; SF 102081. According to JA's undated minutes,
a reference was "declined." Adams Papers, Microfilms, Reel No. 185. The case
arose out of the winding up of the affairs of Joseph Green, deceased, who had run
a business which his son, the defendant, had apparently managed after Joseph's
death. The plaintiff, as administrator of Joseph's widow, sought to question the
son's management.

The action of account, to require one who holds money or goods of another to
render the balance due, was rarely used in England at this time, its functions
having been largely superseded by the less cumbersome device of proceedings in
equity. Fifoot, *History and Sources* 275–276. See JA's minutes, cited above. Since
there was no court of equity in Massachusetts, resort either to account or to the
simpler indebitatus assumpsit for money had and received (note 20 above) was
necessary. Although in later English practice assumpsit seems to have been available
in all cases where account would lie, in the 18th century there was authority to
the effect that it was not proper in the case of an actual account current between
the parties, because of the complexity of the computation involved. See cases cited
in James Barr Ames, *Lectures in Legal History* 117–119 (Cambridge, Mass., 1913).
See also Lincoln v. Parr, 2 Keble 781, 84 Eng. Rep. 494 (K.B. 1671); Gilbert,
Evidence 192; 2 Duncombe, *Tryals per Pais* 494 (London, 8th edn., 1766); 1
Dane, *Abridgment* 165. This authority may explain the use of the action of account
here. At common law the question whether the defendant was liable to account at
all was for the jury, but determination of the sums actually due was submitted
by the court to auditors. Fifoot, *History and Sources* 273–274. In this suit, at the
Inferior Court the defendant pleaded in bar that he was "never bailiff" as to part
of the declaration and that he had "fully accounted" as to the rest. On amendment
in the Superior Court he pleaded that he was "never receiver" as to the first count
of the declaration and "never bailiff" as to the second. SF 102081. Compare the
forms in John Mallory, *Modern Entries in English*, 1:42–43, 51 (London, 1734);
see also 1 Comyns, *Digest* 99–100; 1 Chitty, *Pleading* 483–484. Since these pleas
presented issues for the jury which in both suits were resolved in the defendant's
favor, the question whether auditors should be appointed was never reached.
Auditors were later expressly provided by statute in Massachusetts. Act of 17 Feb.
1786, [1784–1785] Acts and Resolves 521–522; Act of 20 Feb. 1818, [1818]
Mass. 550–551 (Jan. Sess. 1818); see 1 Dane, *Abridgment* 166.

[40] In 1 Mallory, *Modern Entries* 48–49, appear two forms on which the two
counts of this declaration seem to have been based.

[41] The words "Bailiff and" are lined out in the file copy of the writ. SF 102081.

amounting to Two Thousand, Three hundred and seventy Pounds Thirteen shillings and Ten Pence of lawful Money to render a reasonable Account thereof to the said Anna whenever he should be thereto requested; nevertheless the said George, tho often requested, never rendered such reasonable Account to the said Anna in her Lifetime, nor to the said Joshua Administrator as aforesaid since his Intestates decease, tho requested, but still neglects to do it: And for that the said George at said Boston on the first day of July Anno Domini 1765 and from the said first day of July to the Thirty first day of December Anno Domini 1768, the said Anna being all that Time living, was the said Anna's Bailiff, and during all that Time had the Care and Management of all the Goods, Chattells, Wares, and Merchandise and Cash contained in the Schedule hereto annexed, amounting in the whole to the further sum of 2677 Pounds 11s. 1d. of lawfull Money more to merchandise and make Profit thereof for and to render a reasonable Account thereof to the said Anna when he should be thereto requested; yet the said George (although requested) never rendered such reasonable Account to the said Anna in her Lifetime nor to the said Joshua Administrator as aforesaid, though requested since his Intestate's decease, but still neglects and refuses to do it. To the Damage.

[X]

CASE for a malicious Prosecution.

Needham vs. Kingsbury.[42]

2. Ins. Cler. 53. 4. 5. 6. 7.[43] 1 Mod. Ent. 160.[44]

Attach Seth Kingsbury of Walpole, &c. to answer Ezekiel Needham of Wrentham, &c. in a Plea of Trespass upon the Case, for that the

[42] In JA's hand. Pleadings Book, p. 16. The writ, dated 21 March 1771, returnable at the April Suffolk Inferior Court, was apparently drafted by JA, who entered the action. JA also was Needham's counsel at the July 1771 court, where judgment was given for Kingsbury on a demurrer to the plea, Needham having agreed that the trial of any appeal would be final. In the Superior Court, the case was continued term by term until Feb. 1779, when the suit was dropped. See Min. Bk., Inf. Ct. Suffolk, April 1771, No. 204; July 1771, No. 73; SCJ Rec. 1779, fol. 52; Min. Bk. 95, SCJ Suffolk, Aug. 1771, N–7; Min. Bk. 103, SCJ Suffolk, Feb. 1779, C-1; SF 102598. This suit for malicious prosecution arose out of an action brought by John Needham, Ezekiel's son, against Kingsbury at the July 1768 Suffolk Inferior Court for services performed and for a sawmill saw which Needham claimed that Kingsbury had agreed to buy, or at any rate had used and returned in damaged condition. Needham won a jury verdict for three pounds in the Inferior Court, which was reversed by a Superior Court jury at the Aug. 1768 term, and then on review in March 1769 was restored by a third verdict which included costs in the staggering amount of £79 3s. 7d. JA was Needham's counsel

said Ezekiel, now is a good, honest, true and faithfull subject of Us, and hath all his Lifetime hitherto, carried and behaved himself among all his Neighbours, and other our faithfull subjects, and those of our Predecessors, so as to be esteemed by them of a good Name, Fame, Credit, honest and faithfull Conversation,[45] and good Behaviour; and all his Lifetime hitherto hath lived, remained, and continued, without

at both Superior Court trials. See Min. Bk. 86, SCJ Suffolk, Aug. 1768, N–26; Min. Bk. 89, SCJ Suffolk, March 1769, N–24; SF 101254, 101352.

At the Nov. adjournment of the Aug. 1769 Superior Court term, on Kingsbury's complaint, Ezekiel Needham was indicted on two separate indictments for perjury in his testimony at the Inferior Court trial and at the Superior Court trial in review. His wife, Dorothy Needham, was also indicted for perjury in the Inferior Court. In each indictment the charge was the same, that the witness had testified "that three or four Teeth were broken out of the Saw" in dispute, "and that the same Saw was bent and twisted and entirely spoiled." See SF 102598, 101798, 101799, 101773. According to minutes taken by JA, probably at the trial in review, Ezekiel had testified that Kingsbury "brought the saw to my house and said it did not prove so well as he expected. The Saw was damnified, the Teeth were broke and the Saw was bent." Adams Papers, Microfilms, Reel No. 185. At the March 1770 term two indictments were also brought against John Needham—one for forging the signatures of his witnesses to the accounts of their travel to the Superior Court, and one for subornation of perjury, charging that he had procured Samuel Frost to testify falsely as to the condition of the saw at the trial in review. See SF 101796, 101797. After several continuances, during which Ezekiel was free on bail, he was tried under the indictment covering his Inferior Court testimony at the Feb 1771 Superior Court. (On his other indictment no plea appears and the words "not compleated" are written. SF 101799.) JA's minutes of the trial show that various witnesses testified that the saw was not damaged when Kingsbury returned it, but the saw itself was introduced in evidence and apparently had at least two or three broken teeth. Although some witnesses stated that these were broken before Kingsbury got possession, he testified himself that "This is the Saw that I carryd home to Needhams Mill. Just as it was then. I cant so well tell that the Saw was exactly so at the Time I took it. When I carryd it home, I told him that it was something rusty. There was 2 or 3. Same as it is now." Adams Papers, Microfilms, Reel No. 185. This testimony was apparently conclusive. The jury found Ezekiel not guilty and he was discharged. At the same term Dorothy and John Needham were likewise acquitted. Min. Bk. 91, SCJ Suffolk, Feb. 1771. This prosecution was the basis of Ezekiel's present suit.

At the Aug. 1773 term, Ezekiel was once again cited for perjury as a result of his testimony for John in a suit against the latter by Jeremiah Hall, in which Hall had finally prevailed on review. JA was again counsel for Needham in the civil suit. Min. Bk. 98, SCJ Suffolk, Feb. 1773, C–49; Aug. 1773, N–16; SF 102275, 102252c. Needham gave his recognizance for prosecution at the next term, but no further record has been found. See note 46 below. See also Ezekiel Needham v. Jeremiah Hall, Min. Bk., Inf. Ct. Suffolk, April 1772, No. 243, a default judgment for Needham with JA of counsel.

[43] In 2 Gardiner, *Instructor Clericalis* 53–57 (London, 1724), appears a discussion of malicious prosecution, followed by "A Declaration in Case for malitiously preferring an Indictment of Felony, which the Jury return'd *ignoramus*."

[44] 1 Mallory, *Modern Entries* 160, where there appears the form of a declaration in an action on the case for wrongful prosecution for larceny. JA has followed this form almost exactly.

[45] "Manner of conducting oneself in the world or in society; behaviour, mode or course of life." *OED*.

any Blott, or having committed any Falshood, Perjury, or other Crime or Misdemeanor whatever, and hath [46]

[XI]

CASE. For inticing and seducing an Apprentice from his Master whereby he lost his Service.

Paul Revere vs. James Lowrie [47]

Attach the Goods or Estate of James Lowrie now residing in Boston [48] in our same County Mariner, to answer Paul Revere of said Boston, Gentleman, in a Plea of Trespass on the Case, for that one

[46] The MS breaks off here. The declaration as found in the Superior Court files continued as follows: "always been untouched, unsuspected, and free from the suspicion and imputation of any such execrable and horrible crime, by reason of which good Name, fame, Credit, and honest Conversation, he the said Ezekiel had not only gained to himself the love and favour of all his Neighbours, but hath also reap'd and enjoyed great Advantages arising therfrom. Nevertheless the said Seth, being in no wise ignorant of the premises, but contriving and maliciously intending unjustly to grieve the said Ezekl. and not only to injure and detract him the said Ezekiel in his good name, fame, Credit and Reputation, but also to subject and bring him into danger of the pains and Penalties of Perjury, on the twenty first day of November [1769], at Boston aforesaid *falsly and maliciously laid a charge of perjury* against the said Ezekiel, and afterwards there on the same day, he the said Seth, out of his further malice which he had against the said Ezekiel, falsly and maliciously and *without any true or lawful or probable Cause* at our Superior Court of Judicature, Court of Assize, and General Goal Delivery, held at Boston within and for the County of Suffolk, on Tuesday, the Twenty first day of November [1769], by Adjournment duly made from the last Tuesday of August [1769], being the time by law appointed for holding the same Court, exhibited a Bill of Indictment against the said Ezekiel to the Jury of the Grand Inquest." The declaration then went on to recite the substance of the indictment actually returned by the grand jury, which set out the details of John Needham's declaration against Seth Kingsbury at the July 1768 Suffolk Inferior Court and the proceedings there, including Ezekiel Needham's allegedly perjured testimony. Ezekiel's declaration then gave the proceedings on the indictment leading to his acquittal, concluding, "by reason of which premises the said Ezekiel was obliged to expend and lay out divers great sums of money to obtain his Enlargement from his said Imprisonment, and for the said Ezekiel to acquit himself from the said Crime as above charged upon him. To the damage of the said Ezekiel Needham (as he saith) the sum of five hundred pounds, which shall then and there be made to appear with other due Damages." SF 102598. See forms in Perham, *American Precedents* 205–209.

[47] Caption in JA's hand. Title of the case and remainder of the declaration possibly in the hand of William Tudor, JA's clerk. Pleadings Book, p. 18. The records of this case have not been found. The original of the writ, endorsed Paul Revere, dated 23 Oct. 1772, and returnable to the Jan. 1773 Suffolk Inferior Court, appears in SF 91313. According to JA's Office Book, Jan. 1773 Suffolk Inferior Court, MQA, JA represented Lowrie. At the entry he noted "finished," and wrote the figures £1 6s. 8d., which presumably was his fee. This is an action *per quod servitum amisit* (whereby he lost his services), properly brought in case, although if the servant were injured through force, trespass would also be proper. See 1 Chitty, *Pleading* 137–138. For forms, see 2 *id.* at 317–319; Perham, *Ameri-*

David Mosely of said Boston an Infant was by Indentures made by and between himself, by Consent of his Uncle on the one part, and the Plaintiff on the other part, on the 17th of March AD 1770, lawfully bound an Apprentice to the Plaintiff to serve him faithfully for and during the Term of four Years from the same Date, and the Plaintiff in said Indenture did covenant to teach and instruct the said Apprentice or cause him to be instructed in his the said Paul Revere's Trade [or?] Art of Goldsmith and Engraver and also to find and provide for the said Apprentice sufficient Meat, Drink, Washing, Lodging and Cloathing during the said Term; which said Indenture duly executed by &c. on the part of the said Apprentice in Court shall be produced; of all which the said James Lowrie was well knowing, yet he maliciously contriving and intending to deprive the Plaintiff of the benefits of said Apprentice, and to render it impossible for the Plaintiff wholly to perform his Covenant aforesaid did at Boston aforesaid on 27th of Septr. AD 1771 (the said Lowrie being then Master of an outward bound Vessel) seduce the said David Mosely to leave the Plaintiff's service, and did carry him away and has ever since detained and concealed the said David so that the Plaintiff cannot find, and take him, and the said James Lowrie hath oftentimes since (tho requested) refused to deliver said Apprentice to the Plaintiff and still unjustly detains and conceals the said Apprentice whereby the Plaintiff hath lost the benefit of his said Apprentice and is unable to perform his Covenant aforesaid and hath suffered much Pain and Anxiety of Mind, all which is to the Damage of the said Paul Revere, as he saith, the sum of £[150?].

[XII]

DEBT.

Ruddock vs. Aylwin [49]

2 Mod. Ent. 1. Covenant on a Charter Party.[50] 2 Mod. Ent. 211. Debt on Ditto.[51]

---

can Precedents 209–210. The case and its aftermath are described in Forbes, *Paul Revere* 396; Revere "had only got David Mosely [his apprentice] back by suing the shipmaster who had seduced him away from his goldsmith shop (and considering that Mosely then turned around, married his master's sister, Betsey, although she was much older than himself, drank too much, and was a spendthrift and a thorn in Revere's side forever after, he may have wished he had let the boy go)." For Revere's difficulties in later years as Mosely's guardian, see SJC Rec. 1798–1799, fol. 38; SF 107814.

[48] A note in JA's Office Book, Jan. 1773 Suffolk Inferior Court, MQA, indicates that Lowrie was a mariner from Glasgow.

[49] In JA's hand to text at note 54 below. Remainder probably in hand of Jonathan

Attach Thos. Aylwin &c. and John Scollay, &c. to answer Abiel Ruddock &c. in a Plea of Debt, for that the said Thomas and John, by their Indenture of Charter Party of affreightment made at Boston aforesaid, on the fourth Day of May Anno Domini 1770, executed between the Plaintiff, by the Name of Abiel Ruddock, &c. owner of the Schooner, Two Friends on the one Part and the Defendants by the Names of the several Persons whose Names are subscribed and their Seals fixed to the said Charter Party of the other Part, which Part sealed with the seals of the said Thomas and John, and to which their Names are subscribed, the said Abiel brings into Court,[52] the date being the same Day and Year, he the said Abiel granted and demised

---

Williams, JA's clerk. Pleadings Book, p. 25–26, 30. JA presumably drew the writ, dated 18 Dec. 1770, since he appeared for Ruddock in the Jan. 1771 Suffolk Inferior Court, where a jury awarded JA's client £200. JA also represented Ruddock on appeal, but in the Superior Court the case was referred. At the Feb. 1771 term a report was entered reducing his recovery to £49 14s. 4½d. Min. Bk., Inf. Ct. Suffolk, Jan. 1771, No. 235; SCJ Rec. 1771, fol. 20; Min. Bk. 91, SCJ Suffolk, Feb. 1771, N–29; SF 101820. The suit was on a charter party, a contract for the hire of a vessel. As the authorities cited in notes 50 and 51 below indicate, debt and covenant were alternative remedies in such a case where the agreement was under seal. The difference was that in covenant recovery would be limited to actual damages, while in debt the penal sum actually stated in the contract to be due in the event of breach could be sued for. See 1 Chitty, *Pleading* 112–114. The difference was of slight practical effect, since by Act of 10 Dec. 1698, c. 22, §1, 1 A&R 356, the court was permitted to "chancer" a jury verdict in such a penal sum to the "just debt and damages." Compare No. 13, note 3. Here a similar result was apparently reached by the referees. Admiralty has always claimed jurisdiction of charter parties. Today this claim is conceded because of the maritime subject matter involved, although under the "saving clause," 28 U.S.C. §1333, there is concurrent jurisdiction at common law. In the 18th century the common-law courts held that their jurisdiction was exclusive over virtually all contracts not actually made at sea to be performed at sea and used the writ of prohibition to limit the Admiralty courts accordingly. As a consequence, cases such as this seem to have been tried far more frequently before the courts of law than in Admiralty, at least in Massachusetts. See Wroth, "The Massachusetts Vice Admiralty Court and the Federal Admiralty Jurisdiction," 6 *Amer. Jour. Legal Hist.* 351, 360–364 (1962); Gilmore and Black, *The Law of Admiralty* 21, 170. Compare note 99 below.

[50] 2 Mallory, *Modern Entries* 1–6, contains the form of "A Declaration for Breach of Covenants in an Indenture of Charterparty, in not paying for Demurrage, Primage, the Dover Duty, and for Freight," as well as later pleadings.

[51] 2 Mallory, *Modern Entries* 211–215, setting out a declaration in "Debt for £800 upon a Charterparty of Affreightment."

[52] The foregoing language literally describes the historic form of the charter party, a term derived from the Latin *charta partita*, "divided paper." Although the practice had long been abandoned, originally many kinds of legal documents were written in duplicate on a single piece of paper, which was then cut in half on an irregular line running through a word. The two halves could be fitted together to prove the genuineness of the document. Another survival of this practice is the familiar opening phrase of the deed of realty, "This indenture witnesseth." See Charles Abbott (Lord Tenterden), *A Treatise of the Law Relative to Merchant Ships and Seamen* 121–122 (Phila., 1st Amer. edn., 1802); Plucknett, *Concise History* 612–613.

the said schooner, to freightment to the said Thomas and John, by the Names of them subscribed thereto, and that they in like manner hired the same from the said Master for a Trading Voyage, to be made by the Grace of God, to Chalure Bay, Gaspee &c. and from thence to be delivered at Boston,[53] as follows—vizt. the said Abiel for himself, his Executors and Administrators covenanted, promised and agreed to and with the said Merchants, subscribing said Charter Party, that the said schooner is tight and stanch and strong.[54] And is and shall be during said Voyage with all that is necessary that it shall be lawful for the Defendants or their Correspondents to load and unload and reload the schooner with such Goods Wares and Merchandizes as they shall think proper during said Voyage, and they the said Merchants subscribing the said Charter party for themselves their Executors and Administrators aforesaid, covenanted and agreed with the said Abiel his Executors, Administrators, and Assigns: will not only load unload and reload as aforesaid but that they will in case she is seized in a counterband Trade and condemned pay to the said Abiel his Executors or Administrators the full and just sum of £340, that they will also pay the Port charges and the charges for victualling and manning this said schooner during said Voyage: and that they will well and truly pay or cause to be paid unto the said Abiel his Executors, Administrators, or assigns the sum of £15 per month and so in proportion for a greater or less time and the said Ab[i]el firmly by said Charter party obliged and bound himself his Executors, Administrators, and Assigns, and his said Vessel together with all the furniture and freights to the said Men: subscribing said Charter Party, their Administrators, Executors, and Assigns in the penal Sum

[53] Despite the use of the word "demised" this does not appear to be what is today called a demise or bareboat charter, in which the owner furnishes a crewless, victual-less vessel, and the charterer becomes owner *pro hac vice*. See Gilmore and Black, *Law of Admiralty* 170–172, 215–219. The charter here is described as one of "freightment," and it is for a single voyage. Ruddock, the owner, is also described as "Master," suggesting that he was to retain control of the vessel for the voyage in question. Even today these elements would indicate that the owners were exercising that degree of control which would make this a voyage charter (or "charter party of affreightment," as it is sometimes called). This would be so despite the fact that the charterers here undertook to pay "the charges for victualling and manning" the vessel (text below). See Gustavus H. Robinson, *Handbook of the Law of Admiralty in the United States* 594–598 (St. Paul, Minn., 1939). In the 18th century the term charter party seems to have been limited to a contract with these and other attributes of the modern voyage charter. The transaction that would now be classed as a demise charter was considered an altogether different type of contract. See Abbott, *Merchant Shipping* 76, 121. See also Charles Molloy, *De Jure Maritimo et Navali* 255–258 (London, 8th edn., 1744).

[54] The remainder of the declaration is probably in the hand of Jonathan Williams.

of one hundred pounds and to the true performance of everything in said Charter Party, on the part of the said Merchants subscribing said Charter Party to be performed, they the said Merchants by their Charter Party firmly obliged themselves their Executors, Administrators, and Assigns and the Goods as[55] aforesaid intended to be loaded to the said Abel his Executors, Administrators and assigns in the like penal sum of £100 as by the said Charter Party doth and may more fully appear. Now the said Abiel in fact says that he the said Abiel on his part hath well and truly performed his part of said Charter Party that the said Schooner was tight staunch and strong, and was so during said Voyage and before the voyage was ended as aforesaid four months and more were elapsed, the said Abiel further avers that the said Thomas and John have not nor ether of them paid or caused to be paid to the said Abiel the £15 aforesaid agreed to be paid whereby an action has accrued to the said Abiel to require and have from the said Thomas and John the said £100 nevertheless the said Thomas and John tho requested have never paid the same but neglect &c.

[XIII]

EJECTMENT on a Covenant.

Wendell vs. Williams [56]

Summon Nathaniel Henshaw and Jona. Williams &c., to answer unto Oliver Wendell of Boston Merchant, in a Plea, wherein he demands vs. the said Nathaniel and Jonathan, one undivided third

[55] The remainder of the declaration appears on p. 30 in the MS.

[56] In JA's hand. Pleadings Book, p. 27. In this case JA was of counsel for the defendants, Nathaniel Henshaw and Jonathan Williams, both at the April 1771 Suffolk Inferior Court, where a verdict was entered against them, and at the Aug. 1771 term of the Superior Court, where they lost a second time. The writ, dated 11 March 1771, was probably drawn by Josiah Quincy Jr., who entered the action. See Wendell v. Williams, Min. Bk., Inf. Ct. Suffolk, April 1771, No. 145; Henshaw v. Wendell, SCJ Rec. 1771, fol. 213; Min. Bk. 95, SCJ Suffolk, Aug. 1771, N–2; SF 101887. Both Oliver Wendell, plaintiff here, and his cotenant, Jonathan Jackson, were ancestors of United States Supreme Court Justice Oliver Wendell Holmes. Wendell was Holmes' paternal great-grandfather; Jackson (1743–1810), father of Charles Jackson who sat on the Supreme Judicial Court from 1813 to 1824 and who wrote an important treatise on real actions, was his maternal great-grandfather. See Mark DeWolfe Howe, *Justice Oliver Wendell Holmes: The Shaping Years, 1841–1870* 177–180 (Cambridge, Mass., 1957). The deed under which Wendell claimed was a mortgage deed, the defendants being second mortgagees who had probably entered under their mortgage. Wendell was seeking to foreclose the mortgage as to them; he obtained a judgment for the sum actually owed him, or possession, if the sum was not paid within two months. See No. 13, note 3.

Part of all that Farm or Tract of Land, commonly called and known by the Name of Hog Island, both the greater and the lesser, lying within the Bounds and Limitts of the Town of Boston aforesaid containing by Estimation, 530 Acres and bounded on all Sides by the Salt Water,[57] together with one undivided Third Part of all the Buildings thereon standing, and of all the Appurtenances thereto belonging; whereupon the said Oliver complains and says that on the Nineteenth Day of September A. Dom:1769 one Samuel Sewall Esqr. was seized and possessed of the whole Farm or Tract of Land aforesaid, with the Appurtenances, in his Demesne as of Fee, and being so seized and possessed thereof, the said Samuel by a certain Indenture of Bargain and Sale of that Date, made and duely executed by and between the said Samuel, on the one Part, and the said Oliver and one Jonathan Jackson on the other Part, then, at Boston aforesaid, granted, sold and conveyed the same Farm or Tract of Land with the Appurtenances to the said Oliver Wendell and Jonathan Jackson, to hold the one Third Part thereof to him the said Oliver and his Heirs forever, and the other two Third Parts thereof to him the said Jonathan Jackson and his Heirs forever, one Part of which said Indenture, under the Hand and seal of the said Samuel, duely executed, acknowledged and recorded, is in Court to be produced;[58] by Force whereof the said Oliver Wendell and Jonathan Jackson, then and there entered into and became seized, as Tenants in Common, of the said Farm or Tract of Land with the appurtenances, to wit, the said Oliver of one

---

Jackson, the cotenant, brought an identical suit against these defendants. See Jackson v. Williams, Min. Bk., Inf. Ct. Suffolk, April 1771, No. 124; Henshaw v. Jackson, Min. Bk. 95, SCJ Suffolk, Aug. 1771, N–1; SF 101886. JA's minutes are in Adams Papers, Microfilms, Reel No. 185.

The action here, labeled "ejectment" in accordance with usual Massachusetts practice, was in the nature of a writ of entry, in which the plaintiff declared upon the mortgage deed (or "covenant" as JA has here called it), rather than upon his seisin as mortgagee. This practice was said to be proper where the mortgage condition was part of the deed; the pleader was required to make "profert" of the deed (tender it in court), so that the condition would sufficiently appear. Stearns, citing similar forms printed in *American Precedents* 354–355 (Brookfield, Mass., 3d edn., 1821), criticized the procedure for its length and complexity, adding, "In its structure indeed, it is more like an action *of covenant*, or *on the case*, than a *writ of Entry*." Stearns, *Real Actions* 253–254, 451–452. See note 29 above. See also No. 17, notes 3–7.

[57] Hog Island in Boston harbor, now the district known as Orient Heights in East Boston. *Boston Streets, &c., 1910* 245, 352.

[58] The "profert" of the deed, note 56 above. When profert was made, the defendant could demand "oyer." In ancient practice this literally meant a reading of the deed in court. With written pleadings, however, it merely signified that the plaintiff had to set out in the record the deed or other instrument sued upon. See Sutton, *Personal Actions* 102–104. Compare Metcalf v. Hall, Form XXIII.

undivided Third Part thereof, in Fee Simple, and the said Jonathan Jackson, of the other undivided two Third Parts thereof in Fee Simple, and the said Oliver ought still to be in quiet Possession of his said undivided Third Part thereof; nevertheless, the said Nathl. Henshaw and Jona. Williams have since unjustly and without Judgment of Law entered into the whole of the Premisses, and disseised the Plaintiff of his said undivided Third Part thereof, and still unjustly deforce him thereof, and altogether hold him out of the same. To the Damage &c. £1000.

[XIV]

PLEA OF TENDER. Ind[ebitatus] Ass[umpsit] and Quantum Mer[uit]. 2 Counts.

Jno. Coburn vs. Rob. White.[59]

2 Mall. Mod. Ent. Vid. of pleading a Tender under Tit. Pleadings in the Table.[60]

3 Inst. Cler. 134. 136.[61] Bac. Abr. Tit. Tender.[62] 2 Mod. Ent. 310.[63] 5 Bac. Abr. 1.[64]

[59] In JA's hand. Pleadings Book, p. 28–30. The files of this case have not been located. JA was of counsel for Coburn, and Samuel Quincy for White. At the April 1771 Suffolk Inferior Court, "Tender was admitted by the plaintiff" and the jury awarded him the sum tendered (£7 6s. 8d.), but allowed the defendant costs. Min. Bk., Inf. Ct. Suffolk, April 1771, No. 186. See JA's Office Book, April 1771, MQA. In a companion action, with tender also admitted, the plaintiff recovered £7 12s. 8d. and costs, more than the tender. Min. Bk., Inf. Ct. Suffolk, April 1771, No. 187. The pleas here were drawn by Samuel Quincy, counsel for the defendant. The plea of tender is one in which the defendant admits all or part of the liability, but asserts that he has offered to pay that part and been refused. See 1 Chitty, *Pleading* 473–474; 2 *id.* at 479–482. See also Sutton, *Personal Actions* 160–162. Note that here the declaration apparently alleged two of the common counts (note 31 above), and that a virtually identical plea was offered to both. By way of replication, the plaintiff could deny that tender was made, or offer a variety of technical defenses to the plea. With the tender here admitted, trial must have been only on the matters which the defendant had denied. See 1 Chitty, *Pleading* 552–553; 2 *id.* at 645–650.

[60] 2 Mallory, *Modern Entries*, under the heading referred to by JA contains a reference to p. 310–312, where numerous cases on the subject are digested.

[61] 3 Gardiner, *Instructor Clericalis* 134, 136 (London, 4th edn., 1724), two pleas of tender in the original Latin.

[62] 5 Bacon, *Abridgment* 1, tit. Tender and bringing Money into Court upon the common Rule. The rule, "by which the Money brought into Court is ordered to be struck out of a Declaration, is, from its being more frequently granted than that by which it is ordered that the Proceedings shall be stayed, called the common rule." Of particular application to this case are *id.* at 14–19, 27.

[63] See note 60 above.

[64] See note 62 above.

Plea

Suffolk Ss.[65] Common Pleas April 1771.

Coburn plt.	
vs.	} Defendant's plea of Tender &c.
White Deft.	

And the said Robert White comes and defends &c. and as to seven pounds six shillings and Eight Pence, parcell of said sum of Nine Pounds, 14s. 8d. in the first Count in said Declaration mentioned, saith the said John ought not to recover against him the said Robert any further Damages than the said £7 6s. 8d. because he says that the said Robert from the Time of making his said Promise for Payment of said Sum of £7 6s. 8d. (which promise he made for Cash or Money lent him by the said John and for Eight Weeks board, as severally charged in the Account annexed to the Writ) was always ready and now is ready to pay the same to the said John; and he the said Robert before the day of suing forth the said Johns said Writ, vizt. on the Fifth day of January last, at said Boston, offered to pay and tendered the said sum of £7 6s. 8d., then and there to the said John, and the said John then and there refused to accept the same sum; and the said Robert hath ever since been ready to pay the same sum to the said John, and now brings the same into Court ready to pay the same to the said John if he will accept it: And all this the said Robert is ready to verify: [66] Wherefore the said Robert prays Judgment, if the said John, shall have and recover of him on this suit any further Damages than the said sum of £7 6s. 8d. as aforesaid; and for his Costs.   S[amuel] Q[uincy] for Defendant

And as to the sum of Two Pounds Eight Shillings, Residue of the said £9 14s. 8d. in said first Count in said Declaration mentioned the said Robert says he never promised the said John in manner and Form as he declares against him and thereof puts &c.   S.Q.

And the said John likewise.

And the said Robert White comes and defends &c. and as to the

---

[65] "Ss," commonly used in the statement of venue in pleadings and other forms, is said to be a contraction of *scilicet*, meaning "to wit." Black, *Law Dictionary*.

[66] The "common verification," a requirement in pleadings (other than the declaration) which introduced new matter instead of offering an issue. Sutton, *Personal Actions* 86. The prayer for judgment following the verification is in the form proper for a plea of tender in assumpsit. 1 Chitty, *Pleading* 539–540.

said £7 4s. in said second Count in said Declaration mentioned saith the said John ought not to have and recover any further Damages against him than the said £7 4s. Because he says, that from the Time of making his said Promise for Payment of said sum of seven Pounds, four Shillings (which said Promise he made for Eight Weeks Board in the said John's House) he was always ready and still is ready to pay the same to the said John; and he the said Robert before the Purchase of the said Johns Writ, viz. on the Fifth day of January last, at said Boston, offered to pay, and then and there tendered to the said John said sum of £7 4s., and the said John then and there utterly refused to accept the same; and the said Robert hath ever since been ready to pay the same Sum to the said John, and now brings the same into Court ready to be paid to the said John, if he will receive it; and all this the said Robert is ready to verify; wherefore, the said Robert prays Judgment if the said John shall have and recover against him on this suit any further Damages than the said sum of Seven Pounds four Shillings as aforesaid, and for his Costs.

S.Q. pro Defendente

And as to the sum of £2 8s. in said second Count in said Declaration mentioned, the said Robert White saith he never promised the said John in manner and form as he declared against him and thereof puts &c.[67]

S.Q.

And the said John likewise.[68]

[XV]

Writ of Intrusion

Brayton vs. Robinson [69]

Attach Eliza. Robinson &c. to answer unto Israel Brayton of Swansey &c., in a Plea of Ejectment, wherein he demands against the

[67] This portion of the pleading is in effect a plea of non assumpsit (the general issue) to that part of the plaintiff's claim as to which no tender was alleged. See 2 Chitty, *Pleading* 480 note.

[68] The "similiter," the formal acceptance or joinder of issue required when a plea concluded "to the country." 1 Chitty, *Pleading* 549, 570.

[69] In JA's hand. Pleadings Book, p. 31–[32]. The writ, dated 6 Feb. 1771, was probably drawn by Robert Treat Paine, who appeared for Brayton at the March 1771 Taunton Inferior Court, where the jury returned a verdict in Brayton's favor for possession and costs. On the appeal JA joined Paine as counsel for Brayton. At the Superior Court's Oct. 1773 term, again at Taunton, the prior judgment was affirmed. See Robinson v. Brayton, SCJ Rec. 1773, fol. 152; Min. Bk. 100, SCJ

said Eliza. a Messuage [70] and Twelve Acres of Land in Swansey bounded &c. and is bounded all round by Land now in the Possession of the said Israel, and its appurtenances, which demanded Premises were formerly in the Possession of one John Brayton of said Swansey, and which the said Israel Claims as his Right and Inheritance and into which, the said Elizabeth Robinson had no

Bristol, Oct. 1773; SF 145772. The "writ of intrusion" is a form of writ of entry proper when the plaintiff (or "demandant" as he was technically known) was a remainderman or reversioner after a life estate, who had been ousted by an "intrusion" (an entry by a stranger after the life estate had terminated and before the remainderman had entered). See Stearns, *Real Actions* 49, 143, 179–180. For another form, see *id.* at 443–444. As to the requisites of pleadings in writs of entry generally, see *id.* at 149–161. Compare notes 29, 30, above, and No. 17, notes 3–7. Israel Brayton, plaintiff here, had received a reversionary interest in the lands in suit by devise from his grandfather, Preserved Brayton, who had died in 1761. Preserved in 1753 had assigned a life interest in the lands to his daughter-in-law, Ruth Brayton (Israel's mother), in lieu of her dower interest in certain lands once owned by her husband John Brayton, which she had not released. Previously, in 1736 Preserved had sold or given these lands, which included those in suit, to John under a duly recorded conveyance. John sold them back to Preserved in 1743, but seemingly destroyed the deed before it could be recorded. John then sold the property to William Sherman, but in 1744 Preserved was able to obtain possession in an action of ejectment against Sherman at the Superior Court, in which he was allowed to prove the making of his deed from John and that Sherman had had actual notice of it. In 1770 Ruth Brayton died, leaving her daughter Elizabeth Brayton Robinson in possession of the premises for which Israel sued. See documentation in SF 145772 and a summary of the title in Paine's hand in MHi:Photostats (1768). In opposition to Israel's suit Elizabeth apparently claimed that the 1743 conveyance from John to Preserved was ineffective and that she was entitled to a share in the property under her father's estate. JA's minutes of the argument on this question show that he urged authorities to the effect that Preserved's 1744 judgment could be admitted as evidence of his title, and that, in the alternative, depositions and oral testimony as to the fate of the deed and its contents were admissible. Adams Papers, Microfilms, Reel No. 185. A note with JA's Oct. 1772 Docket records that the "Court determined unanimously that Evidence should be admitted of the Deed from Jno. Brayton to his father and of the Destruction of it," an apparent straightforward application of the so-called best evidence rule. Although this note indicates that the question was decided in Oct. 1772, the Paine Law Notes date the argument in Oct. 1773.

[70] A dwelling house, perhaps including its outbuildings and immediate surroundings. Black, *Law Dictionary.* The restraint of the Massachusetts draftsmen in employing technical terminology is admirable. Compare Mrs. Shandy's marriage settlement in Laurence Sterne, *The Life and Opinions of Tristram Shandy, Gentleman* 41 (N.Y., Modern Library edn., undated): "All that the manor and lordship of Shandy, in the county of ——, with all the rights, members, and appurtenances thereof; and all and every the messuages, houses, buildings, barns, stables, orchards, gardens, backsides, tofts, crofts, garths, cottages, lands, meadows, feedings, pastures, marshes, commons, woods, underwoods, drains, fisheries, waters, and water courses; —together with all rents, reversions, services, annuities, fee farms, knights' fees, views of frankpledge, escheats, reliefs, mines, quarries, goods and chattels of felons and fugitives, felons of themselves, and put in exigent deodands, free warrens, and all other royalties and seignories, rights and jurisdictions, privileges and hereditaments whatsoever."

Entry, but by Intrusion which she made upon the same after the Death of Ruth Brayton who was the Wife of the said John Brayton and which Messuage and Lands were assigned to the said Ruth as her Dower of certain Lands which formerly belonged to the said John Brayton by Preserved Brayton to whom the Reversion of the demanded Premises belonged, and who devised them to the Demandant his Son and his Heirs,[71] Whereupon the said Israel saith, that the said Preserved Brayton in a Time of Peace in the Reign of our late Royal Grandfather[72] was seized of the demanded Premises in his Demesne as of Fee, taking the Profits thereof to the Yearly Value of Ten Pounds by the Year and being so seized afterwards vizt. on the Eighth Day of December Anno Domini 1753 by his Deed of that Date in Court to be produced, assigned and sett off, to the said Ruth Brayton the demanded Premises as her Dower in a certain Messuage of about 100 Acres of Land in said Swansey of which the demanded Premises, is part, and of which same Messuage and Land before that time, and since the Intermarriage of the said John and Ruth, the said John Brayton who was deceased before the date of the same deed, was seized in his Demesne as of Fee, and delivered Seisin thereof to the said Ruth and thereupon the said Ruth, then and there, vizt. at said Swansey in the said Eighth Day of December, A.D. 1753, accepted of said demanded and assigned Premises in full satisfaction of her said Right of Dower and entered into the same, and held them as Tenant in Dower of her said Husband, John Brayton, on the said assignment of the said Preserved Brayton as aforesaid and was seized thereof in her Demesne as of Freehold[73] in a Time of Peace in the Reign of our late Royal Grandfather, taking the Profits thereof, to the amount of Forty shilling by the Year, and afterwards vizt. on the 7. day of Decr. A.D. 1759. the said Preserved Brayton to whom the Reversion in Fee of the demanded Premises belonged, and of which he was then seized at Swansey aforesaid made his last Will and Testament in Writing and therein devised his said Reversion to the demanded Premises, to the Demandant and his Heirs, and afterwards, vizt. on the 21. day of May A.D. 1761 the said Preserved at said Swansey died seized of the said Reversion to the demanded Premises, by Force of which Devise the said Israel became seized of said Reversion in Fee simple, and afterwards vizt. on the 26. day of July A.D.

---

[71] That is, the devise was to Israel (Preserved's son) and to Israel's heirs.

[72] George II (1727–1760). As to these and the following phrases descriptive of Preserved Brayton's seisin, see note 30 above.

[73] Ruth Brayton was seised "as of freehold," rather than "as of fee," because her interest was a life estate, rather than a fee simple. See Stearns, *Real Actions* 153–154.

1770 the said Ruth Brayton at said Swansey died seized of said Estate in Dower, and into which demanded Premisses the said Elizabeth had no Entry, but by an Intrusion therein made by her as aforesaid, after the death of the said Ruth Brayton who held as aforesaid, and after the Death of the said Ruth Brayton, the said Israel Brayton ought to be in quiet and peaceable Possession and Seisin of the demanded Premisses; yet the said Eliza. having intruded therein unjustly holds the Demandant out of the Possession of the demanded Premisses, To the Damage &c.

Quære of this Writ? [74]

[XVI]

TRESPASS. Assault, arrest and Imprisonment.

Palmes vs. Greenleaf [75]

Summon Stephen Greenleaf &c. to answer to Richard Palmes of Boston &c. in a Plea of Trespass, for that the said Stephen at said Boston in the 1st. day of August last with Force and Arms, and without any lawfull Cause did assault, arrest, and imprison the said Richard, and without any lawfull Cause or Warrant did there hold and keep the said Richard in Prison and in his Custody, till to obtain his the said Richards Discharge he was by the said Stephen obliged to enter into a certain Recognizance in the sum of a hundred Pounds to appear at the then next Superior Court of Judicature, Court of Assize and General Goal Delivery to be holden at Boston in and for said County of Suffolk, and other Enormities the said Stephen then and there did to the said Richard contrary to Law and against our Peace and to the Damages &c.

[74] The basis of JA's query has not been determined. It may have been the fact that Israel Brayton was devisee of the reversion, rather than the actual reversioner or his heir. At least in later practice the writ presumably lay in such a case, however. See Stearns, *Real Actions* 2, 143, 179–180, 194. Whatever the problem, it was never resolved; the action went to the jury in both courts without a question of law being formally raised. See note 69 above.

[75] In JA's hand. Pleadings Book, p. [33]. The original, dated 15 June 1771, was drafted by James Otis, who was Palmes' counsel at the July 1771 Suffolk Inferior Court where he lost on a demurrer to the plea. Samuel Quincy represented Greenleaf. Min. Bk., Inf. Ct. Suffolk, July 1771, No. 245. The writ, in Otis' hand, is in the Inferior Court files. At the following Superior Court, with JA and Josiah Quincy now representing Palmes, the case went to the jury, which found for the defendant. SCJ Rec. 1771, fol. 215; Min. Bk. 95, SCJ Suffolk, Aug. 1771, N–10; SF 101891. The case arose from Palmes' status as a material witness in the Boston Massacre trials. See editorial note to Nos. 63 and 64, note 63. Greenleaf was sheriff of Suffolk County. Whitmore, *Mass. Civil List* 79.

[XVII]

CASE vs. Master for not transporting Goods according to Bill of Lading.

McLean vs. McEwen.[76]

Attach James McEwen &c. to answer unto Donald McClean of our City of N. York &c., Physician, in a Plea of Trespass on the Case, for that the said James on the 15th. day of Feb. A.D. 1766 at N. York aforesaid had received in and upon the Snow[77] called the Peggy, whereof the said James was then Master, bound on a Voyage from New York aforesaid to Leith in that Part of our Kingdom of Great Britain called Scotland, in good order and well conditioned, diverse Goods of him the said Donald, vizt. one Tierce containing 255 Pounds Weight of Snake Root of the Value of £43 Lawfull Money &c.—to be transported by him the said James in the said Snow from New York aforesaid to Leith aforesaid and there to be delivered to Hector McClean, or his assigns for a certain Hire, by the said Hector to the said James to be paid, thereupon, vizt. one Pound Twelve Shillings Sterling, in Consideration whereof the said James afterwards vizt. on the same 15. day of Feb. aforesaid at said Boston, promised the said Donald that he the said James would carry and transport for the said Donald the said Goods from N. York aforesaid to Leith aforesaid and the same Goods to the said Hector McClean or his assigns at Leith aforesaid would safely and securely deliver (the Dangers of the Seas only excepted): And the said Donald avers that the said

---

[76] In JA's hand. Pleadings Book, p. [34–35]. The writ, dated 31 Aug. 1770 and returnable to the Oct. 1770 Suffolk Inferior Court, was probably drafted by Samuel Fitch, who entered the action there. The Inferior Court Minute Book indicates that "Ad[ams]" represented the defendant in Jan. 1772, when £80 damages were awarded to the plaintiff on a demurrer to the plea. According to copies of the proceedings below in the Superior Court files, however, JA appeared for the plaintiff, and the defendant was represented by Josiah Quincy Jr. It is probable that the Minute Book entry is a clerical error. On appeal to the Superior Court the matter was referred, and in Feb. 1773 the defendant was awarded costs of £7 8s. 2d. Min. Bk., Inf. Ct. Suffolk, Oct. 1770, No. 280; Jan. 1772, No. 21; SCJ Rec. 1773, fol. 3; Min. Bk. 95, SCJ Suffolk, Feb. 1772, N–10; Min. Bk. 98, SCJ Suffolk, Feb. 1773, C–40; SF 102250b. Papers in the file indicate that the goods in suit were in storage at Greenoch, Scotland, where they had been unloaded at the desire of the majority of the cargo owners when the vessel had been seized in an action against her owner. The declaration is one in special assumpsit that that does not set out a bill of lading in express terms, but in reciting the contract uses the standard language of the bill. For similar forms, see 2 Chitty, *Pleading* 159–161; Perham, *American Precedents* 141–142. For a similar but much simpler form, see Holden v. Conner, Form I.

[77] "A small sailing vessel resembling a brig, carrying a main and foremast and a supplementary trysail mast close behind the mainmast." *OED.*

James after making the Promise aforesaid vizt. on the first day of April Anno Domini 1766 safely arrived in the Snow aforesaid at Grenoch in that Part of our said Kingdom of Great Britain call'd Scotland, from N. York aforesaid with the said Tierce and Barrell safe on board the said snow: And altho the said Hector McClean from the Time of making the Promise aforesaid by the said James, was always ready and still is ready to pay the said James the said Hire agreed to be paid him as aforesaid, for transporting the said Goods as aforesaid: yet the said James did not carry the Goods aforesaid to Leith aforesaid, nor hath he ever delivered the same or any Part of them to the said Hector McClean, or to his assigns according to his Promise aforesaid or in any manner performed his said Promise, tho often thereto requested, but hitherto hath wholly refused and still doth refuse to deliver the said Goods as aforesaid or to perform his said Promise.

To the Damage &c.

[XVIII]

DEBT. For a Legacy.

Loring vs. Loring.[78]

Summon Mary Loring &c. as she is Executrix of the last Will and Testament of [*Policarpus Loring*] to answer Thomas Loring of &c. as he is Administrator of all and singular the Goods and Chattells,

[78] In an unidentified hand, presumably that of one of JA's clerks. Pleadings Book, p. [36–37]. The writ, dated 29 Aug. 1772, was probably drawn by JA, who was of counsel for Thomas Loring at the Plymouth Inferior Court, Oct. 1772, where judgment was entered for Mary Loring on a demurrer to the plea. At Plymouth Superior Court in May 1773, with JA still appearing for Thomas, the case was referred. At the Taunton term in Oct. 1773 the report was read, the referees awarding Thomas his debt of £240 and costs. Robert Treat Paine represented Mary in both courts. Min. Bk. 94, SCJ Plymouth, May 1773, N–5; SF 142520. (No record reference has been located.) As to the iron industry in Massachusetts, see Nos. 18–19, notes 4, 5. The size of the recovery was probably a result of the six-year statute of limitations on "all actions of debt grounded upon any lending or contract, without specialty." Act of 20 Nov. 1770, c. 9, §2, 5 A&R 110.

The action of debt for a legacy stems from a quasi-contractual feature of the action which permitted recovery where one party was under a noncontractual duty to pay money to the other. See Fifoot, *History and Sources* 222–223; 1 Chitty, *Pleading* 91, 102; Shipman, *Common-law Pleading* 134. In England a pecuniary legacy was ordinarily sued for either in chancery or in the ecclesiastical courts. Lord Mansfield's decisions that indebitatus assumpsit lay, because a promise could be implied from the duty to pay imposed upon the executor who had received assets, were rejected toward the end of the 18th century, on the ground that the courts of law could not adequately enforce the wishes of the testator. See Atkins v. Hill, 1 Cowp. 284, 98 Eng. Rep. 1088 (K.B. 1775); Hawkes v. Saunders, 1 Cowp. 289, 98 Eng. Rep. 1091 (K.B. 1782); Deeks v. Strutt, 5 T.R. 690, 101 Eng. Rep. 384 (K.B.

Rights and Credits which were of Lydia Loring late of said Plimton Widow deceased intestate, in a plea of Debt, for that one Caleb Loring, of said Plimton, on the 22d day of January A.D. 1731, at said Plimton, made and duely executed his last Will and Testament in Writing, which Will was afterwards duely proved and approved, which Will and the Probate thereof in Court shall be produced, and in and by said last Will, the said Caleb among other things gave to the said Lydia, who was then living and the said Caleb's wife £40 a year, yearly to be paid her, by his two Sons Ignatius and Policarpus (the said Mary's aforesaid Testator) so long as the Furnace in Plimton should be improved and She the said Lydia remain his the said Caleb's Widow, in Consideration that he did in that his Will aforesaid, give his two Sons aforesaid his eighth part of said Furnace. And the said Caleb in and by his said Will gave and bequeathed unto his two Sons aforesaid (who were then in full Life) their Heirs and Assigns his eighth part of the Furnace in Plimton aforesaid, with the priviledges thereto belonging; and thereby ordered them to pay to his aforesaid Wife, the sum of £40 yearly and every year, so long as the Furnace should be improved, and his said Wife should remain his Widow: And afterwards at said Plimton, viz. on the 22d day of December A.D. 1732 the said Caleb died, living [leaving?] his said Wife and two Sons; and afterwards there the said Ignatius and Policarpus by virtue of the Devise aforesaid in said last Will to them made, entered into and became possessed of the said eighth part of said furnace, as Join-tenants in Fee simple, and thereupon became jointly chargeable to pay the said Annuity or Legacy of £40 a year to the said Lydia as aforesaid. And the said Ignatius and Policarpus continued during their joint lives jointly to improve the said Eighth part of said Furnace: And there afterwards on the 9th day of April A.D. 1742 the said Ignatius died, living his Mother aforesaid the said Lydia and his aforesaid Brother Policarpus, whereupon both the Right to the Eighth part of the Furnace aforesaid and the obligation to pay the Legacy

---

1794). See also Alison Reppy and Leslie J. Tompkins, *Historical and Statutory Background of the Law of Wills* 145–150 (Chicago, 1928); Fifoot, *History and Sources* 408–410, 435 note. In Massachusetts, where there were neither chancery nor ecclesiastical courts, a statute provided that all "certain" legacies might be sued for at common law. Act of 14 July 1693, c. 8, §2, 1 A&R 122. The actions of debt and assumpsit were thus at least partially concurrent remedies of the legatee. As-sumpsit seems to have been more commonly used because of the doctrine that debt lay only for a sum certain, which had to be proved exactly. Debt was a proper remedy, however, where, as in this case, the legacy was in the form of an annuity and only arrears were sought, the right to the annuity having ceased at the legatee's death. See 2 Dane, *Abridgement* 239; 5 *id.* at 103–104, 119–124, 238–239; 1 Chitty, *Pleading* 107–108; Perham, *American Precedents* 274–277.

or Annuity aforesaid, survived to the said Policarpus, who became bound to pay the same to the said Lydia according to the Will aforesaid.

Now the Plaintiff in fact says that the furnace aforesaid in Plimton has been improved from the day of the date of said Caleb's aforesaid Will, untill this day, and the said Lydia lived and remained unmarried, the Widow of the said Caleb, from his death until the 28th day of March A.D. 1771. Nevertheless the said Ignatius and Policarpus never paid the Legacy aforesaid, or any part thereof, to the said Lydia, during the Life time of the said Ignatius and Policarpus, nor did the said Policarpus in his Life time ever pay the said Legacy or any part thereof to the said Lydia, during his Lifetime, nor has the said Mary Loring Executrix as aforesaid since her Testator's decease ever paid the said Legacy or any part thereof, to the said Lydia in her Life time, or to the said Thomas Loring Administrator as aforesaid since his Intestate's decease, but detains it.

To the damage of the said Thomas in his said Capacity as he saith £2000. Adams

[XIX]

[CASE. *Assumpsit against an executor for a legacy.*]

[*Gore et ux. v. Gould*] [79]

Summon J[oseph] G[ould] of &c. Sole Executor &c. to answer J. Gore. and A. his Wife, in a Plea of Trespass on the Case, for that the said J[ohn] G[ould] Testator, at &c. on &c.—made and duely executed his last Will and Testament in Writing and therein among other Things, bequeathed to his daughter the said Abigail the Sum of £13 6s. 8d. lawfull Money, to be paid her in three Years after his decease, vizt. £4 8s. 10d. thereof to be allowed and paid her by the said Testators Son John, £4 8s. 11d. thereof by his son Samuel, and £4 8s. 11d. thereof by his said son Joseph, whom he therein appointed sole Executor, of his said Will: And after making and executing his said Will the said John Gould the father at said &c. on &c.—died seized and possessed of a real and personal Estate sufficient to pay all his funeral Expenses and Debts and to pay and satisfy all his Bequests and Legacies in his said Will and afterwards to wit on &c.—at &c.—

[79] In JA's hand. Pleadings Book, p. [37]. The records and files of this case have not been found. The suit is one in assumpsit against an executor for a legacy based on his implied promise to pay it. See Perham, *American Precedents* 140, 180–181. See generally note 78 above.

Suffolk, ss. GEORGE the Third, by the Grace of GOD, of Great-Britain, France and Ireland, KING, Defender of the Faith, &c.

or to any Constable of Braintree in said County of Suffolk

To the Sheriff of our County of Suffolk, his Under-Sheriff, or Deputy, Greeting.

WE Command you to Attach the Goods or Estate of William Whitmarsh of Braintree in said County Gentleman

to the Value of Nine Pounds, and for want thereof to take the Body of the said William (if he may be found in your Precinct) and him safely keep, so that you have him before Our Justices of Our Inferiour Court of Common Pleas next to be holden at Boston, within and for Our said County of Suffolk, on the Third Tuesday of April next: Then and there in Our said Court to answer unto

John Adams of Braintree in said County, Esqr in a Plea of the Case for that the said William at said Braintree on the Seventh day of July Anno domini 1766 by his Note under his Hand for value received, promised the said John to pay him or order one Pound two shillings of lawfull Money, on demand, with lawfull interest therefor till paid: and for that the said William thereafterwards on the Thirteenth day of July Anno domini 1767, by his other Note under his Hand for value received promised the said John to pay him or order the further Sum of Thirteen shillings of lawfull Money on demand with lawfull Interest therefor till paid: and for that the said William thereafterwards, on the fifth day of January Anno Domini 1768, by his other Note under his Hand for value received promised the said John to pay him Fifteen shillings of lawfull Money on demand with Interest therefor till paid: and for that the said William there afterwards on the Tenth day of this instant March being indebted to the Plaintiff in the further Sum of one Pound four shillings of lawfull Money more as by the Account annexed appears promised him to pay him that Sum on demand. Yet the said William tho' requested, has never paid Either of the Sums aforesaid, nor any of the Interest aforesaid, but still neglects & refuses to do it

90271

To the Damage of the said John as he saith, the Sum of Nine Pounds, which shall then and there be made to appear, with other due Damages: And have you there this Writ, with your Doings therein. Witness Eliakim Hutchinson, Esq; at Boston, this Twenty Third Day of March in the Eleventh Year of Our Reign. Annoque Domini, 1771

Ezek.l Goldthwait Cler

Wm Whitmarsh to John Adams

	£ s d
1769 Oct 1. To Writ, sum &c & adve in J. Tirrell vs Jos Tirell	0:12:0
To Attend 1 day	0: 1:6
To W. S. &S. vs Ed. Blake & att 1 day	0:10:6
	£1: 4: 0

90271

---

3. WRIT AND ACCOUNT

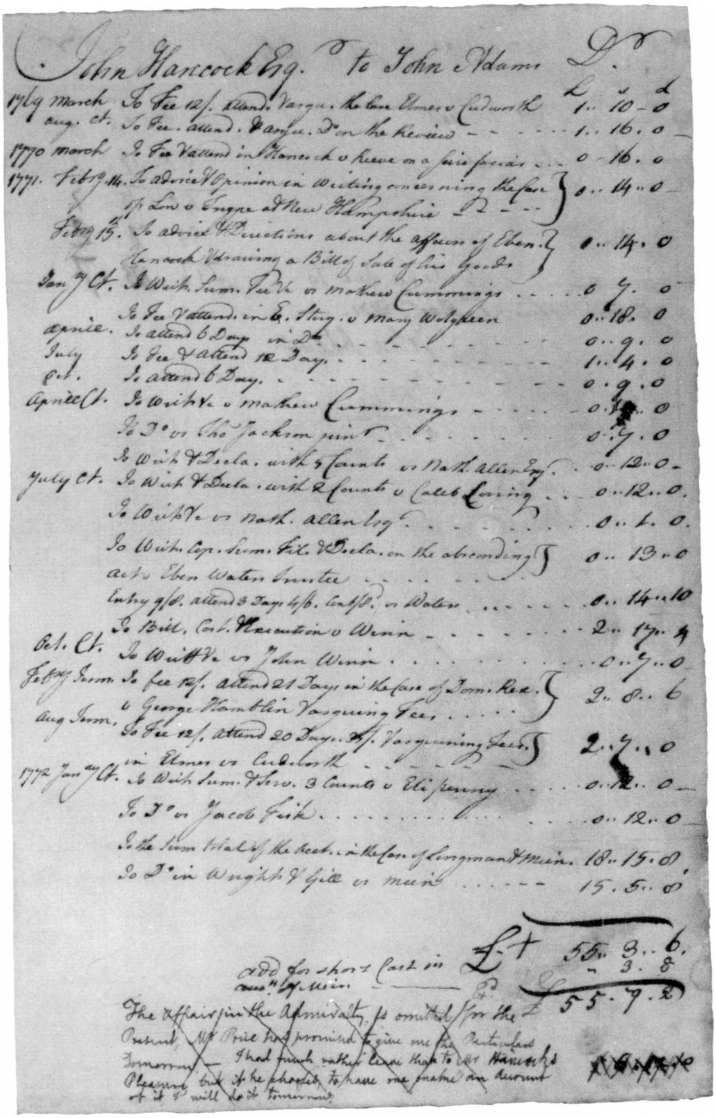
John Hancock Esqr to John Adams Dr

		£	s	d
1769 march	To Fee 12/. attend. & argue. the case Elmer v Cudworth	1	10	0
aug. Ct.	To Fee. attend. & argue. D° on the Review	1	16	0
1770 march	To Fee & attend. in Hancock v Reeve on a Fair Review	0	16	0
1771. Feby 14.	To advice & Opinion in Writing concerning the Case of Low v Tugne at New Hampshire	0	14	0
Feby 15.	To advice & Directions about the affairs of Eben. Hancock & drawing a Bill of Sale of his Goods	0	14	0
Jan Ct.	To Writ. Sum. Decl. v Mathew Cummings	0	7	0
	To Fee & attend. in Ex. Stng. v Mary Wolfpeen	0	18	0
April.	To attend 6 Days in D°	0	9	0
July	To Fee & attend 12 Days	1	4	0
Oct.	To attend 6 Days	0	9	0
April Ct.	To Writ &c v Mathew Cummings	0	[illegible]	0
	To D° v Tho. Jackson junr	0	7	0
	To Writ & Decla. with 2 Counts v Nath. Allen Esqr	0	12	0
July Ct.	To Writ & Decla. with 2 Counts v Caleb Loring	0	12	0
	To Writ &c v Nath. Allen Esqr	0	4	0
	To Writ. Cop. Sum. Fil. & Decla. on the absconding act v Eben Waters Trustee	0	13	0
	Entry 9/6. attend 3 Days 4/6. Cost 5/. v Waters	0	14	10
	To Bill, Cost. Execution v Winn	2	17	4
Oct. Ct.	To Writ &c v John Winn	0	7	0
Feby Term	To Fee 12/. attend 21 Days in the Case of Dom. Rex v George Hamblin & arguing Fee	2	8	6
Aug Term.	To Fee 12/. attend 20 Days. 12/. & arguing Fees in Elmer v Cudworth	2	7	0
1772 Jany Ct.	To Writ Sum. & Serv. 3 Counts v Eli Penny	0	12	0
	To D° v Jacob Fisk	0	12	0
	To the Sum total of the Acct. in the Case of Longman & Mein	18	15	8
	To D° in Wright & Gill v Mein	15	5	8
		£ 55	3	6
	Add for short Cast in accot of Mein		3	8
		55	7	2

~~The Affair in the Admiralty is omitted for the Present, Mr Price has promised to give me the Particulars Tomorrow — I had much rather leave them to Mr Hancock's Pleasure but if he chooses to have me make an Account of it I will do it tomorrow.~~

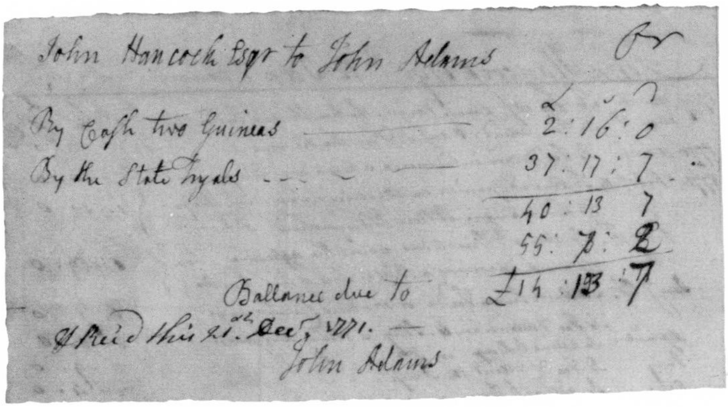
John Hancock Esqr to John Adams Cr

	£	s	d
By Cash two Guineas	2	16	0
By the State Tryals	37	17	7
	40	13	7
	55	7	2
Ballance due to	£14	13	7

Recd this 21st. Decr. 1771. —
John Adams

4. JOHN HANCOCK'S ACCOUNT WITH JOHN ADAMS

the said last Will, was by the said J[oseph] Executor as aforesaid, presented to the then Judge of the Probate of Wills &c. for said County, to whom the Probate thereof appertained, and the same last Will was by the same Judge, then and there duely proved and approved an authenticated Copy of which Will and the Probate thereof in Court shall be produced and the said Joseph then and there accepted the said Trust, and undertook the Administration, of the said Testators Estate, according to the Tenor and Intent of said Will, and received all the said Estate into his Hands for that Purpose and thereby became obliged to pay the Legacy aforesaid to the Plaintiff according to the Will and Intent of said Testator and in Consideration thereof, promised at &c.—on &c., but hath not paid it tho [requested?] often and at &c.—on &c.

To the Damage &c.

[XX]

Debt. For not exhibiting a true Inventory of the Testator's Effects.

Woodward vs. Fisher [80]

Attach &c. D[aniel] Fisher [*i.e.* as executor of Jeremiah Fisher] to answer Richard Woodward and D[eborah] his wife in a plea of Debt, for that the said J. on the 5th Day of Apl. made his last Will and Testament, and therein appointed his Son in Law N. Ames and his Son D. Fisher joint Executors of that his last Will &c. and thereby

[80] In the hand of one of JA's clerks, perhaps Jonathan Williams. Pleadings Book, p. [38–39]. The original writ in JA's hand is in Suffolk Inferior Court Files, Jan. 1773, No. 71. At the end of the declaration JA wrote out a plea of the general issue (nil debet), which the defendant, Daniel Fisher, signed. JA added a joinder of issue, but the plea was apparently withdrawn in favor of a demurrer to a sham plea filed for Fisher by Josiah Quincy Jr. There is no record of the result, but it must have favored Fisher, because the Woodwards' appeal was entered at the Feb. 1773 Superior Court. The case was settled before trial. In JA's Docket for this term, MQA, appears the notation "Ag[ree]d. 10d. Rec'd. £2 2s. 8d. in full." See SCJ Rec. 1773–1774, fol. 6; Min. Bk. 98, SCJ Suffolk, Feb. 1773, N–3. This suit by a residuary legatee against a surviving executor is based on the executor's statutory duties. See note 83 below; see also note 37 above. Dr. Nathaniel Ames, the deceased executor, was the father of Fisher Ames and Dr. Nathaniel Ames Jr., whose political differences epitomized the split between Massachusetts Federalists and Jeffersonians in the forty years after the Revolution. Deborah Woodward, one of the plaintiffs, was Deborah Fisher Ames, daughter of the testator (who had died in 1766) and widow of Nathaniel Ames Sr. She married Richard Woodward on 23 Feb. 1772. Suffolk Files, Births, Marriages, Deaths, 1637–1774, No. 398. See Samuel Eliot Morison, *By Land and by Sea* 200–207 (N.Y., 1953); Charles Warren, *Jacobin and Junto* 4–5, 25 (Cambridge, Mass., 1931). For an earlier JA case between Deborah Ames and Daniel Fisher over Jeremiah Fisher's will, see Fisher v. Ames, Min. Bk. 91, SCJ Suffolk, March 1770, C–60; Feb. 1771, C–84; SF 101627, 101882; Adams Papers, Microfilms, Reel No. 185.

gave and bequeathed to the said D[eborah] among other things an uncertain residuary Legacy and on   died, leaving a considerable Estate there and elsewhere, both real and personal, and among many other things leaving a Bond under the Hand and Seal of S. Laucher,[81] &c. bearing Date, wherein and whereby the said S. Laucher bound himself to the said J.F. who was then living in the Sum of £80, conditiond per the payment to the said J. (his Executors &c.) of the Sum of £40 13 4 of L[awful] m[one]y with law[ful] Interest therefor on &c.; which Bond was the property of the said J.F. at his Death and thin [i.e. then] due and wholly unpaid. And the said Daniel undertook to execute the said Will (the said N. the other Executor in said Will having died before the Testator at said Dedham) and on &c. presented the said Will to the Honble. T. Hutchinson Esqr. Judge and Probate of Wills for the County[82] &c., who on   comitted the Administration of the said J's Estate, accordingly to his Son in Law N. Ames, and his Son D. Fisher Executors in the same Will named, well and faithfully to execute the said Will and to administer the Estate of said Deceased according thereunto, and to make a true and perfect Inventory of all and singular the Goods, Chattles &c. of said Deceased and to exhibit the same into the Registry of the Court of Probate for the County &c. at or before the Day—And also to rendir a plain and true Account of said Administration upon Oath, and the foremention'd Bond then came to the said D[aniel]'s Hands and Knowledge—Yet the said D. did not give Bond pursuant to the Law in that Case provided to pay the Debts and Legacies of the said J. and tho the Judge of Probate &c. did not enlarge the time for the said D's rendering into his Register's Office a full and true Inventory of the said J's whole Estate upon Oath beyound the said Day of &c. and notwithstanding the Honble. T.H. Esqr. on Judge on —— caused the said D to be cited to appear at the Probate Office &c. to exhibit more particularly a full and true Inventory of the Estate of the said J. yet the said D. has not exhibited into the said Office an Inventory of the said Bond, or any Sum of Money due to said Estate for or upon it altho' the said D. before &c. had

<hr>

[81] "Samuel Louchlen" in the file copy of the writ. Suffolk Inferior Court Files, Jan. 1773, No. 71.

[82] Thomas Hutchinson was judge of probate for Suffolk County from 1752 to 1769. In August of the latter year, he was succeeded by his brother, Foster. See Whitmore, *Mass. Civil List* 80; 8 Sibley-Shipton, *Harvard Graduates* 163. The copyist here has omitted Hutchinson's full title, a statement that he "proved and approved" the will, and a repetition of his name. (JA in the original had inadvertently called him "Foster" as well as "Thomas.") Suffolk Inferior Court Files, Jan. 1773, No. 71.

demanded and received the principal and Interest due upon said Bond of the said S. Laucher, whereby and by Force of the Acts of this Province in that case provided [83] the said D has forfeited to the Plaintiff the sum of £3200 for thirty two Months Neglect therein from &c. to —— which he has not paid but unjustly detains to the damage ——.

Adams

[XXI]

CASE. For a false Return.

Pierpont vs. Phipps. [84]

Summon David Phips of Cambridge in our County of Middlesex Esqr. and Sheriff of said County of Middlesex to answer Robert Pierpont of Boston in said County of Suffolk Gentleman in a plea of Tres-

[83] The suit here is based upon the Act of 26 Jan. 1739, c. 23, 2 A&R 977, which provided an "action of debt" for "any uncertain or residuary legatee" against an executor taking up his charge, who "against the tenor of the law in that case provided" should neglect "to give in a full and true inventory of the whole estate of the deceased, so far as is then come to his hands or knowledge, being duly served with a citation from the judge of probate to that purpose." The executor was to forfeit £100 per month for every month's neglect, "over and above the penalty already provided." The earlier statute referred to is the Act of 22 Nov. 1703, c. 12, §1, 1 A&R 536, providing that an executor who submitted a will to probate must within three months thereafter "(or at such further and longer time as the judge of probate shall see meet to allow, the circumstances of any estate requiring the same)" exhibit his inventory, or else give bond to pay the testator's debts and legacies. The penalty was forfeiture of £5 a month for each month's neglect to be recovered in accordance with a still earlier Act that established penalties for not presenting a will. That measure, the Act of 1 Nov. 1692, c. 14, §2, 1 A&R 45, provided for the recovery of forfeitures "by action or information, in the inferiour court of pleas in the same county, and to be disposed of, one moiety thereof to the use of the poor of the town where the deceased person last dwelt, and the other moiety to him or them that shall inform or sue for the same."

[84] In the hand of one of JA's clerks, probably Jonathan Williams. Pleadings Book, p. [40–42]. The records of this case have not been found. According to JA's Office Book, Suffolk Inferior Court, Oct. 1772, MQA, he received a fee of 12s., but the writ was "Not served." The original of the writ, first prepared for the Oct. court but redated 21 Oct. 1772 and altered to the Jan. 1773 court, appears in SF 91338. On its verso are the words, "This action is satisfied, per Robt. Pierpont." Pierpont's original action against William Barber was a suit on a note for £223 os. 4d. sterling. His recovery at the April 1771 Suffolk Inferior Court was affirmed with costs in both courts on his complaint at the Aug. 1771 Superior Court when Barber did not prosecute his appeal. SCJ Rec. 1771, fol. 226; Min. Bk. 95, SCJ Suffolk, Aug. 1771, N–69; SF 101969. No copy of the execution has been found. According to the Minute Book, it was dated 9 Sept. 1771 and was "del[ivered to the] Creditor." For another JA case involving Pierpont, see Pierpont v. Cutler, discussed in 2 JA, *Diary and Autobiography* 8–9. Trespass on the case was the common remedy against the sheriff for his neglect, or that of his deputy, in serving process, levying execution, and the like. See 3 Dane, *Abridgment* 75; 1 Chitty, *Pleading* 69, 73, 140–141; 4 Bacon, *Abridgment* 442. See also Quincy, *Reports* 295–296. For forms, see Perham, *American Precedents* 222–231; 2 Chitty, *Pleading* 352–355.

pass upon the Case, for that the said Robert by the Consideration of our Justices of our Superior Court of Judicature Court of Assize and general Goal Delivery holden at Boston within our County of Suffolk, and for our County of Suffolk, on the lastt Tuesday of August in the eleventh Year of our Reign, recoverd Judgment against William Barber in our County of Middlesex Merchant for the sum of £227 16s. 2d. L[awful] M[one]y of ⟨*Massachusetts*⟩ Great Britain, Damage and for the sum of three Pounds, Seven Shillings and two Pence Lawfull Money of the Province of Massachusetts Bay, Cost of Suit, as to us appears of Record, and thereupon afterwards vizt. on the eleventh Day of September in the eleventh Year of our Reign, took out of the Clerks office of our said Court our Writ of Execution in Form as by the Law of this Province is prescribed [85] directed to the Sheriff of our said County of Middlesex, his under Sheriff or Deputy, returnable to our said Superior Court of Judicature Court of Assize and General Goal delivery holden at Boston within our said County of Suffolk, upon the third Tuesday of February there next and at Boston aforesaid, on the same eleventh day of September, in the said eleventh Year of our Reign, delivered the same to one Joseph Butler, then being and untill the return thereof and ever since continuing to be one of the said David's Deputy Sheriffs, for whose default and misconduct in this said Office the said David is answerable [86] which was by the said Joseph accordingly returned to the same Court in the following words and Figures vizt. "February 18 1772 Received Fifty two pounds Fourteen shillings on this Execution and order the officer to return this Execution so far satisfyed Robert Pierpont.

"Middlesex Feby. 18th 1772 I return this Execution but in part satisfyed as above by order of the Creditor Jos[ep]h Butler, Deputy Sheriff," as to us appears of Record.

[85] The form of the writ of execution in personal actions is prescribed in the Act of 3 June 1701, c. 2, §1, 1 A&R 460, and discussed at length in the dissenting opinion of Trowbridge, J., in Richmond v. Davis, Quincy, *Reports* 279–297 (SCJ Suffolk, March 1768). It called upon the sheriff or his deputy to render to the judgment creditor the cash value of his judgment in "the goods, chattels or lands" of the debtor, if they were acceptable to the creditor; otherwise the body of the debtor was to be taken and held until the debt was satisfied or discharged. This writ combined the features of the English *elegit* and *capias ad satisfaciendum,* but did not contain the provisions of the writs of *fieri facias* and *levari facias,* under which the sheriff could sell the debtor's land or effects and pay the creditor the proceeds. See 2 Bacon, *Abridgment* 348–352. This situation was partially remedied by the Act of 14 July 1772, c. 12, 5 A&R 207, by virtue of which the sheriff was empowered to sell the debtor's chattels, apparently confirming a settled practice. See Quincy, *Reports* 297 note.

[86] The clause beginning "for whose default" is omitted in the file copy of the writ. SF 91338.

Whereupon the said Robert Pierpont, afterwards vizt. on the twenty Third day of March in the twelfth Year of our Reign took out of the Clerks Office of the same Court our Alias Writ of Execution for one Hundred eighty eight pounds five shillings and ten pence Lawfull Money of Great Britain, and said sum of three Pounds seven shillings and two pence Lawfull Money of the Province aforesaid Costs of suit in form as by the Law of this Province is in such Cases prescribed [87] directed to the Sheriff of our said County of Middlesex, his under-sherriff or Deputy returnable to our superior Court of Judicature, and general Goal Delivery holden at Boston within our said County of Suffolk upon the last Tuesday of August then next and the said Robert afterwards at said Boston, on the same twenty third day of March in the twelvth Year of our Reign delivered our same alias Writ of Execution to the said Joseph Butler being then and ever since one of the said Davids Deputy Sheriffs for said County of Middlesex to be by him executed served and returned to our same Court according to our Command therein given: And the said Joseph might and could have executed served and returned the same accordingly, Yet the said Joseph Butler in no wise regarding his said office but contriving and fraudulently intending, him the said Robert in this behalf to injure, and deceive and him to hinder and wholly deprive of the Obtaining his Debt and Damages aforesaid, afterwards viz. on the twenty fifth day of August Anno Domini 1772 falsely and fraudulently made return of the same Execution to our same Court in the Words and figures following vizt. "Middlesex Ss. April [...] Received £100 L[awful] M[one]y in part of the within Execution equal to seventy Five Pounds Sterling." Robert Pierpont. ["] Middlesex Ss. August 25, 1772 Received one Hundred Pounds of Lawfull Money in Part Satisfaction of this Execution and paid the same over to the Creditor and took his Receipt as above therefor, the Creditor declining to levy this Execution on the real Estate of the Debtor [88] and having directed me not to take the Debtor's Body and I not being able to find any Goods or Chattels of the Debtor for the further Satisfaction of this Execution, do return it satisfied in Part as above mentioned. Joseph Butler Deputy Sherriff ["]

[87] The Act of 9 April 1742, c. 22, 2 A&R 1095, provided that, if an execution was returned unsatisfied or partially satisfied, the clerk of court might "*ex officio,* renew or make out an *alias* or *pluries* execution for the whole or the remainder, as the case may be, till the judgment be fully satisfied."

[88] Under the Act of 21 Nov. 1719, c. 9, §1, 2 A&R 150, when a creditor could not be satisfied out of the debtor's personal estate, if he "doth therefore think fit to levy upon the real estate" of the debtor, the sheriff was to proceed to have the lands appraised and an appropriate portion of them set off to the creditor.

And the said Robert avers that the said last mentioned Return is false and fraudulent, and that in Truth, the said Robert the Creditor aforesaid never did direct him the said Joseph Butler not to take the said William Barber the aforesaid Debtor's Body and the said Robert also further avers that after the delivery of the said last mentioned Execution to the said Joseph Butler and before the Return day thereof the said Joseph was able to find and well and easily might and could have found Goods and Chattels of the said Barbers the aforesaid Debtor within his the said Butlers Precinct in the further and full Satisfaction of that Execution by which false and fraudulent return the same Robert is not only deprived of his Remedy for the obtaining of the Damages aforesaid and Costs aforesaid against the said Barber, who always after the return last aforesaid in a place unknown to the said Robert hath been hiding and skulking and hath wholly concealed Person Goods and estate so that they cannot be come at but also the same Robert his Damages yet unpaid being £113 5s. 10d. of L[awful] M[one]y [89] of the Province aforesaid and the further sum of Three Shillings and nine Pence like Money of said Province for the two Executions aforesaid so as aforesaid recoverd both wholly Lost. To the Damage of the said Robert as he saith two Hundred Pounds.

[XXII]

[CASE *for diminution of water in a stream.*]

Clark vs. McCarney.[90]

Attach Michael McCarney, &c. to answer Richard Clark, &c. in a Plea of Trespass on the Case, for that one James Boies of said Milton

[89] The copyist has omitted the words "Of Great Britain and £3 7s. 2d. Lawful Money," which appear in the original writ. SF 91338.

[90] In JA's hand. Pleadings Book, p. [45–47]. The writ was presumably drawn by Samuel Fitch, who entered the action at the Oct. 1772 Suffolk Inferior Court. After Josiah Quincy Jr., representing McCarney, prayed oyer (note 58 above) and filed a plea in abatement (note 93 below), the case was continued for the plaintiff to file a replication. The records do not indicate who won in the Inferior Court, but it was Clark who appealed to the Aug. 1773 Superior Court. There, with Blowers and Fitch representing Clark, and JA and Quincy appearing for McCarney, the plea in abatement was overruled and the case was continued for trial. After numerous additional continuances, the action was finally "dismist the appellant being" dead, in Aug. 1777. Min. Bk., Inf. Ct. Suffolk, Oct. 1772, No. 91; SCJ Rec. 1775–1778, fol. 140; Min. Bk. 98, SCJ Suffolk, Aug. 1773, N–26; Min. Bk. 103, SCJ Suffolk, Aug. 1777, C–47.

This case, a dispute between the owners of two paper mills, illustrates the problem which arises when a stream's water level drops so much that it cannot supply all the riparian users. The plaintiff claimed that his was the earlier mill, and that the defendant consequently was bound to shut down in a time of shortage. Thus the

Gentleman on the Twenty ninth day of June A.D. 1765, was seized in Fee, and possess'd of a certain Paper Mill in said Milton,[91] with its appurtenances, erected and standing upon or near to Neponsit River, and also of the Right and Priviledge of, in, and unto the whole of the Stream of said River, and of the Head or Pond of Water therein, upon which Pond, or near to the same, the said Paper Mill stands, and from which Pond, or Head of Water the same Paper Mill was, and is supplied with Water to carry and work the same: and being then so seized and possessed of the said Paper Mill and its appurtenances, and of the said stream, Pond, and Head of Water, He the said James Boies, on the same 29. June A.D. 1765. at said Milton, by his Deed of that Date under his Hand and Seal, duely executed, acknowledged and recorded, and in Court to be produced, for a valuable Consideration in said Deed mentioned, among other Things, granted and conveyed to the said Richard Clark, and to his Heirs and Assigns forever in Fee simple, *the one Moiety or half Part in Common and undivided of the said Paper Mill, and the Appurtenances thereto belonging, together with the one Moiety or half Part of all the said James's Right and Interest in the Stream of Water aforesaid, the said Paper Mill to have the commanding Part of said Stream, from the first of May to the first day*

plaintiff relied on what has since become known as the rule of prior appropriation: "first in time is first in right." This principle is the law in the arid West today, but it is not now followed in Massachusetts, and was not the rule at common law in England. See Maass and Zobel, "Anglo-American Water Law: Who Appropriated the Riparian Doctrine?" 10 *Public Policy* 109–156 (1960). The common law followed the so-called riparian principle: every bona fide riparian proprietor has an equal right to the use of the stream, and must consequently suffer a proportionate diminution of that right when the stream falls. This point was not raised by the pleadings and was never passed upon in the Superior Court, due to the action's being dismissed. The fact that Clark seemed to rely on a prior appropriation theory suggests two possibilities: (1) he may have sought to assert a right by prescription, which would have had the same effect on the defendant as an application of the prior appropriation rule; (2) the Massachusetts lawyers may have, in substance, if not in form, followed the principle of priority. See note 108 below for a further discussion of this point. For other water cases, see Nos. 14, 18–21.

[91] Hutchinson to Lords Commissioners for Trade and Plantations, Sept. 1769, 25 Mass. Arch. 330: "I must acquaint your Lordships that a paper mill which had been erected in the Town of Milton within this Province having gone to ruin, one James Boies, who had sometimes improved this mill, about three or four years ago erected a new mill upon the same stream, about two miles distance from the former where more paper has been manufactured than had been at the former mill in the course of thirty years, and the undertaker meets with such encouragement that he is preparing to erect another paper mill near to the first mentioned and the owner of the first mill is also rebuilding that." This mill had apparently been the source of paper for John Mein's *Chronicle* (see Nos. 5 and 12). Arthur M. Schlesinger, *The Colonial Merchants and the American Revolution* 164 (N.Y., 1918). See Boies and Clark v. Russell, SF 91619 (Suffolk Inferior Court, 1771), for an action to collect an account for "fine Crown" paper and "foolscap."

of October following Yearly,[92] and the equal half of said stream the remaining Part of the Year forever. To Hold the said granted Premisses to him the said Richard, his Heirs and Assigns forever. By virtue of which said Grant, the said Richard then entered into, and became possessed, of the said granted Premisses, and hath ever since held the same. That since the making the Grant aforesaid to the said Richard, another Paper Mill hath been erected upon the same Stream and is supplied with Water from the same Pond or Head of Water aforesaid: That on the Thirtyeth Day of July last, at said Milton, the Water in said Neponsit River was so low, that it was not sufficient to supply both said Mills, and keep them both going in a proper Manner, at the same Time: Whereupon the said Richard, who was then and there improving his said Mill in making Paper, finding that the Water failed and that there was not sufficient to keep his said Mill going and at Work in a proper Manner, unless the other said Mill last built as aforesaid, which was then going, and the Water drawn off to supply it, was stopped, then and there went to the said Michael, who was then actually in the occupation and Improvement of the said other Mill, and keeping the same going, and drawing off the said Water, to supply the said other Mill, and acquainted him the said Michael with the Premisses, and that there was not sufficient Water to supply both the said Mills at that Time, and that his the said Richards Mill must stop, for Want of sufficient Water to keep it going unless he the said Michael would shutt his Water Gate and stop his Mill in order to give him the said Richard the whole Use and Command of the said Stream for that Time according to the Grant made to him as aforesaid: and he the said Richard then and there requested the said Michael to shut his the said Michaels Water Gate and to stop his said Mill accordingly, for that Time, and for the Purpose aforesaid: that the said Michael then and there absolutely refused to shut his said Water Gate and to stop his said Mill, tho thereto requested as aforesaid; but continued his said Water Gate open and to draw off the Water of said Stream from said Pond, and Head of Water therein and to keep his said Mill going: By means whereof the said Richard had not sufficient Water left to him to keep his said Mill going, and at Work in a proper manner, but was greatly hindered and retarded in the Use of his said Mill and in his Business, and his said Mill was Stopped for want of sufficient Water,

[92] *Boston Gazette,* 22 Feb. 1773, p. 4, col. 1: "To be Sold. The real Estate of Richard Clark, of Milton, near the Slit-Mill, Consisting of . . . upwards of Eight Acres of Land, with Half Part of the Paper Mill, and Utensils thereto belonging, with Half Part of the Negro Caesar and Half Benefit of three Apprentices. The Paper-Mill having the Command of the Water in the Summer Months."

and he could not proceed in his Business of making Paper for the space of 30 days. To the Damage &c. £150.

Plea in Abatement [93]

Suffolk Ss. Court of Common Pleas Octr. A.D. 1772.
  Richard Clark Plaintiff
           vs.
  Michael McCarney

And the said McCarney, by Josiah Quincy Jnr. his attorney comes and defends &c. When [94] &c and prays oyer of the said Deed of the

[93] The plea in abatement was a dilatory plea going to the sufficiency of a particular writ, rather than to the merits. Because of the distaste with which the courts affected to view such pleas, it was necessary under the strict common-law rules that the different causes for abatement be pleaded in proper order or else be waived. The order was: (1) the jurisdiction of the court; (2) the capacity of the plaintiff; (3) the capacity of the defendant; (4) the count or declaration; and (5) the writ. 1 Comyns, *Digest* 1-2. The first two matters pleaded here go to the capacity of the plaintiff. *Id.* at 11-14. The third item in the plea asserted a repugnancy or inconsistency in the declaration. *Id.* at 38-39. The fourth and fifth items seem to raise the defense of nontenure, a lack of capacity in the defendant. *Id.* at 27-28. Joseph Story's comments on similar pleas are a good example of the way in which such indigenous forms were later modified to conform to English practice: "It was the common practice in this Commonwealth, till within a few years, to take all objections to the writ and declaration, by a plea in abatement. The mode of assignment was to pray judgment of the writ; and then state the various objections, however numerous or different in nature, in regular display, (as causes are assigned on special demurrer) and then conclude the whole, united in *a single plea,* praying judgment of the writ, that it might be quashed. In this way misnomer, coverture, infancy, misjoinder, and defects of the count were united, and judgment given according to the prayer of the plea. So that in fact all defects in the declaration, which are now stated as causes of special demurrer, were tried by pleas in abatement. It is apprehended that this practice was irregular, when compared by English rules in many respects." Joseph Story, *A Selection of Pleadings in Civil Actions* 59-60 (Salem, Mass., 1805). The plea here obviously violates the common law principles of order. Moreover, it is faulty in two of the "many respects" which Story went on to enumerate: (1) It was improper to plead more than one matter in the same class. See Zuill v. Bradley, Quincy, *Reports* 6, 7 (SCJ Suffolk, Aug. 1762), apparently permitting such duplicity. (2) Despite older precedents, the 18th-century English view seems to have been that defects in the declaration should be raised on demurrer. See 1 Comyns, *Digest* 70; 5 Dane, *Abridgment* 708; see also 1 Chitty, *Pleading* 438, 442.

[94] The "defense" presented special problems in the plea in abatement. The "full defense," quoted in note 38 above, was in earlier practice considered improper for a plea in abatement, since it admitted most objections to jurisdiction and capacity. The correct usage was the "half defense": "comes and defends the force and injury and says." In the abbreviated form used here the addition of "when" was at first supposed to indicate a full defense, but later cases said that it could stand for either full or half. After three pages of learned discussion, Story concluded, "Indeed, since the common contraction of them is the same, and the Court will intend the abbreviation, either, according to the case in which they occur, ... there seems no objection to use the common form, 'comes and defends the force and injury, *when,* &c.' in all cases whatsoever." Story, *Pleadings* 3-4.

said James Boyes, to the said Richard Clarke, mentioned in the Plaintiff's said Writ and Declaration, and hath it, and the same is read to him the said McCarney in the Words and Tenor thereof, which appear by the said Deed filed in the Case; which said Deed being read and heard, the said McCarney saith that the Plaintiff's said Writ and Declaration are bad and ought to abate.

1. Because by the Plaintiff's own shewing in his said Writ and Declaration, that one James Boies is tenant in Common with the Plaintiff in the said Paper Mill, and in the said Right Priviledge and Interest, of and in the said Stream of Water, mentioned in the Plaintiff's said Writ and Declaration, which said James ought by Law to have joined in the said Action, brought against the said McCarney.[95]

2ly. Because by the said Deed of the said Boies to the said Clark in the Case, it appears, that the said Boies and Clark are Jointenants of the said Paper-Mill and the same Right, Priviledge and Interest in the said Stream of Water, which said Boies ought by Law, to have joined in the said Action, brought against the said McCarney.

3. Because by the Plaintiff's own shewing in his said Writ and Declaration he made a Demand upon the said McCarney for the whole Use and Command of the said Stream for that Time mentioned in the Plaintiff's Writ and Declaration: Whereas the said pretended Grant therein mentioned was only of the Commanding Part thereof; and for this supposed Denial, of this unwarrantable Demand of the said Clark, he hath brought his said Action.

4. Because the said Clark in his said Writ and Declaration, hath not anywhere suggested, or properly set forth, that the said McCarney had any Right or Authority to shut down said Water Gate, or stop said last erected Mill, whereof one Hugh McLean, and the said James Boies were at the Time of the supposed Denial and ever since Tenants in Common in Fee simple, and thereof then and ever since in actual and full Seisin and Possession.

5. Because the said McCarney would have been a Trespasser and Wrong Doer had he complied with and obeyed said Demand of the said Clark, for a Non Compliance of which, he hath brought his said Action. All which the said McCarney is ready to verify: wherefore he prays Judgment of the Writ and Declaration aforesaid; that the same may abate and for his Costs.

[95] See No. 18.

[XXIII]

DEBT upon a Bond.

Metcalf vs. Hall [96]

For Pleadings in a similar Case vid. 3 Ld. Ray. 275 &c.

Defendant pleads as follows.

Suffolk Ss. Common Pleas. July A.D. 1772

Hannah Metcalf Plaintiff vs. Jeremiah Hall Defendant.

[96] In JA's hand. Pleadings Book, p. [49–50]. JA, representing plaintiffs Hannah and Deborah Metcalf, filed a special demurrer to the plea printed here, which was decided in the plaintiffs' favor at the Jan. 1773 Suffolk Inferior Court. At the Superior Court in Feb. 1773 the demurrer was argued again and the previous decision on it upheld. The case was continued for "chancery" (determination of the actual damages). At the next term, one Hannah Messenger, who had related claims against defendant Jeremiah Hall, was admitted an additional plaintiff and the case was referred, the parties agreeing not to "employ any sworn Attorney to appear for them before said Refferees." The referees awarded the plaintiffs £105 damages and costs of £27 12s. 3d. SCJ Rec. 1773–1774, fol. 105; Min. Bk. 98, SCJ Suffolk, Feb. 1773, N–2; Aug. 1773, C–49; SF 102308. The suit was brought on a bond for £213 6s. 8d. given to Hannah and Deborah Metcalf by Hall to secure his performance of an agreement of the same date (the "sarting Articals" of the plea) under which he took control of all their real and personal estate, agreeing to pay certain debts for them and to provide for them until the funds were exhausted. According to Hall's statement in the file, the suit was instigated by Ezekiel Needham, with whose son Hall was currently in litigation. See note 42 above. Needham, seeking to ruin Hall, had first persuaded the ladies to leave the latter's house and had personally removed their household goods, making it impossible for Hall to perform his obligations. The statement continued, "and if this ant a most wicked abusive transaction done to me who have almost put my life in my hand in their troubles and all because I ask them for my Just Right which is as justly due to me Now as ever a Copper was due to any Man on Earth." Hall's account is borne out by the fact that Needham endorsed the Metcalfs' writ, but there was also testimony in the file that Hall had not been taking proper care of his charges. SF 102308.

The plea printed here was presumably drawn by Josiah Quincy Jr., who represented Hall in the Inferior Court. Oyer of the bond and condition (note 58 above) was followed by an affirmative plea of performance. JA's demurrer (SF 102308) began with a clause "protesting" that Hall had not performed his obligation as he had pleaded. This was a *protestando*, used in a plea or replication that traversed only part of a preceding pleading to avoid a conclusive admission of the part not traversed. The device was ordinarily not used in a demurrer, perhaps on the assumption that admissions on demurrer were not conclusive in any event. There was little or no authority to the latter effect in the 18th century, however, and occasional examples of the practice are found. See Shipman, *Common-law Pleading* 282–293, 358–359; Sutton, *Personal Actions* 112–113, 177–179; Story, *Pleadings* 322–323; 6 Dane, *Abridgment* 213; John Lilly, *Modern Entries* 231 (London, 2d edn., 1741); 5 Comyns, *Digest* 115–116, 126–127. See also Lee v. Boothby, 1 Keble 720, 83 Eng. Rep. 1205 (K.B. 1676). The remainder of the demurrer, in form similar to that in Apthorp v. Gardiner, No. 9, Doc. III, asserted that the plea was insufficient because Hall had not "set forth in certain what those Sarting Articals and Agreement indented, and bearing even date with the said Bond, made between

73

And the said Hall comes and defends &c. and craves oyer of the said obligation and it is read to him &c. He likewise craves oyer of the Condition of the same obligation, and it is read to him in these Words, Ss.

"The condition of this obligation is such, that if the above bounden Jeremiah Hall, his Heirs, Executors, Administrators or Either of them, shall and do, for his, or their Part, in all manner and every Thing, or Things, well and truly observe, perform, fulfill, accomplish, all and singular the Covenants and Agreements whatsoever, which on his or their Part are or ought to be observed, as menshened in a sarting Articals and Agreements indented and baring Evin Date with theis Presents made between Jeremiah Hall, on the one Part and Hannah Metcalf and Debory Met[calf] on the other Parte, whose Names are abovementioned, and that in and by all Things, According to the said Articals, with ought Covent,[97] then this present obligation to be void and of none Effect, or else to remain in full Force and vartor [virtue] during there Lives."

Which being read and heard, the said Jeremiah Hall saith that the said Hannah and Deborah Metcalf, their Action aforesaid thereof, against him ought not to have or maintain, because he saith, that he the said Jeremiah Hall, for his Part, in all Manner and in every Thing and Things well and truly hath observed, performed, fullfilled, accomplished, all and singular, the Covenants and Agreements, whatsoever which on his Part, are, or ought to be observed, as menshened in a Sarting Articals and Agreements indented and baring even Date with the said Bond, made between Jeremiah Hall, on the one Part and Hannah Metcalf and Debory Metcalf on the other Parte, whose Names are mentioned in the same Bond, and in and by all Things, according to the said Articals, with ought Covent.[98] And this the said Jeremiah

---

Jeremiah Hall on the One part and Hannah Metcalf and Deborah Metcalf on the other part mentioned in the said Jeremiah's said Plea, were in particular, as he ought to have done." The court's decision upholding the demurrer was in accord with English authority to the effect that when the condition of a bond was to perform the covenants in an indenture, the defendant must set out at least the substance of the indenture. See Stephen, *Pleading* 366–368; 2 Chitty, *Pleading* 530–532; Story, *Pleadings* 240–241; Jevens v. Harridge, 1 Saund. 8, 9, 85 Eng. Rep. 8, 12 (K.B. 1678). The citation in the next line of the text is to Chaloner v. Davis, 3 Ld. Raym. 273, 92 Eng. Rep. 684 (C.P. 1696), a declaration in covenant on a performance bond. See 1 Ld. Raym. 400, 91 Eng. Rep. 1166.

[97] Thus in MS, and in the file copies of the Inferior Court record and the actual bond. The file copy of the plea reads "without covent." SF 102308. The reading in the text here seems the correct one. The meaning is probably "with all things covenanted."

[98] In the text of the file copy of the plea (SF 102308) the passage beginning "for his Part, in all Manner . . ." and ending at this point is in quotes, indicating that the pleader was reciting performance in terms of the condition of the bond. This

Hall is ready to verify: Wherefore he prayeth Judgment, if the said Hannah and Deborah their Action aforesaid thereof against him, ought to have or maintain.

J[osiah] Q[uincy]

[XXIV]

Replevin. Of a Sloop hypothecated.

Rob. Mercer and Jno. Ramsay vs. Edward Moffat.[99]

[SEAL] Suffolk Ss. George the third by the Grace of God of Great Britain, France and Ireland, King, Defender of the Faith &c.

---

would have been sufficient had the condition not referred to covenants in the indenture. See Stephen, *Pleading* 362–366.

[99] In JA's hand. Pleadings Book, p. [53–55]. The writ, drawn by Samuel Fitch, is dated 27 Nov. 1772. It and the bond are in the Suffolk Inferior Court Files, Jan. 1773, No. 268. No record of subsequent pleadings or of the outcome has been found. The action of replevin was unique among common-law forms, in that prior to suit the plaintiff could have redelivery of a chattel alleged to have been wrongfully taken and detained by the defendant. If judgment for the plaintiff then followed, he might be awarded damages for the taking; otherwise the court ordered a return of the goods to the defendant. Unless he had not taken the goods, the defendant ordinarily pleaded a so-called "avowry" in which he justified the taking by stating affirmatively his claim to the chattel. The plaintiff then responded with a plea, and the pleadings proceeded as in other actions, but with the roles reversed. See Sutton, *Personal Actions* 91–94, 166; 1 Chitty, *Pleading* 162. Replevin originally could be brought only by one injured through wrongful distress (the taking of chattels from a wrongdoer to satisfy his liability). Although Blackstone still considered the action as thus limited, it had in fact earlier been expanded by the courts to include other wrongful takings. In 18th-century England there was authority supporting the latter position, but the action seems to have been limited in practice to cases of distress. See James Barr Ames, *Lectures on Legal History* 69–70 (Cambridge, Mass., 1913); 3 Holdsworth, *History of English Law* 285 note; 1 Chitty, *Pleading* 159 note; 3 Blackstone, *Commentaries* *146; 4 Bacon, *Abridgment* 384–385; Sir Geoffrey Gilbert, *The Law of Distresses and Replevins* 157–165, 257–342 (London, 1757).
In Massachusetts the Act of 10 June 1698, c. 6, §2, 1 A&R 322, permitted owners of cattle taken damage-feasant to bring replevin; a later Act, prescribing a form of the writ substantially like that followed here, provided that the action could not be brought against an officer distraining goods for taxes, fines, and forfeitures. Act of 6 Dec. 1720, c. 13, §2, 2 A&R 188. After the Revolution, a Massachusetts statute extended replevin to goods taken other than by distress. Act of 24 June 1789, §4, [1788–1789] Acts and Resolves 430–436. Although this enactment might be construed to mean that the prior practice had been narrower, the fact that the Act of 19 Feb. 1787, [1786–1787] Acts and Resolves 182–187, had established the writ of de homine replegiando, earlier used without statute in a slavery case, No. 40, suggests that the 1789 measure merely codified existing law. The instant case supports this view, since it does not involve a distress.
The use of replevin here is of particular interest because of the maritime nature of the subject matter. The contract of "bottomree" (i.e. bottomry), under which the plaintiffs claimed an interest, was a common device for financing marine ventures, in which the lender was secured by a lien on the vessel, but could receive payment only if she reached port safely. The transaction here was a loan to the master of a

To the Sherriff or Marshall of the said County of Suffolk, his Under-
sherriff or Deputy, or Constable of Boston within the said County
or to any or Either of them, Greeting.

In his Majestys Name you are required, to replevie the sloop or
Vessell called the Industry of the Burden of about Twenty five Tons,
with her Tackle and Apparel belonging to Robert Mercer and John
Ramsay of our City of New York in our County and Province of New
York, Merchants, now distrained kept or impounded by Edward
Moffat, now residing in Boston in our said County of Suffolk Mariner,
and deliver the said sloop or Vessell with her Tackle and Apparell unto
the said Robert Mercer and John Ramsay: And summons the said
Edward Moffat to appear before our Justices of our Inferior Court of
Common Pleas, next to be holden at Boston, within and for our
County of Suffolk aforesaid, on the first Tuesday of January next, then
and there in our said Court to answer to the said Robert Mercer and
John Ramsay, in a Plea of Replevin: For that the said Sloop or Vessell,
on the first day of January Anno Domini 1771 was at New York, a
Place so called vizt. in Boston aforesaid upon a Voyage from New
Providence one of our Bahama Islands, and back again, and was
greatly out of Repair, and in Want of many Necessaries, as well to
repair and refit the said Vessell as to furnish her with stores and other
Things necessary to enable her to prosecute pursue, and finish the said
Voyage, and one John Petty Mariner was then and there legal Master
of said Sloop or Vessell and had the Care and command of her, for
and during the said Voyage, and was thereunto duely authorized and

---

vessel for ship's necessaries in a foreign port, for which the owners were not personally liable; the customary remedy was a libel *in rem* in Admiralty. This was a
proceeding beyond the power of the common law, brought directly against the
vessel, in which she could be seized and sold to meet demands secured by maritime
liens. Although the common-law courts had severely restricted the Admiralty jurisdiction in the 18th century, this was one variety of action which, for want of another
remedy, was excepted from the restriction. See Gilmore and Black, *Law of Admiralty* 480–519; Arthur Browne, *A Compendious View of the Civil Law and of
the Law of Admiralty*, 2:84–85, 195–196 (London, 2d edn., 1802); Charles
Molloy, *De Jure Maritimo et Navali*, bk. 2, c. 11, §11 (London, 8th edn., 1744);
8 Holdsworth, *History of English Law* 261–263. This case came up at a time when
the Massachusetts Vice Admiralty Court was being attacked for its role in enforcing
the Acts of Trade. See vol. 2:102–104, notes 17, 22, 24. The declaration here thus
may represent an ingenious attempt to avoid the necessity of proceeding in
Admiralty by using the only common law form which, like a libel *in rem,* was concerned not with personal liability, but with rights in the *res.* In all probability the
tactic failed. Assuming that replevin lay in a case other than distress, a wrongful
taking from one with possession or the immediate right to possession was nevertheless
a necessary element. See 1 Chitty, *Pleading* 158–160; Abbott, *Shipping* 101; Gilmore and Black, *Law of Admiralty* 480–482.

appointed, and was necessitated to take upon the Adventure of said Sloop or Vessell the sum of two hundred and Eighty four Pounds Twelve shillings and five Pence current Money of our said Province of New York, for making Repairs, and discharging the Repairs made upon said Vessell,[100] and furnishing her with Necessaries to set forth on, and pursue her said Voyage, and without which She could not have proceeded on said Voyage: which said sum the said Robert Mercer and John Ramsay, supplied and paid to the said John Petty, for the Purpose aforesaid, at his Request, at the Rate of Eight Pounds Per Cent for said sum, for and during the said Voyage: And the said John Petty, then and there, vizt. on the said first day of January Anno Domini 1771 at said Place called New York viz. in Boston aforesaid, by a certain Bill, or Instrument in Writing of Bottomree, and Hypothecation[101] of that Date under his Hand and Seal, duely executed and in Court to be produced, in Consideration of the said Sum, supplied and paid him as aforesaid, did covenant grant, promise and agree to and with the said Robert Mercer and John Ramsay that the said Sloop or Vessell should depart from the Port of the said City of New York on her said Voyage to Providence on or before the tenth day of January aforesaid and as Wind and Weather would permit, should proceed on her said Voyage without Delay: And the said John Petty further, by the same Instrument, or Bill of Bottomree and Hypothecation, for the Consideration aforesaid, did then and there, vizt. on the said first day of January aforesaid at said Place called New York vizt. in Boston aforesaid, grant, bind, hypothecate and pledge the said sloop or Vessell, with the Freight, Tackle and Apparel of the same, to the said Robert Mercer and John Ramsay their Executors, Administrators and Assigns to pay them the full sum of £307 currant Money of our said Province of New York in 10 days next after the said Sloop or Vessell Arrived at Providence aforesaid; and the said John Petty did then and there by the same Instrument or Bill, further covenant with the said Robert Mercer and John Ramsay, that the said Sloop or Vessell, with her freight, Tackle, and Apparell, should at all Times after the said Voyage be lyable and chargeable to and with the Payment of the said sum of £307 currant Money aforesaid, to them the said Robert Mercer

---

[100] That is, discharging liens for repairs already made.

[101] A civil-law term meaning a pledge in which the pledgor retained possession of the *res*. Black, *Law Dictionary*. In later usage the term was expressly applied to the kind of transaction here, to distinguish it from ordinary bottomry, in which a loan was made to the owner in his home port and on his personal credit, as well as on the credit of the vessel. 2 Browne, *Civil Law* 196–197. The principal work on maritime law in use before the Revolution did not make the distinction, however. See Molloy, *De Jure Maritimo*, bk. 2, c. 11, §11.

and John Ramsay; and by the same Instrument or Bill it was then and there further provided, declared and agreed by and between the said Parties to the same, that in Case the said Sloop or Vessell should be lost, miscarry, or be cast away before her Arrival at Providence aforesaid, that then the Payment of the said sum of £307 current Money afore-said should not be demanded or be recovered by the said Robert Mercer and John Ramsay; and that the loss thereby should be wholly born and sustained by them; and that every Act, matter and Thing in said Instrument or Bill contained, on the Part and Behalf of the said John Petty, should be void: And the said Robert Mercer and John Ramsay aver, that the said Sloop or Vessell did depart from the said Port of the City of New York as aforesaid, and within the Time limited for her departure as aforesaid: and did proceed on her said Voyage, and arrived safely at Providence aforesaid on the 10th. day of Feby. Anno Domini 1771, and was not lost nor did she miscarry, nor was she cast away: And that the said sum of £307 (which is equal in Value to £230 5s. Lawfull Money of our Province of the Massachusetts Bay) hath never been paid to them the said Robert Mercer and John Ramsay or any Part thereof; whereby the said Sloop or Vessell with her Tackle and Apparel hath become forfeited, and belongs to them, and that they ought to be in Possession of the same. And that the said Edward Moffat, on the 16 day of October last at Boston aforesaid took the said Sloop or Vessell with her Tackle and Apparell belonging to the said Robert Mercer and John Ramsay the present Plantiffs: and the said sloop or Vessell, with her said Tackle and Apparell carried away and kept at a Place called the Long Wharf in Boston aforesaid, and there unjustly detained against Pledges and Sureties till this day; which is to the Damage of the said Robert Mercer and John Ramsay as they say the sum of £300 lawfull Money aforesaid, as shall then and there appear, with other due Damages: Provided the said Robert Mercer and John Ramsay give Bond to the Value of £300 lawfull Money aforesaid, with sufficient surety or sureties to prosecute their said Replevin, at the said next inferiour Court of common Pleas, and so from Court to Court untill the Cause be ended, and to pay such Costs and Damages as the said Edward Moffat shall recover against them. Hereof fail not and make due return of this Writ with your Doings therein unto the said Court. Witness Eliakim Hutchinson Esqr. &c.

[XXV]

DEBT ON JUDGMENT.

[*Palmer v. Noyes*] [102]

Attach &c. to answer unto Joseph Palmer of &c. in our said County of Suffolk Merchant in a Plea of Debt for that the said Joseph by the Consideration of our Justices of our Inferior Court of Common Pleas

[102] Possibly in the hand of Nathan Rice, JA's clerk. Pleadings Book, p. [56]. The action was commenced, with Thomas Flucker, secretary of the Province, as co-plaintiff, in the April 1773 Suffolk Inferior Court; the writ, dated 10 Feb. 1773, is in JA's hand. Suffolk Inferior Court Files, April 1773, No. 217. Noyes defaulted, and judgment of £39 13s. 10d. and costs was entered. (No explanation appears for the two-shilling discrepancy between this figure and the figures in the declaration.) At the Aug. 1773 Suffolk Superior Court, the defendant failed to prosecute his appeal, and judgment was entered for plaintiffs on an affirmation in the sum of £40 9s. 4d. and £4 11s. costs. SCJ Rec. 1773–1774, fol. 113; Min. Bk. 98, SCJ Suffolk, Aug. 1773, N–47; SF 102305. JA represented Palmer; Benjamin Kent, Noyes. The file papers indicate that the original action concerned payment for 69 hats and two pieces of "English duck." The defendant defaulted. Min. Bk., Inf. Ct. Suffolk, Oct. 1771, No. 139.

A recent statute had created a direct "action of debt" on a judgment. Act of 6 March 1773, c. 32, 5 A&R 231, 232. Ostensibly, this statute merely remedied the problem that arose because "when judgment is rendered, if the party obtaining it dies, no execution can be sued out thereon, without a writ of *scire facias* being first brought and prosecuted with effect; and because, upon a writ of *scire facias*, neither the goods or estate of the debtor can be attached, nor his body taken, the debt may be lost." (A *scire facias* had the effect of reviving the judgment, but a new execution was necessary. R. Pound and T. F. T. Plucknett, *Readings on the History and System of the Common Law* 449 [Rochester, N.Y., 3d edn., 1927].) But the statute is very broad, and provides that "when judgment is given in any court of record, and remaineth in force, the party obtaining it, his or their executors or administrators, may, instead of a writ of *scire facias*, have and maintain an action of debt upon such judgment, in the same court where the record thereof remaineth." 5 A&R 232. This is the only Province statute on the point, but the action of debt on a judgment was used in Massachusetts before 1773. See, for example, Tirrell v. Clark, SF 85178 (Suffolk Inferior Court 1764), in which JA drew a writ almost identical to the one here. For later forms, see Perham, *American Precedents* 271–272.

The statute seems to have embodied the English rule that if a plaintiff "hath once obtained a judgment against another for a certain sum, and neglects to take out execution thereupon, he may afterwards bring an action of debt upon this judgment, and shall not be put upon the proof of the original cause of action; but upon shewing the judgment once obtained, still in full force, and yet unsatisfied, the law immediately implies, that by the original contract of society the defendant hath contracted a debt, and is bound to pay it. . . . [But] actions of debt upon judgment in personal suits have been pretty much discountenanced by the courts, as being generally vexatious and oppressive, by harrassing the defendant with the costs of two actions instead of one." 3 Blackstone, *Commentaries* *158–159. The common-law action was also available to an executor. 1 Dane, *Abridgment* 161. Debt was the sole remedy here, because indebitatus assumpsit could not be brought on a judgment. James Barr Ames, *Lectures on Legal History* 160 (Cambridge, Mass., 1913); 8 Holdsworth, *History of English Law* 89. The 1773 Act may have been deemed necessary because the whole process of levy of execution in Massachusetts was statutory. See notes 85, 87, 88, above.

holden at Boston within and for our County of Suffolk aforesaid on the first Tuesday of October Anno Domini 1771 recovered Judgment by the Names and Additions of Joseph Palmer &c. both in our said County, against the said Joseph Noyes for the sum of 36 pounds 14/ and 4 pence of Law[ful] M[one]y Damage and two pounds 17/ and 6d. Costs of Suit, as by the record thereof in our said Court remaining appears which Judgment remains in its full force and Unsatisfied whereby an Action hath arisen to the Plaintiff to recover those sums against the said Joseph Noyes yet he hath not either of them, tho often requested but detains them.

[XXVI]

EJECTMENT by Lease, Entry and Ouster.

Laughton vs. Pitts et als.[103]

Summon James Pitts Esq. Charles Dabney and James Sumner &c. to answer to William Laughton, of Boston &c. Tayler, in a Plea why they the said James Pitts, Charles Dabney and James Sumner, with Force and Arms a Part of a Messuage, Part of a shop and other Buildings, with two certain strips or Parcells of Land, under and adjoining thereto, situate in said Boston and bounded as follows vizt. &c. [*one line blank in MS*][104] with the Appurtenances, which William Warden of said Boston Peruke maker and Sarah his Wife, demised to the said William Laughton for a Term which is not yet past, entered and

---

[103] In the hands of JA and a clerk, possibly Jonathan Williams. Pleadings Book, p. [57]. The writ, dated 21 June 1773, was drawn by Sampson Salter Blowers, who represented Laughton in both the Inferior and Superior courts. The original writ in Blowers' hand, with pleadings signed by JA, is in Suffolk Inferior Court Files, July 1773, No. 286. JA was of counsel for the defendants throughout the litigation. In July 1773 at the Suffolk Inferior Court, Laughton was awarded possession on a demurrer to JA's plea that the defendants "do not know the said William Laughton." At the Superior Court in Aug. Laughton prevailed again on the defendants' confession of judgment for possession and costs. SCJ Rec. 1773–1774, fol. 108; Min. Bk. 98, SCJ Suffolk, Aug. 1773, N–15; SF 102278. This is an action of ejectment in the form commonly employed in the English courts. The declaration alleges a lease, collusive or fictitious, from the party claiming the premises to a straw or nonexistent person, in whose name the proceeding is actually brought. Compare note 18 above; see also No. 17, note 5. Although these proceedings might reflect an arms' length transaction between the parties, that they do not here is indicated by a bill of costs in the file drawn by Blowers as attorney for "Laughton on the Case of Warden et ux. appellees vs. Pitts et al. appellants." SF 102278. Further, on the Inferior Court writ, cited above, the name Warden has been crossed out and that of Laughton written in.

[104] The premises were between Marlboro (now Washington) Street and Bishop's Alley (now Hawley Street). SF 102278.

him from his farm [105] aforesaid ejected, and committed other outrages upon him to the great Damage of the said William Laughton, and against our Peace,

And whereupon the same William Laughton complains and saith that the said William Warden and Sarah his Wife on the Sixteenth day of this present June, in the 13 Year of our Reign at Boston aforesaid in the County aforesaid demised to the same William Laughton the Tenements aforesaid with the appurtenances to have and to hold to the same aforesaid William Laughton and his assigns, the same Tenements aforesaid, with the appurtenances, from the said sixteenth day of June aforesaid for and during the full Term of three Years, from thence next ensuing to be compleat and ended, by Virtue of which demise, the same William Laughton into the Tenements aforesaid with the Appurtenances entered and was thereof possessed; and he the said William Laughton being so thereof possessed, the said James Pitts, Charles Dabney and James Sumner, afterwards, to wit, the same 16 day of June aforesaid with Force and arms &c. into the Tenements aforesaid with the Appurtenances which the said William Warden and Sarah his wife, to the said William Laughton demised in form aforesaid for the Term aforesaid which is not yet passed, entered, and him the said William Laughton from his farm aforesaid ejected, and other outrages they the said James Pitts, Charles Dabney, and James Sumner, then and there did against our peace and to the Damage &c.

[XXVII]

CASE for diverting Water from a Trench, Mill and Land.

Boies vs. Gillespie.[106]

Attach A. Gillespie &c. to answer to J. Boies &c. in a Plea of Trespass on the Case, for that whereas the said J. Boies was on &c. to &c. seized in his Demesne as of fee of a certain Water Mill comonly called

---

[105] Not a reference to agricultural activity, but a literal translation of the original Latin form, meaning the leasehold itself. See 2 Chitty, *Pleading* 442 note.

[106] Possibly in the hand of Jonathan Williams, JA's clerk. Pleadings Book, p. [58–59]. The litigation dragged on for over 20 years. The original writ, bearing Josiah Quincy's name, dates from 21 Sept. 1773. SF 91749. Documentation has not been found for the proceedings at the Oct. 1773 Suffolk Inferior Court (although there is a suggestion that Samuel Fitch represented Gillespie), but Boies apparently prevailed, because the Superior Court and Supreme Judicial Court Records and Minute Books carry the case as "Gillespie v. Boies." Originally entered in Feb. 1774, Gillespie's appeal was continued to Aug. 1777, when it was dismissed for an unspecified "irregularity of the proceedings in the lower Court." SCJ Rec. 1775–1778,

the Slitting-Mill [107] and of a parcel of Land cont[ainin]g by Estimation 13 Acres or thereabouts near adjoining to said Mill with the Appurtenances situate on or near a Trench in a place between the upper and the lower dam so called in Milton aforesaid; and the said J. Boies and all those whose Estate he hath, in the Mill and parcel of Land aforesaid have and ought to have, and from time immemorial have been accustomed and ought to have the Benefit of a certain Water or Water-Course [108] commonly called Neponset River, running from a Spring in

fol. 141; Min. Bk. 103, SCJ Suffolk, Aug. 1777, C–74. Boies recommenced his action, which came to trial for the first time in the spring 1779 Suffolk Inferior Court. Gillespie again appealed, and filed a prayer "that a Jury may go uppon the Spot, in order that real Justis may be done, & the Matter Finish'd this Term." SF 102679b. After assorted continuances, the matter was apparently settled, for in SJC Rec. 1784, fol. 1, is the final notation: "Neither party appears." See also Min. Bk. 2, SJC Suffolk, Feb. 1784, C–1. For another suit between the same parties, see Boies v. Gillespie, Suffolk Inferior Court Files, April 1774, No. 202.

[107] *Boston Gazette*, 5 Nov. 1770, p. 3, col. 2: "The old Slitting Mills at Milton is now in good Repair: At which Place good NAIL RODS may be had at 30s. per Hundred."

[108] A consequence of the riparian system of water rights (note 90 above) is that the right to use of the water inheres in the very ownership of bankside realty. Unlike the prior appropriation system, where the right to water does not exist unless and until the water is actually used, the riparian system confers on the proprietor a perpetual right to the flow of water. A riparian landowner can lose his water right in only two ways: he can grant it to another proprietor; or he can suffer another proprietor to take the right away by prescription (open and long-continued usurpation). To say that a right to water may be lost by prescription is not the same thing as saying that this right may be acquired only by prescription. The first thought is entirely compatible with the riparian system; the second is wholly foreign to it, being in fact another way of expressing the doctrine of prior appropriation. In the debate which has simmered for the past half-century on the issue whether the common law was appropriative or riparian, a focus of inquiry has been the old pleadings, particularly the declarations. Compare Wiel, "Waters: American Law and French Authority," 33 *Harv. L. Rev.* 133 (1919), with Maass and Zobel, "Anglo-American Water Law: Who Appropriated the Riparian Doctrine?" 10 *Public Policy* 109 (1960). It was argued that because so many of the old declarations used language importing prescription, the water rights involved must have depended on prescription; in other words, prior appropriation was the key to those rights. The counter-argument was that no matter how the pleadings read, the facts of the cases and the language of the judges indicated that water rights followed riparian ownership.

In the absence of reported judicial opinions, it is difficult to determine the 18th-century Massachusetts rule. The point was raised in neither the declaration nor the plea in Clark v. McCarney, Form XXII. Language in the present declaration ("from time immemorial have been accustomed and ought to have the Benefit of a certain Water or Water-Course") sounds in prescription; another "water" case in the Wetmore Notes, Symonds v. Traske (Essex Inferior Court? ca. 1771), likewise alleges "that a spring of Water ran thro' [plaintiff's land] for time immemorial . . . and still ought to run." Adams Papers, Microfilms, Reel No. 184. And all the relevant forms in Perham, *American Precedents* 196, 199–200, use similar language. But the Wetmore Notes show that counsel in Symonds v. Traske, at least, knew of English forms noting that the ancientness of the watercourse need not be alleged. See, for example, 1 Mallory, *Modern Entries* 482–483.

said Milton commonly called Charles River from thence to the said place there in said Milton commonly call'd the upper Dam and increases a certain Water-Course River, or Stream of Water, which runs from and by the said upper Dam thro' a certain place there call'd the Trench to the said Mill of the Plaintiff there situate between the said upper and lower Dam as aforesaid; And the said A. Gillespie well knowing the premises but maliciously contriving, and fraudulently intending him the said J. Boies of the profits and Commodity of his said Mill and parcell of Land altogether to deprive, on the Day of the purchase of this Writ and on divers other days and times between the said first day of J[anuar]y and the day of the purchase of this Writ in Dorchester aforesaid the Bank of Inclosure of the Water Course aforesaid which runs from the spring aforesaid and increases the Water-course River or Stream of Water aforesaid which runs as aforesaid from and by the said upper Dam thro' the Trench aforesaid to the Mill of the Plaintiff so much broke, cut, dug, carried away and threw down or caused to be cut, broke, dug, carried away and thrown down, and the Water aforesaid so much diverted or caused to be diverted that by means of the breaking, cutting, digging, carrying away, throwing down and diversion aforesaid, the said Mill of the Plaintiff call'd the Slitting Mill for want of sufficient Water running in the ancient Course thereof, could not slit or work so well or commodiously; and the said parcel of Land was greatly damnified, whereby the said J. Boies lost great part of the profits of the said Mill and parcel of Land aforesaid for a long time viz. on the day of the purchase of the Writ and divers other days and times between the said first day of January and the said Day of the purchase of this Writ, and more especially the Plaintiff lost the Benefit, profit and Advantage of cutting and slitting two Tons of Iron at said Milton on the same day which lay there ready at said Mill to be cut and slit, and the plaintiff avers that every thing was then and there ready for the purpose of slitting and cutting the said Two Tons of Iron excepting water sufficient for commodiously working the said slitting Mill, which water was then and there diverted and turned away out of it's said antient Course by the said A. Gillespie in Manner as aforesaid.

And also for that wheras the said J. Boies on &c. and for three years last past was and now is seized in fee and possessed of, and in an antient Messuage, and a certain other Tract of Land cont[ainin]g by Estimation 13 Acres or thereabouts with the Appurtenances in Milton in the County aforesaid which same Tract lieth contiguous and adjoining on the North Side, to a certain antient Water Course called

Neponset River, which runs and time out of mind hath run and used and of right ought to run from a certain Spring head called Charles River in Milton aforesaid to, in, and by the said last mentioned Tract of Land of the plaintiff and his Messuage aforesaid thro' a certain other Trench there by the same Tract of Land quite up to, by, and beyond the lower Dam there so called adjoining a certain other Tract there being and belonging to the plaintiff, notwithstanding which, the said A. Gillespie (not ignorant of the premises, but contriving and maliciously intending to frustrate and hinder the said J. Boies from the use and Benefit of the same Water Course) on the day of the purchase of this Writ and on divers other days and times between the said 1st Jany. and the said Day of the purchase of this Writ in Dorchester aforesaid dug, broke up, and cut away a certain bank or Inclosure of the said Water-Course and thereby diverted the same Water Course from the Water Course of the said J. Boies; by which the said J. Boies was greatly injured and deprived of and lost a very great part of the use profit Benefit and Advantage of the said Water Course for a long time viz. on the day of the purchase of this Writ and also from the said 1 Jany. to the said day of the purchase of this Writ: Ad damnum £300.

[XXVIII]

TRESPASS.

Ditson vs. Small.[109]

Attach &c. John Small &c. to answer John Ditson &c. in a Plea of Trespass for that the said John Small, at Dunstable &c. on the first

---

[109] In JA's hand. Pleadings Book, p. [61]. The records and files of this case have not been found. The action was one in trespass *quare clausum fregit* — "wherefore he broke the close." ("Close" was a term of art referring to any interest in the soil, whether enclosed or not.) This was the remedy of one in actual possession of land for an injury to the land through or during a wrongful entry. For the remedies of one out of possession, see notes 29, 103, above. The judgment awarded money damages, but the action could be used to determine the right to possession. See 8 Holdsworth, *History of English Law* 467; 1 Chitty, *Pleading* 173–183; Shipman, *Common-law Pleading* 66–82; Perham, *American Precedents* 333–339; 5 Dane, *Abridgment* 567; Act of 20 Nov. 1770, c. 9, §4, 5 A&R 110. That determination of rights rather than recovery of damages was the object of this suit is suggested by the fact that the plaintiff could have obtained damages for injuries to his trees, soil, and grass, through a statutory action in which the defendant bore the burden. Act of 21 June 1726, c. 3, §§1–3, 2 A&R 383–384; Act of 10 June 1698, c. 7, §4, 1 A&R 324. See Perham, *American Precedents* 334. Note that the declaration alleges that the trespass was from its beginning "to the Day of the Purchase of this Writ, at Sundry days and Times continuing." Such an allegation, called a "continuando," was proper when the trespass complained of was a continuing act, rather than a series of independent actions. Some authorities at least might have considered the cutting of

day of January Anno Domini 1771 with Force and Arms, broke and entered the Plantiffs Close in Dunstable aforesaid, containing &c. bounded &c. and being so entered with Force as aforesaid cut down and carried away one hundred Trees the Property of the said John Ditson to the Value of 2s. each, erected a Fence on the said Land of the Plantiffs, dug up the Soil and the Grass of him the said John Ditson in the Close aforesaid then growing with certain Cattle and Teams, oxen and Carts did eat up, tread down and destroy, the Trespass aforesaid as to the cutting down and carrying away the Trees as aforesaid and as to the Eating up, treading down and destroying the Grass aforesaid with the Cattle aforesaid from the aforesaid first day of January Anno Domini 1771 to the Day of the Purchase of this Writ, at Sundry days and Times continuing, and many other Enormities the said John Small did to the said John Ditson against our Peace and to the Damage &c.

[XXIX]

BORROWING.

Stone et al. v. Littlefield.[110]

Attach &c. to answer in a plea of the case for that upon the 4 Octr. &c. at &c. the said J. borrowed and received of the Plaintiffs 11 Gall.

---

trees to be in the latter class. See *id.* at 51–52, 338–339; Sutton, *Personal Actions* 159.

[110] Probably in the hand of Edward Hill, JA's clerk. Pleadings Book, p. [62]. Documentation of this case is fragmentary. The original writ in the hand of Benjamin Kent is dated 6 Jan. 1773, returnable to the April 1773 Suffolk Inferior Court. SF 91649. JA's Office Book, April 1773, MQA, shows that he was retained by Littlefield and carries the notations "Fini[shed]" and "to be abated," which may mean either that the writ was abated, or that JA intended to plead in abatement. No other indication of the result has been found. For a related action in trover for an anchor between the same parties, in which JA was also of counsel for Littlefield, see SF 91671; Office Book, April 1773, MQA.

The problem in the present case was that the transaction was an exchange rather than a sale of goods. By his contract the plaintiff was entitled to eleven gallons of rum, but none of the remedies available to him could provide this recovery. He could not rescind the contract and get back the rum which he had originally given to the defendant, because, in the absence of fraud, title passed to the defendant on delivery. A right to possession was necessary to maintain detinue or replevin, the usual actions for the recovery in specie of wrongfully detained goods. See 2 Blackstone, *Commentaries* *447–448; 2 Kent, *Commentaries* *496, *514; Shipman, *Common-law Pleading* 117–118, 125–128. Detinue and replevin were similarly unavailable for the rum which the defendant had agreed to furnish, because they lay only for specific chattels, and no particular eleven gallons seem to have been intended here. In addition, replevin was not available where, as here, the plaintiff had consented to the original taking. *Id.* at 114–131; note 99 above.

Some legal historians say that debt or indebitatus assumpsit lay to recover un-of Barbadoes Spirit, worth [£] 2–13–4 and in consideration thereof the said J. then and there promised the plaintiffs to repay them 11 Gall. of the same sort of Spirit when he should be requested so to do; Now the said &c. say that afterwards viz. on &c. at &c. they requested the said J. to return and redeliver to them 11 Gall. of the said Spirit, but the said J. then refused and still refuses to deliver to the Plaintiffs 11 Gall. of said Spirit and so has broken his promise aforesaid.   Kent

ascertained chattels due by contract, but 19th-century authorities made clear that in such a case a showing of the value of the chattels would be required and that the recovery would be in money. Ames, *Lectures on Legal History* 89; Fifoot, *History and Sources* 24–28, 243; see 5 Dane, *Abridgment* 308; Mayor of Reading v. Clarke, 4 Barn. & Ald. 268, 106 Eng. Rep. 936 (K.B. 1821); 2 Chitty, *Pleading* 38 (Springfield, Mass., 13th Amer. edn., 1859). Even if recovery in specie might have been allowed under these forms, the action of debt for chattels had fallen into disuse by JA's time. He and his contemporaries could well have concluded that Blackstone meant to exclude the recovery of goods when he said, "The legal acceptation of *debt*, is a sum of money due by certain and express agreement." 3 Blackstone, *Commentaries* *153. Since it was commonly (although erroneously) considered that indebitatus assumpsit lay only where debt lay, it would have been logical for the 18th-century lawyers to assume that neither remedy existed in this case. See Fifoot, *History and Sources* 365. For cases following this logic, see Watson v. M'Nairy, 1 Bibb (Ky.) 356 (1809); Spratt v. M'Kinney, *id.* at 590, 595 (1809).

If the plaintiff could not obtain the rum in specie, he would have to be satisfied with money damages. Trover, the common remedy in damages for the wrongful appropriation or detention of a chattel, would not lie either for the rum originally given by the plaintiff or that owed him by the defendant, on the same reasoning that barred recovery in detinue or replevin. Shipman, *Common-law Pleading* 101–107. The remedy in debt or indebitatus assumpsit on the contract might have sufficed, but there is good reason to think that it would have been held unavailable. Both indebitatus assumpsit on the common count for goods sold and delivered and quantum valebant (note 31 above) were based on a fictitious undertaking of the defendant to pay for goods either their price or their reasonable value, measured at the time of making the contract. Although there was some disagreement, a substantial body of later authority held that these actions were inappropriate where the defendant was to pay in chattels, because the plaintiff had bargained to receive the value of the goods at the time of his demand, which might be higher or lower than the value at the time of sale. According to this authority, the proper form of action was special assumpsit, in which the measure of damages was the loss occurring to the plaintiff through the breach – in this case the value of the rum at the time of the demand. See Mitchell v. Gile, 12 N.H. 390, 395–396 (1841); Harris v. Fowle (N.P. 1787), cited in Barbe v. Parker, 1 H. Bl. 287, 126 Eng. Rep. 168 (C.P. 1789); Shipman, *Common-law Pleading* 156, 253; but see 2 Chitty, *Pleading* 273–275 note (Springfield, 1859); John Wentworth, *A Complete System of Pleading*, 2:121–122, 191–192, 200, 220 (London, 1797). In any event, if the defendant's default had been occasioned by a rise in the price of rum, special assumpsit would be tactically preferable.

For whatever reason, special assumpsit was the form used here.

C. *Torts*

1. Bassett v. Mayhew; Mayhew v. Bassett; Mayhew v. Allen

1762–1768

EDITORIAL NOTE

This complex litigation, a landmark in the history of Martha's Vineyard, arose out of an unhappy family situation. The genealogical as well as the legal involutions of these cases being what they were, a sketch of the members of the great Mayhew clan of Martha's Vineyard mainly concerned, and of their relationships, is almost essential to an understanding of the legal issues.[1] The chief figure on one side was *Dr. Matthew Mayhew* (1721–1805), a physician who was repeatedly a representative to the General Court and, from 1761, a Justice of the Peace at Chilmark, the village where all the action in the cases occurred. Allied with him was his wife's brother, *Robert Allen* (1732–1792), the coroner of the County of Dukes County.

A sister of Dr. Mayhew, *Hannah*, had married into the other and much more extensive family faction.[2] Her husband was *Zephaniah Mayhew* (1715–1751), a son of *Bethiah (Wadsworth) Mayhew*. Among their children who were to play parts in the physical and legal scuffles of the 1760's were *Lucinda* (1739–1815), *Wadsworth* (1741–1829), and another *Zephaniah* (b. 1745). Bethiah, widow since 1733 of an elder Zephaniah, was the embattled "old lady" of the trial records.

The feud seems to have begun after the death of the younger Zephaniah, husband of Hannah, in 1751. Though the details are obscure, his widow appears to have handled her affairs and brought up her numerous children in a manner so irksome to Dr. Mayhew that, it was said by those who disliked *him*, he "sought all occasions, to ruin and destroy them." With the backing of her husband's family, Hannah evidently succeeded fairly well, at least for a time, in fending off the effects of her brother's ill-will.

By 1762 the widowed Bethiah and three of her daughters—*Jerusha* (1717–1793), *Bethiah* the younger (b. 1723), and *Mercy* (1725–1825)—as well as the widowed Hannah and several of her children were

---

[1] All vital data in this sketch are drawn from the genealogies of the Mayhew and related families in Charles E. Banks, *The History of Martha's Vineyard*, vol. 3 (Edgartown, Mass., 1925).

[2] Banks does not show Hannah's relationship to Matthew, but it is stated in Hovey's narrative of the background of Jerusha Mayhew's case against Robert Allen, in Doc. I.

domiciled in the Chilmark household of the elder Bethiah's nephew, *Zaccheus Mayhew* (1723–1775). Zaccheus, the son of the late Colonel (Judge) Zaccheus Mayhew, was one of the most prominent members of a family always prominent in the Vineyard; in the documents he is never called by his Christian name but always deferentially Squire ("Esqr.") Mayhew. Zaccheus was married to *Rebecca*, and had numerous children of his own, including, it seems, *Lucy* (sometimes confused with her cousin *Lucinda*, Hannah's daughter).

Strong-mindedness was evidently endemic among the Mayhew women, notably the elder Bethiah and her daughter Jerusha; but Dr. Mayhew eventually found, or thought he found, a vulnerable point in their defenses. In 1744 Mercy Mayhew had married *Abel Chase*, a hatter of Edgartown. After bearing Chase two sons, Mercy quarreled with him and went to live with her mother, taking her younger son Zeph, who was actually, however, articled to his grandmother until he reached the age of fourteen. Zeph turned fourteen in 1762 and his father wanted him back. The new chapters in the old feud began when Chase applied to Justice of the Peace Doctor Matthew Mayhew for legal help in forcing the women to give up the boy. What happened thereafter is told in the documents printed here.[3]

The case fast became "a quarrell of the most invidious, inveterate and irreconcileable nature." [4] Conflicting testimony abounded. Some of it appears in the minutes which follow; more may be found in a large collection of depositions and processes in the Superior Court Files.[5] Adams remarked years later, "it was impossible for human Sagacity to discover on which Side Justice lay." [6] The years have not resolved the problem. We propose now merely to describe the procedural framework.

Legal matters commenced with Abel Chase's giving the warrant for Zeph's return to Deputy Sheriff Cornelius Bassett. When Bassett went for Zeph at Bethiah's house on 1 June 1762, the boy evaded him. It does not appear that Bassett made any return on the warrant; thus the warrant remained effective, a fact which was to become important later on. Bassett did however formally complain to Justice Matthew Mayhew that Jerusha Mayhew, her sister Mercy Chase, and Lucy Mayhew had rescued Zeph out of his hands. The Justice then issued a warrant, dated 1 June 1762, directed to "one of the Coroners" of Dukes County for the arrest of the three women.

Coroner Robert Allen took the writ. It is not clear whether he attempted to execute it immediately, although there is some evidence that he at least read the process to Jerusha on 1 June. On 9 October 1762 Allen brought

---

[3] Other Mayhews who had lesser roles in what followed were two brothers, "Deacon" Timothy and Simon Mayhew, who were distant cousins of Matthew, Zaccheus, and the elder Bethiah's late husband, Zephaniah.

[4] 3 JA, *Diary and Autobiography* 284.

[5] SF 83471, 85247, 86474, 144133, 144145, 144187, 144233.

[6] 3 JA, *Diary and Autobiography* 285.

Jerusha physically before the Justice, who bound her over to the next Sessions at £5. Jerusha refusing to post the bail, Justice Mayhew ordered her committed and issued a mittimus.[7]

Now began Jerusha's lengthy attempt to foil Allen. On 11 October 1762 he went to take her but forbore when she pleaded illness and when Deacon Timothy Mayhew promised that she would go on the 15th or "the next fare day." [8] Allen returned on the 19th and the 20th, but still Jerusha would not go, even though on the 20th Allen himself agreed to be one of her bondsmen.[9] On the 25th, Allen came to the house once more, this time with Thomas Lothrop as aid,[10] and repeated his offer. Like almost everything else in the case, what happened next is uncertain. One of Jerusha's witnesses said that Allen manhandled Jerusha as she lay in bed and had threatened her with a whip; Lothrop said that Jerusha called Allen a liar and used him "with Uncivility," whereupon Allen told her that if she were a man he would horsewhip her. Allen asked Wadsworth Mayhew to aid him, but Wadsworth, the Mayhews said, was deaf. According to Allen and Lothrop, Wadsworth rescued Jerusha out of Allen's hands.[11]

Now it was Allen's turn to swear out a complaint, this one at the Court of General Sessions of the Peace which was then sitting at Tisbury. A warrant for the arrest of Wadsworth Mayhew issued, dated 26 October 1762 and directed to the sheriff or his deputy.[12] It is clear that Bassett took the warrant, but the evidence is confused as to whether or not he agreed to wait until the next day before executing it.[13] At any rate, he summoned a number of men to aid him and set off at about 9:30 P.M. on the 26th for Bethiah's house, where Wadsworth was supposed to be. To cloud the picture further, there was evidence that he had the old warrant for Zeph in his pocket and intended to execute that as well.[14]

From the depositions of members of the Aid,[15] it appears that Bassett's group stole silently toward the house and surrounded it. Bassett went to the front door, demanded entrance, heard a voice cry "Fire the gun," and received a charge of buckshot in the legs. He and his men then broke down the door and entered the house. Inside, Bethiah Mayhew, although seated in a chair, began belaboring Bassett with a three-foot stave. Seizing it to protect himself, he pulled her onto the floor. More pulling and hauling

[7] SF 144187.
[8] Deposition of Rebeckah Mayhew, SF 144187.
[9] Deposition of Rebeckah Mayhew, SF 144187.
[10] Deposition of Thomas Lothrop, SF 144187.
[11] Depositions of Rebeckah Mayhew and Thomas Lothrop, SF 144187.
[12] SF 83471. The warrant is printed in Quincy, *Reports* 93 note.
[13] Depositions of Ebenezer Smith and John Cottle, SF 85247.
[14] Deposition of William Stewart, SF 85247.
[15] Depositions of Eliakim Norton, Thomas Daggett, Jonathan Cathcart, Silvanus Norton, Jeremiah Manter, and Benjamin Coffin, SF 83471, 85247, and 144133. The Aid was the group of citizens enlisted by an officer to assist him in the performance of a particular task.

ensued before "the People then Grew Moderate."[16] Wadsworth, being securely tied, was then carried to jail and the Sessions.

Wadsworth, Bethiah Jr, and Bethiah Sr. were all indicted for criminal assault by the Grand Jury at the May 1763 sitting of the Superior Court at Barnstable,[17] but only Wadsworth was ever tried. In May 1764 the jury brought in a verdict of guilty, which the court rejected.[18]

Meanwhile, the civil litigation multiplied.[19] Jerusha sued Allen, Bassett sued Bethiah Sr, and Bethiah Sr. sued Bassett. Bethiah Jr. later was admitted as a party in all actions, while Lucinda Mayhew was admitted to the action against Allen, and Wadsworth was admitted to the actions against Bassett. The litigation wound its way from the Edgartown Inferior Court to the Barnstable Superior Court, where finally, in May 1764, all the cases were submitted to three referees: Gamaliel Bradford, Josiah Edson, and Ebenezer Spooner. In August 1764, the referees attempted to hear the cases, but Jerusha interposed a series of objections which succeeded in postponing the hearings for a year.[20] Finally, on 29 August 1765, the hearings commenced.[21] The minutes which follow as Documents I and II, by Adams and Robert Treat Paine respectively, memorialize the proceedings before the referees. Adams was of counsel for Bassett and Allen, and Paine for the Mayhews. It appears from the minutes that the cross actions between Bassett and the Mayhews were tried together.

After hearing the evidence and the arguments, the referees found against Allen in favor of Jerusha, £6; for Bethiah Jr, 20 shillings; and for Lucinda, 20 shillings. They also found against Bassett and awarded Bethiah Sr. £4; Wadsworth, £3; and Bethiah Jr, 20 shillings. In addition, Allen had to pay court and reference costs of £30 16s. 11d. Bassett's costs were £43 8s. 4d.[22] The controversy remained alive until 1768, by which time Bethiah Sr. had died and Bethiah Jr. as her executor prayed execution against Bassett for the £4 damages and costs. Adams interposed a multipart defense, of which the following sentence is sufficiently illustrative to stand as a commentary on the entire case: "And the said Cornelius Bassett comes and defends, &c. and Saith that this Writ is bad and ought to abate for that   1. It is in said Writ alledged that said Bethiah Mayhew before the Justices of the Superior Court of Judicature, &c. holden at Barnstable within said County of Barnstable and for the Countys of Barnstable and Dukes County, on the second Wednesday of May in the Sixth Year of his Majesty's Reign and by the Consideration of said Justices recovered the

[16] Deposition of Eliakim Norton, SF 144133.

[17] SF 144145.

[18] See note 68 below.

[19] Min. Bk. 72, SCJ Barnstable, May 1763, C–3, C–9; *id.*, May 1764, N–3, N–4; Min. Bk. 82, SCJ Barnstable, May 1766, C–3, C–4; Rec. 1766, fols. 28–29; Min. Bk. 89, SCJ Barnstable, May 1768, N–4, N–5; Rec. 1768, fols. 177–178.

[20] SF 144187. Part of the matter was tried at the May 1764 sitting, according to minutes in the Paine Law Notes which are not printed here. It does not appear that JA participated at this stage.

[21] SF 86474.

[22] Min. Bk. 82, SCJ Barnstable, May 1766, C–3, C–4.

Judgment mentioned in said writ which by Law ought not to have been alleged if the said judgment should have been alleged to have been recovered on the Wednesday preceeding the third Tuesday in May in said year." [23]

Apparently Adams never pressed the technicality, for the final Record entry is: "The Defendant makes default"; [24] that is, the defendant allowed the plaintiff to prevail by default.

I. ADAMS' MINUTES OF THE REFEREES' HEARING [25]

Chilmark, Martha's Vineyard, August 1765

Seal. Directed to a proper Officer. The Cause. General Warrant. Martha's Vineyard

Hovey. Justifies by Warrant. Generality. Turning Point, legality of Warrant. Void in itself. Broke open in the dead of Night.

Damages. Thrown down on the Hearth. Stripd of her Cloathing. Not yet got rid of her Wounds as she saith. Fright. Weakness consequent. Bethiah and Wadsworth—Weakly. She never had got over it she says. Wadsworth.

Hovey.

Abel Chase of Nantucket married Mercy Mayhew, Daughter of Bethiah Mayhew. They disagreed and separated 15 or 20 Years ago. They had a young male Child at the Time of separation, which Chase put out by Indentures to the Grandmother Bethiah Mayhew, from 5 to 14 Years of Age. When the Boy come to be 14, his Father wanted him, and complained to Dr. Mayhew,[26] that his son refused to obey him, and had run away from him. Dr. Mayhew made out a Warrant for the Boy, which Bassett was about to serve about to take the Boy, when the Women Bethiah, Jerusha and others, came out and assaulted Basset and held him, till the Boy went out of Bassetts Way. Basset

[23] SF 144233.

[24] Rec. 1767–1768, fols. 177–178; Min. Bk. 79, SCJ Barnstable, May 1768, N–5.

[25] In JA's hand. Adams Papers, Microfilms, Reel No. 185. The minutes are in the form of a paper booklet, with "Martha's Vineyard" in large careful letters on the front cover. The matter beginning "Abel Chase" commences on the second leaf, and the notes set out here between the heading and that matter are written in a hasty hand on the front cover, some of the writing being upside down with respect to the title. These first notes pertain to Bassett v. Mayhew; it is possible that they are not courtroom jottings at all, but at least in part represent a memorandum of a conversation between JA and James Hovey, who was one of the opposing counsel.

[26] Dr. Matthew Mayhew was a Justice of the Peace, commissioned 16 Oct. 1761. Whitmore, *Mass. Civil List* 149.

complains of the Opposition of the Women to Dr. Mayhew. Dr. Mayhew gave a Warrant to the Coroner,[27] upon the Comp[lain]t of Deputy Sheriff, vs. the Women &c., for Resisting him in the Execution of his office. 1st fault directed to Coroner,[28] 2d. no Seal. 3d. general. Allen the Coroner took that Warrant, and went and read it to them, and told em they must go, but they said theyd die first. Another Time, told Jerusha she must go, and she said she would go home first and come, and did. The Justice Dr. Mayhew sentencd to recognise[29] or go to Goal. She refused to find Bond so a Mittimus was made out, directed only to the Goaler.[30] But Allen did not committ her, took her Word for her Appearance on Monday, but then she pretended to be sick from Time to time and pretended to be at one Time set forth in her Writ, when Allen only took hold of her Hand.

At this Time two young Men came up and held her and kept off Allen. Wadsworth Mayhew was the most active. Then Allen goes and complains to the Sessions, that he was opposed and resisted, by Wadsworth Mayhew. Court orders a Warrant[31] to bring Wadsworth vs. all opposition, before them and to enter any House, where the officers should suspect him to be. This directed to the Sherriff. Bassett goes with Aid[32] to the House, and demands Entrance &c. A Gun is fired which wounds him in the foot and Leg. He breaks the House and drags Wadsworth away to the Court.[33]

Jerusha Mayhew vs. Robert Allen.

3 Imprisonments and an assault and Battery. Octr. 1763. Verdict vs. her.[34] Sup[erio]r C[our]t Papers in Justification rejected.[35]

[27] Robert Allen and Thomas Daggett had been commissioned Coroners of the County of Dukes County 16 Oct. 1761. Whitmore, *Mass. Civil List* 160.

[28] The Mayhew interests argued throughout the litigation that the warrant should have been directed to the Sheriff, not the Coroner, and that any actions which Coroner Allen took in pursuance of the warrant were therefore illegal. A statute of the Province provided for service by the Coroner of writs running against the Sheriff and empowered the Coroner to return talesmen to fill up the jury in any case in which a sheriff was concerned or related to the parties. Act of 10 June 1700, c. 3, §10, 1 A&R 429.

[29] That is, to post bond for appearance at the next Inferior Court.

[30] A mittimus was an order of commitment. The Mayhews argued that the mittimus, an attested copy of which is in SF 144187, was illegal, because it merely commanded the jailkeeper to accept Jerusha, but did not order an officer to take and deliver her.

[31] See SF 83471 and Quincy, *Reports* 93 note.

[32] See note 15 above.

[33] The position and handwriting of the preceding two paragraphs in the MS indicate that they constituted JA's statement of the whole litigation, prepared well in advance of the hearing.

[34] Presumably in the Dukes County Inferior Court. No record of the case has

Hovey. Not for bearing hand vs. civil Authority.

Zeph. Mayhew married the sister of Dr. Mayhew. Zeph. died. His Wife administerd and was Guardian of the Children. Widow taken in by J. Webb and Company. J. Webb became Master of the Children and Property. These orphan Children, thrown upon this family. Adonijah pursues his right, his Aunt Jerusha assists him. The Dr. disliked it, and thence sought all occasions, to ruin and destroy them. Chase's marriage, separation, oldest son with the father, youngest with this family.

Dr. Mayhew issues out a Writ, intended for a Warrant for this Boy, delivered to Bassett, who attempted to execute it, but the light-footed Boy made his Escape. Jerusha placed herself between Bassett and the Boy. Basset returns that the Boy was rescued[36] by Jerusha. Now the Coroner in Tow. Sherriff and Coroner shall play into one anothers Hands. Not a Warrant of them will justify an Officer. Jerusha apprehended, carried before the Dr. and sentenced that she was sufficiently guilty of an offence and must give Bail, which she would not do. Dr. makes out a Mittimus, illegal one. How to be carried could not tell. Allen seizes Jerusha to carry her to Goal. 2 June as well as 1st.[37] Then slept till Octr. 25th.[38] Octr. seizes her again by same Warrant at Esqr. Mayhews, seizes her in her Bed, and would have her out, commanding assistance. Wadsworth seeing his Aunt ill used, put up the Cloths on his Aunts Breast. Allen cryd, thats enough Wadsworth has rescued you out of my Hands. Allen makes the most vile and devilish Return.[39] God knows not a Word of Truth in it. The

---

been found. The Barnstable records were destroyed by fire in 1827. Richard L. Bowen, *Massachusetts Records* 20 (Rehoboth, Mass., 1957).

[35] It is not clear whether JA refers to Superior Court papers which were rejected, either in the Inferior Court or before the referees, or whether it was the Superior Court that rejected other papers. Nor is it certain just which papers were intended. Possibly the reference is to Rex v. Gay, Quincy, *Reports* 91 (SCJ Suffolk, Aug. 1763), which held, three judges to two, that in a prosecution for assaulting an officer in the execution of his office, the warrant under which the officer was acting is not admissible as evidence unless it is legal. (Samuel M. Quincy cites Bassett v. Mayhew as contrary authority. *Id.* at 93 note.)

[36] The elements of a rescue include the officer's lawful custody of the prisoner and the forcible removal of the prisoner from that custody. Failure to assist an officer or even impeding him in his efforts are crimes of a different nature. Hovey's point here is that Bassett never had custody of Zephaniah, and, therefore, his return, or account, of a rescue was wrong.

[37] There is no indication that Allen seized Jerusha on either 1 or 2 June; it was Bassett who attempted the seizure on 1 June.

[38] The testimony of one of the Mayhews' own witnesses was that Allen made several peaceable attempts to take Jerusha prior to 25 October. Deposition of Rebeckah Mayhew, SF 144187.

[39] The warrant and return have not been found. In SF 83471, 144138, and

Court then makes out a Warrant to the Sheriff, to take Wadsworth vs. all opposition. Basset comes, and makes the Disturbances of *the* night, and goes and complains again vs. the whole Family, a new Warrant [40] is given to Allen, who comes and seizes and binds &c. them.

Jerushas demands vs. Allen. Assault and Imprisonment. 1st. June. 9th. Octr. 25th. Octr. Besides these she demands Damages for 2d time and for breaking her House on the 26th. Octr. and for imprisoning her on 11th. Octr. and 20th.

Evidence

Deposition of Rebecca Mayhew Wife of Esqr. Allen offered to be her Bail.

Deposition Mary Hunt. Heard Jerusha tell Allen he lyed.

Witnesses

Jane McGee. 25th. at Esqr. Mayhews I went, Jerusha told Allen he lyed. Then he said he'd horse whip her if well. I did not hear her complain of his griping her Hand. I took it, Wadsworth laid his Arm over to hold her and prevent Allen from taking her away. Had hold of her Hand not long.

Zeph. Mayhew. Bro[the]r to Wadsworth. He pull'd her up and about. I thought to hurt her not to take her.

Esqr. Smith. Interlocutory [...].

Simon Mayhew. Mittimus. We gave our Words for Jerusha at Dr. Mayhews. I did not see Allen touch her nor hear him make her his Prisonment [*i.e.* Prisoner?].

D[eaco]n Mayhew. Desir'd to bring her behind him to Dr. Mayhews.

Mrs. Chase. Hall'd out a Paper—at the Door—but laid Hands on no one.

Uriah Tilton. At Dr. Mayhews. She refused to find Bonds. Mittimus written. She unwilling to go that night. He unwilling to carry her. Allen [...] their Words till Monday. D[eaco]n Mayhew then present about making up, that she might stay longer.

144145 are copies of the writ in Allen v. Mayhew which indicates Allen's complaint that while in the execution of his office he attempted to carry Jerusha to jail in Edgartown and was "Opposed in his said Office by one Wadsworth Mayhew of said Chilmark by Violently Seizing the body of the said Jerusha and holding her." The mittimus, SF 144187, has only one return: Allen took Jerusha and brought her before Justice Mayhew on 9 Oct. 1762.

[40] This warrant, dated 27 Oct. 1762, SF 83471, brought before the Court of General Sessions of the Peace at Tisbury Bethiah Mayhew Jr, Lucinda Mayhew, Zephaniah Mayhew, and Jerusha Mayhew Jr. (Zephaniah's sister) to answer for the disturbance of the night before; the file does not indicate what action was taken.

No. 1. Bassett v. Mayhew

John Bassett. Beg[inning of] June. Allen wanted me to go as aid. Esqr. Mayhew would not go. We could not catch them.

Stewart, Wm. Beg[inning of] June. Dr. Mayhew advised me to go as a Friend. Esqr. Mayhew in a great Passion—'tho commanded would not go. We went to the House but could not persuade them to come out, nor could we catch them.

Esqr. Mayhew. Told Allen that it would be little less than Murder to carry her to Goal. I asked Allen if I should take his Prisoner, and he consented.[41]

Jeira Willis. Nothing.

Paine. Ashes raked over these unhappy Coals. Whole Bone picked and the Hatched [Hatchet] for ever buried. Boadicea the deliverer of Britain from the Invasion of the Hunts [Huns?]. Rod however broken, this Warrant however illegal, hung like a bloody Banner, over this family. Poor helpless Women—Walked between his Legs as a ship between those of the Colossus. Touching not of the Essence of Imprisonment.[42] Surrounded the House, lockt up Doors, Windows, stop'd up Chimney, till starvd to death.

Vulgar Custom refuted by a vulgar Proverb. A bad Custom better broke than kept.

Jack ancient or pendant. Stings 1000 times deeper—gives a greater Weight to the Bullet. Going down stream, tide and half Tide. Noahs Dove—wise, Dove—found nowhere after flying about, to set his foot.[43] Many a Case, has sunk like a Millstone to the Bottom of the Ocean, when founded on an illegal Warrant.

Cornelius Bassett vs. Mayhews.

Jeremiah Manter. Aid. Bassett stooped down to see his Wound, and the old Lady, with a stick smites Bassett 3 or 4 times over the Head. Then He took hold of the stick and in pulling it out of her Hand, she fell down, no Hurt done her that I saw. About ½ after 9. Robert Allen came to call me.

Meletiah Davis. Aid. A Deputy Sherriff. Basset came to me and desired I would go and serve the Warrant. The Clerk carried it to the high sherriff, who offerd it to me, I declind. Basset offerd me a Dollar

---

[41] Apparently Squire Mayhew himself agreed to produce Jerusha.

[42] Paine seems to be arguing that laying on of hands is not an element of imprisonment, an argument that could, in the instant case, cut both ways. See note 36 above.

[43] The sense of Paine's metaphors eludes us, as the shape of his phrases seems to have eluded JA.

to go. Esqr. Mayhew advised Basset not to go that Night. Basset said he would not, if he would promise to bring him out in the Morn.

The blood running out of his stocking. The old Woman laid him over the shoulders. He caught the Clubb, and pull'd. She held so fast that the Coll.[44] pull'd her out of her Chair. We were afraid of Murder, and so bound the 2 young fellows. I heard no Noise at the Door but Voices till after the Gun. She fetched Shreve[45] a Blow in the face and gave him a black Eye. The old Woman was laid on the bed. Hardly time for Wadsworth to have fired the Gun.

Eliakim Norton. Aid. About Chase up Chamber and danger of his killing somebody. Gun loaded deeply. He being a friend hoped to prevent difficulty. Heard it said Basset was under a sort of a Difficulty or Engagement to Esqr. Mayhew. I thought not time for Wadsworth to fire the Gun.

Thos. Dagget. Aid. Bethiah said I shall go into a fit. He let her go. She struck him.

Silvanus Norton. Aid. Heard in the House a Womans Voice damn you all, what do you do here. Mrs. Chase wishd to God she had been there, she would have prevented all this.

Ebenezer Allen. 12 Men Aid. Bassett said he had another Writ in his Pocket. Stand off. Two Bethiahs by Voice. It appears to me it was 11 O Clock. Davis and Dagget took Bethiah from out of her Mothers Arms. Old Woman prayd. God not here, more like the devil. Robert Allen said it hurt him to take the old Lady, and agreed to omit it. Basset ordered to search the Chamber, because he did not know what Mischief might be done. Utensils brought to light a Candle. Every one went in and out as they pleasd. No Rigor used.

Robert Hammet. I knew nothing of their Coming to this House till it was over.

Benja. Coffin. Basset told Esqr. Mayhew he would not go if he'd give his Word. But Esqr. would not. But he said he believd he should not. Women cryd begone, or theyd break his Head. Many Threatening Speeches, and one cryd fire the Gun. I thought I heard somebody in the Chamber. A Woman's Voice in this Room, I thought. I take it to be Bethiah Mayhew Ju[nio]rs. The old Lady struck at me. Bethiah Mayhew seemd to look as if she was looking for a Weapon. Some of Us took hold of her Hands and raised her up. I said I thought it would be best to bind her, but nobody did. She said if she died, she hoped

[44] Bassett was evidently a colonel or lieutenant colonel of militia; he is occasionally referred to by title in these minutes and in the deposition.

[45] Possibly a reference to the Sheriff, Bassett, or perhaps to one of the aid.

somebody would prosecute for her. Basset said he did not know but he might take the Boy if he had opportunity. She talkd more than all the rest till Allen came. She laughd heartily and made the Company laugh.

Nathl. Hancock Esqr. The whole Island knows of their Threatnings, keeping Guns, &c. Jerusha reflected on the whole Court[46] as guilty of Intemperance.

Ebenr. Smith Esqr. The People were almost universally for his going.[47] I said I did not know but it was best.

Dr. Mayhew Esqr. Bethiah said that if officers came either from Me or the Authority they would resist them to the last degree.

Mary Mott, and Jer. Manter. Urged them to put in Things that they knew not.[48]

Jona. Foster. The old Women said We keep a Gun, to kill the Man that comes for the Boy and a Clubb too.

Samuel Bradford. The Dr.[49] Basset had a bad Wound such as I should not chuse to have for any Money. I would not have such a Legg for £5000. 5 shot in one Legg and 2 in the other. The shot passing thro the Door, were bruisd, and inflamed. The Legg is not well yet. It swells with Exercise and never will be well.

Dr. Smith. 5 shot in one Legg and 2 in tother. The Wound was bad. One or two shots lodged against the Bone.

Hovey. Incidents. Doors, Windows, Avenues guarded. Jumbled against the door.[50] Who the Persons were that fired the Gun, the Witnesses know not. Wadsworth fire the Gun, fire the Gun. 1st. convince you, that Wadsworth Mayhew could not be the Person, that fired this Gun. Norton, Davis and Manter. At the back door. Broken Way in the Entry.

Witnesses. *Zephaniah Mayhew.* Large Noise as if somebody pulling

[46] The Inferior Court.

[47] That is, for Bassett's going to take Wadsworth on the night of 26 October.

[48] ". . . being present where the said Jerusha was taking evidence [I] have heard said Jerusha mention and urge things to the Deponents to give in which they refused as not knowing the same." Deposition of Mary Mott, SF 85247. No such language appears in either of Manter's depositions, SF 83471, 144133.

[49] Samuel Bradford was a physician. Charles E. Banks, *The History of Martha's Vineyard*, 3:44 (Edgartown, Mass., 1925). It is worth noting that so-called "Golden Rule" testimony ("I would not have such a Legg for £5000") was apparently admissible. See also King v. Stewart, No. 2, text at notes 66, 67.

[50] "Basset came from the window to the door and I heard somebody step from the bed towards the door or fireplace and just as Basset he got to the door and grumbled at it, the gun was fired through the door." Deposition of Jeremiah Manter, SF 144133.

down the broad side of the House. Heard Grandmother and Aunts crying Murder. Bound my Hands quite tort[51] so they hurt me a great while. Basset pulled Grand[mother] out of her Chair. He turnd from her and curs'd and swore, and somebody said God ant here. Basset ordered somebody to go up Chamber and look for Zeph Chase. I waked Wadsworth up and he and I went to the back door. I heard no Gun, nor [fired?].

Lucinda [Mayhew].[52] I went to Wadsworth in Bed. I saw Dagget have Jerusha by the Hands.

Zeph. Chase. Heard swearing too. Never knew there was a Gun shot, that night.

Mercy Chase. My Child, &c. Family in great Distress, Terror and Fright. Mother complained of Jams and Bruises. Sister Bethiah compland that she was mashed, and I saw burns and black spots.

Esqr. Mayhew. Manter forward. Bassetts Word. Old Lady said what have I done to be beat and abused so. Basset said he could not remember whether he mentioned Wadsworth Mayhews name.

Esqr. Hancock said if any Body should break his House he would kill them as soon as a Rabbit.[53]

Mary Hunt. In her Apprehension Bethiah Mayhew had been much hurt by the Persons that broke in.

D[eaco]n Mayhew.

Simon Mayhew.

John Cottle. Basset told me that one Reason of his going that night was to take Chase.

Mary Mcgee. Dr. Mayhew said the best way to get the Boy was to pull the House down. Dr. Mayhew dont remember.

Ruth Mayhew. See Deposition.[54] Bruises, &c.

John Basset's Opinion.

Timothy Mayhew Jnr. Deposition. Heard Basset say he would have the Boy dead or alive,[55] and heard Discourse with James Athearn, about pulling the side of the House down.[56]

[51] Thus in MS, for "taut" or "tight"?

[52] This is presumably the "Lucy Mayhew" who was a party plaintiff only in the action against Allen. She was therefore competent to testify in Mayhew v. Bassett.

[53] The Paine Law Notes (Doc. II) indicate clearly that this is Mayhew's report of what Hancock said. It seems to be hearsay, but neither Paine nor JA indicates that it was excluded.

[54] SF 85247. Ruth Mayhew visited the Mayhews the day after the fracas and deponed in their behalf concerning the disordered state of the house and the poor physical condition of Bethiah Sr.

[55] SF 85247. Timothy Mayhew deponed in Bethiah's behalf to overhearing Bassett state his intention on 6 June 1762.

[56] SF 85247. Timothy also deponed that later in June he had overheard Bassett

Sarah Hatch. Deposition.[57] Discourse with Athern.

Elisha West. Saw the old Womens Bruises. Abel Chase told me he had employd them that he expected would get the Boy.

Jeira Willis. I took it Basset was determind not to come that Night.

Ezra Tilton Jr. Manter told me, that Robert Allen called him up, and he was ready to get up.

Jer. Tilton.

Hovey. Wadsworth could not be the Person. Witnesses perjured. Lucinda, and Zeph. Wadsworth could not get out and in again without waking Zeph.

As little Probability that the others did it as Wadsworth. Bethiah was found in such a Posture that she could not do it. Lucinda heard no Gun.

Bassetts Authority. I hold his Warrant. Vid. 2 Shaw. 382, bottom,[58] will not justify. General Warrant. Law gives no such Power to Justice or sessions. 1. Shaw. 76.[59] Browlow Bordmans.[60] Law of Arrests. C[enter?] of p. 235,[61] vid. §8;[62] p. 186.[63] No Necessity. Late in the Night. Agreement with Esqr. Mr. Bordmans House Damages. Confined till near April. Leg swelld at Barnstable.

Paine. Awful Night, the Æra of Liberty. Pretended Complaint of

---

[57] tell James Athearn he would have to "take the door of its hinges and pull down one side of the house." Athearn was clerk of the Dukes County Inferior Court. His name appears in many of the file papers in these cases.

[57] SF 85247. Sarah Hatch deponed in Bethiah's behalf to Bassett's telling Athearn in June or July 1762 that "he would not go to said house again without a special writ and orders to breake open the house and men enough to gard him."

[58] The editors have not located the precise edition of Joseph Shaw, *The Practical Justice of Peace* involved here. However, 2 *id.* 348 (London, 6th edn., 1756) bears on this point.

[59] See note 58 above. 1 Shaw, *Justice of Peace* 85 notes that "a Justice of the Peace his Warrant will not justify a Constable in breaking into a House to apprehend any Person for a less Crime than Felony or Misprision of Felony."

[60] The citation is unclear and so, at this point, is JA's handwriting. See Woody's Case, 1 Brownl. & Golds, 204, 205, 123 Eng. Rep. 756 (C.P. 1606): "A justice of peace cannot command his servant to arrest one without a warrant in writing in his absence."

[61] *The Law of Arrests* 235 (London, 1742): "No one can justify the breaking open another's door to make an arrest, unless he first signify to those in the house the cause of his coming, and request them to give him admittance; for the law never allows such extremities but in the cases of necessity."

[62] *Law of Arrests* 236 (§8): "[Breaking open the door is justified] where one known to have committed a treason or felony, or to have given another a dangerous wound, is pursued either with or without a warrant, by a constable or private person; but not where one lies under a probable suspicion only."

[63] *Law of Arrests* 186: "Any constable or private person, to whom any justice of the peace directs his warrant to arrest a particular person for felony, or any other misdemeanor, within the justice's jurisdiction, may lawfully execute it, whether the person mentioned in such warrant be in truth guilty or not."

Allen piping Hot. Sessions. Overruled in Sessions, 'tho objected to. Mrs. Jerushas Resignation and Obedience. Crusade. Veterans of death Regt.[64] No Counsel. No Pleadings. Arrests 173.[65] Sir Wm. Pepperells House. No remedy. We dont hear of such Procedings in Boston, nor any where else.[66] Officer must demand a peaceable Entry. Night Time not the proper Time. Something else in his Mind. Zeph Chase. Clashing of Evidence. The mean to be taken.[67] Doubtful whether Either of them fired the Gun. Sup[erio]r C[our]t would not receive the Verdict vs. Wadsworth.[68] Family Witnesses, when none others. Something in human Nature, abandond [...]. Not Partialities &c. Characters of this family. Prejudices of Witnesses on the other side. Cobb whose wife had prompted on this unruly Proceeding.[69] Threats before Hand. Faithful Memory of an Enemy. Family obnoxious to the Government, weigh nothing. [Haulescks?] Law. Widow is wounded in the House of her fri[en]ds. The Report Defamation of keeping a Gun. Cape fly a way. Resisting the sham appearance of Authority is

[64] The allusion is unclear.

[65] *Law of Arrests* 173: A single justice may issue a warrant for an offence "cognizable only by a Session of two or more Justices." JA may have miscopied Paine's citation.

[66] "[W]hile We were at Falmouth waiting to be ferried over to the Island the News arrived from Boston of the Riots on the twenty fifth of August [1765] in which Lt. Governor Hutchinson's House was so much injured." 3 JA, *Diary and Autobiography* 285.

[67] That is, the truth lies between the conflicting versions.

[68] Wadsworth Mayhew was indicted at the May 1763 Barnstable Superior Court, and tried at the May 1764 sitting. The Minute Book entry does not state the verdict. "The Jury bro't in a Verdict which the Court think is contrary to the Evidence. They therefore reject the same and the Indictment is continued to the next term for trial." Min. Bk. 72. It does not appear that Wadsworth was ever retried, however. The Paine Law Notes contain the following minute of his May 1764 trial:

Barnstable Sup[erio]r C[our]t May 1764
Dom. Rex vs. Wadsworth Mayhew

Benja. Coffin. Took it to be the Voice of B[ethiah] junr. did not disting[uish] his telling his bus[iness]: took hold of the Door before.

Norton. Told his bus[iness] full.

Manter. Bethiah junr. call'd, Basset gave orders to open an inner Door.

Davis. Saw Wadsworth immediately after firing Gun. I was at back, not Time eno[ugh].

Allen.

Basset.

Defendant

Esqr. Mayhew.

Lucy. I and Wadsworth opend the Door. Thought of going for a Warrant.

Zepha[niah]. Wadsworth was Sleep, waked scared, went to back door, not to escape.

Mem[orandum]. Wadsworth was cleared at the Inf[erio]r Court for Damages.

Mem[orandum]. He told his bus[iness] but they did not hear it.

[69] The reading is clear, although the meaning is not. This is true of many of the phrases which follow.

laudable. Fire the Gun. No Evidence vs. Bethiah Se[nio]r. Not a Word of the old Woman. Lucindas Cry to Zeph Chase. Damages. Careless of his Legg. Cases at Plymouth.[70] Bulletts in Leggs, &c. Damage without an Injury.

II. PAINE'S MINUTES OF THE REFEREES' HEARING [71]

Chilmark, Martha's Vineyard, August 1765

Dukes County Augt. 1765

Cor[am] Referrees

1762.

1762. June 1. C. Basset complains of Jerus[ha] Beth[i]a[h] junr. Lucinda Mahew and Mercy Chase and a Warrant issues *without Seal* and directed to *Coroner and General* who on said day serves it on all three and *lets them go.*

Oct. 9. Coroner *Allen* serves it again on Jerusha and takes her before M. Mahew who binds her to Court and makes a *Mittimus directed* only to the Goaler.

Oct. 25. Coroner *Allen* takes Jerusha being sick a bed *by Words* Esqrs. said *Mittimus* and Wadsworth hinders.

26. On this Allen complains to Sessions then sitting of Wadsworth and the Warrant goes on which the home was broke.

27. C Basset complains to M M[ayhew] and al. and he grants a Warrant vs. Bethiah, Bethiah junr., Lucinda, Jerusha junr. and Zephaniah [...] for the trespass at the breaking: directed to and serv'd by *Coroner.*

Jerusha brings Act[io]n vs. Allen for serv[in]g said Warrant on June 1 and Octr. 9th and the Mittimus, and Bethiah junr. and Lucinda are admitted Parties and complain of the service of the three Warrants on June 1st. and also of Allen abusing them in *the Night.*

Bethiah brings Action vs. Basset for abusing her that Night and Bethiah junr. and Wadsworth are made Partys complain of Bassets abusing them on *the Nights* and also say Basset's judg[men]t vs. them for the Trespass is wrong or too much.

---

[70] Presumably other cases of personal injury decided during the Plymouth term of the Superior Court. But it could also refer to Inferior Court cases determined there.

[71] Paine Law Notes. The material down to the minutes of Mayhew v. Allen is, from the state of the MS, Paine's pre-trial statement of the litigation.

Jerusha Mahew et al. vs. Robt. Allen

Plaintiff

Rebbecca Mahew. Deposition 11th. Octr. 1762. Came again 20th. Came again 25th. PM came again.

Mary Hunt. Deposition same.

Jane Magee. 25th. Jer. gave defendant the lye about a Death he said if she was well he would horsewhip her tho she was a Woman. Same as Reb[ecca] and Marys.

Zeph. Mahew. Oct. 25. Same. June 1st.

Esqr. Smith. Interlocutory Recognizance.

Simon Mahew. 9th. Octr. mittimus given to Allen. He procured two men to pass word for his forth coming.

Deacon Mahew. The taking on the warrant.

Mrs. Chase. June 1 the taking by the Warrant, on *the Nights.*

Uriah Tilton. The imprisonment before Justice M Mahew and [....] *mittimus* and his ⟨being⟩ giving [word?] for her forthcoming.

John Basset. Went after him in June and could not catch them.

Wm. Steward. Same.

Esqr. Z. Mahew. She was too sick to be carried on the *Mittimus*. I ask'd Allen if I might take his Prisoner and he gave Liberty.

Law Arrests. P. 189 §22. Constable liable in executing General Warrant.[72]

184 §8 Cons[table] can suffer to go at large and retake.[73]

172 §8. Jus[tice of the] P[eace] can't grant General Warrant.[74]

71 §9 Not Murder to slay an officer executing bad Warrant.[75]

---

[72] *Law of Arrests* 189, §22: "And if one Justice of the Peace direct his Warrant to a Constable, to bring the Person before him, to answer all such Matters as shall be objected against him by another, and does not set forth the special Matter in the Warrant, the Warrant is unlawful, because it does not give the Offender Time and Opportunity to find Sureties; and the Constable, if he executes it, is liable to an Action of false Imprisonment."

[73] *Law of Arrests* 184, §8: "And if a Constable arrests an Offender by Virtue of a Warrant from a Justice of the Peace, and afterwards suffers him to go at large, upon his Promise to come again at such a Time and find Sureties, he cannot afterwards arrest him by Force of the same Warrant."

[74] Probably *Law of Arrests* 173–174, §8: "A Justice of the Peace (it is said) cannot justify the Granting a general Warrant, to search all suspected Houses in general for stolen Goods; for such a Warrant seems in the very Face of it to be illegal, because it would be very hard to leave it to the Discretion of a common Officer to arrest what Persons, and search what Houses he should think fit. . . . And yet there is a Precedent of such general Warrant in *Dalton's Justice*, notwithstanding the Unreasonableness, and seeming Unwarrantableness of such Practice."

[75] *Law of Arrests* 71–72, states the facts and holding of Rex v. Cook, Cro. Car. 537, 79 Eng. Rep. 1063 (K.B. 1640).

No. 1. Bassett v. Mayhew

13 §11. Coroner not officer to serve Warrants.[76]

2 Shaw. 382 §3: action lyes vs. person who executes a Warrant who is not legal ⟨Warrant⟩ officer.[77]

1 Shaw. 262 § officer cant execute general Warrant.[78]

Defendant

The Warrant vs. Jerusha et al.

The Mittimus vs. Jerusha.

The Province Law of Coroner. @ Plaintiff and Compl[ainan]t the same. And it doth not appear on the warrant the Sheriff was Compl[ainan]t.[79]

Distroying these Warrants for want of form will open a Door for Actions, As the Sup[erio]r C[our]t has condemned them.[80]

Thos. Lothrop. Deposition.

There was no touching therefore no Arrest. @ there may be Imprisonment without touching.

How Dr. Mahew could be interested. @ resentment.

Cornelius Basset vs. Wadsworth, Bethiah and Bethiah junr. Mahew.

Plaintiff

Last Judg[men]t.

Warrant to take Wadsworth.

Jona. Cathcart. Deposition.

Jer. Manter. Bethiah junr. cry'd Wad. fire the Gun by her Voice, Lucinda, cry'd Zeph. dont fire.

Mela. Davis. I was at Cobb's. Basset offered me a Dollar to go as

[76] *Law of Arrests* 13, 14, §11: "The Coroners are not the proper Officers of the Court in any other Case, but where the Sheriff is absolutely improper."

[77] See note 58 above. This may be 2 Shaw, *Justice of the Peace* 348: "If a Justice of Peace exceeds his Authority in granting a Warrant, yet the Officer must execute it, and is indemnified in so doing; but if it be in a Case, where he has no Jurisdiction, or in a Matter whereof he has no Conusance, the Officer ought not to execute such Warrant, for if he does, he may be punished. . . . And so note, that the Officer is bound to take Notice of the Authority and Jurisdiction of the Judge." See also *id.* at 347: "If a Person says, I arrest you in the King's name, &c. you ought to obey . . . and if it appears afterwards that he was no legal Officer, an Action of false Imprisonment lies against him."

[78] See note 58 above. This may be 1 Shaw, *Justice of the Peace* 260–261: "If a justice sends his Warrant to a Constable, to bring a Person before him to answer to such Matters as shall be objected against him, and doth not specify the Cause in his Warrant, for which he issued the same; this Warrant is unlawful, and the Officer is liable to an Action of false Imprisonment if he executes it; for all Warrants not specifying the Cause, are utterly against Law."

[79] See note 28 above. Paine used the symbol @ to indicate an answer to, or refutation of, an opponent's point.

[80] The cases have not been identified.

officer. Ill press you as assistance. Esqr. Mahew offered to have him forth Coming. 9 oClock when we came from Cobb's; not time eno[ugh].

Elias Norton. Deposition. Basset seemed to say he was obliged to go that Night. Not time eno[ugh].

Thos. Dogget. Some body in house said fire the Gun; told him [try].

Sylv. Norton. Forced the door with billets of Wood. Saw the Gun ly on the Stairs.

Ebenr. Allen. Came from Cobbs about 9 oClock, eat supper at Cathcarts. I think it was 11 oClock when we got to the house.

Robt. Hammet.

Benja. Coffin. Basset promised Esqr. Mahew if he would [have] Wadsworth that he believed he would not go. Bethiah cry'd Wadsworth fire Gun. Near 10 at Cathcarts.

Esqr. Hancock. The reason of the Court's granting such a Warrant and del[ivere]d about 7 oClock. I understood next morning that Basset had engaged me to go that night and [...] his preachments.

Esqr. Smith. I did not like the warrant, it was imagined they were determined to bear down the Authority of the Island.

Dr. Mahew. Bethiah junr. told me if any officers came with warrant they would resist unto the last degree, speaking of Zeph. Chase.

Esqr. Athearn. By the talk they had I concluded they would not go that night.

Nathan Mahew. Deposition. Jerusha said they had a Gun hidden and would shoot April 2 1762.

Mary Mott. Deposition.

Seth Dogget. Deposition. Jerusha shreaking that she was sory she must be the Death of some of their neighbours.

Wm. Stewart. Deposition about F[...] Being threatning.

⟨*Jona. Cathcart. Deposition.*⟩

Jona. Forster. I ask'd to come in 2 or 3 years ago Jerusha came to the Door and bid me come in. Old Woman said we keep a Gun to shoot any officer that comes for the Boy and also a Club.

Saml. Bradford. Col. Basset had bad Legg.

Dr. Smith. Bad for a flesh Wound.

Defendant

Zeph. Mahew. Wadsworth was asleep. I waked him, I heard no report of Gun.

Lucinda Mahew. Wadsworth and Zeph in bed, I waked em and they went with me to the back Door.

Zeph Chase. I was up Chamber and made my Escape and did not know if a Gun fired till next day.

Mercy Chase.

Esqr. Mahew. Warrant ⟨Bassett⟩ I proposed to Basset not to go till morning, Jer. Manter pushed on the thing. Basset then said if you'll undertake to acquaint the Family, I'll let it alone till morning. As I pass'd Defendants house I saw no light, I told Jerusha there was a Warrant on Wadsworth. She said We will Not stop him Against lawful Authority. Allen came with his Warrant. Esqr. Hancock said if any body should Attempt to break his house in the Night he would kill 'em as quick as a Rabbit.

Mary Hunt. Deposition as to the Damage done Bethiah junr.

Deacon Mahew. Bethiah junr. much hurt.

Simon Mayhew. Bethiah junr. much hurt.

John Cottle. Deposition of Basset's promise and intent to take Chase's Boy.

Mary Magee. Deposition of Dr. Mahews Speech about pulling down the house to take Chase Boy.

Ruth Mahew. Deposition. Bethiah junr. much hurt.

John Basset. Talk with Basset.

Timo. Mayhew junr. Deposition about Bassets Zeal in taking Zeph. Chase and said he must take door off hinges.

Sarah Hatch. Deposition of Basset threats to take the Boy Very Strong.

Elisha West. Deposition of Bethiah junr's Bruizes; of Zeph Chase carrying the Gun, Abel Chase said he had employ'd them that would get the Boy.

Jeira Willis. I took it for granted Basset was determined not to come that night, Cobb's Wife advised Basset to go and others back'd him, Basset insulted Wadsworth, late bed time when they [. . . .].

Ebenzr. Smith. Deposition. Bassets promise not to go that Night.

Ezra Tilton. Jer. Manter told me next day how he was desirous to go.

Uriah Tilton.

Objections to Warrant

To search all suspected houses.

Not for sufficient Cause to break house.

If Warrant good, officer could not break in the night.

2. King v. Stewart

1773–1774

EDITORIAL NOTE

This case, an early instance of patriotic violence which disturbed Adams deeply, arose on the night of 19 March 1766 at Scarborough in the District of Maine, when a mob broke into the home and store of Richard King. The rioters terrorized King's pregnant wife and five children (including the future Federalist politician Rufus King), destroyed his windows and furniture, and burned a deskful of papers. The court files and related papers on this and other suits involving King suggest three roots for the townspeople's animus. First, many of them were his customers and owed him money; second, they had suspected that he was a prospective Stamp Act officer; third, they resented his claim that the parish, of which he had been treasurer, owed him money for disbursements.[1]

Despite threats of death if he sought legal redress, King pressed indictments against the mob members and petitioned the General Court for pecuniary relief (Document I). Meanwhile, in the spring of 1767, the mob had burned another house of his and a barn whose alleged size (72 by 32 feet) suggests King's financial position.

Unsuccessful in his efforts to obtain either vengeance or recompense, in March 1773 King finally commenced a civil action at Falmouth Inferior Court (now Portland) against John Stewart and nine others whom he numbered among his tormentors.[2] The subsequent course of the litigation may be traced in King's remonstrance to the Superior Court (Document II) and in the writ of review (Document III) which the defendants obtained after a Superior Court jury at the June 1773 term had awarded King £200 damages for his losses in March 1766. The first Superior Court trial is of interest from the evidentiary standpoint, because testimony

[1] As to King, see JA's comments and the editorial note on this case in 1 *Adams Family Correspondence* 131–134. See also the files of King v. Stewart in SF 139590, 139642, 139645. For King's successful litigation with the Parish, see SCJ Rec. 1768, fols. 219–220; SF 139251, 139254. The undated minutes of a Grand Jury hearing, probably dating from 1766, also suggest that the Stewarts suspected King's servant of killing a horse of theirs. NHi:Rufus King MSS.

[2] See Doc. III. The reasons for King's delay of seven years in bringing this action are not clear. He may have feared the vengeance with which he was threatened, or perhaps he felt that legislative redress was likely to prove more fruitful than an action at law against defendants of doubtful solvency. In any event, King escaped the bar of the statute of limitations by virtue of the Act of 20 Nov. 1770, c. 9, §2, 5 A&R 109, 110, which, extending the period of limitations for trespass to goods from three to six years, provided that such actions might be brought "within six years from the first day of December [1770], or within six years next after the cause of such actions or suits, and not after." The same statute would have barred King's action if it had sounded in assault and battery, since such actions had to be brought "within one year, next after the first day of December aforesaid, or within four years next after the cause of such actions or suits, and not after."

of parties as to whom the action had been dismissed was allowed, as was handwriting evidence both for and against John Stewart.

Adams first appeared in the case as counsel for King at the trial in review, where King's cross-appeal seeking an increase in the damages previously awarded was also tried. Three of the remaining six defendants had defaulted, perhaps pursuant to an offer of settlement made by King (Document XI).

Adams' minutes (Document XIII) are unusual, because they contain not only a summary of the evidence but what appears to be a complete text of his address to the jury. That he considered this case unusual is strongly suggested by a letter to his wife, written at Falmouth on 7 July 1774 (Document XIV), which echoes the vivid phrases of his address. The two are virtually contemporaneous expressions of his distaste for indiscriminate mob action, apparently high on the eve of the Revolution after nearly a decade of participation in the affairs of the patriotic movement.

Despite Adams' rousing argument, the jury saw fit to increase King's recovery by only £60 10s. Moreover, it reversed the former judgment as to defendant Jonathan Andrews, awarding him £40 10s. to be remitted by King. The verdicts thus left the remaining defendants liable in a total of £260 10s., much less than the ad damnum of £2000 which King had alleged in his writ. Even this relatively modest judgment was not soon to be satisfied, however. As late as 1784 King's widow was still trying to realize upon it.[3]

[3] See the judgments in SCJ Rec. 1773, fol. 92; *id.* 1774, fols. 229–231. The actual damages enumerated in the declaration for the night of 19 March 1766 total £1425 3s. 1 1/2d., of which all but £27 was in notes and other obligations destroyed by the mob. The verdict may reflect the fact that King had been able to collect some of the debts represented by the lost papers. He was the successful party in numerous actions appearing in the Superior Court Minute Books for Cumberland and Lincoln counties for the years 1766 through 1774. See also note 12 below. The execution which issued to King after his first victory in 1773 was returned unsatisfied, and no execution in his favor issued after the decision in review in 1774. Execution against King issued in favor of Jonathan Andrews in Nov. 1774, but it was returned unsatisfied in May 1775, King having died earlier in the year. SF 119636, 109174. In 1784, King's widow prevailed in two actions of debt on the judgments recovered by her husband in July 1774. See SJC Rec. 1784, fols. 201–202; SF 139893, 139894. The files contain two executions returned in Nov. 1784 partially satisfied in the amounts of £36 8s. 10d. and £17 9s. 2d. SF 119637, 119638. In June 1790 she recovered upon a note for £50 given to her husband in Aug. 1773 by John, Joseph, Samuel, and Timothy Stewart, SJC Rec. 1790, fol. 140; SF 140140. This note, rather than Doc. XI, may have been the basis of the Stewarts' default in July 1774. See notes 35, 40, below.

I. KING'S PETITION TO THE GENERAL COURT[4]

4 January 1768

Province of the Massachusetts Bay To His Excellency the Governor The Hon[orab]le His Majestys Council and the Honle. House of Reprisentitives in General Court Assembled

Humbly Shews Richard King of Scarborough in the County of Cumberland in Said Province Gentleman That in the Night of the 19th of March AD 1766. a Number of Persons in Disguise with axes Clubbs &c. Broak the windows of the Dwelling House and Wair-House of Your Petitioner, and Entered both Distroyed the kitchen furniture &c. and marred the winscot of the Dwelling House Burnt and Distroyed Robb'd and Carried of from the Dwelling House and WairHouse Great Quantitys of Your Petitioners Papers and writings of Great value among which the Number of Bonds and notes of Hand for money Due which have already Com to Your Petitioners knowlidge togather with the Lawfull Intrest Due on the Same to the Time of the Riot Amount to the Sum of £1104/15/3 lawfull money of said Province Exclusive of other writings of Great value. That in the morning of the second Day after the Riot a writing was found put up at your Petitioners Gate in the name of Sons of Liberty Threatening Your Petitioner and Every other Person in the County that Should be Instrumental of any worrant or Summons to be Served on aney Person on account of the Riot he or they might Depend upon haveing their Houses and Barns Burnt and Consumed and themselves Cut in pices and burnt to Ashes. That in a Short time after another Threatening letter was lodged at the Door of one John Fitts who was a Tenant to Your Petitioner, therein warning him to Depart from that House within twelve Days or he might Expect to be Distroyd for they were Determined to Distroy King and all he had.[5] That Eight Days after the Riot upon Complaint a Warrant was Issued by Several Justices of

---

[4] FC, in an unidentified hand, signed by King. NHi:Rufus King MSS. The chaotic punctuation of the MS has been left undisturbed. A petition from King was presented to the General Court on 20 Jan. 1768 and referred to a committee. No record of action on it has been found. Mass., *House Jour.*, 1767–1768, 2d sess. The list King mentioned in the penultimate paragraph below has not been found. It probably resembled the "schedule" annexed to his writ, discussed in note 12 below.

[5] The anonymous message addressed to King by the Scarborough "Suns of liburty" is printed as Doc. X below. That to Fitts was as follows: "Fits this Is to Give you notice that Wee are all ditirmand If you dont move off and Leave the Place We Will Sarve You as We dide king Cause we are ditirmand to destory him and all he hass. And Wee Give you 12 days to go of in and if you ant gone in that time you may Expect to be destroyed. Samuel oos." NHi:Rufus King MSS.

the County Against such Persons as were Suspected, and Summonses for Such as were Supposed Capable to Prove the Fact. But with little Effect two only of the Persons Suspected Suffering them selves to be taken the others as also the Principal witnesses Either keeping their Doors Shut against the officers Going back into the woods or Going armed avoided being taken or summoned, that while the Justices that were assembled on this Occasion were waiting for the officers to Execute the warrants &c. a Number of the Riotous Party actualy Assembled in order as was Said to Rescue aney Person that might be apprehend, That in May following the House Improved by Fitts above mentioned was Set on fire and had Nigh like to have ben Consumed with the Household Goods therin which so Allaramed him that he soon Quit the Same which House was Soon after almost distroyed by tairing Down the Chimney &c. That Your Petitioner perciveing the Injuerys he had sustained by the Riot appeared to be pointed more at his papers then aney other Part of his Intrest and that maney Persons appeared Determined to take advantage of the Distruction of his Securities for the Discharge of their Debts &c. That sum from whome your Petitioner had Purchased Lands began to threaten a reEntery, upon finding their Deeds were not on Record, alledging for their Justification that your Petitioner had obtained Deeds, Bonds, and Notes by taking the Advantage of People. Wherefore your Petitioner by an Instrument in writing under his hand appointed the Two first Justices in the County togather with a Gentleman of the Law Arbitrators in General between my Selfe and all Persons (if aney there were) who will appear before Said arbitraters within three months and alledge their having Suffered or being lyable to Suffer by means of aney Deed of Sale Deed of mortgage or Bill of Sale Bond note of hand or other Obligation whatsoever, with Three months more to prove the Same was by Your Petitioner fraudelintly Obtained as they alledge.

And if upon a full hearing of the matter aney such fraudes Should appear on the Part of your Petitioner Said Arbitraters were therin Desired to Certifie the same in writing under their Hands which Certificate if refering to a Deed of sale Deed of Mortgage or Bill of Sale Should Intitle the Party to recover the whole Consideration over again or if it referred to aney Bond Note of hand or other obligation whatsoever to be Sufficiant in aney of His Majesty's Courts of record to Barr aney action that might Ever after be brought upon Such obligation respectively, therin also Subjecting himSelfe to pay all Cost and Charge arising by Such Dispuet wherin he Should be found in the wrong which Submission Your Petitioner notified at length in two

[of] the most frequented Taverns in said Town of Scarborough, But no Person Ever appeared, nor Applied for aney redress, That while the officers were Indeviouring to Summon the witnesses to attend the Sup[erio]r Court in this County June 1766. Seven windows in a Dwelling House belonging to Your Petitioner were broak and Distroyed. That in the month of Augt. following Your Petitioner Suffered the Loss of an Ax Stole out of his Pasture Suposed to have ben Taken by Sum of the riotous Party who Imploied them selves back in the woods to be out of the way of an Officer. That in the Night of the 4th March last the Dwelling House last mentioned (which had ben lately refitted) was attacked the Boards and Clapboards Tore off the Sealing beat in, and the Posts and Studds Cutt off and the House rendered Irepairable. That in the night of the fourteenth of May last being a few Days after the apprehending and Imprissoning one Silas Burbank upon an Inditement for the Riot,[6] a Barn belonging to Your Petitioner of more then seventy foot Long and thirty wide Covered and fixed in the best manner togather with a Shedd of Eighty foot Long was burnt and Consumed with sum Hay and most of your Petitioners Utensils for Husbandry. And Two of your Petitioners best Calves Killd and Carried off at the same Time. That your Petitioner has ben at Great Trouble and Expence in Indeviouring to bring those Rioters to Justice that altho a Number were Indited at the Supr. Court in this County June 1766 and warrants against them Given to proper officers and those officers afterwards actualy in Company with Sum of those the warrants were against Yet the same have not ben Executed upon aney Except Burbank above named and not on him till he Grew so Bold as to use the Goalkeepers House as a Tavern, the reason assigned by the officers for not Executing the warrants when both togather were in Companey with Sum that were Indited, was, that they Did not think it safe and were actualy afraid to Execute the same. That During this time the Rioters Party have ben Sending off to Machias and other Places Such as might have ben made use of as Witnesses against them and Greatly Intimidating others So that the obtaining witnesses against them (all Circumstances Considered) must be attended with Great Difficulty if not Impossibillity to your Petitioner. That for a Privat man to bring a Great number of Persons to Justice for such Dissorders as first origenated under a Notion of Publick Utility Committed in a Time of General Dissorder and Confusion

---

[6] Burbank was undoubtedly released when the indictment was not pressed. His subsequent incarceration in 1773 was on a body attachment in King's action of trespass. See note 26 below.

while others who were alike Guilty were Exempt from Punishment by act of Government [7] is a Burthen too Great and attended with too much Hazerd to be Effected by an Individual at this Time. That as it is Evident the Injuryes Your Petitioner has sustained is by a Detachment of the Spirit of Dissorder above mentioned the other Sufforers by which have ben Since Compensated. Your Petitioner thinks it an unhappiness and Misfortune peculer to him Selfe to be obliged Either to Sell [Sett?] down by his Losses or Go through Such an ardous [... undertaking] to Repair them as appear more likely to render his Losses Double Such an undertaking as Even Government it Selfe has though[t] fit to Decline and Yet to be Taxed to the Compensation of others. That Notwithstanding your Petitioner has taken all possible pains to obtain the renewal of the obligations he Lost by the Riot by offering long Credit and Easey Payment, Yet the amount of the Sum that is neither paid nor renewed nor Can be Confided in to be paid renewed, or in aney wise made Good by the respective Debtors is £463/3/5 1/2 Exclusive of the Intrest on the same Since the Riot. A List whereof togather with the other articals of Loss Sustained by your Petitioner as above is herewith presented to Your Excellency and Honours.

Which Losses and Damages togather with the Exposed Scituation of Your Petitioner Your Petitioner Humbly Supplicats Your Ex[cel]-le[nc]y and Honours to take under Your wise and Just Consideration, and that Your Excellency and Honours would be pleased to Compensate and make Good to Your Petitioner the Injureys he has Sustained from the Hands of those Riotus Persons as also that your Excellency and Honours would be pleased to Direct in Such wise with respect to any further Process against them, that the Intrest of your Petitioner may be Secured from any further Distruction at their Hands. All which Your Petitioner Humbly Submitts and Prays. Richd. King Scarbo[rough] Jany. 4th 1768

[7] The reference is apparently to An Act for Granting Compensation to the Sufferers, and of Free and General Pardon, Indemnity and Oblivion to the Offenders in the Late Times, 6 Dec. 1766, 4 A&R 903. This Act, which was later disallowed by the Privy Council, compensated royal officials injured in Boston's Stamp Act riot in Aug. 1765, and extended amnesty for events through 1 May 1766. It contained a clause providing that it should be a good defense to any indictment for rioting and the like. Despite the disallowance, payments to the "sufferers" were made under the Act, and it probably was effective in other respects as well. See 4 A&R 931–945. The Act probably would not have protected King's tormentors, since it was not effective to pardon rioting, "wherein any burglaries, arsons, or thefts were committed against the properties of persons not compensated" by it. But it cannot have made the job of bringing the offenders to justice any easier. For JA's report of popular reaction to the idea of indemnification, see 1 JA, *Diary and Autobiography* 323–326.

II. KING'S REMONSTRANCE [8]

Richd. Kings Remonstrance to the Superr. Ct. July. 1771

To The Honle. His Majesty's Justices of the Supr. Court of Judicature Court of Assize &c. Now Holden in the Countys of Cumberland and for the County of Cumberland and Lincolen

Richard King of Scarborough in the County of Cumberland Humbly remonstrates that by a riot in the night of the 19 of March AD 1766 His Dwilling House and waireHouse were broken up and a great number of his Notes and Bonds for money due and other papers of value were burnt or Carried off by the Rioters, Exclusive of other Damages, that altho' thredened by letter and otherwise that if he was the Cause of any warrants or Summonses being served on any Person or Persons on that acco[un]t he might depend upon it, his Cattle should be killed, his House, and Barns Burnt, and himsilfe Cut to pieces and burnt to ashes. That notwithstanding their many threats and Menaces Your Remonstrant persued the measuers directed by the then attorney General, upon which fourteen Persons were Indicted at the Supr. Court 1766. preparitory to the Supr. Court in 1767. Wittness were summoned and sum persons Indicted were taken, but by reason of a failour of Juriours from said lower County no new Indictments Could be found, nor the olde ones brot On Tryall. Your Remonstrant made the utmost Efforts again preparitory to the Supr. Court 1768. and Caused witnesses to be summoned who if they had appeard and Deposed the Truth must have proved those Guilty who were under Indictment and then before the Court, and ben the means of procuring new Indictments of those that Distroyed his farmHouse and burnt his Barn &c. The Honle. Court ordered a Warrant, and an officer was sent after them, who made return he could not find neither of them. So nothing further was don at that Court nor since til now, in this length of time sum persons have disclosed matters that did not appear before, and other Circumstances which Gave Incouragement to your Remonstrant to make a new attempt. Accordingly on Satterday last Your remonstrant having precured a new warrant for the Persons Indicted, percured Timothy Stuart, one of the Principel actors among them that were Indicted to be apprehended by one Abraham Lavit one of the Counstables of Scarborough. But the officer not being

---

[8] FC, apparently in King's hand and signed by him. The docketing note on verso is printed here as a caption to the document. NHi:Rufus King MSS. It has not been determined whether this "Remonstrance" was ever submitted to the court. No action upon it appears in the Minute Books.

sufficiantly on his Guard, suffered the said Timothy to make his Escape on his way to the Goal.[9] The Loss sustained by Distruction of your remonstrants security for money Due (Exclusive of what has bin since in any wise paid or renewed) togather with the Intrest amounts to £743.0.10 Exclusive of all other matters, which upon the whole must Exceed £1000. LMy. [lawful money] Exclusive of the Great Pain to him Selfe, wife and Children, Trouble and Expence in Endiveouring to bring the Parpitrators to Justice and to hire men to Guard his House[10] against their outrage agreeable to their threats while he was so Doing. Wherefore Your Remonstrant Humbly Supplicates Your Honours to take his Case under Consideration, and that Your Honours would be pleased to Take such Imediate measuers as may Tend to reduce his Distroyers to reason and open the way for his redress.

All which is Humbly Submitted by Your Honours Most Obedient, and most Humble Servant   Richd. King
Falmo[uth] 2d. July 1771.

III. WRIT OF REVIEW—STEWART ET AL. v. KING[11]

Cumberland Superior Court, Falmouth, June 1774

To the Sheriff of our county of Cumberland his under-Sheriff or Deputy, Greeting.

We command You that You summon Richard King of Scarborough in our County of Cumberland Esqr. (if he may be found in your precinct) to appear before our Justices of our Superior Court of Judicature Court of Assize and general Goal delivery to be holden at Falmouth within said county of Cumberland and for the countys of Cumberland and Lincoln on the tuesday next after the fourth Tuesday of June next, then and there in our said court to answer unto

[9] Documentation for this account is in the Suffolk Files. See the indictment, dated June 1766, in SF 87727. Although John Stewart's plea of Not Guilty, dated June term 1766, is on the verso of this document, the Minute Books of the Superior Court show that none of the offenders was ever actually tried. Min. Bks. 76, 87, 92, 99, SCJ Cumberland and Lincoln. Most of the warrants which King describes, including that for Timothy Stewart, with a return reporting his escape, are in SF 87726, 88530, 89145, 90305.

[10] In a letter to King dated 18 May 1767, Col. Samuel Waldo, apparently commander of the Falmouth militia, regretfully informed him that if he wanted a military guard it would have to come from Scarborough, but suggested that if he was leery of entrusting his fortunes to his fellow townspeople, he might hire his own guards and ask the General Court to reimburse him. NHi:Rufus King MSS.

[11] SF 139642. In the hand of Nathaniel Hatch. Caption ("Province of the Massachusetts Bay. . . . George the third," &c.) omitted.

John Stewart Yeoman Jonathan Andrews Blacksmith, Amos Andrews Yeoman *Timothy Stewart Yeoman, Samuel Stewart* Yeoman, and Jonathan Andrews junr. Blacksmith all of said Scarborough In a plea of Review of a plea of Trespass commenced and prosecuted at an inferior court of common pleas held at said Falmouth on the last Tuesday of March seventeen hundred and seventy three by the said Richard against the said John Jonathan, Amos, Timothy, Samuel and Jonathan Andrews junr. and also against Jonathan Wingate Silas Burbank and Benjamin Carl in the words following, to wit, In a plea of Trespass for that the said John, Jonathan Andrews Amos Jonathan Wingate, Silas Timothy Samuel Jonathan Andrews junr. and Benjamin Carl at Scarborough aforesd. on the nineteenth day of March, AD 1766, in the nighttime with force and Arms broke and entered the said Richards house in said Scarborough wherein he and his family then dwelt and then and there with force as aforesaid broke and destroy'd seven of his glass windows of the value of seven pounds and cut and defaced the wainscott stair case within the said house of the value of six pounds bruised and ruin'd three dozen pewter plates and dishes of the plaintiffs of the value of four pounds ten shillings broke and destroy'd the plaintiffs stone earthen and brassware Kitchen chairs table and other household Utensils and furniture there found of the value of six pounds broke open and destroy'd the said Richard's desk in his said house of the value of four pounds, broke and entered the said Richard's shop near his said house, took and carried away from said house and shop and burnt and destroy'd divers deeds, notes of hand bonds and other papers of the said Richards a schedule whereof is to the writ annexed of the value of thirteen hundred ninety eight pounds three shillings and a penny half penny [12] and put the said Richard and his family into great fear and distress and danger of their lives and for that [13] the said John Jonathan Andrews Amos Jonathan Wingate Silas Timothy and Samuel Jonathan Andrews jnr.

[12] The "schedule" lists fifty-four notes of hand, three bonds, eight deeds, five copies of executions and records of pending cases, one lease, and "many other papers which I cannot now ascertain but suffer for the want of in Defending myself against the Suits of many persons," the whole totaling the amount alleged. The schedule also indicated, however, that of this sum £510 1s. 3 1/2d. in notes and bonds had been "paid or Secured to me by Several Debtors." SF 139590.

[13] In the margin of King's writ of review appears a notation that King's motion to strike the second and third counts of his declaration was granted with the defendants' consent. SF 139645. Thus the incidents of 2 March and 14 May 1767 were not in controversy on the trial in review, probably because King's proof was insufficient; on the first trial in the Superior Court in June 1773, the jury had found the defendants "not guilty" of the trespasses alleged in the second and third counts. Min. Bk. 99, SCJ Cumberland and Lincoln, June 1773, N–1.

and Benjamin Carl afterwards on the second day of March, AD 1767, at said Scarborough with force and arms cut down ruin'd and destroy'd another house of the said Richard in said Scarborough of the value of fifty pounds and afterwards upon the fourteenth day of May, AD 1767, at sd. Scarborough, the said John, Jonathan Andrews Amos Jonathan Wingate, Silas, Timothy, Samuel Jonathan Andrews junr. and Benjamin Carl with force as aforesd. burnt and destroy'd the said Richards barn there seventy two feet in length and thirty two feet in width of the value of eighty five pounds and his shed adjoining the same barn of the value of fifteen pounds one load of English hay being in said barn of the value of fifty shillings two bushells of his Flax seed of the value of twelve shillings his hay Cart of the value of twenty four shillings twelve rods of his barnyard fence there of the value of four pounds, and took and carried away two sleds of the value of twenty four shillings each six ox yoaks of the value of thirty six shillings six hay forks of the value of twenty shillings four scythes of the value of twenty four shillings four sickles of the value of six shillings and ten rakes of the value of twelve shillings all the property of the sd. Richard and divers other of his utensils of husbandry there found of the value of forty shillings and also took carried away and kill'd two of his calves there found of the value of thirty six shillings, and other enormities and wrongs did there at the several times aforesaid to the sd. Richard against our peace and to the damages of the said Richard as he says the sum of two thousand pounds, at which sd. inferiour Court Judgment was rendred that the sd. John Stewart Jonathan Andrews Amos Andrews Jonathan Wingate, Silas Burbank, Timothy Stewart Samuel Stewart, Jonathan Andrews junr. and Benjamin Carl recover against the said Richard King cost of Suit;[14] from which Judgment the sd. Richard appealed to the sd. Superiour Court of Judicature &c. held at said Falmouth on the Tuesday next after the fourth Tuesday of June last, when and where the sd. Richard moved the Court that he might be allow'd to strike the names of Silas Burbank Jonathan Wingate and Benjamin Carle, out of the original writ, and it was granted;[15] and their names was struck out accordingly, and the sd. Silas Jonathan and Benjamin in the same court acknowledged themselves satisfied as to their costs

[14] Judgment in the Inferior Court was rendered on the verdict of a jury after pleas of the general issue by the several defendants. SF 139590.

[15] As to this maneuver, designed to make these men competent as witnesses for King, see Doc. IV. The lists of witnesses in the files show that Wingate and Burbank gave depositions and testimony for King in June 1773. SF 139590. All three testified in June 1774. See Doc. XIII.

and Judgment of the same Court was rendred that the said Richard King recover against the said John Stewart, Jonathan Andrews Amos Andrews, Timothy Stewart Samuel Stewart and Jonathan Andrews junr. the sum of two hundred pounds lawfull money damage and costs taxed at twenty two pounds twelve shillings and a penny; which same Judgment the said plaintiffs in this writ of Review say is wrong and erroneous and that thereby they are damnified the Sum of two hundred and fifty pounds wherefore for reversing the same Judgment and recovering back from the said Richard King the sd. Sum of two hundred pounds and the same cost and for recovering Judgment against him for cost of Courts they the plaintiffs in Review bring this Suit. . . .[16]

And the said Richard King comes and defends &c.[17] and Saith that the Said last mentioned Judgment is in nothing erroneous, Saving that it ought to have been for Two Thousand Pounds[18] and thereof puts himself on the Country. John Adams

And the said Plaintiffs in Review likewise.[19]

James Sullivan ⎱
John Sullivan ⎰ their attorneys

IV. CUSHING'S REPORT OF THE ARGUMENT[20]

Cumberland Superior Court, Falmouth, June 1773

Richard King v. Jno. Stewart & al

This was an action of trespass—and on motion of Mr. Bradbury attorney to plaintiff after issue joined—plaintiff was allowed by the Court to strike out the names of several of the Defendants in order that they might be witnesses for plaintiff—on payment of costs—1

---

[16] King's writ of review was substantially identical with this one, except in the relief sought, which was the recovery of an additional £1800, the remainder of the original ad damnum of £2000. SF 139645. (The teste and return of service are omitted.)

[17] For the language used here, see p. 43, note 38 above.

[18] This assertion, perhaps analogous to a counterclaim, might well have been objectionable under ordinary pleading rules. It is obvious, however, that these rules were not observed closely in the rather special situation of the writ of review, which had no English equivalent, and formally raised only the single broad issue whether anything in the prior phases of the action had been erroneous. Since as a practical matter both this action against King and King's action seeking an increase of the judgment would be tried together, a pleading with such an exceptive clause avoided any inconsistency of position. A similar form was employed by the defendants in pleading to King's writ. SF 139645.

[19] Both plea and joinder are in JA's hand, although the Sullivans signed the latter.

[20] Cushing Reports, fol. 4.

Wils. 89, Trials per pais 386, Str. 420, were cited.[21] On the trial of the issue the plaintiff offered to prove, *by comparison of hands* that an anonymous letter which had been found posted on the plaintiff's door was written by Defendant—This kind of evidence was objected to by Sullivan for Defendants—but allowed by the Court as good in civil actions.

Oliver, CJ, Hutchinson, Ropes and Cushing, Justices

Vide Evans' translation of Pothier on obligation Append. 2d vol. No. XVI sec. 6c.[22] 8 Ves. 438 Egleton v. Kingston.[23]

V. KING TO SILAS BURBANK[24]

Mr. Burbank   Scarborough 31. May 1773

Sir

I receved Yours of the 17th. Current, and a Second that appears

[21] It was necessary for King to dismiss his action against those defendants whom he wished to have testify for him, not merely to dispose them favorably toward him, but in order to make them competent as witnesses. At common law, parties to an action could not testify. The authorities cited in the text were as follows:

Noke & Chiswell v. Ingham, 1 Wils. K.B. 89, 90, 95 Eng. Rep. 508, 509 (K.B. 1745): "Lee Ch. Justice: It is agreed on all hands, that in trespass against several, the plaintiff may enter a *nolle prosequi* [an abandonment of further prosecution] as to one, and that will not discharge the other."

2 Duncomb, *Trials Per Pais* 386 (8th edn., 1766): "Trespass against several; after issue joined on motion, one of the defendants name was struck out, that he might be a witness for the plaintiff. 2 [*i.e.* 1] Siderf. 441 and the like done as to a person named in the *simul cum* ["together with," i.e. the phrase linking defendants known and unknown]. 1 Mod. 11."

Bayly v. Raby et al., 1 Str. 420, 93 Eng. Rep. 608 (K.B. 1721): Motion to consolidate four separate declarations in trespass against four separate defendants denied, despite affidavit that the trespass, if any, was committed by all jointly. "The plaintiff may have the benefit of the other's evidence in his action against either, but this will be to deprive him of that."

[22] M. Pothier, *A Treatise on the Law of Obligations or Contracts*, 2:182–186 (London, transl. W. D. Evans, 1806). An essay by the translator on the English law of handwriting evidence. "[T]he practice of the law seems to be clearly settled, that the casual knowledge or belief of a person, who has once seen the witness write, and speaks from the effect of that incident upon his memory, in respect to the character of the writing, is admissible, and a sufficient foundation for reading the disputed paper; but that a direct comparison with the greatest possible number of authentic papers, indicating the similarity to the most obvious inspection, and confirmed by the most critical scrutiny, is wholly inadmissible." *Id.* at 185. This and the citation in note 23 below were obviously added, by someone unknown, at a date much later than 1773.

[23] Eagleton & Coventry v. Kingston, 8 Ves. Jr. 438, 474, 32 Eng. Rep. 425, 438 (Ch. 1803), *per* Lord Eldon, C: "[T]ill very lately, I never heard of evidence in Westminster Hall of comparison of hand-writing by those, who had never seen the party write; though such evidence had been frequently received in the Ecclesiastical Court."

[24] FC, apparently in King's hand. Docketed in same and another hand. NHi:Rufus

to have ben wrote Since. In your first You point out the Horrows of a Goal, and Compair Your present state of Confinement, To that which Succeeds a wicked life in this world unregreted, and unrepented of, with a verry Just Exception. If taken in a spiritul Sense that You are a Prisoner of Hope, Your Pathatic Complaint of being deprived of the Company of an agreeable wife, and the parental Duty You owe to your Innocent Children, is Sufficiant to move a Heart much less Serceptive of Humain Misery then mine. You Conclude with observing, the Time has ben, when our affections mutualy flowed in kindness towards Each other, But that now there is as remarkable a Coldness.

Now Sir as You have opened this Channel of Communication between us, I will Treat the Subject with that unreservedness of mind that I should be glad to have from You. If I shall herein Charge you wrongfully in any Part, I will (when that shall appear) not only aske Your Pardon, but Publickly Confess my Error.

You Justly observe, the Time has ben when there was a mutual flow of Affection between us. I Can only add, that on my part it was Sinceer. Let us now Enquire how the Change Came, and who was first in the Offence, was it not anough on Your part to make use of the law. To Palm The Cabinet wair on me, which our privat Confidence in Each other Should have obliged You to have look'd upon as Sent at Your own Risque.

But having Comminced your Action against me at Oct. Court 1765 in order to make up your own loss, out of the owner that had also lost the Vessell that Carried it: How then Could you think of Joyning in a Plan, and Find [Fiend] like Exerting Your Selfe in adding final Distruction to the remaining Interest of your Confessed old Friend. You now Complain of the Dismel Gloom of a Goal, wherein you are Surrounded, with Massy Barrs of Iron, and thereby deprived of the Peacefull and InExpressable Philicity of Family Connections. This Misfortune You point to me, as tho I was mercyless and Cruell, void of Natural Affection, and delighting in misery. As almighty God has made all men of one Blood, and Given them the Same perseptions of Pain and Pleasure, Love and hatered, life and Death Com back with me to the 18 of March 1766. Here view Your Selfe without the least Cause of affrunt; Engaging others on that and on the Succeding Day to meet at Your House on the night of the 19th. keeping that blackest part of the Designe a Secret from all Such who's humanity you sur-

King MSS. This and the following documents indicate something of the mechanics by which Burbank's testimony was obtained.

spected would Shudder at so Dark a Sceene, Till you had Got them mett at your own House with you and other whoes minds were Proof against all Virtue. Behold Your Selfe using fair Speaches, and threats by Turns, to hold Those that discovered an unwillingness to Joyne in So Horrid an act of Ingratitude, and unjustness. But behold Still the most Horrid Part Consealed in the brest of you and a Select few, that were at the Bottom. In fine behold your Selfe now at the Head of a Banddity of Thieves and Robbers, under the Cover of night, determined to Carry Terror, and Turpitude unprevouked Destruction and Enrich Your selves out of the Spoiles of the Greatest Benefactor in Trade that Ever Dealt in the Place. To Robb and Plunder him of the verry means with which he was to discharge the Debt which he owed for what they and others had Eat, Drunk, wore, bought, and built with and this Too at a Time whin his late Loss would have Excited Pitty from one Enemy Towards another.

Here let the Sceene Change to the House of him whoes doors were allwais open, whoes open Heart had dealt out (tho' Greatly to his loss) as freely to the Necessities of the Poor, as to the Abilities of the Rich. Here behold a General Benifactor Sleeping in Perfect Security, not dreaming of Envy or Mallice, his bosom Frind upon his arm who's months with her at that Time Called for Tender usage, his Young Brood lodged around him. In this state awoaked out of sleep by the dashing in of his windows, behold him in Great amaze opening the Chamber door, Calling aloud to know the matter, his wife holding him by the arme, no humain voice in answer, Except a servant informing that his life was threatened In case he attempted his masters Relief. Here behold a murcyless hand Thorw a hatchet into the windo whence the voice of distress was heard which dashing the Glass about the Naked Bodys Scarce Miss'd their heads. Behold the Tenderer Sexes in untimly Time for flight, faultering, Sinking, Dieing, and the distress'd Husband Conveying her back to her Bead to Die there but being doubly armed with life, Each by Turn recaught the Electrical Fire. Open also your Ears to the Tender Cryes of his Childeren Crying, Father woant they kill me, Father Save me.

View this and much more also, not as an Ammaginary, but as a real Act, and Your selfe as a Principal actor in this, Original Tragedy. Then passby all that past between. Even Your threats uttered to my face Til we Com to the Night of the 14th. May 1767. Here Stop and view the Flaims. Consider well the Spirit that set them on Fire recolect the out Guards Planted there, and near my own Dwilling House also at the Same Time; hear and See a frish the Destress of a mother.

Espessuuly upon hering her outcries Eccoed by one find [fiend] to
another in the Neighbouring bushes. Here again the Cries of helples
Children, Intreeting their pairents to flee as Expecting Every moment
to be Surounded in flaims, but flee wheather. Devowerers had Surrounded us, and were Yelling like finds of H–ll for their prey. Two
fatted Calves did not appear to Suffize them. Take a Back Sight upon
the whole. Look up to God, as looking upon us lay Your hand on Your
brest, and Say Your Innocent of any part of the foregoing Charges,
or that King has Treated you unjustly. In Your Second letter, you
Say "You think the poor Deceased Captive Creaturs have little Sense
of what is Past, and that for all that is past, to the Day Instent, the
portions remaining to all are Equall." I Chuse to leeve it to the Proper
Profession to Instruct how Solomon and other Sacred writers are
to be understood but without Intrudeing; I think this much may be
Clearly asserted that vice only can make us Miserable in this life,
that he that allowedly lives and Delights therein Can never be happy
so long as his mind is So desposed and that on the Contrary the
Virtous and well meaning Can never be Miserable. For the Truth of
this we need only look into our Selves, and Enquire, whether vice
Ever gave us True Pleasure, or Virtue Pain. The Same that we Sow,
that shall we reap, and the Lord of the Harvest will Gather us accordingly.

VI. BURBANK'S RELEASE [25]

28 June 1773

Whereas Richard King Esq. hath released me from Gaol where I
have been sometime confined by having my body attached by a writ
of Trespass in which the said Richard is Plaintiff, and John Stewart
myself and others defendants [26] at my request in consideration there-

[25] In an unidentified hand; docketed by King: "Burbank's Release to Richd. King,
Esq."; signed by Burbank. NHi:Rufus King MSS. This document represents a release by Burbank of any rights against King for false imprisonment.

[26] Burbank was taken and committed in accordance with King's writ on 12
March 1773. SF 139590. Although judgment in his favor was handed down at
the Inferior Court, March term 1773, the attachment apparently remained in force
pending the appeal. By statute, execution on the Inferior Court judgment was stayed.
The process in that court seems to have served also to compel appearance in the
Superior Court, the defendant's protection being the bond which the appellant had
to post. The statutory provision that no person imprisoned on mesne process was to
remain in jail more than 30 days after the rising of the court to which the process
was returnable unless his body had been taken in execution was thus apparently
suspended by the stay of execution on appeal. See Act of 12 June 1701, §§8, 9, 11,
1 A&R 465–466.

of and of five shillings paid me by said Richard I do hereby release unto the said Richard all cause of action whatsoever I have or may have against the said Richard on account of having my body attached and imprisoned as aforesaid.

In witness whereof I have hereunto set my hand and Seal this twenty eighth day of June in the eleventh Year of his Majesty's Reign, An. Dom. 1773. Silas Burbank
Test.
Theo. Parsons

VII. DEPOSITION OF SILAS BURBANK[27]

28 June 1773

I Silas Burbanks of lawful age testify and say, that in the spring of the Year 1766, a few days before the riot at Mr. Richard Kings dwelling house, I was at the house of Mr. John Stewart, and he was talking to me about said King; he asked me if he was not a bad man, and had not done as much hurt to the people here, as Bute had done to the people at home; and afterwards, the day before the riot at Mr. Kings house, I was again at said Stewart's house, when he talked with me about King, and told me he was a bad man; had done a great deal of hurt, had treated him very unrighteously; and that he had killed his Mare; *that they were going to give him a rally*; and the Mischief Mr. Stewart proposed should be done to Mr. King was, *either to destroy him, or destroy his papers, or whip him*, but I am not certain which of them, but am certain it was one of them: Stewart said it was *a good thing*, and would do *King good*, and *make him a better man*; he also encouraged me to go, told me I had better, and used arguments to persuade me to go. I then asked him if he was a going, but am not certain, whether he said he should go or not, but I very well remember he said, if he did not go, his sons should—He said it was the best thing that could be done, and urged me by all means to go; he also told me that King was a favourer of the Stamp Act. I have seen Stewart several times since the Riot, and when we were conversing about it, he always desired me to keep it a secret, and once told me, he would spend his life and fortune before anybody should be hurt by it.

I further testify and say, that the day before the Riot at Mr. King's house, I was talking with *Amos Andrews* near his house, when An-

[27] 28 June 1773, SF 139645. Signed by the deponent.

drews asked me, *if I had heard what they were going to do.* I asked him what? He answered *we are going to pay King a visit and take him down; don't you intend to go? You have a dispute with him, and you see how he ⟨uses⟩ trys to cheat you, and may judge by that, how he uses every body and dont you intend to show some resentment? He is a bad man, and will ruin us all, if he goes on at this rate; if something or other is not done with him, if he is not humbled,* it is not worth while for any of us to live here; and he is hard hearted to the widow and orphan. I asked him who was going? He answered *he was going, and all their people up their road; that every body almost was going*; and that Stewart's family was going. I asked him if he should certainly go; *he said he should certainly go, and gave me his word and promise over and over again, that he would go, for he said it must be done.* I asked him what he proposed to do to King if he went. He answered, *we propose to take him out and cut his ears off.* I told him, that would not do, for it was monstrous; he then said *we will take him out and whip him*; He also talked with me about the Stamp Act, and said that King was a favourer of it, and had the Stamp papers in his house; and that it was probable if that Act took place, he would be Stamp Master for Scarborough. This argument, with a vast many others, he used to persuade me to join them, and be one of them, for says he, *we have already agreed upon it.* He also urged me very much to go with them; said *it was the best thing that could be done and it was no Sin.* After the riot, he told me *he was very sorry he was not there,* for he was prevented by a bad belly ach, but *was a well wisher to it, and would be as faithful as if he had been there*; and always since the Riot, he has been very urgent with me to *keep the affair secret.* I further say, the Evening Mr. King's farm house was cut down which was some time after the riot at Kings dwelling house when some persons were hanging up a dead colt before it, it was proposed to cut the house down, whilst Andrews was present, when somebody asked him if he would lend his axes; he said *his axes were dull, but they might have them,* and they lay on the hill before his door. I was also at Andrews's a day or two after the farm house was cut down, and asked him if he heard them, he said yes; I asked him if he was up, no replied he, I and my wife went to bed, and I will tell you something comical; we had a Molatto, who was a bed upstairs, and when they were cutting the house down, the Noise waked him, and he called to me to know what the noise was. What noise says I. A great noise, answers he, don't you hear it. O says I, a parcel of people are cutting down *Brother Elijah Sellea's house.* What, says he, that poor lame man's house, I will get up and help him. *No don't stir for your life says I*, they will come and cut down our house, I expect, so don't stir for your life, *for you will be killed.*

I further testify and say, that the evening before said riot at Mr. Kings house, I was at Jonathan Andrews's shop. He asked me if I had heard what they were going to do with King. I asked him what? He said *they were going to have a frolic with him, that it was a very good thing* for King was a bad man, and he mentioned several bad things, that he said King had done; that it was *absolutely necessary* something should be done with him, he was grown so arbitrary and bad. He *objected against hurting Mr. King's Interest*, but proposed their *taking him out and whipping him*; and he encouraged the thing very much. I asked him if he was going: he said he did not know, but he believed his son would. Since the riot, he has been very urgent with me to keep the affair secret. I further testify and say, that Joseph Stewart, Timothy Stewart, Samuel Stewart, and *Jonathan Andrews junr. were present aiding and assisting at the riot* at Mr. Kings dwelling house.   Silas Burbanks

[Verification omitted.]

The Deponent adds, It was in the night when I saw the person whom I supposed to be Amos Andrews, but I cannot say it was he otherwise then as I judged it to be him from the voice and appearance of the person and his Dress.   Att. Sam Winthrop Cler.[28]

Sullivan expressly allows that the Witnesses swear that Amos Andrews encouraged them to *mob* King, which includes every supposable species of Trespass.[29]

VIII. DEPOSITION OF JOHN NEWBEGIN [30]

19 January 1773

I John Newbegin of Lawful Age testify and say that the Evening of the 18th Day of March 1766 Silas Burbanks spake to me and told me a number of People were to meet at his House next Evening and

---

[28] The preceding paragraph was added in court at the trial.

[29] This was apparently a stipulation between counsel designed to avoid a time-consuming semantic battle. It appears in an unidentified hand on a separate scrap of paper which was apparently at one time attached to the deposition. SF 139645.

[30] 19 Jan. 1773, SF 139645. Signed by the deponent. Note that this deposition and the one that follows were also "Sworn in Court" at the action of review in July 1774, indicating that the deponent took the stand and reaffirmed the substance of his testimony.

were going to take a walk, that he had wanted to see me a good while and ask'd me if I would come. I promised I would and accordingly I did; *Timothy Stuart, Samuel Stuart, Jonathan Andrews Jnr.* with several others met there the Evening of the 19th of said Month and the said Silas was present, it was then proposed by some of the Company to go down to Mr. Richard Kings to *punish his Body* (because they said he had been a bad Man, destroy'd the poor and taken away Peoples Estates) which was agreed to by the above named Persons and about nine oClock, (I judge it was) they set out I went with them as far as the Road against his House but did not go out of the Road. The Reason I did not was because I found by their talk they were going to carry Matters further than I expected, but the said Silas Burbank, and Timothy Stuart, Samuel Stuart Jonathan *Andrews Jur. with others go into the House and Shop as they told me afterwards and were all active in breaking open the House and Shop and doing the Mischief that was done,* we all return'd to said Burbanks and staid there an Hour or more; there I saw *several of the said Richard Kings Notes of Hand which the said Silas either read or delivered to some of the Company to read and then they were thrown into the Fire and burnt up,* one by one as they were read. Among others I remember a Note against Nathl. Milliken two or three Notes against some of the Stuarts either the Father or Sons or both all payable to said Richard, and there were among other Papers said Burbanks and some of the others shewed which were brought from Mr. Kings—Burbanks said they broke *open Mr. Kings Desk to get his Papers* and some or other of the Company mentioned destroying the Pewter and hacking the Walls of the House. The breaking the Windows I heard; they made a very great Noise breaking in and doing the mischief, but said but little. Further I say that we waited some time before we went to Mr. Kings *for John Stuart the Father of the above named Stuarts, Amos Andrews and Jonathan Andrews,* some of the Company saying they had promised to come, and *Amos Andrews* afterwards *told me he designed to, and should, have been there but he was not well. I have heard the said John Stuart, Amos Andrews, and Jonathan Andrews often say since that they were very glad the Thing was done,* and *let what would come they would bear their part* of the Cost that might arise, and from frequent conversation with them, I ⟨understood⟩ clearly perceived *they were knowing and advising to the said Riot before it was committed. And I know they three did contribute Money* to get Burbanks out of Gaol at York where he was comitted for an Offence in rescuing some Oxen from Benja. Hooper an Officer, and the Reason they paid for him was for fear he should turn Kings Evidence[31] if he could not get out any other Way. The said *John Stuart, Amos Andrews* and *Jonathan Andrews* always appeared *as much concern'd about being discover'd as the others.*   John Newbegin

[Verification omitted.]

And the said Newbegin being asked if he saw Amos Andrews pay any money to get Burbank out of Gaol, answers that he did not, but that he went to Amos Andrews and asked him to pay it, and said Amos say'd he had not the money then but he would get it and pay it shortly.—and some time afterwards said Andrews told him he had paid it.

Sworn in Court at Falmouth July 9, 1774.

Att. Sam Winthrop Cler.

IX. DEPOSITION OF JONATHAN WINGATE [32]

16 June 1773

I Jonathan Wingate of lawful age testify and say that about eight or ten days before Mr. Richard Kings house and shop were broken open in March 1766 I was in a Shoemaker's shop belonging to one Hodgdon not thirty rods from my own house when *Amos Andrews* came into said shop and soon of *his own motion* began to discourse about the mobbing and riots that had lately happened in several parts of the province and then said the Mr. Richard King was reported to be a very bad man, took all advantages of people, was a near neighbour to him and he had found him very troublesome and he thought it would be *a good scheme to mob him,* and that it would do him good that *such a thing had been talked of* for some time *in their road and he would join in it and he asked me if I would too;* some days after this I was going by his door upon my private business. Seeing him standing at his door I stopped and we renewed the discourse on the same subject; which of us then began it I don't remember; but he then said *it was a very good thing to pay Mr. King a visit* and to *mob him;* that he might be made a better man by it, and said *he would go,* and again asked me *if I would go too;* he also *desired me to speak to Mr. John Stewart to ask his advice about it as I was then to go by his house* about my business I accordingly went into Mr. Stewart's house and coming out of it I met him coming in I then related to him what had

[31] Presumably this refers to the Crown and not to the plaintiff.
[32] 16 June 1773. SF 139645. Signed by the deponent.

passed between Mr. Andrews and me about *Mobbing Mr. King* as aforesaid; and that Mr. Andrews had desired me to talk with him about it; and I then asked him whether he thought it was best to do it; to which he replied with earnestness *yes by all means*; which I think he repeated. In my way home from Mr. Amos Andrews to Mr. Stewarts I called at *Jonathan Andrews' Shop* with whom I conversed on the same subject but do not remember which of us began the conversation; he said it would be *a good thing to pay Mr. King a visit* and that he might be made a better man by it. I have frequently conversed with the above three persons about the riot at Mr. King's house, since, and they have frequently *expressed their approbation of and satisfaction in what had been done*; and said Stewart and *Amos Andrews* declared they would *stand by it and every one would be a fool that would* not and from conversation with said Jonathan I have no doubt but he was of the same mind. Said Stewart and Amos Andrews have to my Knowledge used their endeavours by persuasions to prevent any persons from being witnesses for Mr. King and making discovery of any persons concerned and declared that nothing would be too bad for any one that should. And Amos Andrews told me *he was to be* and *should have been present* himself at the Riot, but was prevented by the Colic or the Belly Ach.   Jona. Wingate

[Verification omitted.]

Sworn in Court July 1774
Att. Sam Winthrop Cler.

X. THREATENING LETTER SENT TO KING [33]

ca. April 1766

In Considiration whar of a number of the Suns of liburty have Shun a mordrit resment [*i.e.* resentment] for the repeted abus which they have reseved for many yers past Do herby hartily Signyfy to the Said Riched. King that in Cas the Said riched or any Other parson Within the Couty should us greet or menthen or be insterimental of any Warants or Summen's to be Sarvd on any Pasen or Pasens he ma Depend onit that he not onley will have houses and barnes burnt and Consumed but him Self Cut in Peses and burnt TO ASHES we also think it best for him to Submit to Provadences, and behave beter for the futer and think him Self wel yoused.[34]

[33] The original, on which the handwriting test was conducted, is in SF 139590, marked in another hand: "Produced by Mr. King." For the dating, see Doc. II.

[34] Stewart apparently introduced evidence to discredit this document, because SF

5. HANDWRITING SAMPLES

Hugh McDaniel appellant vs John Channing appellee
The appellant in Court by his Attorney prays leave to dis-
continue this Action granted & the Appellee asks no Costs.

_____

Ezekiel Hearsey, exr appellants vs Mathew Meriam, al.
This Action is Agreed see Agreement on file.

_____

John Gill of Boston in the county of Suffolk, printer
Appellant vs John Mein of said Boston Bookseller appellee
from the Judgment of an Inferiour court of common pleas held at
Boston in & for said county on the third tuesday of April Anno Domini 1769 when & where the Appellant was plt. & the appellee was
Defendant In a plea of trespass for that the said John Mein
at Boston on the twenty sixth day of January last in the evening
of the same with force & arms vi & armis with a large club made an assault upon this
John Gill two violent blows with this club upon the back part of the head of the s John Gill & beat
wounded & evil entreated the said John Gill in so grievous a manner that
his life was dispaired of & other enormities the s John Mein did against
the peace of the Lord the King & to the Damage of the said John Gill
as he saith the sum of two hundred pounds At which said Inferiour court Judgment was rendred that the said John Gill
recover against the said John Mein the sum of one hundred
& thirty pounds Lawfull Money Damage & Costs This appeal
was brot foward at the superiour court of Judicature court
of Assize & general goal Delivery held at Boston in & for the
County aforesaid on the last tuesday of August last when & where
& their said appeal was continued to the last term of the said
Superiour court by order of Court at the appellees motion when
& where the partys appeared & the case after a full hearing was
committed to a Jury sworn according to law to try the same
who returned their Verdict therein upon oath that is to say
they find for the Appellant Seventy five pounds Money
Damage & Cost. Whereupon the Appellee moved for a new
tryal & said appeal was continued to this court on that motion

6. RECORD, SUPERIOR COURT OF JUDICATURE

XI. KING'S OFFER OF SETTLEMENT[35]

27 May 1774

Richard King To those Imediately Consirned in his action of review against them Depending &c. and any others that the matter of that action may Consern

I am Sensable that when a man has Entered the field in order to do him Selfe Justice against those from whom he has receved an Injury then To offer Terms to his adversary is often Constered a weakness of mind, or want of abillity, notwithstand[ing] its being hild fourth in the highest authority as a Duty. But well knowing that you must be Sensable that the Witnesses produced on the former Tryall are produced again (if no other) and that their Evidence alone would have ben Sufficant in point of Proof, Even had not a duty of the [highest?] Authority Indused Two of you to make a Confession (partial as it was) Sufficant for my purpous.—Matters standing thus I think it Safe Honourable and frindly to acquaint you that I now stand ready to accept of a much less Sum then the damages and Charges I have sustained amounts to rather then put my Selfe to further Cost to Effect the future [...] of [...] and that upon proper Security Given for such Sum as may be agreed on. Time also shall be given upon simple Intrest for the payment thereof; If I have no answer within Seven days I shall Take it for granted you Treat this as a waist paper, and hold my Selfe at liberty to do the Same. Yours,

Richd. King

Scarborough May 27th. 1774

XII. DEPOSITION OF JONATHAN SAYWARD[36]

29 June 1774

Jonathan Sayward of York in Said County of York, Esqr. Testifys and Says that He very well knew Josiah Beal who ⟨lately⟩ some years Since was an Inhabitant of the Town of York, but now if liveing re-

---

139590 contains a sample of his handwriting marked, in another hand, "Produced by Mr. Stuart."

[35] FC, in King's hand and signed by him. NHi:Rufus King MSS. Perhaps in response to this appeal, the three Stewarts defaulted. Min. Bk. 99, SCJ Cumberland and Lincoln, June 1774, N-4, N-6. See the beginning of Doc. XIII below. See also note 3 above.

[36] York, 29 June 1774, SF 139645. In a clerk's hand, signed by Sayward. Presumably "Deacon" Jonathan Sayward, a loyalist sympathizer, who retained his

sides in some part of Novaskhotia Government as the Deponent Supposes That he was in poor circumstances with respect to Substance when he left York, which is 8 or 10 year ago, and He has never heard that He said Beal has since his remove from York mended his Worldly circumstances.   Jonathan Sayward

Querys put by Mr. King,
   Do you Know that Josiah Beal has now any Estate Real or personal in the Town of York?
   Answer. The deponent says He does not Know that He Has, any, or that He has not.
   Have you heard that said Beal has a grant of two Thousand acres of land in Novascotia Government? [37]
   Answer The Deponent has no remembrance that he has ever heard of such a Grant of land to said Beal.
[*Verification omitted.*]

XIII. ADAMS' MINUTES OF THE REVIEW [38]

Cumberland Superior Court, Falmouth, July 1774

King vs. Stewart—Review

Scurlogging.[39]
3 Stewarts defaulted. 3 Andrews appear. By the Sullivans.[40]
Bradbury.[41]
Silas Burbank. About 10 days before the Affair, I was informed that a Number of Persons from 2 Roads, were about making an Onset on Mr. Kings House. Stewarts and Andrews's were joined in it. I was coming down by Amos Andross's House. He asked me if there were not a Number about making Sir Richard a Visit. He said he should

---

power in the community after the Revolution. See 1 *Adams Family Correspondence* 111 note. Sayward had earlier refused an offer of preferment for fear of the Sons of Liberty; see Sayward to Thomas Hutchinson, 22 Aug. 1769, 26 Mass. Arch. 328.
   [37] King seems to have been trying to bring out that Beal had been bribed by the defendants to leave the Province. Beal was probably one of the rioters; his note of hand for £139/12/1 had been among those destroyed. SF 139590.
   [38] In JA's hand. Adams Papers, Microfilms, Reel No. 185.
   [39] Apparently a heading, but the meaning is uncertain; probably mobbing or rioting.
   [40] As to the default, see notes 3, 35, above. The Andrews' counsel were John and James Sullivan, New Hampshire and Maine lawyers respectively. See JA to AA, 29 June 1774, 1 *Adams Family Correspondence* 113.
   [41] Theophilus Bradbury, JA's co-counsel, opening the case for King.

128

go, and thought he deservd a good Whipping and to have his Ears cutt of, because he had treated him ill and others. This was the Afternoon before the Affair happened. He said K[ing] had kill'd these Creatures &c. and he deserved to be checked and corrected. He advised me to go, thought it was proper for me to go, and others. He has wrongd me and is endeavouring to wrong you and he will ruin us all if not humbled. It will be for our good and for his. There was one Person there, I believe to whom he gave a strong Encouragement to go. I know there was one. He said twice he would absolutely go. Afterwards he said he did not go, because he was taken with a bad Belly Ach. He said he was as good a Friend and or Well wisher or both, as any that was there.

Some nights before the Church Meeting A. Andross told me the Belly Ach was relentment of Mind that he had encouraged so bad a Thing. About the same Time, the day before saw Jona, Andross senr. Said he believd he should not go, but believ'd his son would. It would be the best Way for Somebody to go, and whip him with small sticks, as he was weak and frail in Body. Jona. mentioned a great many bad Things that K. had done—killing Creatures, and would drive the poor People away, if not checked. A Person that he advised and encouraged to go, did go. Something was mentiond about the Stamp Act, this was Amos, that King was a favourer of it.

Jona. Andrews Jnr. was in the Affair. I first saw the Party in the Road near my House near a mile and an half. Jona. Jnr. was in the Company, near and at Kings House. He went from near my House with the Company to K's House, in the night. He said he did not know whether his father would come. Dont know that I saw him in K's House, but saw him after the Affair was over with the Company at the Meeting House.

Several Windows were broke.

The Person I mention, I am inclin'd to think, would not have gone if he had not been encouraged by Men of Estates and Character.

Neither Amos nor Jona. advised to breaking the Windows, stealing Papers breaking Desks, to cut down the House or burn the Barn. It was proposd that night to go and take him out of his House, and whip him.

I know there was a Number of Papers destroyed. Bonds, Notes, Deeds, a great Number burnt in his House upon the Hearth and others thrown out of Doors. Many torn to Pieces, Bills of Parcells &c. dont know the Names, Dates, nor Sums. Jona. Jnr. was present and saw many of em burnt.

Jona. Wingate. 8 or 10 days before, at Hodgdons shop, Amos Andross came in and talk'd about the Riots in the Prov[ince] and said he thought it would be a very good Thing to make Mr. King a visit and to mob him and that he ought to be mobbed. A few days after, I saw him by his House, and he said he thought it would be a very good Thing, and said he would go. After the Riot, he told me he should have been there but for the Belly Ach. He spoke very encouraging, and said it was a good Thing. When I was going by his House, he said he would have me go and see Mr. Stewart and take his Advice about it. I did and Stewart advised to it.

I knew of a Person that he advised, who was in the Mobb.

I call'd at Jona. Andross's. Cant tell who begun. He reckoned it would be a good Thing to make Mr. King a Visit.

Windows were broke, and Papers destroyd. Papers were burnt. Near 20 People at the House. After 9 O Clock.

John Newbegin. Saw K's House next Day. It was very much damnified. Jona. Andross Jnr. was There and he told me he was in the House. I never heard of it till the Night before. I was asked, by one Person the Night before to go.

One Note vs. D. Millikin was destroyd and several vs. the Stewarts and deeds and all the Papers there were destroyed.

Heard Amos say he was prevented from going by the belly Ach. He said he never would be behindhand in Advancing Mony, to screen it. And he has advanced Money. He really appeard to me to be very glad.

Jona. appeared to be *well pleased with the Notion,* and Jona. Junior was there. Did not hear Jona. say any Thing about it beforehand. He afterwards *laugh'd and was merry about it.*

A Year or two after I heard Jona. say, that it was a bad Thing.

The House, Windows, Desk, Wainscot, Walls, Pewter damagd. About a Year after Amos said he could take a few Bundles of flax and a Coal of fire and put under his Warehouse, and put a stop. Have heard Amos laugh about the Ladder that they could not get it together. 2 Men and one want willing, it was difficult.

Benja. Carl. The Talk was that about 70 men were to go and talk with him and tell him that he had said he would fill Falmouth Goal with Debtors next C[our]t. 20 or 30 did assemble. 6 went into the Windows. A desperate Outcry in the House. Heard Mr. K. cry to his servant.

I saw a Peck of Papers or more. I said it is a Pity to destroy these Papers. They said they had got what they wanted. I said are not you a Parcell of ungratefull Writches. Burbank came to me. Cant tell who burnt the Papers. Burnt at Burbanks House.

Such a Noise in the House as I never heard in my House.[42] Jona. Andross Jnr. was one of the Company. Thumping, Yelling, Hooping —I thought K. was in the Extremity of Death.

3 Stewarts there.

Jona. Junr. proposed the whole Parish should go to the Justices, and let him take whom he pleased. There was some Meeting for that, at old Mr. Stewarts.

Nat. Jose. Met Amos Andross, and we got discoursing about the Mob which had been at K's. I said I was glad ont. Amos said if we had thought so We should have invited you to have gone [with] us. K. had my Note and I hoped mine was destroyed.

Nath. Carl. At Amos's Mill, he said to me, how easy a Thing it would be for a youngster that lived as near as I, to put a Coal of Fire to his Buildings. This after the Riot but before the Barn was burnt. He did not seem to me to be in earnest.

Paul Tompson. Heard Jona. say the best Way for K to find who had mobb'd him is to go to his Books and see who he has wrong'd. He has wrongd me out of 300£. He mentiond Graffam, but did not understand him to quote Graffam.

Lem. Millikin. K. sent to my Fathers just after the Mobb, and desird sum of Us to come. A large Quantity of Papers burnt to Ashes. K. answered they have undone me [then?] Mrs. K. was then fainted away, could but just keep Life in her. She lay in.

Windows of House and Store dashd all to Pieces. An Hatchet thrown into a Chamber Window and lying on the Flooer. His Desks broke to Pieces, his Wainscoat, Plaistering &c. broke to Pieces.

Rob. 1st. I knew was the Windows coming in. Master called to me, and went back into his Chamber. I attempted to go, but the People were there, and I could not go. I went to my Gun, and she was not loaded. I said I would stop some of them. I met Master coming down to get something for Mistress. She was faint. He bid me go and get his Gun. I went and went up Chamber and found the Maid holding Mistress who was faint. Plate, Earthen Ware, Chairs, Desks, broke, Papers burnt. Stair Case hacked, Wainscot Wall hacked. 7 or 8 Windows. They broke into the shop. Window broke open.

Mistress said Lord of Mercy where shall I go?

John Porry. Some days after the Mob at Mr. Andross's Jona.'s. Saw Mill, he said he was not in it, but if there was ever another he would

[42] Perhaps an inadvertence for "life."

be in it. For it was justifiable in the sight of God and Man. The Common Law could not take hold of a Mob. If he [43] man was injured and could not get his Remedy at common law, he might take it himself.

John Augur Millikin. April at Millikins Tavern 10 o Clock at Night. Saw the Barn burnt. Ladder was to Pieces. Amos Andrews at the other End. The Ladder would fly to Pieces 10 times—as if by Witchcraft.

Somebody ripd the Boards off at the End, and let the Air in.

Jona. said he believd the D——l was in the People.

Abraham Tyler Junr. Cost about £80 to repair what has been done. £10 L.M. to repair the Wainscoat, and staircase.

Daniel Moulton. Saw the House and Furniture.

Schedule of Notes, Bonds, &c. annexed to the Writ.

Hawk. P.C. 315. No Accessories in Trespass. §16. Hire, Command, Council or Conspiracy. Approbation unless they countermand and retract their Encouragement. [44]

King vs. Stewart et al.   Defence

James Sullivan, for Amos Andrews.

Abhors Mobs.

Wingates Deposition. Taking K. out of Bed and Whipping him or cutting his Ears is not cutting his Ears.

Law of Evid. 254. [45] All must be Principals. None guilty but he who Acts in it.

Hawk. 311. § 4. [46] Woods Inst. 407. [47] 4. Bac. 179, top. [48] Foster 372, 369. 70. [49] 372. § 1. 2. 3. [50] Hawk. 310. [51]

[43] Inadvertence for "a."

[44] 2 Hawkins, *Pleas of the Crown* 315: "It seems to be agreed that those who by Hire, Command, Counsel, or Conspiracy; and it seems to be generally holden, that those who by shewing an express Liking, Approbation or Assent to another's felonious Design of Committing a Felony, abet and encourage him to commit it, but are so far absent when he actually commits it, that he could not be encouraged by the Hopes of any immediate Help or Assistance from them, are all of them accessories before the Fact, both to the Felony intended, and to all other Felonies which shall happen in and by the Execution of it, if they do not expressly retract and countermand their encouragement, before it is actually committed."

[45] Gilbert, *Evidence* 254: "In Trespass all the Defendants must be Principals, for no Man can by commanding a Trespass, give any Man Authority to do it, Therefore no Man is guilty but that he acts in it, and any other Person is not guilty at all."

[46] 2 Hawkins, *Pleas of the Crown* 311: "*Sect.* 4. It seems agreed, That whosoever agrees to a Trespass on Lands or Goods done to his Use, thereby becomes a Principal in it. But that no one can become a Principal in a Trespass on the Person of a Man by any such Agreement. Also it seems agreed, that no one shall be adjudged a Principal in any common Trespass, or inferior Crime of the like Nature,

No. 2. King v. Stewart

Omnis Ratohabitio retrotrahitur, and Mandato precedenti antecedenti æquiparatur.[52]

No Intention to break House or burn Papers, in Amos.

---

for barely receiving, comforting and concealing the Offender, though he know him to have been guilty, and that there is a Warrant out against him, which by Reason of such Concealment, cannot be executed. And if he cannot be punished as a Principal, it is certain that he cannot be punished as an Accessary; because in such Offences, all who are punished as Partakers of the Guilt of him who did the Fact, must be punished as Principals in it, or not at all."

[47] See Wood, *Institute of the Laws of England* 397 (London, 9th edn., 1763): "In *Petit Larcenies, Trespasses Vi et armis,* there are no Accessories. For as in the highest Offense there is no Accessory, so it is in the lowest Offenses, or in all Offenses under Felony, as in Riots, Routs, forcible Entries, and other Trespasses *vi et Armis.* Here all are Principals as before observed. He that Receiveth a Trespasser on Lands and Goods, after the Trespass is Committed, is no Trespasser, unless the Trespass was done to his Use and Benefit, and He agreeth to it afterwards; for then his subsequent Agreement amounteth to a Commandment, and makes him a Principal. Yet if the Trespass was on the Person of any one, such After-Agreement will not make Him a Trespasser." *Id.* at 407, contains references to statutory measures concerning accessories.

[48] Probably 5 Bacon, *Abridgment* 179: "All who are Parties to a Trespass with Force are liable to this Action; for there can be no Accessary in such Trespass."

[49] Foster, *Crown Cases* 372: "Did the Principal Commit the Felony He standeth Charged with under the Influence of the flagitious Advice, and was the Event in the ordinary Course of Things a probable Consequence of that Felony? or did He, following the Suggestions of his own wicked Heart, Wilfully and Knowingly commit a Felony of Another Kind or upon a Different Subject?"

[50] Foster, *Crown Cases* 369–370:

"Much hath been said by Writers who have gone before Me, upon Cases where a Person supposed to commit a Felony at the Instigation of Another hath gone beyond the Terms of such Instigation, or hath in the Execution varied from them. If the Principal totally and substantially varieth, if being solicited to commit a Felony of One kind He *wilfully and knowingly* committeth a Felony of Another, He will stand single in that Offence, and the Person soliciting will not be involved in his Guilt. For on *his* part it was no more than a fruitless ineffectual Temptation. The Fact cannot with any Propriety be said to have been Committed under the Influence of that Temptation.

"But if the Principal in Substance complieth with the Temptation, varying only in Circumstance of Time or Place, or in the Manner of Execution, in these Cases the Person sollicting to the Offence will, if Absent, be an Accessary Before the Fact, if Present a Principal. For the Substantial, the Criminal part of the Temptation, be it Advice, Command, or Hire, is complied with. A. Commandeth B. to Murder C. by Poison, B. doth it by a Sword, or other Weapon, or by any other Means. A. is Accessary to this Murder. For the Murder of C. was the Object principally in his Contemplation, and that is Effected.

"So where the Principal goeth beyond the Terms of the Solicitation, *if in the Event the Felony committed was a probable Consequence of what was Ordered or Advised,* the Person giving such Orders or Advice will be an Accessary to that Felony. A. upon some Affront given by B. ordereth his Servant to way-lay Him and give Him a sound Beating; the Servant doth so, and B. dieth of this Beating. A. is Accessary to this Murder.

"A. adviseth B. to Rob C., He doth Rob him, and in so doing, either upon Resistance made, or to conceal the Fact, or upon any other Motive operating at the Time of the Robbery, Killeth him. A. is Accessary to this Murder.

"Or A. soliciteth B. to Burn the House of C., He doth it; and the Flames taking

133

The Ladder. The axes, and Presence when the Colt hung up.

Depositions to be treated with more care, because taken when Amos not present.[53]

The whole 12 Jurors must agree.[54]

Damages. A melancholly Tragedy. Pewter, China, &c.

Papers.

Fright. Pain of Mind for 1/4 of an Hour.

Prov[ince] in an Uproar, on Account of Stampd Papers.

Shall Amos and family be beggared, and reduced to Distress for Life.

John. Sullivan. J. Hale said it was difficult to distinguish between Crime and Person.[55]

No Damages to make Reparation to the Public.

The Thought of killing sovereign is Treason.

Ever and *Never* in Gilbert.[56]

---

hold of the House of D. that likewise is Burnt. A. is Accessary to the Burning of this Latter House.

"These Cases are all governed by One and the Same Principle. The Advice, Solicitation, or Orders in Substance were pursued, and were extremely flagitious on the Part of A. The Events, though possibly falling out beyond his original Intention, were *in the ordinary Course of Things the probable Consequences of what* B. *did under the Influence, and at the Instigation of* A. And therefore in the Justice of the Law He is answerable for them."

[51] 2 Hawkins, *Pleas of the Crown* 310–311: "It seems to have been always an uncontroverted Maxim, that there can be no Accessaries in High Treason, or Trespass. Also it seems to have been always agreed, That whatsoever will make a Man an Accessary before in Felony, will make him a Principal in High Treason and Trespass; as Battery, Riot, Rout, Forcible Entry, and even in Forgery and Petit Larceny. And therefore, where-ever a Man commands another to commit a Trespass, who afterwards commits it in Pursuance of such Command, he seems by necessary Consequence to be as guilty of it, as if he had done it himself; from whence it follows, that being in Judgment of Law a Principal Offender, he may be tried and found Guilty, before any Trial of the Person who actually did the Fact."

[52] Presumably, "Omnis ratihabitio retrotrahitur et mandato priori æquiparatur," *i.e.,* "Every ratification relates back and is equivalent to a prior authority." Black, *Law Dictionary.* If the point is that Amos' subsequent approval of the riot which he had encouraged constituted participation, the maxim would appear to have been a note by JA of a possible rebuttal argument to Sullivan's preceding citation of authority.

[53] Note that depositions were admissible, even though taken out of the presence of the opposing party, if he had been notified or lived more than twenty miles away. Act of 12 Dec. 1695, c.15, §1, A&R 225.

[54] "The Jury must be kept together without Meat, Drink, Fire or Candle, till they are agreed. . . . If there be eleven agreed, and but one dissenting, who says he will rather die in Prison, yet the Verdict shall not be taken by eleven. . . ." 3 Bacon, *Abridgment* 269.

[55] Presumably Sullivan refers to Hale, *Pleas of the Crown.* The reference has not been identified.

[56] Probably Gilbert, *Evidence* 255: "and in Trespass, the Intent to trespass was

Hawk. 311.[57]

The Evidence comes from Persons who were original Defendants. Burbank was Captain General.—Answer. The Andrewss were King and Ministry and Privy Council.[58]

Page 316.   Read §22d [59]

Defendants Witnesses.

D[eaco]n Millikin. Heard Wingate threaten to mob Millikin [60] 6 Months before it was done. If I could perswade any Body to join me, I would mob him immediately.

Ben Durgan. Neither of the Defendants there when the Colt hung up. In the Night I saw nor heard any thing of them. Dark overcast night. Jona. was at home when the House was torn down.

John Gookin. King told me, as I understood him, he lost nothing of any Value. His Books, Bonds and Notes were all safe. Waste Papers destroyed. If they had put their Hands round they would have ruined him. Principal Part of the Papers they took were waste Papers and Memorandums. Dont remember his saying about the desk in the House. All in Confusion.

James Boothbay. Had a Note there not destroyd, King Joked.

Jotham Libby. Paid his Note.

Mr. Graffam. The best Notes were in the draw which they never touched.

Dr. Southgate. Saw Dr. Southgate. Gookin told me that they

---

ever reckoned a Trespass, and therefore there are no Accessories." JA's minute suggests that Sullivan was arguing that the word "ever" should be "never." See quotation at note 45 above. But in Gilbert, *Evidence* 255 (2d edn., 1760), the passage is reprinted without change.

[57] See note 46 above.

[58] This phrase is apparently a rejoinder noted down by JA for use in rebuttal.

[59] 2 Hawkins, *Pleas of the Crown* 316–317: "But it is observable, That *Plowden,* in his Report of *Saunder's* Case, which seems to be the chief Foundation of what is said by others concerning these Points, in putting the Case of a Command to burn the House of *A.* which shall not make the Commander an Accessary to the burning the house of *B.* unless it were caused by burning that of *A.* states in this Manner, *If I command a Man to burn the House of such an one, which he well knows, and he burn the House of another, there I shall not be Accessary, because it is another distinct Thing, to which I did not give Assent,* &c. By which it seems to be implied, That it is a necessary Ingredient in such a Case to make *B.* no Accessary, that he knew the House which he was commanded to burn; for if he did not know it, but mistook another for it, and intending only to burn the House which he was commanded to burn, happen by such Mistake to burn the other, it may probably be argued, That the Commander ought to be esteemed an Accessary to such Burning, because it was the direct and immediate Effect of an Act wholly influenced by his Command, and intended to have pursued it."

[60] An apparent inadvertence. See Dr. Southgate's testimony below for a similar error.

destroyed a valuable Number of Papers and sustained a very great Loss, and he should have been ruined, if they had not missed a valuable File of capital Notes.

John Sullivan. What is the meaning of Mobbing. There was not one Thing done that Jona. advised to. Dont urge that mobs being in other Places, is any Justification.

There is Evidence that Jonathan Junr. was with the rest.

Under c[ommon] l[aw] a Person wants understanding, to make him guilty of a Crime.

3 Bac.[61]

The Stewarts have confessed themselves guilty, by their Default.[62]

People was divided about the Destruction of the Tea.

Jona. has pd. a sixth Part of £200 which should be returned to him Exemplary Damages, not known to the Legislators.[63]

1. Damage to the House. 2. Furniture. 3. Papers. 4. Credit in Trade. 5. To his Character. 6. Indignity. 7. Children. 8. Wife. 9. The Terror, Cruelty and Horror of that dismal Scene. 10. Consider what the Crime was and what King might have done. He might have killed em all and been justified.[64]

Damages.

1. To the House.
2. To the Furniture.
3. The Papers.
4. To his Credit in Trade.
5. To his Reputation and Character in generall. Such popular Hurricanes always scatter Dust upon a Man. They make the World suspect very often where there is no just Cause or Ground for Jealousy. The Maxim with many is that where there is so much Smoke there is always some fire, and under the Influence of this Opinion they take up a Prejudice vs. a Man with[out] exam[in]ing into the Truth. These popular Commotions always set ill humours afloat. They put

---

[61] 3 Bacon, *Abridgment.* The exact citation has not been identified.

[62] Sullivan was reminding the jury that even if it brought in a verdict for the Andrewses King could still mulct the Stewarts in damages.

[63] "Exemplary damages," or "smart money," are damages over and above the plaintiff's actual loss, in circumstances aggravated by the defendant's malice. Black, *Law Dictionary.*

[64] These are notes for JA's closing address to the jury, which follows and may have been written during a recess in the trial or possibly afterwards in the heat of fresh recollection.

licentious Tongues and Pens in Motion, as they did particularly in this Case. These Andross's hired a Paper to be printed even in a Newspaper and to be scatterd also in Hand Bills, to asperse and blacken his Character. Every Man has Enemies. Every Enemy takes Advantage of such a season, and becomes industrious to propagate Reports true or false, to the Injury of a Man's Character. Besides every one of the Persons who is concerned in such an Outrage has a Number of Friends, who are at once alarmed, and become anxious least the Perpetrators should be discoverd and punished, and least the World should condemn the Action as unjust. These therefore instantly join the Cry, and say in all Companies the most bitter, cruel, and often false and deceitfull Things they can think of. In short I know of nothing that happens in society which is such a Nursery of Scandal, and Calumny, of obloqui and Defamation as a Mob. Besides it is such a Gratification to the Envy and Revenge, of the most sordid, base and groveling among the Vulgar, that it gives them a Triumph and they always become insolent, impudent, and abusive to such a Man— swallow down greedily all the Lyes and dirty Tales that are told and propagate them far and wide.

Apply this to Mr. King and to those Rioters.

6. The Indignity offered to the Plaintiff. The Insult and Affront.

An Englishmans dwelling House is his Castle. The Law has erected a Fortification round it—and as every Man is Party to the Law, i.e. the Law is a Covenant of every Member of society with every other Member, therefore every Member of Society has entered into a solemn Covenant with every other that he shall enjoy in his own dwelling House as compleat a security, safety and Peace and Tranquility as if it was surrounded with Walls of Brass, with Ramparts and Palisadoes and defended with a Garrison and Artillery.—This covenant has been broken in a most outragious manner. We are all bound then to make good to the Plaintiff his Damages.

Every English[man] values himself exceedingly, he takes a Pride and he glories justly in that strong Protection, that sweet Security, that delightfull Tranquillity which the Laws have thus secured to him in his own House, especially in the Night. Now to deprive a Man of this Protection, this quiet and Security in the dead of Night, when himself and Family confiding in it are asleep, is treat[ing] him not like an Englishman not like a Freeman but like a Slave—like a miserable Turk, or Tartar. Is not this a base Affront? No Man who has a Soul, who has the Spirit of a Man in him can ever after during his whole Life, ever forget such an Indignity, tho he may forgive it. He can never think of it without Pain of Mind, without Impatience, Anger, Resentment, Shame and Grief.

7. The Damages and Danger to his Children.

5 young Children, all suddenly awakend, by the Dashing of Glass, the Yells, and Noises. Sudden Terror it seems is dangerous to Children. We had the last Week at York Instances. A Gun—a rap.[65] This Danger arises from the Constitution of all Animals. A Colt once thoroughly affrighted never gets over it. A sudden fright destroys the natural Tone and Vigour of the Nerves and turns the Animal Spirits into such Channells that they never can be brought back.

There is a natural Courage in Children, which once abated, and Habits of Fear fixed in their Minds, they never can be cured. Instances are common. Fill a Childs head with stories of Ghosts, Apparitions and Hobgoblins, and You fix such Habits of fear upon them, that all the force of their Reason shall never be able to make them walk in the dark without fear.

8. The Danger, the real Damage and actual Cruelty, to his amiable Wife. She was at that Time far gone in her Pregnancy. She run 1000 Chances of her Life, and still greater Risques of the fruit of her Body. What had the innocent Babe in her Womb done to this abandon'd Mob, that its Existence should be put at Hazard, by their Fury, Malice, Madness and Revenge.

9. The Cruelty the Terror, the Horror of the whole dismal scene. It would be affectation to attempt to exaggerate, it is almost impossible to exagerate, the distresses of this innocent Family, at that Time. The Excellency of a Tryal by Jury is that they are the Partys Peers, his equalls—men of like Passions, feelings, Imaginations and Understandings with him. If your Passions are not affected upon this Occa-

[65] See JA to AA, York, 1 July 1774, 1 *Adams Family Correspondence* 118: "In a Tryal of a Cause here to Day, some Facts were mentioned, which are worth writing to you. It was sworn, by Dr. Lyman [Isaac Lyman, Yale 1747; see 12 Sibley-Shipton, *Harvard Graduates* 182], Elder Bradbury and others, that there had been a Number of Instances in this Town of fatal Accidents, happening from sudden Noises striking the Ears of Babes and young Children. A Gun was fired near one Child, as likely as any; the Child fell immediately into fits, which impaired his Reason, and is still living an Ideot. Another Child was sitting on a Chamber floor. A Man rapped suddenly and violently on the Boards which made the floor under the Child [tremble?]. The Child was so startled, and frightened, that it fell into fits, which never were cured.

"This may suggest a Caution to keep Children from sudden Frights and surprizes."

The case referred to is probably Moulton v. Swett, SCJ Rec. 1773–1774, fol. 219; Min. Bk. 99, SCJ York, June 1774, N–6; SF 137483. Moulton was a constable who had taken Swett's gun away from him after Swett had wrongfully discharged it. Swett sued, but lost in the Superior Court. Unfortunately the file does not list the Superior Court witnesses.

sion, you will [not] be the Plaintiffs Peers. It is right and fit, it is reasonable and just that you should feel as he did, that you should put yourself in his Place, and be moved with his Passions.[66]

Be pleased then to imagine yourselves each one for himself—in bed with his pregnant Wife, in the dead of Midnight, five Children also asleep, and all the servants. 3 Children in the same Chamber, two above. The Doors and Windows all barrd, bolted and locked—all asleep, suspecting nothing, harbouring no Malice, Envy or Revenge in your own Bosoms nor dreaming of any in your Neighbours. In the Darkness, the stillness the silence of Midnight.

All of a sudden, in an Instant, in a twinkling of an Eye, an armed Banditti of Felons, Thieves, Robbers, and Burglars, rush upon the House. Like Savages from the Wilderness, or like Legions from the Blackness of Darkness, they yell and Houl, they dash in all the Windows and enter. Enterd they Roar, they stamp, they Yell, they houl, they cutt break tear and burn all before them.

Do you see a tender and affectionate Husband, an amiable deserving Wife near her Time, 3 young Children, all in one Chamber, awakened all at once, ignorant what was the Cause, terrifyd, inquisitive to know it. The Husband attempting to run down stairs, his Wife, laying hold of his Arm, to stay him and sinking fainting dying away in his Arms. The Children crying and clinging round their Parents—*father will they kill me*—father save me! The other Children and servants in other Parts of the House, joining in the Cries of Distress.

What sum of Money Mr. Foreman would tempt you, to be Mr. King, and to let your Wife undergo what Mrs. King underwent, and your Children what theirs did for one Night?

I freely confess that the whole sum sued for would be no temptation to me, if there was no other Damage than this.[67]

But how can the Impression of it be erased out of his Mind and hers and the Childrens. It will lessen and frequently interrupt his Happiness as long as he lives, it will be a continual Sourse of Grief to him.

10. Such an Event establishes and perpetuates Rancour, Animosities and Hatreds among Families. One of these Children will never recollect ⟨the⟩ see one of the Family of Stewart and Andrews without Pain of Mind. Is it not a damage to a Man to have Quarells entailed

---

[66] It would be questionable today for a lawyer so to address a jury. See Callaghan v. A. Lague Express, 298 F. 2d 349 (2d Cir. 1962). JA may have based the next three paragraphs on King's own account, p. 119 above.

[67] In this and the preceding paragraph JA seems to exceed the bounds of permissible argument. See note 66 above.

upon him and his Family, forever, with all his Neighbours and their Families.

11. It's of great Importance to the Community that sufficient that exemplary Damages should be given in such Cases. King might have kill'd em all.[68] If a Man has Humanity enough, to refrain, he ought to be fully compensated.

12. It would be a stain of this excellent and noble Tryal by Jury, if it should not afford Justice in such Cases. There are Levellers, but they disgrace Jurys.

XIV. JOHN ADAMS TO ABIGAIL ADAMS [69]

Falmouth, 7 July 1774

I am engaged in a famous Cause: The Cause of King, of Scarborough vs. a Mob, that broke into his House, and rifled his Papers, and terrifyed him, his Wife, Children and Servants in the Night. The Terror, and Distress, the Distraction and Horror of this Family cannot be described by Words or painted upon Canvass. It is enough to move a Statue, to melt an Heart of Stone, to read the Story. A Mind susceptible of the Feelings of Humanity, an Heart which can be touch'd with Sensibi[li]ty for human Misery and Wretchedness, must reluct, must burn with Resentment and Indignation, at such outragious Injuries. These private Mobs, I do and will detest. If Popular Commotions can be justifyed, in Opposition to Attacks upon the Constitution, it can be only when Fundamentals are invaded, nor then unless for absolute Necessity and with great Caution. But these Tarrings and Featherings, these breaking open Houses by rude and insolent Rabbles, in Resentment for private Wrongs or in pursuance of private Prejudices and Passions, must be discountenanced, cannot be even excused upon any Principle which can be entertained by a good Citizen—a worthy Member of Society.

[68] Compare with the argument in Rex v. Richardson, No. 59.
[69] 1 *Adams Family Correspondence* 131.

3. Cotton v. Nye

1767

EDITORIAL NOTE

This suit, as Adams noted in his diary, "arose from Ambition" [1] and (apparently) from competition for the favors of the voters of Sandwich. Rowland Cotton, the town's representative in the General Court since 1758, had lost his seat to Stephen Nye in 1761, but had then obtained the sinecure of Clerk of the House of Representatives. [2]

In February 1763, Nye presented a petition to the General Court on behalf of "Jabez Joseph, Indian Man of Plymouth Setting forth That he served as a Soldier ... at Crown Point in 1761, and that in his way home he froze both his feet, and lost part of both, so that he is like to be a Cripple all his days, And Praying an Allowance." The court voted a total of £4 to be paid to Nye "to be by him delivered to Mr. Elisha Tupper for the use of" Joseph. In addition Tupper, who had apparently been Joseph's master, was to receive £4 annually for three years, if Joseph lived so long, for Joseph's use. [3]

In the summer of 1763, Cotton appears to have "presented a Memorial to the General Court ... suggesting ... a mistake" in the grant of the pension because of the court's "supposing the said Jabez to be a legally mustered Soldier when probibelly he was not so." [4] The court then appointed John Murray of Rutland and Thomas Foster of Plymouth to investigate the matter. Nye told the committee that Cotton had obtained an order from Joseph's master to receive Joseph's wages from the Province Treasurer. When Cotton denied this, Nye said that he had seen in the Treasurer's office not only the order but also Cotton's receipt for the wages. The Treasurer, however, supported Cotton, and certified to the committee that Nye's declaration was "altogether false and Groundless." [5] The committee then reported in Cotton's favor.

According to depositions in the file, Nye accused Cotton of reading the committee's report to a group in a Boston or Cambridge barbershop and then taking it to the General Court where the Speaker read it aloud. Early in January 1767 Cotton invited Nye to call a general town meeting, "that the Inhabitants thereof might judge of the Difference between Them." Nye failed to accept the invitation, and on January 12, before a group of townsmen at Nathaniel Bassett's blacksmith shop in Sandwich, told Cotton: "That is a false, lying paper which you made yourself and forged the Committee's name to it." [6]

[1] 1 JA, *Diary and Autobiography* 333 (4 April 1767).
[2] Resolve of 22 Feb. 1762, 17 A&R 160.
[3] Resolve of 16 Feb. 1763, 17 A&R 349.
[4] Declaration, SF 144208.
[5] Certificate (copy), SF 144208.
[6] Depositions of Nathaniel Bassett, John Jennings, and Thomas Clapp; Declaration, Cotton v. Nye, SF 144208.

Cotton, represented by Paine, thereupon commenced an action for slander in the Barnstable Inferior Court which Adams defended on Nye's behalf. The cause was tried on 7 April 1767, and after the jury found for Cotton in the sum of twenty shillings and costs,[7] both parties appealed to the Barnstable Superior Court.

There, on 14 May 1767, the case came on anew. After trial, the jury brought in a general verdict for Cotton for £7 and costs, and Nye's motion in arrest of judgment, argued at Boston in August 1767, was overruled.[8] Admitting that Nye had uttered the words, Adams had sought to argue that they were not actionable. The notes set out below suggest that his point was technical: the act of which Nye accused Cotton not being criminal, plaintiff could not recover without a showing of special (i.e. provable) damages. It is not clear whether this argument, which found considerable support in the authorities which Adams collected,[9] was addressed to the court as well as to the jury. Adams' diary entry (Document VII) shows that he attempted vainly to argue the question to the jury. His minutes (Document V) show that the court unanimously upheld the actionability of the words. It cannot be determined whether the judges gave this ruling as part of the usual seriatim charge; whether they intended it as a determination binding the jury, as in the English criminal libel practice; or whether the ruling was made upon the motion in arrest of judgment.[10]

There are four separate Adams minutes or notes for this case (Documents II, IV, V, VI). Their exact dating is uncertain, but the present arrangement is supported by Paine's dated minutes of the Inferior Court proceedings (Document III).

[7] Inferior Court record, Barnstable, April 1767 (extract copy), SF 144208.

[8] SCJ Rec. 1766–1767, fols. 228–229; Min. Bk. 82, SCJ Barnstable, May 1767, N–2. As to the motion, see the file wrapper and bill of costs. SF 144208.

[9] See 8 Holdsworth, *History of English Law* 353–356, which discusses the practice whereby 17th-century judges sought to discourage actions for slander by holding that "in these actions the words complained of must be construed not in their natural sense, but, whenever possible, in 'mitiore sensu.' That is, they must be held not to be defamatory if a non-defamatory sense could be twisted out of them." *Id.* at 355.

[10] As to criminal libel and instructions to the jury generally, see No. 12. The motion in arrest of judgment was a means of attacking the legal sufficiency of the declaration after verdict, as on a demurrer. See Sutton, *Personal Actions* 129–131. Compare William Sheppard, *Actions upon the Case for Slander* 275 (London, 2d edn., 1674). If the court chose to regard actionability as matter of law only, it could overturn the jury's finding by this device. Few examples of the motion have been found in Massachusetts. Its use here and in No. 36, another defamation action, suggests that the independence of Massachusetts juries may have given it a special utility in such cases. See No. 36, note 7.

No. 3. Cotton v. Nye

I. ADAMS' DIARY[11]

4 April 1767

Poor Nye of Sandwich, seems dejected. I should suspect by his Concern that Cotton gained Ground vs. him. He seems to be hipp'd.[12] It fretts and worries and mortifies him. He cant sleep a Nights. His Health is infirm.

Cotton is insane, wild. His Proposal of giving his House and Farm at Sandwich to the Province is a Proof of Insanity.... His sitting down at the Council Table with his Hat on and Calling for his Deed and a Justice to acknowledge it when the Council was sitting.

Cottons Method of Getting Papers Signed by Members, in order to demolish poor Nye is new. The Certificate from Murray and Foster if genuine is a mean, scandalous Thing. It was mean in Murray and Foster to sign that Paper. For one Rep[resentative] to give a Constituent a Weapon to demolish another Rep., is ungentlemanlike.

II. ADAMS' MINUTES OF THE TRIAL[13]

Barnstable Inferior Court, April 1767

Cotton vs. Nye

Hovey.[14] Certificate.[15]

Benja. Fessenden. Bassetts Shop. Lying Papers. *Set* their Names to it.

D[eaco]n. Forster. Signd the Certificate,[16] &c.

Dr. Smith. Cotton said in Barbers Shop that he had a Certificate from Com[mittee] to prove Nye a Lyar. Understood that it was agreed[17] and to be destroyd.

---

[11] 1 JA, *Diary and Autobiography* 333–334.

[12] "To affect with hypochondria, to render low-spirited." *OED.*

[13] In JA's hand. Adams Papers, Microfilms, Reel No. 185. The dating is based on similarity with Paine's minutes (Doc. III).

[14] The position of this name in the MS and the Minute Book entry suggest that James Hovey was not of counsel and that his name appears inadvertently or inexplicably.

[15] "Deft. objects to it, there ought to be an Attestation of the Clerk [of the House]. The committee have no right to sign." Paine Law Notes, Barnstable Inferior Court, April 1767. See note 22 below.

[16] Deacon Thomas Foster was a Justice of the quorum and of Plymouth Inferior Court. Whitmore, *Mass. Civil List* 142, 96.

[17] That is, the dispute was settled.

John Jennings. False lying Paper, which you made yourself, and forgd their Names to it.[18]

Prince Tupper. A False lying Paper. Had stolen it or forgd it. Might as well do it as to put Turners Name to it. Annual Meeting, had been reading several Papers.

Nathl. Bassett. Cotton said he had read a Certificate about Nyes lying.[19]

Mathias Ellis. Whether he stole that, or made another just like it he could not tell.[20]

Nehemiah Webb. Made out of his own Head. Had stolen it or forged it, as he did some other. Mr. Spooners Name.

Paine. Wherever Words tend to the slander of a Mans Reputation I shall be for maintaining an Action to preserve the Peace.[21]

Court of Law a substitute in the Place of Passion.

III. PAINE'S MINUTES OF THE ARGUMENT[22]

Barnstable Inferior Court, April 1767

Defendant

It may be part of a great plan to get Representat[ion over?] that Paper.

It is true he made the Story for he drew it up.

Plaintiff put in memorial to cross Col. Cotton.[23]

The Committee had no business to sign said Certificate.

The design of the Paper was to fix a Lye upon Nye and was a parlimentary paper.

"A lying Paper," no Slander.

---

[18] Jennings' deposition, to which he also swore in the Barnstable Superior Court, 14 May 1767, is in the file. SF 144208.

[19] See to this effect deposition of Thomas Clapp. SF 144208.

[20] Ellis' deposition, sworn to in the Barnstable Superior Court, 14 May 1767, is in the file. It contains the exact wording here set out. SF 144208.

[21] See 4 Bacon, *Abridgment* 506: "and *per Holt* Ch.J. 'It is not worthwhile to be very learned on this point [i.e., the rule of *mitiore sensu* discussed in note 9 above]; for, wherever Words tend to slander a Man and to take away his Reputation, I shall be for supporting Actions for them for the Preservation of Peace,'" citing Baker v. Pierce, 2 Ld. Raym. 959, 960, 92 Eng. Rep. 139, 140; 6 Mod. 23, 24, 87 Eng. Rep. 787, 788 (K.B. 1704).

[22] Paine Law Notes, Barnstable Inferior Court, April 1767. A portion of Paine's minute has been omitted because of its similarity to JA's (Doc. II). See note 15 above.

[23] The sentence is clear in the MS, but makes no sense as it stands because Cotton was the plaintiff and had submitted the memorial.

This was not Forgery. 485 Bac. 4.[24] HPC 185 [25]
The House [of] Repres[entatives] would have votd he was crazy.
Cotton's Character is not so imaculate.

IV. ADAMS' NOTES OF AUTHORITIES [26]

Barnstable Superior Court, May 1767

Cotton vs. Nye

4. Bac. 485. "All Words are actionable which import the Charge of such a Forgery, as is within any of the statutes against this offence." [27]

"An action also lies for charging a Man with Forgery, although it is not said to be of such a Record, Deed, Writing, or Instrument as is within any of the statutes; for Forgery is an offence indictable and punishable at common Law." [28]

"But no Action lies for saying of J.S. he hath forged the Hand of J.N., these Words being too general; for unless it had been said to what Deed or Instrument, this is no offence under any of the statutes or at Common Law." [29]

1. Roll. Abr. 66. Pudsey and Pudsey.[30] 1. Roll. Abr. 65. Garbritt and Bell.[31] 3. Leon. 231.[32] 1 Roll. Abr. 65 pl. 4.[33]

3. Leonard. 231. Hill. 31. Eliz.[34] "An Action upon the Case was brought for these Words vizt. Thou hast forged my Hand: It was holden by Gawdy and Wray Justices that such Words are not actionable, because too general, without shewing to what Writing. And by Wray, these Words Scil. Thou art a Forger, are not actionable because it is not to what Thing he was a Forger. Godfrey, Between Warner and Cropwell Scil. She went about to kill me; an Action lyeth for them: for if they were true, she should be bounden to the good Behaviour.

"And by Gawdy, for these Words scil. 'Thou hast forged a Writing':

[24] See note 27 below.
[25] See note 40 below.
[26] In JA's hand. Adams Papers, Microfilms, Reel No. 185.
[27] 4 Bacon, *Abridgment* 485. Quotation marks supplied.
[28] 4 Bacon, *Abridgment* 485. Quotation marks supplied.
[29] 4 Bacon, *Abridgment* 485. Quotation marks supplied. The citations at notes 30–33 below appear as notes in Bacon.
[30] See text at note 46 below.
[31] Garbritt v. Bell, 1 Rolle, *Abridgment* 65 (K.B. 1639): Action lies for saying of B: "I have found Records which he hath forged, and he shall dearly pay for it. I have catched the forger."
[32] See note 34 below.
[33] See note 43 below.
[34] Anonymous, 3 Leon. 231, 74 Eng. Rep. 652 (Q.B. 1589).

145

They are not actionable because they are uncertain Words; which Wray concessitt:[35] But if the Declaration had been more certain, as "innuendo,[36] such a Deed," then it had been good enough.

"Fuller, a Case was betwixt Brook and Doughty, Scil.; He hath Counterfeited my Lord of Leicesters Hand unto a Letter against the Bishop of London; for the which he was committed to the Marshalsea for it. And it was holden, not Actionable. And afterwards in the principal Case, Judgment was, Nihil capiat Per Billam."[37]

Hawk. P.C. 1st. Part. chap. 70. Page. 184. §8. "and first it is clear, that one may be guilty thereof by the Common Law, by counterfeiting a matter of Record." §9. "any other authentic matter of a public Nature," &c.[38]

§11. "As to other Writings of an inferiour Nature, [...] the Counterfeiting them is not [properly] forgery," rather Cheats.[39]

§12. Forgery by Statute. §13.[40]

Cheats.

Page 188, §4. Offences of this Kind &c. falsely and deceitfully obtain Money, Goods Chattells, Jewells by counterfeit Letter.[41]

Libel, Lye to Damage.

1. Roll. Abr. 65. pl. 4. "Si home dit al Auter [42] he hath forged the Queens Evidence and I would not be in his Coat for £1000. Nul Action gist pur ceux Parols, par le Generality de eux."[43]

1. Roll. 66. [pl.] 8. "Si home dit al Auter "Thou hast made forged

---

[35] "Conceded."

[36] "Meaning." The innuendo was that part of a declaration for libel or slander which explained or pointed out the defamatory nature of the words. Here Gawdy was noting that not all forgeries were crimes (as forgery of a deed was), and that therefore an imputation of an undifferentiated forgery would not be actionable.

[37] "He takes nothing by his writ." That is, judgment for the defendant. Quotation marks supplied.

[38] 1 Hawkins, *Pleas of the Crown* 184. Quotation marks supplied.

[39] 1 Hawkins, *Pleas of the Crown* 184. Quotation marks supplied. At the ellipsis JA has omitted the words: "it seems to have been generally laid down as a rule that."

[40] 1 Hawkins, *Pleas of the Crown* 184–185. The statute is 5 Eliz., c. 14 (1562). See note 45 below. (The section numbers refer to the treatise, not the statute.)

[41] 1 Hawkins, *Pleas of the Crown* 188: "Offenses of this kind by statute depend upon 33 Hen. VIII c. 1 [(1541)] by which it is enacted, 'That if any person or persons shall falsely and deceitfully obtain or get into his or their hands or possession, any money, goods, chattels, jewels, or other things of any person or persons, by colour and means of any privy fake token, or counterfeit letter made in another man's name,' " he or they shall upon conviction be liable to suffer imprisonment or any corporal punishment other than death.

[42] "If a man says to another."

[43] "No action lies for these words, because of their generality." 1 Rolle, *Abridgment* 65. Quotation marks supplied.

Writings and thou shouldest have lost thy Ears for it. Null Action gist pur ceux Parols, pur ceo que est tout ousterment uncerten queux Writings, il intend par le[s] primer Parols, car peradventure il intend ascuns Writings le Forgerie de que ne violent deserver le perder de ses Aures et donque les d'arren Parols ne explaneront son Intention, entant que Poet estre que ceo fuit forsque un male Conclusion sur le[s] Premisses." [44]

"9. Si home dit al J.S. Thou didst Forge an Acquittance, and I will prove it, Action gist, car n'est material pur quel Chose L'Acquittance fuit, car tiel Forgerie est deins l'Estatute." [45]

"10. Thou has caused a Deed to be forgd and a dead Mans Hand to be put to it, and cheated and couzened my Husband of his Land. Action gist. [...] Pudsey and Pudsey." [46]

"11. Si A. dit, This is B. his Writing and he hath forged this Warrant (innuendo, &c.) B. n'avira ascun action pur ceux Parols par ceo le Parol Warrant est de un uncertain sense et le innuendo ne ceo aidera." [47]

Sheppards Actions on the Case for slander.[48]

"It is said to be adjudgd not to lie for this thou are a forger of false Writings."

"Nor as it seems for this Thou hast made false Writings, thereby to get my Land from me." [49]

Croo. 1. Shep. Page. 166.[50]

---

[44] "No action lies for these words, because it is completely uncertain which writings he meant by the first words; for peradventure he meant some writings the forgery of which would not cost one the loss of his ears; and thus the last words would not disclose his intent, so that perhaps it would be a wrong conclusion in the circumstances." 1 Rolle, *Abridgment* 66. Quotation marks supplied.

[45] "If a man says to J.S. ... an action lies, for it is not material by what means the acquittance came, for such a forgery is within the statute." 1 Rolle, *Abridgment* 66. Quotation marks supplied. The statute referred to is 5 Eliz., c. 14 (1562), "An Act Against Forgers of False Deeds and Writings," especially §3.

[46] 1 Rolle, *Abridgment* 66. Quotation marks supplied.

[47] "If A says ... (meaning &c.) B shall not have any action for these words because the word 'warrant' is of uncertain sense and the *innuendo* will not aid it." 1 Rolle, *Abridgment* 66. Quotation marks supplied.

[48] Sheppard, *Actions upon the Case for Slander.* The two following paragraphs appear at p. 166 of this treatise.

[49] Sheppard cites "Croo. 1 part last publisht 855," probably an inadvertence for Perkinson v. Bowman, Cro. Eliz. 853, 78 Eng. Rep. 1079 (1600), which indeed seems to hold as the treatise suggests. Quotation marks supplied in this and the preceding paragraph.

[50] Notes 48, 49, above.

V. ADAMS' MINUTES OF THE ARGUMENT [51]

Barnstable Superior Court, May 1767

Otis.[52] Certificate of General Assembly.

Law very much altered of late Times.

To prevent Gothic Contentions and single Combats.

High Proceedings.

Strange 747.[53] Order for Allom. Forgery at common Law.

Protection from a Member.

Possibility of Damage.

Reason of the Thing. Injury.

Paper indictable.

Public Record.

Q. If Cotton had forgd this Paper, whether he would have been liable to an Indictment for a Misdemeanor? [54]

4. Bac. 506.[55]

Made a false Record. Forgery of a Writ.

Great Slander and Defamation.

Court unanimous Nyes Words actionable.

VI. ADAMS' MINUTES OF THE EVIDENCE [56]

Barnstable Superior Court, May 1767

Cotton vs. Nye

Certificate [57]

Mr. Fessenden. A Lye of his own making, and he had set their Names to it.

Jennings.[58] Memento.

Bassett.[59]　　　　　　　⎫ Deps.

Ellis.[60]　　　　　　　　⎭

[51] In JA's hand. Adams Papers, Microfilms, Reel No. 185.

[52] James Otis, counsel for Cotton.

[53] Rex v. Ward, 2 Str. 747, 93 Eng. Rep. 824 (K.B. 1727): Trial for forging an order for a quantity of alum. *Held*: a criminal forgery even though it did not appear that defendant had actually obtained any alum as a result of the forgery.

[54] This is apparently JA's query.

[55] 4 Bacon, *Abridgment* 506. The treatise at this point catalogues the actionability of various words, but does not mention forgery; see note 21 above.

[56] In JA's hand. Adams Papers, Microfilms, Reel No. 185.

[57] See text at note 5 above.

[58] See note 18 above.

[59] See text at note 19 above.

[60] See note 20 above.

No. 4. Burnam v. Mugford

VII. ADAMS' DIARY [61]

16 May 1767

The Court was fixed in the Sandwich Case. Cotton is not only a Tory but a Relation of some of the Judges, Cushing particularly.... Cushing was very bitter, he was not for my arguing to the Jury the Question whether the Words were Actionable or not. He interrupted me—stopped me short, snapd me up.—"Keep to the Evidence—keep to the Point—dont ramble all over the World to ecclesiastical Councils —dont misrepresent the Evidence." This was his impartial Language. Oliver began his Speech to the Jury with—"A Disposition to slander and Defamation, is the most Cursed Temper that ever the World was plagued with and I believe it is the Cause of the greatest Part of the Calamities that Mankind labour under." This was the fair, candid, impartial Judge. They adjudged solemnly, that I should not dispute to the Jury, whether the Words were actionable or not.

4. Burnam v. Mugford

1770–1771

EDITORIAL NOTE

In the spring of 1770 the schooner *Hitty*, John Burnam, master, sailed from her home port of Marblehead to Philadelphia. As she lay at the wharf in the latter port, Burnam spent a night ashore. Next morning, a small locked trunk in which he kept gold coin was missing from its place inside a larger chest in his cabin. Two or three days later the empty trunk was found floating in the harbor with the bottom knocked out of it. The Captain's suspicions lighted upon James Mugford, a member of the crew. When the *Hitty* was about three days out of Philadelphia, homeward-bound, he undertook an inquiry to verify those suspicions. In the course of his investigations Burnam found a sum of money in gold dollars and johannes, amounting to about £20, part wrapped in a handkerchief and part in a purse, both of which were in a pair of Mugford's breeches hidden in some straw in the latter's quarters. After questioning the rest of the crew, Burnam confronted Mugford with his find and accused him of the theft. Mugford denied his guilt and insisted that the money was his, saying that the Captain had most likely come back aboard and taken the money himself. Angry words and threats followed between the two, but the net result was that Burnam kept the money.[1]

[61] 1 JA, *Diary and Autobiography* 335.

[1] See the depositions of the mate and two members of the crew in SF 132064. Mugford was probably the Massachusetts naval hero, who was killed in action in

Mugford brought suit against Burnam within a few days after their return to Marblehead. His declaration in trespass alleged a taking "at said Marblehead," a fictitious allegation intended to overcome any objection to the venue based on the fact that the incident had not occurred within Essex County.[2] At the July 1770 term of the Inferior Court at Salem, after a plea of the general issue, the jury found a verdict for Mugford of £22 damages and costs.[3]

On the appeal which followed, Adams joined John Lowell as counsel for Captain Burnam. Adams' minutes of testimony at the trial in the Superior Court in June 1771 offer some interesting views of life aboard ship and indicate what a slender thread of circumstantial evidence there was to justify Burnam's taking. These witnesses and the depositions on file in the case were agreed that Mugford had had money when he got to Philadelphia, and that Burnam had taken money from Mugford's possession. Burnam could offer no direct evidence that the money was his, or that Mugford had come by it wrongfully. Thus, Mugford's title, as well as his possession, was made out. In this state of the case it is hardly surprising that the jury returned a verdict affirming the former judgment for Mugford.[4]

ADAMS' MINUTES OF THE TRIAL[5]

Essex Superior Court, Ipswich, June 1771

Burnam vs. Mugford.

Jno. Melzond. Was on board the Vessell with Captn. Burnam and Mr. Mugford. Burnam took an Hankercheif and a Purse and 1/2 Jo[hannes][6] in it, and some small Money. B. askd Mugford is that your Money? Yes. M. said Do you intend to keep it. M. claimed it as his Money. Said it was his Money and asked C[aptain] B[urnam] if he want going to let him have it. B. said No. Cant say if the Handkerchief was his. 1/2 Jo. in the Purse. B. did not claim any Thing but the Money. I had seen M. have such a Purse and wear such a Pair of Breeches. He had a Chest on board. Dont know how M. came by the M[oney].[7] M. said he brought the Money from Spain. He had a Watch which he used to keep in the Coopers Chest. C.B. was out that

---

Boston Harbor, 19 May 1776. See AA to JA, 27 May 1776, 2 *Adams Family Correspondence* 417–419. His status aboard the *Hitty* cannot be clearly determined. He is described as "⟨Mate⟩ a Seaman," yet he shared a cabin with the mate. Deposition of George Wellford, note 8 below.

[2] Writ and declaration are in SF 132064. As to the venue, see p. 35, note 28, above.

[3] The judgment of the Inferior Court is in SF 132064.

[4] Min. Bk. 93, SCJ Ipswich, June 1771, C–13; SCJ Rec. 1771 fol. 95.

[5] In JA's hand. Adams Papers, Microfilms, Reel No. 185.

[6] A Portuguese gold coin worth about 36s. sterling. *OED.*

[7] MS torn.

Night. Fortnight or 3 Weeks before. I went and made the C[aptain]s Cabbin. Dunlop the officer, and Mugford playd a Game of Cards. I saw the Cabbin open and his Trunk next Morning. B had Money in that Trunk. Mugford had Money, with him when he went to Phyladelphia. *He lent 2 1/2 Jos. and said his father gave em to him to buy Pork.* M. a foremast Hand. B. when he found his Trunk was broke he said he had lost about £450 0. [...]. The Trunk was found between the Wharfe and ship. The Trunk was generally lockd the Chest Unlock'd. 2 Hds. Molasses rolled off the Wharf that Night.

James Mugford—father of Plaintiff. The Voyage before this, he went to Spain, and he carried with him Fish &c. which sold for £60 L.M. He had a Months pay of C.B. and the neat Proceeds of an Hogshead of Molosses, which might amount to £70 L.M. He told me he brought Money from Spain. He brought from Phyladelphia 5 Barrels flour and 1000 Wt. Bread. I gave him no Johannes to buy Pork, or anything, before he sail'd.

Lowell.

George Wilfords Deposition vid.[8]

Grist. M. told me that C. Mugford[9] accused him with stealing Money, which he was innocent of, as the Child in the Womb. He said He carried 10 Jos. which his father gave him, to buy Pork. He did not buy it because the Pork was so dear.

Mr. Grist. M. told me he was clear, &c.

5. Gill v. Mein

1768–1769

EDITORIAL NOTE

In the bitter verbal battling which rumbled beneath the physical violence of the pre-Revolutionary years, the heavy advantage rested with the radical press. Led by such pseudonymous journalistic swordsmen as Samuel Adams, Joseph Hawley, and Joseph Warren, the patriots skewered

---

[8] The deposition of George Wellford, dated at Marblehead, 10 April 1771, is in SF 132064. Wellford testified that, on the voyage to Philadelphia, Mugford had told him "that he had got seven or eight small pieces of gold which he said he would if he could pass them for dollars." At Philadelphia, Mugford had said "that he brought eighteen Jos. which his father sent by him to buy pork, but pork being dear, he would not buy it, but would [lay?] out the money in flour and bread." The deposition also substantiates the other accounts of the theft of the trunk and Burnam's confrontation of Mugford.

[9] An inadvertence for Captain Burnam.

the administration and the loyal faction without restraint, and almost without opposition.[1] Only one tory printer possessed sufficient journalistic skill and courage to brave the muscular threats with which Sam's Mohawks imposed their ideas of liberty. That man was John Mein, printer of the *Boston Chronicle*. It was Mein, for example, who crippled Adams' non-importation campaign by publishing authenticated lists of the self-styled "well-disposed" merchants who, having signed the agreement not to import, were quietly landing and selling forbidden goods.[2]

Mein's combative nature and his journalistic skill plunged the *Boston Chronicle* into controversy from the very start of its brief existence. In the first issue, under a London dateline, Mein ran a sharp attack on William Pitt, Earl of Chatham, the idol of the Sons of Liberty.[3] A violent response by "Americus" appeared in Edes and Gill's *Boston Gazette*, indirectly accusing Mein, among other things, of Jacobite leanings.[4]

[1] The best treatment of this subject is Arthur M. Schlesinger, *Prelude to Independence* 84–109 (N.Y., 1958); see also John C. Miller, *Sam Adams, Pioneer in Propaganda* 174–176 (Boston, 1936); E. F. Brown, *Joseph Hawley* 63–68 (N.Y., 1931); John Cary, *Joseph Warren* 60–63 (Urbana, Ill., 1961).

[2] On Mein's life, see Alden, "John Mein: Scourge of Patriots," 34 Col. Soc. Mass., *Pubns.* 571–599 (1942), and Bolton, "Circulating Libraries in Boston, 1765–1865," 11 Col. Soc. Mass., *Pubns.* 196–200 (1907). See also No. 12. On the *Boston Chronicle*, see Matthews, "Bibliographical Notes to Check List of Boston Newspapers, 1704–1780," 9 Col. Soc. Mass., *Pubns.* 403, 480–483 (1907); Schlesinger, *Prelude to Independence* 107; Andrews, "Boston Merchants and the Non-Importation Movement," 19 Col. Soc. Mass., *Pubns.* 159, 227–230 (1917).

[3] "It is confidently reported that the E. of C——'s gout is only political, and that notwithstanding his late indisposition he will soon appear on the scene of action and struggle hard to guide the reins of government, but having lost the confidence of the people, whom he has deceived by his contradictions and changes, and never having been a favorite with the nobility, whom he always affected to dispise, he will while he exists be considered by every disinterested man as a miserable monument of wrecked ambition." *Boston Chronicle*, 21 Dec. 1767, p. 5, col. 1. In the same piece, the Marquis of Rockingham received praise for having "quieted the commotions which shook the state by the repeal of the American Stamp Act; while he preserved the constitution in full vigour by the act for securing the dependence of the colonies."

[4] "When I read the Proposals, for publishing the Boston Chronicle, I tho't on the Plan with Satisfaction, hoping thereby much good would accrue to America in general, and to this province in particular; with Pleasure I also noted the judicious Advice given Messi'rs Mein and Fleeming by their Friends of Taste. It runs thus:

" 'We suppose you intend to study your own Interest; if you would do it effectually, be of no Party, publish and propagate with the greatest Industry whatever may promote the general Good. Be Independent—Your Interest is intimately connected with this noble Virtue—If you depart from this, you must sink from the Esteem of the Publick, to the partial Praise of a Party, who, when their Purposes is serv'd or defeated, may perhaps desert you, and then how can you expect that those whom you have revil'd will support you'—To which at that Time they answer'd.—'Whenever any Dispute claims general Attention, the Arguments on both Sides shall be laid before the Publick with the utmost Impartiality.'

"But to the Surprize of many, how are they fallen off from their own Purposes, and the excellent Caution of their Benefactors—Instead of giving impartial Accounts concerning Affairs at Home, and the unhappy Disputes lately arisen between the

No. 5. Gill v. Mein

Storming into the *Gazette's* office, Mein unsuccessfully demanded that the editors name the author; returning the next day, he repeated his inquiry and was again repulsed.[5] Finally, that evening, Mein met Gill and, by his own admission, caned him.[6]

greatest Men of the Nation; they have made Choice of, or printed under Guise of being taken from the London Papers, the most infamous and reproachful Invectives, that ever was invented against the worst of Traitors to their King and Country, and who are these that are thus censur'd? Why, men held in the highest esteem and veneration in the British Parliament. Patriots and Friends and Deliverers of America from Oppression. He who nobly vindicated her Cause, almost against the whole Senate, who cast behind him all Lucre of Gain, when it came in Competition with the Good of his Country, and sacrific'd his Family-Connections and Interest to the publick Welfare. He that through real Infirmities hardly stood, (not to cover his politic Schemes and Ambition as his Enemies would insinuate) but stood though tottering, and in the Cause of Liberty made that heroic Speech before the august House of Commons, in Opposition to the Stamp-Act, sufficient to eternize his Fame, and ought to be written in Letters of Gold to perpetuate his Memory. Could the Sons of America be ingrateful, or countenance the greatest Falsities, rais'd only to prejudice their best Friends and Benefactors—God forbid! Let that Dishonor stain with the blackest Infamy the Jacobite Party—And though Invectives should be daily thrown out, let us keep our Integrity to the Confusion of our Enemies; who, for a long Time have exerted their Power to shake the Props of our Constitution, and bring a free people into Bondage, thereby to satisfy their more than common Avarice, &c." *Boston Gazette,* 18 Jan. 1768, p. 1, col. 3.

Benjamin Edes (1732-1803) and John Gill (d. 1785) had been partners since 1755. Isaiah Thomas, *The History of Printing in America,* 1:136-140 (Worcester, 2d edn., 1874). "Gill was a sound whig, but did not possess the political energy of his partner. He was industrious, constantly in the printing house, and there worked at case or press as occasion required." *Id.* at 140.

[5] "In consequence of a piece signed *Americus,* published in the last Monday's Gazette, Mr. Mein came to our office between 4 and 5 o'clock the same afternoon, and there being a number of persons present, he desired to be spoke with in private, accordingly I withdrew with him to another room—when he said, I suppose you know what I am come about. I told him I did not. Well then, said he, I am come to demand the author of the piece you printed against me; and if you will not tell me who he is, I shall look upon you as the author, and the affair shall be decided in three minutes. In reply to which I said, Mr. Mein, above all persons in the world, I should not have thought a Printer would have ask'd such an impertinent, improper question; and told him that we never divulg'd authors; but if he would call on the morrow between 9 and 10 o'clock, being then very busy, I would let him know whether I would tell the author or not,—and added,—if we have transgress'd the law, it is open, and there he might seek satisfaction. He said he should not concern himself with the law, nor enter into any dispute; but if I did not tell the author, he should look upon us as the authors, and repeated it, the affair should be settled in three minutes. I then ask'd him, if what he said with regard to settling the affair in three minutes, was meant as a challenge or threat? which he declin'd answering, but said he would call at the time appointed, and then departed.

"Accordingly the next morning, I was at the office precisely at 9 o'clock, where I found Mr. Mein, who immediately after my entrance, and saying your servant, ask'd whether I would tell him the author of the above piece or no. I told him I would not. He then said he should look upon me and Mr. Gill as the authors. I told him he might and welcome. I then ask'd him what he meant by saying the last night he would settle the affair in three minutes, whether as a challenge or threat? He answered, if I would take my hat, and take a walk with him to the

153

Gill sued Mein for £200 at the April 1768 Suffolk Inferior Court, where with Adams as Gill's counsel the case was tried on 28 April 1768; after a "long hearing" the jury brought in a verdict for Gill of £130 and costs.[7] Both parties appealed. Meanwhile, Mein had been cited criminally for the assault, and at the April sitting of the Court of Sessions, had been fined forty shillings.[8]

At the March 1769 Suffolk Superior Court, the civil matter went to trial on Mein's appeal, with Kent and Auchmuty defending Mein, while Otis and Adams (whose minutes appear below) represented Gill. This time Gill won again, but the verdict was reduced to £75 and costs. A motion for a new trial was made in Mein's behalf, but later withdrawn.[9]

From the state of Adams' minutes, it seems probable that he opened for the plaintiff and was followed by Kent for the defendant. Plaintiff's evidence then went in, but defendant did not introduce any. Auchmuty closed for defendant, and Otis for plaintiff.

Although Mein's plea had traversed (denied) the assault, and had not attempted to justify it, the Adams minutes suggest that Mein conceded the striking but sought to minimize the damages by arguing provocation.

ADAMS' MINUTES OF THE TRIAL[10]

Suffolk Superior Court, Boston, March 1769

Gill vs. Mein.

News Paper. Jacobite Party.

Kent. Odd that Edes and Gill should desire him to be of no Party. Pitt is a fallen Angell, and given up by his Partizans, since he dwindled into a Lord. Lost. Lucre of Gain. Gain of Gain. Did not come from Salem.[11] Mem. no Witchcraft in it. Jacobite Party, ungenerous base Insinuations. Kick upon the A–se.

---

southward, he would let me know. I told him I was not to be at every fellow's beck, and did not regard him. He then said, I shall look upon you as the author. I reply'd, you may. Your servant, and your servant.   B. Edes." *Boston Gazette*, 25 Jan. 1768, p. 2, col. 1.

⁶ See note 11 below.

⁷ *Massachusetts Gazette*, 5 May 1768, suppl., p. 1, col. 3; SF 101491.

⁸ Rex v. Mein, Sess. Min. Bk., Suffolk, April–May 1768.

⁹ Min. Bk. 89, SCJ Suffolk, Aug. 1769, C–12; SCJ Rec. 1769, fol. 235.

¹⁰ In JA's hand. Original not found, but a photostat of the MS, originally in private hands, is preserved in MHi:Photostat Coll. under date of 1768. Quotation marks supplied by the editors. See note 4 above.

¹¹ A paper in Mein's hand in 3 Bernard Papers 45, 46, MH, explains this allusion: "Jemmy [Otis] is fond of dating his pieces from Salem, being the town where he has the fewest Adherents. And he is suspected from good Authority of being the author of the abusive piece in Edes & Gill against me when our Chronicle was first published, which obliged me to call on the Printers, and on their refusal to name the Authors to ask them one after another to take a short Walk; and on their

B. Edes. No Conversation past between Us, about agreeing not to abuse one Another, nor to mention one Another. The Account I published is true, all but one Word, and I am uncertain whether I said *Fellow, Rascall* or *Scoundrel.*

Anthony Oliver. Do not remember Meins desiring Edes and Gill, not to mention him in their Paper, Mein said he would get the Printers to meet, so that they might have no Dispute.

Auchmuty. I shall confine myself to one single Object, the Quantum of Damages. To view a Case of this sort thro the Flames of Passion, must give you a dissagreable Turn against the Rules of Justice.

The Passions are sometimes, excused by Law. Son killing the Assailant of his father. The Husband killing An Adulterer, with his Wife, not guilty of Murder, Jury not to punish in Terrorem. Feeling, &c. Tendency to take away his Bread by publishing that a Man publishes Falsities. Sporting and wantoning with Characters. Not from Man to Man, but scattered thro whole Countries. Have not been so civil as to [give?] his Name. If Printers will not tell the Author they must be treated as the Authors themselves.

Auchmuty. Uncandid and uncivil, not to tell the Author. An Indication of some little Guilt, in the Mind of Mr. Gill when he desired Witnesses beforehand, to take Notice if Mr. Mein should Assault him.

Virulence of Representation, high Colouring Rather that Mr. Adams has given it in Opening.

"But how are they fallen off," &c. This is to catch and byass the Reader.

Accuse Mein of taking out of "Choice ... the most infamous and reproachfull Invectives" vs. the Patron of the Country. By his Profession depends vastly upon the public Smiles. The Insult vastly greater, upon Us, than upon Gill.

Encomiums and Panegyricks upon Mr. Pit or the Person alluded to. 1st to be guilty of infamous Lying, and for no other End but to abuse the "best Friends and Benefactors" of the Country. A Lyar, a Traytor, and a Jacobite. Assassin, Ruffian, Spaniards Sticking and Stabbing.[12]

---

declining it to cane the first of them I mett which has already cost me about £100 St." On the resistance of Salem to the nonimportation agreement, see Miller, *Sam Adams* 222.

[12] "The Freedom of the PRESS has been deservedly esteemed an important Branch of our LIBERTY. We hold it dear, and look on all those as our Enemies who endeavour to deprive us of it. The Dispute therefore between Messieurs Gill and Mein, cannot be looked upon barely as a Dispute between two private Persons, but is of the highest Importance to the Community. If we suffer the Printers to be abused, for resolutely maintaining the Freedom of the Press, without discovering our just Resentment against those who endeavour to force them from their Duty, we shall

Henshaw and Tyng.[13] Lye, the high Provocation. If I was to call Assassin, and Ruffian, I would in some other Place. A Man must be made of Oakum, not to feel Cutting, and tearing Characters. It is one of the greatest inconveniences, and may be attended with public Mischief.

Otis. Weight and Bulk of the Stick. Observations a cool deliberate Action. No sudden Heat, or Ruffle of Passion. Went once and twice to the office, and took an Opportunity afterwards to beat. Gill pretends not to be a Boxer, Bruizer, Man of the sword or any Prowess whatever. I would not engage Mein, but I would beat 2 of Gill.

He was assaulted for carrying on a Paper, in the Course [of] his Business. No Man I think ought to publish an Opinion that he is not able nor willing to defend.

Mr. Cooke[14] who lived and died in the Service of the Town whose last Words expressed Wishes for our Welfare, and Fears of the very Things that are now coming upon Us.

Chaind between two Posts. Odd Idea of Liberty of the Press.[15] A Fashion to raise a vast Outcry vs. this Paper. Scurrillity of Grandees. Dream or Vision, of a mutual Compact between Mein and Gill.

Green & Russell[16] go on in pe[a]cable quiet, harmless, dovelike, inoffensive Manner. Distinction between Bump and Tumour. Note the Diversity.

Paper set up above all Criticism. This is but a Criticism [of?] impartial History.

---

soon find the Press shut against us—For it cannot be expected that one or two Men who will be subject to the Malice of the publick Enemies, bear to be bruised, and run the Hazard of being assassinated, if the Public, whose Cause they are fighting do not zealously patronize their Cause. The People in this Province, and this Town in particular, must for the foregoing Reasons, be justified in their general Disapprobation of, and Disgust to Mr. Mein, for his late Spaniard-like Attempt on Mr. Gill, and in him, upon the Freedom of the Press." *Boston Gazette,* 1 Feb. 1768, p. 2, col. 2.

[13] The reference is unclear.

[14] Elisha Cooke (1678–1737), "the masterly hand from School Street," politician and court clerk, of "a fixt enmity to all Kingly Governments," had led the fight against the royal prerogative in the 1720's. He even sailed to England to argue the cause before the Privy Council. *DAB.* Ironically, a transcript of the Privy Council proceedings had appeared in the *Boston Chronicle,* 11 Jan. 1768, p. 33, cols. 1–3. Cooke was the father of Middlecott Cooke (1705–1771), clerk of the Suffolk Inferior Court. See vol. 2:248–249, notes 4, 5, and 7, below.

[15] "Otis at my trial for caning Gill, bandied about this Liberty of the Press as the Salvation of America, and said, that in beating him I had endeavoured to shutt up that great Source of freedom." Mein, "A Key to a Certain Publication," 3 Bernard Papers 45, 47, MH.

[16] John Green and Joseph Russell, publishers of the pro-Administration *Boston Post-Boy.* Matthews, "Bibliographical Notes," 9 Col. Soc. Mass., *Pubns.* 403, 470.

Little nibbling quibbling Decisions in our Books about Libells and Actions of Defamation.[17] All these decisions cannot make the Words "leave these Things to the Jacobite Party" applicable to Mein.[18] Interlard and interlace with Innuendo's.

6. Gray v. Pitts

1771

EDITORIAL NOTE

This was an action brought by John Gray for injuries inflicted upon him by Lendall (or Lindall) Pitts in a scuffle outside Dehon's barber shop in Boston. Adams' minutes indicate that the underlying cause was an earlier incident in which Pitts had "gallanted" what he assumed to be an attractive young lady, only to learn that feminine clothes covered a masculine form—either Gray himself or another male procured by him. Pitts blamed Gray in any case and, after unsuccessfully demanding an apology, opened Gray's scalp with a walking stick.

Gray sued in the July 1771 Suffolk Inferior Court for £300; Josiah Quincy was able to win him only a £5 verdict, which Gray appealed to the August 1771 Suffolk Superior Court.[1] There, the jury awarded him £18 damages and costs of £10 8s. 8d. Adams, who had been specially appointed guardian *ad litem* for Pitts (a minor), was his counsel at both trials.[2]

From a technical standpoint, the case is interesting because, although the plea was not guilty, that is, a flat denial of the assault, Adams was allowed to introduce evidence in justification of the blow.[3]

[17] See the discussion of this point in 8 Holdsworth, *History of English Law* 355–356, cited in No. 3 at note 9.
[18] The words are apparently Otis' paraphrase for "Let that Dishonor [i.e. falsities and prejudice of friends] stain with the blackest Infamy the Jacobite Party," from the Americus letter, note 4 above.

[1] SCJ Rec. 1771, fol. 216. SF 101911. Pitts' cross appeal was dismissed, the merits having been determined in Gray's appeal. Min. Bk. 95, SCJ Suffolk, Aug. 1771, N–11.
[2] SF 101911. JA's wealthy client, James Pitts, had a son named Lendall. If the dates (1747–1784) given for him by Shipton are correct, however, he could not have been a minor in 1771. See 9 Sibley-Shipton, *Harvard Graduates* 81; Francis S. Drake, *Tea Leaves* 141–145 (Boston, 1884). The Pitts here involved may be the Pitts referred to in the deposition of Sergeant John Eylery, dated 25 Aug. 1770, 12 Gay Transcripts 93, MHi. On 17 Oct. 1769, Eylery said, a mob gathered before the Guard Room door—on the south side of King Street, across from the Town House—and began insulting the sentinels "in a most abusive manner, and particularly one Pitts who said if he had the Scoundrels elsewhere and without Arms he would thresh them as long as his cane would last."
[3] See note 14 below.

Adams' minutes suggest that James Otis spoke at the trial on 2 and 3 December 1771, although he was not counsel of record for either party.[4] In fact, on the latter date Otis, having been certified "a distracted person" by the Selectmen of Boston, was "carried off . . . in a post chaise, bound hand and foot."[5] If the remarks recorded by Adams were actually made in court, they not only offer a striking glimpse of Otis on his way to the madhouse, but suggest a very informal court room atmosphere.

I. ADAMS' MINUTES OF THE TRIAL[6]

Suffolk Inferior Court, Boston, July 1771

Gray vs. Pitts.

James Melvin. Saw Pitts push Gray off with one Hand and give him a stroke with his Stick. G. no Hatt on. Saw the Blood run. A knotty Stick—big as the Thumb. Bigger than [Wallaces's?]. Did not strike so hard as he could.

Wm. Winter. Gray came into Dehons shop.[7] Pitts and he went out. Pitts demanded Satisfaction. I ask your Pardon you chuckle headed son of a Bitch. Pitts held up his Fist and Gray held up his, and then Pitts pushed him off with one hand and struck him with the other.

Mr. Hutchinson.[8] Pitts told me, he had sent a Lad to demand Satisfaction for the Insult he had received. Saw Gray stand holding his Coat, the Blood dropping from his Head.

Odin. ⟨Pitts sa⟩ Gray said you woolly headed Rascall. Pitts said you shall—The Blow did not seem very hard. Saw Blood.

Mr. Molineux.

---

[4] Min. Bk. 95, SCJ Suffolk, Aug. 1771, N–11, N–17. The dates are fixed by the foregoing entries. The trial began on the "18th day" of the Aug. term, which, after an adjournment, had reconvened on 26 Nov., the 14th day. The subpoena and bill of costs in the file confirm this determination. SF 101911.

[5] Selectmen's Minutes, 26 Nov. 1771, 23 Boston Record Commissioners, *Reports* 103–104 (1893); letter of Thomas Hutchinson to Francis Bernard, 3 Dec. 1771, 27 Mass. Arch. 260.

[6] In JA's hand. Adams Papers, Microfilms, Reel No. 185. The trial took place 26 July 1771, according to a summons in the Inferior Court file.

[7] William Winter, "peruke maker," was also a witness in the Superior Court. SF 101911. "Dehons" is probably the shop of Theodore Dehone, Perukemaker. See Thwing Catalogue, MHi.

[8] Godfrey Hutchinson, "infant," was also a witness in the Superior Court. SF 101911.

To the Constables of *Pembrook*
or any or either of them, Greeting.

YOU are Required in His Majesty's Name, forthwith to assemble the Freeholders and other Inhabitants of your Town, qualified according to the Royal Charter, and to signify unto them, that they are Required to choose *three* good and lawful Men of your Town, each whereof to have a Real Estate of *Forty Shillings* per Annum, or other Estate worth *Fifty Pounds* Sterling: *one* whereof to serve on the Grand Jury, and *two* on the Jury of Trials, at the next Superiour Court of Judicature, Court of Assize and General Goal Delivery, to be Holden at *Plymouth* for the County of *Plymouth* on the *Third* Tuesday of *May* next, which Persons so chosen you are to Summon and Warn to attend the Service of said Court, at Nine o'Clock in the Morning of said Day, and make Return of your Doings herein, with the Names of the Persons so chosen to the Sheriff of said County a Day at least before the Sitting of said Court. Dated the *sixth* Day of *March* 1765. In the *fifth* Year of his Majesty's Reign.

Sam Winthrop Cler

142058

7. VENIRE FACIAS, SUPERIOR COURT OF JUDICATURE

8. JURY LIST, SUPERIOR COURT OF JUDICATURE

4. CAMBRIDGE IN 1775

II. ADAMS' MINUTES OF THE TRIAL[9]

Suffolk Superior Court, Boston, December 1771

Gray vs. Pitts. Assault and Battery.

J. Quincy.

We had done nothing but what was justifiable by the Laws of our Country.

J. Whitworth.[10] Pitt said in the forenoon, that Gray had used him very ill, and he would beat him whenever he met him. About 1 1/2 Hour before, he did [...] Very ill in Speaking Reports of him.

Mr. Hutchinson.[11] Pitts told me he had sent a Lad to the Custom house to call Gray out to demand Satisfaction of him. And I saw em at it, and the Blood dropping from G's Head. Stick knotty, 1/2 Inch Diameter.

Tim. Odin. Pitts went into the Barbers shop, and asked Gray if he would ask his Pardon. No, you wooly headed Rascall, I wont. D—n you you shall, running his Fist up says Pitts. I could not hear the rest of the Conversation till Pitts struck him. The stick did not seem to be struck hard. But Gray said, Ile set this down to your everlasting Account.

Melvill.[12] Gray had no stick nor Hatt. Gray and Pitts were coming from Dehones shop, to Carpenters. Pitts in a Passion. Pitts shoved him off first with his Hand, and then a stroke with a stick. Saw the Blood.

Isaac Pierce. Heard a Blow at the Town House steps. About 3. Rods.

Dr. Roberts. 2 Wounds, one about 3/4 of an Inch, the other between 1/3 and 1/2 on the scalp, Top of the Head. Both done at one blow. About 12 or 14 days. Every other day. Bill a Guinea. No more than a flesh Wound.[13]

J. Quincy. If he had a Mind to discover his Manhood as much as he had at other Times he would have taken another Weapon.

Knows Gentlemen who have a Talent of diminishing or exagerating just as they please.

[9] In JA's hand. Adams Papers, Microfilms, Reel No. 185.

[10] John Dean Whitworth, Boston merchant. SF 101911. See Jones, *Loyalists of Mass.* 295.

[11] See note 8 above.

[12] Probably the "James Melvin" whose testimony is set out in Doc. I above. James Melvil, "infant, peruke maker," was a witness in the Superior Court. SF 101911.

[13] This concession may have emerged on cross-examination. Dr. Roberts was apparently a reluctant witness, since a capias for him appears in the file. SF 101911. Peter Roberts had a shop "near the Town House" in 1767. Thwing Catalogue, MHi.

Pain, of Body, Expences, Ignominy.

Of great Importance that Juries should be uniform and steady in their Decisions, and that Capriciousness and Humour should not prevail.

Atrocious, inhuman, Injury &c.

Our Witnesses

Shaw. No you woolly headed Rascall dam ye you woolly headed Rascall, I ask your Pardon. And Gray run his Fist up at his face in a threatning manner. Cant say which fist was up first, Grays or Pitts's.

Jones. Pitts told me Gray had used him ⟨at⟩ in a Rascally Matter. Gray called him chucklehead, and put his fist up to Pitts's face, cant say he touched him. 1636 upon the Head of it. The stick was like a fishing Cane. I ownd it—lent it to P. 2 or 3 Months before. Very light stick and hollow I thought.

Mr. Plaisted.

Mr. Molineux.[14] I saw him dressed in Womens Cloaths. He had the outward Appearance of a Woman, a Gown and Womens Cloaths. I saw a Couple of young Gentlemen gallanting him. Pitts was one. I was very sensible they were taken in. Plaisted was the other. They appeared to be very loving—she rather Coy. I called out to Pitts at New Boston.[15] He turnd a deaf Ear. He came back and said he had a very clever Girl, and went to her again.

Otis. Clodius, dressed in Womans Apparell, broke in upon the Sacrifices of the Bona Dea.

Orat. pro Milone beginning.[16]

[14] According to the file, this was William Molineux Jr, son of the patriot leader. SF 101911. See Samuel A. Drake, *Historic Fields and Mansions of Middlesex* 424 (Boston, 1874). This evidence, presumably in justification, was apparently not objected to, although it was inadmissible under the plea of the general issue entered here. See 1 Chitty, *Pleading* 491–493.

[15] The Beacon Hill area. See 2 JA, *Diary and Autobiography* 46–47.

[16] "Clodius . . . being in love with Pompeia, Caesar's wife, got privately in his house in the dress and attire of a music-girl; the women being at that time offering there the sacrifice which must not be seen by men." Plutarch, *Lives* 1057 (Dryden transl., Modern Library edn.). This was the sacrifice to the Bona Dea, or Good Goddess, "worshipped by the women of Rome as the goddess of chastity and fertility." C. T. Lewis and C. Short, *A New Latin Dictionary* 243 (N.Y., rev. edn., 1907). When in 52 B.C. Titus Annius Milo stood trial for Clodius' murder, Cicero defended him. Otis' second reference is to an expanded version of Cicero's address, *Pro T. Annio Milone Oratio* (Speech on Behalf of T. Annius Milo). Cicero, *Speeches* 6–123 (London & N.Y., transl. Watts, 1931). For a reference to the Bona Dea incident, see *id.* at 68 note. The passage cited by Otis seems to be: "When arms speak, the laws are silent; they bid none to await their word. . . . And

No. 6. Gray v. Pitts

J. Quincy. No smart saying, no pointed Turns. Amorous Rencounter.

Judge Hutchinson. Prov. Law Page 61. last Clause of the Act to prevent Incestuous Marriages.[17]

---

yet most wisely, and, in a way, tacitly, the law authorizes self-defense. . . . The man who had employed a weapon in self-defence was not held to have carried that weapon with a view to homicide." *Id.* at 17.

[17] Act of 19 June 1696, c. 2, §7, 1 A&R 208, 210: "[I]f any man shall wear women's apparel, or if any woman shall wear man's apparel, and be thereof duly convicted, they shall be corporally punished or fined, at the discretion of the quarter sessions not exceeding five pounds, to the use of the county where the offence is committed, towards the defraying of the county charges."

D. Contracts

7. Porter v. Steel

1770–1772

EDITORIAL NOTE

This action was the climax of a series of clashes between James Steel of Haverhill, Massachusetts, and Asa Porter, a merchant and trader from the upper Connecticut Valley Coös region of New Hampshire.[1] In September 1767 Steel had sold Porter and his partner Andrew Savage Crocker a consignment of 1600 barrel hoops. After Porter accepted settlement against him in another matter, Steel sued out a writ for the value of the hoops returnable at the December 1769 term of the Essex County Inferior Court.

Porter traveled south into Massachusetts in the fall of 1769, settling his accounts with various correspondents. At the beginning of November he told Jacob Rowell to leave a note of Porter & Crocker, which he held, at Walker's Inn in Haverhill, where Porter would settle it. On 29 November Porter stopped at Walker's and left Rowell a letter, reporting that he was unable to pay the note now but that satisfaction could be had from a correspondent in Newburyport. On the next day Porter and Steel met at Harriman's Inn at Plaistow, New Hampshire. Here, Porter paid Steel's claim for the hoops and, according to Porter, also gave Steel the sum owed to Rowell with instructions that it be paid over to the latter. Porter took a receipt and then departed for Coös.[2]

Whatever the agreement, Steel did not make payment to Rowell. Accordingly, Porter & Crocker brought suit against Steel at the July 1770 Essex Inferior Court. The declaration contained two counts: (1) That Steel had "received of the Plaintiffs the sum of five pounds ten shillings and in consideration thereof promised the plaintiffs to pay the same sum to one Jacob Rowell on their account and to procure the same sum to be endorsed on a note of hand which the said Rowell had of the plaintiffs payable to the said Rowell." (2) A count in *indebitatus assumpsit* for the same amount, "had and received by said James for the use of the Plaintiffs." On

---

[1] The following statement of the case is derived from the testimony on review in the Superior Court (Doc. I), and the files of the case, SF 132063, 132246, pertinent extracts of which appear in footnotes below.

[2] The receipt on file in the case provides, "Plastow 30th Novr. 1769. Received of Porter & Crocker five pounds ten shilling which I promise to pay to Jacob Rowell of New Salem on their Account and to endorse it on their note payable to him, and also received of said Porter & Crocker five pounds eighteen shillings & 8d. LM in full for hoops and all demands. James Steel." SF 132246.

a plea of the general issue entered by Nathaniel Peaslee Sargeant, counsel for Steel, the case went to the jury, which returned a verdict for Porter in the sum sued for and costs.[3]

Steel appealed to the Superior Court, where at the June term 1771 he obtained a verdict reversing the prior judgment.[4] Porter now sought a writ of review. In November 1772 the case came on in the Superior Court at Salem, with Adams joining Sargeant as Steel's counsel, and John Lowell appearing for Porter. The form of Steel's receipt and the nature of the pleadings suggest some interesting possibilities in the law of contracts, but no issues in this field seem to have been raised.[5] Adams' minutes of the evidence (Document I), and minutes of a portion of the argument in Wetmore's hand (Document II) indicate that Steel's basic contentions were factual: he had not signed the memorandum of the contract urged against him; he had not received the sum sued for. As to the first point, the plaintiffs introduced the original memorandum and a handwriting sample to establish Steel's signature. Steel then urged that the instrument had been altered after he had signed it, but the court ruled that he bore

[3] See pleadings and judgment, SF 132246.

[4] SCJ Rec. 1771, fols. 94–95; Min. Bk. 93, SCJ Ipswich, June 1771, C–12. The following minutes of the trial appear in the Wetmore Notes, No. 2, Adams Papers, Microfilms, Reel No. 184:

"Steel and Porter. Assumpsit. Special declaration, and Count for money received to plaintiffs use.

"The 1. Count is for a promise to pay a Sum he had received of the plaintiff on their account to B. [apparently an inadvertence for Rowell] and to procure it to be indorsed on a Note given by the Plaintiffs to said B. yet he hath not paid it to said B. nor procured it to be indors'd on said note tho requested.

"The written promise is that he had received £— of Plaintiffs which I promise to pay to B. of ——— on their account and to endorse it on their note payable to him. Sewl. objects the variance between Count and writing." ("Sewl." is David or Jonathan Sewall, of counsel for Steel with Sargeant at this stage.)

[5] The theory of the first count seems to have been that the action lay on Steel's promise to pay over the money and procure the endorsement, with Steel's receipt of the money as consideration. Such a contract has been upheld against a defense of no consideration on the theory that there was detriment to the promisee in handing over the money and trusting the promisor. Wheatly v. Low, Cro. Jac. 668, 79 Eng. Rep. 578 (K.B. 1624), cited with approval by Holt, C.J., in Coggs v. Bernard, 2 Ld. Raym. 909, 920, 92 Eng. Rep. 107, 114 (Q.B. 1703). Modern theorists have sought to limit this recovery to bailment situations, indicating that otherwise the remedy lies in tort, but it is analogous in at least some respects to the remedy provided by the Restatement of Contracts, §90, for breach of a gratuitous promise which induces a reasonable reliance. See Samuel Williston and George J. Thompson, *Selections from Williston's Treatise on the Law of Contracts* §138 (N.Y., rev. edn., 1938); G. C. Cheshire and C. H. S. Fifoot, *Law of Contract* 68–71 (London, 4th edn., 1956). There is the further possibility that the receipt as proved, but not pleaded (note 2 above), might have been read to recite a consideration in Porter's settlement of Steel's claim for the hoops, although there is serious question whether payment of an existing debt is consideration. See Williston and Thompson, *Selections* §120. Since the approach under the first count could have involved problems of proof of negligence, damages, and perhaps even reasonable reliance, it is quite possible that the case went off on the count for money had and received, in which the equities of the plaintiff's case were more directly in point. See Fifoot, *History and Sources* 365–367.

the burden of proof on this issue. The jury apparently found that he had not met this burden and that circumstantial evidence indicated that he had received the money, because the verdict was for Porter & Crocker.[6]

I. ADAMS' MINUTES OF THE REVIEW[7]

Essex Superior Court, Salem, November 1772

Porter vs. Steel.

J[ohn] L[owell].[8] Receipt. Wm. Wingate.[9]
Serjeant.

Mr. Webster. P[orter] said S[teel] owed him. Sued him for 100 dollars. S. paid ½ of it, and was sued again for the other 50. S. said he was never paid for Hoops. P. said he cheated me out of 6 dollars in the 1st settlement of the 50 dollars, if there was some Hoops. S. then sued Porter, for the Hoops.

Writ. S. vs. P. & C[rocker] for Hoops.[10]

Jona. Serjeant. 1600 Hoops. S. deliverd.

Amos Mullikin. C. received the 50 dollars. C. paid the 6 dollars for my fees,[11] generously, and treated Us too, upon our representing Poverty. Rather than S. should have gone to Goal, Mr. Wallace would have paid the whole 100 dollars. Dont think that S. knew that Wallace had any more Money.

S. Harriman. P. came into my House, and call'd for Drink, and Sat by the fire. P. moved to S. to walk into another Room. Moved it twice. At last they went into a cold Room. Saw em at the Table with Pen and Ink. Porter took up the drink and drank but never asked S. to drink, and never bid him farewell.[12]

[6] SCJ Rec. 1772, fol. 190; Min. Bk. 93, SCJ Salem, Nov. 1772, C–12.

[7] In JA's hand. Adams Papers, Microfilms, Reel No. 185.

[8] The MS could be read "J.Q." (Josiah Quincy), but the Minute Book lists only Lowell as counsel for Porter. Min. Bk. 93, SCJ Salem, Nov. 1772, C–12.

[9] See Steel's receipt to William Wingate, in Nov. 1771, for certain goods received in payment for buildings conveyed by Steel to Wingate, SF 132246. This document was apparently put in evidence by Lowell to prove Steel's signature on his undertaking with Porter. See text at note 20 below.

[10] See writ dated 16 Sept. 1769 for the Essex Inferior Court, Dec. 1769 term, in an action of the case brought by Steel against Porter & Crocker, with counts on an account annexed and in *quantum valebant* for 1600 hoops sold to the defendants by Steel in Sept. 1767 to the value of £5 6s. 8d. SF 132246. No documentation on the other litigation referred to has been found.

[11] Mullikin was a Deputy Sheriff in Essex County, who served the writ cited in note 10 above, and apparently also acted in Porter & Crocker's earlier action against Steel.

[12] Harriman appeared in person on this occasion. In his deposition dated 7 July 1770, apparently taken at Steel's request, he had testified "That some time within a

Moses Cushing. They sat at Table settling as I thought. No freedom between em.

Nat. Walker. Jacob Rowell lodged his Note with me. The young Man said P. was to be along and pay it. P. came along and asked me, about the Note, twice. He said he was bound [on] his Journey and could not take up that Note. He after left a Letter at my House, for Rowell. I am not in a Capacity to take up that Note now, but I have left a Letter to let him know when and where to receive it. Rowell came, and opend the Letter. The day I remember by the difficulty of passing the River.

Jos. Dodge. The River froze over 28th. Novr. 1769.

James Walker. Rowell left the Note. P. came down and left a Letter and then went and led his Horse over the Ice. There had not been any Horse over before. S. at N[ewbury]port offered P. to pay the Money, if you will give your Oath, that you gave me that Money. P. said I have your Receipt and nothing to say to you.

Letter left at Walkers, 29 Novr. 1769. Dated a day before it was left.[13]

Jacob Rowell. P. down from Cohoss. 1st Novr. 1769. Told me to leave my Note at Mr. Walkers. And he would pay. I did. Some time after I call'd, but Note not paid. Some time after called again and found the Letter. Sometime the next June after Balch told me, that he had wrote that he had left the Money with a Man but never said who nor where. In March he wrote me that his Money holding out better than he expected he had left it upon the Road.

---

year past Asa Porter of Coors [i.e. Coös] so called and Mr. James Steel of Haverhill was at my house in Plastow and it appeared to me that they had agreed to meet at my house at that time in order to settle sum Law Bisness which had hapned between them in times past. I took notice that their seemed to be sum dispute between them with sum disafection in Countinence &c. and after Mr. Porter departed my house I saw Mr. Steel have in his hands a quantity of money which said Steel told me he receiv'd of said Porter on account of a Law sute which had hap'ned between them or to that porpose. But I never heard neither of them say anything concerning any money said Porter delivered said Steel in Order to pay or deliver anybody else on said Porter's Accompt nor anything else to that effect. But I cannot say it was not so for Mr. Porter seemed to have a mind to be in Privet, and accordingly had a room to themselves almost the hole of the time they were at my house together and it did not appear to me at that time that either said Porter or Steel was in the least disguised with liquor." SF 132246.

[13] See Porter to Rowell, Haverhill, 29 Nov. 1769, SF 132246: "I was not able to procure the Money for you as I expected but was oblig'd to sue a man's note in order to get you Money and supose the Money will be paid soon if you have opportunity to send your note to Mr. Benjamin Balch of Newburyport in about three weeks I expect he will be able to get the Money for you as the Court is near at hand." The letter continues with mention of other commercial matters between Porter and Rowell.

P. when he took up the Note, he askd me if Steel had got the Letter he wrote to me.

S. Chadwick. P. left Money with me for Rowell, fore Part of Summer before the suit. P. said nothing to me about S's ill treating him. He asked what sort of a Man S. of Haveril was accounted. I said [little?]. Brother in Law. P. resumed. S.'s Character. Nothing. Heard Webster say, if he had opportunity to talk with Ingalls before he should have got better Evidence from him.

S. Whites Deposition.[14]

Number of Gentlemen to Character.

Mr. Balch. I told Mr. P. the Money was not indorsed. He said he was surprized. [...] Steel offerd P. to pay if he would swear, he was very much in a Rage with P. and abusive. Quite in a Passion, and much beside himself. P. said Yes you did pay me that Money. S. said if you'l swear it, I'le pay it.

[...] *Fitz.* S. in a great Passion. Said the Receipt was forged. S. said he should prove he was used to doing such Things. His father had not brought him up to Colledge for Nothing.[15] I told P. he would give S. an Advantage if he [went?] to Swear.

Moses Littles Deposition. Good Character.[16]

Jacob Chase Deposition. Went thro Chester.[17]

Susanna Hale and other.[18]

[14] Deposition of Samuel White, "Sworn in Court, Novr. Term 1772": "That being in the Town of Newbury Port, some time between the Month of July and Month of November, in the Year 1770, where I saw James Steel and Asa Porter together, and heard Steel tell Porter, that if he would go before a Justice, and give Oath that he let him have that Money (which Money I understood said Porter had recover'd at the then last July Court) that he the Said Steel would pay the Debt and Costs." SF 132246.

[15] Porter was Harvard 1762, A.M. 1765. See 12 Sibley-Shipton, *Harvard Graduates* 166–168; MH–Ar. No record has been found of Steel's attendance at "Colledge." He may thus mean that Porter learned to forge receipts at Harvard.

[16] Deposition of Moses Little, 2 Nov. 1772, SF 132246: "that he has been acquainted with Asa Porter when he lived in Newburyport and since he has Lived at Haverhill in the Province of New Hampshire and has dealt confidently with Said Porter and allways found him Punctual and fair in his dealings."

[17] Deposition of Jacob Chase, Chester, N.H., 2 Nov. 1772, SF 132246: "That Asa Porter Esqr. in Haverhill in New Hampshire Came to my house in the last of November or the first of December in the year 1769 to Enquire for one Daniel Wiot and one Purkins Coth of Campton which men the said Porter parted with in Newburyport and they told me that He the said Porter told them he was Going through Haverhill in the Massachusetts to Do Some Business he had there. He likewise told me he traveled through Haverhill and Came and Lodged at Capt. Hales tavern in Hampstead and the Next morning about Eleven o Clock the said Porter came to my house and after Dinner they all went on their journey Home which was Expedient for them on account of its being Remarkable Bad traveling."

[18] Deposition of Susanah Hale and John Emmory, 30 Oct. 1772, SF 132246: "That on or aboute the firste of December AD 1769 Asa Porter of Haverhill in the

II. WETMORE'S MINUTES OF THE REVIEW [19]

Essex Superior Court, Salem, November 1772

Porter [and] Steel. Case for money received and promise to pay it. Plea no promise. Proof. Produced a Receipt and the signing was denied. The Clerk of Inf[erior] Court produced the original receipt.[20]

Sarge[ant] for Steel. The Qu. is (as this is a review) whether the former Judgment be wrong.

Adams. The principal query is whether the Receipt was sign'd.

Oliver J. Steele owns his subscribing the paper but say[s] a part has been added at the top. This must be proved by him else of no consequence save to his own disadvantage.

---

province of New Hampshire Esqr. on his jorney to Cooss (as he informd us) took a Lodging at the House of Capt. Ebenezer Hales Husband of the said Susanah who keeps a Publick House in Hampstead in said Province and after Breack faste the next morning Sat oute for his intended jorney as aforesaid."

[19] In William Wetmore's hand. Adams Papers, Microfilms, Reel No. 184.

[20] The original does not appear in the files.

E. *Commercial Law*

8. Alcock v. Warden

1766

EDITORIAL NOTE

In June 1765 at Boston, James Warden endorsed two bills of exchange drawn on a New York mercantile house and delivered them to Joseph Alcock of Portsmouth, New Hampshire. In September the bills were presented on Alcock's behalf to the drawee in New York, who refused to accept or pay them. Alcock's New York correspondent immediately procured a "protest," the affidavit of a notary public to the presentment and refusal. At the April 1766 term of the Inferior Court at Boston Alcock sued Warden in an action of assumpsit on the bills. The court ruled for Warden on a sham demurrer to the defendant's plea of the general issue.[1]

Alcock appealed to the Superior Court, where, at the August term 1766, the case was tried to a jury, with James Otis and Jeremy Gridley as counsel for Alcock, and Robert Auchmuty arguing for Warden. Adams was not involved, but was present to make what amounts to a report of the

---

[1] See the bills, protest, writ, and Inferior Court judgment in SF 100780. The bills were in identical amounts, payable to James Warden or order, one at 32, the other at 33, days after sight. The declaration contained a count on each bill, setting forth the instrument and alleging that on the "8th day of June A.D. 1765 at Boston aforesaid the said James Warden before the payment of the said sum or any part of it, made his Indorsement on the said Second Bill of Exchange [i.e. second copy of this bill] and thereby for value received ordered and directed the said sum of one hundred and ninety three pounds six shillings and eight pence New York currency to be paid to the said Joseph Alcock, and afterwards, viz, on the Sixteenth day of September A.D. 1765, at New York aforesaid, the said Second Bill of Exchange was presented to the said John Alexander & Company [the drawee] and they were then and there requested to accept the said Second Bill of Exchange and to pay the said sum ... to the said Joseph Alcock according to the tenour of the said Bill of Exchange and indorsement, and the said John Alexander & Company then and there refused to accept the said Second Bill of Exchange or to pay the said sum ... tho the said first Bill [i.e. the first copy] was not accepted or paid, wherefore afterwards, that is to say on the same sixteenth day of September A.D. 1765 the said Second Bill of Exchange was for want of acceptance and payment at New York aforesaid in due form protested, and of all this the said James Warden at Boston aforesaid by the same Joseph Alcock had notice and thereupon became chargeable to the said Joseph Alcock for the said sum ... equal to the sum of one hundred forty five pounds lawful money with all damages costs interest and charges whatever amounting with the principal to the sum of two hundred pounds lawful money, and in consideration thereof the said James Warden then at Boston aforesaid promised the said Joseph Alcock to pay him the same sum ... on demand." *Ibid.* The form is very similar to that given in Joseph Chitty, *A Treatise on the Law of Bills of Exchange* 239–241 (London, 1799).

argument and decision on an interesting point of law which the case raised. Alcock had asked for damages beyond the face amount of the bills. In England, upon protest special damages could be awarded in an action against a drawer or indorser for nonpayment of a "foreign" bill, that is, one drawn on a merchant or banker outside the realm. No such recovery was allowed on an "inland" bill (one drawn on an English house), at least at common law. The damages on a foreign bill were not very clearly defined in the authorities, but they consisted principally of interest and what was called "re-exchange," the cost to the holder of procuring a new bill for the same amount in the drawee's country.[2]

In the colonies a practice had developed of allowing the plaintiff on a foreign bill an additional flat percentage of its face value in lieu of re-exchange,[3] and this had been the custom in Massachusetts. Although there were no written reports of decisions to rely on, the court in Alcock's case was able to follow its own precedents on this point. Samuel Fitch, whose role in the case is unclear, because he was not counsel of record for either party, pointed out that the local practice had been approved in a case on a New York bill argued in 1755. Samuel Winthrop, Clerk of the Superior Court, Ezekiel Price, a notary public, who had been Clerk pro tem in 1755, and Ezekiel Goldthwait, also a notary and Clerk of the Inferior Court, confirmed the custom.[4]

Argument followed on the question whether the percentage should be allowed in this case. It was urged by Otis and Gridley that no distinction was made in England between foreign and inland bills as to damages, or that in the alternative a bill drawn on New York should be treated as a foreign bill, the same considerations of distance and difference in practice being present. Auchmuty contended that there was a distinction at common law but does not seem to have argued directly on the question whether New York bills were to be regarded as foreign.

The court decided that 10 percent should be allowed, and the jury brought in a verdict which complied with this ruling.[5] According to Adams' note, Justice Benjamin Lynde found that the bills involved were not inland bills. It is not clear whether he was articulating the opinion of the court on this point, or whether the majority held that damages were available regardless of the nature of the bill. This would have been the

[2] As to the common law rule, see note 18 below. For interest and re-exchange see Chitty, *Bills of Exchange* 213–218; *Brannan's Negotiable Instruments Law* 1263–1264 (Cincinnati, 7th edn., F. K. Beutel, 1948); John W. Daniel, *Treatise on the Law of Negotiable Instruments*, 3:1749–1762 (N.Y., 7th edn., T. H. Calvert, 1933).

[3] For the rule in other colonies, see note 17 below. The practice was not followed in England, except for bills returned from India. See Chitty, *Bills of Exchange* 217.

[4] See note 14 below.

[5] Min. Bk. 81, SCJ Suffolk, Aug. 1766, N–4; SCJ Rec. 1766–1767, fols. 93–94. The verdict was for £336 17s. 6d. and costs of £7. This figure was the sum of the face value of the bills, £290; 10 percent of the sum, £29; and interest at 6 percent from the date of protest, £17 17s. 6d.

result by statute in England, but it was doubtful that the Acts in question applied in the colonies, and the issue does not seem to have been raised in argument.[6]

Alcock v. Warden was consistent with later developments in the American law of negotiable instruments. In 1809 the Massachusetts Supreme Judicial Court, in an opinion by Chief Justice Theophilus Parsons, recognized the rule of damages followed here as "a part of the law-merchant of the commonwealth," and applied it in the case of a protested bill payable in England.[7] A similar rule, awarding percentage damages on bills drawn or endorsed within the Commonwealth and payable outside the United States, was adopted by statute in 1826, and many other states followed suit.[8] The question of damages on a protested bill drawn in one state and payable in another was rendered doubtful in the first years of the 19th century by a split of authority as to whether such a bill was "foreign" or "inland." No early decision on this point has been found in the Massachusetts *Reports*, but in view of *Alcock v. Warden* an ambiguous passage in Dane's *Abridgment* should probably be read to mean that damages could be had, whatever the label applied to the bill.[9] An Act

[6] For the statutes, see note 18 below. Although damages could be had on an inland bill under these Acts in England, re-exchange would not have been included, because there was no currency exchange factor in the transaction. See John Bayley, *A Short Treatise on the Law of Bills of Exchange* 45–46 (London, 1789). The flat percentage used in Massachusetts was not tied to re-exchange, however, so that on a broad reading it could have been awarded as damages even on an inland bill. But compare note 9 below. Since there was a difference between the currencies involved, when the bill was payable in another province, such a rule was not inequitable in this case, whether the bill was called "inland" or "foreign."

[7] See Grimshaw v. Bender, 6 Mass. 157, 161 (1809): "But the rule of damages, established by the law-merchant [i.e. interest, charges, and re-exchange], is in our opinion absolutely controuled by the immemorial usage in this state. Here the usage is, to allow the holder of the bill the money for which it was drawn, reduced to our currency at par, and also the charges of protest, with *American* interest on those sums from the time when the bill should have been paid; and the further sum of one tenth of the money for which the bill was drawn, with interest upon it from the time payment of the dishonoured bill was demanded of the drawer. But nothing has been allowed for re-exchange, whether it is below or at par. This usage is so ancient, that we cannot trace its origin; and it forms a part of the law-merchant of the commonwealth. Courts of law have always recognized it, and juries have been instructed to govern themselves by it in finding their verdicts."

[8] The statute provided 5 percent damages if the bill was drawn on a country not in Asia or Africa, otherwise 20 percent. See Act of 4 March 1826, c. 177, §1, Mass. Laws, 1826, p. 315–316. For the practice in other states, see *Brannan's Negotiable Instruments Law* 150, 200–201, 1263–1264; Theophilus Parsons, *A Treatise on the Law of Promissory Notes and Bills of Exchange*, 1:655–661 note (Phila., 2d edn., 1876); Annotation, 27 A.L.R. 1189 (1923).

[9] See 1 Dane, *Abridgment* 420 (1823): "*The amount recovered on a protested bill*. . . . This sum in Massachusetts [before the 1819 Act, note 10 below] was principal, interest, ten per cent. damages, and costs on foreign bills generally, and interest and costs on inland bills, and this rule extends to bills drawn in one State on merchants and others in another State." The split of authority was finally resolved by Buckner v. Finley, 27 U.S. (2 Peters) 586 (1829), holding an interstate bill "foreign" for purposes of a statute limiting federal circuit court jurisdiction of

of 1819 settled the matter, providing that on bills drawn in Massachusetts and payable in another state a percentage varying according to the distance of the state from Massachusetts should be awarded as damages. Similar rules were adopted by statute and at common law in other states.[10]

Although somewhat atrophied in use, the Massachusetts statutes just referred to remained in force until 1958, when they were repealed in the adoption of the Uniform Commercial Code.[11] The Code does not deal expressly with the question of damages raised here, but it does provide that "Unless displaced by the particular provisions of this chapter, the principles of law and equity, including the law merchant . . . shall supplement its provisions." [12] Perhaps *Alcock v. Warden* is again good law in Massachusetts.

ADAMS' REPORT OF THE ARGUMENT [13]

Suffolk Superior Court, Boston, August 1766

Alcock vs. Warden.

On a Bill of Exchange, drawn on N. York, protested.

Q. made was whether Bill on N. York was a foreign Bill? So as to

choses in action to foreign bills. See also 3 Kent, *Commentaries* 63 note (N.Y., 1828). Massachusetts soon followed *Buckner*. Phoenix Bank v. Hussey, 12 Pick. (Mass.) 483 (1832) (Interstate bill is "foreign" and drawers could not be charged without a protest). The rule was expressly adopted in the Uniform Negotiable Instruments Law. NIL, §129; Mass. G.L. (Ter. edn., 1932), c. 107, §152. See William E. Britton, *Handbook of the Law of Bills and Notes* 583–585 (St. Paul, 2d edn., 1961).

[10] The Massachusetts Act of 1819, ch. 166, Mass. Laws, 1819, p. 263–264, was entitled "An Act regulating Damages on Inland Bills of Exchange." Its terms embraced "any Bill of Exchange drawn or endorsed within this Commonwealth" and payable in another state, which had been "regularly protested." For practice in other states, see sources in note 8 above.

[11] See Mass. G.L., c. 107, §§9, 11, repealed effective 1 Oct. 1958 by Acts, 1957, c. 765, §2. No case has been found construing or applying c. 107, §11, the interstate bills provision. As to §9, the overseas provision, see Foreign Trade Banking Corp. v. Cosmopolitan Trust Co., 240 Mass. 413, 134 N.E. 403 (1922).

[12] Uniform Commercial Code, §1–103, Mass. G.L., c. 106, §1–103 (as amended, 1957). The Code shows an intent to abandon distinctions between interstate and intrastate instruments by requiring protest only for bills drawn or payable outside the United States. The holder of other kinds of instruments may protest at his option, however. UCC, §3–501(3). There would thus seem to be no obstacle to an award of damages on an interstate bill if some rule of law expressly provided for it. The Code provisions limiting the drawer's and endorser's undertakings to the face of the instrument merely adopt prior provisions of the NIL, which in Massachusetts, at least, had existed side by side with the damages provisions until 1958. See UCC, §§3–413, 3–414; NIL, §§61, 66, Mass. G.L. c. 107, §§84, 89. See also Carmen v. Higginson, 245 Mass. 511, 140 N.E. 246 (1923). According to a leading commentator, the question of damages on foreign bills of exchange was relegated to the Law Merchant by NIL, §196 (Mass. G.L. c. 107, §22), the predecessor of UCC, §1–103. *Brannan's Negotiable Instruments Law* 1263.

[13] In JA's hand. Adams Papers, Microfilms, Reel No. 185.

carry 10 Per Cent damages and 6 Per Cent Interest, as a Bill on London.

Fitch reminded Court of the Case of Wimble and Bayard, in which he Said 10 Per Cent was allowed, upon Argument.[14] Auchmuty recollected the Case by Pratts introducing a little Book, which no Body else knew. It was Marius on Bills of Exchange, which Holt calls a good Book.[15] Winthrop, Price, Goldthwait &c. were enquird of and agreed that 10 Per Cent was allowd.

Otis. Viner. Title, Bills of Exchange. Goldsmith's Note indorsed, is a Bill of Exchange.[16] We dont find any Distinction, between inland and foreign Bills, even in England, and the Inconvenience which is the Reason, is greater, in the Case at Bar, than in a Bill in Eng[lan]d protested in any Part of Europe.

Auchmuty. The Custom is not the same in all the Provinces. In Phyladelphia, they allow, 20 Per Cent.[17] Here 10.

[14] Wimble v. Bayard was an action by the payee against the drawer of a bill for £10 drawn in Boston, which had been dishonored by the drawee at New York in June 1754. The endorsee, who had presented the bill, protested, and the payee paid him £12 2s. at New York. In the Superior Court at the Feb. 1755 term, with Auchmuty and Fitch (but not Prat) as counsel, the jury awarded the payee £12 8s., which would seem to be damages of £2 (20 percent) and interest of 8s. (6 percent for eight months). SCJ Rec. 1755, fol. 22. Min. Bk. 69, SCJ Suffolk, Feb. 1755, N–39. If this analysis is correct, it may be that the award was based on the actual damages sustained by the payee in reimbursing the endorsee under New York practice, which provided a 20 percent premium. See note 17 below. *Wimble* thus recognized the principle of a flat percentage recovery on a New York bill. Fitch erred in his recollection of the actual figures in the case, but the clerks (text at note 4 above) were probably correctly testifying as to the usual practice in Massachusetts.

[15] John Marius, *Advice Concerning Bills of Exchange*, first published at London in 1651, was considered one of the leading treatises from the practical point of view. See 8 Holdsworth, *History of English Law* 155–158. For Holt's comment, see Ward v. Evans, 2 Ld. Raym. 928–929, 92 Eng. Rep. 120–121 (Q.B. 1703); compare 3 Kent, *Commentaries* *125–126. Its later editions were published as part of the 1656, 1685, and 1686 editions of Gerard Malynes, *Consuetudo vel Lex Mercatoria* (published in Islip), a leading treatise on maritime and mercantile law. 1 Sweet & Maxwell, *Legal Bibliography* 523–524. JA's copy of the 1686 edition of Malynes, which had belonged to Jeremy Gridley, thus contained the 1684 edition of Marius. *Catalogue of JA's Library* 158–159. Prat may have cited the work for another purpose, but it does assert the general rule that the drawer or indorser is liable for "Rechange and Costs" on protest for nonacceptance. Marius, *Bills of Exchange* 28 (London, 4th edn., 1684).

[16] 4 Viner, *Abridgment*, tit. Bills of Exchange, Notes, &c., A, pl. 3: "Goldsmiths Bills are govern'd by the same Laws as other Bills of Exchange, and every Indorsement is a new Bill," citing Holt's opinion in Hill v. Lewis, 1 Salk. 132, 91 Eng. Rep. 124 (K.B. 1693). Otis' point seems to have been that bills drawn on London goldsmiths, although necessarily inland bills, were not distinguishable from foreign bills. In the cited case Holt had actually been dealing with the questions of the liability of an endorser upon the default of the drawer and the length of time that should be allowed the holder before presentment.

[17] The rule in Philadelphia was established for bills drawn or endorsed upon

Bacons Abridgment. Title Merchant and Merchandize. Of Inland Bills. Page 603.[18]

Cunninghams Law of Bills of Exchange.[19]

Gridley. The Foundation of this Damage is, that no Proscess runs from one Kingdom to another—and the Disappointment. Bills of Exchange, saving the Risque and Expence of Carriage, are of such Convenience that the whole commercial World is come into it.[20]

Court all of a Mind that 10 Per Cent should be allowed. Lynde thought this was not an Inland Bill.

England or Europe by the Act of 27 Nov. 1700, c. 70, 2 Pa. Stat. 86, which provided that when such bills were returned "unpaid with a legal protest," the parties liable should pay the face of the bill, "together with twenty pounds per cent advance for the damage thereof." See Francis v. Rucker, Ambl. 672, 27 Eng. Rep. 436 (Ch. 1768); Morris v. Tarin, 1 Dall. 147 (Pa. C.P. 1785). Similar practice seems to have been followed in Rhode Island by statute and in New York by custom. The premium in the former colony was 10 percent, and in the latter 20 percent. See Brown v. Van Braam, 3 Dall. (3 U.S.) 344, 346–348 (1797); Hendricks v. Franklin, 4 Johns. (N.Y.) 119 (1809); Herbert Alan Johnson, *The Law Merchant and Negotiable Instruments in Colonial New York, 1664 to 1730* 39–40 (Chicago, 1963).

[18] 4 Bacon, *Abridgment* 603: "Inland Bills of Exchange are those drawn by one Merchant residing in one part of the Kingdom, on another residing in some City or Town within the same Kingdom; and these also being found useful to Trade and Commerce, have been established on the same Foot with foreign Bills: but at Common Law they differed from them in this, that there was no Custom of protesting them, so as to subject the Drawer to Interest and Damages in Case of Non-payment, as there was on foreign Bills." Bacon went on to quote at length the statutes, 9 & 10 Will. 3, c. 17 (1698), and 3 & 4 Ann., c. 9, §§4–8 (1704), which remedied the latter "Inconveniency" by providing for the payment of "costs, damages, and interest," by the drawer on bills over £20 if protest was duly made. Since the Act of 9 & 10 Will. 3 was expressly limited to bills drawn in England, Auchmuty is apparently arguing on the assumption that the common law rules as to inland bills still applied in Massachusetts. As to the effect, see note 6 above. See generally J. Milnes Holden, *The History of Negotiable Instruments in English Law* 52–55 (London, 1955).

[19] Timothy Cunningham, *The Law of Bills of Exchange* (London, 2d edn., 1761). At p. 15–20 Cunningham quoted Bacon, note 18 above, and stated a case construing the statutes. Since much of Cunningham's text is similarly drawn from Bacon, Auchmuty may have cited him here merely by way of confirmation.

[20] Compare the dictum of Parker, C.J., in Adams v. Cordis, 8 Pick. (Mass.) 260, 265–266 (1829): "The ground upon which the original usage and the statute provisions have been adopted [i.e. those in note 8 above], is the great inconvenience and derangement of business which may occur, in consequence of the disappointment in regard to funds relied upon, where a bill is drawn upon a foreign country."

9. Apthorp v. Gardiner
1766–1768

EDITORIAL NOTE

This case throws some light on the conduct of business in Boston in the middle 1760's, but it is primarily of interest for the pleading problem which it presents. James Apthorp, younger son of a leading Boston mercantile family, and William Gardiner, in the course of breaking up their business partnership in 1763, had made an agreement under seal which provided among other things that Apthorp would "pay all debts that are now or may hereafter become due from said company to any person or persons whomsoever for any matter, cause or thing whatsoever, and [would] forever hereafter indemnify and save harmless the said William Gardiner, his Executors and Administrators, of and from all debts and demands now due or that hereafter may become due from said company on any account whatsoever." [1]

Apparently Apthorp had not succeeded in meeting all of the "company's" obligations, for early in 1765 Trecothick & Thomlinson, London merchants, advised Gardiner that his old firm owed them £6949 7s. 11d. sterling, plus interest. The letter pointed out that no remittance had been received on the account, "Mr. Apthorp's efforts having as we apprehend been bent to reduce other ballances," and added that "we have good reason to believe that the greatest part if not all the other demands on Messrs. Apthorp & Gardiner are paid off." This rather knowing tone is perhaps explained by the fact that the Apthorp family had had a long commercial and personal relationship with Trecothick & Thomlinson. Apthorp's father and brother were at different times in partnership with the firm, and his sister Grizzel was married to Barlow Trecothick, once a Boston merchant, soon to be Lord Mayor of London.[2]

In 1766 Gardiner brought suit against Apthorp in the Suffolk Inferior Court, alleging that the "demand" from Trecothick & Thomlinson was a breach of the foregoing covenants, in that "the said James though requested hath not paid all the debts that were then and [are] now due from the company nor hath he the said James though requested indemnified and saved harmless him the said William of and from all debts and demands that were then . . . and are now due from said company . . . and the said William is still held and obliged to pay the [debt] and never discharged or indemnified therefrom by the said James . . . to the damage of the said William as he says the sum of twelve thousands pounds lawful money of Great Britain" (Document I).

---

[1] SF 101250. See text at notes 9–12 below.

[2] For the correspondence, see SF 101250. As to the Apthorps, see Wendell D. Garrett, *Apthorp House 1760–1960* 4–8 (Cambridge, Mass., 1960); John Wentworth, *The Wentworth Genealogy*, 1:512–520 (Boston, 1878). See also a mortgage assigned by James Apthorp to Barlow Trecothick for £151, on 15 Dec. 1767, in SF 145409.

Apthorp's plea to the declaration was a form of specific traverse technically known as *non damnificatus*, in which he asserted "that the said William hath not been damnified by any demand made upon him by Messrs. Trecothick & Thomlinson or in any manner" (Document II). Gardiner demurred to the plea in a lengthy special demurrer (Document III). The gist of his attack was that the plea did not answer the separate allegation of a breach of the promise to pay debts. In the alternative he asserted that if the plea were taken as an answer to this breach, it was bad because it was not a direct contradiction of the allegation. It thus violated the rule that pleadings must not be argumentative and must not contain a "Negative Pregnant." [3]

After several continuances the court in July 1767 found for Gardiner on the demurrer.[4] On appeal to the Superior Court the point was argued again at the March term 1768, with Robert Auchmuty and James Otis appearing for Gardiner, and Samuel Fitch and Jonathan Sewall for Apthorp. Although Adams was not of counsel, the questions involved apparently interested him greatly, for he made extensive minutes of the arguments and of the court's ruling (Document IV). That his minutes were taken down on the spot appears in the verbatim phrases from cases read to the court by counsel, which Adams copied with a keen ear, but often without regard to relevance.

The issue argued was a rather fine point of pleading, but it is a good demonstration of the way in which such heroic struggles over form could often represent the actualities of the case. In pleading *non damnificatus,* Apthorp was trying to put in issue the only point which he could hope to establish on trial, that Gardiner had not been harmed because he had never actually paid or even been sued for the debt due to Trecothick & Thomlinson. Behind the barrage of technical arguments there thus lay one substantial question: did Apthorp bind himself only to indemnify and save Gardiner harmless, either by reimbursing him after he had paid a debt, or by defending any suit brought on it? Or was Apthorp to pay the debts as they arose? If the former, then *non damnificatus*, amounting to performance of the covenant,[5] was a good plea, for Gardiner had in fact been indemnified. If the latter, then the plea was subject to all the technical defects which Auchmuty ascribed to it.

In spite of Fitch's very modern-sounding argument that, whatever its language, the real purpose of the agreement was only to indemnify, the court found that, notwithstanding its generality, the contract embodied a separate promise to pay debts. Since the mere breach of the promise to pay debts would give rise to damages without a showing of special harm, the absence of harm would have served no better as a defense on the trial than it did as a pleading.

On the subsequent trial of the issue of damages, the jury brought in a

---

[3] That is, an affirmative implication. See No. 13, note 9.
[4] See the Inferior Court judgment in SF 101250.
[5] See Stephen, *Pleading* 364.

special verdict which raised this question in another form. They awarded Gardiner £12,000 sterling, the full amount set forth in his *ad damnum*, if the court found that he was "entitled to recover full damages for the debt . . . though [he] was not actually sued therefor nor paid the same." If he was not entitled to full damages, then the jury found that he should receive the amount of the debt, plus interest, which amounted to £8,290 2s. 5 2/3d. At the August term 1768 the court held that the damages were in the lesser amount.[6] The facts that Apthorp had sought to plead in bar to the action thus at least served to limit Gardiner to a recovery for the breach of the promise to pay debts, with no additional damages for a failure to indemnify. While even this result may seem to give Gardiner a windfall, it is in accord with modern authority.[7]

Gardiner's victory seems to have been a hollow one. After a motion for new trial on the grounds of excessive damages that was either denied or withdrawn, Apthorp's counsel entered an action of review, which remained on the docket of the Superior Court until February 1778 when it was finally discontinued by agreement on terms which do not appear. After the 1768 decision, execution had issued, but the court files show that it was returned unsatisfied. Apthorp had been declared an insolvent debtor in February 1768 and had apparently succeeded in winding up his affairs in time to evade Gardiner's demands.[8]

I. WRIT, DECLARATION AND RETURN[9]

Suffolk Inferior Court, Boston, October 1766

[SEAL] Suffolk Ss. George the Third by the Grace of God of Great Britain France and Ireland King Defender of the Faith &c.

To the Sheriff of our county of Suffolk his Undersheriff or Deputy Greeting. We command you to Attach the Goods or estate of James Apthorp of Boston within our county of Suffolk merchant to the value

[6] See SCJ Rec. 1767–1768, fols. 352–356. For the special verdict, see SF 101250.
[7] Samuel Williston and George J. Thompson, *A Treatise on the Law of Contracts* §§1408–1409 (N.Y., rev. edn., 1937).
[8] Fitch's motion "That the Verdict may be set aside for Excessive Damages, and no Judgment Entered thereon, That a new Tryal may be granted—and that he may be heard thereon," is in SF 101250. It was filed, but no action was noted. See SCJ Rec. 1767–1768, fol. 350; for the review, see Min. Bk. 86, SCJ Suffolk, March 1769, N–42; Min. Bk. 103, SCJ Suffolk, Feb. 1778, C–1; SF 102582. For the execution, see SF 115949. As to Apthorp's insolvency, see 4 A&R 798; compare the assignment mentioned in note 2 above. He later settled in Braintree, where he died in 1799. 1 Wentworth, *Wentworth Genealogy* 520; Pattee, *Old Braintree and Quincy* 60, 416, 623.
[9] SF 101250. Subscribed: "Copy examined, Middlecott Cooke, Cler." Minimal punctuation has been supplied.

of ten thousand pounds lawful money of Great Brittain and for want therof to take the Body of the said James if he may be found in your precinct and him safely keep so that you have him before our Justices of our Inferior Court of Common pleas next to be holden at Boston within and for our said county of Suffolk on the first Tuesday of October next, then and there in our said Court to answer to William Gardiner late of said Boston merchant in a plea of covenant broken, for that by a deed of Indenture made and executed at Boston aforsaid on the first day of January A.D. 1763 by and between the said James of the one part and the said William by the name of Wm. Gardiner of Hartford in the county of Hartford and Colony of Connecticut merchant on the other part, one part of which said Deed of Indenture of that date sealed with the seal of the said James shall be in court produced,[10] he the said William in consideration of the sum of twenty six hundred pounds lawful money of the Province of the Massachusetts Bay to him in hand paid by the said James in notes of hand payable to the said James and William in company, and in consideration of the covenant in said Deed contained on behalf of the said James, did release and quit claim to the said James as well all the agreements and covenants contained in certain articles of copartnership between him the said James and the said William as well as all his the said Williams right title claim Interest and demand of in and to the Goods, Moneys, effects, debts (except the notes aforsaid) that were then belonging or due to the said James and William in company. And further the said William by said deed of Indenture did then and there covenant to and with the said James that he the said William would pay one half the expences attending the shipping of all the English goods that then were at Hartford aforsaid belonging to the said company to Boston aforsaid and would in case of any loss [that] should arise on such Goods by shipping the same as aforsaid bear one half of all such losses, and that he the said William would deliver to the said James all the monies notes papers books and goods belonging to said company (except the notes before excepted) as soon as he the said William conveniently could that were then in his possession, and

---

[10] A copy of the agreement, signed, sealed, and delivered by Apthorp in the presence of witnesses on 1 Jan. 1763, is in SF 101250. It begins with a recital that "Whereas there has been and still is subsisting between [Apthorp and Gardiner] a Copartnership as may appear by the Articles of Copartnership duly executed between the said partners on the tenth day of January Anno Domini 1759, and whereas by the mutual consent of [Apthorp and Gardiner] and in consideration of the covenants and agreements hereinafter mentioned said Copartnership is from the [date] of these presents to be dissolved—Now this Indenture witnesseth." The remainder is in substance as pleaded, with exceptions noted below.

would from time to time deliver to the said James all such moneys, notes, bonds, papers, and goods (except the notes before excepted) as should come to his the said Williams hand and possession that belonged to the said company, he the said James paying the charges thereof, if any there should be. In consideration whereof the said James did then at Boston aforsaid by said deed of Indenture among other things covenant with the said William that he the said James would on or before the first day of January A.D. 1764 pay and deliver to the said William the further sum of three thousand five hundred and thirty three pounds six shillings eight pence like money in good notes on interest that should then be due and payable on demand, and that he the said James would make good and pay to the said William all such sums of money as should not be recovered by and paid to the said William in the same notes which he the said James should put into his the said Williams hands for the payment of the said sum of three thousand five hundred and thirty three pounds six shillings and eight pence; that he the said James would make good and pay to the said William all losses that should or might arise on any or all of said last mentioned notes, and *also that he the said James would pay all the debts that were then or should thereafter become due from said company to any Person or persons whomsoever for any matter cause or thing whatsoever and would for ever thereafter indemnify and save harmless the said William* of and from all debts and demands then due or that might thereafter become due from the said company on any account whatsoever.[11] And the said William did at said Boston on the said first day of Jany. A.D. 1763 by said deed of Indenture further covenant with the said James that he the said William, in case the money due on any of the said notes should not be paid within six months after the same should be demanded by the said William, that then he the said William would cause the same to be sued for and would prosecute all such suits and obtain Judgment as Soon as he could for the recovery thereof, and would do his endeavour to obtain satisfaction of all such Judgments, and in case he the said William should neglect to prosecute as aforsaid then he should take the risque of the payments of all such notes upon himself and bear the loss, if any, accrued. And that the said James by said deed of Indenture then, viz., on the first day of Jany. A.D. 1763 at Boston aforsaid, did further covenant with the said William that in case the

[11] For the wording of this passage in the actual agreement, see text at note 1 above. The agreement adds: "and the said James Apthorp doth Hereby release and quit claim unto the said William Gardiner all the Agreements and covenants contained in the said Articles of copartnership." SF 101250.

said William should put any of the last mentioned notes in suit and should not finally obtain full satisfaction thereof in money but should be obliged to levy his the said Williams execution on and take real estate in discharge of all or any part of the same, then he the said James would after notice thereof pay to the said William at said Williams election other notes on interest due in the year A.D. 1764 the amount of what he the said William should so take in real estate as aforsaid. And the said William then, to wit on the said first day of Jany. A.D. 1763 at Boston aforsaid, by said deed of Indenture did further covenant with the said James that he the said William would quit claim to the said James all the right and title that he the said William should have in any such real estate so taken as aforesaid, the said James requiring it and being at the cost of the conveyance.[12] Now the said William in fact saith that he hath well and truly performed and fulfilled all and singular the covenants contained in said deed of Indenture on the part of the said William to be performed and fulfilled according to the true Intent and meaning of the same, yet the said James tho requested *hath not paid all the debts* that were then and now due from the company, nor hath he the said James tho requested *indemnified and saved harmless him the said William* of and from all debts and demands that were then, to wit on the said first day of Jany. A.D. 1763, and are now due from said company. For that on the twenty fifth day of Jany. A.D. 1765 there was due from said company to Messrs. Trecotheck and Thomlinson the sum of six thousand nine hundred and forty nine pounds eleven shillings and seven pence sterling with interest from the said James and William in company as aforsaid, which said sum and the interest thereof then at Boston aforsaid by the said Messrs. Trecothick and Thomlinson was demanded of the said William as one of the said first mentiond company, and the said William is still held and obliged to pay the same and never discharged or Indemnified by the said James therefrom. So the said James his covenants aforsaid hath not kept but broke the same to the damage of the said William as he says the sum of twelve thousand pounds lawful money of Great Britain which shall then and

[12] The agreement adds: "And the said James Apthorp doth hereby further covenant with the said William Gardiner that he the said James Apthorp will if required sign and duly execute to the said William Gardiner good and sufficient power or powers of Attorney in Law if required by the said William Gardiner to enable him the said William Gardiner to recover any of the last mentioned notes and in case any suits should be commenced in his the said James Apthorp's name or in the name of the said William Gardiner upon any of the last mentioned notes the said James Apthorp will pay the reasonable expence of prosecuting the same to final Judgment." SF 101250.

there be made to appear with other due damages. And have you there this writ with your doings therein. Witness Eliakim Hutchinson Esq. at Boston this twelfth day of September in the sixth year of our Reign Annoque Domini 1766.   Middlecott Cooke Cler.
Auchmuty [13]

Suffolk Ss. Boston Septr. 12th 1766

For want of Goods or estate to Attach of the within named James Apthorp I took his Body and have taken bail to Respond the action at time and Court within mentiond.

per Benja. Cudworth Dep. Sheriff

II. PLEA [14]

Suffolk Inferior Court, Boston, July 1767

And the said [James] comes and defends &c.,[15] and saith that the said William hath not been damnified by any demand made upon him by Messrs. Trecothick & Thomlinson or in any manner as the said William in his Declaration hath alledged and supposed and thereof the said James puts himself on the countrey.   Saml Fitch

III. SPECIAL DEMURRER AND JOINDER [16]

Suffolk Inferior Court, Boston, July 1767

William Gardiner v. James Apthorp

And the said William says that the plea aforsaid pleaded by the said James in manner and form afore pleaded and the matter in the same contained are insufficient in Law and that he the said William to that plea in manner and form aforsaid pleaded hath no necessity nor is bound by the Law of the Land in any way to answer and this he is ready to verify wherefore for want of a sufficient plea in this behalf the said William prays Judgment and the damages by reason of the premises to be adjudged to him and costs.

And for causes of demurrer in Law in this behalf according to the

[13] That is, the writ was endorsed by Robert Auchmuty.
[14] SF 101250. On the same page with the return (Doc. I). Dated from the Inferior Court judgment, *ibid.*
[15] See p. 43, note 38, above.
[16] SF 101250. Subscribed: "Copy Examined. Middlecott Cooke, Cler." Dated from the Inferior Court judgment, *ibid.*

form of the Statute in such case made [17] he sets down and to the Court here expresses the causes following

First   Because the said James in his plea aforsaid hath not answered one of the breaches assigned in said declaration by said William in the words following to wit "yet the said James tho requested hath not paid all the debts that were then or now due from the said company."

Secondly   Because the said James in his said plea hath pleaded "that the said William hath not been damnified by any demand made upon him by Messrs. Trecothick & Thomlinson or in any manner as the said William in his declaration hath alledged and supposed and thereof the said James put himself on the countrey" but hath not in his said plea given any answer to the breach of covenant contained and set forth at large in the said Williams declaration against the said James for not paying all the debts that were due from the said James and William in Company

3dly.   Because the said William in his said declaration alledges that the said James covenanted with the said William "that he the said James would pay all the debts that were then or should thereafter become due from said company to any Person or Persons whomsoever for any matter cause or thing whatsoever" and the said William afterwards in his said declaration further alledges as a breach of said covenant that the said James tho requested hath not paid all the debts that were then or now (meaning at the time of making said covenant and the purchase of said writ) due from the said company and the said William further alledges in said declaration that on the twenty fifth day of January AD. 1765 there was due from said company to Messrs. Trecothick & Thomlinson the sum of six thousand nine hundred and forty nine pounds eleven shillings and seven pence sterling with interest from the said James and William in company as aforsaid yet the said James in his plea aforsaid hath not in any manner answered the said breach of covenant declared on in manner as aforsaid by the said William in his said declaration.

4thly.   Because the said James in his said plea hath not alledged that

[17] That is, the statute, 4 Anne, c. 16, §1 (1705), which provided that on demurrer the courts would look to defects of form only when expressly stated with the demurrer.

he hath paid all the debts that were due from the said company and shewn in particular how and when as by Law he ought to have done

5thly. Because the said William in his said declaration hath alledged that the said James tho requested hath not paid all the debts that were then or now due from the said company nor hath the said James tho requested indemnified and saved harmless him the said William of and from all debts and demands that were then to wit on the first day of January AD. 1763 and are now due from the said company for that on the twenty fifth day of January AD. 1765 there was due from said company to Messrs. Trecothick & Thomlinson the sum of six thousand nine hundred and forty nine pounds eleven shillings and seven pence sterling with interest from the said James and William in Company as aforsaid which said sum and the interest thereof then at Boston aforsaid by the said Messrs. Trecothick & Thomlinson were demanded of the said William as one of the first mentioned company and the said William is still held and obliged to pay the same and never discharged or indemnified by the said James therefrom and the said James in his said plea hath pleaded that the said William hath not been damnified by any demand made upon him by Messrs. Trecothick & Thomlinson or in any manner as the said William in his said declaration hath alledged and supposed and thereof the said James puts himself on the countrey and so the said James in his said plea hath given a negative answer only to the aforsaid breach assigned by the said William in his said declaration which is also in the negative and therefore the said James hath not tendred to the said William any proper issue to join and yet the said James hath concluded his said plea to the countrey. Which he ought not to have done but ought to have concluded his said plea with a verification of the same and prayed Judgment if the said William ought to have and maintain said Action against him the said James whereupon the said William might have replied and shewed forth other and special damnification.

6thly. Because the plea of the said James is too general and argumentative and informal and not direct and certain for in said plea the said James alledges that the said William hath not been damnified by any demand made upon him by

Messrs. Trecothick & Thomlinson or in any manner as the said William in his declaration hath alledged and supposed which is not a direct and positive negation of a demand made upon the said William by the said Messrs. Trecothick & Thomlinson as set forth in said declaration but is an argumentation and too general an answer to the said declaration because if there was not a demand made upon the said William as aforsaid then he could not be damnified thereby and if there was then the said James in his said plea traverses the damnification resulting therefrom to the said William. And the said William further says that the plea of the said James by him recorded as aforsaid is inconsistent incertain not issuable and wants form.   Robt. Auchmuty

And the said James says that the plea aforsaid by him in manner aforsaid pleaded and the matter therein contained are good and sufficient in Law to preclude him the said William from his action aforsaid against him the said James which plea the said James is ready to Verify &c. and because the said William doth not answer to that plea nor hitherto any ways deny the same he the said James prays Judgment that the said William may be precluded from his action aforsaid against him and he be allowed his Costs.   Saml. Fitch

IV. ADAMS' MINUTES OF THE ARGUMENT [18]

Suffolk Superior Court, Boston, March 1768

James Apthorp vs. Gardiner, William.

Covenant Broken. Plea.

Special Demurrer. 1. 2. 3. 4.

Joinder in Demurrer.

Auchmuty. 2 Breaches assigned in Declaration by Plaintiff. 1. 2. not indemnifying. Plea is that Plaintiff was not damnifyd by any Demand from Trecothick & Thomlinson.

The 3 first Reasons in the Special Demurrer, are to the same Point. —Tro.[19]

Holts Reports. Page 206. Annersley vs. Cutter. 2nd. Exception is that he did fit him to be Master of Arts. As to the first the Plea is good.

[18] In JA's hand. Adams Papers, Microfilms, Reel No. 185.
[19] A comment from the bench by Edmund Trowbridge, J.

Scismaticus inveteratus. Pleas adjudgd bad because not shewn who maintained him, from the Time of Batchelor till Master. Incompleat Plea.[20]

1. Salk. 179. Weaks vs. Peach. Replevin for. Plea an Answer to Part and whole.[21] 2 Breaches in the Declaration, but one answerd in the Case at Bar. They come and defend &c. i.e. take the whole Defence upon them, and then go on, and answer but one Cause of Action. All Declarations must have compleat Answers.

4th. Objection to the Plea—that he has not in his Plea set forth that he had paid the Debts, and how and when and where &c. 3d. Inst. Cler. 522. Covenant to indemnify and save harmless, ought to shew how he saved harmless.[22] Our Breaches are that he hath not paid, and hath not saved harmless. An Issue cannot be made out of two Negatives any more than out of two Affirmatives.

Infregit Conventionem. 3. Levinz. 19. Pitt vs. Russell. Breach assigned in the Negative and Plea in the Negative.[23]

[20] Annesley v. Cutter, Holt K.B. 206, 90 Eng. Rep. 1013 (1706). An action of debt on a bond conditioned on the defendant's educating and maintaining his son "until he had passed all his degrees, and was a Master of Arts." Plea that the defendant had maintained his son "until he had passed all the degrees that were requisite to fit him to be Master of Arts ... and *postea* such a Day he became Master of Arts." Demurrer, asserting (1) uncertainty, in the failure of the plea to detail the degrees obtained prior to that of Master of Arts, and (2) the failure of the plea to state who maintained the son during the three years between his Bachelor's and his Master's degrees. Held, *per curiam*, that the plea was bad on the second ground asserted. The phrase "*schismaticus inveteratus*" appears in the report of the case as part of defendant's argument on the first point. It is drawn from a case in *quare impedit* in which it was held insufficient for a bishop to plead that he had rejected one presented for a benefice merely because the presentee was, literally, an inveterate schismatic. Specot's Case, 5 Co. Rep. 57a, 77 Eng. Rep. 141 (K.B. 1590). The point has some relevance to later portions of the argument in the present case, but is bare dictum in *Annesley* and is not at all the point for which Auchmuty is citing the case.
[21] Weeks v. Peach, 1 Salk. 179, 91 Eng. Rep. 164 (K.B. 1701). Replevin for taking chattels from two different places. Avowry justifying the taking from one place only. Held, per Holt, C.J., that the avowry was demurrable if it purported to answer the entire declaration and answered only part.
[22] 3 Gardiner, *Instructor Clericalis* 522, citing Ellis v. Box, Aleyn 72, 82 Eng. Rep. 921 (K.B. 1648). Condition that third party perform covenants and that defendant save plaintiff harmless. Plea: Performance and that he did save harmless. Demurrer. Held: Plea insufficient, because it should have set forth the covenants, some of which might have been negative, and because it should have set forth with particularity how the defendant saved the plaintiff harmless. Robert Auchmuty's copy of *Instructor Clericalis* is in the Harvard Law School Library, but throws no further light on this case. See JA's reference to the work in his Autobiography as "used dayly for Precedent." 3 JA, *Diary and Autobiography* 271. His own copy of Gardiner's work, 5 parts, London, 1713–1727 (pt. 2 missing), is in the Boston Public Library. See *Catalogue of JA's Library* 100.
[23] Pitt v. Russell, 3 Lev. 19, 83 Eng. Rep. 555 (C.P. 1681). Covenant on a lease, assigning breaches in not repairing the premises. Plea: *Non infregit conven-*

Cro. Car. 316. Non Debet. Oyer. Payment at Day. Court if issue joined aided by Statute Jeofails, 'tho upon Demurrer bad.[24]

Informal, argumentative, &c. Too general, not direct and certain. A Negative Pregnant. Cro. Jac. 559. Lee vs. Luther. Pleaded in the Negative that he had not, &c. Plaintiff demurred.

Negativa pregnans. 1st. Argument. 1st. Cause.[25]

Ours is non Payment, we in the Reason of the Case and therefore the Case must uphold us. These are the Exceptions and these the Authorities to support them. Negative answers to Negative Breaches. All the Entries, all the Precedents shew the Plea to be bad. Law abhors and detests a negative pregnant. Double Pleadings by the Statute and the Leave of the Court, may be, but no Statute allows of a Negative pregnant.

This Plea concludes to the Country too, which it ought not.[26]

Fitch. For Defendant Apthorp. Honors have heard Declaration,

---

tiones (he did not break the covenants). Demurrer. Held: Plea too general, first, in that several breaches were alleged; second, in that the breach is in not repairing and the plea is not breaking, thus opposing a negative to a negative, which does not make an issue.

[24] Parker v. Taylor, Cro. Car. 316, 79 Eng. Rep. 876 (K.B. 1632). Debt upon a loan and upon a bond conditioned on payment at a certain day. As to the loan, the plea was *non debet*, the general issue; as to the bond, after oyer, the plea was payment at the day. Issue was tendered and joined on each count and the case tried to a jury which found for the plaintiff on the bond and for the defendant on the loan. On writ of error it was argued that the plaintiff should have replied, denying payment and thus properly creating an issue out of an affirmative and a negative. Held: Since issue had been joined on the case as pleaded, and the jury had found that the defendant had not paid, "it is good enough, and aided by the Statute of Jeofayles." *Id.* at 317. Auchmuty's apparent conclusion that the plea would have been bad on demurrer is only implicit in the report of the case. The various Statutes of Jeofails provided that certain nonsubstantial pleading defects should not be fatal. See Sutton, *Personal Actions* 118–120.

[25] Lea v. Luthell, Cro. Jac. 559, 79 Eng. Rep. 480 (K.B. 1618). Debt upon a bond on four conditions, one in the negative, to make no further grant of certain premises without the plaintiff's consent. Plea: As to the first three, performance; as to the last, that no grant had been made. On demurrer plaintiff objected, first, that since one of the covenants was the act of a stranger and an act of record, it should have been pleaded specially; second, that, since there were several covenants, performance of each ought to have been pleaded; third, that the plea that no grant was made is a negative pregnant. Held: Plea bad for all these causes, "wherefore it was adjudged for the plaintiff, upon the first argument, especially for the first cause." *Id.* at 560. In noting this last phrase, JA may be querying the applicability of the case.

[26] That is, it concludes with the form for tender of issue, upon which the plaintiff could only demur or join issue and go to the jury. Auchmuty seems to have the right of this question, since the plea in essence raised new matter that required an answer. See 1 Chitty, *Pleading* 536; 2 *id.* at 528–529; Stephen, *Pleading* 251–253, 364.

185

Plea and Exceptions. We have answerd that Gardiner Plaintiff hath not been damnified by any such Demand as he has set forth in his Declaration. The whole Effect of the Covenant is, to indemnify Gardiner, from certain Debts and Demands. 2 Ways of indemnifying, are by Payment, by procuring a Discharge.

This Covenant is only a Covenant to save harmless, and the Effect is the same as a Bond with a Penalty conditioned to save harmless. Non Payment is no Breach, and would be bad upon a general Demurrer.

Saville. Page. 90. Case 167. Anonimous. Debt upon an Obligation. Ought to plead not damnified. Bound to discharge pay and save harmless from Rent. Had Defendant pleaded that Plaintiff was not damnifyed, it would have been good.[27] Nothing to distinguish this Case from that of Savilles. This exempts this Case from the Force of every Authority the Gentleman has [presented?].

1. Salk. 196. Griffith vs. Harrison. In some Cases the Intention is traversable. Plaintiff did not shew a Disturbance. Counterbond cannot be sued without a Special Damnification.[28]

If Plaintiff can support an Action now without a special Damnification, he might have supported one Eo Instante that the Covenant was executed.

Cro. Jac. 634. Horseman vs. Obbins. Debt on obligation Conditiond for Indemnification. Demurred because not shewn quo modo indemnem &c. Being a Plea in the Affirmative, should have shewn quo modo, but if he had pleaded generally that he had not been damnified non damnificatus, it would have been good.[29]

Cro. Jam. [Jac.] When one pleads a discharge and that he saved

---

[27] Anonymous, Saville 90, 123 Eng. Rep. 1029 (C.P. 1588). Debt on a bond conditioned on a promise to discharge and save harmless from payment of rent, and to pay, discharge, and save harmless from any action brought for rent. Plea: No rent due. Demurrer. Held: Plea bad, because the condition was to save harmless from paying any rent. The proper plea would have been that the plaintiff had not been damnified by the payment of any rent.

[28] Griffith v. Harrison, 1 Salk. 196, 91 Eng. Rep. 176 (K.B. 1693). Action on covenant to discharge or indemnify from all arrears of rent, alleging that a certain sum of rent was in arrears. Plea: Payment of part to lessor and part to plaintiff with the intention that it be applied to the lease. Demurrer. Held: Plea probably good, over objection that intention was not traversable. Judgment for defendant because special damages not pleaded. Where the condition is to save harmless from an obligation that will not fall due on a certain day in a certain way, such as "a single Bill without a Penalty, there the Counterbond cannot be sued without a special Damnification. So here, Rent remaining in arrear, and not paid, is not a Damage, unless the Plaintiff be sued or charged." *Id.* at 197.

[29] Horseman v. Obbins, Cro. Jac. 634, 79 Eng. Rep. 546 (K.B. 1621). The defendant had pleaded that he had indemnified the plaintiff. The court upheld the demurrer on the grounds paraphrased in the text.

him harmless he ought to shew how, but if he had pleaded generally non damnificatus it had been good &c.[30]

3. Mod. 252. Mather vs. Mills. Non Damnificatus and Demurrer. Negative Parish not damnified. Good.[31]

2. Mod. 305. Shaxton vs. Shaxton. Condition to save harmless, &c. Defendant pleads not damnified, &c.[32] Same Principle.

Negative Answer to Negative Breach. This is a wrong Representation. The Words of the Declaration. Covenant. Will save harmless from all Debts due from the Company of Gardiner & Apthorp to Trecothick & Company. They have made use of negative Words, but not to the Purpose. What is our Answer to their Declaration. That they have not been damnified, by any such Demand, which is the only Breach they have alledgd that could support their Action. Concluding in Bar, when the Matter is brought to a plain Affirmation and Negation would be ill, because it tends to protract Pleadings in Infinitum, therefore we concluded properly to the Country.

Jenkins's Centuries Page 110. Case 12. Non Damnificatus a general Issue.[33]

Sewall run over the same Ground.

Otis. Read Several Authorities, one from Leonard[34] and several others, to shew that where there is a Covenant or Bond to save harm-

---

[30] That is, Codner v. Dalby, Cro. Jac. 363, 79 Eng. Rep. 311 (K.B. 1611), cited in margin in Horseman v. Obbins, note 29 above. Debt on a bond conditioned to save harmless from bail in a certain action. On demurrer to the plea the court found for the plaintiff substantially in the language reported by JA.

[31] Mather v. Mills, 3 Mod. 252, 87 Eng. Rep. 166 (K.B. 1688). Debt on a bond conditioned on acquitting, discharging, and saving harmless a parish from a bastard child. Plea: *Non damnificatus.* Demurrer. Held: Judgment for defendant, over argument that "acquit and discharge" required a showing as to how the defendant had acquitted and discharged.

[32] Shaxton v. Shaxton, 2 Mod. 305, 86 Eng. Rep. 1088 (C.P. 1678). Condition to save the plaintiff and the mortgaged premises harmless and to pay interest. Plea: Plaintiff not damnified because defendant had paid the principal and all arrears of rent due. Demurrer. Held: Plea bad. Goes only to the person of the plaintiff, not to the premises.

[33] Anonymous, Jenk. Cent. 110, Case XII, 145 Eng. Rep. 77 (Exch. Ch. 1457). Condition to save harmless. Plea that defendant did save harmless. Demurrer. Held: Plea bad, because the manner of discharge not shown. *Non damnificatus,* the general issue, would have been a good plea.

[34] The case "from Leonard" is undoubtedly Bret v. Audars, 1 Leon. 71, 74 Eng. Rep. 66 (C.P. 1587), an action of debt on an obligation conditioned "to acquit, and discharge and save harmless." Plea: *Non damnificatus.* Demurrer. Held: Plea insufficient. The defendant ought to have shown the manner of discharge, since the condition was to discharge. If, however, the condition were to save harmless only, "then *non damnificatus* generally is good enough." *Id.* at 72.

less only, there Non Damnificatus will do for a Plea. But where there is Covenant or Bond to pay Rent, to pay Debts, &c. and to save harmless from that Rent, those Debts &c., there Non Damnificatus will not do.

C. J.[35] There is no Time sett, when the Payment of the Company Debts shall be made, in the Covenant.

To pay, and shall pay all the Debts, due or that shall hereafter become due.

Difference between an Undertaking, by Covenant or Bond, to pay and save harmless, And an Undertaking to save harmless only.

The Judges of England make a strong Inference from the Silence of Precedents.

Tis a Duty as much when there is no Day fixed as when there is a Day fixed, and the Law says it shall be done in a reasonable Time.

10. Bancroft v. Lee

1768–1772

EDITORIAL NOTE

On 22 November 1762, Jeremiah Lee, prominent Marblehead shipowner and merchant, obtained a policy of marine insurance upon one half the cargo of the schooner *Merrill* for a voyage "from Marblehead to any and all the Islands in the West Indies to Windward of St. Croix, St. Thomas, Havannah and Jamaica until the cargo is sold and delivered." The *Merrill* was then 79 days out of Marblehead. The eight underwriters, of whom Jonathan Bancroft was one, did not know that on October 17th, while making for Martinique, she had been taken by a Spanish privateer. When Lee subsequently presented his claim for the loss the underwriters refused payment on grounds of fraud. About a year later, the claim was submitted to arbitration in accordance with a provision of the policy. In November 1763 the arbitrators, Foster Hutchinson, John Rowe, and Melatiah Bourne, returned their unanimous report that Bancroft and six of his fellow underwriters, who had agreed to the submission, were liable in the amounts which they had subscribed.[1] These seven made payment

---

[35] Thomas Hutchinson, C.J. Hutchinson's construction is borne out by later authorities, but it seems harsh where the promise to pay debts is in such general terms. See Stephen, *Pleading* 364–366; 2 Chitty, *Pleading* 528–529 notes.

[1] See the papers in the case, including the policy with the arbitration agreement and report on the verso in SF 131791, 132239. As to Lee, who in dying of a chill contracted while evading the British at Lexington became surely the first politician to give his life in the patriot cause, see 2 JA, *Diary and Autobiography* 61, 172;

accordingly. The eighth underwriter, William Shillaber, was less tractable. He had not agreed to the arbitration, and Lee was forced to bring suit against him on the policy. In June 1767 Shillaber finally prevailed in an action of review in the Superior Court.[2]

Thereafter Bancroft and two other underwriters brought actions against Lee, claiming that the policy was void and demanding return of the payments made under it.[3] Bancroft's case, in which Adams was of counsel for Lee, provides some useful insights into the conduct of maritime and mercantile affairs. It also raises an interesting problem of the effect of an arbitration proceeding upon subsequent litigation between the same parties and shows bench and bar applying English authority of most recent date to this question.[4]

Bancroft's declaration in an action on the case in deceit alleged that Lee had induced the underwriting by his deliberate false affirmation that the insurance was a "fair chance," and that he had knowingly concealed two circumstances which materially altered the risk: (1) that the master's sailing orders had directed him to proceed to "the Island of Martineco (if he could get in there)"; and (2) that Lee, before the policy was written, "had received certain Intelligence that the said Schooner had not arrived at Martineco . . . when she had been gone from Marblehead . . . by the space of thirty three days." [5] After Lee prevailed in the Inferior Court on a sham demurrer, Bancroft appealed to the Superior Court, where at Ipswich in June 1769, upon waiver of the demurrer, the case was tried to a jury. Document I is Adams' memorandum of authorities on the issues presented by the fact that the vessel was actually lost at the time of the underwriting. Since Lee's policy included the words "lost or not lost," the underwriters were liable unless Lee had sought the insurance with knowledge of the loss. This question was apparently determined adversely to Lee, because the jury found for Bancroft in the amount paid out, plus interest.[6]

Samuel Roads, Jr, *The History and Traditions of Marblehead* 113–114, 351 (Boston, 1880); compare Oliver, *Origin and Progress* 120.

[2] Lee v. Shillaber, Min. Bk. 77, SCJ Salem, Oct. 1764, N–2; Min. Bk. 85, SCJ Ipswich, June 1767, N–14. SF 131138, 131503.

[3] The other actions were Crowningshield v. Lee, No. 11, and Goodhue v. Lee. In the Crowningshield case JA was also of counsel for Lee. In Goodhue's case JA has left us no minutes, but the Minute Book of the Superior Court indicates that he was of counsel for Goodhue on the appeal, in which the latter obtained a verdict. Lee v. Goodhue, Min. Bk. 85, SCJ Ipswich, June 1770, N–4. While this change of allegiance may not have been inconsistent with the legal ethics of the time, there is evidence to suggest that it is actually a clerical error. At the trial of the case in the Inferior Court, John Lowell, who had been counsel for Bancroft and Crowningshield, was Goodhue's lawyer, and William Pynchon, who had been Lee's counsel in the other actions, represented him in this one. SF 131923.

[4] The first edition of 1 Wilson, note 35 below, did not appear until 1770. 2 Burrow, note 36 below, was first published in 1766, with a second edition in 1771. See 1 Sweet and Maxwell, *Legal Bibliography* 294, 310.

[5] See the declaration in SF 131791, 132239.

[6] Min. Bk. 85, SCJ Ipswich, June 1769, N–1. The pleadings and judgment in the Inferior Court, Salem, Dec. 1768, are in SF 131791, 132239.

Lee then obtained a writ of review, which was first brought on for trial in November 1770, but was continued on the withdrawal of a juror.[7] In June 1771 at Ipswich the case came on again, but after Bancroft had put in at least a part of his evidence, it was continued on Lee's motion, the ground not appearing.[8] Adams' minutes of this phase (Document II) are largely a summary of the testimony. John Lowell, counsel for Bancroft, after expounding authorities in his favor, produced evidence tending to show that the *Merrill* had in fact sailed for Martinique. He then sought to establish his allegations as to Lee's concealment of knowledge of the vessel's loss and as to his calling the risk a "fair chance." The question of knowledge turned on the deposition of one Captain Howard, who had returned to Marblehead two weeks prior to the writing of the policy, reporting that he had heard nothing of the *Merrill*. Did this report amount to "certain intelligence" of her nonarrival, and was it known to Lee or to the underwriters?

The case was brought to trial a third time in November 1771. Here Adams' minutes (Document III) suggest that after Lowell had concluded his case the court on its own motion raised the problem of the effect of the 1763 arbitration report. In any event the jury was again dismissed and the action continued, this time by order of court.[9] While Adams may have raised this question himself, it is interesting to note that this was the first occasion on which Foster Hutchinson, newly appointed to the court, had sat on the case, that he was one of the referees in 1763, and that he seemed to take the lead in dealing with the issue.[10]

After this continuance Adams and Jonathan Sewall, who with Lowell was of counsel for Bancroft, entered into a stipulation to the effect that if the court found that the report (which had not been pleaded) could be admitted in evidence under the general issue, and found that, if admissible, the report was a bar to Bancroft's action, then Bancroft would default. In June 1772 the court found the report admissible and once again ordered a continuance, doubtless for argument on the second point.[11] At Salem in

---

[7] Min. Bk. 85, SCJ Ipswich, June 1770, N–5; Min. Bk. 93, SCJ Salem, Nov. 1770, C–10. Withdrawal of a juror was a means of continuing, or terminating short of judgment, an action in which a jury had been empaneled. It was generally done with consent of all the parties, but, at least in later practice, might be done on the motion of one party on grounds of surprise and the like. The practice also might be allowed where the jury, upon deliberation, could not reach a verdict. See Wood, *Institute of the Laws of England* 600; cases collected in annotation, 48 L.R.A. 432 (1900). The reason for its use here and the distinction between this practice and the later continuance (note 8 below) are not known.

[8] Min. Bk. 93, SCJ Ipswich, June 1771, C–9.

[9] Min. Bk. 93, SCJ Salem, Nov. 1771, C–7.

[10] Hutchinson first took his seat on the court at the Aug. 1771 term in Suffolk County, although he had been appointed in March. SCJ Rec. 1771, fol. 207. See 2 JA, *Diary and Autobiography* 39.

[11] Min. Bk. 93, SCJ Ipswich, June 1772, C–4. See the stipulation in JA's hand and the order (on the wrapper) in SF 132239. The decision to admit the report under the general issue seems in accord with authority. See 1 Chitty, *Pleading* 486–487; compare 4 Bacon, *Abridgment* 60–65.

November 1772, according to William Wetmore's minutes (Document V), Hutchinson disqualified himself, and, with the other referees, gave evidence concerning the arbitration proceedings. Their testimony as minuted by Adams (Document IV) shows that the questions of the *Merrill's* actual destination and Lee's knowledge of her apparent non-arrival had been raised at the hearing in 1763. The court had at first held that the award without more was not a bar, but on this showing they found that the action could not be maintained, applying the doctrine known today as collateral estoppel.[12] A jury which had been empaneled was dismissed, and Bancroft's default was entered in accordance with the agreement.[13]

I. ADAMS' NOTES OF AUTHORITIES [14]

Essex Superior Court, Ipswich, June 1769

Bancroft vs. Lee.

Bac. 3. 599.[15] Tit. Merchant. "Where a Policy is a *perfect Cheat* as where a Person, having *certain Intelligence* that a Ship is lost, insures so much, this shall not bind the Insurer."

Molloy. B. 2, c. 7, §5, bottom.[16] "A Merchant having a *doubtful Account* of his Ship, insures her, without acquainting the Insurers of her danger; Chancery relieved against the Policy of this *fraudulent Insurance.*"

Ditto. "If the Party, that caused the Assurance to be made *saw the ship was lost,*[17] or had *certain Intelligence,* such subscription will not oblige, the same being accounted a mere fraud."

But Yet,

Molloy. B. 2, c. 7, §5. "Those Assurances are most dangerous when these Words are inserted 'lost or not lost'; which is commonly done when a ship hath been long missing and no Tidings can be had, the Premio (especially in Time of War) will run very high, sometimes

---

[12] See the opinions in Doc. V. The present case is distinguishable from Moses v. Macferlan, note 36 below, because the issues here not only were available to the underwriters, but were raised and determined. For cases in which an award was held to bar the action of the original plaintiff on the same cause of action, see Matthew Bacon, *The Compleat Arbitrator* 245–249 (London, 2d edn., 1744). The Harvard Law School's copy of this work is inscribed "J. Lowell, 1765."

[13] Min. Bk. 93, SCJ Salem, Nov. 1772, C–4. SCJ Rec. 1772, fol. 189.

[14] In JA's hand. Adams Papers, Microfilms, Reel No. 185.

[15] 3 Bacon, *Abridgment* 599. Quotation marks supplied. Italics are JA's.

[16] Charles Molloy, *De Jure Maritimo et Navali* 289 (London, 8th edn., 1744). Quotation marks supplied. Italics are JA's.

[17] The original reads "wreckt," rather than "was lost."

30 or 40 per Cent, and though it happens at the Time that the subscription is made, the ship is cast away, yet the Assurers must answer."

II. ADAMS' MINUTES OF THE TRIAL[18]

Essex Superior Court, Ipswich, June 1771

Lee vs. Bancroft. Ipswich June 1771.

Lowell. Cun. 173. Concealment of Intelligence, a Fraud. Each Party ought to know all the Circumstances.[19]

178.—179. 184.[20]

79 days from G[ordon's] sailing to the Insurance,[21] which was a good Chance to have heard of her Arrival at any Part of the W. Indies.

J. Pedricks Deposition. Gordons Protest. Jab. Harlow's Deposition.[22]

Captn. Jos. Howard.[23] Arrived from M[artinique] 7th. Novr. Saild, 7. Octr. Frenchman arrived from Guadaloupe. Deposition vid.

Mr. Shillibeare.[24] I asked whether the Vessells were in Time or

---

[18] In JA's hand. Adams Papers, Microfilms, Reel No. 185.

[19] Timothy Cunningham, *The Law of Bills of Exchange, Promissory Notes, Bank Notes, and Insurance* 174 (London, 3d edn., 1766). The language here was drawn from two cases in which the facts favored the insurers rather more than in the instant case. See De Costa v. Scandret, 2 P. Wms. 170, 24 Eng. Rep. 686 (Ch. 1723) (Insured had heard that ship looking like his was taken); Seaman v. Fonereau, 2 Str. 1183, 93 Eng. Rep. 1115 (K.B. 1743) (Insured had intelligence that vessel had been leaky and was lost sight of just before a hard gale).

[20] That is, Cunningham, *Bills of Exchange* 178–179, 184, citing Rooke v. Thurmond (unreported, K.B. 1743) (Dictum that policy void if insurers could prove that insured knew that another vessel, which sailed from Carolina ten days after the insured vessel, arrived in England seven days before the underwriting); Green v. Bowden (unreported, K.B. 1759) (Policy void where insured had informed insurers that his ship, which was lost on 25 Aug. between Naples and Leghorn, had been safe in Naples on 8 Aug., when in fact she had been safe there on the 3d).

[21] That is, 79 days from 4 Sept., the date on which the master, Nicholas Gordon, sailed from Marblehead, until 22 Nov., the date of the underwriting.

[22] The deposition of Joseph Pedrick, owner of the other half of the enterprise; the protest of the master, Nicholas Gordon, on the loss of the *Merrill*; and the deposition of Jabez Harlow, master of the vessel which finally brought Gordon and his crew home, may be found in SF 132239. This evidence supports the allegation that the master's orders were to proceed to Martinique. For relevant portions of the protest and other evidence on this question, see No. 11.

[23] Captain Howard's deposition, "Sworn in Court, June 19, 1771," states in part that "About 14 days before I left Martineco one Monsr. Misinaire arrived there from Guadeloupe of whom I inquired if any vessels was there belonging to Marblehead or Salem. . . . As to vessels he told me there was none belonging to Ither of those places. . . . When I arrived at Marblehead I was inquired News of by Sundry persons and at Salem when I Entered but can't Remember any persons Particularly. I heard no news of Capt. Nichols Gordon belonging to Marblehead from the time I left it to my return [3 Nov. 1762]." SF 132239.

[24] William Shillaber, the underwriter whose successful defense to Lee's action

whether the Chances were fair. A few days after Mr. Hooper[25] came into the office and enquired if Lee said nothing of his having a Chance. Then he has taken you in, &c. From 20 to 26 or 27 days a common Chance.[26] I would not have wrote under 50 Per Cent. I did not know there was such a Man as C[aptain] Howard. Never heard of his going to the W. Indies. I have been Master, but never was strictly bound up.

C. Hodges. 3 Vessells together.[27] Dont remember any Questions put to him. No dispute—all seemd fair. Hooper came in and said We were taken in. Somebody said We should have looked to our Title. Never knew a Policy underwrote without enquiring when the Vessell sail'd. *Something said in the office about the Vessells being over[set] before she sail'd.* At the Time when Lee was in the Office and Cabbit[28] present talking with Lee. It appeared to me to be in Time and a customary Præmium. One said she was fair, in season, in Time. They often take it from the 1st. underwriter [who] enquires the Circumstances. Those that follow sometimes take it for granted.

Jos. Hodges.[29] Lee wrote the Minutes himself. Cabbit said fair Chances I suppose. Yes. I Asked how long those Vessells had been out. Lee made a Pause. Lee said the 1st. Advice will give an Account of 2 of em. And it did. 2 were taken. I relyed upon Lees Honour that he would not put in an unfair Chance. 30 days a Chance. I did not know of the Arrival of Howard. I would not have wrote upon any Consideration. Dont remember Powers[30] being mentiond. Fellows not mentiond that I remember. Many Vessells at that time had long Passages. Knew Howard was an [Eastern?] Master. But should not have thought to enquire W. India News of him.

Jona. Gardiner Junr. Nothing said of Howards Arrival. I did not know of it. Coll. Lee once scratched his Name out once and said he

---

started the litigation. See note 2 above. Shillaber's deposition of 3 Nov. 1770, with some further details of the underwriting and of the conversation with Hooper, is in SF 132239.

[25] Robert "King" Hooper, Marblehead's wealthiest merchant, and Lee's brother-in-law, Roads, *History of Marblehead* 350, 354; Stark, *Loyalists of Mass.* 222–223.

[26] That is, a chance to have heard news of the vessel's safe arrival. Here the "Chance" was 34 days, the interval between the departure of the *Merrill* from Marblehead on 4 Sept. and Howard's departure from Martinique.

[27] Presumably John Hodges (the "C" standing for "Captain"), whose deposition in the file of Goodhue v. Lee indicates that he was present in the insurance office at the time of the underwriting. SF 131923. Lee insured two other vessels with the *Merrill.* See Shillaber's testimony, text at note 24 above.

[28] Josiah Cabot, one of the underwriters.

[29] Joseph Hodges, one of the underwriters.

[30] Another Marblehead captain who departed in one of Robert Hooper's vessels at about the same time that the *Merrill* sailed. See Shillaber's deposition, cited in No. 11, note 7.

never took desperate Chances, and never put in unfair ones. A Man of Character declaring it is a fair Chance is generally satisfactory.

Jona. Ropes Junr. I underwrote for Pedrick, and was a good Mind to take £20 more for Lee but did not. I did not know of Howards Arrival. I knew when she sailed. But it might be because, We must write on all 3 or none. The Risque not so great when a Number, as on one. Dont know that ever I underwrote first without enquiring when the Vessell sailed, and the Circumstances.

George Dodge.[31] C[ol.] Lee said fair Chances. I had underwrote upon Gordon before, and did not know of Howards Arrival. I have made several Voyages in 14 Weeks. Hoopers News was received in the Office with surprise, and uneasiness.

Warwick Palfry. She might have returned and made her Voyage in 79 days. I knew a Vessell that performed 3 Voyages [nearly?] in 10 Weeks and 3 or 4 days.

Saml. Ward. Lee said he never put a Vessell in out of Time and never took a desperate Chance.

Gordons Sailing Orders.[32]

III. ADAMS' MINUTES OF THE ARGUMENT[33]

Essex Superior Court, Salem, November 1771

Salem. Novr. 1771. Lee vs. Bancroft.

Lowell. 24 or 25 days a Chance. Passages from 17 to 25.

Vessell in Time. A fair Chance. Did not mention how long she had been out, nor Howards arrival.

C[ol.] Lees Character so respectable, and Knowledge so perfect, that "a fair Chance" &c. from him would preclude all Enquiry.

1764 Jany. 28. Receipt for Money.[34]

Judge Hutch[inson] mentiond a Case in Wilson[35] that the Court

---

[31] One of the underwriters.

[32] Gordon's orders are in SF 132239. In his deposition, sworn in court in Nov. 1770, also in SF 132239, he contradicted their impact. See the relevant parts of each as set out in JA's minutes in No. 11.

[33] In JA's hand. Adams Papers, Microfilms, Reel No. 185.

[34] That is, Lee's receipt to Bancroft for £20 paid out on the loss of the *Merrill*, in SF 132239.

[35] Kill v. Hollister, 1 Wils. K.B. 129, 95 Eng. Rep. 532 (1746). The case held that an action lay on the policy since there had been no reference and none was pending.

will not sustain an Action when the Policy is or has been under Ref-
ference. But the Clause in the Policy, that it shall be left to Arbitration, shall not preclude an Action.

Moses vs. Macfarlan. Burrows. Vol. 2d. 1009.[36] Money paid upon
a Risque deemed to be fair.

IV. ADAMS' MINUTES OF THE ARGUMENT [37]

Essex Superior Court, Salem, November 1772

Lee. vs. Bancroft.

Lowell. 25 days a Chance.

Judge Hutchinson. The Underwriters charged Lee with concealing
some Circumstances—the Arrival of a Vessell—but I cant recollect
all the Particulars. The Arbitrators agreed. An Account of a Vessell
and I think it was Howard, and Col. Lee told 'em it was possible she
might be gone to some other Island. The main dispute whether she
was gone to Martinico or some other Island. Heard something about
Pedrick but cant say whether his Deposition was before us.

Mr. Rowe.[38] Cabot and Crowningshield.[39] No Evidence from Pedrick. They thought L[ee] had not said what was necessary, that he
had concealed something which he should have communicated. The

---

[36] Moses v. Macferlan, 2 Burr. 1005, 97 Eng. Rep. 676 (K.B. 1760). In this
famous case the defendant had recovered against the plaintiff in the Court of Conscience upon notes indorsed by the plaintiff under an agreement that the defendant
would not hold him liable on them. The latter court refused to hear evidence of
the agreement, and the plaintiff brought an action at law in assumpsit for money had
and received to recover the sums thereby awarded. While Lord Mansfield's decision
that the action lies on the implied promise is the point for which the case is best
known, the defendant had also argued that there could be no recovery of money
awarded by the judgment of a court of competent jurisdiction. Mansfield held that
the action was not inconsistent with the prior judgment because the Court of
Conscience had properly concluded that the agreement was not before it. In the
process he enlarged upon the theme that a new action could always be brought to
attack a judgment on a ground that was not available as a defense against that judgment. The phrase noted by JA, which is from that portion of the opinion, appears in
the following passage: "Suppose a Man recovers upon a Policy for a Ship *presumed to
be lost*, which afterwards comes Home;—Or upon the Life of a Man *presumed to
be dead*, who afterwards appears;—Or upon a Representation of a Risque *deemed
to be fair*, which comes out afterwards to be grossly fraudulent." 2 Burr. 1009–1010.
As to the case, see C. H. S. Fifoot, *Lord Mansfield* 141–157 (Oxford, 1936).

[37] In JA's hand. Adams Papers, Microfilms, Reel No. 185.

[38] John Rowe notes in his diary under date of 2 Nov. 1772, that "I attended Mr.
John Adams this morning about Colo. Lee's affair." Rowe, *Letters and Diary* 235.

[39] John Crowningshield, one of the underwriters. See No. 11.

Underwriter[s] thought she was bound first to Martinico, and they complaind that she went to some other Island.

Mr. Bourn. The Objection was that Lee had concealed Howards Arrival. Howard I know very well. The other Matter was spoke off, his being bound to one Island and going to another. I am not positive it was considerd.

V. WETMORE'S MINUTES OF THE ARGUMENT[40]

Essex Superior Court, Salem, November 1772

Novemr. 1772

Lee–Bancroft. Review. Some Terms agon the parties agreed (Nov. 1771) to make 2 questions—1. Whether the reference to Rowe &ca. can be given in Evidence, and if not[41]

Objected to Judge Hutchinson that he had sat in the Cause as referee. Answerd that the same will lie in reviews and new hearings but J[udge] Hut[chinson] then utterly refused to Judge in the Cause. Then Two of the other 3 Judges (there being but 4. in Court) determined the award to be no barr.

The Court determind that the Plaintiff B[ancroft] shoud not be admitted to offer evidence of any fraud not mentioned in the declaration and therefore the former referees must be the proper persons to settle the facts of fraud laid before them and any previous to their award. Quin[cy] alledges that[42]

was not laid before referees.

2. That the affair of the joint Orders being altered was not laid before them.

Low[el]l: 1. Query is this award a barr to the action and it must appear that the party must be heard in Person or by attorney and Ban[croft] was not there either way. Answered that plaintiff consented becaus he paid the Money in consequence of the award.

Cushing.[43]

---

[40] Wetmore Notes.

[41] As to the second question, see note 11 above.

[42] Thus in MS. Quincy (who had replaced Sewall as Bancroft's counsel) may have referred to Pedrick's deposition mentioned by the referees in Doc. IV. The Minute Book does not specify whether this is Samuel or Josiah Quincy. Min. Bk. 93, SCJ Salem, Nov. 1772, C–4.

[43] A blank space of several lines follows in the MS. It is therefore difficult to tell whether the opinion that follows is Justice Cushing's, but presumably it is.

As to the new evidence. I think this supposed that it's not sufficient to set aside the award.

Ropes. As to the intelligence of arrival its not clear to me that it was laid before the ref[eree]s. I think the Matters submitted I think 'em the same as now complained of.

And as to Plaintiffs Consent to the award I agree with Bro[ther] Cushing.

J[ustice] Oliver. It appears that there was sufficient time to have produced all the Evidence needful before the referees and for this and other Reasons mentioned the action is not maint[aina]ble and according to Parties agreement made before the [*review*] Ban must be defaulted.

11. Crowningshield v. Lee

1768–1770

EDITORIAL NOTE

This is a companion case to *Bancroft v. Lee*, No. 10. John Crowningshield was one of the underwriters on the marine insurance policy taken out by Lee in 1762 upon one half the cargo of the schooner *Merrill*. He had submitted to the arbitration of Lee's claim, and in 1765 he finally paid his share of the *Merrill's* loss after Lee had recovered judgment against him upon the arbitration award in the Inferior Court. Crowningshield thereafter died, but in March 1769 his widow, perhaps inspired by the success of other underwriters in reopening the matter, brought an action against Lee in the Salem Inferior Court, alleging a false affirmation and the concealment of material circumstances in language virtually identical with that used in Bancroft's declaration. At the July term 1769 she obtained judgment after a jury trial,[1] and Lee appealed to the Superior Court, where Adams and James Putnam served as his counsel.

Adams' short minutes of the trial in November 1769, printed below, deal almost entirely with the evidence presented on the question whether Lee's failure to reveal his orders to the master, Nicholas Gordon, amounted to concealment of a material circumstance. Lee's written application sought insurance for a voyage "from Marblehead to any and all the West India Islands to Windward of St. Croix, St. Thomas, the Havana, and Jamaica till said Cargo is sold and delivered." Although this description is not without ambiguity, read literally it would seem to include both Guadeloupe, to which the master testified that Lee had directed him orally, and Martinique, the destination in Lee's written orders. Both islands lie

[1] See writ and judgment in both Inferior Court actions in SF 131857. Bancroft's declaration is quoted in No. 10.

generally in the direction of the prevailing easterly trade winds from the named points. The plaintiff presumably accepted this reading, since she did not plead and does not seem to have argued either that this language, which was substantially repeated in the policy, was a warranty breached by a voyage to Martinique, or that a voyage to Martinique was outside the policy's coverage. Her point may have been that failure to disclose orders to Martinique was a concealment despite the literal meaning of the description of the risk, because the island had just been captured from the French and was still in a dangerous zone.

Lee apparently relied on the master's testimony that the final orders were to Guadeloupe. His position may have been that such orders were not a material circumstance, since the latter island had been in English hands since 1759.[2] More simply, Lee may have urged that Mrs. Crowningshield's action failed because her declaration alleged concealment of orders to Martinique and the proof was that the orders had been to Guadeloupe. Whatever the argument, Lee prevailed. The judgment of the Inferior Court was reversed with costs.[3]

Mrs. Crowningshield entered an action of review at the November 1770 Salem Superior Court, with Adams now alone as Lee's counsel. At this term three of the other underwriters joined Mrs. Crowningshield in a rule to refer their claims. The referees brought in a unanimous report in Lee's favor, awarding him costs both of the action and the reference.[4]

ADAMS' MINUTES OF THE TRIAL[5]

Essex Superior Court, Salem, November 1769

Crowningshield vs. Lee. Salem S. Ct. Novr. Term.

Receipt for the Money, "and Costs of C[our]t." [6]
1762. Aug. 9. Sailing orders. To proceed to *Martineco or any other*

---

[2] On the war in the West Indies, see sources cited in Knollenberg, *Origin of the American Revolution* 24 note. As to trade with the French islands, see Goebel, "The 'New England Trade' and the French West Indies, 1763–1774," 20 *WMQ* (3d ser.) 331–335 (1963). As to the trade winds, see William Falconer, *An Universal Dictionary of the Marine*, tit. Wind, 6th–7th (London, 1769). Guadeloupe, Martinique, and the chain of islands south and west of them, were known as the Windward Islands.

[3] *Sub nom.* Lee v. Crowningshield, Min. Bk. 85, SCJ Salem, Nov. 1769, N–1; SF 131857.

[4] Min. Bk. 93, SCJ Salem, Nov. 1770, N–4; SCJ Rec. 1770, fol. 226; SF 131988. The parties entering the reference were Joseph Hodges, George Dodge, and Elizabeth Cabot, widow of Josiah. Joseph Ward, the only underwriter who does not appear in litigation, may have settled his claim. See his receipt on the policy. SF 132239. Compare No. 10, notes 2, 3.

[5] In JA's hand on verso of his notes for No. 10, Doc. I. Adams Papers, Microfilms, Reel No. 185.

[6] That is, Lee's receipt to Crowningshield for "fifty pounds he underwrote . . .

Island—"*and sell, at said Island, or any other Island in the West Indies.*"

1762. Novr. 4. Grand terre. Nick Gordon, the Masters Protest, that they saild 4. Septr. *from Marblehead bound to Martineco.* 17th. Octr. taken.

1769. July 10. Gordons Testimony. "By particular verbal Directions, from Lee, a few Hours before sailing, I proceeded for Guadaloupe, and because Lee told me, that R. Hooper had orderd Captn. Power to Martineco, &c. After trying to get to Guadaloupe and could not, I thought it best to try for Martineco. My Written orders to proceed to Martineco or any other Island."[7]

Rob. Hooper Esqrs. Test[imony].

The Mate's.[8]

12. Longman v. Mein; Wright & Gill v. Mein

1770–1771

EDITORIAL NOTE

John Mein's stormy career was cut short by two actions brought against him by John Hancock under a power of attorney from Mein's London creditors. That Mein infuriated the "well-disposed" and the Sons of Liberty is certain; that they rejoiced in his difficulties, including these protracted lawsuits, is equally clear.[1] It is more doubtful whether Mein was correct in attributing to Hancock the responsibility for initiating the litigation. The evidence tends somewhat the other way.

To begin with, there is no question that by late 1768, Mein had run up sizable debts to two major London suppliers, Thomas Longman, the

---

and costs of court." This document, as well as the sailing orders and protest, extracts of which follow, are in SF 131988.

[7] This is a substantially accurate extract of Gordon's deposition in Bancroft v. Lee. See No. 10, note 32. Closing quotation marks have been supplied. As to Hooper, see No. 10, note 25. The files of the Crowningshield case contain his voucher for his expenses as a witness, as well as his order for insurance upon the schooner *Dove*, Thomas Power master, "to Martineco and from thence to any and all the Leeward Islands to Windward of Sambreo." SF 131857.

[8] See the deposition of the mate, George Gordon, sworn in court, Nov. 1769, substantially concurring with the master's testimony. SF 131988.

[1] Note JA's view in 1775: "There never was before, in any part of the world, a whole town insulted to their faces, as Boston was by the Boston Chronicle. Yet the printer was not molested for printing. It was his mad attack upon other printers with his clubs, and upon other gentlemen with his pistols, that was the cause, or rather the pretence, of his flight. The truth was, he became too polite to attend to his business; his shop was neglected; procurations were coming for more than two thousand pounds sterling, which he had no inclination to pay." "Novanglus," No. iii, 4 JA, *Works* 29, 30. Yet JA apparently bought books of Mein. See 1 JA, *Diary and Autobiography* 338. As to Mein, see also No. 5.

bookseller of Paternoster Row, and a firm of stationers, Thomas Wright & William Gill.[2] Mein did swear that his credit would have remained good had not Hancock "with an intent as this deponent believes to distress him the more wrote home letters to . . . Longman . . . importing that the aforesaid Hancock would willingly accept of a power of Attorney from . . . Longman to whom this deponent was indebted as . . . Longman alledges in the sum of one thousand six hundred pounds or thereabouts in order to seize or attach the effects of this deponent in Boston."[3]

But the other sources suggest that whatever zeal Hancock may ultimately have thrown into the prosecution of the case, the initial impulse came from Longman, who in a letter of 22 July 1769 invited Hancock's assistance in recovering the debt.[4] It is not certain just when this letter reached Hancock, nor has his reply survived. Apparently he responded affirmatively on 24 October 1769, requesting a formal power of attorney as well as Mein's account with Longman.[5]

Between 22 July and 24 October, Mein's standing with the patriot

[2] See the accounts in SF 101964. The debt to Longman was £1,643 19s. 3 1/2d.; that to Wright & Gill was £315 3s. 6d. Mein had written Longman on 28 Sept. 1768, forwarding a part payment and assuring prompt settlement of the outstanding accounts. MHi:Hancock Papers. Longman's firm was the direct ancestor of the present London publishing house of Longmans, Green & Co., Ltd. Unfortunately, a wartime bomb destroyed the firm's records for the period in question. Letter to the editors, 30 April 1963, V. L. Ripley (secretary to Mr. Longman).

[3] Copy of Mein's affidavit, 22 Feb. 1770, MHi:Hancock Papers. See also Alden, "John Mein: Scourge of Patriots," 34 Col. Soc. Mass., *Pubns.* 571, 590 (1942), which notes that the John Carter Brown Library copy of *The Letters of Sagittarius* (Boston, 1775), a book attributed to Mein, bears on its flyleaf an inscription accusing Hancock of buying up Mein's English debts and, by making "a sudden demand upon honest Mein," bringing on his ruin.

[4] Thomas Longman to John Hancock, 22 July 1769:

"Your haveing several times offered me your kind assistance induces me now earnestly to request it in the following affair.

"Mr. John Mein of Boston (Bookseller) is Indebted to me a very considerable sum of Money, the greatest part of which has been due near three Years, which upon my remonstrating to Him He has several times promised to make such Remittances as w'd be satisfactory, but this He has yet neglected to do, nor now even so much as writes to me by way of appology. I should therefore be greatly obliged to you if you could recommend a proper Person to me to whom it would be safe to send a power of Attorney and to Act for me in the most adviseable manner in this unfortunate affair. I know your time and attention is at present much taken up in Public Affairs, but as the recovery of this Debt is of great consequence to me, hope you will not deny my request but favour me with your answer by the first opportunity which will be ever gratefully acknowledged by Sr. Your much obliged Humble Servant, Thomas Longman." MHi:Hancock Papers.

It was at Longman's instance that Wright & Gill, too, made Hancock their attorney over a year later. Longman to Hancock, 4 Dec. 1769, MHi:Hancock Papers.

[5] "I received your favour of the 24th of October (per Capt. Bryant) on Wednesday last, and shall ever acknowledge my self under the greatest obligations for your readiness to undertake the settling of my Account with Mr. Mein, and for that purpose have inclosed a state of it properly Attested, with a Letter of Attorney impowering you to act for me in this unfortunate Affair." Thomas Longman to John Hancock, London, 4 Dec. 1769, MHi:Hancock Papers.

party had deteriorated even more sharply. On 21 August he had begun publishing the manifests which incriminated many of the ostensible non-importers.[6] On 5 September, John Robinson had caned James Otis in the British Coffee House, and Mein had defied a mob to stand surety for W. S. Brown, accused of aiding Robinson.[7] Enraged, the patriots had on 10 September censured Mein for treating "the whole body of merchants and traders in the most haughty, imperious, and insulting manner." [8] "Mr. Mein at present is so obnoxious to the People on account of his publishing the Manifests that he's obliged to go Arm'd" a contemporary wrote, "and tis but a few Nights since that two Persons who resembled him pretty much were attack'd in a narrow Alley with Clubs, and would in all probability have lost their lives if the Mistakes had not been timely discover'd." [9]

Shortly after Hancock accepted Longman's commission, the final storm broke around Mein. On 28 October, as he was walking up King Street, a threatening crowd began to surround him. Pulling out his pistol, he faced down his assailants and slowly backed his way toward the guardhouse at the head of King Street. There he gained safety, but not before Thomas Marshall had laid the sharp edge of a shovel to Mein's back, and Mein's pistol had somehow gone off. Hidden in the guardhouse, Mein managed to elude the mob, even though Samuel Adams and William Molineux obtained a warrant and personally searched the premises for him. Finally, he escaped to a ship in the harbor,[10] while ashore his effigy became the hate figure of the annual Pope's Day festivities.[11]

It was impossible for Mein to return to Boston. When he asked Governor Hutchinson for military protection to enable him to press his civil remedies against those who had mobbed him, Hutchinson refused. "In Ireland perhaps where the people have been long used to the military upon an apprehension only of violence from the populace such a measure might have

[6] Andrews, "The Boston Merchants and the Non-Importation Movement," 19 Col. Soc. Mass., *Pubns.* 159, 228 note (1918). The publishing stopped temporarily on 19 Oct. 1769. *Ibid.*

[7] Letter, Thomas Young to ——, Sept. 1769, reprinted in Edes, "A Memoir of Dr. Thomas Young," 11 Col. Soc. Mass., *Pubns.* 2, 5–6 (1910); James Murray, however, indicates that Murray himself was the sole surety. N. M. Tiffany and S. I. Lesley, eds., *Letters of James Murray* 160 (Boston, 1901). Mein had apparently been present at the affair: the capias for Brown and Ralph Dundass lists Mein as among the witnesses. SF 89228.

[8] Andrews, "Boston Merchants," 19 Col. Soc. Mass., *Pubns.* 228 note.

[9] George Mason to Joseph Harrison, 20 Oct. 1769, 3 Bernard Papers 53, MH.

[10] Alden, "John Mein: Scourge of Patriots," 34 Col. Soc. Mass., *Pubns.* 571, 587–589 (1942) vividly uses the sources to describe the near-lynching. See also Rowe, *Letters and Diary* 194; Tiffany and Lesley, *Letters of James Murray* 168; John Miller, *Sam Adams, Pioneer in Propaganda* 205 (Boston, 1936); George Mason to ——, 28 Oct. 1769, 3 Bernard Papers 47, MH; Mein to Joseph Harrison, 5 Nov. 1769, *id.* at 51; Gailer v. Trevett, p. 41, note 35, above.

[11] Celebrated on 6 Nov., because 5 Nov. 1769 fell on a Sunday. The effigy carried an acrostic which included the homonymic line "Mean is the man; M–N is his name." Bolton, "Circulating Libraries in Boston, 1765–1865," 11 Col. Soc. Mass., *Pubns.* 196, 198 (1910).

been advisable. In the present state of the colonies I could not think so; and rather thought it advisable for him to forebear prosecuting his complaint for some time." [12] Only one thing remained for Mein to do, and he did it: return to Britain.[13]

Longman meanwhile, having received Hancock's undertaking to act as attorney, immediately himself executed and caused Wright & Gill to execute certified powers of attorney which, together with bookkeepers' affidavits, were promptly sent to Boston. These arrived on 1 March 1770; that very day, John Adams filled out the writs and had the deputy sheriff seize Mein's property, which included his stock of books and, most important, "Seven frames on which are sixty-five Cases with the Types &c. Two Printing Presses with all the Materials thereto," and "One composing Stone." [14]

As Mein later swore, "On the afternoon of said day it was propos'd to Mr. Hancock's Lawyer (Mr. Adams) to give undoubted security to stand the issue of the suit, he discharging the attachments. This proposal was refused and Mr. Murray (Mr. Mein's friend who made the proposal) given to understand that nothing would be satisfactory but an absolute security for the debt independent of any suit. The day following, Mr. Murray sent proposals of accomodation in writing to Mr. Hancock to which he receiv'd Mr. Hancock's answer on the 3d of March. On the 7 of March Mr. Murray sent other proposals of accomodation to Mr. Greenleaf the Sheriff which Mr. Greenleaf answer'd in a letter to Mr. Fleeming the Friday following [9 March]. On the 25th Mr. Murray again wrote to the Sheriff and receiv'd an Answer the 4th of May." [15]

[12] Hutchinson to Hillsborough, 11 Nov. 1769, 3 Bernard Papers 53, MH.

[13] See George Mason to Joseph Harrison, 11 Nov. 1769, which refers to Mein's taking "his passage home in one of His Majesty's Armed Schooners," and is docketed "Per Mr. Mein. Recd Jany 3d." 3 Bernard Papers 54, MH. Compare Arthur M. Schlesinger, *The Colonial Merchants and the American Revolution* 160 note (N.Y., 1918).

[14] Longman to Hancock, 4 Dec. 1769 (docketed "Rec'd by [i.e., via] Paddock March 1st, 1770"): "By this Ship believe you will Receive Letters from Messers Wright & Gill requesting the same favour of you, and as it was by my persuasion they opened an account with Mr. Mein, I could not with Honour take any steps without acquainting them with it." MHi:Hancock Papers. The writs and the deputy sheriff's return are in SF 89428 and 101964. The powers of attorney are also in SF 101964. Adams' Office Book for the April 1770 Suffolk Inferior Court lists both cases, and notes for each: "Copying acct, at J. Hancock Esq's. Instance," and "7s posted to J. Hancock Esqr." MQA.

[15] Deposition of John Mein (copy), 22 Nov. 1770, MHi:Hancock Papers. The correspondence between Murray, Greenleaf, and Fleeming appears as Doc. I below. Murray, a Scot like Mein, attracted the ire of the Liberty Party as much for his ancestry as for his tory leanings. "It may not perhaps lessen your opinion of Mr. Murrays good Qualities to inform you that he is a Scotchman and has continually caball'd with his loyal Countreymen in this Town, and the other Governmental tools against the Charter and liberties of this Province." William Palfrey to John Wilkes, ca. 23–30 Oct. 1770, in Elsey, "John Wilkes and William Palfrey," 34 Col. Soc. Mass., *Pubns.* 411, 422 (1941). Anti-Jacobite feeling was apparently strong in Boston in the late 1760's and early 1770's. Adams' notes in No. 5 are headed "News Paper. Jacobite Party." And the *Boston Gazette* of 5 Sept. 1768, p. 4,

The texts of Murray's original proposals to Hancock have not been found. Charles Bolton, who appears to have examined them in the early 1900's, when what are now the Hancock Papers at the Massachusetts Historical Society were still in the possession of Charles Pelham Greenough, reported that Murray wanted "to have the attachment withdrawn, allow the suit for £1600 to go on in the King's Bench and abide by the judgment of the Court, the property meanwhile to be appraised upon oath and to be delivered up to Hancock as attorney when executions came to be issued." [16] The reference to the Court of King's Bench may be inadvertent; on the other hand, perhaps Murray contemplated a discontinuance of the Massachusetts action in favor of proceedings in London, before an English jury instead of an American one. If it was the local jury which Murray feared, later events proved his doubts well-founded. And, as it turned out, Longman started a suit in the King's Bench anyway.

Despite the failure of the preliminary settlement negotiations, Murray was able, by a means still unexplained, so to manage matters "with the Sheriff as to get him to accept of a pledge for the value of Mr. Mein's Interest attached at the printing office. This set the press a going again, much to the Surprize and Disappointment of Mr. H—— and his party, with whom this was the Capital Object in this Stroke of his. A method has been since hit on to relieve the books also by a tender of other Goods." [17]

It is not clear whether the method of relieving the books ever went into operation. On 18 May 1770, Hancock reported to Longman that Mein's "Effects are in the hands of the Sheriff, and as soon as it has gone thro' the Law, and the Effects turn'd into money, the neat proceeds shall be remitted you, and you will determine the settlement between you and Messrs. Wright & Gill. Tho' I fear even the Whole of his Effects will fall vastly short of the Debts, but I have got all and could get no more." And Hancock urged Longman to "get further Security of Mr. Mein in London." [18] This Longman had already done, commencing an action in the King's Bench against Mein for the amount of the debt and having him arrested and committed to prison "in hopes of His having some Friends that would appear in His behalf." Friends did appear, but none apparently with funds sufficient to release the attachment and free Mein.[19]

---

col. 1, ran a violent letter on the subject. It is difficult to estimate how this spirit affected the jury's attitude toward Mein's litigation, but the effect was probably not favorable.

[16] Bolton, "Circulating Libraries in Boston, 1765–1865," 11 Col. Soc. Mass., *Pubns.* 196, 199. Hancock denied that the proposal would have "fully secur'd" Longman; he insisted that he "waited for Security and finally could obtain none." Hancock to Longman and Wright & Gill, 10 Jan. 1771, MHi:Hancock Papers.

[17] James Murray to Elizabeth Smith, 12 Mar. 1770, in Tiffany and Lesley, *Letters of James Murray* 169–170. "Relieve the books" means to lift the attachment on them.

[18] Hancock to Longman, 18 May 1770, MH–BA:Hancock Letter Book, in A. E. Brown, *John Hancock, His Book* 94 (Boston, 1898).

[19] Longman to Hancock, undated. MHi:Hancock Papers.

Meanwhile, back in Boston, Fleeming, who had been keeping the *Chronicle* going, at last gave up. On 25 June 1770, he put out his final number, "shut up his printing office and fled to the castle for protection." [20] And the lawsuits droned on, having been entered at the April 1770 Suffolk Inferior Court, but continued from term to term. As Hancock explained to Longman, "by a law of the Province, when an Action is brought against a man who is out of the Province, the action must be continued in the Inferior court six months. This was the reason why the action against Mr. Mein was continued at first and when the six months were expired, Mr. Kent, the lawyer, appeared for Mr. Mein at the request of Mr. Fleeming who had a power of attorney from Mein, and moved in Court that these actions might be continued three months longer, because he said Mr. Mein had since been arrested in London for the same debt and was a prisoner in the King's Bench for them and therefore desir'd time that they might get evidence of it, in order that the suits here might be discharged. The Court granted the motion." [21]

Finally, on 15 January 1771, the actions came on for trial in the Suffolk Inferior Court, with Adams representing the creditors, and Benjamin Kent defending Mein. Our account of what took place is conjectural, for Adams' trial notes have not survived; we have only a list of authorities which he used in argument. The reconstruction which follows has been based on the Hancock correspondence and the court files.

In both actions, the writ had originally sounded in ordinary *indebitatus assumpsit*, based on an account annexed to the writ, which set out in rudimentary double entry form the amount of Mein's purchases over the years, the sums he had paid on account, the balance due, and (in Wright & Gill's case) the interest.[22] When the cases came on, according to Hancock, "an objection was made by Mr. Mein's Council to the Generality of [Longman's, and, presumably, Wright & Gill's] account, that it was not sufficiently explicit, and that the particulars should be Exhibited." This was, Hancock assured his London correspondents, a mere delaying ruse. None-

---

[20] Christian Barnes to Elizabeth Smith, 29 June 1770, in Tiffany and Lesley, *Letters of James Murray* 178. The "castle" was Castle Island in Boston Harbor where the troops were quartered.

[21] Hancock to Longman, 19 Nov. 1770, MH–BA:Hancock Letter Book, in part in Brown, *John Hancock, His Book* 95–96. Hancock's report is confirmed by Min. Bk., Inf. Ct. Suffolk, April 1770, Nos. 178, 179; July 1770, Nos. 113, 114; Oct. 1770, Nos. 67, 68. The statute in question was "An Act to Enable Creditors to Receive Their Just Debts out of the Effects of Their Absent or Absconding Debtors." 4 A&R 168, 169, Act of 13 Feb. 1759: "and such attorney, factor, agent or trustee, upon his desire, shall be admitted to defend the suit on behalf of his principal throughout the course of the law, and an imparlance shall be granted of course at two terms successively, that he may have an opportunity to notify his principal thereof, and at the third term, without special matter alledged and allowed in bar, abatement or further continuance, the cause shall peremptorily come to trial." Originally, a prayer for leave to imparl meant that the defendant "wanted time to talk matters over with the plaintiff out of court. Later on all that it meant was that he wanted to have until the next term to plead." Sutton, *Personal Actions* 104.

[22] SF 101964.

theless, "it is best at the next Trial to be ready to answer and remove their objections." So he forwarded "Mr. Adams's (my attorney) minutes to me in order to Transmit you, by which you will see what is necessary for you to do, and I pray you will so soon as possible after the receipt of this prepare the necessary papers and accounts and be as explicit as possible. . . . You will Communicate this to Messers. Wright & Gill." That Adams considered the accounts essential to the case may be deduced from the fact that Hancock sent his letter in duplicate by two separate vessels.[23]

It is not certain whether by 16 January 1771, the date of Hancock's letter, the trials had been held; the court files contain a summons in Adams' hand to "Alexander Reid Stationer, and William Miller both of Boston," dated 17 January 1771; the return indicates that these witnesses were actually subpoenaed on 19 January.[24] Possibly the court heard the preliminary objections and then continued the matters for trial later on in the term; the cases were certainly tried at this term.[25] At the trial Adams apparently put into evidence the depositions of the respective bookkeepers which established the facts of the debts; he may also have called Reid and Miller for evidence on the reasonableness of the Wright & Gill prices or even to prove that Mein had actually received the goods in question.[26] Whether the defense adduced any evidence is an open question.

From Adams' authorities (Document II) and Hancock's letter of 16 January, referred to above, it appears that the court, on whatever evidence the plaintiffs had brought forward, or perhaps on the basis of defendant's objections to the legal sufficiency of the accounts, had directed a finding for the defendant in one or perhaps both of the actions, and that the

[23] Hancock to Longman and Wright & Gill, 16 Jan. 1771, MHi:Hancock Papers. The copy is docketed: "To Mr. Thos. Longman to be Communicated to Messers Wright & Gill abt Mein's affairs with Mr. Adams Minutes respectg the Objections to the Accots. Jany 1771. By Jarvis. By White."

[24] SF 101964.

[25] See copy of the Inferior Court record, SF 101964. The *Longman* trial was on the fifth day of the term, and the *Wright & Gill* trial on the eighth day. Min. Bk., Inf. Ct. Suffolk, Jan. 1771, Nos. 43, 44. The court convened on Tuesday, 1 Jan., but apparently did not sit regularly thereafter, if the assumptions in the text are correct.

[26] The depositions actually should have sufficed, under the provisions of "An Act for the More Easy Recovery of Debts in His Majesty's Plantations and Colonies in America," 5 Geo. 2, c. 7 (1732): "[I]n any action or suit . . . brought in any court of law or equity in any of the said plantations, for or relating to any debt or account, wherein any person residing in Great Britain shall be a party, it shall and may be lawful to and for the plaintiff or defendant, and also to and for any witness to be examined or made use of in such action or suit, to verify or prove any matter or thing by affidavit or affidavits in writing upon oath, or . . . affirmation, made before any mayor or other chief magistrate of the city, borough or town corporate in Great Britain, where or near to which the person making such affidavit or affirmation shall reside . . . ; and every affidavit or affirmation so made . . . shall in all such actions and suits be allowed to be of the same force and effect, as if the person or persons making the same . . . had appeared and sworn or affirmed the matters contained in such affidavit or affirmation *viva voce* in open court." All the depositions met the statutory requirements; the attestations specifically referred to the Act. SF 101964.

respective juries had notwithstanding brought in plaintiff's verdicts. The material at the end of the Adams notes suggests that the objection reported by Hancock had been the basis for the court's charge that the accounts lacked particularity.

At any rate, the juries seem to have treated the cases individually. In the Wright & Gill action, the account annexed had listed every single shipment which made up the debt; the verdict was for the net balance, plus the claimed interest. Longman, on the other hand, had sued on an account whose first item was simply "To a Ballance due as per Account then sent ... £1453:10:0," the other items being individual shipments.[27] In reaching its verdict for Longman, the jury deducted the pre-existing balance from the balance on the account, thus in a sense giving some effect to defendant's objection and the court's direction. As Adams noted: "Verdict for Longman for about £200, far short of the whole. Apld. both sides." [28]

It is clear that the defendant moved for a new trial in the Inferior Court, possibly in both actions, although Adams' collection of authorities on this point bears only the title "Wright and Gill vs. Mein—The Jury." In his quasi-brief (Document II), the simple point of commercial evidence on which the cases really turned quickly became obscured in the constitutional argument over the sacred right of jury trial, an argument which Adams expounded even more vigorously in the apparently contemporaneous fragment reprinted here from his diary as Document III.

Whether the "free speech" theme which underlay Adams' references to current English political turmoil echoed some of the bitterness of the Boston journalistic controversy, and whether Adams was attempting to inject contemporary local partisanship into an otherwise quiet legal dispute are matters well beyond the scope of the present note. Certainly in Boston, free speech and the power of the jury were related subjects. Three years before, after a series of vicious attacks on then-Governor Bernard had stimulated Chief Justice Hutchinson to a detailed charge upon the subject of criminal libels to the Grand Jury,[29] the jurors refused to indict—because they were tampered with, Bernard claimed; because they were "worthy and independent," the Sons of Liberty boasted.[30] And the inter-

---

[27] SF 89428.

[28] See JA, Docket, Suff. Inf. Court, Jan. 1771, Adams Papers, where the entry for "Wright v. Same" is "Verdict for Ptf., Deft. appld." Both cases were "Posted to Hancock & pd."

[29] Quincy, *Reports* 262–270 (Suffolk SCJ, March 1768).

[30] Bernard to Shelburne, 12 March 1768, 6 Bernard Papers 278, MH: "[A]s soon as [the Jury] came out of Court they sent for the Attorney General, and directed him to prepare a Bill against the next Morning. But in the Interval the Faction who conducts that Paper was indefatigable in tampering with the Jury; so that when the Business was resumed the next day, the Bill was opposed so effectually that it passed in the negative by a small Majority, some say of only one. Upon this occasion the Managers of the Papers were seen publickly to haunt the Grand Jury Men wherever they went; and the Arguments which were used in the Grand Jury Chamber were almost word for word the same which Otis had before used in Publick." The *Boston Gazette*, 21 March 1768, p. 3, col. 1, reported that

weaving of press and jury, as the issues had arisen in England, was brought vividly to Boston's attention at the very time of the Mein cases, for the *Boston Gazette* of 28 January 1771 had reprinted the "Junius" letter to Lord Mansfield which Adams quoted in his brief; and the battle between Lord Camden and Lord Mansfield was reported in the *Boston Gazette* of 4 February 1771.[31]

Of course, the Bernard libels and the Junius-Mansfield-Camden imbroglio all dealt with the power of a criminal jury to decide law as well as fact. The interesting features of the Mein litigation are that it was an ordinary civil action, and that the court agreed with Adams and allowed the verdict to stand, a point to be considered more fully later in this note.

In view of the right of appeal, why did Mein's attorneys bother to resist the outcome at the Inferior Court stage? Perhaps they felt that some tactical gain would result from a delay. It is noteworthy that Adams did not seek a new trial in the *Longman* case, where the jury had returned a verdict so much less than the amount sued for. The explanation for that seems to lie in the court's not having directed a larger verdict; thus the smaller verdict did not (so far as plaintiff was concerned) contravene a favorable direction.

The double appeals in the Longman case and Mein's appeal in the Wright & Gill case were entered at the February 1771 Suffolk Superior Court, whence they were continued, possibly because the additional accounts were still in London.[32] By August they had arrived, full of enough bibliographical detail to support a doctoral dissertation. Hancock "immediately" delivered them to his "Attornies . . . in full Expectation of the

---

at a celebration of the repeal of the Stamp Act, one of the toasts was: "The worthy and independent Grand Jurors."

[31] *Boston Gazette*, 28 Jan. 1771, p. 1, cols. 1–2, p. 2, cols. 1–2; 4 Feb. 1771, p. 2, col. 3. The arguments for and against rejecting the verdict may even have taken place on 4 Feb.; the appeal bonds in these cases all bear that date, and their execution may well have followed immediately upon the court's upholding the verdicts. See SF 101964.

[32] At this stage there were three cases: Longman, appellant, v. Mein; Mein, appellant, v. Longman; and Mein, appellant, v. Wright & Gill. The Feb. 1771 term of the Suffolk Superior Court commenced on 19 Feb., according to the Minute Book, which gives the following history for Longman's appeal: "4th Day. The 1st Jury half fees. 25th Day. Continued to next Term by consent." Min. Bk. 91, SCJ Suffolk, Feb. 1771, N–13. The other two cases were not called until the twenty-fifth day, at which time they, too, were continued to the next term by consent. Min. Bk. 91, SCJ Suffolk, Feb. 1771, N–19 and N–20. A paper inserted in Min. Bk. 91 at the March 1770 term in Benjamin Kent's hand and signed by him shows that the original plaintiffs were allowed to file new declarations "paying Costs."

The reference to half fees suggests that the jury had been empaneled, if not sworn, and then the case continued. A statute of 1739 had provided that in such cases, the party responsible was to pay half the normal jury fee. Act of 24 June 1739, 2 A&R 938, 939. This Act, which applied to all courts in the Province, had by its terms expired in 1742. The successor legislation, however, had been limited to the Inferior Courts and Courts of General Sessions of the Peace. Act of 15 Jan. 1743, 3 A&R 28, 29. No similar legislation covering the Superior Court appears to have been enacted, which suggests that the Superior Court may have been extending the statute by analogy.

matter being Determined at our August Term, but the Judges saw fit to Refer it to November." [33]

At the November adjournment, Adams chose not to rely solely on the fortified evidence. On 26 November 1771, he filed new declarations, alleging, in addition to the promise to pay, language comprising what Massachusetts lawyers then and now would call "the common counts," a phrase which is shorthand for stereotyped language stating the debtor-creditor relationship in every conceivable way. Moreover, Adams increased the amount of the alleged debt; instead of suing merely for the net amount due, he stated as damages the total of Mein's purchases. [34]

It is impossible accurately to calculate the date of trial from the minute books. Hancock's letter to Wright & Gill of 30 November says: "The Jury yesterday at Superior Court gave in their Verdict in our favor in Mein's Affairs, but Mr. Mein's Council mov'd for a New Trial. How that will be Determined, I know not, but will inform you and as soon as I obtain Execution will turn the Effects into money as soon as possible. Please to inform Mr. Longman of this as I have not time now to write him." [35]

The jury, which had been the same in both cases, although they had been tried separately, brought in verdicts in the amount of the outstanding balances. It is worth noting, in view of the earlier arguments concerning the right of the jury to bring in a general verdict, that the verdicts as the jury originally returned them read, in each instance, "the jury find for the appellant [in *Longman*—"for the appellees" in the other action] the net amount sued for." Each verdict was then amended to conform with the pleading in assumpsit to read: "the jury find that the [original defendant] made the promise alledged in the Declaration & assess damages." [36]

[33] Hancock had not received the accounts by 24 April 1771. Hancock to Longman, 24 April 1771, MH–BA:Hancock Letter Book, in Brown, *John Hancock, His Book* 96. Hancock to Wright & Gill, 24 April 1771, MH–BA:Hancock Letter Book. The accounts and the supporting affidavits appear in SF 101964. Longman's account is of special interest, being a listing of every title shipped to Mein from 1765 to 1769. *Ibid.* Hancock, who had been ill since April, did not report their arrival until 14 Nov. 1771. Hancock to Longman, Hancock Letter Book. There was no Nov. term of the Suffolk Superior Court. Hancock refers to the action of the court on 10 Sept. adjourning the Aug. term (which had commenced 27 Aug.) to 19 Nov. and again to 26 November. Presumably a long trial list coupled with the imminence of sittings in other parts of the Province provoked the adjournment.

[34] The declarations, one in Adams' hand, the other not, are in the file, both docketed as being "filed in the Superior Court at Boston November 26th 1771," the one in Adams' hand adding "by leave of the Court." The new language alleged that Mein owed his creditors: (1) for the reasonable worth of the goods; (2) for money had and received; (3) for money laid out and spent; and (4) for goods sold and delivered. SF 101964.

[35] The respective Minute Book entries are Min. Bk. 95, SCJ Suffolk, Aug. 1771, C–64 and C–66. Mein's appeal against Longman, which was docketed as C–65, was dismissed on the fourteenth day, its merits having been tested in Longman, appellant, v. Mein. See note 36 below. The Hancock letter appears in MH–BA:Hancock Letter Book.

[36] The verdicts are in the file, SF 101964. On the back of each, in a hand not JA's, is a calculation converting the sterling amount to lawful money (by raising it one third). This is why the Minute Book, Record, and executions give the figures

There is no indication when, if ever, motions for new trials were heard. If they did come on for hearing, they were apparently denied because, on 23 December 1771, executions were issued.[37] Then began the problem of trying to realize on the security. As far back as 24 April 1771, Hancock had warned Longman that despite the assurances of Mein's friends about the adequacy of Mein's effects to cover the claim, "you will find on the settlement of the matter here, it will fall vastly short of their Expectation and manifest their suggestion to be utterly groundless." [38] Now the event proved his prophecy. Longman's original attachment had covered "a large number of books, a parcell of Stationery Ware, an Iron Stove, a Wooden press, some Patent medicines, magazines, Reviews and other pamphlets, pewter plates for Engraving, forty five trunks with a variety of other articles," which had been stored during the litigation in a house owned by Samuel Fitch, and upon which the Sheriff levied on 27 December 1771. The appraisers were three Boston bookseller-stationers, Henry Knox, the future Secretary of War (appointed by the Sheriff), Joseph Edwards (appointed by Hancock), and John Langdon (appointed by Fleeming). After ten days' contemplation, the appraisers valued the assortment at £1,038 8s. 10d. Massachusetts money. Deduction of various costs (including an appraisement fee of £32 15s. 5d.) brought the figure even lower: on 18 February 1772, all outstanding fees having been deducted, Hancock signed a receipt for "books, other goods and Effects" valued at £956 4s. 6d.[39]

The dividend on Wright & Gill's claim was similarly slight. On 10 November 1770, three printers—Richard Draper, John Green, and Thomas Fleet—had appraised the printing plant at £185 17s. 4d., of which half belonged to Fleeming. After Sheriff Greenleaf levied execution upon this equipment on 26 December 1771, they again appraised it at the same figure. Some bookbinding equipment being caught within the execution, Langdon and Edwards returned to appraise it, too. Once again, costs were deducted, and Hancock receipted for £94 11s. 6d. worth of bookbinder's tools and printing gear.[40]

Liquidating the collection was difficult. Not until the fall of 1772 was Hancock able to remit anything to England and even then he had to confess that "to this Day have not Received the Whole Money. There is now outstanding about £100 Lawful Money. However, rather than keep them any longer, I have taken it upon myself and now close the whole." [41]

---

as £2191 19s. 0 2/3d. for Longman, and £420 4s. 8d. for Wright & Gill. *Longman*: Min. Bk. 95, SCJ Suffolk, Aug. 1771, C–64; SCJ Rec. 1771, fol. 210; SF 120432. *Wright & Gill*: Min. Bk. 95, SCJ Suffolk, 1771, C–66; SCJ Rec. 1771, fols. 210–211; SF 129636.
[37] SF 129636.
[38] Hancock to Longman, 27 April 1771, MH–BA:Hancock Letter Book, printed in part in Brown, *John Hancock, His Book* 96.
[39] SF 120432.
[40] SF 129636.
[41] Hancock to Longman, 7 Nov. 1772, MH–BA:Hancock Letter Book. The letter enclosed bills and orders totaling £757 2s. 4 1/2d., but it is not clear whether

Whether the underlying motive in these suits was financial or political, they did raise questions of broader significance than Mein's inability to pay his debts or even the patriots' desire to close his newspaper. The issue of a jury's right to decide the law independent of the court's direction or in violation of it (and the closely related question, whether or not counsel could argue law to the jury) claimed much attention in 18th-century England and America. It was present not only in this case, but also in *Cotton v. Nye,* No. 3, and in *Rex v. Richardson,* No. 59. The problem arose also in the Massacre Trials (Nos. 63, 64) where Adams very carefully urged the jury to rely on the authorities which he was citing (and which the prosecution did not dispute), in order to enable the jury correctly to determine the law itself.[42] Josiah Quincy, on the other hand, more "carried away by zeal for his client," [43] argued that the law was the court's concern, and that on the facts, the accused must be acquitted.

The extent of the jury's power and the means by which the judges may impose and maintain bounds on that power agitate the profession even today.[44] At early common law, a court at Westminster, when considering the result of proceedings at nisi prius, could, if it "thought that there had been irregularity in the proceedings . . . decline to proceed and leave the parties to start proceedings afresh. In other words, there was a new trial." [45] In the 17th century, "it became the practice for the judge, with the consent of the parties, to give leave to move the court to enter a verdict for the other side, if they considered that his direction to the jury had been erroneous." [46]

By the beginning of the 18th century, the idea of granting a new trial for misdirection had become rooted in the supervisory functions of the Westminster courts.[47] Other grounds for the granting of new trials included the judge's error in admitting evidence or excluding it,[48] and a "wrong" finding by the jury. This latter phenomenon divided itself into

this all stemmed from the Mein affair or if some was for Hancock's own account. The total net from the executions was £1050 16s., lawful money, or approximately £787 2s. sterling. This approximates the amount Hancock sent, allowing for liquidation shrinkage and attorney's fees. "I have charged no commission, as I promised," Hancock wrote Longman. "What little service I may have rendered you, if it be acceptable will give me pleasure." JA's account with Hancock, receipted 21 Dec. 1771 (p. lxx above), shows for the Jan. 1772 Superior Court: "To the Sum total of the Account in the Case of Longman and Mein—£18 15s. 8d. To Ditto in Wright & Gill v. Mein—£15 5s. 8d."

[42] Quincy, *Reports* (Appendix) 564–565. See also 3 JA, *Diary and Autobiography* 295–296.

[43] Quincy, *Reports* (Appendix) 564.

[44] Statement of Black and Douglas, JJ., on the Rules of Civil Procedure and the Proposed Amendments, *Amendments to the Rules of Civil Procedure for the United States District Courts* 31–33 (Washington, 1963).

[45] 1 Holdsworth, *History of English Law* 282.

[46] 1 Holdsworth, *History of English Law* 282–283.

[47] "A new trial shall be granted if the Judge of Nisi Prius misdirect the Jury, because those Trials are subject to the Inspection of the Court." Anonymous, 2 Salk. 649, 91 Eng. Rep. 552 (Q.B. 1702), per Holt, C.J.

[48] See cases collected in 2 Viner, *Abridgment* 485.

two classes, verdicts "contrary to the evidence" or "against the evidence" and verdicts "against the weight of the evidence." The distinction does not always emerge clearly from the reports and the abridgments, but the difference seems certain. A verdict contrary to evidence was one in which all the evidence adduced, no matter by whom, tended toward one party and none toward the other. A verdict against the weight of the evidence was one in which, although favorable evidence had been produced for both parties, the evidence, taken as a whole, preponderated for one side or the other. The difference may be illustrated by an anonymous case of 1743. At the trial there had been six witnesses for each side, and the judge certified "that the jury found for the defendant, which was against his opinion, but that he could not take upon himself to say that this was a verdict against evidence, because there was evidence on both sides." [49]

Generally, "if the Jury have found a Verdict contrary to the Evidence, the Court will grant a new Trial," [50] the theory being "that the Jury ought to ground the Verdict intirely upon the Evidence given in Court." [51] But, where the trial had seen evidence for both sides, the problem was more difficult. After all, a certification by the trial judge that the verdict was against the weight of the evidence was (and is today) nothing more than a judicial evaluation of the testimony, a difference of opinion between one man and twelve. Which estimate, or rather whose estimate, should prevail, seriously troubled the English judges: "It has been held in some Cases, that if the Jury have found a Verdict which is in the Opinion of the Judge before whom the Cause was tried contrary to the Weight of the Evidence this is a good Reason for the granting of a new Trial. . . . But it has been held in other Cases that the Court ought not to grant a new Trial; because the Jury have in the Opinion of the Judge before whom the Cause was tried found a Verdict contrary to the Weight of the Evidence." [52]

An unreported case set out in Bacon's *Abridgment* sums up the state of the law on this point. On the motion in the Common Pleas for a new trial, Chief Justice Pratt, before whom the trial had been held at nisi prius, said: "If I had been upon the Jury, and had known no more of the Witnesses than I did when this Cause was tried, I should have thought that the Verdict which is for the Plaintiff ought to have been for the Defendant; but I do not chuse to declare myself dissatisfied therewith: Because wherever there is a flat Contrariety of Evidence as to the principal Matter in Issue, and the Characters of the Witnesses on both Sides stand unimpeached, the Weight of Evidence does not altogether depend upon the Number of Witnesses: for it is the Province of the Jury who may know them all to determine which Witnesses they will give Credence to; and in my Opinion no Judge has a Right to blame a Jury for exercising their Power of determining in such a Case."

[49] Anonymous, 1 Wils. K.B. 22, 95 Eng. Rep. 470 (1743). See Angier v. Jackson, Quincy, *Reports* 84–85 (Mass. SCJ, 1763), which also demonstrates the distinction.

[50] 5 Bacon, *Abridgment* 244.

[51] 5 Bacon, *Abridgment* 292.

[52] 5 Bacon, *Abridgment* 245.

Clive, J., said: "The granting of a new Trial in this Case would be taking away that Power which is by the Constitution vested in the Jury. It has been said that it is the Duty of the Judge to enlighten the Understanding of the Jury, but that he ought not to lead the Jury by the Nose."

Bathurst, J.: "As there was in this Case strong Evidence for the Plaintiff a new Trial ought not to be granted, although the Weight of the Evidence was in [the trial judge's] Opinion with the Defendant."

Gould, J.: "It is very difficult to draw a Line between the Cases in which there ought or ought not to be a new Trial; and perhaps the granting of a new Trial must in every Case depend upon the particular Circumstances of the Case. In the present Case there is no Reason to grant one." [53]

And in so-called "hard" cases, that is, actions which the court felt should not in conscience have been prosecuted, new trials were denied after verdicts for the defendant, even though against evidence.[54] As Bacon put it: "It has been held in divers Cases that the Court will not grant a new Trial unless the Justice of the Case requires it, although the Jury have found a Verdict contrary to the Evidence." [55]

No consideration of the judge-jury problem in English law could properly omit some mention of *Bushell's Case*,[56] which established the principle that a jury which refused to convict, in defiance of the judge's direction, could not be fined and imprisoned.

Shortly after it was decided, the case was cited in support of the argument that the jurors need not respect the court's direction in anything pertaining to their verdict. In a chapter entitled "That Juries are not Finable, or any way to be punish'd, under Pretence of going contrary to Evidence, or against the Judges Directions," Henry E. Care, the author of *English Liberties*, set out large portions of the opinion "to satisfy you that a Jury is in no way punishable for going according to their Conscience, though against seeming Evidence." [57] A close reading of Chief Justice Vaughan's holding indicates, however, that it very narrowly restricts and qualifies the jury's role. Because of the significance of the case, and because Adams apparently cited it in his argument in the instant cases,[58] a reappraisal of *Bushell's Case* is worthwhile here.

Bushell had been one of the jurors who had disregarded the court's instructions and had refused to convict the Quakers Penn and Mead at their

[53] Francis v. Baker, 5 Bacon, *Abridgment* 246 (C.P. 1763).

[54] Smith v. Bramston, 2 Salk. 644, 91 Eng. Rep. 543 (K.B. 1695); see also Dunkly v. Wade, 2 Salk. 653, 91 Eng. Rep. 556 (Q.B. 1707) and Sparks v. Spicer, 2 Salk. 648, 91 Eng. Rep. 550 (K.B. 1698). Another case which appears to approve a jury finding against evidence, Deerly v. Dutchess of Mazarine, 2 Salk. 646, 91 Eng. Rep. 547 (K.B. 1696), really rests on a theory of estoppel, that a woman who is reputed to be a feme sole and lives as one may not set up her coverture as a defense to payment of her debts.

[55] 5 Bacon, *Abridgment* 244, which cites all the cases referred to in note 54 above.

[56] Vaughan 135, 124 Eng. Rep. 1006 (C.P. 1670).

[57] Henry E. Care, *English Liberties, or The Free-Born Subject's Inheritance* 123, 124-127 (London, 1703).

[58] Text at note 89 below.

trial in the Old Bailey. As a result, the judges had imprisoned the jurors and literally starved them. Finally, Bushell's lawyers obtained a writ of habeas corpus from the Court of Common Pleas, and the Sheriffs of London, bringing Bushell with them, came into Court to justify the imprisonment. The main reason was "That the Jury acquitted those indicted against the direction of the Court in matter of Law, openly given and declared to them in Court." [59] Vaughan admitted that "no Issue can be joyn'd of matter in Law, no *Jury* can be charg'd with the tryal of matter in Law barely, no Evidence ever was, or can be given to a *Jury* of what is Law, or not; nor no such Oath can be given to, or taken by, a *Jury* to try matter in Law." But he denied that the judge "having heard the Evidence given in Court (for he knows no other)" could tell the jury "upon this Evidence, the Law is for the *Plaintiff*, or for the *Defendant*, and you are under the pain of Fine and Imprisonment to find accordingly."

However, he said plainly that the judge could before verdict ask the jury whether it had found a particular fact and, depending on the answer, could "declare 'The matter of Fact being by you so found to be, the Law is for the *Plaintiff*, and you are to find accordingly for him.' " And a finding for the defendant "may be thought a *finding in matter of Law against the direction of the Court*; for in that case the Jury first declare the Fact, as it is found by themselves, to which fact the Judge declares how the Law is consequent."

And even after verdict, the judge may "ask, 'How do you find such a Fact in particular?' And upon their answer he will say, 'then it is for the *Defendant*,' though they found for the *Plaintiff*, or *e contrario*, and thereupon they rectifie their Verdict."

It was also proper, Vaughan said, to put the matter to the jury hypothetically: "*If you find the Fact thus* (leaving it to them what to find) *then you are to find for the Plaintiff; but if you find the Fact thus, then it is for the Defendant.*"

But, because the law of the case depended on the facts, and because the jury alone could find the facts, it was impossible for any judge to direct the jury. "If the Jury were to have no other Evidence for the Fact, but what is depos'd in Court, the Judge might know their Evidence, and the Fact from it, as equally as they, and so direct what the Law were in the Case." But the jurors, the neighbors of the parties, have knowledge of their own, going either to the issues or to the credibility of the witnesses. It is, therefore, "absurd a *Jury* should be fined by the *Judge* for going against their Evidence, when he who fineth knows not what it is. . . . [F]or the better and greater part of the Evidence may be wholly unknown to him; and this may happen in most Cases, and often doth." "[T]he evidence in Court is not binding evidence to a Jury."

Finally, Vaughan noted, although in some situations, such as demurrers to the evidence, the decision goes "upon the *Judge's Opinion* of

[59] Vaughan at 143, 124 Eng. Rep. at 1006. For background see 1 Holdsworth, *History of English Law* 345. In the quotations which follow, the original emphasis has been retained.

the Evidence given in Court, [and] the *Plaintiff* becomes *Nonsuit,* when if the matter had been left to the *Jury,* they might well have found for the *Plaintiff,*" in all general issues, the jury merely "find for the *Plaintiff* or *Defendant* upon the Issue to be tryed, wherein they resolve both Law and Fact complicately, and not the Fact by itself."

Bushell's Case thus rests principally on a concept of the jurors as quasi-witnesses, an idea which remained very much alive down to Adams' time, as the quotation from Chief Justice Pratt demonstrates. To the Vaughan-Pratt view, which is unanswerable once its major premise be accepted, the Massachusetts lawyers added an interpretation of *Bushell's Case* which had come to them through Care's book, that the jury should always decide the law as well as the fact. On 13 March 1769, the *Boston Gazette* ran an unsigned letter setting out a long passage from *English Liberties,* including this sentence: " 'Tis by applying Matter of Fact and Law together, and from their due Consideration of, and right Judgment upon both, that a Jury brings forth their Verdict." [60]

The author of Appendix II to Quincy's *Reports* thought that, until the 1800's, Massachusetts civil juries had the right to decide both law and fact, in support of which position he cited *Stickney v. Atwood.*[61] From Dane's digest of this unreported case, it appears that one of the purported grounds for a new trial was that the verdict was against the court's opinion. The court apparently overruled the motion, however, holding that the verdict was "not against the court's opinion, if the facts be true, of which the jury must judge." Thus the case seems to stand only for the proposition that if court and jury disagree over the *facts,* the jury's mind will control.

The distinction between (1) the jury's disregarding the court's direction in a matter of law, and (2) the jury's disregarding the court's opinion of the facts was not entirely clear in 18th-century Massachusetts, although the English decisions, even the *Junius* cases, made the difference plain. In each of those criminal libel cases, the jury had been asked to find only the bare fact of publication, with the legal effect of publication—the guilt or innocence of the accused—to be decided then by the judge. That is, the court was asking the jury to respond to a kind of special interrogatory: "Did the defendant publish the statement in question?" Or, to put it another way, the courts were attempting to force the jury to return a special verdict (a verdict in which the jury found certain specific facts, leaving it to the court to determine which party should prevail). In a general verdict, on the other hand, the jury found "generally," that is, for the plaintiff (with assessed damages), or for the defendant according to the plea. It was the juries' insistence on bringing in a general verdict (not guilty) which, combined with judicial attempts to regard these general verdicts as special ones, touched off the controversy. But not even Lord Mansfield himself ever *directed* a jury to find the simple fact of publication.

Inability to distinguish between the differences stemmed in part, as

---

[60] *Boston Gazette,* 13 March 1769, p. 3, col. 1; Care; *English Liberties* 121.
[61] Quincy, *Reports* (Appendix) 567; 6 Dane, *Abridgment* 252 (Mass. 1784).

Adams himself noted, from the practice of styling anything the court said a "direction." [62] Thus what today would be considered a judge's summing up, or perhaps his commentary on the evidence,[63] might, in Adams' time, be regarded as an attempt to direct a jury's finding. Expressions like "contrary to the mind of the Court," [64] or "against the mind of three in four of us Judges," [65] could be interpreted either way.

Of course, no one took the position that all questions whatsoever were for the jury. Even Adams admitted that there were numerous classes of litigation whose intricacies "would confound a common Jury and a decision by them would be no better than a Decision by Lott." [66] But Adams' point was that the jury would recognize its own limitations and would voluntarily bring in a special verdict in such cases. He argued that it should be the jury's decision rather than the judges' whether or not a special verdict should be employed, and that the jury, if it liked, could decide to determine the law, no matter what the court thought. The opposing view found expression in a letter to *The Censor*, signed "A.Z.," which insisted that the losing party receive a new trial "when a jury will pertinaciously determine matters of law directly against the opinion of the Court." [67] A middle view came from Robert Auchmuty and Chief Justice Hutchinson. Arguing against a new trial in a 1763 case, Auchmuty had said: "I confess I wish for a Power in the Court to set aside Verdicts, but not for an unlimited one. . . . The Court is not to be Judge of the Law and Fact too absolutely; if it should be, it takes away all Verdicts but such as are agreeable to the Mind of the Court." And Hutchinson asked: "Are you not agreed, that, were it evidently against Law and Evidence, there the Court may grant a new Trial, but not where there is Evidence on both sides?" [68]

Whatever the division of powers and function between court and jury, it is apparent that in Massachusetts anyhow, after a verdict the judges could not enter up judgment for the losing party, no matter how strong they thought his case to be. The most he could get was a new trial. Even

[62] Doc. II. For an example of the use of the word "direct" in this context, which does not, however, resolve the question of the binding effect of the direction, see William Torrey v. Joseph Torrey, Min. Bk. 89, SCJ Suffolk, Aug. 1769, N–59, SCJ Rec. 1769, fol. 248, an action on an account, in which JA had obtained judgment for the defendant on a sham demurrer at the July 1769 Suffolk Inferior Court. Josiah Quincy joined JA for the defendant in the Superior Court, where he again prevailed. A note from the file in the hand of Judge Trowbridge explains why: "Nothing being offered by the plaintiff in Support of his Declaration but the account in the Case Signed by Joseph Torrey The Court Were of opinion That That was not sufficient Evidence to support the plaintiff's Declaration and Directed the Jury Accordingly." SF 101517. See JA, Docket, SCJ Suffolk, Aug. 1769, Adams Papers.

[63] In Massachusetts today, the judge is not permitted to charge the jury "with respect to matters of fact." Mass. G.L., c. 231, §81.

[64] Angier v. Jackson, Quincy, *Reports* 84 (Mass. SCJ, 1763).

[65] "At Superiour Court at Salem, Eliza Ames and her son Eames tried for poisoning his wife. They were acquitted, tho' against the mind of three in four of us Judges." Lynde, *Diary* 193 (14 Nov. 1769).

[66] Doc. III.

[67] *The Censor*, 14 March 1772, p. 1, col. 2.

[68] Angier v. Jackson, Quincy, *Reports* 84–85 (1763).

"A.Z." asked for nothing more than that. It was not until the middle of the 19th century that the Massachusetts Court ruled that if a civil plaintiff's evidence was so weak that "the Court would set aside any number of verdicts rendered upon it, *toties quoties*, then the cause should be taken from the jury by instructing them to find a verdict for the defendant." [69]

I. CORRESPONDENCE OF JAMES MURRAY,
JOHN FLEEMING, AND SHERIFF STEPHEN GREENLEAF [70]
March–May 1770

Sir   Boston March 7 1770

In order to prevent as much as may be any damage to any of the parties in the said suits or to the Officers who laid the attachments the defendants friends propose that you cause the effects attached to be appraised you chusing the appraisers for the defendant and that his friends will shew you other effects of his to the full amount of the Value appraized less perishable than those now attached on which you may lay the attachment to lie forthcoming for the judgment which shall be obtained in the said suits.

They request the favour of you that the appraisement may be as soon as possible and that Mr. John Fleeming the defendant's Attorney may have notice to attend by himself or Agent during the appraisement. I beg an answer to these proposals in *writing* and am in behalf of the defendant and his friends Sir Your most obedient Servant,

(Sign'd) Ja Murray

Stephen Greenleaf Esq. High Sheriff of said County

Sir   Friday morning [9 *March* 1770]

I yesterday saw Mr. Hancock who consents to have the Goods of Mr. Mein which were attached appraiz'd. I have therefore appointed Mr. Leverett and Mr. Edwards Booksellers to join with any one appointed by Mr. Hancock to execute that business. Mr. Hancock promised to nominate his Man this Morning and then Mr. Cudworth who made the attachment will attend them and give you notice to attend also if you please. *The late disorders of the Town have a little delayed this affair* which Mr. Mein's friends will excuse. Yours,

(Sign'd) S Greenleaf

Mr. John Fleeming

[69] Denny v. Williams, 5 Allen 1 (Mass. SJC, 1862).
[70] Copies attested by John Fleeming, as attorney for John Mein, his former partner in Boston, before Justice Edmund Quincy, 29 Sept. 1770. MHi:Hancock Papers. See note 15 above.

No. 12. Longman v. Mein

Sir   Milton April 25 1770

It is with much concern for my friend Mr. Mein that I learn his Bookstore is still shut up notwithstanding the fair proposal I had the honor to make you of the 7th. of last Month, where the fault is I know not. *It is not at present convenient for me to go to Town to enquire,* but I have too good an opinion of you as a Gentleman and an Officer to imagine it lies at your door. I shall be much oblig'd to you for accelerating the business. I am ready to comply with my engagement. In the meantime give me leave briefly to state my friends case in confidence for the Truth of which I appeal to you. A Bookseller and printer for daring to oppose and attempting to expose a combination of several Merchants and others in the Town of Boston is hurt in his trade by many underhand practices. An attempt is made upon his life. He is driven off. Letters of procuration are obtained from his Creditors at home to a *Champion* of the combination. His Stock in Trade and all tools of trade are attached in his absence. His Stock is shut up from Sale. Undoubted security is offered that the Stock or the value of it should be forthcoming to satisfy the judgments that shall be obtained. That offer is rejected. A second offer is made to shew other effects of the debtors less perishable. That proposal too equitable to be flatly refused is evaded by procrastination and the Debtor thus treated in his absence is to be liable for the prime cost, accruing interest and charges of Goods which he is utterly debarr'd from selling. Is not this what was understood of Old by being compelled to make Bricks without straw. I have the honor to be respectfully Sir Your most obedient Servant,   (Sign'd Ja Murray)

To Stephen Greenleaf Esq. High Sheriff of Suffolk in Boston

Dear Sir   Boston 4 May 1770

Your obliging Letter relative to Mr. Meins affair would have been sooner replied to had I not waited to have it in my power to have given a more pleasing Account than I am yet able to do. Various reasons may be assigned for the delays in the Appraisers. The constant attention which I have been oblig'd for Six Weeks past to pay to the Courts of Justice may serve as some part of an apology for me if any was necessary but when I assure you that nothing has been left undone by me which could be legally done in order to get Mr. Mein's Shop opened and in a course of business your goodness I am sure will lead you to excuse every thing on my part. You have been doubtless informed by Mr. Fleeming that after a considerable delay the [three?] appraisers were got together and Mr. Cudworth (whose business it was) appointed [his?] Son to attend de Die in Diem to make out a compleat Catalogue and Inventory of the whole. Mr. Reid also attended. The appraisers finding it would take a long time ⟨*to make out a Compleat Catalogue*⟩ thought it quite unnecessary for them to be there during the Inventory being taken but agreed as they informed me that as soon as it was done they would set down the price against the several Articles. Cudworth promised to furnish them with a Copy for that purpose which I am told he delivered to Mr. Fleeming. I have since often spoke to the Appraisers but have always found a backwardness, whether owing to an influence, Business of their own or a natural disinclination I am not to say, but so it is. Mr. Leverett (one of them) has been laid up some time with the Gout. I see him this day and he hopes to be able to attend the affair the beginning of the Week when I shall push the matter having obtained a fresh promise from the other two Gentlemen to wait upon him at his own house for that purpose. Whether it won't be still delayed 'till Mr. Hancock can hear from England I know not. His constant business at Cambridge with my unwillingness to be further importunate with a *Gentleman of his great superiority* has really kept me from applying to him on the Subject and if I know your mind imagine you would not desire me to supplicate the favour. What I can with honor to myself and friendship to Mr. Mein get accomplished will certainly be done. Being with all possible respect Sir Your most obedient Servant,

(Sign'd) S Greenleaf

James Murray Esq.

II. ADAMS' NOTES OF AUTHORITIES [71]

Suffolk Inferior Court, Boston, January 1771

1771. Jany. Court. Wright and Gill vs. Mein—The Jury.

The Jury found a Verdict for the Sum sued for. Kent moved that the Verdict should be rejected. I deny'd the Power of the Court to reject it, and said if he would move for a new Tryal, that would not be without a Precedent in the Superiour Court tho it would in an inferiour Court.[72]

[71] In JA's hand. Adams Papers, Microfilms, Reel No. 185. These notes were written on several sheets which may once have formed a gathering but are now loose and worn. JA partly paged them, but the order of the material, written at different times and hurriedly, is not always clear.

[72] In the margin appears the following: "See, however, The several Titles of

13 Ed. 1. c. 30. Barrington Obs. on Stat. 103. "Item ordinatum est quod Justitiarii ad Assisas capiendas assignati, non compellant Juratores dicere precise, si sit disseisina vel non; dummodo voluerint dicere Veritatem facti, et petere Auxilium Justiciariorum; *sed si sponte velint dicere quod Disseisina sit, vel non, Admittatur eorum Veredictum sub suo periculo*—The latter part of this Chapter shews, that the Contest between Judges and Juries was of a very different Nature at this Time, from what it hath been of late Years. The Reason of this arises from what I have before observed, with regard to it being very common anciently to bring Attaints against Juries, and an Angry or dishonest Judge therefore drove them to the finding an improper Verdict in order to subject them to the Prosecution by Attaint; Admittatur eorum Veredictum sub suo periculo—*As this Law is unrepealed, there can therefore be no doubt but a Jury may find what Verdict they please*, and the Misfortune is, that they run no Risque at present of an Attaint; there is however generally that Moderation in Juries, that they seldom abuse this Liberty. This Chapter is generally called the Statute of Nisi Prius; it relates to Actions depending in Utroque Banco, without any Notice of the Court of Exchequer."[73]

"If you will take upon you to determine the Law, *you may do it,* but you must be very sure that you determine, according to Law, for it touches your Consciences, and you Act at your Peril." Lord Mansfield in Baldwins Case. Junius to Lord M.[74]

3 Black. 378. "The Jury may, if they think proper, take upon themselves to determine at their own hazard, the complicated Question of fact and Law; and without either Special Verdict or Special

---

Mistrial, New Tryal &c. Verdict may be set aside and a venire facias de novo [new jury, that is, new trial] awarded." The precise treatise or treatises to which JA here refers have not been identified. See, however, 5 Bacon, *Abridgment* 240, tit. Trial: "A new Trial ought not to be granted by an inferior Court, and if the Judge thereof does grant one a Mandamus lies for a Procedendo ad Judicium upon the first Verdict."

[73] Barrington, *Observations upon the Statutes* 103–104. Quotation marks supplied. The Latin expression is from the Statute of Westminster II, 13 Edw. 1, c. 30 (1285): "And also It is Ordained, That the Justices assigned to take Assises shall not compel the Jurors to say precisely whether it be Disseisin or not, so that they do shew the Truth of the Deed [fact] and require Aid of the Justices; but if they of their own head will say, that it is [or is not] Disseisin, their Verdict shall be admitted at their own Peril." 1 *Statutes of the Realm* 86 (London, 1810).

[74] This paragraph is written in the margin. Quotation marks supplied. Rex v. Baldwin (K.B. 1770) was apparently never reported. See 20 *State Trials* 922; Frederick Siebert, *Freedom of the Press in England* 387–388 (Urbana, Ill., 1952). The quotation here is taken, with only pronominal changes, from Junius' letter to Lord Mansfield, 14 Nov. 1770 (No. XLI), 2 *Letters of Junius* 159, 174–175 (London, ed. Woodfall, 1814).

Case may find a Verdict absolutely, either for Plaintiff or Defendant. Vid. page [....]." [75]

5. Bac. Abr. 285. 286. relating to general and Special Verdicts. [76]

1. Inst. 228. a. Littleton §368. "Also in such Case where the Enquest may give their Verdict at large, if they will take upon them the Knowledge of the Law, upon the Matter, they may give their Verdict generally, as is put in their Charge; as in the Case aforesaid they may well say, that the Lessor did not disseise the Lessee, if they will &c." [77] Note. "Altho the Jurie, if they will take upon them (as Littleton here saith) the Knowledge of the Law, may give a general Verdict, yet it is dangerous for them so to do, for if they mistake the Law, they run into the Danger of an Attaint, therefore to find the Special Matter, is the safest Way, where the Case is doubtfull." [78]

4. Rep. 53. b. Rawlins Case. 29-30. Eliz. B.R. "And in such Case the Jury ought, if they will, not find the Special matter, and leave it to the Judgment of the Law, [to] find it at their Peril according to Law." [79]

2. Ld. Ray. 1493. Oneby's Case. "The Court are Judges of the Malice and not the Jury." Page 1494. "Upon the Tryal of the Indictment the Judge directs the Jury thus 'if you believe such and such Witnesses, who have sworn such and such Facts, the Killing the deceased was with Malice prepense express, or it was with Malice implied, and then you ought to find the Prisoner guilty of Murder; but if you do not believe those Witnesses, then you ought to find him guilty of Manslaughter only.'" [80]

Foster. 255. "In every Case where the Point turneth upon the Question, whether the Homicide was committed willfully and maliciously, or under Circumstances justifying, Excusing, or alleviating; the Matter of Fact, vizt., whether the Facts alledged by Way of Justification, Excuse, or Alleviation are true, is the *proper* and *only* Province of the Jury. But whether upon a Supposition of the Truth of Facts such Homicide be justified, excused, or alleviated must be submitted to the Judgment of the Court. For the Construction the Law putteth

---

[75] 3 Blackstone, *Commentaries* *378. Quotation marks supplied. This paragraph is also written in the margin.

[76] 5 Bacon, *Abridgment* 285–287. This collects the authorities, many of which JA cites or quotes later in the present minute.

[77] Coke, *Littleton* 228a. Quotation marks supplied.

[78] Coke, *Littleton* 228a. The note is Coke's. Quotation marks supplied.

[79] Rawlyn's Case, 4 Co. Rep. 52a, 53b, 76 Eng. Rep. 1007 (K.B. 1585). Quotation marks supplied. JA has erroneously inserted a comma between "they will" and "not find"; also "it" between "find" and "at their Peril."

[80] Rex v. Oneby, 2 Ld. Raym. 1485, 1493–1494, 92 Eng. Rep. 465, 470–471 (K.B. 1727). Quotation marks in part supplied.

upon Facts stated and agreed or found by a Jury is, in this, as in all other Cases, undoubtedly the Proper Province of the Court. In Cases of Doubt and real Difficulty it is commonly recommended to the Jury to state Facts and Circumstances in a Special Verdict. But when the Law is clear, the Jury under the Direction of the Court in Point of Law, Matters of Fact being still left to their Determination, may, and if they are well advised always will find a general Verdict conformable to such Direction. Ad Quæstionem Juris non respondent Juratores." [81]

[1] Burrows 393. Bright Exr. vs. Eynon.[82] Lord Mansfield, "Tryals by Jury, in civil Causes could not subsist now, without a Power somewhere, to grant new Tryals, &c. &c.[83] If an erroneous Judgment be given in Point of Law, there are many Ways to review and set it right. Where a Court judges of Fact upon Depositions in Writing, their Sentence or Decree may, many Ways, be reviewed and set right.

"But a general Verdict can only be set right by a new Tryal," &c.[84] "The Writ of Attaint is now a mere Sound, in every Case: in many, it does not pretend to be a Remedy."

Vid. page 3 of this Statute.[85]

Holt. Rep. 702. Argent vs. Darrell. Holt. "We must not make ourselves absolute Judges of Law and fact too."[86]

1 Tr. pr. Pais 283 [87] Littleton quoted, and then a Note. "The Court cannot refuse a general Verdict, if the Jury will find it; it was so held before Justice Wyndham, Lent Assizes 1681 in Verdons Case at Cambridge."

Whether a Jury may give a Verdict on their own Knowledge, or on the Knowledge of any one of them, without being sworn as Witnesses?

---

[81] Foster, *Crown Cases* 255–256 (1762). Quotation marks supplied. The Latin phrase means, roughly: "The jurors do not answer questions of law."

[82] Bright, Executor v. Eynon, 1 Burr. 390, 393, 97 Eng. Rep. 365, 366 (K.B. 1757). Quotation marks supplied. Action on note to testatrix; defense: discharge in defendant's hand, signed by testatrix; reply: forgery. No evidence of the forgery being introduced, the trial judge (Lord Mansfield) left it to the jury to say whether there had been (1) forgery or (2) fraud. The jury found for the defendant. On motion for new trial, *held*, rule to set aside verdict made absolute, because by "the Evidence on both Sides, the Transaction to get her Hand to this Writing must have been *fraudulent*." 1 Burr. at 396, 97 Eng. Rep. at 368.

[83] The "&c.'s" do not appear in the printed text.

[84] JA omits: "which is no more than having the Cause more deliberately considered by another Jury; when there is a reasonable Doubt, or perhaps a Certainty, that Justice has not been done."

[85] Marginal note. The reference is obscure.

[86] Argent v. Sir Marmaduke Darrell, Holt K.B. 702, 90 Eng. Rep. 1288 (1699). Quotation marks supplied. This paragraph appears in the margin of the MS.

[87] Duncombe, *Trials Per Pais* 283 (1766). The quotation from *Littleton* appears in the JA minutes, at note 77 above.

Vid. 5. Bac. Abr. 292. Tit. Verdicts.[88] Vaughan 147. Bushells Case.[89]
1. Salk. 405.[90] Farr. 2.[91] 1. Sid. 133. Fitz James vs. Moys.[92] Cro.
Eliz. 616. Graves vs. Short.[93] Obs. on Stat. 74.[94]

Holt 701. 2. Ash vs. Ash. Jury shy of giving Reasons "thinking they
have an absolute Despotic Power, but I did recti[fy that] Mistake for
they are to [try] Causes with the Assistance of the Judges; and ought
to give Reasons when required, that if they go upon any mistake they
may be set right." [95]

Holt 703. 704. Gay vs. Cross. A general Verdict, and Jury would
give no Reason for it. Holt said, "he never had known the like, and
that he would have but little regard for the Verdict of a Jury on a
Tryal that would not at a Judges desire declare the Reasons which
had induced them to give it; for as the Judges of the Courts do publickly declare the Reasons of their Judgments and thereby expose themselves to the Censure of all that be learned in the Law; yet [there is]
no Law obliges them to it, but it is for public Satisfaction. So the Jury
ought [likewise]" when requir'd by the Court to make known the
Reasons but the Court would not grant a new trial tho the Judges
were very much dissatisfy'd with the Jury. It was a trial at Bar.[96]

[88] 5 Bacon, *Abridgment* 292. The general subject is "In What Cases a Verdict
is Bad Upon the Account of a Misdemeanor in One or More of the Jurors"; and
at the page cited Bacon collects authorities (including those in the next four footnotes) on the question whether the jury's verdict must rest solely on evidence adduced in court.

[89] Bushell's Case, Vaughan 135, 147, 124 Eng. Rep. 1006, 1012 (C.P. 1670):
"[The jurors] may have Evidence from their own personal knowledge, by which
they may be assur'd, and sometimes are, that what is depos'd in Court, is absolutely false. . . . The jury may know the Witnesses to be stigmatiz'd and infamous,
which may be unknown to the parties, and consequently to the Court." For a discussion of Bushell's Case see text at notes 56–60 above.

[90] Anonymous, 1 Salk. 405, 91 Eng. Rep. 351 (K.B. 1696): "If a jury give a
Verdict on their own Knowledge, they ought to tell the Court so, that they may be
sworn as Witnesses; and the fair Way is to tell the Court before they are sworn,
that they have evidence to give."

[91] Note, Farr. (7 Mod.) 2, 87 Eng. Rep. 1056 (Q.B. 1702), a paraphrase of the
case in note 90 above.

[92] Fitz-James v. Moys, 1 Sid. 133, 87 Eng. Rep. 1014 (K.B. 1663): One of
the jury, having heard the evidence, was himself sworn as a witness, testified, and
yet continued on the jury.

[93] Graves v. Short, Cro. Eliz. 616, 78 Eng. Rep. 857 (Q.B. 1598). No error
for juror to show his fellows a paper not otherwise in evidence but favoring one of
the parties. The case is cited in 5 Bacon, *Abridgment* at 291.

[94] Barrington, *Observations upon the Statutes* 74.

[95] Ash v. Lady Ash, Holt K.B. 701–702, 90 Eng. Rep. 1287 (1696). Quotation
marks and words JA omitted are supplied. This paragraph appears in the margin
of the MS and is partly worn away.

[96] Gay v. Cross, Holt K.B. 703, 90 Eng. Rep. 1288 (1702). Quotation marks
and words JA omitted are supplied. This paragraph was inserted in the margin and
between paragraphs written earlier in the MS.

Province of ye } Anno Regni Regis Georgii tertii magnæ
Massachusetts Bay } Britanniæ Franciæ et Hiberniæ &c[a]
Suffolk ss }

At this Majestys superior Court of Judicature
Court of Assize and general Goal Delivery
begun & held at Boston, within & for the County
of Suffolk on the last tuesday of August
(being the 29th day of said month) January
D[omi]ni 1769

By the Hon[bl]e Thomas Hutchinson Esq chief Just[ice]
        Benjamin Lynde   }
        John Cushing   } Esq Justices
        Peter Oliver   }
        Edmund Trowbridge }

#118   119. Amos Bowney ad[m]o v Thom. Bayley &[al]
                as prayed for &c[a] for
                affirmation &c[a] costs indeps with two magns
                whereof the partees to raise costs of the sam
                pay to said & Thomas & Elizabeth
                pay to raise costs of the sam
                £3.8..0 Confill moneys & costs £4.18..5

January 20. Miles Mansfield v Samuel Peirce
                affirmation &c[a] as prayed for
Execution   5£..o Damna & £3.2.10 cost
14.3½(1769)
2/2
        21. The petition of Anne M[c]William adm[x] of M[r]
                M[c]William late of Boston
                Fox the Estate of James M[c]William late of Boston
                dec[d] for sale of his real Estate; granted

        22. Petition of David Marsh adm[or] of the estate of
                Amos Jones late of Weymouth dec[d] for sale of
                his real Estate; granted

        Boston April 17 1769 Judgment is entered up according
                to the verdicts and the Court is adjourned
                without Day Att Sam: Winthrop Cler

Capt Part K[i] Jn Winslow Wright v Edw Trowbridge Esq &[al]
  any   Cont under said Rule to next Term
                by consent

3e   2. Benj. Hallowell Esq[r] v Rich[d] Dana Esq[r] apples (of
                Continued to next term under the same Rule
                at the motion of the appelles, the appellant
                not objecting—

Ent   3. Nath[l] Porter Esq[r] v George Kent
        12 day Thes (1st) surryfied for the appellant Cost[a]
                Thes (1st) surryfied for the appellant Cost[a]

3e   4. Ch: Wm Apthorp Esqr v Hen[ry] Bromfield apples
        23 day Continued to next term by consent

Anno Regni Regis Georgii tertii Magnæ Britanniæ &
Franciæ et Hiberniæ Nono.

At a Court of General Sessions of the Peace begun Held
at Boston within & for the County of Suffolk on the Second Tuesday of
April being the Eighteenth day of Said Month being Anno Dom. 1769
Being the first Session in the new Court House in Said County.

His Majesty's Justices Present

Samuel Welles Esq
Joshua Winslow
Robert Auchmuty
Josiah Quincy
Nath. Hatch
Edmund Quincy
Jno. Hill
Edmund Quincy
Josiah Williams
Samuel Miles
Benj. Miller

} Esq

Nath. Warner
Richard Dana
Joshua Hay
Josiah Sewall
John Avery
John Ruddock
Jos. Metcalf
Wm. Fletcher
John Jones
Sam. Winthrop
Edgar Gautier

} Esq

Clerk by Cox.

Ordered that the Clerk ... for the present year ...
the several Warrants for the Several Towns of ... Boston, Roxbury, Dorchester, Braintree, Medfield, Walton,
Brighton, Natick, Needham, Chelsea, Weymouth, Medway, Abington, Bristton
in a County Treasurer for the present year being Chosen, Hopkinston
... them, Mark Jackson, Benjamin ... Esq. is unanimously chosen into
that office, & he being in Court took the Oaths required by Law to qualify
him to Execute Said Office. —

Ordered that the Clerk of Warrants & other Persons ... Shillings ... be allowed
and Paid out of the County Treasury ... viewed Neck & one of the Warrens
of this County, & being by himself and ... for an ... by him taken
... late of Braintree ... Deceased, whereas ...
that a Warrant is ... but he having left no Estate nor Relations
obliged by Law to pay the Same, an ... allowed for on file. —

Braintree April 18 1769. —

Ordered that the ... Five Shilling of Champion
be allowed & Paid unto the County Treasury unto William Warner in full of
his due to ... unto ... supplied the County of ... as by his due on file. —

Dorchester April 18 1769. —

Joseph Winslow of Boston Brazier is appointed a Measurer of Iron ...
Northampton within the Town of Boston, and he being in Court took the Oath ...
was required to qualify him for executing Said office. —

Ordered that Mr. Alexander Young of ... the County of Hampton ...
to take the Care of the Poor ... being taken in ... Street, and he
being in Court declared his ... of the Same. —

May 8 May 22 1769. —

Ordered that the ... of Citer ... Eighteen Shilling ... be
... Paid out of the County Treasury unto Nathaniel ... 18
being his Bonds ... the Said Butland house, as by his Acc.
on file will appear. —

Attaint. Cun. Dict. Tit. Attaint. In what cases an Attaint lies.[97]
Gilb. H.C.B. 128.[98]

Obs. on Stat 74.[99] Stat. West. 1st. 3. E. 1. A.D. 1272, chap. 38.[100]
Le Roi (de son office) donera[101] Atteint sur enquestes en pleint de
terre, ou de franchise, ou de chose qui touche frank Tenement.

"[It is generally agreed, that] No Prosecution by Attaint hath been
carried on against a Jury for the last 300 Years." (Note this. Lord
Coke lived 150 Years ago, so that the Attaint had been disused 150
Years when he wrote.) "This arises partly from the more modern
Practice of granting new Tryals, and partly from the great Difficulty
there is in convicting, as the Jury may give their Verdict upon what
is known to themselves, though it hath not appeared in Evidence
during the Course of the Tryal. It is indeed said, that a Juror having
such private Knowledge of a Fact should disclose it, in open Court;
but what signifies the mere Advice of a Judge, which cannot be
inforced?"[102]

"It may [therefore] deserve Consideration, whether this method of
Punishment, being now totally disused may not have occasioned a most
material Alteration, and Deviation from the Principles, upon which
Juries were originally instituted.[103]

"The Attaint [was trial by twenty-four jurors, of double the substance with the first jury; and it is to be observed that it] lay only in
civil Cases, either by common Law or by this Statute. The Reason is,

[97] Cunningham, *Law Dictionary*, tit. Attaint: "[S]o this is the only curb that
the law has put in the hands of the judges to restrain jurors from giving corrupt
verdicts."

[98] Gilbert, *Common Pleas* 128: "Now the Jury may be attainted two Ways;
First, where they find contrary to Evidence, *2dly*, where they find out of the Compass
of the *Allegata*; but to attaint them for finding contrary to Evidence is not easy,
because they may have Evidence of their own Conuzance of the Matter by them, or
they may find upon Distrust of the Witnesses on their own proper Knowledge."

[99] Barrington, *Observations upon the Statutes* 74. Quotation marks are supplied
throughout the passages from Barrington, text at notes 102, 103, and 107, below.

[100] Thus in MS and Barrington, *Observations upon the Statutes* 58. The correct
date is 1275, 1 *Statutes of the Realm* 36 (1810). Statute of Westminster II, 3
Edw. 1, c. 38: "[T]he King, of his office, shall from henceforth grant Attaints
upon Enquests in Plea of Land, or of Freehold, or of anything touching Freehold,
when it shall seem to him necessary."

[101] Thus in MS. "Durra" in Barrington, *Observations upon the Statutes* 74, and in
the statute. Barrington, *Observations upon the Statutes* 74 note, says: "*De son
office* should be translated of right . . . ; *durra*, which follows, is put corruptly
for donera."

[102] Barrington, *Observations upon the Statutes* 74. Quotation marks and words
JA omitted are supplied. JA omits Barrington's footnote: "It should seem to have
been understood in the time of Henry the Third, to have been the duty of the
judge to control the verdict of the jury," citing Bracton, lib. iv, c. 19.

[103] Barrington, *Observations upon the Statutes* 75.

a [104] strong Presumption, that no Jury would condemn a criminal contrary to the Evidence: and that it would be inconsistent with the Principles of Liberty to permit the Crown [(when it might intend oppression)] to call in Question a Verdict of Acquittal.[105] Since [that glorious æra] the Revolution, [the] Kings [of England] have [only] prosecuted as Pater Patriæ [when punishment hath been necessary for the safety of the whole]; but when we look into Tryals during preceeding Reigns, we cannot but revere the wise and noble Constitution established by our Ancestors against the vindictive Prosecution of a Plantaganet and [106] a Stewart." [107]

Common Law.

Black. 63. bott. "[But, with us at present,] The Monuments and Evidences of our legal Customs, are contained in the Records of the several Courts of Justice, in Books of Reports, and judicial Decisions and in the Treatises of learned Sages of the Profession, preserved and handed down to us, from the Times of highest antiquity." [108] Page 73. "[And thus much for] the 1st. ground and chief corner Stone of the Laws of England, [which] is, general immemorial Custom, or common Law from Time to Time declared in the Decisions of the Courts of Justice; which Decisions are preserved among our public Records, explained in our Reports and digested for general Use, in the Authoritative Writings of the venerable Sages of the Law." [109]

Question 1st. "Does the Opinion mean to declare, that upon the general Issue of Not Guilty, in the Case of a seditious Libel, the Jury have no Right by Law to examine the Innocence or Criminality of the Paper, if they think fit, and to form their Verdict with such Examination?

"2. Does the Opinion mean to declare, that in the Case above mentioned, when the Jury have delivered in their Verdict, Guilty, that this Verdict has found the Fact only, and not the Law?

[104] Thus in MS. The text reads: "The reason of which seems to have been grounded upon the strong Presumption." Barrington, *Observations upon the Statutes* 75.

[105] Beside the words in brackets, JA omits: "It is for the same reason when a crime is prosecuted by appeal (the remedy of a private person) and not by indictment (which is the suit of the crown), that there is no intervention of a grand jury to find the bill. Happily for this country . . ."

[106] Thus in MS; "or" in Barrington.

[107] Barrington, *Observations upon the Statutes* 75. Words JA omitted are supplied.

[108] 1 Blackstone, *Commentaries* *63–64. Closing quotation marks supplied.

[109] 1 Blackstone, *Commentaries* *73. Closing quotation marks supplied.

"3. It is to be understood by this Opinion, that if the Jury come to the Bar, and say, that they find the printing and publishing, but that the Paper is no Libel, that in that Case the Jury have found the Defendant, guilty, generally and that the Verdict must be so entered up?

"4. Whether the Opinion means to say, that if the Judge, after giving his Opinion of the Innocence or Criminality of the Paper, should leave the Consideration of that matter, together with the printing and publishing, to the Jury, such a Direction would be contrary to Law?

"5. I beg Leave to ask, whether dead and living Judges, then absent, did declare their Opinions in open Court, and whether the noble L—d has any Note of such opinions?

"6. Whether they declared such Opinions, after solemn Arguments, or upon any Point judicially before them?"

Questions put by Lord C——n to Lord M——d in answer to a Paper his Lordship left with the Clerk of the Room the day before. M——d refused to answer these Questions, saying he would not answer interrogatories. Newspaper.[110]

4. Blackstone 354.[111] "[But] An open Verdict may be either general, guilty, or not guilty; or Special, setting forth all the Circumstances of the Case, and praying the Judgment of the Court, whether for Instance, on the Facts stated, it be murder, Manslaughter, or no Crime at all. This is where they *doubt* the matter of Law, and therefore *chuse* to leave it to the determination of the Court; though they have an unquestionable Right of determining upon all the Circumstances, and finding a general Verdict, if they think proper so to hazard a Breach of their Oaths: and, if their Verdict be notoriously wrong, they may be punished and the Verdict set Aside by Attaint at the Suit of the King; but not at the Suit of the Prisoner, 2. H.P.C. 310.[112] But the Practice, heretofore in Use of fining, imprisoning, or otherwise punishing Juries merely at the discretion of the Court, for finding their

---

[110] Quotation marks supplied. Lord Mansfield's conduct of the trial of Woodfall for the publication of the Junius letters having been the subject of Parliamentary debate, Mansfield deposited with the Clerk of the House a copy of his charge to the jury in that case. The next day, 11 Dec. 1770, Lord Camden propounded these questions, which Mansfield never answered. 16 *Parliamentary History* 1312–1322 (London, 1813); C. H. S. Fifoot, *Lord Mansfield* 44–46 (Oxford, 1936); James Stephen, *History of the Criminal Law of England*, 2:325–326 (London, 1883). Camden was a legal hero to the patriots, Quincy on one occasion referring to him as "undoubtedly the first common lawyer in England." Josiah Quincy, *Josiah Quincy, Jr.* 272. Which "Newspaper" JA took these "Questions" from is not known.

[111] 4 Blackstone, *Commentaries* *354–355. Quotation marks in part supplied.

[112] 2 Hale, *Pleas of the Crown* 310, discusses the means of punishing a jury for finding against evidence.

Verdict, contrary to the direction of the Judge, was arbitrary, unconstitutional, and illegal: and is treated as such by Sir Thomas Smith, 200 Years ago; who 'accounted such doings to be very violent, tyrannical, and contrary to the Liberty and Custom of the Realm of England.'[113] For as Sir Mathew Hale well observes 2. H.P.C. 313.[114] 'it would be a most unhappy Case, for the Judge himself, if the Prisoners Fate depended upon his Directions: unhappy also for the Prisoner; for, if the Judges opinion must rule the Verdict, the Tryal by Jury would be useless.' Yet in many Instances, 1 Lev. 9,[115] T. Jones 163,[116] St. tr. 10. 416,[117] where contrary to Evidence the Jury have found the Prisoner guilty, their Verdict hath been mercifully set aside, and a new Tryal granted by the Court of Kings Bench: for in such Case as hath been said, it cannot be set right by Attaint. But there hath yet been no Instance of granting a new Tryal, where the Prisoner was acquitted upon the first. 2. Hawk. 442."[118]

4. Black. 431.[119] The establishment of New Tryals, with the abolition of feodal Tenures, and the Act of Navigation, came out of the Times of Confusion.

5. Rep. 104.[120] Bakers Case. "Upon Evidence in an Ejectione firmæ between Middleton and Baker, it was resolved by the whole Court, that if the Plantiff in Evidence sheweth any matter in Writing, or of Record, or any Sentence in the ecclesiastical Court, upon which a Question in Law doth arise, and the Defendant offereth to demurr in Law upon it, the Plantiff cannot refuse to join in Demurrer, but he

---

[113] Thomas Smith, *Commonwealth of England and Manner of Government Thereof* 203 (London, 1640).

[114] 2 Hale, *Pleas of the Crown* 313: "And to say the truth, it were the most unhappy case that could be to the judge, if he at his peril must take upon him the guilt or innocence of the prisoner, and if the judge's opinion must rule the matter of fact, the trial by jury would be useless."

[115] Rex v. Read, 1 Lev. 9, 83 Eng. Rep. 271 (K.B. 1661): No new trial in the event of an acquittal.

[116] Rex v. Smith, T. Jones 163, 84 Eng. Rep. 1197 (K.B. 1682): Verdict of guilty, against the judge's direction, set aside and new trial awarded.

[117] Ashley v. Simons the Jew, 10 State Trials 411 (K.B. 1752); reported also from MS *sub nom.* Rex v. Simonds, 5 Bacon, *Abridgment* 243. The facts appear in No. 59, note 180.

[118] 2 Hawkins, *Pleas of the Crown* 442: "[I]t hath been adjudged, That if the Jury acquit a Prisoner of an Indictment of Felony against manifest Evidence, the Court may, before the Verdict is recorded, but not after, order them to go out again and reconsider the Matter; but this is by many thought hard, and seems not of late Years to have been so frequently practiced as formerly."

[119] 4 Blackstone, *Commentaries* *431.

[120] Baker's Case, 5 Co. Rep. 104a, 77 Eng. Rep. 216 (Q.B. 1600). Quotation marks supplied.

ought to join in the Demurrer or waive his Evidence. So if the Plantiff produceth Witnesses to prove any matter in Fact, upon which a Question in Law doth arise, if the Defendant admitteth their Testimony to be true, there also the Defendant may demurr in Law upon it, but then he ought to admit the Evidence given by the Plantiff to be true; and the Reason hereof is, *that matter in Law shall not be put to Laymen.* So may the Plantiff demurr upon the Defendants Evidence, mutatis mutandis; But if Evidence be given for the King, in Information or other suit, and the Defendant offer to demurr upon it, the Kings Council are not tied to join in Demurrer, but in such Case *the Court ought to direct the Jury to find the Special matter, and upon that they shall adjudge the Law* as it appeareth 34. H. 8. Dyer 53.[121] But that is by the Kings Prerogative who also may waive a Demurrer, and take issue at his Pleasure quod Nota."

Mem. every Thing that is said by the Court to the Jury, is uniformly styled in our Books a Direction. So the Court give a Charge to the grand Jury to present a particular offence, &c. But the Question is whether the Jury are bound, in Point of Conscience, or of Law, to observe that Direction and find according to it? Are they subject to any Penalty, or Fine, or Imprisonment, or corporal Punishment, if they find contrary to that Direction? No Man will say that they are.[122]

Question. Whether Ind[ebitatus] Ass[umpsit] may be maintained for "Sundries" or "Sundry Goods Wares and Merchandizes," or "sundry Goods Chattells and Articles," without any Account or Schedule of Particulars annexed to the Writ, or enumerated in the Declaration. Saunders 69. Peacock vs. Bell & Kendal, 70, 71.

"Ind. fuisset pred. Ri. and Ben. in £39 L.M." "Pro *diversis Merchandizis et Mercimoniis,* per pred. Ri. and Ben. eidem Johanni Peacock, ad Specialem instanciam et Requisitionem ipsius Jo. Peacock, ante Tempus i[llud] vendit et deliberat. Et sic &c."[123]

---

[121] Rex v. Muschampt, Dyer 52b, 53a, 73 Eng. Rep. 116 (Exch. 1543): Information for maintenance and buying of pretended titles. "[T]he Court charged the jury to enquire of the whole matter, and to find it, and upon such finding the Court would adjudge upon the law."

[122] The state of the MS suggests that this paragraph was written at a later time than the one which precedes it. The observations are apparently original with JA.

[123] Peacock v. Bell and Kendal, 1 Saund. 69, 71, 85 Eng. Rep. 81, 82 (K.B. 1667). Quotation marks supplied. "[Peacock] was indebted to the said Richard [Bell] and Benjamin [Kendal] for £39 lawful money . . . for divers merchandises and wares which the said Richard and Benjamin had before that time sold and delivered to the same John Peacock at his special instance and request." There is

2. Instructor cler. 161, 2. "If one be indebted unto another upon simple Contract, and the Plantiff sue for it upon a Promise to pay it, he must shew how the first Debt grew due and for what; as upon an Ind[ebitatus] Ass[umpsit] where the Debt is the Consideration of the Promise." [124]

Sed Vid. [...] [125] is not said how particular you must be. See 2. Ins. Cler. 157 a Declaration for diverse Merchandizes sold and deliverd. [126]

III. ADAMS' DIARY NOTES ON THE RIGHT OF JURIES [127]

1771. Feby. 12.

At a Time, when the Barriers against Popery, erected by our Ancestors, are suffered to be destroyed, to the hazard even of the Protestant Religion: When the system of the civil Law which has for so many Ages and Centuries, been withstood by the People of England, is permitted to become fashionable: When so many Innovations are introduced, to the Injury of our Constitution of civil Government: it is not surprizing that the great Securities of the People, should be invaded, and their fundamental Rights, drawn into Question. While the People of all the other great Kingdoms in Europe, have been insidiously deprived of their Liberties, it is not unnatural to expect that such as are interested to introduce Arbitrary Government should see with Envy, Detestation and Malice, the People of the British Empire, by their Sagacity and Valour defending theirs, to the present Times.

There is nothing to distinguish the Government of Great Britain, from that [of] France, or of Spain, but the Part which the People are by the Constitution appointed to take, in the passing and Execution of Laws. Of the Legislature, the People constitute one essential Branch—And while they hold this Power, unlimited, and exercise it frequently, as they ought, no Law can be made and continue long in Force that is inconvenient, hurtful, or disagreable to the Mass of the society. No Wonder then, that attempts are made, to deprive the Freeholders of America and of the County of Middlesex, of this troublesome Power, so dangerous to Tyrants and so disagreable to all who

---

dictum in the report that the declaration as here set out was faulty for failure to allege where the goods had been sold and delivered.

[124] Gardiner, *Instructor Clericalis* 161–162. Quotation marks supplied.

[125] This is a marginal note, with a tear in the MS.

[126] Gardiner, *Instructor Clericalis* 157. The declaration there set out does not allege the place where the goods were delivered.

[127] 2 JA, *Diary and Autobiography* 3–5. As to the genesis of this material, see *id.* at 5 note.

have Vanity enough to call themselves the better Sort.—In the Administration of Justice too, the People have an important Share. Juries are taken by Lot or by Suffrage from the Mass of the People, and no Man can be condemned of Life, or Limb, or Property or Reputation, without the Concurrence of the Voice of the People.

As the Constitution requires, that, the popular Branch of the Legislature, should have an absolute Check so as to put a peremptory Negative upon every Act of the Government, it requires that the common People should have as compleat a Controul, as decisive a Negative, in every Judgment of a Court of Judicature. No Wonder then that the same restless Ambition, of aspiring Minds, which is endeavouring to lessen or destroy the Power of the People in Legislation, should attempt to lessen or destroy it, in the Execution of Lawes. The Rights of Juries and of Elections, were never attacked singly in all the English History. The same Passions which have disliked one have detested the other, and both have always been exploded, mutilated or undermined together.

The british Empire has been much allarmed, of late Years, with Doctrines concerning Juries, their Powers and Duties, which have been said in Printed Papers and Pamphlets to have been delivered from the highest Trybunals of Justice. Whether these Accusations are just or not, it is certain that many Persons are misguided and deluded by them, to such a degree, that we often hear in Conversation Doctrines advanced for Law, which if true, would render Juries a mere Ostentation and Pagentry and the Court absolute Judges of Law and fact. It cannot therefore be an unseasonable Speculation to examine into the real Powers and Duties of Juries, both in Civil and Criminal Cases, and to discover the important Boundary between the Power of the Court and that of the Jury, both in Points of Law and of Fact.

Every intelligent Man will confess that Cases frequently occur, in which it would be very difficult for a Jury to determine the Question of Law. Long Chains of intricate Conveyances; obscure, perplext and embarrassed Clauses in Writings: Researches into remote Antiquity, for Statutes, Records, Histories, judicial Decisions, which are frequently found in foreign Languages, as Latin and French, which may be all necessary to be considered, would confound a common Jury and a decision by them would be no better than a Decision by Lott. And indeed Juries are so sensible of this and of the great Advantages the Judges have [to] determine such Questions, that, as the Law has given them the Liberty of finding the facts specially and

praying the Advice of the Court in the Matter of Law, they very seldom neglect to do it when recommended to them, or when in any doubt of the Law. But it will by no Means follow from thence, that they are under any legal, or moral or divine Obligation to find a Special Verdict where they themselves are in no doubt of the Law.

The Oath of a Juror in England, is to determine Causes "according to your Evidence"—In this Province "according to Law and the Evidence given you." It will be readily agreed that the Words of the Oath at Home, imply all that is expressed by the Words of the Oath here. And whenever a general Verdict is found, it assuredly determines both the Fact and the Law.

It was never yet disputed, or doubted, that a general Verdict, given *under the Direction of the Court* in Point of Law, was a legal Determination of the Issue. Therefore the Jury have a Power of deciding an Issue upon a general Verdict. And if they have, is it not an Absurdity to suppose that the Law would oblige them to find a Verdict according to the Direction of the Court, against their own Opinion, Judgment and Conscience.

[It] has already been admitted to be most advisable for the Jury to find a Special Verdict where they are in doubt of the Law. But, this is not often the Case—1000 Cases occur in which the Jury would have no doubt of the Law, to one, in which they would be at a Loss. The general Rules of Law and common Regulations of Society, under which ordinary Transactions arrange themselves, are well enough known to ordinary Jurors. The great Principles of the Constitution, are intimately known, they are sensibly felt by every Briton—it is scarcely extravagant to say, they are drawn in and imbibed with the Nurses Milk and first Air.

Now should the Melancholly Case arise, that the Judges should give their Opinions to the Jury, against one of these fundamental Principles, is a Juror obliged to give his Verdict generally according to this Direction, or even to find the fact specially and submit the Law to the Court. Every Man of any feeling or Conscience will answer, no. It is not only his right but his Duty in that Case to find the Verdict according to his own best Understanding, Judgment and Conscience, tho in Direct opposition to the Direction of the Court.

A religious Case might be put of a Direction against a divine Law.

The English Law obliges no Man to decide a Cause upon Oath against his own Judgment, nor does it oblige any Man to take any Opinion upon Trust, or to pin his faith on the sleve of any mere Man.

F. *Property*

13. Prout v. Minot

1761–1766

EDITORIAL NOTE

Although there was no court of equity in provincial Massachusetts, the law courts were able to develop the real estate mortgage into an effective and flexible instrument of finance. In the usual transaction the mortgagor gave the mortgagee an obligation in the form of a bond or note for the amount borrowed; this obligation was secured by the mortgage itself, a deed to the mortgaged premises in fee simple, conditioned on the repayment of the sum covered by the obligation. Both the liability of the land and the general personal liability of the mortgagor were thus established. In the event of default the mortgagee could bring an action on either obligation or mortgage, but he could proceed only at law.[1] If common law forms had been followed literally in these suits, injustice might have resulted. In some cases at least, the plaintiff could have recovered both land and money, and, in an action on a sealed obligation such as a bond, payment other than according to the precise terms of the instrument would not have been a bar. Further, the common law did not recognize the mortgagor's right, protected by the court of equity in England, to redeem the lands by tender of the debt and costs after the time for payment had run.[2]

Such defects might have discouraged potential borrowers from offering their lands as security, had it not been for a Massachusetts Act of 1698 which gave the common-law courts the equity powers necessary to overcome them. Under the statute in actions brought on sealed instruments and on mortgages when judgment or verdict was for the plaintiff, the court was empowered "to moderate the rigour of the law and on consideration of such cases, according to equity and good conscience to chancer the forfeiture, and enter up judgment for the just debt and damages." In real

---

[1] Even today a mortgage may be given without a note, thus freeing the mortgagor from personal liability. Dual liability is the general rule, however, as it was both in Massachusetts and England in the 18th century. See note 6 below. See also Symes v. Hill, Adams Papers, Microfilms, Reel No. 185, Quincy, *Reports* 318 (SCJ Middlesex, 1771); Ivers v. Hooper, et al., 4 Dane, *Abridgment* 184 (SJC Essex, 1801); Charles A. Jackson, *A Treatise on the Pleadings and Practice in Real Actions* 50–51 (Boston, 1828); Garrard Glenn, *Mortgages, Deeds of Trust and Other Security Devices as to Land*, 1:25–28 (Charlottesville, Va., and N.Y., 1943).

[2] As to the nonavailability of the equitable defenses of payment and accord and satisfaction at common law, see James Barr Ames, *Lectures on Legal History* 109–111 (Cambridge, Mass., 1913). As to the equity of redemption, see 1 Glenn, *Mortgages* 11–17, 234–313; R. W. Turner, *The Equity of Redemption, passim* (Cambridge, 1931).

actions on mortgages the judgment was "to be conditional,—that the mortgager or vender, or his heirs, executors or administrators do pay unto the plaintiff such sum as the court shall determin to be justly due thereupon, within two months time after judgment entred up for discharging of such mortgage or sale, or that the plaintiff recover possession of the estate sued for, and execution to be awarded for the same." [3] By the same Act, "where any mortgagee or vendee of any houses or lands granted on condition hath recovered, or entred into and taken possession of the same for the condition broken," the mortgagor within three years after entry could tender the unpaid balance and costs and disbursements in court and have possession restored by quitclaim deed from the mortgagee or a purchaser, or by judgment.[4]

Thus, under the statute if the mortgagee sued upon his bond, he could recover the actual debt, but not the penalty of double the face value usually attached to such instruments; moreover, the debtor presumably was credited with any partial satisfaction which he had made. If the mortgagee wished to proceed against the land, he might either enter peaceably, or sue for it in ejectment, asserting his title under the mortgage deed. In the latter event he could enter under a judgment in his favor if the mortgagor did not pay the debt within two months. In either case the mortgagee's title became absolute if the mortgagor did not redeem within three years after entry. This was the process of strict foreclosure, still substantially in effect in Massachusetts. It resembled the procedure at equity in England, with the significant difference that there the court had unlimited discretion to open up the foreclosure for redemption if justice required.[5]

There was the further difference that in England, if the mortgagee re-

---

[3] Act of 10 Dec. 1698, c. 22, §1, 1 A&R 356. See Watts v. Hasey, *Quincy, Reports* 194 (SCJ Suffolk, Aug. 1765). This statute was the first to provide specifically for mortgages, although after 1648 the judges of the Court of Assistants in the Massachusetts Bay Colony had had power to determine "any matter of apparent equitie, as upon the forfeiture of an Obligation, breach of Covenant without damage, or the like." *The Laws and Liberties of Massachusetts* 32 (Cambridge, Mass., 1929). Under this act the court would "chancery" a bond, presumably to the actual amount of the debt. See, for example, Bennet v. Gridley (1677), *Records of the Court of Assistants of the Colony of Massachusetts Bay, 1630–1692*, 1:82 (Boston, ed. John Noble, 1901); Dyre v. Hutchinson (1684), *id.* at 261. After 1692 in several Province Acts, rejected by the Privy Council on various grounds, the common-law judges were given power to chancer penal bonds. See, for example, Act of 25 Nov. 1692, c. 33, §14, 1 A&R 75. Relief on penal bonds was accorded at law in England by 8 & 9 Will. 3, c. 11, §8 (1698). See Samuel Williston and George J. Thompson, *A Treatise on the Law of Contracts*, §§774, 775 (Boston, rev. edn., 1936).

[4] Act of 10 Dec. 1698, c. 22, §§4, 5, 1 A&R 357, as amended by Act of 25 March 1713, c. 8, §2, 1 A&R 703.

[5] For the present Massachusetts provisions, which carry forward without substantial change much of the Act of 1698, see Mass. G.L., c. 244, §§1–10, 18–36. Foreclosure may also be had by sale when the mortgage contains a power of sale. *Id.* at §§11–17c. The Massachusetts courts now have broad equitable powers, but the essentially equitable remedy given at law by these statutes is deemed adequate, except in unusual cases. See 1 Glenn, *Mortgages* 435. For the English practice of opening up a foreclosure for redemption, see *id.* at 403–405.

covered the land through foreclosure, a subsequent action against the mortgagor on his personal obligation opened up the right to redeem, although the land might be worth less than the debt. The cases are not clear, but there even seems to have been some 18th-century authority for the proposition that foreclosure barred an action on the bond altogether, unless the premises had been sold by the mortgagee. In England and in many of the United States, these problems were ultimately met by the device of foreclosure by sale, the usual modern practice, in which on a bill to foreclose the court will order a sale of the property and adjudge any deficiency against the mortgagor, but will allow him to take a surplus.[6] *Prout v. Minot* shows that, although provincial Massachusetts had not developed foreclosure by sale, the courts were able to accommodate the conflict between recovery on the land and recovery on the debt through flexible use of the statutory procedures just discussed.

The case arose out of a complicated series of transactions. Timothy Prout borrowed £100 from Christopher Minot in December 1753, giving a mortgage of his real estate on Milk Street in Boston and a bond in the penal sum of £200 to secure the loan. In October 1755 Prout gave a second bond and mortgage on the same property to one William Brown for a loan of £184. Two years later Brown foreclosed in an action on the second mortgage and was awarded possession in December 1757. In December 1758 Minot assigned to Brown his rights in Prout's first bond and mortgage for a consideration of £112, the sum of the principal and unpaid interest. Brown, having rid himself of this encumbrance, was apparently content with his bargain until the house on the mortgaged premises was destroyed in the great fire of March 1760, which significantly reduced the value of his investment.[7]

---

[6] For the development of foreclosure by sale, see 1 Glenn, *Mortgages* 405–407, 460–467. The Massachusetts practice of sale under a power of sale in the mortgage, also utilized in England and elsewhere, achieves similar results. *Id.* at 433–434, 610–614. See note 5 above. As to the action on the bond after foreclosure, it was first held that since a mortgage was a pledge, the mortgagee had to be content with the land while he held it, but that if he sold it and it produced a deficiency he could proceed on his bond. Tooke v. Hartley, Dickens 785, 21 Eng. Rep. 476 (Ch. 1784). Later the position was reversed and an action on the bond permitted only before sale, on the theory that since the action opened the right to redeem, the mortgagee could bring it only if he was still capable of reconveying the premises to the redeeming mortgagor. Perry v. Barker, 8 Ves. Jun. 527, 32 Eng. Rep. 459 (Ch. 1803); Lockhart v. Hardy, 9 Beav. 349, 50 Eng. Rep. 378 (Ch. 1846); see Dashwood v. Blythway, 1 Eq. Cas. Abr. 317, 21 Eng. Rep. 1072 (1729). If there had been provision for the award of a surplus of the sale proceeds over the debt to the mortgagor, these problems need not have arisen. See John J. Powell, *A Treatise on the Law of Mortgages*, 2:1001–1006 (London, 6th edn., T. Coventry, 1826). Even without such a provision, they did not arise in Massachusetts. See note 15 below.

[7] For the facts, see Doc. II and SF 100777. The lot, on the northerly side of Milk Street, and bounded by lands belonging to Andrew Oliver Jr. and Joseph Dowse, measured about 63 × 128 × 48 × 138 feet. *Ibid.* Brown's foreclosure action is in Min. Bk., Inf. Ct. Suffolk, Oct. 1757, No. 44. No files have been located. The fire of 20 March 1760 destroyed 349 houses and other buildings in the area bounded by the present Washington, State, and Milk streets, and the waterfront (Commercial

At the July 1761 Suffolk Inferior Court an action of debt on the first bond was commenced against Prout in Minot's name, a procedure made necessary by the common-law rule against assignments of "choses in action," that is, rights legally accrued but not reduced to possession. That Brown, rather than Minot, was the real party in interest seems certain from the fact that the instrument by which the bond was assigned gave the former power to sue upon it and keep the proceeds. At the April 1762 term, after argument on the pleadings, the court held Prout's plea in confession and avoidance bad and awarded Minot "chancery" of £136 6s., the actual amount of the debt plus interest.[8]

Prout appealed to the Superior Court, where at the August 1762 term argument was again had on the lower court pleadings. Prout's plea, which had been filed by Oxenbridge Thacher, averred Minot's assignment of bond and mortgage to Brown, and alleged that on the day of the assignment Brown had elected to enter upon the premises for nonpayment of the sum secured, rather than to sue upon the bond. Minot's replication, by Richard Dana, denied that the entry was for nonpayment as alleged. Thacher demurred, asserting that the replication contained a negative pregnant (a denial of a particular allegation which implicitly admits the rest). Dana, joined by Jeremy Gridley, countered by attacking the plea, a permissible tactic at common law, because a demurrer at any stage made all of the pleadings fair game for either side. The ground of the attack was that Brown's election was not a bar to the action, since an entry under the

Street), extending along the latter to the South Battery, near the corner of present Broad Street and Atlantic Avenue. No lives were lost, but damage was estimated at £100,000 sterling. Drake, *History and Antiquities of Boston* 649–653. As to compensation for the sufferers, see note 21 below. For the consequences of a later fire, see No. 33.

[8] For authorities on the assignability of choses in action, see notes 23, 24, below. The bond and Inferior Court judgment are in SF 100777. The reasons for Brown's proceeding on Minot's bond, rather than on his own, are not known but may include the following: Brown had entered under the judgment on his own mortgage in Dec. 1757, so that the process of foreclosure was complete in Dec. 1760, before he had brought suit. If the English theory which deemed recovery on the bond tantamount to redemption (see note 6 above) were observed in Massachusetts he may have feared that, since under the local statute redemption was absolutely barred, he would not now be allowed to recover on the bond. Further, even if the court had permitted such a recovery, it might also have permitted redemption, and Brown, for reasons unconnected with the land's present market value, may have wished to retain possession. Even if the court had denied redemption because the land was worth less than the debt, it might have allowed Prout to set off the value of the foreclosure in "chancery," limiting Brown's total recovery to the face value of his bond. A suit on Minot's bond was not subject to these drawbacks. Although Brown, being already in possession, could be said to have "entered" peaceably under Minot's mortgage on the day he took the assignment, this entry would not ripen into a foreclosure until Dec. 1761. Since the right to redeem was still open, there was no bar to recovery. Redemption was not a danger, however, because Brown as junior mortgagee could effectively block it on the grounds that the mortgagor was primarily liable for the debt to the first mortgagee and thus had a duty to save the land harmless (see note 13 below). Finally, since the foreclosure was not yet ripe, there was no recovery that could be set off against this bond.

mortgage did not discharge the bond. The court in a unanimous opinion upheld this contention and found the plea bad. Prout, however, was not content with the usual procedure by which the court chancered the bond to the debt appearing in the record. He asked for and was granted leave to be heard further "in chancery" at the next term.[9]

Accordingly, he filed a "Bill in Chancery" (Document I), at the February 1763 session of the court, setting forth the facts and praying relief from what he urged was an inequitable double recovery in Brown's behalf. The matter was continued term by term until it finally came on in August 1766. Samuel Fitch now argued for Prout against Dana and Gridley. Adams was not of counsel, but made brief minutes of the argument and opinion, which are printed as Document II.

Fitch produced authorities to show that assignments of choses in action are invalid at law but convey a right which the assignee alone can enforce in equity. His point seems to have been that since this was in effect an equitable proceeding, the court should treat Brown as the real party in interest, even though the action was in Minot's name. This position could have been the basis for an argument that Brown should not recover because he did not have a claim to the bond which a court of equity would recognize. His acquisition of the mortgagee's title by assignment after he had acquired the mortgagor's equity through foreclosure could be said to have effected a merger which extinguished the debt. Adams' notes do not show whether Fitch pressed such a contention, but he must at least have argued that if Brown had an equitable claim, his entry on the land had satisfied it, and there could be no recovery in his behalf against the bond. Implicit in these positions was the basic equitable argument, expressly made in Prout's bill (Document I), that, even if merger and entry were not absolute bars, the action should not lie because at the time of entry the land had been worth more than both bonds together.

According to Adams, Gridley "Seem'd to conceed" that the action was really in Brown's behalf, probably because there were ample grounds on which to argue that he was not barred. The court apparently found these grounds adequate, since, despite the concession, it entered judgment against Prout for £176 10s., the principal of the bond, with 6 percent interest from the date of the last payment in 1756.[10]

Although it is not clear that the merger argument was raised, the result in this case is consistent with later authority on the question. In 1849 Chief Justice Shaw of Massachusetts, in an opinion synthesizing earlier English and American decisions, announced the proposition that a merger of the

---

[9] SCJ Rec. 1766, fol. 78; Min. Bk. 79, SCJ Suffolk, Aug. 1762, N–8; SF 100777. The 1762 argument and pleadings are reported *sub nom.* Minot v. Prout, Quincy, *Reports* 9. Compare Burnell v. Martin, 2 Doug. 417, 99 Eng. Rep. 268 (K.B. 1780). As to the negative pregnant, see Stephen, *Pleading* 381–384; No. 9. For the rule that on demurrer the court will look to the whole record, see Stephen, *Pleading* 162–164.

[10] SCJ Rec. 1766, fol. 78; Min. Bk. 81, SCJ Suffolk, Aug. 1766, C–1. For the computation of interest, see the bond in SF 100777.

equity and the mortgage takes place when the purchaser of the mortgage is under a duty to clear the equity from the encumbrance, or, in the absence of such a duty, the purchaser has no proper interest in keeping mortgage and equity separate.[11] Under this theory one who purchases the equity of redemption at its actual value and then takes an assignment of the mortgage cannot maintain an action on the obligation against the mortgagor, because the gist of the purchaser's bargain is that, having bought the equity for less than the full value of the land, he will pay the rest of the price by indemnifying the mortgagor against the debt. This he does either by paying to the mortgagee the amount due, or by allowing the land to be taken in satisfaction. He is doing no more than fulfilling his bargain when he pays the mortgagee for an assignment. It would be inequitable if he could also recover the amount so paid against the mortgagor personally, because he would end up with clear title, but would be out of pocket only what he had bargained to pay for an encumbered title.[12]

Brown, however, did not purchase the equity outright, but obtained it only in an effort to satisfy the mortgagor's debt to him. The bargain out of which that debt arose was that Brown should get back the money which he had loaned, not that he should become obligated to pay out further sums. Thus, when Brown bought the first mortgage, he was not performing a contractual duty to the mortgagor, but was acting to protect his own investment from the effects of the mortgagor's default. Since he had not bargained to pay the debt, it would have been inequitable if he could not have recovered what he had paid out both on his own loan to Prout and for the assignment from Minot.[13] If the value of the land had been

[11] Brown v. Lapham, 3 Cush. (Mass.) 551 (1849). For earlier American cases basing merger on the purchaser's duty, see Tice v. Annin, 2 Johns. Ch. (N.Y.) 125 (1816); Eaton v. George, 2 N.H. 300 (1820). These cases cite no authority. They are in effect a particular application of the interest theory, since if the purchaser has a duty to redeem, equity would not recognize as valid a contrary interest in pursuing the mortgage. See Gibson v. Crehore, 3 Pick. (Mass.) 475 (1826); Gardner v. Astor, 3 Johns. Ch. (N.Y.) 53 (1817); compare Bassett v. Mason, 18 Conn. 131 (1846). The latter cases, which are based on interest, rely on English authority espousing the general equitable doctrine that where the holder of any equitable charge on an estate acquires the legal title, there will be a merger, unless the party has a valid interest in preserving the equitable title, usually for protection against intervening interests. See Forbes v. Moffatt, 18 Ves. Jun. 384, 390, 34 Eng. Rep. 362, 364 (Ch. 1811); Powell v. Morgan, 2 Vern. 90, 23 Eng. Rep. 668 (Ch. 1688); Thomas v. Kemeys, 2 Vern. 348, 352, 354, 23 Eng. Rep. 821, 822–823 (Ch. 1697); compare 15 Viner, *Abridgment* 369.

[12] See 2 Glenn, *Mortgages* 1159–1160; George E. Osborne, *Handbook on the Law of Mortgages* 770–771 (St. Paul, 1951); Tice v. Annin, 2 Johns. Ch. (N.Y.) 125 (1816); Lydon v. Campbell, 198 Mass. 29 (1908). Compare Darcy v. Hall, 1 Vern. 49, 23 Eng. Rep. 302 (Ch. 1682).

[13] Although few cases in point have been found, modern authorities agree that a second mortgagee can insist that, as between himself and the mortgagor, the latter rather than the land shall bear primary liability for the mortgage debt, on the theory that the second mortgagee has received no reduction as consideration for the prior encumbrance. See A. James Casner, ed., *American Law of Property*, vol. 4, §16.127 (Boston, 1952); Osborne, *Mortgages* 697; Herbert T. Tiffany, *The Law of Real Property*, 5:371 (Chicago, 3d edn., 1939); Glenn, "Purchasing Subject to

sufficient to provide this recovery, there still would have been a merger, because Brown would have had no valid interest in preserving the obligation. If there was a deficiency, however, the obligation would survive as a basis for action against the mortgagor.[14]

Adams' notes show that the court did deal with the question of recovery against the bond after recovery of the land. Justice Benjamin Lynde apparently recalled the court's earlier ruling on demurrer that an entry under the mortgage did not bar an action on the bond. The result here carried the principle further, asserting the mortgagee's right not only to pursue both remedies, but to take satisfaction out of both sources up to the amount of the debt. The complexities of English practice were rejected in favor of a simple rule, focused on the debt rather than the security, which was characteristic of later American mortgage law.[15]

Mortgage. First Phase: Mortgagor's Rights Against Grantee," 27 *Va. L. Rev.* 853, 855 (1941). Compare Samuel Carter, *Lex Vadiorum* 100–103 (London, 2d edn., 1728). In holding that even where a second mortgagee had assumed the senior mortgage debt by express agreement, the senior mortgagee could not join him as defendant in a deficiency suit, the Court of Appeals of New York stated as a general proposition underlying this result that "Where a party, taking from his debtor a lien on property subject to prior liens, assumes and pays them off, he is certainly entitled to add the amounts so paid to his original debt; the payments, though made in pursuance of his agreement, are made for the benefit of the debtor, and upon his debts, and to protect him and his property." Garnsey v. Rogers, 47 N.Y. 233, 240 (1872). In Bassett v. Mason, 18 Conn. 131 (1846), however, the court held the mortgagor entitled to an injunction barring a junior mortgagee who had foreclosed his own mortgage and then had bought in two prior encumbrances from suing on the note secured by the first mortgage. This result may be reconcilable with *Prout.* Although the Connecticut court seems to have assumed that the land was worth less than the face value of the encumbrances, the amounts which the mortgagee actually paid for them do not appear and may well have been less than the land value. If the cases are not reconcilable, *Prout* is more consistent with the general principles of strict foreclosure. In *Bassett* the court seems to have based its conclusion that the land was the primary fund for payment of the debt upon New York cases, cited by counsel, in which the junior encumbrancer had acquired his title by buying in at his own foreclosure sale, rather than through entry and foreclosure. 18 Conn. 131, at 134, 137. See Cox v. Wheeler, 7 Paige 248 (N.Y. Ch. 1838); McKinstry v. Curtis, 10 Paige 503 (N.Y. Ch. 1844). A similar result has been reached in a modern view, on the theory that by virtue of the conditions of sale the junior encumbrancer in such a situation is like any other purchaser and so agrees that the land will be primarily liable. See Osborne, *Mortgages* 768–769. Compare text at note 12 above.

[14] In Bassett v. Mason, note 13 above, the court indicated that it would have found no merger if the value of the land had been less than the note sued upon.

[15] See Amory v. Fairbanks, 3 Mass. 562 (1793); Coit v. Fitch, 1 Kirby (Conn.) 254 (Super. Ct. 1787); 1 Glenn, *Mortgages* 436–437. Since 1836, a Massachusetts statute has provided that if the mortgagee recovers on a deficiency after foreclosure, the right to redeem is reopened for a year. Mass. G.L., c. 244, §35. Later construction of this Act indicates that it created a right not previously known at common law. Fennyery v. Ransom, 170 Mass. 303, 49 N.E. 620 (1898). It has not given rise to the difficulties about deficiency suits found in England. See note 6 above; compare Ely v. Ely, 6 Gray (Mass.) 439 (1856). By Act of 1818, now Mass. G.L., c. 244, §36, it was provided that a mortgagor could recover a surplus in an action at law. Presumably at common law any surplus was a windfall to the mortgagee. Thus,

The questions whether Prout's personal obligation survived in Brown's hands and, if it did, whether Brown could pursue it despite his entry under the mortgage, both turned on the value of the land. If this figure exceeded the amount of the debt, Prout's complaint was justified and Brown should have been barred. If there was a deficiency, however, it was equitable for Prout to be responsible for all of his indebtedness. The total of principal and interest on the two debts was at least £481.[16] Prout alleged in his bill (Document I) that in 1758, when Brown entered, the premises were worth more than the debt, but the only figures which he set forth were 1760 values of £200 for the house and "at least" £133 6s. 8d. for the land. Accepting these figures and adding in Prout's figures of £50 for rent at £20 a year from Brown's first entry in December 1757 until the fire in March 1760, there would still have been a deficiency of nearly £100.[17] Thus, even by Prout's calculations, Brown was entitled to recover against the bond, and the only question open was the amount. The court's actual award of £176, the maximum possible on the bond, was probably based on the value of the land after the fire, when the deficiency would have been nearly £300. This valuation seems harsh from Prout's standpoint, but it could have been justified by the fact that Brown's title was subject to Prout's right to redeem until December 1761. It might have been argued that in the determination of a deficiency the mortgagee's interest cannot fairly be valued until foreclosure is complete and his title is absolute in equity as well as at law.[18]

---

the mortgagor could not ordinarily open the foreclosure merely because of a surplus. See John J. Powell, *Mortgages* 457–461 (London, 1st edn., 1785).

[16] As to the right of the assignee to interest, see Darcy v. Hall, 1 Vern. 49, 23 Eng. Rep. 302 (Ch. 1682); compare 1 Glenn, *Mortgages* 542–544. The sum might have been increased by a rule that interest paid by the assignee to the mortgagee could be asserted as principal (and so itself subject to interest) against the mortgagor. Under the English rule this could not be done without the consent of the mortgagor, but it was done without consent in a later Massachusetts case. See Swinerton v. Fuller, 4 Dane, *Abridgment* 185 (SJC Essex, 1792); compare *id.* at 176; Carter, *Lex Vadiorum* 108–110.

[17] By the Massachusetts Act of 1698, note 4 above, the mortgagee was required to account for rents and profits on redemption. It has been assumed that the successor of this statute, Mass. G.L., c. 244, §20, is equally applicable in a suit on a deficiency. See Hadley Falls Trust Co. v. United States, 22 F. Supp. 346, 352 (D. Mass. 1938), reversed on other grounds, 110 F. 2d 887 (1st Cir. 1940).

[18] The Massachusetts courts have held that foreclosure is not complete until the three-year redemption period has run, and have stated that the value of the land for purposes of deficiency is to be taken as of that time, West v. Chamberlin, 8 Pick. (Mass.) 336 (1829); McLaughlin v. Cosgrove, 99 Mass. 4 (1868); Morse v. Merritt, 110 Mass. 458 (1872). In one early case, however, in which a barn on the mortgaged property was destroyed after entry, although in determining a deficiency the property was appraised after the time for redemption had run, the value of the barn was included in the appraisal. Amory v. Fairbanks, 3 Mass. 562 (1793); SF 106460.

No. 13. Prout v. Minot

I. PROUT'S "BILL IN CHANCERY" [19]

Suffolk Superior Court, Boston, February 1763

Province of the } To the honble. his Majesty's justices of the
Massachusetts bay } Superior Court of judicature &ca. to be holden
Minot v. Prout } at Boston within and for the county of Suffolk
Bill in Chancery } on the third tuesday of February A.D. 1763

Humbly petitioning showeth Timothy Prout of Scarborough in the county of Cumberland Esqr.

1. That well and true it is that the said Timothy on the said tenth of December A.D. 1753 became bound unto the said Christopher Minot in the sum of two hundred pounds lawfull money of this province conditioned to pay the sum of one hundred pounds like money with lawfull interest on or before the tenth of December A.D. 1754. And the said Timothy as a collateral security to the said Christopher for payment of the same sum and interest by deed of mortgage bearing date the said tenth of December A.D. 1753 conveying to the said Christopher a certain messuage in Milk Street in Boston aforesaid bounded as in the same deed recorded in the registry of deeds in the said county of Suffolk copy whereof duly attested your orator hath ready to exhibit to hold to him the said Christopher and his heirs if the said sum of one hundred pounds and interest should not be paid.

2. That afterwards your orator upon the first of October A.D. 1755 became bound unto one William Brown of Beverly in the county of Essex Esqr. in a penal sum conditioned for the payment of the sum of one hundred and eighty four pounds lawfull money and interest on or before the first of October A.D. 1756 and more fully to secure to the said William the payment of the Same sum and interest according to the tenor of the same condition your said orator on the day of the date of the last mentioned bond and collateral thereto executed a deed of Mortgage to the same messuage and land which had before been mortgaged to the said Christopher to him the said William and in the same Mortgage expressly mentioned the said former mortgage made to the said Christopher as by a copy of the said mortgage made to the said William which the said Timothy hath ready to exhibit to this honorable court may appear.

[19] In an unidentified hand, signed and attested as shown in text. The paragraph numbers appear in the margin of the MS. SF 100777.

3. That afterwards the said William Brown put in suit the mortgage made by your orator to him as aforesaid and at the inferior court of common pleas held at Boston aforesaid on the first Tuesday of October A.D. 1757 recovered judgment for possession of the said mortgaged premises and cost of court taxed at three pounds fifteen shillings and five pence unless the said Timothy should pay the sum of two hundred and seven pounds lawfull money within two months from the rendring of the same judgment and the same sum not being paid the said William soon after the expiration of the said two months actually entred into the said mortgaged premises and became seised thereof in his demesne as of fee and hath ever since held and possessed the same and still does so and the cost aforesaid was paid by your orators attorney.

4. And your said orator further humbly suggests to your honors *that the said William* after he had actually entred into the said mortgaged premises as aforesaid *the better to strengthen his title thereto he on the thirteenth of December A.D. 1758 purchased of the said Christopher the prior mortgage aforesaid* and at the same time the obligation now sued on both which were in reality for one and the same debt and the said Christopher assigned them both to the said William.

5. And your said orator doth in fact affirm allege and say and is ready to prove that the said mortgaged premises were worth on the same thirteenth of December much more than the sums equitably due on both the mortgages aforesaid, that the said William reserving good part thereof in his own care rented the residue for twenty pounds a year lawfull money and the same William held himself well content with the said mortgaged premises in satisfaction of the same debts.

6.[20] Further after that on the twentieth of March A.D. 1760 the dwelling house on the said mortgag'd premises was burnt down the said William estimated his loss thereby at the sum of two hundred pounds lawfull money and actually made a claim to the committee for distributing the charitable contributions made for the sufferers by the said fire to be considered as suffering so much loss.[21]—That the said William sold the bricks in the ruins for six pounds lawfull money and the loft and land are worth at least the sum of one hundred and thirty three pounds six shillings and eight pence more.

[20] In the margin: "Quere."

[21] As to the fire, see note 7 above. A fund made up of sums appropriated by the General Court and donated by other provinces and private persons was given to the Selectmen and Overseers of the Poor for distribution among those who had suffered losses. See Drake, *History and Antiquities of Boston* 651–652.

7. And now after the said mortgage recovered on by the said William in his own name hath become irredeemable, and that the fire hath consumed the said house he the said William pursueth your orator in the name of the said Christopher on the said obligation given to the said Christopher and would compell the Entire payment of the same [notwithstanding] *that he hath in manner aforesaid received full satisfaction therefor contrary to equity and good conscience.*

And all these things your orator is ready to prove when your honors shall appoint wherefore in as much this suit is manifestly litigious your orator prayeth that the penalty of the said obligation which your honors on the pleadings in law have adjudged to be forfeited may be chancered down to the *sum of one penny and that* your orator's reasonable cost *may be decreed him.*   Tim. Prout Attorney to Tim. Prout Esqr.

Jany. 8 1763 fil'd in the Office.
Att. Nat. Hatch Cler.

II. ADAMS' MINUTES OF THE ARGUMENT [22]

Suffolk Superior Court, Boston, August 1766

Prout vs. Minot.

Fitch.

2 Vernon 539. 540. Payment to Obligee, after Notice of an Assignment is not good. The Assignee alone is entituled to the Money.[23]

Choses in Action are assignable in Equity, 'tho not in Law.

Jones's Reps. Page 223. 223. Lewis vs. Wallis.[24]

Tho the Action must be in the Name of Assignor, yet it is considered in Equity and even in Law, as the Property of the assignee.

The real Interest in the present Case is in Brown.

---

[22] In JA's hand. Adams Papers, Microfilms, Reel No. 185.

[23] Baldwin v. Billingsley, 2 Vern. 539, 23 Eng. Rep. 950 (Ch. 1705). Baldwin had borrowed £200 from a trust, giving the trustees a bond in that amount which recited the trust. The bond was delivered to Mrs. Billingsley, the beneficiary. Baldwin paid £100 to one of the trustees who gave him a receipt in the name of the trust, then absconded. The Lord Keeper ruled for Mrs. Billingsley, saying, *id.* at 540, "Mr. Baldwin ought to have been cautious how he paid the Money; it being in Equity the Money of *Billingsley,* as much as if the Bond had been assigned to her; and Payment to the Obligee after Notice of an Assignment is not good: In the Case of an Assignment of a Bond the Assignee alone becomes intitled to receive the Money."

[24] Lewis v. Wallis, T. Jones 222, 223, 84 Eng. Rep. 1228 (K.B. 1683), held that attachment in an action of debt did not lie against an asset assigned by the debtor to a third party.

Gridley. Seem'd to conceed.

Judge Lynde. The Court has determin'd that if the Land mortgaged is insufficient to pay the Debt, mortgagee may have recourse to his Bond, and may sue both, i.e. Bond and Mortgage.[25]

1753, Bond and Mortgage was given to Minot.

1755, Bond and Mortgage of the same Land was given to Brown.

After, Brown sued his Mortgage had Judgment and enterd on Possession and

After, Minots Mortgage was assignd to Brown.[26]

The great Fire in March 1760, burning the House occasiond this Dispute.

14. Keen v. Turner

1768–1769

EDITORIAL NOTE

This case and Nos. 18–21 reflect some of the legal problems arising from the dependence of the New England economy on running water as a source of industrial power. They fall into two categories: defendant either blocked a running stream entirely or so diverted the flow as to diminish the amount available to plaintiff; or defendant caused the stream to overflow plaintiff's land. Plaintiffs in both sorts of cases had first to prove a right to the water, the land, or, sometimes, both. Some of the Adams minutes are thus largely concerned with chain-of-title evidence. And, as in most provincial litigation, technical points of pleading were usually never far from the surface.

Like *Wilkins v. Fuller*, No. 20, the instant litigation arose from the flooding of plaintiff's meadow by back water from defendant's dam, this one being across Pudding Brook in Pembroke. Here, however, there was no pleading issue to delay the proceedings. The action was entered at the Plymouth Inferior Court in March 1768,[1] and was continued to July 1768 where, after a jury view of the land in question, Adams won a "Verdict for Defts." with costs, and a fee of 28s.[2] We have no Adams minutes of the Inferior Court trial, but Robert Treat Paine's notes include

[25] That is, the earlier decision of the court on this point at the Aug. 1762 term of the Superior Court. See text and note 9 above.

[26] Commas supplied in this and the preceding three paragraphs for clarity.

[1] The writ is endorsed "Otis," SF 142297, although Paine seems to have tried the action. A note on JA's list of cases for this term reads: "I have promised to be for Defts. Recd. 12s, Recd. 22s. Continued." JA, Docket, Adams Papers. Counsel of record in the SCJ were Paine and Otis for plaintiff, JA and Leonard for defendant. Min. Bk. 82, SCJ Plymouth, May 1769, N–2. See also Clark v. McCarney, p. 68 above.

[2] JA, Docket, Adams Papers.

the former's argument (Document I). Adams' own minutes (Document II) date from the Plymouth Superior Court, May 1769, where once again his clients won.[3]

I. PAINE'S MINUTES OF THE TRIAL[4]

Plymouth Inferior Court, July 1768

Mr. Adams. The grass was good till it was pastured and the bushes grew up; if the mill had not been built, his neglect would have filld up the natural Course and spoil'd the Meadow.

Why did not he bring his action in the time of it?[5]

He has no damages for what he bought 5 years ago.[6]

The fall of water. I knew a meadow. [...] Duke of Bridgwater's Cannel.[7]

II. ADAMS' MINUTES OF THE TRIAL[8]

Plymouth Superior Court, May 1769

Keen vs. Turner.

Keens Witnesses.

Ed. Thomas. Known Georges Meadow 30 Years. Carted the Grass 2 Years. It was a very good Piece of fresh Meadow. I went in with a full Team without miring. Last August I saw it. The Meadow very much altered. The Meadow wet. Ditching and clearing the Brook could not wholly prevent the Damage.

Wm. Cox. Deposition. Vid.[9]

Elisha Barker. Both Sides lay open to a Pasture 7 Years. Sold it since the Mill was built.[10] Liable to great freshets.[11] All a Pond. My

---

[3] SF 142297; Min. Bk. 82, SCJ Plymouth, May 1769, N–2; SCJ Rec. 1769, fol. 183. Costs were £13 8s. 10d.

[4] Paine Law Notes.

[5] The writ alleged the flooding to have commenced five years prior to 24 March 1768 (the date of the writ) and to have continued until that date. The applicable statute of limitations was five years. Act of 7 July 1740, 2 A&R 1020. Compare No. 20.

[6] Last two words unclear in MS.

[7] Francis Egerton, 3d Duke of Bridgwater (1736–1806), commissioned James Brindley (1716–1772) to construct a canal from Worsley to Manchester. The canal was one of the major engineering achievements of the century.

[8] In JA's hand. Adams Papers, Microfilms, Reel No. 185.

[9] This deposition is not in the file. "I hired it 2 or 3 yr. ago. 20 or 30 yr. ago. Good crops and good grass next to English." Paine Law Notes.

[10] On the significance of this evidence, see 2 Blackstone, *Commentaries* *403:

father who owned the Meadow consented to sett up this Mill. Mills 100 Years. Drand off 10. Apl.

Saml. Tayler. 1764, 5, 6. I got the Hay. One Year it Spoilt the Hay. I understood that Turner said he would stop his Mill one day. But at Night let it go.

Amos Witherel. Subject to freshits, the Water grows the Weeds. I cant tell whether, occasiond by the Mill.

Wm. Hetherd. Ditto.

Mr. Soper. Brook worn away. Meadow much damaged by the Water, coming repeatedly upon it.

Eliazer Hamlen. Boggy Land, bad fodder. Mill set agoing and I saw the Channell fill, and overflow the Meadow. Water has not so good a passage as it might have. Must dig lower than the Bottom of the Brook.

James Cox. The Brook not filled by the natural Stream.

Isaac Keen. Deposition. Vid.[12]

Fra. Keen. Deposition. Vid.[13]

Leonard. Our Witnesses. An unfavourable Case.

Coll. Turner. 1738, 9, 40, 41. I hird it. I was told I must be carefull and watch my Time. Once I went after a Rain and my Cocks [14] were half leg deep in Water. It is rather wetter, than it was when I cutt it. It was miry from End to End. A great deal more Grass now

---

"If a stream be unoccupied, I may erect a mill thereon, and detain the water; yet not so as to injure my neighbor's prior mill, or his meadow: for he hath by the first occupancy acquired a property in the current." Blackstone may not have accurately stated the English law. Compare Wiel, "Waters: American Law and French Authority," 33 *Harv. L. Rev.* 133 (1919), with Maass and Zobel, "Anglo-American Water Law: Who Appropriated the Riparian Doctrine?", 10 *Public Policy* 109 (1960).

[11] Sudden flooding, as from rain or melting snow.

[12] "Isaac Keen of full age testifieth and saith that I have been well acquainted with a certain piece of meadow called by the name of George's meadow, lying upon a brook called Pudding Brook, and a little below the grist-mill called Turner's mill and have been acquainted with said meadow this forty odd years past, and have mowed in the meadow for a great many years past, and then the meadow was hard enough to go in with a cart, and the grass very good, a large burden and very good fodder, and never knew any failure till since the abovesaid grist-mill was set up, and since that I have been across it very often, and I look upon the meadow is much damaged by reason of the above said mill being there, which occasions the meadow to be much overflowed, and very difficult working in it, it being to miery, and the hay that is cut of but very little value, and further saith that the bank of the meadow very much broke away by reason of said stream. Isaac Keen. Sworn to in open court." SF 142297.

[13] This deposition, which substantially duplicates that of Isaac Keen, was also sworn to in open court. SF 142297.

[14] Hayricks.

than when I had it. Next the Brook as good. The rest not. The Brook might be easily cleared so as to convey all the Water off.

Aaron Sole. Of Opinion the Meadow is betterd by the flow. I have some Meadow that grows worse without overflowing. The Saw Mill went Winter and summer many Years.

Barker. Very full. The flow an Advantage. Ton to an acre last Year, glad to cutt by Halves.

Mr. Hatch. Viewed it, and the Brook. My opinion that the Brook cleard out and Meadow ditched, the flow would be a great Advantage. Offer to clear it out. Answerd that would not Answer any Purpose. 2 Men in a day would clear the Brook, and by stopping a few Places in the Banck, one Rod would not be flowed.

Seth Briggs. Logs across the River, almost buried in sand. A bridge about 30 Years, furrd [15] with Sand, so that Weeds grow quite across the Brook. A good Crop last Year and good Grass. 4 foot fall, in 40 Rod.

Barnab. Briggs. Juror.[16]

David McGoon. Offered to help clear the Brook.

Jno. Chapman Jnr.

Mr. Palmer. Such Meadows generally as good again for the water.

Jno. Turner Jnr. 5. Bushells in 24 Hours.

15. Clap's Will

1767–1768

EDITORIAL NOTE

The litigation arising from Samuel Clap's will is illustrative of two very important features of the Massachusetts system of distributing decedents' estates: the necessity that wills be executed under conditions of capacity and formality similar to those required in English law; the interaction and conflict between the Province probate court system and the courts of common law in dealing with contested wills.

Clap, a resident of Scituate in Plymouth County, died on 8 December 1766. On 25 October of that year he had made a new will in order to disinherit his eldest living son, William, whom he accused of a variety of unfilial acts. After a life estate to his wife and a token for William, he left the bulk of his realty to another son, Samuel Jr., and the rest of it to his

[15] "Fur." "3. To coat or cover with fur or morbid matter. *To fur up*: to stop up or 'clog' with this." **OED.**

[16] "A Juror who is a Witness, must be also sworn in open Court to give Evidence, if he be called for a Witness; for the Court and Council are to hear the Evidence as well as the Jury." 2 Duncombe, *Trials Per Pais* 384. See No. 12, notes 90–92.

grandson, Samuel Randall, at age 21. Clap's daughter, Sarah Randall, was to receive certain household goods, and there were small cash legacies to Sarah's daughters, as well as to Michael Clap, another grandson, whose father had predeceased the testator. Samuel Clap Jr. and Sarah Randall were nominated as executors and were bequeathed all of the testator's bonds and notes under a direction to pay debts, legacies, and funeral expenses.[1]

In April 1767, before Plymouth County Probate Judge John Cushing, William Clap attacked the will, and it was disallowed. Samuel Clap Jr. appealed in August to the Governor and Council sitting as the Supreme Court of Probate. There, Commissioners appointed for that purpose proceeded to administer interrogatories and take depositions in February 1768.[2] At the end of that month a hearing was held in which Adams argued for the will and Robert Auchmuty opposed it. Adams' notes for his own address and his minutes of Auchmuty's argument, which are printed below, show that there were two lines of attack. Clap's testamentary capacity was called in question by a series of witnesses who reported that he had not been himself for the last year of his life, and that on at least two occasions he had given vent to expressions indicative of an unsound mind. Certain unusual features of the will itself were also pointed to as indicative of lack of capacity. In addition, Auchmuty argued that the will was invalid for noncompliance with the formalities of execution. The will was in writing and signed by the testator and three witnesses, as required by the Statute of Frauds, but it was written on several sheets stitched together in a "paper book," and Clap had left numerous blank pages, which he allegedly planned to fill in later.[3] Auchmuty thus con-

---

[1] For the will, see Supreme Ct. Probate Rec. 1760–1830, p. 57–60. The devises to William and the testator's wife are set out in notes 14 and 15 below. The date of Clap's death appears in the writ in Clap v. Randall, SF 142299. See No. 16, note 3.

[2] See Supreme Ct. Probate Rec. 1760–1830, p. 57–61; SF 129912. In the files one Benjamin Jacob appears as "appellee" in the subscription of two depositions taken at Samuel Clap's request. *Ibid.* Jacob has not been further identified but may have been a representative of William Clap at the taking of the depositions. Interrogatories were a civil law practice, perhaps adopted on the recommendation of Governor Thomas Pownall, who reorganized the court in 1760. See his Message to the Council, Quincy, *Reports* (Appendix) 572–579. As to the probate system generally, see p. xliv above; No. 16, note 1.

[3] As to the Statute of Frauds, see No. 16, note 12. The blank pages are noted in the copy of the will in Supreme Ct. Probate Rec. 1760–1830, p. 57–60. See testimony of Joshua Jacob, SF 129912, and Thomas Clap, SF 142299; No. 16, note 9. The execution of the will is described in "The deposition of Elisha Barrel relating to a paper Book purporting [to be] the will of Samuel Clap Lat of Scituate in the County of Plymouth decesd dated October 25 ad 1766, taken upon interrogatories as follows viz. Question. Did you see the said Samuel sine and seal the Last written Leaf of said book and hear him Declare the same to be his Last will and testament. Answer. Yes. Question. Did you with David Jacob and Ja[mes] Jacob subscribe as witness thereto at the same time in his presence, and was he then of sound mind. Answer. Yes as I apprehended. Question. Did you obsarve any blank or clean unwritten leavs in said paper book when you set your hand as a witness there

tended that the will offered in probate could not positively be identified as the will attested by the witnesses.

Adams seems to have concentrated his argument on the question of capacity. His review of the depositions is a witty and effective resolution of conflicting testimony in favor of Clap's sanity. His notes also show that he cited authority indicating that only the literal requirements of the Statute of Frauds need be adhered to, and that, the Statute aside, a will such as this one was good. His arguments were apparently convincing. On 2 March 1768 the court ordered that the decree of the probate judge should be reversed and so upheld the will.[4] Clap's heirs were not yet out of difficulty, however. The will was soon to be tested at law in the action of *Clap v. Randall*, No. 16.

ADAMS' ADDRESS AND MINUTES OF THE ARGUMENT[5]

Supreme Court of Probate, February 1768

SAMUEL CLAP TESTATOR, LEFT[6] a Grandson Michael Clap, Son of the Eldest Son of the Testator, whose Name was Michael Clap, deceased.

⟨William Clap, the oldest Son Living dis⟩

Sarah Randall Widow of Samuel Randal deceased who left by her, four Children, 2 Sons and 2 Daughters, the Names Samuel, Mary, Sarah and Elijah.

William Clap the Eldest son living. Disinherited.

Samuel Clap, the Executor, and principal Legatee. Mrs. Randall Ex[ecutri]x too.

The Testator in his Life time, had allowed large Priviledges to his eldest son Michael in his Life time, whereby he had acquired a pretty Estate of his own, and young Michael being young but six or seven Years old, might die and then whatever he might have would go to his Mother, entirely out of the Family and Name of Clap.

---

to. Answer. I did not observe it. Question. Were all the Leavs stiched to gether as they now are when you signed as a witness as aforesaid. Answer. The book appeared in the same shape as it does now, but whether there was so many leaves I cannot say. Question. Was what now appears in the several leaves of said book wrote before you subscribed as a witness. Answer. I am not abel to say." Dated 19 Feb. 1768. SF 129912.

[4] Supreme Ct. Probate Rec. 1760–1830, p. 61. For Adams' authorities, see note 17 below. They are further discussed in No. 16, note 7.

[5] In JA's hand. Adams Papers, Microfilms, Reel No. 185.

[6] These three words, and the headings and names of deponents printed in large and small capitals below, were written by JA in a hand much larger than that in the rest of the MS, perhaps as a device to call his attention to important points as he spoke.

SAMUEL CLAP'S WILL.
EVIDENCE VS. THE WILL

Joseph Jacob. Testifies that he looked upon him, *for several Years before his Death, not to be a Man of a sound Mind.* But Jacob gives no Reason, relates no Fact on which to ground his Opinion. Informs the Court of no Action nor Expression of the deceased, to satisfy the Court that his Opinion was just—excepting the Will itself. He refers you to the Will to prove him mad. But I say his Referring you to the Will as Proof of Insanity, is a much stronger proof of his own, for the Will itself is a sensible wise and judicious one. Will cant be proof of Insanity for years before it was made.

Bezaliel Curtis. Did not look upon him for *some time,* before he made his Will, *to be in such a Frame of Mind, as a Man ought to be in when he makes his Will.* This is mere Opinion, Judgment, Conjecture again, without any Word or Deed to support it. Besides no Man can tell this Witness's meaning by *Frame of Mind.* He does not tell Us what Frame of Mind a Man ought to be in ⟨when he⟩ in his Judgment and Opinion when he makes his Will. He does [*i.e.* does not] say that he ever heard him speak a silly or an idle Word, or do a wild or inconsiderate Action. He dont so much as say that he ever perceivd him Unsound in his Mind, deficient in his Memory or weak in his Understanding, but not in a suitable Frame of Mind to make a Will. And I suppose his Meaning was really this. This Word Frame is a technical Term among the Visionaries and Enthusiasts in the Country and signifies the moral and religious state of the soul, rather than the Conduct of the Understanding, the Government of the Passions and Appetites, rather than the command of the intellectual Faculties.[7] So I suppose Mr. Curtis thought that the [testator]

---

[7] For examples of "frame" used in this sense, see RPB: Diary of Isaac Backus, vol. 4, 20 July 1755: "One thing that has burden'd my Soul of late is having my mind and my hands too much cumberd with earthly things, So that I've greatly neglected private reading meditation and prayer. By reason of which I've often come before Gods people very unprepar'd both as to matter, and also as to a sutable frame of mind to treat with Souls about eternal Things." *Id.,* 21 July 1755: "I visited Sister Elizth. Show who has been sick this fortnight with the long fever, and she complain'd much of a confus'd and stupid frame of mind; but while I pray'd her Soul was bro't forth so that as soon as I had done she broke forth in the praises of the Lord, and did admire his great goodness to such a vile Backslider, O! said she 'I have found him whom my Soul Loveth.' And I left her in a sweet frame and went to see some others, and found Some engagement of mind to labour to stur up Souls to mind their Spiritual concerns." For this and other similar references to the Backus Diary the editors are indebted to Professor William G. McLoughlin of Brown University. Professor McLoughlin points out that the term was in very general use among the pious. Letter to the editors, 16 Dec. 1963. See, for example, the following stanza of a Watts hymn, quoted in Backus, Diary, vol. 4, 27 June 1756: "My

Clap was not meek and patient and humble and devout enough, but was too peevish and passionate for so solemn an Action. But the Law makes no Enquiry about the Frame of his soul, and the vilest Sinner living has as good a Right in Law to make a Will and may be as capable of it as the most emminent saint in the Calender.

Zecharias Daman is the next Witness and he testifies, he was intimately acquainted with Saml. Clap for many Years, and that *for about a Year before his Death, it appeared to him he was not in a sound Mind, nor capable of disposing of his Estate by Will.* That he found *visible and material Alterations in him* from what he formerly was, and that he perceived *these Alterations and this Unfitness to make a Will, at 4 or 5 Conversations he had with him, within about 2 months before he died.*

This Testimony is like the two former. The Deponent barely gives his Opinion, not founded on any facts, Words, or particular Observations, not that the Testator was unsound ⟨*Non Compos, delirious, lunatic, &c. but that he was*⟩ unfit to make a Will, and incapable of disposing of his Estate by Will. The Deponent indeed informs us that he always made use of *odd Expressions* in all his Discourse, ever since he knew him.

Anna Cothrel testifies, that she was well acquainted with Samuel Clap, and always for many Years, looked upon him of sufficient Understanding to dispose of his Estate, till the June before he died, when I looked upon him in *a Case tending to Distraction.* Some Weeks before his Death, I perswaded him to come in but I could not get any other Words from him, than these *God blast the Corn,* which he often repeated.

This Witness has come to particulars. Has sworn to one Expression tending to convince the Court, of Claps Insanity. But before I consider that Expression I should Observe that she differs widely totally from one of the former Witnesses Dr. Joseph Jacob in her general Opinion of him. Dr. Jacob swears that for several Years before his Death, he looked upon him *not to be a Man of a sound Mind.* She Anna Cothrell swears that she was acquainted with him for many Years, and *always looked upon him of sufficient Understanding to dispose of his Estate till June before he died.* Here is a Difference in Opinion which I shall leave them to reconcile. She is willing to allow him his Reason till June before he died, Jacob strips it all away from

---

willing soul would stay, / In such a frame as this, / And sit and sing herself away / To everlasting Bliss." See Isaac Watts, *Hymns and Spiritual Songs* 106 (Boston, 37th edn., 1774).

him for several Years before, ay and all for the small offence of making a wise, sensible tho an odd Will. Anna Cothrell in June looked upon him in a Case *tending to Distraction,* I was mistaken I thought she gave her Opinion that he was distracted, but she does not go so far, she only says *tending to distraction.* I must own I like this Witness better than Jo. Jacob. He deals in *Distraction* by wholesale and inferrs several Years of it, from one sensible Will. She only infers a Tendency to Distraction from a strange Expression, and that is *God blast the Corn.* This as it stands in her Deposition is a *strange Expression.* One knows not what to make of it. But it is so loosely and uncertainly related to us by her that we can conclude nothing from it with Safety. She says it was some Weeks before his Death—how many is uncertain. I am told that before the Commissioners[8] she said Three. But this is impossible, as we shall shew presently. But the Time is not ascertaind when these Words were spoken. Nor is there any one Circumstance that accompanied them related. We are not told what went before or after, We know not what he was doing whether he was on Horseback or a foot, whether looking on the Cornfields or contemplating the Heavens. If these Circumstances were known we might perhaps see that the Words were sensible. He might be a looking towards a Cornfield and see young Ears of it blasted. And he might say to some body or to himself *that God blasts the Corn.* I say to himself, because many a sensible Man is frequently found talking to himself alone. So that no Inference of Insanity can be drawn from his talking with himself, nor are the Words insensible. Blasts are a Part of the Constitution and Course of Nature, the whole of which is under the Providence of God, and he may be said to blast the Corn as well as to send Rain on the just and unjust.

There is but one Deposition more against the Will and that is of JAMES LAMBARD, who was intimate with Clap 35 Years. Several Years before his Death he was not as *rational as usual,* particularly the last Year, when he was not *of a sound And disposing Mind* because he knew him to be out one morning and cry out, with a loud Voice *I am King I am King* and at another Time I heard him cry *Murder Murder* no Body near him as he saw and he at 80 Rods Distance, both in the High Way.

This Mr. James Lambard, your H[onor]s will remember is the Grandfather of Michael Clap, a Child of 7 Years old, who is the Representative of his father, who was the Eldest son of the Testator,

---

[8] That is, the Commissioners to administer interrogatories and take depositions for the Supreme Court of Probate. See note 2 above.

so that necessary Allowances will be made for the Affection of a father to his Child and fatherless Grandchild. For this Grandchild of his will be intituled to a double share in the Estate if the Will is disapproved.[9] Mr. Lambard differs from all the other Witnesses in one Particular and agrees with Jos. Jacobs that for several Years before his death he was not as rational as usual particularly the last Year, and that he was not of a sound mind, because he cryed *I am King*. In order to satisfy the Court about this odd Expression We shall presently read some Depositions to shew that This Rebellious son Wm. was often wrangling with his father and abusing him, and that the father used to say to him I am King yet in my own House and over my own Estate And will be obeyed. This son used to steal his fathers oxen and cutt his Timber, and sell it, which the old Gentleman thought was an Usurpation, and a taking by Violence, the Reigns[10] of Empire from his Hands. The other Cry of Murder, if true, was owing I suppose to the same Cause, for his son used to strike and beat his father as well as steal and destroy his substance and it is most likely he had been beating of him when he ran out and cryed *Murder*.

EVIDENCE FOR THE WILL.

JOHN JACOB. We begin with his Barber who shavd him constantly for six Weeks before he died and saw nothing in his Conversation or Behaviour, but he had the free Use of his senses and Reason, as well as ever for 10 Years, and he thought him to be of a sound Mind, and all the Time thought it impossible he should go out, which shews the Probability and Incredibility of Anna Cothrells story, that she saw him a broad some Weeks before his death, and heard him say *God blast the Corn*. This Witness in 6 Weeks Attendance must have had Opportunity to observe his Wildnesses, if he had been wild. He swears he saw none.

JAMES CUSHING. Looked upon him a *cunning subtle Man* in Managing his Affairs the last Year of his Life, which he did with much *Prudence* and *Discretion. Trouble in his family* put him into a *Passion*, but when out of a Passion a *reasonable Man*, of a *sound Mind* and capable of disposing of his Estate.

DAVID KENT. Took Care of his Cattle and got his Firewood for the Winter for his Victuals, lived with him till his Death, and always looked upon him capable of disposing of his Estate. Deceased told

[9] See No. 16, note 3.
[10] Thus in MS.

Deponent that Wm. would undo him, that he stole his oxen and carted his Wood in the Night Time, to prevent which he ordered his Yokes to be locked up, and that he *shoved him about House, and struck him* and that he could not go out for 5 Weeks.

ISRAEL SILVESTER. Acquainted 20 Years. Clap told him, that his son William had *broke his Corn House open and stole his Corn*. Hasp to keep him out. Told him he was going to *alter his Will*—that he had *made two Wills*. That this was the Third, that he was about to make and this the last. And that he *determined to cut his son* William ⟨off⟩ short, for he had behaved badly and had *got enough out of his Estate. Visited him 4 or 5 days before death, and talked* with him and did *not find or perceive but that he was as reasonable as usual.*[11]

ELISHA JACOB. In June 1766 a Controversy between Saml. Clap and his son Wm. Was called in as a Witness. Clap appeared very rational, then and always. Said Wm. would not go off according to Promise, but took oxen and carted Wood, without Leave. Said *He would be King Yet*. Of sound Mind and Memory and capable of conducting his affairs and disposing of his Estate.[12]

---

[11] The deposition of Israel Silvester, taken for the Probate appeal at Samuel Clap's request on 18 Feb. 1768, was as follows: "That I have been Well Acquainted with Samuel Clap Late of Scituate Deceased for About Twenty Years Passed and that Sometime In August AD 1766 According to the best of My Remembrance I Exchanged Some Rye with Said Clap for Indian Corn and at That Time he Told me that his Son William had broke his Corn House Open and had Stole his Corn and that he would Undo him and Desired me that I would make him a Good Strong hasp for he Said he had Got a Sufficient Lock to keep him out. I accordingly made him a hasp. Some time after this as I was Riding the Road with Said Samuel In Conversation with Said Samuel he Told me that he was Agoing to Alter his Will and that he had made Two Wills and that this Was the Third that he was about to make and He hoped this Would be the Last and that he Determined to Cut his Son William Short for he had behaved Badly and had already Got Enough out of his Estate. After this I heard that Said Clap was Very Poorly and Not Like to go Abroad again. I went to See him According to the best of My Remembrance about four or five days before his Death and talked with him and I did not find or perceive but that he was as Reasonable as usual." SF 129912. See William Clap v. Samuel Clap, SF 142364, Min. Bk. 82, SCJ Plymouth, May 1769, N–7, SCJ Rec. 1770, fol. 77, an action by the executor of the testator's estate on William's promise to deliver £60 worth of farm goods.

[12] The deposition of Elisha Jacob, taken for the Probate appeal at Samuel Clap's request on 17 Feb. 1768, was as follows: "Some time in June 1766 Theare was a Controversy Arose Between Samuel Clap Late of Scituate [Deceased?] and His Son William Clap and I Was Called in as an Evidence to Some of Their affairs and the said Samuel Appeared to be Very Rational at that and at other times Ever Since the Year 1750 and More Espesally the Latter Part of his Life as I Was More Entimately a Quainted With his affairs. He appeared The Mane [*i.e.* in the main?] Rational for He Said his Son William Would Not goe off according to agreement But Continued Theire and Took his oxen and Carted wood Without Leave. Said Samuel Said he Would Bee King yet and he Still Apered of Sound Mind and Memory By his Conducting of his affairs The Latter Part of his Life. For he Repaired his

Here it seems that he was fond of the Expression that he would be ⟨*Master*⟩ King, which shews the Probability that I was right in my Conjecture about James Lambards Deposition. Lambard heard him say *he would be King* and no doubt there had been then a Dispute between Wm. and him and He said then as he said upon this occasion that he would be Master Yet.

Joshua Jacob Jnr. Acquainted 15 Year, conducted with Prudence, the last Year as well as ever, and that in his Opinion he was capable on mature Consideration of making a Will. And heard Wm. own he *had struck his Father with as good a Will as he ever did a snake.*

Desire Clap. Vizited him a Week before he died. Told her, he had not long to live, that he had made a new Will and cutt Wm. off or given him but a Trifle.[13]

Mr. Auchmuty.

Exhibit. 3 or 4 Reasons. Not sound Mind. Blanks liable to be filled. No Proof that Will the same.

Inconsistencies. Absurdities and Nonsense. Devise to Sarah his Wife, that I have not given belonging to.[14]

Wm. Clap, Chubbuch's [15]

3d Mod. 263. 3 Witnesses—one never saw this Will. Court if Witnesses saw the last Paper and never saw the first. Wm. & Mary.[16]

Buildings and fences Which he Said his Son William would Not Do. Furthermore I Looked upon him Capable of Disposing of His Estate as Ever I Knew him in all My Life." SF 129912.

[13] See Desire Clap's deposition, taken for use at the Superior Court in Clap v. Randall, No. 16. SF 142299.

[14] Samuel Clap's will: "I give to mi wife Sarah Clap for her support one half of my improved Lands and and one third part of the House I now Dewil in and also one third part of my quick Stock of Cattel and Sheep to improve for her suport, also I give one third part of all my Household Goods as long as she lives, and I also give to improve that part I have not given to my son Samuel Clap, and I also give my wife Two pounds a yearely as long as she lives if wanted and called for from them or Her who it belonging tow." Supreme Ct. Probate Rec. 1760–1830, p. 57.

[15] Samuel Clap's will: "Item, I give to my son William Clap one part of a House and part of a Barn and one fourth of a acres of Land lying in Hingham lying at Thomas Chubbuck and if not disposed or Sold in my life time. If sold then I give my Son William Clap ten shillings in lawful money forever." Supreme Ct. Probate Rec. 1760–1830, p. 57.

[16] Lea v. Libb, 3 Mod. 262, 87 Eng. Rep. 173 (K.B. 1689), a case in which there were two witnesses to the will and two to a codicil, one of the latter having also been one of the witnesses to the will. It was asserted that the will was valid, there being three witnesses in all. The court held otherwise, stating, at 3 Mod. 263, 87 Eng. Rep. 174, that "If a Man make a Will in several Pieces of Paper, and there are three Witnesses to the last Paper, and none of them did ever see the first, this is not a good Will." The last phrase noted by JA is an incomplete reference to the date of the case, given in the report as the first year of the reign of William and Mary.

Vid. Lex Testamentaria Page 529.[17]
1 Sid. Stephens vs. Gerard 315.[18]
5th Bacon 502.[19] Godolphins Orphans Legacy Page 23. 24. 25.[20]

[17] This and the following citations were written by JA in a heavier hand similar to that in his address, suggesting that these are authorities for his position. The work cited here is William Nelson, *Lex Testamentaria* 529 (London, 2d edn., 1724), a passage setting out the Statute of Frauds, 29 Car. 2, c. 3, §6 (1677), (No. 16, note 12), as well as cases on the signing of wills to the effect that under the statute a will need not be signed at the end, and that before the statute unsigned wills could be valid in certain circumstances. One of the cases on the latter point is Stephens v. Gerrard, note 18 below. JA's spelling, "Gerard," which is that used in *Lex Testamentaria*, suggests that the latter work, rather than the report, was his source. See also No. 16, note 7.

[18] Stephens v. Gerrard, 1 Sid. 315, 82 Eng. Rep. 1128 (K.B. 1666), was an action in ejectment in which "le title del defendant fuit le volunt [will] de Sir Edward Worsley . . . et ceo volunt fuit escrite per un Bainham de Greys-Inn, et come il jure publy per luy mes ne fuit subscribe per Sir E. W. sed remain in loose sheets." The case was heard "Sur trial al Bar" and various "excepc̄ons" were taken to Bainham's testimony on the grounds of his interest in the will and the lands in suit. The court allowed his evidence, however, "et le jury done verdit p̄le [pour le] volunt." The discussion of the case in Nelson, *Lex Testamentaria*, upon which JA probably relied, concludes: "and this was adjudged to be a good Will." See note 17 above. The report indicates, however, that the issue of informality was not directly raised.

[19] 5 Bacon, *Abridgment* 502, a section dealing with capacity to make wills, includes this passage: "A mad or lunatick Person, during the Time of his Insanity of Mind, cannot make Will of Lands or Goods; but such a one as hath his *lucida Intervalla*, clear or calm Intermissions, may, during the Time of such Quietness and Freedom of Mind, make his Will and it will be good."

[20] John Godolphin, *The Orphan's Legacy* 23–25 (London, 4th edn., 1701). The pages cited deal with the capacity of "mad persons." In addition to the passage quoted by JA from Bacon, note 19 above, the pages contain a discussion of the manner of proof of insanity, including the following: "And here note, that every Person is presumed to be of perfect Mind and Memory, until the contrary be proved. So that he that objecteth Insanity of Mind, must prove the same, for which it is sufficient if he prove, that the Testator was beside himself, or had lost his Reason but just before he made his Testament, though he prove not the Testator's Madness at the very time of making the same, unless the contrary be proved, or Circumstances to induce a contrary presumption. For it is a very tender and difficult point to prove a Man not to have the use of his Reason and Understanding; therefore it is not sufficient for the Witnesses to depose that the Person was mad, unless withal they render upon knowledge a sufficient reason thereof. Neither is one Witness sufficient to prove a Man mad, nor two, in case the one depose of the Testator's Madness at one time, and the other of his Madness at another time; but both agreeing in time, if then the one Witness deposeth of one mad Act, the other of another mad Act at one and the same time, these sufficiently prove that the Testator was then mad, though they do not both depose of one and the same mad Act." Godolphin goes on to state presumptions in favor of sanity, including the propositions that if the testator is known to have intervals of lucidity, or if the will is "wisely and orderly made" it will be presumed to have been drawn during such an interval. Godolphin, *Orphan's Legacy* 24. JA copied some of this discussion into his diary, Feb. 1763, when dealing with another will case. 1 JA, *Diary and Autobiography* 243–244.

Hampshire ss.

An Inquisition Indented, Taken at
Springfield within the Said County of Hampshire the Eighth
Day of August, In the first year of the Reign of our Sovereign
Lord George the third by the Grace of GOD. of England
France & Ireland King Defender of the Faith &c Anno Dom:
1761. — Before Robert Harris Gentn one of the Coroners of our
Said Lord the King. within the County of Hampshire aforesaid,
upon view of the Body. of Timothy Mirick of Springfield aforesaid.
then and their being dead; by the oaths of Isaac Brewer, Samll Warner
Ezra Barker, Phinehas Newton, Moses Burt, Nathl Bliss, Henry Chapin
Stephen Stebbins, Aaron Bliss, Danl Warner, John Hitchcock junr Moses Wininer
Henry Wright Noah Alvard, Moses Alvard aaron Alvard, Danl Cadwell, Willm King.
Good and Lawfull men of Springfield aforesaid within the County
aforesaid, Who being charged and Sworn to Enquire for our Said
Lord the King, when, and by what means, and how the Said
Timothy Mirick came to His Death: upon their oaths Do Say:
that aforesaid Timothy Mirick Came to His Death by the misfortune of
the Bite of a Rattle Snake, and So the Said Jurors aforesaid Say that
the Said Timothy Mirick aforesaid Came to His Death of

In witness whereof, as well I the Said Coroner aforesaid, as the Jurors
afore Said, to this Inquisition — have

82197

Have

14. SAMUEL WINTHROP, BY JOHN SINGLETON COPLEY

13. JEREMIAH LEE, BY JOHN SINGLETON COPLEY

16. Clap v. Randall

1769

EDITORIAL NOTE

In England the probate of wills of personalty was within the jurisdiction of the ecclesiastical courts, although many related questions, both of administration and distribution, had to be tried at law or in equity. The ecclesiastical courts had no power over wills of realty, because the common law claimed exclusive jurisdiction of title questions. Such wills were proved only if an action at law was brought to test the devisee's right.

One result of this division of jurisdiction was that the validity of a will might be brought again into question in an action at law despite presumably conclusive probate proceedings. In Massachusetts the confusion was relieved somewhat by Province statutes which gave to the judges of probate many powers in the administration and distribution of both real and personal estates.[1] Title was still a question for the common law, however, and in *Clap v. Randall*, the validity of Samuel Clap's will, previously allowed by the Governor and Council sitting as Supreme Court of Probate (No. 15), was reopened and argued anew, apparently without objection. The action may have been permitted either because lack of notice to the plaintiff, or his guardian, was held to relieve him from the bar of the prior probate decree, or because the English practice of not giving conclusive effect to such a decree was followed.[2]

---

[1] As to the English practice, see 12 Holdsworth, *History of English Law* 686–689, 695–697; Atkinson, "The Development of the Massachusetts Probate System," 42 *Mich. L. Rev.* 425–426 (1943). The basic provision in Massachusetts was the Act of 1 Nov. 1692, c. 14, 1 A&R 43–45, which provided that all lands held in fee might be disposed of by will and that wills were to be submitted to probate under penalty of law. In the event of intestacy administration of both realty and personalty was to be granted and supervised by the judge of probate. Later provisions are summarized in Atkinson, "Massachusetts Probate System," 42 *Mich. L. Rev.* 440–447. Atkinson, *id.* at 445, states that the Act of 17 June 1723, c. 3, 2 A&R 284–285, gave the lands of the deceased directly to the heirs at death, thus removing them from administration. The 1723 act, however, seems to provide only that an administrator *de bonis non* (*i.e.* "of the goods not" administered by a previous administrator or executor), appointed for a supplemental administration, was to have no power over unadministered real estate, which descended to the heirs automatically. Subsequent legislation indicates that the provisions of the 1692 act as to administration and distribution of realty by the original administrator were not altered. See Act of 1 Jan. 1735, c. 16, 2 A&R 738; Act of 12 April 1750, c. 20, 3 A&R 495.

[2] Under later Massachusetts law, a probate decree was conclusive in an action at law, except as to matters of jurisdiction, such as lack of notice, which could be collaterally attacked. See Smith v. Rice, 11 Mass. 507 (1814); Dublin v. Chadbourn, 16 Mass. 433, 441–442 (1820); Daniel A. White, *A View of the Jurisdiction and Proceedings of the Court of Probate in Massachusetts* 26–30 (Salem, Mass., 1822); Alger, "Conclusiveness of Decrees of a Domestic Probate Court in Massachusetts," 13 *Harv. L. Rev.* 192–193 (1899). That the probate decree was

The action was a plea of partition brought by the guardian of Michael Clap, minor son of Samuel's deceased eldest son, against the testator's three surviving children, Sarah Randall, William, and Samuel Jr. Under the will, Michael had received only a £60 legacy, apparently because the testator had made *inter vivos* gifts to his father. The lands in suit had gone to Samuel Jr. and Samuel Randall, Sarah's son. William Clap, who had contested the will in probate, had been virtually disinherited. Michael's declaration ignored the will completely, setting forth that Samuel had died intestate while seized of the lands and that Michael and the defendants, Samuel's only heirs, were thus tenants in common in the premises. Although in form the writ sought money damages for failure to partition, the suit was brought under a Province statute permitting a cotenant to compel division of lands in an action at law.[3]

---

not conclusive is made more likely by the fact that probate jurisdiction was by the Charter of 1691 vested in the Governor and Council, who created the county courts solely by commission, without legislation. It is thus possible that the probate courts were not considered "courts of record." See Coke, *Littleton* 260a.

[3] Act of 14 July 1693, c. 8, §1, 1 A&R 122. For the will, see No. 15, note 1. The declaration set out "a plea of partition, for that one Samuel Clap late of said Scituate yeoman deceased, in his life time, in a time of peace, in the sixth year of our reign, was seized in his demesne as of fee, of two parcels of land [description], taking the esplees thereof to the amount of three pounds lawful money by the year. And on the eighth day of December 1766, the same Samuel dyed so seized at said Scituate, and intestate, leaving the above named [defendants] his only surviving children, and the plaintiff, his grandson, the only child of Michael Clap late of said Scituate yeoman deceased, who was the eldest son of the said Samuel the intestate, and died on [the] tenth of June ad. 1760. Whereupon at the death of the said Samuel, the intestate, the premises by the law of our province of the Massachusetts Bay, descended to the plaintiff [and the defendants], the only heirs of the said Samuel the intestate, to wit two fifth parts thereof to the plaintiff, the only child and legal representative of the said Michael, deceased, the eldest son of the said intestate, and one fifth part thereof to [each of the defendants], and they and the plaintiff are accordingly seized of the same two parcels of land in their demesne as of fee, and do hold the same together in common and undivided. Whereof it appertains that the plaintiff [and the defendants] ought to hold, possess, and enjoy their respective parts thereof in severalty.... Yet [the defendants] tho' often requested, do utterly refuse to divide or make partition of the same parcels of land, that so they, and the plaintiff, may hold and enjoy their respective parts and interest in the premises in severalty as aforesaid, contrary to the said law of the said province in that case made and provided, and to the damage of the said Michael Clap as he by his said guardian saith, the sum of forty pounds." SF 142299.

Under the Province intestacy law (note 1 above) the eldest son took a double share. In England partition lay among coparceners (cotenants by inheritance) at common law, and among joint tenants and tenants in common by statute. See 6 Dane, *Abridgment* 478–480; 3 Holdsworth, *History of English Law* 19. The Province Act of 1693, 1 A&R 122, cited above, established the writ of partition as an action at law for all three classes of cotenancy. Note that the declaration used here states the title of the cotenants in the form followed in real actions, although it was apparently the rule in partition that title could be stated briefly, as being "of the inheritance of" the predecessor, since the action was for possession, not property. See Fitzherbert, *New Natura Brevium* 142 note (London, 1755); 16 Viner, *Abridgment* 240; see also Perham, *American Precedents* 313–314 (1802). As to the form in real actions, see Charles Jackson, *A Treatise on the Pleadings*

The case came on for trial at Plymouth Inferior Court in April 1769, where Adams entered a plea of not guilty for the defendants. Daniel Leonard's demurrer was overruled and judgment entered on the plea. On appeal to the Superior Court at Plymouth in May 1769 the lower court pleadings were waived and Adams averred that the defendants "and the Plantiff do not hold the said Premises together in common and undivided, as the Plantiffs have above declared." The case went to the jury.[4] Adams' minutes of the evidence and arguments, printed below, indicate that the validity of the will was the principal question argued. Witnesses for the plaintiff testified both as to Samuel Clap's mental state and to the informal character of the document itself. The authorities cited by Leonard are on these points, and James Otis, also arguing for the plaintiff, directly raised the Statute of Frauds. That Act required only that a will be written, signed, and witnessed, but Otis apparently argued that its policy of preventing frauds through proof of the testator's actions should be extended to bar a will with blank pages, which would give great opportunities for later changes.

Adams, as he had in *Clap's Will*, brought forward authority dating from before the Statute of Frauds, to the effect that wills with defects other than those covered by the Act were good at common law. His principal source seems to have been Nelson's *Lex Testamentaria*, a treatise of doubtful value in which two of the three cases which Adams cited are misstated in his favor, revealing the pitfall, not unknown today, that awaits one who relies upon secondary sources. No objection seems to have been made to Adams' authority, however, either because no one in the Province had the original reports from which Nelson's work could be refuted, or because Adams' position was accepted as good law despite dubious precedent. The jury returned a verdict for the defendants, and Samuel Clap's estate was finally at rest.[5]

---

and Practice in Real Actions 348 (Boston, 1828); No. 17, notes 4–6; p. 36, notes 29, 30. Although in form the writ sought damages, it was the rule at common law that no damages would be awarded, and that the judgment was in fact for partition. See 16 Viner, *Abridgment* 236–237, 240; 6 Dane, *Abridgment* 491. The procedure followed in this case is to be distinguished from the proceeding by original petition in the Superior Court, provided by Act of 1 Feb. 1749, c. 12, 3 A&R 426–428. The latter was not an adversary proceeding, no provision being made for trial of issues under it. In 1787 the defect was remedied by a provision for pleading and trial to a jury in such cases. See 6 Dane, *Abridgment* 483.

[4] See the pleadings in both courts and the Inferior Court judgment, in SF 142299. Adams' plea of not guilty in the Inferior Court was probably an informal one designed to implement the sham demurrer which was evidently intended. See p. xlvi above. The plea was in general use for real actions in Massachusetts, and thus would arguably have been proper in partition. See Joseph Story, *A Selection of Pleadings in Civil Actions* 333 (Salem, Mass., 1805). In this case, however, it might have been subject to the logical flaw that it seemed to deny the refusal to partition. JA's Superior Court plea was in literal translation, "non tenent insimul," a proper plea in partition. See 5 Comyns, *Digest* 274; Coke, *Littleton* 167; compare 6 Dane, *Abridgment* 491.

[5] Min. Bk. 82, SCJ Plymouth, May 1769, N–5; SCJ Rec. 1769, fols. 183–184.

ADAMS' MINUTES OF THE TRIAL[6]

Plymouth Superior Court, May 1769

Lex Test., Page 576. Stephens vs. Gerard, 1. Sid. 315. Page 571, Sackville vs. Brown. Page 576, Chadron v. Harris, Noy 12.[7]

Randal et als. vs. Clap.

Leonard.

Witnesses.

Zechh. Daman. In the latter Part of his Life, he seemed not so capable, intosticated[8] and Passionate. Good Ideas.

Bezaliel Curtis. A good deal of Judgment once. He seemed to be in a hurry, a fury, &c. I did not look upon him the Man he used to be. One time he seemed cool, and calm. At other Times he said that Bill would not catch his Horse and Sam. had promised to do it. Will the Eldest. He said Will had wronged him, and had Creatures and not returned 'em.

Josa. Jacobs. Fortnight before he died, Saml. gave me the Will to keep. The old Man told me, he had sent it by Saml. December Court delivered [to] me. He left Blanks that Coll. Clap might view it and

---

[6] In JA's hand. Adams Papers, Microfilms, Reel No. 185. The minutes were written with a haste and carelessness unusual even for JA's courtroom jottings, and both words and sense in a few passages are beyond recovery. Among other things, JA's titling of these minutes "Randal et als. vs. Clap" seems to be a misnomer. Sarah Randall and her brothers were defendants below and appellees in the Superior Court. See note 4 above. No other action by this name has been found in the files.

[7] As to "Stephens v. Gerard," see No. 15, notes 17, 18. The latter case and the others cited here are presumably drawn from William Nelson, *Lex Testamentaria* (London, 2d edn., 1724). This work, at p. 576, first compares the common-law rule of two witnesses for a will of goods and three witnesses for lands, to the varying rules of the civil law, the law of nations, and the canon law. It then cites Chadron v. Harris, Noy 12, 74 Eng. Rep. 983 (K.B., ca. 1605), apparently as holding an unsigned and unsealed will good where three witnesses were produced, two of whom "deposed on the Report of others, but the third had subscrib'd his Name to the Will." According to the actual report, however, this case involved questions of the validity of a will in which no executor was named, and the power of the common-law courts to issue a writ of prohibition to the ecclesiastical court in a suit by a legatee under such a will, when administration had been granted despite the defect. The citation seems to have been misplaced in the margin of *Lex Testamentaria* by the printer, since the immediately preceding paragraph deals with prohibition in a similar matter. Sackville v. Brown, Keilw. 209, 72 Eng. Rep. 389 (C.P. 1558) was a case in which, according to *Lex Testamentaria* 571, "the Testator on his Death-bed desir'd another to *write* his Will, who took short Notes of it, and went Home to write it in Form, and soon return'd with it *written*, but before he came the Testator was *dead*; yet this was adjudg'd a good Will within the Statute 32 H. 8 [32 Hen. 8, c. 1 (1541)]." The report confirms this account.

[8] Thus in MS—the result of a natural and amusing confusion of associations.

alter it. He said so.[9] I did not see but what his Mind was as usual. He never [. . . .].

Hawk. Cushing. Unreasonably prejudiced vs. his son Wm. Whenever Wills Name was mentiond he was in a Passion. He would talk about common Affairs, he would talk well eno. I [swore?] to Man it shall be £4000 out of his Pockett.

Abigail Sylvester. I should venture to trade with him as well as ever. In a Passion, always hasty.

He left Blanks to alter when he had occasion for it, he said.

Leonard.

Swing. 522.[10] 82. Become a Child.[11] Proof of it.

[9] The deposition on interrogatories of Joshua Jacobs in the files of the Supreme Court of Probate substantiates this testimony as to the delivery of the will. SF 129912. "December Court" presumably refers to the sitting of the Inferior Court at Plymouth on the second Tuesday in December. Act of 19 Feb. 1765, c. 20, §1, 4 A&R 737. Since this date was 9 Dec. in 1766, and Clap died on 8 Dec., the witness may mean that Clap informed him of his intent two weeks before his death, but the will was not delivered until later. "Coll. Clap" may be Thomas Clap, perhaps a relative, who was a judge of the Plymouth Inferior Court. Whitmore, *Mass. Civil List* 96–97. The files include the deposition of one "Thomas Clapp," 10 May 1769, that in the spring of 1766, Samuel Clap had shown him an old will in a paper book with stitched leaves and many blanks, and had asked him to "write" a new will. This Thomas did. In Oct. 1766, Samuel asked him to write still another will to disinherit his son William, producing as a draft the document now in controversy. Thomas could not comply, because he "was bound on a Jorney . . . not because he [Samuel] was not compus mentis." SF 142299.

[10] Error for "Swinb." See Henry Swinburne, *A Treatise of Testaments and Last Wills* 522 (London, 6th edn., 1743): "What if a Writing be found written indeed with the Hand of the Testator in Manner of a Will, wherein he hath disposed his Goods, and appointed an Executor, but the Writing is neither sealed with the Testator's Seal, nor subscribed with his Name, nor by him acknowledged before Witnesses to be his Last Will? Whether shall this Writing be accounted to be a Draught of the Testator's Will, or the Testament it self? I suppose that the Solution of this Question resteth in the Variety of Circumstances. For if the Writing be unperfect, for that perhaps the Testator doth leave off in the Midst of a Sentence, and without any Date, or if the same be written with strange Characters, or if the same be written in Paper, and great Distance betwixt every Line, divers Emendations and Corrections made betwixt the Lines; if also the same be found amongst other Papers of finall Value or Account; by these Circumstances it seemeth rather a Draught or Preparation to a Testament, than the Testament it self. But on the contrary, if the Writing be perfect or fully finished, having a certain Date of the Day, Month, and Year, and be written with usual and accustomed Letters in Parchment, without Corrections, and with small Distance betwixt the Lines, and also found in some Chest of the Testator, among other Writings of the Testator of great Value and Moment; by these Circumstances it seemeth rather to be the very Testament it self than a Draught only."

[11] Swinburne, *Testaments and Last Wills* 82 (1743): "Yet if a Man in his old Age do become a very Child again in his Understanding, (which Thing doth happen to divers Persons, being as it were worn away with extreme Age, and deprived not only of the Use of Reason, but of Sense also,) such a Person can no more make a Testament than a Child."

Will itself.

Otis. Statute of Frauds, requires the Subscription of 3 Witnesses.[12] Many Frauds were found to be committed, concerning Wills. The design that the Witnesses may be able to swear to the Identity of the Writing.

This Method lyable to Fraud and Interpolation.

17. Hill v. Whiting

1770–1772

EDITORIAL NOTE

In August 1770, with Adams and Jonathan Sewall as his counsel, John Whiting had prevailed in an action of trespass which he had brought against his neighbor Ichabod Ware for a tract of land near Smoking Hill in Wrentham. Referees, under a rule of the Superior Court directing them to fix a boundary between the litigants, had reported that no line could be drawn, because Ware had no claim to any portion of the lands which Whiting claimed.[1] Whiting traced his title to Ebenezer Hill, who had died in 1732 owning substantial real estate in Wrentham. In his lifetime Hill had conveyed fifty acres at Smoking Hill to his brother Jabez. William Bollan and Henry Laughton, grantees of Jabez, had conveyed the same premises to Eliphalet Whiting, John's father. Ware's unsuccessful claim had been based on a conveyance of several parcels in the same vicinity made in 1734 by Ebenezer's administrator, Jonathan Whitney, to one Joshua Morse. The claim had failed, apparently because Ware could produce no evidence of the passage of title to him from Morse.[2]

Perhaps as a result of this decision, Abiel Hill, posthumous daughter

---

[12] That is, the Province Statute of Frauds, Act of 22 Oct. 1692, c. 15, 1 A&R 46–47 (patterned after the English statute, 29 Car. 2, c. 3 [1676]), which provided that "For prevention of many fraudulent practices which are commonly endeavoured to be upheld by perjury and subornation of perjury .... [§3] all devises and bequests of any lands or tenements shall be in writing, and signed by the party so devising the same, or by some other person in his presence and by his express directions, and shall be attested and subscribed in the presence of the said devisor by three or four credible witnesses, or else shall be utterly void and of none effect." The Act further provided that no devise in writing should be revoked or altered other than by destruction by the testator, or "by some other will or codicil in writing, or other writing of the devisor, signed in the presence of three or four witnesses, declaring the same." *Id.*, §4.

[1] Min. Bk. 91, SCJ Boston, Aug. 1770, C–1. SF 101696.

[2] See the various deeds, extracts from the Wrentham Proprietors' records, and the deposition of Ebenezer Fisher in the files of Hill v. Whiting. SF 102137. An abstract of Whiting's title in JA's hand, based on the foregoing materials, and apparently used in the action against Ware, is in Adams Papers, Microfilms, Reel No. 185.

and only heir of Ebenezer, brought an action against Whiting, claiming possession of the tract formerly in suit, which she alleged to be 99 1/2 acres in extent. Her declaration purported to be in "ejectment." [3] In England, this form of action, originally the remedy of a lessee turned out of the leased premises, had, through an elaborate fiction, become the usual method of trying title to land. The pleadings, which echoed the origin of the action, told a tale in which John Doe, a fictitious lessee of the actual plaintiff purported to sue Richard Roe, an equally nonexistent ejector, in whose name the real party in interest was called upon to defend. If the actual plaintiff succeeded in his suit, he was awarded possession of the land. Since the action was in form only for a single trespass, it could have been brought repeatedly by an unsuccessful plaintiff for later trespasses, but the courts tended to discourage such suits when the title in question was the same. This drawback was rendered of such little effect that by the 18th century ejectment had largely replaced the numerous ancient real actions, with their cumbersome process, technical rules, and narrow scope.[4]

While the fictional form of ejectment was not unknown in Massachusetts, it seems to have been little used, apparently because of the lack of conclusiveness and a feeling that the adventures of Doe and Roe led to unnecessarily complex and wordy pleading. Instead, "ejectment" was a generic term for a form of action which could embrace any of the ancient real actions and attendant rules that a given case demanded, but which embraced them within a simple form of writ and process that avoided medieval mysteries and led to a trial like that in any other civil suit.[5] Abiel's

[3] A copy of her declaration is in JA's Pleadings Book, p. 36–37 above. Although "Abiel" might ordinarily be a man's name, JA was correct in characterizing her as female in the title to her pleading. *Ibid.* See a copy of her birth record in SF 102137.

[4] See 7 Holdsworth, *History of English Law* 4–23; Sutton, *Personal Actions* 52–56.

[5] As to the Massachusetts action and some of the advantages seen in it, see Perham, *American Precedents* 288–290; Charles Jackson, *A Treatise of the Pleadings and Practice in Real Actions* 11–13 (Boston, 1828); Asahel Stearns, *A Summary of the Law and Practice of Real Actions* 91–94, 396–398 note (Boston, 1824). For an example of the use of the fictional form of the action in Massachusetts, see Johnson, Lessee of Stevens v. Hewes, Min. Bk. 81, SCJ Suffolk, Aug. 1765, C–33; review, *sub nom.* Hewes v. Johnson, *id.*, March 1766, N–23; SF 100633, 100729. In this complicated action arising out of the Land Bank scheme, JA was of counsel for Hewes. The declaration, apparently drafted by Robert Auchmuty, gave no label to the action, but set forth a lease from Timothy Stevens to one "Samuel Johnson, scrivener," whose name does not appear elsewhere in the file. The actual defendants were alleged to have "Entered, and him the said Samuel from his farm aforesaid ejected." SF 100729. The form is essentially that given in Sutton, *Personal Actions* 53–54. The name of the real defendants was probably used either because this was the new declaration served upon them after they had been notified to defend (*id.* at 54), or because the formality of the completely fictional declaration had been dispensed with. After a demurrer for Hewes in the Inferior Court, Johnson won both the appeal and the review in the Superior Court. Hewes then moved for an appeal to the Privy Council, but it was denied, "there being no provision in the Royal Charter for an appeal in this Case." (The Charter provided an appeal only "in any Personal Accion wherein the matter in difference doth exceed" £300 ster-

suit shows that there were situations in which the Massachusetts form was an improvement upon the English.

Her declaration was a form apparently unique to Massachusetts which had some attributes of the ancient assize of *mort d'ancestor*, but was in effect a variety of writ of entry.[6] Even in England one of the ancient forms would have been necessary in her case, because ejectment depended upon a right of entry in the actual plaintiff. Abiel's right had accrued in 1732, at the death of her father, or at best in 1733, when she was born. Under the applicable statute of limitations, an entry upon lands had to be made within twenty years after the right accrued, or if it had expired during the minority of the claimant, within ten years after his majority. Abiel's right of entry was thus lost, and with it her right to proceed in ejectment as that action was known in England.[7]

At the trial in the July 1771 Suffolk Inferior Court, with Adams once again of counsel, Whiting obtained judgment on a demurrer to his plea of not guilty. On appeal to the Superior Court in February 1772 the demurrer was waived and the case went to the jury, which brought in a special verdict. The declaration had alleged that Abiel's father died seised on 30 October 1732. The jury found that the actual date of his death was 21 October 1732; that if the court should hold that this discrepancy was not a bar to the action, then Abiel could recover 21 acres and 31 rods of

---

ling. 1 A&R 15.) JA's minutes of the argument, or arguments, which show that the existence of the fiction was recognized, are in Adams Papers, Microfilms, Reel No. 185. For another such action, see Laughton v. Pitts, p. 80–81 above.

[6] See p. 36, note 30, above. The usual writ of entry was brought for a disseisin (wrongful entry during the life of one seised). This was a case of an "abatement" (wrongful entry between the death of the seised ancestor and the entry of the heir). Ordinarily in an abatement the plaintiff still had a right of entry under which he could enter, thus momentarily obtaining seisin. Continued possession thereafter by the wrongdoer amounted to a disseisin and the plaintiff could bring a "writ of entry in the quibus," the usual remedy of the disseised against the disseisor. Abiel had lost her right of entry, however, so that neither entry in the quibus nor the English form of ejectment was available to her. See note 7 below. The assize of *mort d'ancestor*, an ancient remedy for an abatement, had fallen into disuse, because it did not lie for lands devisable by will. JA in argument seems to have regarded the suit as one on a writ of right, and such a writ would have been appropriate here. The actual form used more closely resembles that in a writ of entry, however, and Stearns definitely classified it as such. See Stearns, *Real Actions* 146–169, 176–179, 350–359; p. 36, note 30 above. See also 2 Pollock and Maitland, *History of English Law* 56–74; George Booth, *The Nature and Practice of Real Actions* 174–178 (London, 1701); Jackson, *Real Actions* 2–3, 195–196; 3 Blackstone, *Commentaries* *186–187.

[7] The statute is 21 Jac. 1, c. 16, §§1, 2 (1623). Ejectment might also have failed because some of the lands in dispute had apparently been conveyed under the administrator's deed to Joshua Morse. Whiting might have raised the defense of *ius tertii* (a superior right in a third party), which was good in ejectment, but not in a real action. Moreover, since Whiting in all likelihood was not the original wrongful entrant, Abiel's right of entry might also have been "tolled by descent," that is, lost by the passage of the property to the heir of the original abator. See 3 Holdsworth, *History of English Law* 89–90; 7 *id.* at 20–21, 61–69; Charles Runnington, *Action of Ejectment* 12–13 (London, 1781); Jackson, *Real Actions* 5–6.

the land sued for (apparently a parcel which had not passed under the grant from Ebenezer to Jabez); that otherwise she took nothing.[8]

At the August 1772 session of the court Adams for Whiting, and Josiah Quincy Jr. for Abiel, argued the question presented. Adams' minutes (Document I) set out authorities for his position that the date of Ebenezer's death was a material allegation. Treating the action as a writ of right, he apparently argued that the time in which the ancestor was seised must always be set out, and that the exact date was material because of the statutory periods of limitation for the bringing of actions for the recovery of lands. At the end of these notes, which were probably before him as he argued, he took down the cases cited in opposition by Quincy and made a notation of the court's unanimous opinion that Abiel could recover in accordance with the verdict.[9] The files of the case contain the actual opinion of Judge Trowbridge on this and another point apparently raised by Adams, the validity of a verdict for less land than was sued for.[10] This unusual item appears as Document II.

The court's decision seems sound. Even Adams' authority indicates that only the fact of seisin, not the precise date, is material. As for the statute of limitations, although in real actions entry or seisin within the required time had to be established by the plaintiff, the discrepancy in dates was not material here.[11]

I. ADAMS' MINUTES OF THE ARGUMENT[12]

Suffolk Superior Court, Boston, August 1772

Hill vs. Whiting

In this Case the Plaintiff has alledged that her Father died seized on the Thirtyeth of the Month. But the Jury have found that he died seised on the Twenty first of the Month.

1. Inst. 293. a.[13] "Also where a Man will sue a Writ of Right, it behoveth that he counteth of the Seisin of himself or of his ancestors, and also that the Seisin was in the same Kings Time, as he pleadeth in his Plea. For this is an ancient Law used, as appeareth by the Report of a Plea in the Eire[14] of Nottingham."

[8] Min. Bk. 95, SCJ Suffolk, Feb. 1772, C–63. See the proceedings in the Inferior Court where Whiting had made an unsuccessful effort to vouch in his grantors, and the special verdict, with a draft in JA's hand, in SF 102137.

[9] Min. Bk. 95, SCJ Suffolk, Aug. 1772, C–41; SCJ Rec. 1772, fols. 109–110.

[10] The decision for Abiel on this point was in accord with authority. See Runnington, *Ejectment* 109–110, 130–131.

[11] See Stephen, *Pleading* 311–314; Stearns, *Real Actions* 241–242. Compare 3 Bacon, *Abridgment* 518–519.

[12] In JA's hand. Adams Papers, Microfilms, Reel No. 185.

[13] Coke, *Littleton* *293a. Quotation marks supplied.

[14] The court of justices in Eyre, royal judicial officials who held court on circuit in medieval times. Plucknett, *Concise History* 144–146.

Fitz. N.N.B. page. 69.[15] Writ de Droit. "In this Writ he ought to count of his own Possession, or of the Possession of his Ancestor; otherwise the Writ doth not lie, and he ought to alledge Esplees" &c.[16]

From these Authorities it seems, that the Demandant must count of a Seisin at some certain Time as upon a certain Day, or within some certain Time as within such a Kings Reign, or within some other certain Time, and must prove accordingly.

32. H. 8. and 21 Jac. 1. Limitation of Real Actions.[17] Bac. Abr. Vol. 3. 501.[18]

Holbeck vs. Bennett, 2. Lev. 11.   2. Saund. 317.[19]
Blackwell vs. Eales, 5. Mod. 286.[20]
Rex vs. Bishop of Chester, Skin. 660.[21]
Lane vs. Alexander, Cr. Ja. 202.[22]
Cro. Car. 360.[23]
2. Comyns's Rep. 12. 13.[24]

[15] Fitzherbert, *New Natura Brevium* 69 (London, 8th edn., 1755) Quotation marks supplied. The quotation is actually from a section on writs of right of advowson, a special variety of the writ dealing with the right to present a candidate for a church or benefice. In the section dealing with writs of right generally there is a similar statement, with the qualification, perhaps dangerous to JA's position, that "If he count the Seisin of his Ancestor, he may alledge the Seisin in the Time of King Richard the First." *Id.* at 11.

[16] That is, the products of the land. It was alleged here. See the declaration, p. 36, note 30, above.

[17] The statute, 32 Hen. 8, c. 2, §2 (1540), provides that no writ of entry may be maintained upon the seisin of an ancestor or predecessor which was not in effect within fifty years prior to the date of the writ. As to the statute of 21 Jac. 1, see text and note 7 above.

[18] 3 Bacon, *Abridgment* 501–504, setting out the statutes cited in note 17 above.

[19] Holbeck v. Bennett, 2 Lev. 11, 83 Eng. Rep. 429; *sub nom.* Bennet v. Holbech, 2 Saund. 317, 85 Eng. Rep. 1113 (K.B. 1682) (Time and place of lease pleaded in avowry in replevin held not traversable, per Hale, C.J.). This citation and the remainder of the minutes, written in a hastier hand with a heavier pen, are JA's on-the-spot notes of Quincy's argument and the court's ruling.

[20] Blackwell v. Eales, 5 Mod. 286, 87 Eng. Rep. 660 (K.B. 1696) (Time but a circumstance, where evidence of a thing done must be given; traverse taking issue thereof would be bad, and declaration alleging trespass on a day not yet come held aided by verdict).

[21] Rex v. Bishop of Chester, Skin. 651, 660, 90 Eng. Rep. 291, 295 (K.B. 1696) (Failure to deny exact time of seisin in *quare impedit* does not admit it, because exact time immaterial; seisin generally in time of peace, &c. is enough).

[22] Lane v. Alexander, Cro. Jac. 202, 79 Eng. Rep. 177 (K.B. 1607) (In ejectment, where one copyhold is pleaded as being before another, denial of exact date of earlier copyhold held bad on demurrer as immaterial where question is which came first).

[23] This citation has not been identified. In all editions of Croke's *Reports in the Time of Charles I* ("Cro. Car.") consulted by the editors, page 360 is blank.

[24] An inadvertence for —— and Blackall v. Heal et al., 1 Com. 12, 92 Eng. Rep. 933 (K.B. 1696), another version of Blackwell v. Eales, note 20 above.

3. Lev. 193. W[he]r[e] Day is made Parcell of the Issue it is ill.[25] Brooke Trav. pl. 40.[26]

2. Mod. 145. Brown vs. Johnson.[27] Time is not traverseable. Plaintiff must alledge a Time for Forms sake but Defendant ought not to make Time Parcell of the Issue.

Court unanimous that the Day is not material, and therefore the Plaintiff recover.

II. OPINION OF JUDGE TROWBRIDGE [28]

Suffolk Superior Court, Boston, August 1772

In the Case of Hill Agt. Whiteing in Ejectment,

Whether Hills Father died on the 21st or 30th day of October 1732, He [*i.e.* she] is alike intitled to recover the 21 acres and 31 Rods of Land, and to recover the same by an Action of Ejectment; therefore on which of those Days he died seised, is an Immaterial Circumstance and not Traversable. Holbeck vs. Bennet, 2 Lev. 11, 2 Saunders 317. Blackwell vs. Eales, 5 Mod. 286. Rex vs. Bishop of Chester, Skin. 660. Lane v. Allexander, Cr. Ja. 202. And the Plaintiff may recover so much as he is Intitled unto, tho it be less Than he demands in Ejectment. 1 Burrows 329.[29] I think the Plaintiff Ought to have Judgment for the 21 Acres and 31 Rods, and Costs.

Edm: Trowbridge

[25] An inadvertence for Dring v. Respass, 1 Lev. 193, 83 Eng. Rep. 364 (K.B. 1666) (Traverse to declaration in debt on a judgment held bad on demurrer where it had effect of putting date of the judgment in issue).

[26] Apparently an inadvertence for Robert Brooke, *La Graunde Abridgement*, tit. Traverse per sans ceo, pl. 140 (London, 1586) (Debt on condition that defendant enter peacefully before Michaelmas; plea that he entered peacefully on such a day before the feast. Replication bad that he entered forcibly on another day, because day not traversable).

[27] Brown v. Johnson, 2 Mod. 145, 86 Eng. Rep. 991 (K.B. 1688) (In action of account, dates during which defendant was bailiff are matter of form, not issue).

[28] In Edmund Trowbridge's hand. SF 102137.

[29] Denn v. Purvis, 1 Burr. 326, 329, 97 Eng. Rep. 335, 336 (K.B. 1757) (Mansfield, C.J.).

18. Prescott v. Keep
1771–1776

19. Prescott v. Priest
1771–1773

EDITORIAL NOTE

Prescott v. Keep, in which Keep, Adams' client, was the original plaintiff, began with a complicated argument on a pleading point. The defendants sought to bar the action on the ground that the plaintiff had failed to join (bring in) his cotenants as coplaintiffs. The issues which seem to have been argued were whether defendants should have raised the point at the outset (that is, by plea in abatement), and whether, having pleaded the general issue, they would at the trial be prevented from introducing evidence bearing on the failure to join. If the court followed the authority set out in Adams' minutes (Document I), the answer was that, since plaintiff's writ had not averred the cotenancy, defendants would not be allowed to raise the issue at the trial. In the related case of *Prescott v. Priest*, the initial question was Adams' contention that the death of one of the original plaintiffs might cause the action itself to die. As Justice William Cushing's report (Document IV) shows, the court ruled that it did not; Adams was then allowed to file an answer on the merits.

Once the technicalities clear away, the *Prescott* cases illustrate neatly the legal problems that could arise over the right to use flowing water, here, Stony Brook in Westford. The Prescott family had long maintained a gristmill and a sawmill on the stream, near its source.[1] In 1720, old Jonas Prescott, his two sons, Jonas and Benjamin,[2] and three others had formed a joint venture to erect and maintain an iron forge on land owned by young Jonas slightly upstream from the mills.[3] The forge, of course, depended on water power to operate its bellows.[4]

[1] Westford was until 1730 a part of Groton. " 'June 15, 1680, on a training day, granted unto Jonas Prescott, that he should take up a piece of land at Stony brook, in reference to the setting up of a mill there.' " " 'At a general town meeting at Groton, June 13, 1681: Then granted to Jonas Prescott liberty to set up his corn mill at Stony brook.' " " 'An agreement made between Jonas Prescott and the town of Groton, that he, the said Prescott, have liberty to set up a saw mill at Stony brook, and to have the use of the stream ... always provided, the saw mill do not hinder the corn mill.' " Caleb Butler, *History of the Town of Groton* 37–38 (Boston, 1848). Later, it seems, a fulling mill was added. Deposition of Nathaniel Prentice, SF 148100.

[2] Father of William Prescott (1727–1795), who commanded troops at Bunker Hill. Samuel A. Green, *Three Historical Addresses* 105–107 (Groton, 1908).

[3] Young Jonas (actually he was 42 years old at the time) played the major role in and took the major profits from the enterprise, which was "the fourth or fifth of the kind in New England. The ore used was the variety known as bog-iron, and was procured in Groton. The 'Groton iron,' produced at the forge, was not of very

By a complicated and sometimes obscure series of conveyances, a five-eighths interest in the forge had come to Jonathan Keep,[5] who apparently attempted to maintain and even improve the ironworks without the consent of the Prescott interests. The latter had other plans for the use of the available water, because in 1771, according to Keep, they altered the dam previously shared with the iron works and erected a new dam some thirty or forty rods upstream.

There were several issues between the parties. First, the Prescotts insisted that the original articles of 1720 governing the ironworks ought not to be construed to permit the holder of a majority interest to keep the works in operation without consent of the minority. Second, the Prescotts impugned Keep's title to the five-eighths interest; he was, they argued, merely leasing the use of the works from the Prescotts, a relationship which could terminate if the Prescotts so desired. Finally, it appears, the Prescotts claimed that, inasmuch as title to the land on which the forge stood, as well as to the relevant part of the stream itself, remained in the Prescott family, Keep had no right to the water. Keep denied all these contentions and instituted the first of the actions documented here (Document I).

Meanwhile, Keep's apprentice, Joel Priest, had on various occasions removed the flume (or sluice) lever from the Prescotts' new dam, had shut down their mill gate (thus preventing diversion of the water), and had even broken the mill dam itself. The Prescotts thereupon sued Priest directly (Documents II–IV).

In both cases the Middlesex Inferior Court judgments resulted from sham demurrers.[6] Pleadings being reopened in the Superior Court, the technical arguments were determined, and after the usual continuances the matters went to trial. Adams, with Jonathan Sewall, represented Keep and Priest. The verdict for Keep was £40, but the Prescotts moved in arrest of judgment, and the matter did not conclude until 1776 when a file paper indicates that the parties settled the action.[7] In the other case the jury awarded the Prescotts damages of 40s. and costs of £19 16s. 10d.[8]

---

good quality, being brittle, and it was not extensively used. The business was carried on until the year 1865, when the Forge Company ceased to exist." Edwin R. Hodgman, *History of the Town of Westford* 243 (Lowell, Mass., 1883). The JA materials here set forth seem to refute Hodgman's thesis that during the life of the company its control rested in the hands of old Jonas' descendants. The articles of association are preserved in the file papers of Prescott v. Keep, SF 148227.

[4] See the description of a contemporary ironworks, in which "The bellows ... are very large, and moved by water." John Harris, *Lexicon Technicum*, tit. Iron (London, 1736).

[5] Andrew Oliver prepared a list of forges and furnaces in Massachusetts in 1758, which shows the forge at Westford to be in the possession of "Keep." Arthur C. Bining, *British Regulation of the Colonial Iron Industry* 126 (Phila., 1933).

[6] SF 148100, 148227.

[7] Min. Bk. 96, SCJ Middlesex, Oct. 1773, C–13; SF 148227. No record reference has been found.

[8] Min. Bk. 96, SCJ Middlesex, April 1773, C–20; SCJ Rec. 1773–1774, fols. 18–19.

I. ADAMS' MINUTES OF THE TRIAL[9]

Middlesex Superior Court, Cambridge, October 1773

Prescott vs. Keep.

See 1. Inst. 200 b.[10] to maintain this Action.

Litt. §315.[11] T[enant]s in Common shall have personal Actions jointly.

[2] Cro. 231. Some vs. Barwish.[12] They shall join in Trespass and for Nusance.

2 Vent. 214.[13]

May be taken Advantage of under the general Issue.[14]

1 Vent. 214.[15] Cant be given in Evidence unless one Tenant in common brings Action vs. another.

1 Mod. Ent. 31.[16] If it appears on the Writ, Defendant may take Advantage of it under the general Issue.

Latch. 152, 3.[17]

Defendants Witnesses.

Ebenr. Hadley. Worked at the framing and raising of the new forge. Only a frame in 1770. No new Wheels. The Prescotts forbid Captn. Keep from improving. About 2 foot bigger. Captn. Keep

David Goodhue. Saw Captn. Keep pay Rent. 1/8th Part. Keep and

[9] In JA's hand. Adams Papers, Microfilms, Reel No. 185.

[10] "If two several owners of Houses have a River in Common between them, if one of them corrupt the River, the other shall have an action upon his Case." Coke, *Littleton* 200b, §323.

[11] Coke, *Littleton* §315: "By this it appeareth that Tenants in Common shall have personal Actions jointly. And it is to be observed, that where damages are to be recovered for a wrong done to Tenants in Common ... and one of them shall dye, the survivor of them shall have the action."

[12] Some v. Barwish, Cro. Jac. 231, 79 Eng. Rep. 200 (K.B. 1610): "Where a Nusance is made to the land of two Tenants in Common, ... they shall joyn in the Action; for it is personal."

[13] Apparently an inadvertence for 1 Vent. 214; see note 15 below.

[14] This does not relate to the preceding citation, but the state of the MS suggests that it may pertain to the citation to Mallory, *Modern Entries*, note 16 below.

[15] Anonymous, 1 Vent. 214, 86 Eng. Rep. 144 (K.B. 1673): "In Trespass Quare clausum fregit 'tis a Plea in Abatement to say, That the Plaintiff is Tenant in Common with another: But cannot be given in Evidence upon Not Guilty, as it may where one Tenant in Common brings Trespass against the other."

[16] 1 Mallory, *Modern Entries* 31: "If there be two Tenants in Common, and one only brings an Action where they ought to join; if this appears by the Plaintiff's own shewing, the Defendant may take advantage of it upon the General Issue, but if it does not appear, then it ought to be pleaded in Abatement. *Latch* 153."

[17] Harman v. Whitchlow, Latch 152, 82 Eng. Rep. 321 (K.B. 1627): If one joint tenant or tenant in common brings an action alone, and general issue pleaded, and the tenancy in common appears by the verdict, judgment for the plaintiff; the plea should have been in abatement.

Prescot ballancd Accounts. Keep gave a Note. Rep[ai]rs and Improvement and Forge, Land and Water. K[eep] has often told me that he paid Rent for the whole that he improved and had always paid Rent to Coll. Prescott, and had Receipts till this Contention and since then they would not receive it.

Oliver Parker. Keep said he had Money for the Rent of the old Iron Works. 4 years ago. Prescot came in and Keep paid him Rent for one Year 8 dollars. Prescot said he was obliged to pay it to others. Eben. and Dr. Prescott.

Caleb Woods. K[eep] said they had paid Rent to the Prescotts to their Satisfaction.

Tim. Prescott. Heard Captn. Keep Say he had paid Rent for 5/8ths and had Receipts. And Jona. K[eep] Said he had been and tendered the Rent and they would not take it.

Gershom Fletcher. Keep told of paying Rent to the Prescotts for the Water. Keep said Prescott had a Bond and he paid untill the Bond was so full, that they could enter no more.[18] Then they made Receipts.

1719. Jonas Prescots deed to Jonas the Grandfather of the Defendant,[19] and the Grandfather granted one half to Ebenezer.

1749. Aug. 17. Deed from Jonas Prescott to Ebenezer, one of the defendants. 1/2 of all my homestead. 200 Acres.[20]

1727. Shipley to Eb. Prescot of 1/8 of the forge.[21]

Putnam.[22] Plaintiff has not made out his Title to 5/8ths with any certainty. Answer his fathers Deed to him is of 5/8ths.[23] Kent conveys to J. Keep 1/4—i.e. 2/8ths.[24] Kent to Lyman 3/8ths.[25] Lymans Will[26] and his Widows Deed i.e. Saml. Hunt and his Wifes Deed.[27]

---

[18] The witness refers to the entry of payments on the back of the bond (or lease). This document is not in the file.

[19] Deed, Jonas and Mary Prescott to Jonas Prescott Jr, 8 Oct. 1719; Middlesex Reg. Deeds, Lib. 19, fols. 456–457; SF 148227.

[20] Deed, Jonas Prescott [Jr.] to Ebenezer Prescott, 17 Aug. 1749; Middlesex Reg. Deeds, Lib. 48, fols. 621–622; SF 148227.

[21] A receipt for this deed, John Shipley to Ebenezer Prescott, 21 Oct. 1727, is in SF 148227.

[22] James Putnam, counsel for the Prescotts.

[23] Deed, Jabez Keep to Jonathan Keep, 22 May 1771; Middlesex Reg. Deeds, Lib. 72, fol. 1; SF 148227. JA was noting that this deed answered Putnam's argument.

[24] Deed, Samuel Kent to Jabez Keep, 19 Nov. 1729. Middlesex Reg. Deeds, Lib. 71, fols. 56–57; SF 148227.

[25] Deed, Samuel Kent to Caleb Lyman, 20 Mar. 1735. Middlesex Reg. Deeds, Lib. 36, fol. 120; SF 148227.

Plaintiff has not proved any Right in Hunts Wife, i.e. Lymans Widow. Answer Saml. Kent sold to Caleb Lyman. See the deed.[28]

B. Prescott sells all his Right.[29] Dont appear what it was.

Articles.[30] To be kept up so long as the Major Part should agree to carry on these Works.[31] Never the design that if one Purchased more than half the shares that he should have Power to controul the rest.

The Action must be brought upon the Articles. No support of this Action.

Keep went on in opposition to other Proprietors who forbid him going on. If he can do this he can continue them forever.

The Deed produced by Us comprehends both the Dams *and* both the Mills.

Whoever owns the Land on both sides, owns the Land under the stream.

By the same Reason an Action would have lain, if he had put up a Dam, a mile of[f].

A Dam above, may be of great Advantage. Putnam knows an Instance.

Damages. Only 1 1/2 Ton lost making. Mem. Coal lost. And our [loss?][32] As Priest says.

An hole in the old Dam. Nothing more.

One Witness swears that a Passage Way has been left open there for fish. Then the sluice was made by one of the owners of this Dam—some say to set up a Malt Mill. But none set up.

---

[26] Will, Caleb Lyman, dated 18 March 1737. SF 148227.

[27] Deed, Samuel and Susanna Hunt to Jabez Keep, 11 Sept. 1770. Middlesex Reg. Deeds, Lib. 72, fol. 317; SF 148227.

[28] See note 25 above.

[29] Deed, Benjamin Prescott to Samuel Hartheway, 29 June 1728. Middlesex Reg. Deeds, Lib. 72, fols. 479–480; SF 148227.

[30] Articles dated 6 Feb. 1720, between Jonas Prescott, Jonas Prescott Jr. Benjamin Prescott, John Shaple, John White, and Caleb Trowbridge. The parties agreed "to build, Erect and set up, a Good strong Sufficient and Substantial Forge, Building or Works for the making of Iron by one Fire on, or by, the Brook called Stoney Brook in the Township of Groton almost at the same Place where the said Jonas Prescott has a sawmill not long in standing." SF 148227.

[31] "We the Parties above-named do Covenant consent and agree that when and so soon as the Greater part of the Owners abovesaid their heirs, or Assigns shall conclude and agree to Let alone and cease Improving of the said Forge, or Iron Works for the Use aforesaid. The Irons, other Tools and materials, shall be sold and the money that shall be received for them shall be Divided, and Shared betwixt us, our heirs &c. In Proportion, to what Each one is to Pay, as aforesaid or Otherwise disposed of as the Major Part of us shall Agree and conclude upon." SF 148227.

[32] MS unclear. But probably in response to Putnam's argument that the damages were only the iron lost when the bellows stopped, JA contended that the damages ought to include the value of the wasted fuel and (possibly) the lost profits.

Law obliges the owner of Dam to keep open a passage for fish.[33]

Water carried to the fulling Mill, by a sluice Way or Ditch, at the End of the Dam.

Co. Lit. §324. Notes 200b. Tit. Tenants in Common. If one Tenant in common corrupts the River, the other may have his Action on his Case.[34]

J. Trowbridge.

2. Black. 209.[35] Fee simple conditional, base or qualified fee. Tenants of the Manor of Dale.

Ld. Ray.[36] Judge Powell. A Grant so long as Bow Church stands. Or so long as J.S. has Heirs of his Body.

P. Williams. Macclesfield.[37] So long as such a Tree stands.

II. ADAMS' ABSTRACT OF TITLE [38]

Middlesex Superior Court, Cambridge, October 1772

Prescott vs. Priest.

1756. Novr. Deed from Jonas Prescott to Jonas Jnr. of Gift. 1/4th.

1749. Aug. 17th. from Jonas to Ebenr. 1/2 of all my Homestead. Free Liberty to pass and repass by Gates and Barns.

1719. Octr. 8th. from Jonas to Jonas Jnr. All my Right in an old Dwelling House, &c. excepting

1727, 8 Jany. 28. Jonas to Jonas. 1/2.

---

[33] Probably a reference to the Act of 15 Jan. 1742, set out in No. 34, note 14.

[34] See note 10 above.

[35] Probably this should be 2 Blackstone, *Commentaries* *109: "A base, or qualified, fee is such a one as has a qualification subjoined thereto, and which must be determined whenever the qualification annexed to it is at an end. As in the case of a grant to A and his heirs, *tenants of the manor of Dale*; in this instance, whenever the heirs of A cease to be tenants of that manor, the grant is intirely defeated."

[36] Presumably this refers to a case in Lord Raymond's Reports, and to a dictum by John Powell (1645–1713), puisne judge of the Court of Common Pleas (1695) and the Court of Queen's Bench (1702). *DNB*. The editors have not been able to identify the case.

[37] This also is from an opinion, presumably printed in Peere Williams' Reports, which the editors have not been able to identify. Thomas Parker, first Earl of Macclesfield, was Lord Chief Justice (1710) and Chancellor (1718). *DNB*.

[38] In JA's hand. Adams Papers, Microfilms, Reel No. 185. Dated by reference to adjacent minutes on MS, Smith v. Child, which was tried *sub nom.* Child v. Smith at the Cambridge Superior Court Oct. 1772. Min. Bk. 96, SCJ Middlesex, Oct. 1772, N–6. Many of the deeds are in the file of Prescott v. Keep. See text at notes 19–29.

David Goodhue. Jonas Esq. in Possession of Part, and Prescott that is dead of another Part.

III. ADAMS' MINUTES OF THE TRIAL[39]

Middlesex Superior Court, Charlestown, April 1773

Prescot vs. Priest.

8 Mod. page 115, 16.[40] Hardwick's Cases.[41]
Gilbert's Hist. of Common Pleas.[42]

Dana.[43]

Gershom Fletcher. 55 Years, Prescott the Grandfather of Plaintiffs, have possessed it, and Plaintiffs since and knew they possessed the Grist mill and fulling Mill,[44] *Keep in Possession of the Forge where the Saw mill was.*

David Goodhue.[45] Priest 30 Jany. 1771. took lever out of Prescotts Gate, and tossed it into the Stream. The Gate shut down. Knows Possession 8 years. Dam broke but cant say, who broke it. *Heard Priest say the dam would not stand long,* a Week before it was tore up.

Jona. Pierce. Priest told me that the upper Dam would not stand, that it would be tore down—*the night before it was done.* Plaintiffs have been in Possession. Upper dam built in 1771. Upon Prescotts Land—about 30 or 40 Rods above the other. A benefit to all alike when let out.

Moses Goodhue. Forgot what Priest said, but think he said it would not stand long. The Forge had the longest Use of the Stream, when not Water eno. for all the Mills.

[39] In JA's hand. Adams Papers, Microfilms, Reel No. 185.
[40] Lowther et ux. v. Kelly, 8 Mod. 115, 88 Eng. Rep. 91 (K.B. 1722): Husband and wife sued on an indenture. The wife dying, the husband was allowed to proceed under the statute 8 & 9 Will. 3, c. 11 (1697), note 52 below.
[41] Judge Cushing's report of the present case (Doc. IV) suggests that the case cited was Middleton v. Croft, Hardw. 395, 95 Eng. Rep. 255 (K.B. 1737): When husband and wife declare in prohibition, and take a partial judgment, and the husband dies before costs allowed, the widow may take her costs upon suggestion of the husband's death.
[42] Gilbert, *Common Pleas* 242–248, treats at length the subject of abatement by the death of parties.
[43] Francis Dana, counsel for the Prescotts.
[44] Fulling is the process of cleansing and thickening cloth by beating and washing. OED.
[45] Goodhue was a clothier (cloth maker) who operated the fulling mill next to the Prescotts' gristmill. Deposition of Nathaniel Prentice, SF 148100.

Nat. Prentice.[46] A Lever, Joel kicked off into the Stream. Joel came into Mill without leave, and shut down the Gate.

IV. CUSHING'S REPORT OF THE TRIAL[47]

Middlesex Superior Court, Charlestown, April 1773

Middlesex—Charlestown. April Term 1773.

Prescott et al plaintiffs vs. Priest.

Trespass quare clausum fregit—Defendant pleads in abatement that one of the plaintiffs died since the last continuance. Demurer and joinder.

Mr. Adams in support of the plea cited Gilb. prac. Com. pleas. 242. 248[48]—Hardwicke's cases 395.[49]

Dana for plaintiff—cites 8 Mod. 115. 116.[50]—Bac. abr. Abatement. F. p. 7.[51]

Per Cur[iam] Oliver, C.J., Hutchinson, Ropes and Cushing, J. The action survives; and by 8 & 9 W. 3., Cap. 11. "where the action survives, and one of the plaintiffs dies—it shall go on and not abate."[52] Respondeas ouster awarded unâ voce.[53]

[46] Prentice, who was approximately 15 years old at the time of the events in question, was then David Goodhue's apprentice. His deposition indicates that the Prescotts encouraged him to "shadow" Priest's activities around the dam and the mill. Deposition of Nathaniel Prentice, SF 148100.

[47] Cushing Reports.

[48] Note 42 above.

[49] Note 41 above.

[50] Note 40 above.

[51] 1 Bacon, *Abridgment* 7: "(F) *Of Abatement by the Death of the Parties.* The general Rule to be observed in this Case is, that where the Death of any Party happens, and yet the Plea is in the same Condition as if such Party were living, there such Death makes no Alteration or Abatement of the Writ. A difference has been held with Respect to Real Actions, where there are several Plaintiffs, and there is Summons and Severance (as there is in most Real Actions) that in these the Death of one of the Parties abates the Writ, but not in Personal or Mix'd Actions, where one intire Thing is to be recovered." The word "Severance" refers to the right of several defendants to answer severally. See Stephen, *Pleading* 270.

[52] 8 & 9 Will. 3, c. 11, §7 (1697): "And be it ... enacted ... That if there be two or more plaintiffs or defendants, and one or more of them should die, if the cause of such action shall survive to the surviving plaintiff or plaintiffs, or against the surviving defendant or defendants, the writ or action shall not be thereby abated; but such death being suggested upon the record, the action shall proceed at the suit of the surviving plaintiff or plaintiffs against the surviving defendant or defendants."

[53] That is, the court unanimously ruled that defendant would file a new answer, or "answer over."

20. Wilkins v. Fuller

1771–1772

21. Smith v. Fuller

1770–1778

EDITORIAL NOTE

Jonathan Wilkins owned a pasture and apple orchard on Mill Brook in Middleton, near the Great Pond. On 10 March 1762, Timothy Fuller erected a dam which on 28 March 1762 and thereafter at intervals until February 1770 caused the stream to overflow part of Wilkins' land, allegedly damaging his trees and spoiling his grass. For unexplained reasons, Wilkins waited until 1771 before bringing an action of trespass on the case for the damage. Apparently he was then suing for damage to land which he no longer owned. The writ alleged that Wilkins "on the twenty-eighth Day of February A.D. 1770 was and for nine years then last past had been seized in his Demesne as of Fee" of the land in question.[1] In the Wetmore Notes under the heading "Issues November Term Salem 1771" appears the entry "Wilkins v. Fuller—case for flowing before sale," that is, before Wilkins sold the property.[2] That this was the situation is confirmed by the statement of Samuel Porter, counsel for Fuller, that "Trespass could not be maintained because the Plaintiff not now owner of the land" (Document II).

It is not clear that Adams was ever of counsel. He does not appear in the earliest phase of the case, Ipswich Inferior Court, March 1771, where the jury found for Wilkins £6 damages and costs.[3] Accurate dating of Adams' minutes (Document II) has been difficult. In the manuscript, it appears on the reverse of a copy of the writ in *Hoyt v. Brown,* a case which was entered at the March 1771 Ipswich Inferior Court, and continued term by term to the July 1772 Salem Inferior Court, when the matter was determined on a sham demurrer.[4] It is therefore possible that Document II dates from the March 1771 Ipswich Inferior Court. The docu-

---

[1] SF 132243.

[2] See Wetmore Notes, No. 2, Adams Papers, Microfilms, Reel No. 184. If the quoted phrase means instead that the flowing occurred before a sale *to* Wilkins in 1770, his declaration may reflect an effort to evade the familiar common-law rule that a person who came to an established nuisance had no cause of action. See 2 Blackstone, *Commentaries* *402–403; 7 Holdsworth, *History of English Law* 331. Such a reading seems unlikely, since proof of the title pleaded was necessary to maintain the action. See Shipman, *Common Law Pleading* 209–210. A deed of the property to Wilkins was put in evidence (Doc. II) but it has not survived in the file of the case.

[3] SF 132243.

[4] SF 132296. An appeal was taken, but not prosecuted, at the Nov. 1772 Salem Superior Court.

mentary evidence, however, suggests a later date, either in the June 1771 Ipswich Superior Court, to which both parties appealed, or before referees later. At the June 1771 sitting, the court continued the matter to the Salem Superior Court, November 1771, at which time the case was sent to referees. Mention of the jury view in June 1771 (Document I) suggests that the case may have been partially tried at the Superior Court, although the Minute Book does not so indicate; and indeed current English practice permitted the taking of a view before the trial jury was even impanelled.[5]

But the most probable attribution of Document II is the referees' hearing, the likeliest forum for the sort of testimony there included. One of the original referees having died, a substitute was appointed at the June 1772 Ipswich Superior Court; the report itself is dated 2 July 1772.[6]

The Minute Book contains no mention of counsel, but Document II suggests that Nathaniel Sergeant and Porter appeared for Fuller, with John Lowell for Wilkins. Adams, too, may have appeared for Wilkins. In November 1772, the court read and accepted the referees' report that "there is nothing due from either Party to the other."[7]

Elias Smith had also commenced an action against Fuller alleging straight trespass rather than case,[8] and claiming that Fuller had built a dam on Smith's land in March 1766, "flowing" two and a half of Smith's acres. There are no minutes in Adams' hand, except the solitary title "Smith v. Fuller" in the booklet containing cases from the Ipswich Superior Court, June 1771.[9] The Wetmore Notes, however, contain what appear to be minutes of certain legal points which arose at the trial in the latter term (Document III). Apparently, plaintiff tried to introduce evidence of the actual building of the dam in 1762; defendant objected

[5] Min. Bk. 93, SCJ Ipswich, June 1771, N–2, N–3; Salem, Nov. 1771, C–12, C–13. On the English practice, see Buller, *Nisi Prius* 300–301: "[W]here it shall appear to the Court to be proper the Jury should have a View, the Court may order special Writs of *Distringas* or *Habeas Corpora* to issue, by which the Sheriff shall be commanded to have 6 out of the first 12 of the Jurors named in such Writs, or some greater Number of them, at the Place in Question some convenient Time before the Trial, who shall there have the Matters in Question shewed to them by Persons appointed by the Court. . . . [W]here a View shall be allowed, 6 of the Jurors who shall be named in such Panel, or more who shall be mutually assented to by the Parties, or in Case of their Disagreement, by the proper Officer of the Court, shall have the View, and shall be first sworn to try the Cause before, drawing out of the Box." For the Province statute, see Act of 28 June 1746, 3 A&R 300, periodically renewed.

[6] See the rule and report in SF 132243.

[7] Min. Bk. 93, SCJ Salem, Nov. 1772, C–7, C–8; SF 132243.

[8] For the classic formulation of the distinction between trespass for an immediate injury and case for a consequential injury, see 1 Chitty, *Pleading* 126: "[W]here the damage or injury ensued not directly from the act complained of, it is termed *consequential* or mediate, and cannot amount to a trespass. . . . So if a person pour water on my land, the injury is immediate; but if he stop up a watercourse on his own land; or if he place a spout on his own building, in consequence of which water afterwards runs therefrom into my land, the injury is consequential." See also Reynolds v. Clarke, 2 Ld. Raym. 1399, 92 Eng. Rep. 410 (K.B. 1726).

[9] Wetmore Notes, No. 2, Adams Papers, Microfilms, Reel No. 184.

on two grounds, first, that the dam was not built during the "continuando," or period of continuing flowage alleged in the writ, and, second, that the applicable statute of limitations barred such evidence. From Wetmore's minutes it appears that the court sustained both objections.

The action was initially commenced at the Salem Inferior Court, July 1770, Fuller winning a verdict and costs. The case was appealed to the Salem Superior Court, November 1770 (where Adams first entered the litigation as counsel for Smith, associated with Jonathan Sewall; John Lowell and Samuel Porter appeared for Fuller), and was continued to Ipswich Superior Court, June 1771, where it was at least partly tried before a juror was withdrawn,[10] probably as a result of the court's decision on the evidence questions. At the November 1771 Salem Superior Court, the case was retried, and the jury returned a verdict for Smith for £5 and £30 16s. 7d. costs.[11] Fuller sought review, and the matter dragged on until 1778, when a final entry, "neither party appears," closed the litigation.[12]

I. WETMORE'S MINUTES OF THE WILKINS TRIAL[13]

Essex Superior Court, Ipswich, June 1771

June [1771].

Wilkins v. Fuller. Trespass on the case for flowing land &c. Motion first day of the term for view by Jury and 4 of them sent. Officer and of each side sent.

II. ADAMS' MINUTES OF THE REFEREES' HEARING
IN WILKINS' SUIT[14]

Middleton, July 1772

Wilkins. vs. Fuller

Deed.   Wm. Fuller to Jona. Wilkins.

Archelaus Fuller. Known the Place there 30 years. Wilkins mowed the Land, 1 or 2 Years. Orchard, runs down to the Edge of the Brook.

[10] Min. Bk. 93, SCJ Salem, Nov. 1770, N–8; SCJ Ipswich, June 1771, C–14. SF 132061. On withdrawing a juror, see No. 10, note 7.

[11] Under the heading "Issues November Term Salem 1771" in the Wetmore Notes appears the entry: "Smith v. Fuller. Trespass for Flowing Land." See SCJ Rec. 1771, fol. 194.

[12] Min. Bk. 102, SCJ Ipswich, June 1774, N–1; SCJ Salem, Nov. 1777, C–10; SCJ Salem, Nov. 1778, C–7. SCJ Rec. 1778–1780, fol. 47.

[13] Wetmore Notes, No. 2, Adams Papers, Microfilms, Reel No. 184. This minute appears in the MS several pages after the minutes of Smith v. Fuller, Doc. III below.

[14] In JA's hand. Adams Papers, Microfilms, Reel No. 185.

The Water used to help the Land. But Fullers Dam and Mill there, immediately flowed this Land of Wilkins's and flowd over an high Way that we used to pass to Meeting. It flowd up into Wilkins's an Acre and 1/2 and round several Apple Trees—8 or 10. The Ice would tear the Turffs off, and threw it in Heaps and another sort of Grass and flaggs [15] came in the room of it. A fine Apple tree, was killd by it, as I suppose. 3 Barrells of Cyder a Year. They cutt a 2d Crop, of good Hay before the flowage. There is a Load of Hay odds,[16] worth 9 or 10 Pounds on an Average. The ground when the Water is drawn off is black as a Hat, and a bad Smell the latter End of May. No Mill there since my Remembrance.

Andrew Fuller. 8 or 9 Years since Fuller erected his Mill. Blue Grass before and the want of fresh Grass since. Apple trees, as good bearing Trees as ever known in an orchard. A Number of Trees gone to decay. A Sound Tree, that died. A large Body of Ice froze round it, and as the Water rose and fell the Ice rubbed the Bark off in several Places. The trees are all upon the decay, and now of little Value. Grass not half so good, as it was. Wilkins got about 2 Load, a Year. I suppose the Trees have been planted 40 Years. I remember before a[n]y of them Trees bore [...] of apples.

Jacob Smith. Very good Grass better than 2 Load at 1st and 2d Crop. It has been flowd every Season, better than an Acre. The year before last and every Year before, I mowd it. The 1st Year after it was flowd there was little or no Hay, and very little at any Year since, not a Load. Imagine the Water kill'd the Trees. Bore 2 Barrells a Year upon an Average. A Load we put round the Edges.

Robert Pierce. The Ice tore up the Ground, about the Roots and the Tree died soon. The large Tree had the bark torn off, quite thro.

2 Witnesses about Cyder, Apples, Trees &c.

Porter. Trespass could not be maintained because the Plaintiff not now owner of the Land. Credibility of Witnesses &c.

Mr. Andrews. 69 years ago I helpd draw some Timber to that Mill dam. The Mill sawd Boards for our Meeting House and that is all I know. No Mill there these 50 or 60 years.

Mr. Chandler. It does not look as if any Thing grew on it.

Saml. Cheever.

Rob. Indian. Damages Land, to flow and not keep up the Pond all Winter.

[15] Presumably the marsh plant known as cattail.
[16] "Oddments" or "more or less" are equally valid interpretations.

Bart. Buxton. 1/2 an Acre flowd now [...] as dam up. And the flowing the 1/2 Acre does more hurt than flowing the whole would all Winter.

Thos. Hart. About an Acre flowd.

Andrew Fuller. The freshit has removd a stick and Gravel and made a stop.

Porter. Persons interested not to be credited, and the most credible Witnesses to be believd.

Trees tarr'd. Denyd it.

Law regards not Trifles.

Serjeant. Uncertainty of the Witnesses about the Number of Years. Not the stench to Mr. Smith nor the damage to the High Way.

1st. as to damnifying the Grass. It may be attributed to the upper Mill. Jam [17] Tree, overated.

C[ol.?] Fuller set it at 2 dollars a Year.

III. WETMORE'S MINUTES OF THE SMITH TRIAL [18]

Essex Superior Court, Ipswich, June 1771

June 1771

Smith and Wilkins [v.] Fuller. Bacon Trespass 212. Contin[uand]o in trespass may be waved and evidence given of any trespass before the action. [19]

See 2 Barn[ardisto]n 120. Trespass for disturbance in freehold; title allow'd to be given in evidence by defendant and Com[yn]s said that any possession longer than 7 or 8 years was evidence of it. [20]

This action is trespass for erecting a dam on plaintiffs land and flowing it from 1765. Evidence was offered of erecting dam in 1762,

[17] MS is fairly clear, but the meaning remains obscure.

[18] Wetmore Notes, No. 2, Adams Papers, Microfilms, Reel No. 184. The minutes seem to refer only to Smith's case. The reporter's title, "Smith and Wilkins [v.] Fuller," suggests, however, that he deemed the cases to be related. The relationship is borne out by the fact that the Wetmore minutes of Wilkins' case (Doc. I) appear in the MS several pages after these minutes.

[19] 5 Bacon, *Abridgment* 212: "If the Trespass charged in this Action is laid with a *Continuando* for the whole Time, from a Day on which the first Trespass is charged in the Declaration until a subsequent Day therein mentioned, it is not necessary for the Plaintiff to prove a Continuance of the Trespass for this whole Time: But he must prove a Trespass within it; unless he chooses to waive the *Continuando* entirely, in which Case he may give Evidence of any one Trespass committed before the Action was brought."

[20] Baynes v. Reeves, 2 Barn. 120, 94 Eng. Rep. 394 (Lent Assizes 1732), tried before Baron Comyns.

but objected to it as excluded by limitation Act. Answered that it's repealed. J[udge] Trowb[ridge] seem'd to think it not repeal'd by the tempo[rary] law,[21] and that on declaration for trespass done between 2 days certain, evidence was not admissible without[22] those days.

[21] The Act of 7 July 1740 had set limitation periods for various personal actions; that for "trespass upon lands" was five years. 2 A&R 1020. A clarifying Act of 1 Feb. 1749 established a four-year limitation period for "actions of account, or upon the case, grounded on any lending or contract." 3 A&R 444, 445. In a series of "temporary" Acts, subsequent legislatures successively extended the deadline for existing causes of action. Act of 5 June 1752, 3 A&R 609; Act of 19 April 1754, 3 A&R 727; Act of 31 Oct. 1755, 3 A&R 886; Act of 31 Aug. 1757, 4 A&R 26, 27; Act of 16 Jan. 1760, 4 A&R 280. And in 1767, the limiting date was made 1 July 1770. Act of 20 March 1767, 4 A&R 920. But the legislature did not consider the problem again until the fall of 1770, at which time it passed an Act repealing every previous limitation statute and providing that "all actions of trespass *quare clausum fregit*; all actions of trespass [*de bonis asportatis*] . . .; all actions of account and upon the case, other than such accounts as concern the trade of merchandize" brought after 1 Dec. 1770 should be commenced as follows: "the said actions upon the case (other than for slander), and the said actions of account, and the said actions of trespass [*d.b.a.*] . . . and trespass [*q.c.f.*], within six years from [1 Dec. 1770], or within six years next after the cause of such actions or suits, and not after." Act of 20 Nov. 1770, 5 A&R 109–110.

The "tempo[rary] law" referred to by Trowbridge in the minute was apparently the 1770 Act. According to Lieutenant Governor Thomas Hutchinson's letter transmitting the legislation of the session just concluded to England for approval, the 1770 Act was "not a Temporary Law but placed among them [i.e. in the compilation of all laws passed at the session] through inattention which must be corrected." Hutchinson to Lords of Trade, 21 Dec. 1770, in 5 A&R 143 note. The plaintiff seems to have argued that under the 1770 Act matters arising at any time prior to 1 Dec. 1770 were not barred until 1 Dec. 1776. Trowbridge's point was probably that the 1770 Act did not repeal the 1740 Act as to causes of action on which suit had been brought before 1 Dec. 1770. Since the 1740 limitations on trespass q.c.f. had not been among those extended by later legislation, the 1762 evidence was clearly barred when this action was brought in 1770. For JA's role in the passage of the 1770 Act, see p. lxxxvii, note 204, above.

[22] That is, "before or after." The comma following "certain" has been supplied.

G. Domestic Relations

22. Broadstreet v. Broadstreet

1771–1774

EDITORIAL NOTE

At twenty-four Adams could ask, "But Quere, if Dissonance of Dispositions is a sufficient Reason [for allowing a divorce]? This may be known, if sufficient Caution is taken beforehand." [1] Some twelve years later as counsel for Abigail Broadstreet in a divorce case involving domestic discord of the type dear to the readers of women's magazines today, he may well have had cause to ponder this proposition again.

Abigail Fuller had married Dr. Joseph Broadstreet of Topsfield in February 1770. Although Abigail had recently bought a small farm in nearby Middleton, the town in which her family lived, the couple, apparently for financial reasons, chose to move in with her brother Jacob. Within a few months Broadstreet became extremely restive, proclaiming to all who cared to hear that he had made a poor choice of wife in marrying a woman with no fortune but some unprofitable real estate. He said that "he was a damned fool for having of her and that he should rather have married a Negro if She had money." [2] Such pronouncements were accompanied by frequent threats to sell all that Abigail had and to depart with the proceeds to a more desirable location.

By the fall of 1770 Abigail was well along with child. Her mother, hearing that Broadstreet was "very uneasy" with his wife and still threatening to leave her, summoned him to the matriarchal presence. There followed a stormy scene in which she tried to persuade her son-in-law to stay with his wife "in her difficult circumstances, she being very unwell and unfit to care for herself." Pleas and offers of assistance were of no avail. All that Broadstreet would say was "that he was a fool for having her and that he would not tarry with her for he had much rather be in the Mines." [3]

Perhaps in reaction to this interview, Broadstreet then left home. He soon returned, however, and, repenting past excesses and promising future good behavior, persuaded Abigail to move with him into her own house, about half a mile distant. Almost at once he began to threaten abandonment again. According to Abigail's sister Mehitabel, who helped her to move, "He appeared very ill-natured, cursed his wife and cursed himself

[1] Diary, Summer 1759. 1 JA, *Diary and Autobiography* 111.

[2] See the deposition of Mehitabel Fuller, 21 Sept. 1771, in the file. SF 129762. The account which follows is pieced together from numerous depositions found there.

[3] Deposition of Abigail Fuller, widow, 21 Sept. 1771. SF 129762.

280

and behaved like a man in distraction, wishing that he was in Salem Gaol or in the Spanish Mines, or in the worst place in the world other than there, and screaming and hallowing and slapping his hands together." [4] There were moments of respite, but on the whole Broadstreet's unsettled and unsettling conduct worsened during the next two weeks. He would waken Abigail in the middle of the night, ranting of money or screaming that the devil was coming, so that periodically she was forced to take refuge with her mother, who also lived nearby, just to get a night's sleep. Finally, early in December, Broadstreet departed once more, taking his possessions and vowing never to see his wife again.

After waiting a few days for her husband's return, Abigail took up permanent residence at her mother's in order to obtain the bare necessities of existence. Here, Broadstreet, accompanied by friends who sought to reunite the couple, visited her on several occasions. In these interviews she conceded that he had not harmed her, other than by his nocturnal outbursts and perhaps a certain overinsistence on his connubial prerogatives. She remained adamant in her refusal to rejoin him, however, at least until winter and her pregnancy had run their courses, for she feared that an irremediable lack of funds sufficient to maintain Broadstreet in his desired style would quickly reawaken all the old dissatisfaction and lead to a resumption of his rantings. Without some security for his good behavior, which was not forthcoming, she "durst not [return], for he behaved like a madman and . . . he would infallibly be the death of her: not in laying violent hands upon her, but by worrying and frighting her and hindering her from sleep." [5]

On several occasions Abigail agreed to go to some other location, away from her family, which Broadstreet saw as the evil influence upon her. His efforts to find a place for them to live were inconclusive, however, and each meeting seemed to end on a similar note. Broadstreet would formally invite his wife to come and live with him again, but in the same breath aver that he did not care if she ever did. In March 1771 Abigail's child was born. Thereafter, her husband grew increasingly embittered. In calmer moments he blamed the separation on family influence, but more and more frequently he stated that he wished wife and child were dead and expressed his seeming hatred of them in a series of drastic epithets. It was reported that in February he had rented Abigail's house, sold off her hay, and "advertised" her—that is, publicly disclaimed responsibility for her debts.

As her strength returned, Abigail sought a divorce in a proceeding before the Governor and Council, who had jurisdiction of such questions under a Province Act of 1692.[6] In England, questions of divorce were within the competence of the ecclesiastical courts, which applied the canon law. These courts could decree an absolute divorce, *a vinculo matrimonii* (from the bonds of matrimony), only when the marriage itself

---

[4] Deposition of Mehitabel Fuller, note 2 above.
[5] Deposition of Archelaus Fuller, 21 Sept. 1771. SF 129762.
[6] Act of 3 Nov. 1692, c. 25, §4, 1 A&R 61.

was a nullity because of such defects as consanguinity or impotence. In such a case the parties were free to remarry. When the grounds were adultery, cruelty, or the like, the marriage itself was held valid and un-breakable, and the ecclesiastical courts would grant a divorce *a mensa et thoro* (from bed and board). This was in effect only a decree of separation and maintenance, each party being barred from remarriage during the other's lifetime. If the aggrieved party in a divorce *a mensa* wished further relief, he or she might, at least in a case where the grounds had been adultery, apply to the House of Lords, which would, upon appropriate investigation, order the marriage dissolved, permitting remarriage.[7]

In Massachusetts, because of the power of the Governor and Council, the location of jurisdiction to grant divorces *a vinculo* was ambiguous. The Court of Assistants in the old Colony seems to have granted this relief in cases of desertion, bigamy, and adultery, acting in its judicial capacity; [8] but after 1692 the Governor and Council did not follow suit. From 1755 to 1757 the General Court took to itself the powers of the House of Lords, granting divorces *a vinculo* in cases in which the Governor and Council had previously granted decrees *a mensa*.[9] It was perhaps in response to these proceedings that Governor Pownall in a 1760 message to the Council raised the question whether that body had jurisdiction of divorces *a vinculo* as a civil, rather than a spiritual, court under the Province Act of 1692. "If not," the Governor continued, "the Doubt then remains whether this Power lies with the Legislature of this Province or only with the Parliament of Great Brittain." [10] The Board of Trade had referred this question of legislative power to the Privy Council, but, although hearings were scheduled in 1759, none of the private acts granting divorces seems to have been disallowed.[11] Perhaps through Pownall's influence, however, the General Court granted no further divorces, and the Divorce Records of the Governor and Council show that the latter body thereafter issued numerous decrees *a vinculo* in cases of adultery.[12] The relief which in

[7] See Richard Burn, *Ecclesiastical Law*, 2:428–431 (London, 2d edn., 1767); 1 Holdsworth, *History of English Law* 622–624; 10 *id.* at 608; 11 *id.* at 622–623; 12 *id.* at 685–686. Compare Quincy, *Reports* (Appendix) 577. See also No. 23, note 5.

[8] See George L. Haskins, *Law and Authority in Early Massachusetts* 195 (N.Y., 1960); Petition of Mary Sanders (1674), 1 *Records of the Court of Assistants 1630–1692* 30 (Boston, ed. John Noble, 1901); Petition of Hope Ambrose (1678), *id.* at 127; Petition of Susannah Goodwin (1680), *id.* at 168.

[9] See Act of 10 Jan. 1755, No. 81, 6 A&R 165; Act of 10 June 1755, No. 82, *id.* at 169; Act of 15 April 1756, No. 83, *id.* at 170; Act of 18 April 1757, No. 84, *id.* at 173; Act of 22 April 1757, No. 85, *id.* at 174; Act of 14 June 1757, No. 86, *id.* at 177.

[10] Supreme Court Probate Rec. 1760–1830, fol. 1, printed in Quincy, *Reports* (Appendix) 577.

[11] Preface, 6 A&R v–vi; Smith, *Appeals to the Privy Council* 582–585.

[12] See, for example, No. 23. There were at least thirty-five divorce proceedings in Massachusetts between 1760 and 1775, of which twenty were decrees *a vinculo* for adultery; five were annulments for prior marriages; and seven were divorces from bed and board for cruelty and the like; in at least two cases a decree was denied for insufficient evidence. Divorce Recs. In the latter category was Shank

England could be had only by the petitioner who could afford to go to the House of Lords, was thus available in Massachusetts in the ordinary course.

Abigail's libel, filed by Jonathan Sewall in July 1771, alleged Broadstreet's departure in December of the preceding year, his failure to support his wife since that time, and his constantly expressed threats to her fortune and wishes for her death. It concluded with a prayer "that by your Excellency's and Honors' Decree she may be divorced from Bed and Board with the said Joseph and thereby be intitled to the separate and sole use and improvement of her own Estate for the maintenance of herself and Child." Broadstreet's answer, propounded by Josiah Quincy Jr., denied Abigail's allegations and attributed the separation to the efforts of "dark and mercenary Enemies to his household," who by "insinuating arts withdrew the affections of his Wife." Two justices of the peace were assigned to take testimony for both sides, and on 17 October, before the Governor and Council, the depositions were read and the parties heard.[13]

Adams' notes of the proceedings, printed below, indicate that he argued Abigail's case, probably with Sewall. The authorities which he collected show that the canon law, as applied in the ecclesiastical courts in England, was an important source of the Massachusetts law of divorce. He thus limited himself to questions concerning the divorce *a mensa* as the canon law defined it, seeking to establish that desertion and cruelty were grounds, and were present in this case.

Under canon law the husband could be required to pay alimony after a divorce from bed and board, the theory being that, since the marriage still existed, he was merely continuing to perform the duty of support which he would have had in normal course. Since the wife by her conduct could forfeit alimony, Adams also endeavored to lay the groundwork for an argument that Abigail had not done so in this case, despite her coolness toward Broadstreet's attempts at reconciliation. The arguments were apparently successful on all counts, for with the sole dissent of Governor Hutchinson, who did not agree "that there was a sufficient cause for a separation," the Council decreed a divorce from bed and board. Abigail was awarded alimony of £25 per year, payable in quarterly installments, plus the costs of the proceedings.[14]

That the separation which Abigail sought ensued seems clear. What is less clear is her success in obtaining alimony. In 1774 she was forced to

---

v. Shank (1772), in which a divorce *a vinculo* sought for adultery was denied on evidentiary grounds. The libel in the file is in JA's hand. SF 129766. The first Massachusetts Divorce Act after the Revolution empowered the Supreme Judicial Court to grant divorces *a vinculo*, not only on the traditional canon-law grounds, but for bigamy and adultery as well, thus adopting what seems to have been the pre-Revolutionary practice. The court could also decree divorce *a mensa* for extreme cruelty. Mass. Acts 1785, c. 64, §3 (1786).

[13] Divorce Recs., fols. 68–70. See the libel and answer in SF 129762. The Commission to Andrew Oliver Jr, and William Brown, dated 12 Sept. 1771, and a deposition of Daniel Bixby, 5 Oct. 1771, are in MHi:Photostats; for other depositions, see notes 2–5 above; note 27 below.

[14] See Divorce Recs., fols. 68–70. JA received a fee of 48s. JA, Office Book, MQA.

petition the Council again, because Broadstreet had paid her nothing. In accordance with the statutory procedure for the enforcement of its decrees, the Council ordered a warrant to issue for Broadstreet's arrest.[15] He could be held in prison until he chose to comply. Whether he was actually taken, and whether the pains of incarceration eventually triumphed over his enmity toward Abigail do not appear in the record.

ADAMS' NOTES OF AUTHORITIES AND MINUTES OF THE HEARING[16]

Governor and Council, Boston, 17 October 1771

Abigail Broadstreet vs. Joseph Broadstreet

Godolphin's Repertorium Canonicum 507.[17]

"Wife libelled Husband in the Ecclesiastical Court for Alimony because he beat her so as she could not live with him. A Prohibition was prayed, but denied by the Court; and it was held in this Case, that the Wife might have the Peace vs. her Husband for unreasonable Correction." Sir Thos. Simmonds Case. Mores Rep.[18]

508. §13. Definition of Alimony, and Elopement.[19]

509. §14. Vid.[20]

---

[15] See her petition in SF 129762. The statutory authority is that cited by JA, note 24 below.

[16] In JA's hand. Adams Papers, Microfilms, Reel No. 185.

[17] John Godolphin, *Repertorium Canonicum* 507 (London, 3d edn., 1687).

[18] This notation appears in the margin in Godolphin, *Repertorium Canonicum* 507, cited in note 17 above. JA's quote from Godolphin is in turn an almost verbatim borrowing by Godolphin of the report of "Sir Tho. Simonds Case" in *An Exact Abridgment in English of the Cases Reported by Sr. Francis More Kt.* 263 (London, ed. Hughes, 1665). The original report of the case is found *sub nom.* Sir Tho. Seymours Case, in Moore K.B. 874, 72 Eng. Rep. 966 (K.B. undated).

[19] That is, Godolphin, *Repertorium Canonicum* 508. The definitions are "*Alimony* .... that proportion of the Husbands Estate, which the Wife sues in the Ecclesiastical Court, to have allowed her for her present subsistence and livelyhood, according to Law, upon any such separation from her Husband, as is not caused by her own *elopement* or *Adultery*.... *Elopement* ... that voluntary departure of a Wife from her Husband to live with an Adulterer."

[20] Godolphin, *Repertorium Canonicum* 509. A qualification of the passage in note 19 above, to the effect that, although in most cases of separation not occasioned by elopement, adultery, or a legal impediment to marriage, the husband is held to pay alimony, he need not pay if the wife departs of her own accord through no default of his, even where she is not chargeable with adultery. When the reason of her departure is some default in the husband, such as cruelty, she is then entitled to alimony, if she is blameless. If the wife repents of any flight save elopement, adultery, or a legal impediment, the husband must take her back or pay alimony. Conversely, where a blameless wife has fled, if the husband repents and offers security that will assure his good behavior, he need not pay alimony if his wife then refuses to return.

510. §16.[21]
511. §18.[22]
Prov. Law, page 59, 60. An Act to prevent incestuous Marriages.[23]
Prov. Law. 8 G. 2, c. 10, page 371. Impowered to inforce their decrees by Imprisonment.[24]
Burn. Ecc. Law. Vol. 2. 430. 431.[25]
Woods. civ. Law. 124. middle[26]

Drs. Wit[nesse]s.[27]

J. Wilkins
E. Knight
[J.] Town.

[21] Godolphin, *Repertorium Canonicum* 510, setting out John Owen's Case, Hetley 69, 124 Eng. Rep. 349 (C.P. undated) (Prohibition granted to the Council of the Marches of Wales, which had seized Owen and sequestered his property for non-payment of a decree of maintenance made in a case where the husband was living apart by the Bishop of Bangor and confirmed in the Council. *Semble*, the only remedy for disobedience of an ecclesiastical decree is excommunication). This case and the following one were apparently cited by JA as examples of the action of the Ecclesiastical Courts, rather than for the precise holdings on the prohibitions.

[22] Godolphin, *Repertorium Canonicum* 511–512, setting out Cloborn v. Cloborn (cited incorrectly as Clobery v. Clobery), Hetley 149, 124 Eng. Rep. 414 (C.P. 1631) (Prohibition to the Ecclesiastical Court refused in award of alimony for cruelty including physical violence and insults, where the husband had merely denied the allegations. His grounds for the prohibition were that he had chastised his wife for reasonable cause and that there had been a subsequent reconciliation. The court held that it could not "examine what is cruelty," and that moreover the actions here were cruelty. If the husband had pleaded some justification and it had been refused, then the prohibition might lie).

[23] *Acts and Laws, Of His Majesty's Province of the Massachusetts Bay in New-England* 59–60 (Boston, 1759); Act of 19 June 1695, c. 2, 1 A&R 208. Section 3 provides in part that "it shall be in the power of the justices of the superiour court of judicature to assign unto any woman so separated [*i.e.* divorced or marriage annulled] such reasonable part of the estate of her late husband as in their discretion the circumstances of the estate may admit, not exceeding one-third part thereof." *Id.* at 209. For a case of JA's illustrating the operation of the statute, see the petition of Sarah Griffin (Gould), SF 91716; Min. Bk. 98, SCJ Suffolk, Aug. 1773, N–47. This arose from Gould v. Gould, SF 129772; Divorce Recs., fols. 78–79.

[24] *Acts and Laws* 371–372 (1759); Act of 8 Jan. 1755, c. 15, 3 A&R 782. The Act provides that upon refusal or neglect of any person to obey the decree of Governor and Council in a controversy concerning marriage and divorce, the secretary of the Province, upon their order, may issue a warrant for the arrest and commitment to prison of that person without bail until he complies with the decree.

[25] 2 Burn, *Ecclesiastical Law* 430–431. The passage deals with the nature and incidents of divorce *a mensa et thoro*. See text at note 7 above.

[26] Wood, *New Institute of the Civil Law* 124, a passage setting forth the grounds of divorce under the civil law, which include irreconcilable hatred, intolerable cruelty, and "when one party shall unjustly forsake and live apart from the other." Wood then states that the law of England, following the canon law, will not permit divorce from the bonds of matrimony, but does not raise the question of divorce from bed and board.

[27] That is, evidence presented on behalf of Dr. Broadstreet. See note 13 above.

23. Dougherty v. Little

1768

EDITORIAL NOTE

Today we would probably call this action tort for loss of consortium by seduction. In 18th-century England and Massachusetts, the cuckold's remedy was an action of trespass for an assault on his wife, better known as "criminal conversation," or just "crim. con." [1] Adams represented the defendant Little in the Inferior Court, and the testimony recorded in his minute fairly states the story. Further details emerge from the file of the divorce suit which Dougherty was prosecuting simultaneously with his action at law. [2]

Dissatisfied with the £60 verdict in the Inferior Court, Dougherty appealed to the April 1768 Charlestown Superior Court; there, with Adams no longer representing Little, the jury awarded Dougherty £400 and £27 4s. 9d. costs. [3] Meanwhile the grand jury indicted Mrs. Dougherty and Little twice, once for adultery and once for lewd, lascivious, and wanton behavior. [4] Finally, the Governor and Council, sitting in exercise of their exclusive jurisdiction in divorce, on 15 June 1768 granted Dougherty an uncontested divorce *a vinculo*, a copy of the Superior Court judgment being a part of the evidence "by which it appears that the said James [Dougherty] hath fully proved his libel." [5]

See the depositions of Joshua Wilkins, Enos Knight, and Jonathan Town in SF 129762. Wilkins testified that the hay sold by Broadstreet was not actually Abigail's. The other two depositions describe the Jan. 1771 meetings between the parties in terms favorable to Broadstreet.

[1] F. Buller, *Introduction to the Law relative to Trials at Nisi Prius* 26–28 (London, 1772); 3 Bacon, *Abridgment* 581.

[2] "The proponent doth alledge that in August A.D. 1764 he sailed for the Island of Newfoundland and that he continued there 'till the month of December last. . . . That when your proponent returned from the said Island of Newfoundland, to his great grief he found his said Wife Mary big with Child, and has great reason to suspect that the said Thomas Little is the Father thereof your proponent not having cohabited but been absent from his said Wife for the space of three years last past." The libel was filed 26 Feb. 1768. SF 129750. See also note 10 below. For Dougherty's disclaimer of his wife's debts, dated 24 Dec. 1767, see *Boston Gazette*, 7 March 1768, p. 4, col. 3.

[3] Min. Bk. 88, SCJ Charlestown, April 1768, N–13; Rec. 1768–1769, fols. 163–164; SF 147615.

[4] SF 147605. No record of the disposition of Mrs. Dougherty's case seems to have survived. Little's case was called at the Cambridge Superior Court, Oct. 1768, but he defaulted and was fined £200 and costs. Min. Bk. 88, SCJ Cambridge, Oct. 1768, N–15.

[5] Divorce Recs. 45–48 (1768). See also *Boston Gazette*, 25 April 1768, p. 3, col. 2. As to the divorce jurisdiction see No. 22. In England in a proceeding for divorce *a vinculo* in the House of Lords (No. 22, text at note 7), the applicant had to establish that he or she not only had obtained a divorce *a mensa* in the ecclesiastical courts but had recovered for criminal conversation at law. 1 Holdsworth, *History of English Law* 623.

ADAMS' MINUTES OF THE TRIAL [6]

Middlesex Inferior Court, Charlestown, March 1768

Dougherty vs. Little

Sewall. [7]

Dougherty at Newfoundland, 3 Years, Little breakfasted dined suppd and lodgd there. Lodgd with her, got her with Child, and was seen in the Act of Copulation with her.

Revd. Whitney. Rode to Meeting with her.

Thos. Nicholls. Frequently there. Candle put out and two Persons went out, and Little and she came in.

Wm. Little. Was left with the Care of Mrs. Dougherty and got his Brother to bring her up from Charlestown and desired his Brother to take some Care of her and her Negro when I was sick. Talk about the Parson. Am not knowing to her being with Child. The Woman poorly at Meeting. But I know not the Cause. The last Time I saw her it did appear to me, that she was belyed. He always denyd it to me.

Mrs. Little. I thought her with Child. Have not seen her since.

Thos. Trowbridge. He told me that he could have as good a Lodging with Mrs. Dougherty, as I should have with that Woman. Hints. Infirmations. [8]

Chaise coming from Boston.

Mrs. Nicholls. Never saw any Indecency, any unhansum Carriage. Seen his Horse stand there. Common fame, that he used to frequent the House. Not common Report that he staid o Nights. Common Report that she with Child. I thought she was with Child 7 months gone, not sure she was.

Mrs. Nicholls lodged with her. I discoverd [9] that I thought she was pregnant. It seemd like a living Child.

Negro's. Riding a trotting Horse. Into Bed. Saw em twice in Bed. Moonlight went thro the Room once. [10]

---

[6] In JA's hand. Adams Papers, Microfilms, Reel No. 185.

[7] Jonathan Sewall, Dougherty's counsel. See Inferior Court record, SF 147615.

[8] The MS is clear. JA may have meant "Informations," or perhaps he actually intended "Infirmations," "the action of weakening or invalidating (evidence)." *OED.*

[9] That is, disclosed.

[10] This is probably the testimony of one Jacko, whose deposition in the divorce proceedings, dated 6 May 1768, is as follows:

"Jacko twenty-two years of age Testifys and says that In the winter Season in the year 1767 he Came to the house of Mr. James Dougherty in Sherly District and that Soon after he Came there, Thos. Little of said Sherly Came to said Doughertys house Mary the wife of said Dougherty being and liveing at said house

Dinah. Saw the same. Man upon the Woman.

Children. Boy. Saw em on the Bed, with Arms round each others Necks.

Sewal.

Actually with Child. Mrs. Little and Mrs. Nicholls.

[...]. And carnally knew.

⟨*about a fortnight after he said Jacko Came*⟩ said Little Came and put his horse into the Chase and road with said Mary and used freequantly so to Do and also Breakfast Dine and Drink Tea with the said Mary, in the ⟨*month of*⟩ beginning of the Summer in the year 1767 the said Jacko says he saw said Little and said Mary ⟨*Standing against said fence*⟩ standing by the fence said Mary, Back to the fence said Littles Belly to her Belly, Some time after said Little Came to said Doughertys house and in the Evening said Little sent him said Jacko to said Littles house with his horse and Told him he must lodge there that night, between nine and ten o Clock that same Evening he said Jacko Came back from said Littles house said Little asked why he Came back, he answered he would not lye out of the house that night, said Little Bid the people in the house a Good night and went out of the house, said Jacko went out after him, then said Little went round to another Doar where said Mary met said Little and opened the Doar with a Candle in her hand and let him said Little in, and Shut up the house, which obliged said Jacko to go in at a Celler window, and when he Came up into the Entry way he said Jacko Saw said Littles Cloaths lye on the floar by said Marys bed, and then he said Jacko went up Chamber over her said Marys Bedroom, there being only some Boards thrown Down loose for a floar, there being Considerable Distances between the Boards saw said Little and said Mary in Bed together ⟨the moon shining that nite⟩, a few nights afterwards ⟨the moon shining⟩ the said Jacko being in said Chamber he heard Some body Come into the said Marys Bedroom before Discribed, she then being in Bed, Saw said Little In the Bed with said Mary, and upon her, and the Bed Cloaths in Constant motion. Some time after said Little Came to said Doughertys house aforesaid in the Evening the said Jacko being then in bed, and Called him up and asked him where said Mary was, and said Mary and said Little went out of the house and Tarryd about one Quarter of an hour, then said Mary Came in, ⟨*and went to bed*⟩ and Early next morning found said Little in said house, and said Little Told him said Jacko that he Came over to ask said Mary whether she wanted his plow that Day. Some time after said Jacko took a lite in the Evening to go Down Seller to Draw Drink, and saw in the Entry said Mary ⟨*leaning over*⟩ setting against a Chest, and said Little on his Knees ⟨*. . . her*⟩ before her.   Jacko"

H. *Administrative Law*

24. Roxbury v. Boston

1766

EDITORIAL NOTE

As in England, the Massachusetts justices of the peace, singly and in their joint capacity as the Court of General Sessions of the Peace for each county, formed a kind of all-purpose administrative tribunal with jurisdiction in a wide variety of local government questions. Matters within their power included tavern licensing; the construction, repair, and use of highways; militia service; assessment and collection of taxes; regulation of weights and measures, as well as the quality of food and other products; shipbuilding; land use; violation of the Sabbath; support of the ministry and schools; and welfare. In the last category were two important problems which produced substantial amounts of litigation—the settlement and removal of paupers, and the support of illegitimate children. John Adams had a number of cases in both of these fields, which demonstrate the early operation of administrative law in Massachusetts.[1] The present case and Nos. 25–27 concern paupers. Nos. 28–30 are examples of bastardy proceedings, as they were called.

The poor relief system rested on the principle that a town was responsible for the support of all indigent persons having a "settlement" within it. Under statutes in force until 1767 a pauper gained a settlement if he remained within a town for twelve months without being "warned" by the selectmen to depart. Once the pauper had been warned, he could be removed to another town by the constable under the warrant of a justice of the peace. Litigation over those provisions generally concerned the contention of the town to which a pauper had been removed that it should not be charged with his keep. The town would apply to the county Court of General Sessions for decision of the question, a matter within that court's statutory jurisdiction.[2] Usually the court would determine the town of set-

---

[1] For a summary of the jurisdiction of Massachusetts Justices of the Peace and Courts of General Sessions, see p. xxxix–xl above; see note 14 below. For the English practice, see Edith G. Henderson, *Foundations of English Administrative Law* 18–25 (Cambridge, Mass., 1963). For another JA case under the poor laws, see "the Case of Dumb Tom the Pauper" (Scituate v. Pembroke), 17 May 1767, 1 JA, *Diary and Autobiography* 336; SF 142416. For a pioneering discussion of such matters, see Charles F. Adams, *Three Episodes of Massachusetts History*, 2:722–781 (Boston and N.Y., 1892).

[2] For the principal statutory provisions involved, see notes 11–13 below; No. 25, notes 4, 6; No. 27, note 16.

tlement and would order that town to pay all charges incurred by the other town on account of the pauper.

Although a statute provided an appeal to the "court of assize and general gaol delivery" from "sentences" of the General Sessions,[3] there was no specific provision for review of orders in cases under the poor laws. The courts had developed the remedy of certiorari, following English practice in this and other cases in which no other appellate relief was provided.[4] On writ of certiorari, the Superior Court limited its review to matters appearing on the face of the record, except for jurisdictional questions. The procedure on appeal in the Superior Court, however, as it was applied in civil actions and presumably in appeals from the Sessions, involved a trial *de novo* before a jury at which new evidence and matters outside the record could be freely offered.[5] In the case of *Roxbury v. Boston*, the party aggrieved at Sessions sought to obtain this broader measure of relief.

The case concerned the status of one Rebecca Choate, who had allegedly been warned from Roxbury with her husband in 1738. On 31 December 1763, having at some point returned, she was removed from Roxbury to Boston by warrant of a justice of the peace. There she became and remained a public charge, except for a brief stay in Roxbury occasioned by a small-pox epidemic in Boston.

In January 1765 the Selectmen of Boston petitioned the Suffolk County Court of General Sessions for her removal to Roxbury and the return of their expenditures for her, urging that the original warrant of removal had been issued by a justice who was a Roxbury inhabitant, and therefore interested, and that Rebecca was in fact an inhabitant of Roxbury. Jeremy Gridley, who appeared for Roxbury at the April 1765 Sessions, denied that Rebecca was an inhabitant as alleged. After several continuances the case was heard in July 1766. The court found that Rebecca was not an inhabitant of Boston at the time of her warning in Roxbury or afterward, but was an inhabitant of Roxbury, and ordered the latter town to pay her

[3] See note 16 below.

[4] The earliest use of the writ found in Massachusetts for a case under the poor laws is Waltham v. Weston, SCJ Rec. 1760–1762, fol. 161 (Middlesex, 1761). The writ, in the form printed in No. 27, Doc. V, was issued in 1759.

The first certiorari of any kind known to have issued from the Superior Court is that in Boxford Parish v. Rogers, SCJ Recs. 1753–1754, fol. 101d (Essex SCJ, Oct. 1753), a case involving a minister's salary. Edith G. Henderson, *Certiorari and Mandamus in Massachusetts and Maryland* 3–4 (Unpubl. paper, Harvard Law School, 1955). Prior to 1720 at least, appeals from Sessions seem to have been allowed in such matters, as well as in poor law, bastardy, and highway cases. *Id.* at 4–5. In 1747, however, the Superior Court dismissed the appeal in Bodfish v. Barnstable, a case under the poor laws. See note 12 below. The use of certiorari may have developed in response to this decision. The English practice is covered in Henderson, *Foundations of English Administrative Law* 83–116, 143–159.

[5] The procedure and scope of review on certiorari are discussed more fully in No. 27. As to appeal in civil cases, see generally p. xlii above. That there was to be a jury in appeals from Sessions appears in the provision that the appellant in such cases should pay the same fee to jurors required in a civil appeal. Act of 16 June 1699, c. 1, §3, 1 A&R 368. For a case in which the Superior Court may have gone outside the record, see No. 30.

charges and costs of court to Boston. The record reflects that the Selectmen of Roxbury "appealed" to the Superior Court, giving bond as the statute provided.[6]

The precise reason why an appeal was sought instead of certiorari cannot be determined. It is possible that Gridley wanted the case tried to a jury rather than by the court. Suffolk jury panels included jurors from the country towns, who might tend to favor Roxbury's cause against the larger Boston.[7] The reason might also have been a desire to offer evidence or raise issues not in the record. It is not clear whether "the record" for purposes of certiorari was merely the usual formal statement of pleadings and proceedings below taken from the record book of the lower court or whether it also included other papers from the files. If the former, there was evidence in the file from the trial in Sessions, which probably would not have been admissible on certiorari. Since this evidence tended to show that Rebecca Choate was not an inhabitant of Roxbury, Gridley may have wanted the Superior Court to consider it in reaching a decision.[8] Whether or not this evidence was thought part of the record, it is also possible that Gridley was seeking the admission of oral testimony or additional documentary material not preserved in the file.

Whatever the reasons for taking an appeal, the case came on in the Superior Court at the August 1766 term, with Adams and Gridley arguing for Roxbury and Otis and Fitch for Boston. Adams' notes, printed below, indicate that the only question raised was whether an appeal lay. The Province statute providing an appeal from the Sessions seems to have

[6] See the warrants of warning and removal, the petition of Boston, and the record of the Court of Sessions in SF 100839. For the requirement of bond with two sureties in appeals from "sentences" of the Sessions, see Act of 16 June 1699, c. 1, §3, 1 A&R 368, discussed further in note 16 below. Boston's charges, "allow'd by the Court," amounted to £47 3s. 1d. for Rebecca's board in the Alms House until her death in March 1766 and for medical care. SF 100839.

[7] See, for example, the Suffolk venire, Aug. term 1766, which included 48 petit jurors, 16 from Boston, 6 from Roxbury, the rest in ones and twos from 16 other towns. SF 100784.

[8] As to "the record" in certiorari, see No. 27, note 8. The evidence included Rebecca Choate's own deposition, dated 28 Jan. 1766, and those of three other witnesses, dated 20 May 1766, which indicated that she and her late husband had lived in Roxbury until some time in the fall of 1735, but during the next two and a half years had lived successively in Dedham, Stoughton, Dorchester, and Boston. SF 100839. The dates are somewhat vague, but it would have been possible to conclude that the Choates had lived without being warned in either Dedham or Boston for the year necessary to gain a settlement. In March or April 1738 they moved back to Roxbury but a copy of a warrant in the file shows that they were warned from that town in May 1738. *Ibid.* The file also contains an attested list of the selectmen of Roxbury for 1763, showing that Joseph Williams, the justice of the peace who ordered Rebecca's removal, held the former office as well. *Ibid.* This document had presumably been put in evidence for Boston on the trial, to support the contention that Williams was interested. The list would also have been admissible on an appeal, but Gridley may have intended to contest this point on legal rather than factual grounds, since he had not denied the allegation to this effect in the Sessions. The issue had not yet been ruled upon against the jurisdiction by the Suffolk Court of Sessions. See No. 27, text at note 11.

been offered as the basis for the proceeding, but Otis and Fitch argued that this Act did not include determinations under the poor laws, presumably because it was limited to criminal matters. The judges apparently agreed, because they dismissed the case, "being of the opinion that an appeal does not ly, by the Province Law in this case." [9]

ADAMS' MINUTES OF THE ARGUMENT AND DECISION [10]

Suffolk Superior Court, Boston, August 1766

Town of Boston vs. Roxbury.

Fitch. 1st Question whether Appeal will lie?
Page 33 of tem[porary] Acts. Art —.[11]
Otis. Case of Barnstable vs. Bodfish. June 1747, in Sessions. Superior Court, Barnstable July 1747.[12]
Prov. Law 21. Relations.[13]

---

[9] Min. Bk. 81, SCJ Suffolk, Aug. 1766, N–24. See SCJ Rec. 1766–1767, fol. 98. Boston was allowed costs of £1 0s. 2d.

[10] In JA's hand. Adams Papers, Microfilms, Reel No. 185.

[11] Presumably a reference to the Act of 15 Jan. 1743, c. 18, §1, 3 A&R 37, which appears at p. 33 of a volume supplementary to the *Temporary Acts and Laws* (Boston, 1763), entitled *The Acts Contained in this Book were ordered to be left out of the last Impression of Temporary Laws and printed by themselves* (Boston, 1763). The section provided that all doubts or controversies concerning which town was liable for a pauper's support, or whether a pauper's condition was sufficiently "necessitous" to entitle him to relief, "shall be determined by the justices of the court of general sessions of the peace, in the county to which such poor person doth belong; and the said justices are hereby fully authorized and impowered fully to determine the same, upon application to them made for that purpose."

[12] A reference to Bodfish et al. v. Selectmen of Barnstable, SCJ Rec. 1747–1750, fol. 3 (Barnstable, July 1747), an appeal from an order of the Court of General Sessions of the Peace for Barnstable County in June 1747, directing the appellants to pay to the selectmen £2 17s. 6d., which the latter had advanced to one Thomas Haddeway, an indigent person. The appeal was dismissed with costs of £3 2s. 6d. to the selectmen. The proceeding was probably one against the relatives of the indigent, who were liable for his support under the provision next cited by Otis (note 13 below). That Act was apparently construed as giving the justices sitting in sessions jurisdiction in such matters without regard to their powers under the Act of 1743, cited in note 11 above. See Tomlin's Petition (1735), *Records of the Court of General Sessions of the Peace for the County of Worcester, Massachusetts, from 1731 to 1737* 133 (Worcester, Mass., ed. F. P. Rice, 1882); Petition of Southboro (1737), *id.* at 177. Any doubt that this procedure was correct was removed by Act of 12 June 1764, c. 2, 4 A&R 705.

[13] The reference is to the Act of 16 Nov. 1692, c. 28, §9, 1 A&R 67–68, which appears at *Acts and Laws, Of His Majesty's Province of the Massachusetts Bay in New England* 21 (Boston, 1759). The section, which is set out at length in No. 25, note 4, provided that a person who had been in a town for three months without being warned out, should be considered "the proper charge of the same in case through sickness, lameness, or otherwise they come to stand in need of relief, to be born by such town, unless the relations of such poor impotent person in the

Lynde. Bastardy, Highways—Ministers and Paupers, no Appeal has been allowed.[14]

Gridley. This not taking up the Law upon the sense of it: but is taking up one Part of the Law to make it militate vs. another. This is nothing but an Apex Juris,[15] that never occurrd to the Legislature.

Otis. The Q. is whether an Appeal will lie, from an order of Sessions, concerning the Maintenance of a Pauper.

No Appeals lie at Common Law. No Appeal in England upon Facts, nor ought there to be here.

This is not an Appeal from a Sentence, but an Order.[16]

Judicium i.e. quasi Juris dictum. Ld. Coke.[17]

Court unanimously, The appeal must not be allowed.

---

line or degree of father or grandfather, mother or grandmother, children or grandchildren be of sufficient ability; then such relations respectively shall relieve such poor person in such manner as the justices of the peace in that county where such sufficient persons dwell shall assess."

[14] These were the principal areas of the General Sessions' administrative jurisdiction. See Act of 1 Nov. 1692, c. 18, §5, 1 A&R 52 (Sessions to determine paternity and order father to pay maintenance of bastard; see No. 28); Act of 19 Feb. 1757, c. 18, 3 A&R 1001 (appeal to Sessions on damages for highway land-taking); Act of 4 Feb. 1734, c. 14, 2 A&R 834 (Sessions may award damages for town's refusal to allow a private way); Act of 7 June 1698, c. 2, 1 A&R 311, as amended by Act of 4 July 1734, c. 2, 2 A&R 711 (Sessions may order removal of structures encroaching on highways; see No. 33, note 11); Act of 4 Nov. 1692, c. 26, §§1, 2, 1 A&R 62 (Sessions may order town to provide and maintain a minister and charge inhabitants; see Parsons' Petition [1732], *Worcester Sessions Records* 47); Act of 14 Nov. 1706, c. 9, 1 A&R 597 (Grand jury to present delinquent towns to Sessions. If towns do not comply with Sessions' orders, General Assembly will provide minister). As to the last two acts, see No. 37, note 2.

[15] Literally, the summit of the law. Here used in the sense of a legal subtlety or technicality that carries a rule to an extreme beyond even strict application. Black, *Law Dictionary.*

[16] The Act of 16 June 1699, c. 1, §1, 1 A&R 367, established the justices of the peace for each county as the Court of General Sessions "impowred to hear and determin all matters relating to the conservation of the peace, and the punishment of offenders, and whatsoever is by them cognizeable according to law, and to give judgment and award execution therein." The act provided in §3, p. 368, "That it shall and may be lawful for any person agrieved at the sentence of the justices in any court of general sessions of the peace, to make his appeal from such sentence (the matter being originally heard and tryed in said court) unto the next court of assize and general goal delivery to be held within or for the same county, there to be finally issued," if the appellant gave security, and filed reasons of appeal and copies of the sentence appealed from and the evidence with the clerk of the court to which the appeal was taken.

[17] Probably Coke, *Littleton* 39a: "*Judgement. Judicium quasi juris dictum,* the very voice of Law and Right, and therefore, *Judicium semper pro veritate accipitur.* The ancient words of Judgment are very significant, *Consideratum est, &c.,* because that Judgment is ever given by the Court upon due consideration had of the Record before them." Compare *id.* at 168a, 226a. Otis may mean that in the absence of statute providing an appeal the court is bound by the record.

25. Plympton v. Middleboro

1766

EDITORIAL NOTE

Josiah Marshall had lived in Plympton from 1747 until 1753, and had then spent five years at Middleboro as master of the grammar school. In 1758 he returned to Plympton, but in either 1760 or 1762 moved again, to teach school at Pembroke. According to his own testimony, he remained in the latter town for two years and two months. His next stop cannot be determined with certainty, but at some point in his wanderings he was warned and removed from Plympton. It was Plympton, however, which petitioned the Plymouth County Court of General Sessions in July 1766 for a determination of his status.[1] Since such petitions were usually brought by the town in which a pauper was actually residing, it is probable that Marshall went from Pembroke to Middleboro and was removed from the latter town to Plympton, and that his removal from Plympton had occurred earlier in his career. It is also possible that he went from Pembroke to Plympton and that Plympton then removed him, subsequently petitioning to recover its charges for the period prior to his departure.

Whatever the facts, the case was tried at the October 1766 Sessions, with Adams as counsel for Middleboro and Paine apparently arguing for Plympton. According to their minutes (Documents I, II), the principal issue was the validity of Marshall's removal from Plympton. Adams argued against both the warrant of warning and the warrant to remove. Against the former he raised a series of formal objections, including the failure of the selectmen to make return of the warning to the clerk of the Court of General Sessions within the time required by statute. He also attacked the removal warrant on formal grounds and raised an issue that was to be important in later cases (No. 26, No. 27), that the justice who issued it was an inhabitant of Plympton, and so interested in the outcome. The court ruled in favor of Middleboro, according to Adams' account, because of the lack of a timely return to the warrant of warning.[2]

[1] See JA, Docket, Plymouth Inferior Court, July 1766, a listing covering both the Inferior Court and General Sessions, which sat together. Adams Papers, Microfilms, Reel No. 182. The facts of the case cannot be stated with certainty because the only sources of information available are the docket and JA's and Paine's minutes (Docs. I, II), which are incomplete and not entirely consistent with one another.

[2] Middleboro received its costs. See JA, Docket, Plymouth Inferior Court, Oct. 1766. Adams Papers, Microfilms, Reel No. 182. This entry and the docket for July 1766 show that JA received a retainer of 6s. and a fee of £1 10s.

No. 25. *Plympton v. Middleboro*

I. ADAMS' MINUTES OF THE ARGUMENT[3]

Plymouth Court of General Sessions, October 1766

Plymton vs. Middleborough.

Benja. Shurtliff. Decr. 21st 1753. Marshall went from Plympton to Middleborough.

Josa. Marshall. 25 Aug. 1747 came to Plympton first, to 10 Novr. 1753. 7 July 1758, returned to Plympton from Middleborough, where I went first 21st Decr. 1753.

2 Years and 2 months at Pembroke. Came from there 4 Years ago last Spring.

Mem. This Cause was decided in my favour, who was for Middleborough, by a great Majority of the Court, upon this single Point, vizt. that Caution was not entered in the Clerks office within the Year. The Q. was upon the Words of Prov. Law. 4. Wm. & Mary, C. 12, the Act for Regulating Townships &c. The 9th Clause in the Act is "if any Person &c. sojourn or dwell &c. 3 months, &c. not having been warned by the Constable, and the Names, Abode and Warning returnd unto the Court of Quarter Sessions, &c. shall be reputed an Inhabitant, &c."[4] Not having been warned, and the Warning &c. not having been returned, within 3 months, in [is?] the obvious and grammatical Construction.

'Tho many other Points were stirred by me, particularly the Warrant to carry out, was given by Justice Bradford of Plympton, and so

[3] In JA's hand. Adams Papers, Microfilms, Reel No. 185.

[4] Closing quotation marks supplied. JA is citing "An Act for Regulating of Townships, Choice of Town Officers, and Setting Forth Their Power," 16 Nov. 1692, c. 28, §9, 1 A&R 67: "[I]f any person or persons come to sojourn or dwell in any town within this province or precincts thereof, and be there received and entertained by the space of three months, not having been warned by the constable or other person whom the selectmen shall appoint for that service to leave the place, and the names of such persons with the time of their abode there, and when such warning was given them, returned unto the court of quarter sessions, every such person shall be reputed an inhabitant of such town or precincts of the same," so as to charge the town for his support if he stands in need of relief, subject to a proviso if there are relatives, set out in No. 24, note 13. By the Act of 12 March 1701, c. 23, §§4, 5, 1 A&R 453, no town was to be charged with a newcomer unless his presence had been approved by the selectmen of the town, or "unless such person or persons have continued their residence there by the space of twelve months next before, and have not been warned in manner as the law directs, to depart and leave the town, any law, usage or custom to the contrary notwithstanding." The requirements for approval were made more stringent by the Act of 5 Jan. 1740, c. 9, §1, 2 A&R 995. The time period was eliminated altogether and approval made the only basis for gaining a settlement in the Act of 19 March 1767, c. 17, §6, 4 A&R 911.

a Person interested, and I produced the Case of the two Parishes of Great Charte and Kennington B.R. 16. G. 2. Strange Rep. 1173. Order of 2 Justices quash'd, because one was an Inhabitant of the Parish from whence the Pauper was removed.[5]

Making an order of removal a Judicial Act, and the Party interested is tacitly excepted out of 13 & 14th C[harles] 2d, c. 12, which gives the Power to any 2 Justices of Peace, as our Prov. Law does to the next Justice.[6] Lord Raymond went off the Bench when an order of Abbotts Langley the Parish where he lived came before the Court.[7]

[5] Here and in the following paragraph, JA has paraphrased the case of Parish of Greate Charte v. Parish of Kennington, 2 Str. 1173, 93 Eng. Rep. 1107 (K.B. 1742). The order of the two justices had been quashed in Sessions. In favor of the order it was argued before the King's Bench that the practice was authorized by statute (note 6 below), was necessary because there might be a corporation with only two justices, and was saved because there was an appeal on the merits to the Sessions. For the result, see note 7 below.

[6] In Greate Charte v. Kennington, note 5 above, it had been argued that the practice complained of was authorized by the statute, 13 & 14 Car. 2, c. 12, §1 (1662), which provided that upon complaint made to a justice by the church-wardens of any poor person within forty days after his arrival, it should be lawful "for any two justices of the peace, whereof one to be of the *quorum*, of the division where any person or persons that are likely to be chargeable to the parish shall come to inhabit, by their warrant to remove and convey such person or persons to such parish where he or they were last legally settled." By §2, an appeal to the Quarter Sessions was provided for any person aggrieved. The "Prov. Law" referred to by JA is the Act of 16 Nov. 1692, c. 28, §10, 1 A&R 68: "That any person orderly warned as aforesaid [under *id.*, §9, note 4 above] to depart any town whereof he is not an inhabitant, and neglecting so to do by the space of fourteen days next after such warning given, may by warrant from the next justice of the peace be sent and conveyed from constable to constable unto the town where he properly belongs or had his last residence at his own charge, if able to pay the same, or otherwise at the charge of the town so sending him." This provision was also eliminated by the Act of 19 March 1767, note 4 above, which, in §7, authorized removal of all persons not approved by the town. There is evidence, however, that the practice of warning was still followed. See 5 A&R 260.

[7] This paragraph is based on the conclusion of the court's opinion in Greate Charte v. Kennington, note 5 above: "But the court held, that this was a judicial act, and the party interested is tacitly excepted. Lord *Raymond*, who lived in the parish of *Abbotts-Langley*, went off the Bench, when one of their orders came before the court. They said the practice could not overturn so fundamental a rule of justice, as that a party interested could not be a Judge. And as to the case of corporations, they said that if it appeared that there were no other justices, it might be allowed; to prevent a failure of justice. And therefore they confirmed the order of sessions." The reporter adds, "*Vide* the act 16 Geo. 2, c. 18. to remedy this." For this statute, see No. 27, note 28. The court's last point is an interesting contrast to the absolute force given the proposition that a man may not be judge in his own cause in the authorities cited in the argument on the writs of assistance in 1761. See No. 44, note 71. For another Massachusetts case in which both *Greate Charte* and the latter authorities were cited, see Jeffries v. Sewal (Suffolk Inferior Court, Nov. 1762), reported in 1 JA, *Diary and Autobiography* 230–231. As to the parish of Abbotts Langley, see King v. Inhabitants of Abbots Langley, 1 Barn. K.B. 148, 94 Eng. Rep. 103 (1729), in which Lord Raymond, "being of this parish, . . . said he would give no opinion."

II. PAINE'S MINUTES OF THE ARGUMENT [8]

Plymouth Court of General Sessions, October 1766

Plympton vs. Middleborough

Warning.

Shurtleffe. J. Mar[shall] went from Plym[pton] to Mid[dleborough] 21. Dec. 1753.

Mr. Josiah Marshal. Came to Plymp[ton] Augt. 1747 till 20th Novr. 1753.[9] Then to Midd[leborough], returned to Ply[mpton] 7th July 1758. Was Grammar School Master at Midd[leborough]. I went to Pembroke 4 yr. ago and kept school there 2 yr. and 2 months.

Capt. Sprout. Mr. Marshal kept School at Midd[leborough] 5 years.

Adams

Pity there should be a dispute.

Warrant of Warning no Seal no mention made of his Wife and children, not to depart within 14 days. A man and his family means nothing more than the man; Marshals Wife was born at Plymton.

Warrant to remove, not setting forth the cause, given by a Justice in the same Town

Strange. 1163.[10]

26. Chelsea v. Boston

1769

EDITORIAL NOTE

In August 1768, William Dix, a pauper, was removed from Boston to Chelsea by virtue of the warrant of John Hill, a Boston justice of the peace. The selectmen of Chelsea petitioned the Suffolk General Sessions in April 1769 for his return to Boston and for reimbursement of their expenses in his behalf. The petition, which was drafted by John Adams and is printed below, urged that Dix was not an inhabitant of Chelsea, and had not been alleged or adjudged to be such in the removal proceedings. Adams also raised the point that Justice Hill was disqualified by virtue of his residence in Boston.

The case was heard at a May adjournment of the court and then continued. In August, at an adjournment of the July term, the court was "unanimously of opinion that Justice Hill who granted the warrant men-

[8] In Paine's hand. Paine Law Notes.

[9] Thus in MS. JA's notes read 10 November.

[10] That is, Greate Charte v. Kennington, note 5 above. Paine has erroneously written "1163."

tioned in said Petition, being at that time an inhabitant of said town of Boston had no legal power so to do and therefore that the prayer of the Petition be granted." Boston was accordingly ordered to pay Chelsea its charges of £20 7s. 4d. and costs of £5 18s. 2d., and to accept Dix back.[1]

ADAMS' PETITION [2]

Suffolk Court of General Sessions, Boston, April 1769

Suffolk Ss. To the Honorable his Majestys Justices of his Court of General Sessions of the Peace held at Boston in and for the County of Suffolk on the Third Tuesday of April in the Ninth Year of his Majestys Reign Annoque Domini 1769.

Humbly Shew Thomas Pratt, Gentleman, Samuel Sprague, Yeoman, Samuel Serjeant, Gentleman, Samuel Watts Jnr, Gentleman, Samuel Pratt, Gentleman, all of Chelsea in said County and Select Men and overseers of the Poor of the Said Town,

That on the Twenty third day of August Anno Domini 1768, one William Dix, a poor impotent Man, was, by Force of a Warrant given by John Hill Esqr. a Justice of the Peace for Said County, on the Twentyeth day of August A.D. 1768, ⟨at the prayer of⟩ on the Complaint of John Sweetser, by order of Joseph Jackson Esq. and other the select Men of the Said Town of Boston, removed from thence into the aforesaid Town of Chelsea, as the proper Place of his Abode, there to be relieved and Supported, at the Charge of the Inhabitants of Said Town of Chelsea. That the Said William is poor, lame, and utterly unable to support himself, and has been relieved and supported by the Inhabitants of Said Chelsea ever since his Removal to that Town at the Expence of Twelve Pounds six shillings and Eight Pence of lawfull Money.

Now your Petitioners apprehend and aver that the aforesaid Removal was and is contrary to Law for these Reasons among many others.

1. Because the Said William Dix was not at the Time of his said Removal an Inhabitant of Chelsea nor had any legal settlement there, nor was the Poor of that Town, nor was Chelsea the Town where he had his last Residence.

---

[1] Sess. Min. Bk., Aug. 1769. As to the question of an interested judge, see No. 25, notes 5–7; No. 27, text at notes 11–14.

[2] In JA's hand, and signed by him "for said Pet[itioner]s." SF 88992. The court's April 1769 order of service on the Selectmen of Boston in the hand of Ezekiel Goldthwait, Clerk, which follows JA's signature on the last sheet, has been omitted here.

2.   Because the said Dix is not alledged in the aforesaid Complaint of John Sweetser by order of the select Men of said Boston, to be an Inhabitant of said Chelsea, or to have a legal settlement there, or to be the proper Poor of that Town or to have had his last Residence there nor are any of these Things alledged or averred in the said Warrant of the said Justice.

3.   The said Dix is not adjudged, by said Justice in said pretended Warrant, to be an Inhabitant of said Chelsea, nor to have a legal settlement there, nor is there in said Warrant any Adjudication that said Dix had his last Residence in said Town of Chelsea.

[4.]   The said worshipfull John Hill Esq. was at the Time when said pretended Warrant was given an Inhabitant of said Town of Boston, and Rated for the support of the Poor there, and therefore interested in Said Removal, and disqualifyed for that Reason for giving a Warrant in such Case.

For these Reasons and many others your Petitioners say that the said William Dix was illegally removed from Boston aforesaid into Chelsea aforesaid, and that the Inhabitants of Chelsea aforesaid ought not to be at that Charge and Expence of relieving or Supporting him, but that the Inhabitants of Boston aforesaid ought to be at that Charge: And your Petitioners humbly pray your Honours would accordingly order that the said William Dix be removed back again from said Chelsea to Boston aforesaid, there to be relieved and supported at the Charge of the Inhabitants of said Boston for the future and that the Inhabitants of Chelsea may be reimbursed the Expences they have been been at and may be at for such support untill such Removal back into Boston aforesaid, together with the Costs and Charges of this supplication.

And your Petitioners as in Duty bound will ever pray.

John Adams for said Pet[itioner]s

27. Brookline v. Roxbury

1767–1772

EDITORIAL NOTE

The constable of Roxbury had conveyed John Chaddock (alias Chadwick, Chattuck, or Shattuck), his wife, three children, and assorted household goods, to Brookline in January 1767, pursuant to a warrant of removal issued by a Roxbury justice of the peace. In 1760 the selectmen of Roxbury had warned a John Chaddock, or Chadwick, and family, out of the town after a two months' stay. They now asserted that these families were the same, so that the statutory prerequisite of warning within a year after arrival had been complied with.[1]

Brookline contested the removal, petitioning the Suffolk General Sessions in May 1767 for the return of Chaddock to Roxbury and for the town's expenses. Jeremy Gridley signed the petition, but Adams' list of questions presented (Document I) and notes of authorities (Document II) indicate that it was he who argued the case when it finally came on after numerous continuances in November 1768, Gridley having meanwhile died. The petition, which sets forth other documents in the case, appears below as part of the record of the Sessions proceedings (Document III). It urges ten grounds for quashing the removal order, which are principally attacks upon the formal sufficiency of the warrants of warning and removal. Gridley had also contended, however, that the man removed was not the man warned, and that the removal warrant was void because the justice issuing it was an inhabitant of Roxbury and thus interested in the outcome.

Adams' questions presented (Document I) correspond with the grounds of the petition, with two additions: (1) whether a Justice in such a case acted ministerially or judicially (which was related to the problem of interest); (2) whether evidence beyond what Adams called "the Records of this Court" (the warrants and returns) was admissible. Probably Roxbury sought to establish the identity of various persons named in the warrants and thus to cure the alleged defects in them.[2] It is not clear why Adams raised this point. In *Roxbury v. Boston*, No. 24, depositions and other documentary evidence seem to have been at least offered in the trial at Sessions, and were probably accepted, since they formed part of the file of the case. The issue was not reached on the trial in the present case, however, in view of the court's ruling on the merits, to be discussed below.

The three groups of authorities which Adams had prepared for the trial (Document II) give some indication of the issues which he sought to emphasize in argument. The first group deals with the necessity for particularity in naming persons ordered to be warned or removed. The second group consists principally of the forms followed in English removal proceedings, which were based upon a statute similar in its generality to the Province Act here involved, but which set forth in detail just those matters which were unclear in the warrant now before the court. Finally, Adams raised the issue of the interested justice, citing authorities which he had used in *Plympton v. Middleboro*, No. 25.

At the trial, Robert Auchmuty, counsel for Roxbury, in effect demurred to the petition. Upon motion the court gave its opinion, set out in the

---

[1] The warrants are set out in Doc. III. As to the statutory requirement, see No. 25, notes 4, 6.

[2] The files contain subpoenas to the Aug. term of the Suffolk Sessions and its Oct. adjournment, summoning six witnesses, including John and Martha Shattuck of Brookline, and William Borrough of Roxbury, the Chaddocks' alleged host there in 1760. SF 102089. See Doc. III.

record (Document III), that Brookline's allegations were not sufficient to entitle the town to a trial of the question whether Chaddock and family had a settlement there or in Roxbury. This ruling in effect meant that the 1760 warning was effective to prevent the Chaddocks from gaining a settlement in the latter town. Roxbury then moved to dismiss, but on further argument the court instead upheld the petition, presumably on the ground that the removal warrant was in some way faulty. Roxbury was ordered to pay Brookline Chaddock's charges and costs of court; and the Chaddocks were to be returned. Brookline's account for £67 16s. 4 3/4d., which was approved by the court in January 1769, is set out as an example of the scope and quantity of 18th-century poor relief (Document IV). Execution issued for the sum there stated and costs of £6 3s. 4d. on 9 March 1769.[3]

At the March 1769 term of the Suffolk Superior Court, Fitch moved in Roxbury's behalf for a writ of certiorari. This process, by which a higher court could command an inferior court to certify and send up the record of its proceedings, had been used in England since some time in the 17th century to quash an order of Sessions, but had been adopted in Massachusetts at a relatively recent date.[4] The documents involved in this case, which are an interesting example of the adoption of English forms to local needs, are set out below. The writ issued in July, returnable at the August term (Document V). Return was duly made both of the Sessions record (Document III) and of copies of other formal papers from the file.[5] Fitch then filed an assignment of errors sometime before March 1770 (Document VI). This form, not used in the English practice, suggests that in Massachusetts certiorari was viewed as not differing materially from the writ of error, in which the assignment was part of the proceedings both in England and in the Province.[6]

The errors which Fitch assigned are of interest in light of the 18th-century English limits on the scope of review in certiorari to quash. In the English practice, through an accident of historical development, only matters denominated "jurisdictional" had to appear on the face of the record, but an order could be quashed if such matters did not appear. If jurisdictional matter was set out, however, evidence outside the record, in

---

[3] Sess. Min. Bk., 7 Nov. 1768. A copy of the bill of costs in SF 102089 shows a total of £6 3s. 8d. It is not clear whether the discrepancy is due to a copyist's error or represents a reduction by the court. See also note 48 below.

[4] The motion and the court's order granting it appear in Min. Bk. 89, SCJ Suffolk, March 1769. For the development of the writ in England, see Edith G. Henderson, *Foundations of English Administrative Law* 83–116 (Cambridge, Mass., 1963). As to the Massachusetts development, see No. 24, note 4.

[5] These included copies of Brookline's account (Doc. IV), the Sessions bill of costs, two subpoenas (note 2 above), the two warrants, Brookline's petition, and the court's opinion on the question of dismissal. The last three items appear virtually verbatim in the Sessions record (Doc. III).

[6] As to the proceedings in error in England, see Sutton, *Personal Actions* 136–144. See also note 8 below. For other evidence that little distinction was seen between error and certiorari, see Edith G. Henderson, Certiorari and Mandamus in Massachusetts and Maryland 9–10 (Unpubl. paper, Harvard Law School, 1955).

the form of affidavits, was admissible to attack it. Matter of record that was not "jurisdictional" could be attacked if on its face it was not consistent with the order, but no additional evidence was admissible for this purpose. Naturally enough, this practice gave rise to much doubt as to the meaning of "jurisdictional," and the term was often expanded to include issues which might not ordinarily seem to be within it. It should further be noted that the "record" in the English practice was only the formal statement of the court's judgment and order, not the entire pleadings and proceedings below, which the term usually signifies.[7]

The first four errors assigned by Fitch (Document VI) were jurisdictional in the broadest sense. Together they were to the effect that only the merits of the question of a pauper's settlement, and not errors of law in the proceedings had with regard to him were within the court's jurisdiction. This order had to fall, because it granted the petition not only in the absence of necessary allegations or findings on the merits, but despite a specific finding that there was no question on the merits. The second assignment of error, attacking the petition, would presumably have been irrelevant under the English practice whereby jurisdiction had to appear in the judgment or order itself.[8] The fifth error assigned attacked the absence of various findings in the record. In the English view, if any of these had been "jurisdictional" the order would have been fatally defective for lack of them.[9]

After notification of Brookline to appear in March 1770 (Document VII), the case was further continued until February 1772, when with Adams and Fitch arguing, it finally came on for hearing. According to a note in Adams' docket, the matter was "determined for Brooklyne, 7th d[ay] upon Arg[ument] of all the Errors filed." The Superior Court affirmed the judgment, with further costs of £9 13s. 3d.[10] In the narrowest view this decision held only that the Court of General Sessions had jurisdiction to deal conclusively with errors of law in the record before it and that the matters set forth in the fifth assignment as omitted from the order were not "jurisdictional." But it is possible, in light of Adams' description of the

[7] See Henderson, *Foundations of English Administrative Law* 143–145. That this practice was not strictly followed in Massachusetts is suggested by Josselyne v. Harrington, No. 30. Compare No. 28.

[8] This would seem to be a natural result of the fact, already noted in the text at notes 5, 7, above, that in England only the judgment and order were sent to the higher court on certiorari to quash, while in Massachusetts, the whole record (including the pleadings), as well as other formal documents, was sent up. It is not clear whether all of this material would be considered of "record." See No. 24, text at note 8. Pond v. Medway, Quincy, *Reports* 193 (SCJ Suffolk, 1765), SF 100637, is ambiguous on this point. For indications that the "record" for review purposes meant only the document containing pleadings, procedural steps, and judgment, see No. 28.

[9] For examples of fatal defects in English practice, see Henderson, *Foundations of English Administrative Law* 149–154.

[10] See JA, Docket, Suffolk, Feb. 1772, Adams Papers, Microfilms, Reel No. 183; Min. Bk. 95, SCJ Suffolk, Feb. 1772, C–9; SCJ Rec. 1772, fol. 2. "7th day" is the seventh day of the court's sitting.

result, that the court, in examining "all the Errors," looked to the record itself and affirmed the decision of the Sessions on the legal questions.

Whatever the force of the court's holding, the decision in this case seems to be related to a statutory change made several months later. In *Chelsea v. Boston*, No. 26 (1769), the Suffolk Sessions, after its decision in the present case, had expressly held that a removal warrant was void because issued by a Justice who was an inhabitant of the removing town. The court must have followed this rule in other cases as well, because in June 1771 the Selectmen of Boston petitioned the General Court for a change in the law, complaining "that the Court of General Sessions of the Peace for this County have of late construed said Acts [11] in a different manner, by adjudging that a removal by virtue of a Warrant from a Justice of the Peace of this Town is not a legal removal as said Justice is some-what interested therein, and that it properly lays with one of His Majesty's Justices of the Peace of a Neighbouring Town to grant said Warrant—That in consequence of this novel construction of said Acts this Town has already been put to considerable charge and difficulty, which from its peculiar situation and circumstances, and the great number of Vagrants and other poor Strangers which dayly flow in upon us, is like greatly to increase." [12]

The Committee to which this petition was referred recommended that it be put over until the next session.[13] On 14 July 1772 an act was passed which recited that the practice of which Boston had complained was fol-lowed in "the courts of general sessions of the peace for several counties . . . whereby a number of towns in the province, more especially the town of Boston, have been put to much inconvenience and charge, and the expence of the province is likely to be greatly encreased." The act went on to provide that "the removal of any person, by a warrant obtained from one of his majesty's justices of the peace residing in the town from whence the person is to be sent or conveyed, to any other town, either in or out of the province, shall, to all intents and purposes, be deemed as legal a removal as if the warrant had issued from a justice of the peace living in any other town." [14]

On the trial of *Brookline v. Roxbury* at the Sessions in 1768, Adams had urged the invalidity of the warrant on the grounds of the Justice's resi-dence, but the issue had not been expressly referred to by the court as part of the basis for its decision. The question was an important one, however, and may well have been the principal defect which the court found in the warrant of removal. If this was so, it is possible that legislative action was deferred pending the outcome of the proceedings on certiorari, with the hope that the Superior Court might overrule the Sessions on the point. When, instead, the result was a holding which at least recognized the

[11] That is, the removal provisions, set out in No. 25, note 6.
[12] Printed in 5 A&R 261, from 47 Mass. Arch. 551.
[13] 5 A&R 261.
[14] Act of 14 July 1772, c. 4, 5 A&R 198. A similar English provision is set out in note 28 below.

power of the Sessions to rule on such questions without interference from above, and may even have gone so far as to indicate approval of the rule followed in the lower court, the only remedy left was the legislation which was forthcoming.

I. ADAMS' LIST OF QUESTIONS PRESENTED [15]

Suffolk Court of General Sessions, Boston, November 1768

Town of Brooklyne vs. Town of Roxbury

A great Number of Questions arise upon this Petition.

1st. Whether a Justice of the Peace, can by Law, issue a Warrant for the Removal of a Pauper, from the Town where the Justice is an Inhabitant?

2. Whether a Warrant from the Select Men or Overseers of the Poor in a Town, to warn Strangers to depart, is good without warning those Strangers particularly?

3. Whether the Person warned in this Warrant of the Select Men is the Same Person, named in the Return of the Constable, and whether the Person named in the Justices Warrant is not a different Person from that named in the select Mens Warrant, and different also from him named in the Constables Return?

4. Whether the Justices Warrant, commanding the Constable ⟨*of Roxbury to deliver the Pauper to the Cons*⟩ of Brooklyne to receive the Pauper, and deliver him to the Select Men, is good, not being directed to the Constable of Brookline or Select Men of Brookline, or any Body else, but to the Constable of Roxbury?

5. Whether the Justices Warrant can be good, as it admits that the Pauper had lived Six Years in Roxbury, and only Says under Warning. I.e. when it appears upon the Face of the Warrant, that the Pauper had lived in the Town long enough to gain a Settlement by Law, whether the Particulars of his Warning out should not be set forth, i.e. the Time when, and the Authority by which, he was warnd to depart.

6. Whether a Warrant of Removal can be good, without setting forth with Certainty, one of these Things, vizt. Either that the Paupers legal settlement was at the Town he is to be removed to, or that he is an Inhabitant of that Town, or the Poor of that Town, or

---

[15] In JA's hand. Adams Papers, Microfilms, Reel No. 185. In the MS there is a plus sign or dagger at the beginning and end of each numbered paragraph. These may be notations made by JA as each question was reached and considered. They are not here reproduced.

had his last Residence in that Town? Now in this Warrant it is only set forth disjunctively, Either that the said Pauper properly belongs to Brookline, or had his last Residence there.

7. Whether there is any Authority in Law for a Justice to command a Constable in his Warrant to remove the Goods and Effects of the Pauper?

8. Whether a Warrant of Removal should by Law be made returnable to the Clerk of the Peace, or the Justice who issued it.

9. Whether, in the Discussion of this Case, we must not be confined to the Records? Or Whether Roxbury shall be admitted to give any Kind of Evidence in Explanation or Reconciliation of these Records, i.e. these Warrants and Returns? For these Warrants and Returns are all of them Records. Even the Warrant of the Select Men must by Law be returned to the Clerk of the Peace and made a Part of the Records of this Court.[16]

10. Whether a Justice of the Peace, in granting a Warrant of Removal, is a Judicial or merely a ministerial officer? [17]

11. Whether a Justices Warrant of Removal ought not to be quashed for Uncertainty when it orders the Removal of a Person and his family, without naming Wife or Children, or when it orders the Removal of a Pauper and his Children or 5 Children, without naming those Children or ascertaining their ages.

12. Whether the Select Men in their Warrant for Warning, requiring the Constable to warn John Chaddock and Family, Jonathan Smith, Jona. Smith Jnr. and Mrs. Cammell all and every one of the above said Persons, to depart in 14 days, or give security, from all Charge that may arise by means of any or Either of the said Persons, have not renderd their own Warrant void? For by Law, no Person warned out is obliged to give security for 20 other Persons, it is sufficient if he gives security for him self and his own family.[18]

[16] By virtue of the Act of 16 Nov. 1692, c. 28, §9, 1 A&R 67, set out in No. 25, note 4.

[17] See Greate Charte v. Kennington, discussed in No. 25, note 5.

[18] No provision of the Province law on warning and removal has been found which permits the selectmen to take security from the pauper himself in lieu of removal. As the Act is worded, however, removal after warning is not mandatory, so that presumably security would be permissible. See Act of 16 Nov. 1692, c. 28, §§9, 10, 1 A&R 68, set out in No. 25, notes 4, 6. Such a practice was sanctioned by the English statute, 13 & 14 Car. 2, c. 12, §1 (1662), set out in part in *id.*, note 6, which provided that two Justices could give their warrant to remove any poor persons to their place of last abode, "unless he or they give sufficient security for the discharge of the said parish, to be allowed by the said justices." There was a Massachusetts provision that a person "entertaining" someone for nursing, education, or medical care should be "the town's security" for any charges. Act of 16 Nov. 1692, c. 28, §9, 1 A&R 68. Although the warrant (text at notes 36–38 be-

II. ADAMS' NOTES OF AUTHORITIES [19]

Suffolk Court of General Sessions, Boston, November 1768

Brooklyne vs. Roxbury.

Prov. Law. Page 23. Names returned.[20]

2. Salk. 482. Anonimous. 3 Men and families.[21]

2 Salk 485. Sylvanus Johnson.[22]

Foleys Poor Laws 427. Lenham vs. Peckham.[23]

Foley 426. Flixton vs. Roston.[24]

Form of an order of Removal, Burn V. 3, P. 378. V. 3, Page 377.[25]

---

low) is ambiguous enough to have been addressed to the persons named as keeping the paupers, there is no evidence that the latter fell within this provision.

[19] In JA's hand. Adams Papers, Microfilms, Reel No. 185. The present dating is based on the fact that the MS appears on a leaf with cases decided in April 1768 and May 1769 at Plymouth.

[20] The reference is to the Act of 16 Nov. 1692, c. 28, §9, 1 A&R 67. JA is here citing *Acts and Laws, Of His Majesty's Province of the Massachusetts Bay in New England* 23 (Boston, 1742). Compare the citation to the same act in the 1759 edition, No. 24, note 13. The section cited, set out in full in No. 25, note 4, provided that persons remaining in the town for more than three months without being warned to leave, "and the names of such persons with the time of their abode there, and when such warning was given them, returned unto the court of quarter sessions," should be reputed inhabitants for relief purposes. The time period was extended to twelve months in 1701 and eliminated altogether in an Act of 1767 passed too late to be applicable to this case. *Ibid.*

[21] Anonymous, 2 Salk. 482, 91 Eng. Rep. 415 (K.B. 1698): "An Order made to remove three Men and their Families was quashed, *quia* too general; for some of their Family might not be removeable."

[22] Case of Sylvanus Johnson, 2 Salk. 485, 91 Eng. Rep. 417 (K.B. ca. 1698). At sessions, "ordered that *Johnson* and his Wife and Family, should be removed to Sandherst, which was quashed; because *Non constat* what is meant by his Family, and some of them may have a legal Settlement [in the town removing], tho' J. had not."

[23] Robert Foley, *Laws Relating to the Poor* 427 (London, 4th edn., 1758), citing the unreported case of Inhabitants of Lenham v. Inhabitants of Peckham (Q.B. 1711): "Upon Complaint that A. was likely to become chargeable, the Justices make an Order to remove the Pauper, his Wife and Family; quash'd as to the Family." There follow citations of the cases in notes 21 and 22 above.

[24] Foley, *Laws Relating to the Poor* 426, citing the unreported case of Flixton v. Roston (Q.B. 1710): "This was a Motion to quash an Order of two Justices, which was made for the Removal of one *Jane Smith* and her five children. *Exception.* It's too uncertain; for it neither tells the Name or Ages of the Children: Wherefore the Order was quash'd as to the Children."

[25] The precise edition of Richard Burn, *The Justice of the Peace and Parish Officer*, cited by JA has not been located. "The form of a general order of removal" appears both in the 6th edition, London 1758, at 3:83–84, and in the 11th edition, London, 1769, at 3:432–433. It is here set out from the latter:

"**Westmorland. To** *the churchwardens and overseers of the poor of the parish of* Orton *in the said county of* Westmorland, *and to the churchwardens and over-*

13 [&] 14 Car. 2, Chap. 12, cited in Burn V. 3, P. 375.[26]
Prov. Law, 4 W. & M. c. 12.[27]

Justice shall not act in his Town.
2 Strange 1173 Great Charte and Kennington. Foley Page 104.
Statute, 16 G[eorge] 2d, c. 18. Act to impower Justices.[28]

seers of the poor of the parish of Penrith *in the county of* Cumberland, *and to each and every of them.*

"*Upon the complaint of the churchwardens and overseers of the poor of the parish of* Orton *aforesaid in the said county of* Westmorland, *unto us whose names are hereunto set and seals affixed, being two of his majesty's justices of the peace in and for the said county of* Westmorland, *and one of us of the* quorum, *that* John Thomson, Mary *his wife,* Thomas *their son aged eight years, and* Agnes *their daughter aged four years, have come to inhabit in the said parish of* Orton, *not having gained a legal settlement there, nor produced any certificate owning them or any of them to be settled elsewhere, and that the said* John Thomson, Mary *his wife, and* Thomas *and* Agnes *their children, are likely to be chargeable to the said parish of* Orton; *We the said justices, upon due proof made thereof, as well upon the examination of the said* John Thomson *upon oath, as otherwise, and likewise upon due consideration had of the premisses, do adjudge the same to be true; and we do likewise adjudge, that the lawful settlement of them the said* John Thomson, Mary *his wife, and* Thomas *and* Agnes *their children, is in the said parish of* Penrith *in the said county of* Cumberland: *We do therefore require you the said churchwardens and overseers of the poor of the said parish of* Orton, *or some or one of you, to convey the said* John Thomson, Mary *his wife, and* Thomas *and* Agnes *their children, from and out of the said parish of* Orton, *to the said parish of* Penrith, *and them to deliver to the churchwardens and overseers of the poor there, or to some or one of them, together with this our order, or a true copy thereof, at the same time shewing to them the original; And we do also hereby require you the said churchwardens and overseers of the said parish of* Penrith, *to receive and provide for them as inhabitants of your parish. Given under our hands and seals the* day of *in the* year of the reign of his said majesty king George the third.*"

On the preceding pages are forms of summonses to paupers lacking settlement and to the churchwardens of a parish to which removal is sought to appear before a justice or justices for examination and adjudication of removal. *Id.* at 430–432.

[26] 13 & 14 Car. 2, c. 12, §1 (1662), set out in Burn, *Justice of the Peace* 428–429 (1769), appears in pertinent part in No. 25, note 6.

[27] That is, the Act of 16 Nov. 1692, c. 28, 1 A&R 64–68, the basic Province poor law. Sections pertinent to removal are set out in No. 24, note 13; No. 25, notes 4, 6. JA's point here and at note 26 above seems to be that the English forms cited in note 25 above are not dictated by statute, because the English and Massachusetts acts are similarly general in their language.

[28] For the case of Greate Charte v. Kennington, set out from Strange's *Reports* in Foley, *Laws Relating to the Poor* 104, see No. 25, note 5. The statute, 16 Geo. 2, c. 18, §1 (1743), noted by the reporter as passed "to remedy this" (i.e. the ruling in the case that the order of a Justice was void when it concerned his own town) is set out here from a copy in JA's hand in the Adams Papers: "16 G. 2, c. 18. Statutes at large. V. 6th, Page 501. An Act to impower Justices of the Peace to act in certain Cases relating to Parishes and Places, to the Rates and Taxes of which they are rated or chargeable. [§1 . . .] 'It shall be lawfull to and for all and every Justice or Justices of the Peace for any County, Riding, City, Liberty, Franchise, Borough, or Town Corporate within their respective Jurisdictions, to make, do, and execute all and every Act or Acts, Matter or Matters, Thing or Things,

III. RECORD [29]

Suffolk Court of General Sessions, Boston, November 1768

Suffolk Ss: At a Court of General sessions of the peace held
                  at Boston within and for the county of Suffolk by ad-
[SEAL]   journment on Monday the seventh day of Novr. A.D.
                  1768.

The Petition of the Selectmen of the Town of Brookline in the
county of Suffolk, setting forth [30] that on the thirtieth day of January
1767 the worshipful Joseph Williams Eqr. issued a warrant in these
words, vizt., Suffolk Ss. [31] Complaint being made to me the Subscriber, one of his Majestys Justices of the peace for said county, by
Mesrs. John Child, Aaron Davis, and Eleazer Weld, Gentlemen and
Selectmen of Roxbury and overseers of the poor in said Town, that one
John Chaddock alias Chadwick alias dictus Chattuck or Shattuck late
of Brookline with his family, vizt. a wife and four Children, all [32] in
distressed circumstances, the said John being delirious so as to become
chargeable to the Town of Roxbury where they have resided and [33]
under warning between six and seven years, praying that a Warrant
may issue forthwith to remove the said John and family back to
Brookline from whence they came. These are therefore in his Majesty's
name to will and require you and either of you to apprehend the Body
and Bodies of the said John Chattuck and family with their effects
and them safely remove and convey by the best way and means you
can to the constable of the Town of Brookline who is alike required
to receive them and take all due care to notify the Selectmen of Brook-

---

appertaining to their office, as Justice or Justices of the Peace, so far as the same
relates to the Laws for the Relief, Maintenance and settlement of Poor Persons,
&c. Not with standing any such Justice or Justices of the Peace is or are rated to
or chargeable with the Taxes, Levies, or Rates within any such Parish Township
or Place affected by any such Act or Acts of such Justice or Justices as afore Said.' "
At the "&c." JA has omitted provisions covering vagrants, highways, and taxes.
JA must have argued or assumed that this Act was not applicable in the colonies.
For a similar Province Act, passed in 1772, see note 14 above.

[29] SF 102089, in unknown hand. Minimal punctuation supplied. The last page is
missing from the files. The final words of the record have been supplied from the
original in Sess. Min. Bk., Suffolk, Nov. 1768. See note 45 below.

[30] A separate copy of the petition in the files is addressed "To the Honorable
his Majestys Justices of the Court of General Sessions of the Peace in the county of
Suffolk," and begins, "The Selectmen of the Town of Brookline in said county
humbly Shew." SF 102089.

[31] The file copy of the warrant is headed, "to each or either of the constables of
Roxbury within said county of Suffolk, Greeting." SF 102089.

[32] In the file copy of the warrant the reading is "are." The file copy of the petition reads "all." SF 102089.

[33] Word omitted in the file copy of the warrant. SF 102089.

line or overseers of the poor of said Town to which he properly belongs or had his last residence, that such care may be taken and provision made for their support as may be needful. And you are to remove the said Chattuck and family &c. at his own charge if able to pay the same, otherwise at the charge of the Town of Roxbury, for all which this shall be a Sufficient warrant. Fail not and make due return of this warrant and your Doings thereon to the Clerk of the Court of General Sessions of the peace for said county of Suffolk as soon as may be. Given under my hand and Seal at Roxbury this thirtieth day of January A.D. 1767 and seventh year of King Georges reign. Joseph Williams. Which was afterward delivered to John Wood a constable of the said Town of Roxbury to be executed who returned his doings thereon in these words, viz. Suffolk Ss. Roxbury January 30 1767. By virtue of this warrant I have taken the Body of the within written John Shattuck and his wife and a Bed and beding and delivered them to William Davis constable of Brooklyn. February the 3 & 4th, I have further taken three children of the said John, viz. Martha and John and Mary and two beds and beding, a Pork tub, pots and kettles, brass and pewter knives and forks, corn and meal tubs, Chairs, Cyder, Cyder-barrels &c. being all the Indoor moveables of the aforesaid John Chattuck alias John Shattuck and conveyed them to the Town of Brooklyn and delivered them to the wife of the said John Shattuck at Brooklyn aforesaid. John Wood constable. And the said William Davis constable of the Town of Brooklyn made his Indorsement on said warrant in these words: Suffolk Ss. Brooklyn, January the 30. 1767. By virtue of this warrant I have received the within written John Shattuck and his wife and bed and beding and delivered them [to] Isaac Gardner Esqr. one of the Selectmen of Brooklyn aforesaid. William Davis constable.[34] And the said John Shattuck his wife and three children are now in consequence of said warrant resident in said Brooklyn at the expence of the same Town for their maintenance which ought not to be for that it is acknowledged in said warrant that the said poor had lived above six years at said Roxbury and by Law therefore were their poor and ought not to have [been] removed then[35] unless lawfully warned from the same Town. Tis true there was a warning in the year 1760 hinted in the said warrant which the said Town of Roxbury relies upon for good and sufficient warning in this case, the warrant for which and the Return of it are

---

[34] On the file copy of the warrant is the additional notation, "Returned Feby. 7, 1767." SF 102089.
[35] The file copy of the petition reads "thence." SF 102089.

in these words, viz. Suffolk Ss.[36] In his Majestys name you are hereby required forthwith to warn John Chaddock and family at Mr. Bourroughs, Jonathan Smith at Mr. Ebenezer Whitings, Jonathan Smith junr. at Thomas Lyons, and Mr[s?]. Campbel at Mr. Whitings, also all[37] and every one of the abovesaid Persons to depart the Town of Roxbury in fourteen days or give Security to the Selectmen to Indemnify the Town from all charge that may arise by means of any or either of the said persons, and you are to make Return hereof[38] to the Clerk of the General Sessions of the peace in said county together with a certificate of the place of their last abode and the time [of their] residence here as the Law directs. By order of the Selectmen of Roxbury aforesaid, Samuel Gridley Town Clerk, Augt. 1st, 1760. Suffolk Ss. August the 1st. 1760. By virtue of the within I have warn'd the[39] John Chadwick and family, viz. his wife and four children, to depart this Town who came from Brooklyn and had resided in Roxbury about two months, Jonathan Smith and Jonathan Smith junr. who had resided in Town three or four months and came last from Woodstock, and Mrs. Mary Campbel who had resided in Town two months and came from Boston. All and every of the above I have warned to depart the Town in fourteen days or give bond to Indemnify the Town. Attest. per Nathaniel Davis constable.[40] Whereupon the complainants say that one John Chadwick was the Person warned to depart the said Town of Roxbury by force of the first of said warrants and John Shattuck was the Person removed by force of the second of said warrants which are two different names and denote two different familys. The first of said warrants requires John Chaddock and his family to be warned to depart said Roxbury or give Security but does not mention the Persons of his family ordered to be so warned by name as it ought to have done, and the constable in his return to it says that he has warned the [said] John Chattuck and family, viz. his wife and four children, to depart said Town but has not returned their names as he ought to have done. The constable of the said Town of Roxbury is required by the first of said warrants to warn diverse persons and John Chattuck among the rest, as therein is set forth, all and every one of them to depart the said town of Roxbury in fourteen days or give security to the Selectmen to indemnify the

[36] The file copy of the warrant is headed, "To Mr. Nathaniel Davis constable of Roxbury in said county, Greeting &c." SF 102089.

[37] Word omitted in the file copy of the warrant. SF 102089.

[38] "Thereof," in the file copy of the warrant. SF 102089.

[39] Thus in MS. The file copy of the warrant omits "the." SF 102089.

[40] On the file copy of the warrant is the additional notation, "Filed Octr. 21. 1760." SF 102089.

Town from all charge that may arise by means of any or either of the said persons. The constable of the Town of Brookline is required by the second of said warrants to receive the persons so removed and to notify the Selectmen of said Brooklyn, and yet the warrant which requires it is not directed to him as it ought to have been. The same warrant does not mention either of the three children thereby required to be removed by name as it ought to have done. The same warrant admits that John Chattuck required [41] to be removed has resided in said Roxbury more than six years last past and alledges it to be under warning but does not set forth of what nature this warning was. The same warrant as the Gist of it sets forth disjunctively that the said John Chattuck properly belongs to the said Town of Brookline or had his last residence there but does not set forth either of them in certain as it ought to have done and is not traversable. The constable of said Roxbury is by the same warrant ordered to take the effects and deliver them with the Body of the owner of them which is against Law.[42] The said Joseph Williams who subscribed and issued the same Warrant as a Justice of the peace was then, had been many years before and is now an Inhabitant of the said Town of Roxbury and rated for the taxes set for the poor there. The said warrant issued by Joseph Williams Esqr. is therein made returnable to the Clerk of the Court of the General Sessions of the peace and it ought to have been made returnable to the said Joseph Williams Esqr. the Justice of the peace who issued it. Wherefore the Selectmen of the said Town of Brooklyn, inasmuch as its confessd above that the said John Shattuck had lived more than six years last past before said removal in the said Town of Roxbury, for want of any sufficient warrant for warning him to depart said Town of Roxbury or giving security to the Selectmen of it, and for want of any sufficient warrant to remove him to the said Town of Brooklyn, and for the illegality of said warrant and the return thereupon, prays judgment that the said John Shattuck, his wife, and children, Martha, John, and Mary, so removed, may be returned to the said Town of Roxbury, and for the said Town of Brooklyn's expences for his wifes and three children, maintenance and other incidental necessary expences for them since their said removal, and for the costs.[43] This Petition was pre-

---

[41] The file copy of the petition reads, "The said John Chattuck thereby required." SF 102089.

[42] Perhaps "against law" in the sense that the statutory provision for removal does not refer to effects. Act of 16 Nov. 1692, c. 28, §10, 1 A&R 68, set out in No. 25, note 6.

[43] The file copy of the petition shows that it was signed by "Jer. Gridley for the Selectmen of said Brooklyn."

ferred to the Court at its Sessions by adjournment on the fifth day of
May A.D. 1767 when it was read and then ordered that the Selectmen of the Town of Roxbury should be served with a copy thereof,
that they appear on Wednesday the tenth day of June following to
shew cause if any they had why the prayer thereof should not be
granted. And they being served with a copy appeared and by Robert
Auchmuty Esqr. their Council said first that this honorable Court
ought not to take cognizance of the matters and things shewn forth
herein by the said Selectmen of the Town of Brooklyn because the
same are only such matters as are properly enquirable into as error
and not appertaining to the merits of the cause, and secondly that the
matters and things offered and objected by the said Selectmen of
Brooklyn aforsaid are not sufficient for this Court to grant the prayer
of said Selectmen of Brooklyn on. Wherefore the Selectmen of said
Roxbury pray the Court to dismiss this petition and for their reasonable costs. And then the same was continued to the next sessions in
July following and from thence to the next Court and so from Court
to Court until this time by order of Court and with the consent of
parties. And they being now heard upon said pleas,[44] the Council
for the Town of Roxbury moved that the opinion of the Court may
be taken whether there is Sufficient matter alledged in the petition of
the Town of Brooklyn for the Court to proceed to the tryal of the
merits, and thereupon the Court deliver it as their opinion that there
is not matter sufficient in said petition whereby the Court may proceed
to an hearing of the merits so far as to determine whether said Shattuck and family are the proper poor of Roxbury or Brookline. Then it
was moved that said petition be dismiss'd, but the Court are of opinion
that it be not dismiss'd and upon a further hearing of the parties it
is Considered by the Court that the prayer of said petition be and
hereby is granted and ordered that the Inhabitants of the Town of
Roxbury pay and refund unto the Selectmen of the Town of Brooklyn
all such charge and expence as has arisen to them for the support
and Maintenance [45] of said John Chadock alias Chadwick alias Chattuck or Shattuck and his said wife and children untill this time and
that they be returned to the said Town of Roxbury and also pay to
said Selectmen of Brookline all the Costs that have been occasioned
on their application to this Court in this matter.

[44] The file copy of the court's opinion, "filed by consent of both the parties,"
begins, "After long debate." SF 102089.

[45] The remainder of the record is supplied from Sess. Min. Bk., 7 Nov. 1768.

No. 27. Brookline v. Roxbury

IV. BROOKLINE'S ACCOUNT [46]

Suffolk Court of General Sessions, Boston, November 1768

Brookline Novr. 7. 1768

1767   The Town of Roxbury to the Town of Brookline Dr.

Jan. 30	To Isaac Gardner Esqr. for boarding Jno. Shattuck and wife 3 days to two mens watching and Attendance		18	
Feby.	To 2 days spent upon said Shattuck [account?]		8	
	To 1 Day Ditto		3	
6	To Deacon Ebenr. Davis for supplying to said Shattuck family		5	8
	To keeping said Shattuck's horse 18 days		7	8
	To cash to said Shattuck's wife		6	
	To 1/2 day his mans attendance on said Shattuck		4	
	To sundry to said Shattucks Family		3	1
	To 2 1/2 days Attendance on said Shattuck		10	
Mh. 2	To keeping said Shattucks horse 13 weeks @ 3 per week	1	19	
	To Danl. Sanders for watching 4 Nights with said Shattuck		6	
	To Fish and Greenwood for watching with Ditto 1 night		3	
	To Antho. Marion for watching with Ditto 4 nights		6	
	To Edward Williams for Ditto 2 nights		3	
	To George Brown for Ditto 3 nights		4	6
	To Micah Grout for Ditto 1 night		1	6
	To Capt. Parker for 2 [...] candles for Shattuck		1	5¾
Feby. 12	To Benja. White for time and expence to Andover with said Shattuck		14	
22	To time and expence to Ditto		12	11
	To 2 days on Shattucks Account		8	
	To his mans Attendance on Shattuck		4	

[46] SF 102089.

12th	To Majr. Robert Sharp for time and expence to Andover and cash to the Doctor for said Shattuck	1	13	4
	To 2½ days Attendance on said Shattuck		10	
	To his sons Attendance on Ditto		1	6
	To keeping Shattucks horse		3	
	To Mr. John Harris for time and expences to Andover with Shattuck	1	9	
22	To time and expence to Andover and cash to the Doctor for Ditto	1	18	
	To Wood and other Supplies to said Shattuck and family		18	5
	To Docr. Eliphalet Downer for keeping said John Shattuck and Attendance 8 weeks from the 23d. Feby. 1767 @ 13 per week	5	6	8
	To Alexdr. Young for Bread and milk for Breakfasts for said Shattuck while in Goal 17 weeks @ 2 per week	1	14	
		£22	2	3¾[47]

1767				
July 29	To Mr. Enoch Brown for 2 check shirts for said Shattuck	0	15	
Apl. 19	To Benja. White for boarding Mrs. Shattuck and daughter Mary 26 weeks at 10 per week	13	0	
	To keeping Ditto 21 weeks @ 7/4 per week	7	14	
	To keeping Shattuck 24 weeks from the last Octr. @ 8 per week	7	4	
	To keeping said Shattucks horse 25 weeks to grass @ 2 per week	2	10	
1768				
March 15	To keeping Ditto 11 weeks to hay @ 5/4 per week	2	18	8
	To keeping Mrs. Shattuck and Daughter Mary 23 weeks @ 6 per week	9	18	

[47] Subtotal taken at the end of the first page of the MS account.

To nursing said Shattucks daughter Mary in Sickness	o	6	8
To keeping Shattuck himself 8 weeks @ 5/4 per week	2	2	8
To nursing Ditto in his late sickness	o	5	4
To Stephen Brewer for house rent for said Shattucks goods and damages done to His house	1	16	
To Docr. Jona. Davis for medicine and Attendance for Jno. Shattuck wife and daughtr. Mary from Octr. 2. 1767 to Apl. 29, 1768	4	9	8
To Ditto for 1 weeks board	o	12	
	53	12	
Brot from the other side	22	2	3¾
	75	14	3¾
Deduct by order the whole keeping of the horse	7	17	11
Allowd by the Court and Costs.	£67	16	4¾

Brookline Novr. 8. 1768. Errors Excepted per Benja. White Isaac Gardner, John Harris, Jno. Goddard, Thos. Griggs } Selectmen of Brookline

Boston January 31. 1769
We the Subscribers having Attended the Selectmen of Roxbury and considered the Account exhibited by the Town of Brookline relative to the Pauper Shadwick who was removed from Roxbury to Brookline do report that the Town of Roxbury pay to the Town of Brookline Seventy one pounds fourteen shillings and 3 3/4 [48] being in full for their charges in maintaining and supporting said Pauper with their legal costs of prosecution in behalf of John Hill, Samuel Pemberton Esqr. and self John Avery.

[48] This figure is £0 1s. 7d. less than the amount for which execution issued in March 1769, perhaps reflecting an incomplete computation of costs at this stage. See note 3 above.

V. WRIT OF CERTIORARI [49]

Suffolk Superior Court, Boston, July 1769

| [SEAL] | Province of the
Massachusetts Bay
Suffolk Ss | } | George the third by the grace
of God of Great Britain France
and Ireland, King Defender of
the Faith &c. |

To our trusty and well beloved Samuel Welles Esqr. first Justice of our Court of General Sessions of the peace for the said county, Greeting.

Willing for certain causes to be certified of the Record of the process Order and Sentence of a Court of general Sessions of the peace held at Boston in and for said county by adjournment on the seventh day of November last, upon a petition of the selectmen of Brooklyn in said county, then and there heard and adjudged (as it is said) before you and your Companions Justices of the same court: We therefore command you that the said Record, with all things touching the same fully and entirely as the same remains before You, You send before Us in our Superiour court of Judicature, Court of Assize and general Goal Delivery, to be held at Boston in and for the county of Suffolk on the last tuesday of August next, under your Seal together with this writ: hereof fail not; Witness Thomas Hutchinson Esquire, at Boston the twenty seventh day of July in the ninth year of our Reign, Annoque Domini 1769.   Nat. Hatch Cler.

To the Honorable His majesty's Justices of His Superior court of Judicature &c. above mention'd I herewith send the Record within mention'd with all things touching the same.   Samuel Welles

VI. FITCH'S ASSIGNMENT OF ERRORS [50]

Suffolk Superior Court, Boston, March 1770

In the Case of the Select-Men of the Town of Brooklyn against the Town of Roxbury heard and adjudged at the Court of General Ses-

[49] SF 102089, in unknown hand. The form seems to translate literally the Latin form used in England. See, for example, 1 Gardiner, *Instructor Clericalis* 157. It may be a local product, since it varies in detail, though not in substance, from the translated forms found in English books. See William Bohun, *The English Lawyer* 221–243 (London, 1732); Michael Dalton, *The Country Justice* 476 (London, 1746); compare Thomas Chitty, *Forms of Practical Proceedings* 651 (London, 2d edn., 1835).

[50] SF 102089, presumably in Fitch's hand. The document is dated by the reference to it in Doc. VII.

sions of the Peace held at Boston in and for the County of Suffolk by Adjournment on Monday the Seventh Day of November A.D. 1768. The Errors assigned by the Select-Men of the Town of Roxbury, which appear by the Records and Proceedings of said Court in said Case, on the Certiorari are as follows Vizt.

First, For that it appears by the Records of said Court of Sessions in said Case, that the Matters and things set forth and alledged in the Petition of the Select-Men of the Town of Brooklyn to the said Court were only Matters of supposed Error, and enquirable into as such; and that therefore the said Court; which is not a Court for the Tryal of Errors, could not by Law take Cognizance of, or determine upon the same.

2dly. The said Select-Men in their said Petition do not alledge that the Paupers therein mentioned, were not the Poor of the said Town of Brooklyn, and properly belonging to them to Maintain, nor do they shew forth any Facts whereon that Matter could be properly Enquired into and determined, or desire that it should be: And yet they pray that the said Paupers may be removed from Brooklyn to Roxbury and that the Town of Roxbury should Repay to Brooklyn the Expences they had been at in Supporting said Paupers with their Costs and the said Court Granted the said prayer of their Petition as appears by their Records of Proceedings in said Case.

3dly. The Select-Men of the said Town of Roxbury in their Answer to the said Petition Alledged, first that the said Court ought not to take Cognizance of the Matters and things shewn forth therein by the said Select-Men of said Brooklyn; Because the same were only such Matters as were properly enquirable into as Error, and not appertaining to the Merits of the Cause: and secondly that the Matters and things offered and objected by the said Select-Men of Brooklyn, were not sufficient for said Court to Grant the Prayer of said Select-Men of Brooklyn on: And the said Court Thereupon Determined and delivered their Opinion, that there was not Matter sufficient in said Petition whereby the said Court, might proceed to an hearing of the Merits so as to determine whether the said Paupers were the proper Poor of Roxbury or Brooklyn; but yet notwithstanding, the said Court, would not dismiss the said Petition (when it was moved that it should be dismissed) but sustained the same, and Granted the Prayer thereof as aforesaid; which is absurd and Contradictory: All which appears by the Records and Proceedings of said Court in said Case.

4thly. The said Court of Sessions cou'd not with any propriety or Consistancy grant the said Prayer of said Petition without Enquiring into the Merits of said Cause and Determining whether the said Paupers were the proper Poor of the said Town of Brooklyn, or of the said Town of Roxbury: And yet the said Court did Grant the said Prayer of said Petition as aforesaid, without Entering into, or making any such Enquiry or Determination, as appears by their Records and Proceedings in said Case.

5thly. There appears by the said Records of the said Court of Sessions to be no Adjudication that the said Paupers or any of them are or were the proper Inhabitants of the said Town of Roxbury, or that they be, or should be, or ought to be supported and maintained by said Town; or that they had been illegally or improperly removed from said Town, to the said Town of Brooklyn or that the Order for removing them be Quash'd: and yet it appears, by the same Records that the said Court ordered, that the said Paupers should be returned to the said Town of Roxbury, and that the Inhabitants of said Town should pay and Refund unto the Select-Men of the Town of Brooklyn all such Charge and Expence as had arisen to them for the support and Maintenance of said Paupers; therefore the said Order of the said Court of Sessions for the Removal of said Paupers and for Refunding said Charges, is not founded on any direct Adjudication, but at best is founded on an uncertain adjudication, by Implication only; and it is repugnant and Contradictory to and inconsistant with the other Parts of said Record as beforementioned, and is altogether illegal and Erronious in Substance.

Wherefore the said Select-Men of the Town of Roxbury pray that the Order, Sentence, Judgment and proceedings of said Court of Sessions, may be Quashed, and the said Town of Roxbury restored to what they have suffered and paid in Consequence thereof and be allowed their Costs.   Saml. Fitch for the Select Men of Roxbury

VII. NOTIFICATION[51]

Suffolk Superior Court, Boston, ca. 1769–March 1770

[SEAL] Province of ⎱ To the Selectmen of the Town of
Massachusetts Bay ⎰ Brooklyn in said County Greeting
Suffolk Ss

You are hereby notified that by his Majestys Writ of Certiorari bearing Test the 27th. day of July last, the Record of the Process

[51] SF 102089, signed and subscribed as printed.

Order and Sentence of the Court of general Sessions of the peace held at Boston in and for said County of Suffolk by adjournment on the 7th day of November last[52] upon your petition relating to the Charge and Expence of supporting John Chaddock with his Wife and Children, paupers, are removed before his Majesty in his Superior Court of Judicature &ca. now holden at Boston aforesaid for said County of Suffolk: and that the Town of Roxbury have alledged certain Errors in the said Record, and pray'd that the said Order and Judgment may be reversed annulled and vacated: and further that the same be tried and finally adjudged before his Majesty in his superior Court of Judicature &ca. now holden at Boston aforesaid for said County and that you may be present and heard thereon if you see meet.

Done at Boston the 31st. day of March in the tenth year of his Majesty's Reign Annoque Domoni 1770.

By order of Court,

Saml. Winthrop Cler.

Suffolk Ss Bosto April the 3d. 1770
I have Notified Benja. White and Isaac Winchester the Select men of the town of Broockline to be present a Cording to this Sitation By Reading and Suffering them to Read the Same.

Per Benja. Cudworth Deputy Sheriff

The Services 2/

28. Essane v. Dotey
1767–1768
EDITORIAL NOTE

The jurisdiction of the Court of General Sessions of the Peace in cases of bastardy originated in its role as a conservator of public morals. The effect of bastardy proceedings, however, was less to punish the guilty than to provide for the support of the innocent and save the town from charge; thus they may properly be viewed as a phase of the court's administrative powers in welfare matters. The jurisdiction was established by a statute dealing with a number of noncapital offenses, including swearing, drunkenness, burglary, breach of the peace, forgery, and perjury. The section on bastardy, after establishing pecuniary and corporal penalties

---

[52] An inadvertence for Nov. 1768, the date of the Sessions hearing. See Doc. III. The error is probably accounted for by the language of the writ itself, dated 27 July 1769, which referred to the hearing in "November last." See Doc. V.

for fornication, provided, "And he that is accused by any woman to be the father of a bastard child, begotten of her body, she continuing constant in such accusation, being examined upon oath, and put upon the discovery of the truth in the time of her travail, shall be adjudged the reputed father of such child, notwithstanding his denial, and stand charged with the maintenance thereof, with the assistance of the mother, as the justices of the quarter sessions shall order; and give security to perform the said order, and to save the town or place where such child is born, free from charge for its maintenance and may be committed to prison until he find sureties for the same, unless the pleas and proofs made and produced on the behalf of the man accused and other circumstances be such as the justices shall see reason to judge him innocent and acquit him thereof, and otherwise dispose of the child." [1]

Cases under this Act were a frequent item on the dockets of the Courts of General Sessions (successors to the quarter sessions), and Adams tried a substantial number of them.[2] They are of interest both for the social problem which they reveal and because of the procedural steps adopted for its solution.

Jane Dotey, of "Duxborough" (Duxbury) in Plymouth County, gave birth to an illegitimate child in September 1767. In July she had been examined by Gamaliel Bradford, a Justice of the Peace, and had made oath that one Manuel Essane was putative father of the child with which she was then pregnant (Document I). On Bradford's warrant, Essane, a minor apprenticed to Rouse Bourne of Marshfield, was brought before the Plymouth Court of General Sessions then sitting and was apparently bound over to abide the event by virtue of another provision of the statute.[3] Finally at the December Sessions, Jane appeared, was fined for the crime of fornication, and again made oath that Essane was responsible for her

---

[1] Act of 1 Nov. 1692, c. 18, §5, 1 A&R 52. See also notes 3, 5, below.

[2] Other JA cases in addition to No. 29 and No. 30, include Johnson v. Hunter (Concord Sess. Sept. 1768), and Turner v. Reynolds (Taunton Sess. Aug. 1769). His minutes for both are in the Adams Papers. See also his diary entry for 29 July 1766: "At Boston.... Heard some Cases of Bastardy in the Sessions. William Douglass was charged by a Dutch girl with being the father of a Bastard Child born of her Body." 1 JA, *Diary and Autobiography* 317. This was the case of Susanna Strater, who was presented for and convicted of fornication at the Suffolk Sessions on 29 July 1766. She then swore that William Douglass of Boston, a minor, was the father and produced witnesses to the fact. Douglass was ordered to pay maintenance. Sess. Min. Bk., 29 July 1766. See also Hewet v. Clear, *ibid.* For some indication of the number of such cases, see *Records of the Court of General Sessions of the Peace for the County of Worcester, Massachusetts, from 1731 to 1737* (Worcester, Mass., ed. F. P. Rice, 1882). As to the state of morality generally, see Charles Francis Adams, "Some Phases of Sexual Morality and Church Discipline in Colonial New England," 6 MHS, *Procs.* (2d ser.) 477–516 (1890–1891).

[3] For the warrant, dated 6 July 1767 and returned to the Sessions on 11 July, see SF 142245. The section of the bastardy statute quoted above, text at note 1, also provided that "every justice of the peace upon his discretion may bind to the next quarter sessions him that is charged or suspected to have begotten a bastard child; and if the woman be not then delivered, the sessions may order the continuance or renewal of his bond, that he may be forthcoming when the child is born."

plight. The court adjudged Essane "reputed father of the said child," and ordered him to pay maintenance and costs, and to give bond to indemnify the towns of Plymouth, Duxbury, and Marshfield from charges for the child (Document II).[4]

On the motion of Adams, who had represented Essane at Sessions, the Superior Court at its March 1768 Suffolk Term ordered a writ of certiorari to issue returnable at Plymouth in May.[5] Adams filed an assignment of errors (Document III), in which he attacked the Sessions proceedings on six grounds. The first three errors assigned alleged the absence from the record of any findings of compliance with the statutory requirements of accusation and examination before and during delivery. The other assignments were that the order for maintenance was either beyond the court's jurisdiction, or void for uncertainty; that as a minor Essane could not be ordered to give bond; and that the portion of the order requiring Essane to indemnify the three towns was void because there was no finding or evidence as to the child's birthplace, and because, in any event, only the town in which the birth occurred was liable for his charges.

When the case was heard at Plymouth in May, the Court quashed the order of Sessions and filed a memorandum of its reasons, an unusual item, which is printed as Document IV.[6] The first reason, the omission of the child's birthplace from the record, was probably considered "jurisdictional"; that is, the fact omitted was necessary to a valid order, at least one requiring that indemnity be given to a town.[7] In its second reason, that the judgment was based only on the complainant's oath, the court avoided a direct confrontation of the jurisdictional issues in Adams' first three assignments of error, stating in effect only that the facts alleged were insufficient, without saying what particular additional facts would have been necessary.[8] The final reason, that the order should have required the father to indemnify only the town of the child's birthplace, could either be said to go to an excess of jurisdiction or could be considered the correction of an order inconsistent on its face.[9] The presence in the Superior

[4] The order to give bond for all three towns was probably based on Bradford's warrant of 6 July, which gave as a reason for Essane's apprehension that "the said Child when Born May be Chargeable to the said Mother, or to the Towns of Plymouth, Duxborough or Marshfield." SF 142245.

[5] Min. Bk. 86, SCJ Suffolk, March 1768. The writ and notification to Jane Dotey, both dated 8 April 1768, are in SF 142245. They are substantially similar in form to those printed in Brookline v. Roxbury, No. 27, Docs. V, VII. The penalty for fornication provided by the section of the statute at note 1 above was a fine not to exceed £5, or whipping not to exceed ten stripes, in the discretion of the Sessions. JA received a fee of "12" (presumably shillings) from one Elisha Ford. JA, Docket, Plymouth Inferior Court, Dec. 1768. Adams Papers.

[6] Min. Bk. 82, SCJ Plymouth, May 1768, N–12; SCJ Rec. 1767–1768, fol. 189. See note 14 below. See also JA, Docket, Plymouth SCJ, May 1768, Adams Papers, where JA's fee is noted as "12," again presumably shillings.

[7] As to the scope of review on certiorari, see No. 27, notes 7–9.

[8] For further discussion of this point, see No. 30.

[9] See Edith G. Henderson, *Foundations of English Administrative Law* 144–145 (Cambridge, Mass., 1963).

Court file of Jane Dotey's examination (Document I), and the warrant issued by Justice Bradford on the basis of it, suggest an unsuccessful attempt to cure some of these errors by material not strictly speaking in "the record." [10]

I. JANE DOTEY'S EXAMINATION [11]

Plymouth, 6 July 1769

Plymouth Ss. The Information of Jane Doty now Residing in Duxborough single woman taken before me Gamaliel Bradford Esqr. one of his Majestys Justices of the Peace for the said County this ⟨*Eighth*⟩ Sixth Day of July 1767.

Q. Are you now with Child.

A. Yes.

Q. Who is the father of the Child you are now Big with.

A. Mannuel Essane of Marshfield servant to Rouse Bourne ⟨*Between*⟩ on the ⟨*Seventeenth and*⟩ twenty seventh and thirtyeth Days of January Last did enter and had Carnal Knowledge of her Body two several times.

Q. Had any other man Carnal Knowledge of your Body aboute that time.

A. No nor Never in all her Lifetime.

Q. Where was the place he had Carnal Knowledge of your Body.

A. In the House My Gradmother now Lives in in Duxborough.

her
Jane   X   Doty
Mark

Sworn the Day and year above said before Me, Gaml. Bradford Justice of peace.

II. RECORD [12]

Plymouth Court of General Sessions, Plymouth, December 1767

Plymouth Ss. At his Majesty's court of general sessions of the peace, began and held at Plymouth within and for the county of Plym-

---

[10] For Bradford's warrant, see SF 142245; notes 3, 4, above. As to "the record," see No. 27, notes 6–8.

[11] SF 142245. The document seems to be the original in the hand of Justice Bradford.

[12] SF 142245. Subscribed: "A true copy of record examined per Ed. Winslow Junr. Cler." In the MS the numbers of the paragraphs are written in the margin.

outh on the second tuesday of december being the eighth day of said month, in the eighth year of our Sovereign Lord George the third by the Grace of God of Great-Britain, France and Ireland, King, Defender of the Faith, &c. annoque Domini 1767.

Jane Doten [Dotey] a late resident in Duxborough in the county of Plymouth single woman, appeared at this court and confessed that she had been guilty of the crime of fornication. The court having considered her offence (she being poor) sentence her to pay a fine of twelve shillings to his majesty, or be whipped ten stripes on her naked body, to pay costs of prosecution, and stand committed until sentence be performed.

At said court Jane Doten late residing in Duxborough in the county of Plymouth single woman appeared, who having while pregnant, and now before this court made oath that Manuel Esseane was the father of the bastard child born of her body in September last. And after a hearing of the parties in the case. It is considered by the court that the said Manuel Esseane be adjudged to be the reputed father of the said child, that he stand charged with the maintenance thereof, that he pay the sum of three pounds, it being one half of the charge of her lying in, &c., for the first month. And also that he pay the sum of twenty one shillings, it being for keeping said child to the eleventh of december instant, that he pay costs of prosecution taxed at one pound, thirteen shillings and two pence. And also that the said Manuel enter into recognizance with two sureties in the sum of forty pounds that he shall pay quarterly until the further order of said court, at the rate of three shillings a week towards the support of said child. And also that he recognize in the like sum of forty pounds with sureties to secure and save harmless the towns of Plymouth, Duxborough and Marshfield from all charges and damages that may arise by said child. And that he stand committed until sentence be performed.

III. ADAMS' ASSIGNMENT OF ERRORS[13]

Plymouth Superior Court, Plymouth, April 1768

In the Case of Jane Dotey vs. Manuel Essane heard and adjudged at the Court of General Sessions of the Peace held at Plymouth within and for the County of Plymouth on the ⟨first⟩ second Tuesday of December being the Eighth day of said Month in the Year of our

[13] In JA's hand. SF 142245.

Lord 1767, the Errors assigned by said Manual, on the Certiorari are as follow viz.

1st. It does not appear by the Record of the Judgment or Sentence of said Court of General Sessions of the Peace in said Case that Manual Essane was ever accused by the said Jane, to be the Father of the Bastard Child born of her Body, in September last, before the said Child was born.

2d. It does not appear by the Record of said Judgment or Sentence, nor by any other Record of any Proceedings in the Case, that the said Jane, continued constant in her Accusation, of the said Manual to be the Father of said Bastard Child.

3d. It does not appear by said Record of said Sentence, or Judgment, that said Jane was ever examined upon oath while she was pregnant with said Bastard Child, nor that she was put upon the Discovery of the Truth in the Time of her Travail, all of which by Law ought to have appeared.

4. The said Court have, by their Sentence aforesaid, ordered the said Manual, "that he pay the sum of Three Pounds it being the one half of the Charge of her lying in &c. for the first Month, and allso that he pay the sum of Twenty one shillings, it being for Keeping said Child to the Eleventh Day of December," in which the said Court have exceeded their Jurisdiction they not having Authority by Law to make such an order, and if they had such Authority, in this Case the order is uncertain, insensible and void, the said Court not having ordered the said Manual to pay the aforesaid Sums to any Person whatever in certain.

5. The said Court has ordered the said Manual to enter into Recognizance with two sureties, &c. which the said Manual was then and still is by Law incapable of doing as he then was and still is an Infant under the Age of Twenty one Years

6. The said Court have by the sentence aforesaid ordered the said Manual, that he recognize in the sum of Forty Pounds with two sureties to Secure and Save harmless the Towns of Plymouth, Duxborough and Marshfield from all Charges and Damages that may arise by said Child which the said Court had no Authority by Law to do, for it does not appear by said sentence, or any Record in said Case, that said Bastard Child was born in any of those Towns, and if it did, it would still be certain that said ⟨Town⟩ Child could not be born in more than one of said Towns, and therefore in that Case, said Manual could be obliged only to give security to Save that Town harmless where said Bastard Child was born.

Where fore the said Manual prays that the aforesaid order, Sentence, Judgment, and Proceedings of the said Court of Sessions may be quashed.   John Adams for said Manual

IV. REASONS FOR THE JUDGMENT[14]

Plymouth Superior Court, May 1768

In Superior Court at Plymo[uth] May 1768.

Order'd that the aforesaid Judgment and proceedings of the Court of General Sessions of the peace be quash'd—1st. Because it doth not appear in the Record aforesaid where the Child aforesaid was born.

2. It appears by the Record aforesaid that the aforesaid Judgment was founded on the Oath of the said Jane and on that only.

3. The said Manuel is ordered to recognize in £40 with Sureties to save the Towns of Plymouth Duxborough and Marshfield from all Charge and Damages that may arise by the said Child. Whereas the said Court of General Sessions of the peace, if the said Manuel has been duely adjudged the reputed Father of the Child abovesaid could only have ordered the said Manuel to give Security to save the Town or Place where the Child was born from Charge for its maintenance.   S. Winthrop Cler.

29. Gage v. Headley

1768

EDITORIAL NOTE

This was a proceeding at the Middlesex General Sessions for September 1768, in which Lydia Gage accused Josiah Headley of being the father of her bastard child. Adams' docket for this term shows that he took Headley's case and that he "rec'd £1 4s. at one Time and 12s. more at another."[1]

---

[14] SF 142245, in the hand of Samuel Winthrop, Clerk of the Superior Court. This is evidently the document referred to in the court's decision: "After a due inspection of the Record of the order complained of, and a full hearing of the Parties upon the Errors assigned: Judgement that the Order of the Court of Sessions be quashed for the Reasons on file on the back of the Writ." Min. Bk. 82, SCJ Plymouth, May 1768, N–12; SCJ Rec. 1767–1768, fol. 189. The reasons actually appear on the verso of the notification to Jane Dotey, cited in note 5 above.

[1] JA, Docket, Concord Inferior Court, Sept. 1768. Adams Papers. The two were also bound over on the charge of fornication. See recognizances in Files, Middlesex Court of General Sessions, 1768. Office of the Clerk, Middlesex County Superior Court, East Cambridge, Mass. The child was a son born 30 March 1768 and

Adams did not note the result, however, and, although some of the files of the case have survived, the records of the Middlesex Sessions for this term cannot be located. His minutes of the trial are printed here as an example of the testimony and argument in such a case. James Putnam appeared for Lydia.

In the files of the Middlesex Sessions, there remain five depositions in this case, none of them given by the witnesses in Adams' minutes.[2] The depositions contain conflicting testimony as to whether Headley or Zachaus Parkes had offered Lydia £300 to accuse the other. The deponents also reported that she had at various times accused Parkes, Headley, and one Simeon Hagar, and that before Colonel Jones, presumably a Justice of the Peace,[3] she had accused an unknown transient. It also appeared that she had earlier had an illegitimate daughter by Parkes, which was now being "kept" by the latter's brother Ephraim. According to one witness, she at one point threatened to accuse Ephraim because he was going to "put out" her first child, then stated that she had been forced to accuse someone other than Zachaus Parkes, lest Ephraim turn the child out.[4] The pattern of instability suggested in these depositions and in the testimony in Adams' minutes is borne out by the fact that an order of the General Court dated 25 February 1762 had given Theophilus Mansfield of Weston (a deponent here) power to sell the real estate of his ward, Lydia Gage of Lincoln, a *non compos mentis*.[5]

ADAMS' MINUTES OF THE TESTIMONY [6]

Middlesex Court of General Sessions, Concord, September 1768

Lidia Gage vs. Josiah Headley.

Sarah Garfield.

D[eaco]n Farrar.[7] Last of Decr. It is Josiah Headleys. The next Saturday, she said she was sorry she had told me what she did. Not

---

named Josiah, doubtless in honor of the putative father. *Vital Records of Lincoln* 38 (Boston, 1908).

[2] See Files, Middlesex Court of General Sessions, 1768. The depositions are those of James Adams, Lydia Farrar, Moses Underwood, Sarah Mansfield, and Theophilus Mansfield.

[3] Both Elisha and John Jones were Justices of the Peace and of the Quorum in Middlesex County. See Whitmore, *Mass. Civil List* 138.

[4] Deposition of Sarah Mansfield. Ephraim Parkes' testimony to the contrary appears in JA's minutes.

[5] The order empowered Mansfield to sell real estate for his ward's support. See Order of 25 Feb. 1762, c. 390, 17 A&R 166. Mansfield's deposition in the Middlesex Files (note 2 above) seems to favor Headley.

[6] In JA's hand. Adams Papers, Microfilms, Reel No. 185.

[7] Probably the Humphry Farrar in whose family Lydia's child was at the time of his baptism, 31 Oct. 1773. *Vital Records of Lincoln* 38. The names of most of the other witnesses, including Hosmers ("Horsemores") and Hagars, are found in the *Vital Records*, showing the local nature of the affair.

because it want true, but because he said he'd get her whipped. 10 days after she said if the Promisses were not fullfilled, she would tell the whole Truth. Afterwards she said Headly [hired?] her to lay it to Zack Parkes, Simeon Hagar, or some body else. Said she had 2 or 3 meetings, with Headley. Parkes told me, that Headly said he would come and settle it. At the Groaning, I heard her say that it was Josiah Headleys of Weston the Miller and Tavernkeeper. Knew that she had chargd Parkes but never mentiond it to her.

Rebecca Brown. ⟨Deposition vide—Aug.⟩ I talked with her before and after she went before Coll. Jones. A Month before. She said she had Promisses of £300 and other Gifts, and her Brother Robert was to receive it. That Headly asked her to lay it to Zack Parkes, Simeon Hagar, or a transient Person unknown. She had wronged her soul, by clearing Headley. She lived with me 20 Year, never afraid to Trust her. Not given to lying. Robert Gage told me a week before his death, Mr. Headly a friend of his, and he did not choose to say any Thing unless under Oath.

Mrs. Horsemore. Last Winter, Lidia said she was sorry she had been to clear him up before his Wife. Headly had perswaded her in the shed under the Tree, nobody present. She said that it was Headleys to Deacon Farrar, and got soon after the Trooping at Sudbury. I've seen him, and you never see any poor Creature take on so. Deacon Farrar asked her how she came to lay it to Zach Parks.

Susannah Gage. Wife of Robt. Gage. January. I shant tell. Tis not a Man I can have, but a Man that can pay. Headly ta[l]ked so, that he convinced my Husband she had wronged Mr. Headley. She said that it was Headleys as true as a God in Heaven. That he perswaded her, and promised her Money. She came and asked my Husband if Money was left for her.

Lidia Parks. At Mr. Underwoods as she came from Horsemores. Lidia Gage said she would not damn her own Soul any longer for any Body. Headley told me, she had better take what she had and go off, or else he'd Send her to the Devil. Sister in Law to Zach. Parks. If he had not rid her skimmington [8] he had some other Way.

Sufferana Hagar. Lived in the House with Lidia Gage. I knew She

---

[8] "To ride skimmington" in rural England was to hold "a ludicrous procession" of villagers intended to ridicule a shrewish woman, an unfaithful husband, or, alternatively, the victim of such a person. *OED.* Here the term is apparently extended to include the conduct which would cause such ridicule to fall either upon Headley's wife or upon Lydia. In Massachusetts, the word also seems to have connoted "mobbing." See 1 JA, *Diary and Autobiography* 291; JA's minutes, Hodges v. Gilmore, Adams Papers, Microfilms, Reel No. 185.

was with Child, as soon as she did. She said she never had accused him of this Child, and was not a going to. Middle of July, I knew she was with Child. Never knew H[e]adley at the House. She never told me, who was the father, but she gave me two Hints, she said if Headleys family were affronted with her for such Things, they should be affronted worse before long. Latter End of Octr. or Beginning of Novr. I told Headley. He said he would take his Gun and shoot her. But I did not think, he intended to shoot deeper than some People think he had done. His General Character very good, till this came out.

Sarah Garfield. I asked her who was the father, 30 March, in Extremity, she said Headley and no Man else. I asked her how she came to clear him before Coll. Jones. She said He promised her Money and that she should never want. As she expected to answer it before God.[9]

Mrs. Allen. At the Travel [Travail]. She came in to our House a few days before her Travel. I charged her. She said she was told, that if she laid it to Parks she should get nothing, that Daniel Parks had been to a Lawyer, and told her those stories. That all Zack had was made over to maintain Phoebe, i.e. her last Child. Robert Gage told me there was no Truth in the story, that Headly had never offerd a farthing.

Mrs. Gage. At the Travel, as before. Headly came to our House and said he had an Arrant [Errand?] to do to Lidia from a Gentleman. She said Twas a transient Person, and Hagar and Pucker, a poor Toad. In January Headley calld her out under the shed, and talked with her. The family suspected Headley, before she chargd any Body. Under Guardian.

Ephraim Parks. Brother to Zach and Guardian. Zach denyd it. I went to her, and Asked her if she could clear him. She said Zack is clear, and I never laid it to him and ant a going to. He has had nothing to do with me. Did not threaten to put away Phoebe, nor say that she could get nothing.

Wm. Horsemore. Town ant so devilish good to me. They need not concern themselves. She did not lay it to any Body.

Simeon Hager. James Parks. Week before Trav[ail] talked with ⟨Lidia Gage⟩ Headley. Said he was going to Deacon Farrar to settle that Affair. Would you have me pay, if clear? No. I'm as clear as the sun.

[9] According to the deposition of Lydia Farrar in the Middlesex Files (note 2 above), "Mrs. Sarah Garfield" was a midwife present at Lydia's labor, who asked her who the father was. 30 March 1768 was the date of the child's birth. See note 1 above.

Putnam. If the Inconstancy can be accounted for, from a natural Source, so that she is believed, it is within the Law. The only Question is whether her Charge is true.

Her weakness, no Impeachment of her Veracity.

She would tell Deacon Parks the Truth. And she told him, it was Headley. Deacon Farrar meets with Headley. Headley said it was a Matter he would consider of. Tho he denied the Charge.

A Difficulty arises, and a great deal is to [be] made of it. The next Time she told the Deacon she was sorry she had laid it to Headley. She did not pretend to say she had chargd him wrongfully. A Temptation—a snare—a Trap.

Another Objection, she is not the most chaste Woman. A common Strum.[10] She may know, notwithstanding her Inchastity, who is the father. The law does not confine it, to any Number of Times.

Another Objection that being a Lyar, will discredit her Testimony.

30. Josselyne v. Harrington

1769–1771

EDITORIAL NOTE

Ann Josselyne of Marlborough claimed that John Harrington of the same town was the father of her illegitimate child born in June 1768. At the Middlesex General Sessions, Concord, September 1769, she was fined five shillings for fornication, and her accusations were tried.[1] After hearing evidence and the oath of the complainant that Harrington was the father, the court ordered him to pay support for the child and give bond to indemnify the town (Document I).

In the same month Samuel Fitch, acting for Harrington, moved the Superior Court sitting at Worcester for a writ of certiorari returnable at the October 1769 Cambridge term. The writ issued and the case was docketed in Middlesex County.[2] The first two errors assigned by Fitch (Document II) are the same kind of omission from the record of findings of statutory requirements which Adams urged in *Essane v. Dotey*, No. 28. The third error, seemingly based on the reasons stated by the court for its decision in the latter case, was that the judgment of the Sessions had been founded only upon the complainant's oath. Finally, Fitch urged that the complainant

[10] "A handsome wench or strumpet." *OED.*

[1] See her recognizance, dated 9 Aug. 1769, and bill of costs. Rex v. Joslin, Files, Middlesex Court of General Sessions, Sept. 1769. Office of the Clerk, Middlesex County Superior Court, East Cambridge, Mass.

[2] Min. Bk. 90, SCJ Worcester, Sept. 1769, following N–79; SF 147733; Harrington v. Josselin, Min. Bk. 88, SCJ Middlesex, Oct. 1769, N–10.

had not in fact been examined in her "travel" (travail), and that she had not accused Harrington until after the event. He had previously assigned as error the failure of the record to recite these facts, but he now seemed to be going behind the record and asserting a failure of proof.

The case was continued from term to term until April 1771, when the court held "that there is no Error either in the Record and proceedings aforesaid, or in the Rendition of the Judgment aforesaid, and that the said Record is in no wise vitious, or defective." The judgment of the Sessions was affirmed with costs.[3] After *Essane v. Dotey*, the question of what recitals, in addition to the complainant's oath, were necessary to the record had remained open. *Josselyne v. Harrington* indicates that none of the requirements of the statute were considered "jurisdictional" in the sense that the record was faulty without them. Fitch had apparently urged that the court read the record (Document I) so that the word "thereupon" in the phrase "they do thereupon adjudge" referred back to the oath only.[4] The record also recites that the Sessions heard "Evidence," a statement not present in *Essane*. This distinction may have been the basis upon which the Superior Court rejected Fitch's reading and upheld the record in the present case.

Adams' minutes (Document III) present the further interesting possibility that the Superior Court heard evidence on at least one of the points raised by Fitch's fourth assignment of error, despite the fact that it had seemed to find the matters there asserted nonjurisdictional in the sense that they need not appear of record. This is a possibility only, because Adams' minutes cannot be dated precisely by either internal or external evidence. The fact that they are headed "Ann Josselyne vs. John Harrington. Bastardy," and the English rule that on certiorari nonjurisdictional questions were to be dealt with only on the basis of the record, suggest that the document dates from the Sessions.[5]

On the other hand, there is much to support the theory that it is a minute of proceedings in the Superior Court. It opens with a question asked by the "C.J.," or Chief Justice, relative to the validity of circumstantial evidence as a substitute for the statutory requirement of examination during travail. Since this was precisely one of the points which Fitch had raised on certiorari, the question was a logical one to be asked at those proceedings. Moreover, the usage "Chief Justice" indicates the Superior Court. The statutes establishing the court system expressly provided such an officer for that tribunal, but did not so provide for the Inferior Court of Common Pleas, or the Court of General Sessions. In fact the presiding justice of those courts was usually known as "First Justice," a reference to the position of his name in the commission appointing the court.[6] Finally

---

[3] Harrington v. Josselin, SCJ Rec. 1771, fol. 72. See also Min. Bk. 88, SCJ Middlesex, April 1771, C–8. Compare the decision of the court in No. 28, note 14.

[4] See text at note 9 below.

[5] As to the English rule, see No. 27, text at note 7. The court refused to hear evidence outside the record without indicating whether the matter was jurisdictional in Pond v. Medway, Quincy, *Reports* 193 (Mass. SCJ, 1765).

[6] See Act of 26 June 1699, c. 1, §1, 1 A&R 367; Act of 26 June 1699, c. 2,

the language of the court's decision, already quoted, is not inconsistent with the view that the court had gone behind the record as Fitch had asked. The finding of no error in "the rendition of the judgment" is stated disjunctively from the findings regarding the record,[7] indicating a separate finding that there was evidence to support the judgment.

If Adams' minutes are in fact from the Superior Court, the procedure followed can be rationalized with the usual understanding of the scope of review on certiorari only on the assumption that the court ignored the English view that "jurisdictional" facts had to appear of record, but went into the questions here raised because they were "jurisdictional" in the sense that they reflected the requirements of the statute.

I. RECORD [8]

Middlesex Court of General Sessions, Concord, September 1769

[SEAL] Middlesex Ss. Anno Regni Regis Georgii Tertii magnæ Brittanicæ Francæ et Hiberniæ nono.

At a Court of General Sessions of the Peace begun and Held at Concord within and for the County of Middlesex on the Second Tuesday of September being the twelfth Day of said Month Annoque Domini 1769.

John Harrington of Marlborough in the County of Middlesex Husbandman being bound by Recognizance for his Appearance at this Time to answer to the Complaint of Anna Josslin of Marlborough aforesaid Spinster for begetting her with Child of a Bastard, (of which she was delivered in Marlborough aforesaid on the twenty fourth Day of June AD 1768) And the said John being now in Court and charged by the said Anna with being the Father of the said bastard Child born of her Body as aforesaid, denied the said Charge and Accusation; and after a full hearing of the Parties and their Evidence, it appears to the Court and they adjudge that the said Anna Josslin be admitted to her Oath, and she being Sworn, upon her Oath, in Court, says that the said John Harrington is the Father of the bastard male Child born of her Body as aforesaid.

It's thereupon Considered by the Court *and they do thereupon adjudge*[9] the said John Harrington to be, and he is hereby adjudged

---

[7] Text at note 3 above.

[8] SF 147872. Subscribed: "A true Copy as of Record. Examined per Thad. Mason Cler. Pac." (Clerk of the Peace).

[9] Italics in MS. See text at note 4 above.

§1, 1 A&R 369; Act of 26 June 1699, c. 3, §1, 1 A&R 370. As to the usage "First Justice," see No. 27, Doc. V. See also the writ of certiorari in Harrington v. Jocelin, SF 147872; Whitmore, *Mass. Civil List* 79.

331

to be the reputed Father of the same Child and order that he stand chargeable with the Maintenance thereof with the Assistance of the said Anna Josslin the Mother; and that he pay the said Anna the Sum of forty eight Shillings for the first four Weeks next after the Birth of the Said Child towards the defreying the Charges and the Maintenance of the Same Child to that Time, and that he also pay her two Shillings per Week from thence to this Time, and also that he the said John pay to the said Anna from hence forward two Shillings per Week, weekly, towards the Maintenance of the Same Child untill the further Order of this Court. Also it's Ordered by the Court that the said John Harrington give Security, himself as Principal in the Sum of one hundred Pounds with two Sureties in the Sum of fifty Pounds each for his Performance of the above Order with Respect to the Maintenance of the said Child. And also that he give Security, himself as Principal in the Sum of fifty Pounds with two Sureties in the sum of twenty five Pounds each to save the Town of Marlborough, where the same Child was born, harmless and free from any Charge for the Maintenance of the said Child; And that he pay Fees and Costs of this Prosecution; Standing committed 'till performed.

II. FITCH'S ASSIGNMENT OF ERRORS [10]

Middlesex Superior Court, Cambridge, October–November 1769

In the Case of Ann Jocelin against John Harrington heard and Adjudged at the Court of General Sessions of the Peace held at Concord within and for the County of Middlesex on the Second Tuesday of September in the Year of our Lord 1769. The Errors Assigned by the said John on the Certiorari are as follows vizt.

1. It doth not Appear by the Record of the Judgment or Sentence of said Court of General Sessions of the peace, or by any part of the Record in said Case That the said John Harrington was ever accused by the said Ann Jocelin of being the Father of the Bastard Child born of her Body in June 1768 before the said Child was born nor 'till more than Twelve Months after:

2. It doth not Appear by the Record of said Judgment or Sentence nor by any other Record of any proceedings in said Case That the

---

[10] SF 147872, presumably in Fitch's hand. The paragraphs are numbered in the margin. The date has been supplied from the fact that the notification to Ann Josselin issued on 2 Nov. 1769. Min. Bk. 88, SCJ Middlesex, Oct. 1769, N–10. Compare No. 27, Doc. VII.

said Ann Continued Constant in her Accusation of the said John to be the Father of the said Bastard Child, or That She was ever Examined upon Oath while She was pregnant with said Bastard Child, touching the same, nor that she was put upon the Discovery of the Truth relative thereto, in the Time of her Travail, all which by Law ought to have Appeared; [11]

3. It doth Appear by the Record of the said Judgment and Sentence of said Court in said Case, That The said Judgment was founded upon the Oath of the said Ann in said Court, That the said John was the Father of said Bastard Child, and upon that only;

4. The said Ann was not put upon the Discovery of the Truth relative to said Bastard Child during the Time of her Travel nor did she Charge the said John with being the Father of said Child during said Time, nor till long after.

Wherefore the said John prays That the said Order Sentence Judgment and proceedings of said Court of General Sessions of the peace, may be quashed and That he be allowed his Charges occasioned thereby and Costs.   Saml. Fitch for the said John Harrington

III. ADAMS' MINUTES OF THE TESTIMONY [12]

Middlesex Superior Court, Charlestown, April 1771

Ann Josselyne vs. John Harrington. Bastardy.

Putnam.

C.J. If there is other Evidence of Circumstances that tend to render it probable, will not that answer the End of that Prerequisite, of Examination in the Time of Travail? [13]

Jerusha Newton. In feby. she sent for the Man and Jno. Harrington came. She was very suddenly taken in Travel, and very bad. Midwife not there till an Hour after the Child was born. That very day before her Delivery she said Jno. Harrington was the father. She was then very comfortable and well. No Question was put, in the Time [*of*] her Travail. She said she wonderd how any Man could serve any Woman as Jno. Harrington did.

---

[11] The statutory requirements. See No. 28, text at note 1.

[12] In JA's hand. Adams Papers, Microfilms, Reel No. 185. The date is only tentatively assigned. See text at note 6 above.

[13] Evidently a question by Chief Justice Benjamin Lynde, put at the beginning of Putnam's argument, as recorded by JA. See text at note 6 above. The Minute Book and files do not indicate for whom Putnam appeared, but if the witnesses that follow are his, he must have been for Ann.

Mary Morse. Did not examine her. There was Something Said after the Birth, of the Childs looking like Jno. Harrington.

Adonijah Newton. I went and found him at a Burying. All I had to do was to ask him to come, I did not know she was with Child. Some time after she wanted to see him again. Then I mistrusted she was with Child. He wonderd what she wanted to see him for. She told me, before the Child was born, that she was like to have a Child by Harrington.

Thos. Josselyne. Harrington Said, I f——d her once, but I minded my pulbacks. I sware I did not get it.

Rebecca Drummond. 2 Months ago. He denyed it, &c. That all the Money they had of him was for work.

Joshua Newton. I think he said she should not have no more Money than she had got. 3 or 4 Pistareens, and 10 dollars.

Gershom Newton. Knew of his coming to see her often and staying all Night. I carried a Letter from her [to?] [14] the Monadnocks. [15] He admired she should send to him for Money for he had left her some. He gave me a Note for £20 which I gave him up again, because he said his father would cut him off.

Never knew him there but two Nights.

Solomon Wheeler. Jno. Harrington was there once, and laid on the Bed alone. He afterwards called me a fool for telling of it. He said it would make a Talk.

[14] MS torn.
[15] "The Monadnocks" was a term commonly used for Mount Monadnock, or Grand Monadnock, near present Jaffrey, N.H. See 3 JA, *Diary and Autobiography* 268–269.